THE ENGLISH NEWSPAPER

The development in format of the English newspaper from the seventeenth to the nineteenth century

THE ENGLISH NEWSPAPER

SOME ACCOUNT OF THE PHYSICAL DEVELOPMENT OF JOURNALS PRINTED IN LONDON BETWEEN 1622 & THE PRESENT DAY

BY

STANLEY MORISON

Sandars Reader in Bibliography 1931-2

CAMBRIDGE

AT THE UNIVERSITY PRESS

1932

CAMBRIDGE UNIVERSITY PRESS
Cambridge, New York, Melbourne, Madrid, Cape Town, Singapore, São Paulo, Delhi

Cambridge University Press
The Edinburgh Building, Cambridge CB2 8RU, UK

Published in the United States of America by Cambridge University Press, New York

www.cambridge.org
Information on this title: www.cambridge.org/9780521122696

First published 1932
This digitally printed version 2009

A catalogue record for this publication is available from the British Library

ISBN 978-0-521-12269-6 paperback

CONTENTS

Preface *page* xi

CHAPTER I

THE NEWS-PAMPHLETS, PREDECESSORS OF THE NEWSPAPERS, 1622–1664

Introductory; § 1 Corantos; § 2 Diurnalls; § 3 Passages; § 4 Mercuries; § 5 Intelligencers; § 6 Posts; § 7 Spies, Scouts, &c.; § 8 The Official Intelligencer & News *pages* 1–40

CHAPTER II

THE FIRST NEWSPAPERS, 1665–1695

The London Gazette 1665; The Currant Intelligence, &c. 1681; Dawks's News-Letter, &c. 1695 41–52

CHAPTER III

THE THRICE-WEEKLY POSTS, 1695–1702

The Post Boy; The Post Man; The Flying Post; & their Postscripts 53–70

CHAPTER IV

THE FIRST DAILY NEWSPAPER AND THE DEVELOPMENT OF THE THRICE-WEEKLY EVENING POSTS, 1702–1715

The Daily Courant; The Evening Post; The St James's Post 71–80

CHAPTER V

THE WEEKLY JOURNALS, I, 1713–1725

Mawson's 1713 (?); Read's 1715; Mist's 1715, 1725; Applebee's 1713 (?); The Shift Shifted 1716; The Charitable Mercury 1716 81–105

CHAPTER VI

THE WEEKLY JOURNALS, II, 1727–1742

The Craftsman 1727; The Grub-street Journal 1730; The Weekly Miscellany 1732; The Westminster Journal 1742 107–118

CHAPTER VII

DAILY JOURNALS, POSTS & ADVERTISERS, &c.
1719–1741

The Daily Post 1719; Parker's London Post 1719; The Daily Journal 1720; Parker's Penny Post 1725; The Daily Advertiser 1730; The London Daily Post 1741 119–128

CHAPTER VIII

EVENING JOURNALS, 1739–1758

The Champion 1739; The Evening Advertiser 1754; The London Chronicle 1757; Lloyd's Evening Post 1757; The Universal Chronicle (Payne) 1758; The New Weekly Chronicle (Owen) 1758 129–140

CHAPTER IX

THE MID-EIGHTEENTH-CENTURY PAPERS, 1748–1770

The Gazetteer 1748; The St James's Chronicle 1761 & other Evening Posts; The Public Ledger 1769; The Independent Chronicle 1769; The Middlesex Journal 1770 141–158

CHAPTER X

THE MATURE EIGHTEENTH-CENTURY NEWSPAPER, § 1, 1770–1781

The Morning Chronicle 1770; The Morning Post 1772; The English Chronicle 1779; The Morning Herald 1780; Aurora 1781; Noon Gazette 1781 159–172

CHAPTER XI

THE MATURE EIGHTEENTH-CENTURY NEWSPAPER, § 2, 1786–1789

The English Chronicle 1786; The World 1787; The Daily Universal Register: The Times 1785: 1788; The Star 1788; The Oracle 1789; Woodfall's Diary 1789 173–202

CHAPTER XII

THE NINETEENTH-CENTURY DAILY
1803–1846

The Times (*continued*); The Standard 1827; The Daily News 1846 203–224

CHAPTER XIII

THE NINETEENTH CENTURY. SUNDAY NEWSPAPERS TO 1861

British Gazette, and Sunday Monitor 1779; The London Recorder 1783; Sunday London Gazette 1783; The Review, and Sunday Advertiser 1789; The Observer 1791; Bell's Weekly Messenger 1796; Bell's Weekly Dispatch 1801; The News 1805; The Albion 1807; Bell's Life in London 1828; Bell's New Weekly Messenger 1831; Bell's Penny Dispatch 1841; The News of the World 1843; Lloyd's Penny Sunday Times 1843; Reynolds's Weekly Newspaper 1850; The London Halfpenny Newspaper 1861 225–262

CHAPTER XIV

THE MID-VICTORIAN PENNY AND HALFPENNY PAPERS, 1855–1881

The Daily Telegraph 1855; The Pall Mall Gazette 1865; The Echo 1868; The St James's Gazette 1880; The Evening News 1881 263–276

CHAPTER XV

THE 'NEW JOURNALISM', 1883–1896

The Pall Mall Gazette (under W. T. Stead) 1883; The Star (under T. P. O'Connor) 1888; The Times (under G. E. Buckle); The Morning 1892; The Morning Leader 1892; The Evening News (under Kennedy Jones); Daily Mail 1896 277–296

CHAPTER XVI

THE NEWSPAPER OF TODAY, 1898–1931

London Morning 1898; Morning Herald 1900; Daily Mail; Daily Express 1901; The Tribune 1906; The Times— 297–319

Appendix: Francis Hoffman 321–324

Index: to Journals cited 327

to Proper Names and Subjects 331

ILLUSTRATIONS

Composite photograph (reduced) displaying the development (in size of folded sheet) from the seventeenth-century Mercury to the standard nineteenth-century format of *The Times* *Frontispiece*

Postscript to *The Post-Boy*, September 26, 1706, in actual size of the original in the University Library, Cambridge *facing p.* 64

Postscript to *The Post-Man*, August 11, 1710, in actual size of the original in the Burney Collection (B.M.), shewing watermark THE POST MAN in the right-hand margin 67

The Daily Courant, 1702 74

The Westminster Gazette, 1893 296

Appendix: Portrait of Francis Hoffman 321

There are upwards of 156 line blocks in the text. It is regretted that owing to the rigidity of the binding of the respective files and the consequent photography of a curved instead of a flat surface, a number of reproductions are distorted in their left-hand columns.

Figures 1–57 are in the size of the type-area of the originals. Headings and pages from fig. 58 are consistently reduced to a measure of 6½ inches across the columns. Small pieces, devices, and fractions of a page are in their original size.

The factotum initials in the chapters are, with one or two exceptions, recuttings on wood from characteristic originals. In several instances enlargement has been necessary to accommodate them to the present purpose.

PREFACE

The following pages represent, not a history of journalism, but a first attempt to interest students of bibliography in the history of newspaper development. If bibliography is to be considered, in the terms of a recent authoritative definition, as the department of scholarship concerned with the material transmission of thought, the newspaper, essentially ephemeral thing as it is, yet has a place, though humble, beside the codex and the printed book—the most permanent records of human thought and experience.

My matter, being designed for delivery as a series of six lectures in the Sandars Readership, is more discursive than formal; trying to give, by a series of rapid sketches, a consecutive account of the physical side of the English newspaper. The lectures in book-form may, in spite of many omissions, serve the purpose of drawing attention to a neglected subject, and perhaps make a slight contribution to the preliminary studies without which the urgently needed History of British Journalism is impossible. I have added a number of footnotes and restored some subsidiary sections, but the printed text is, substantially, that read at Cambridge in February 1932. The book, in confining its scope to main tendencies, takes only incidental account of illustration in newspapers and omits all consideration of 'picture', trade and technical journals. So far as possible I have worked from original sources. The available reference books, with the notable exception of Mr J. B. Williams's painstaking work on the seventeenth century, are inexact as well as incomplete. I have made constant, though cautious, use of *The Times Tercentenary Handlist*, and I have occasionally been helped by the manuals, all out of print, of Andrews, Knight Hunt, Grant, and Fox Bourne. Reference to Timperley has elucidated several points. In the absence of any modern work on the subject, I made my own notes (and, I do not doubt, errors—though I have been as careful as possible) from the Burney, Thomason and Bagford Collections in the British Museum, supplementing these with the Nichols Collection in the Bodleian Library, the files in the University Library at Cambridge, the specimens in the St Bride Technical Library and one or two collections in the Press Club and other private hands. To the authorities of these institutions I tender my acknowledgments. My thanks are also due to Messrs Birrell and Garnett for adding, by their inquiries, to my own collection of newspapers. Mr Ronald Horton assisted me by searching the Burney files for a period of thirty years, thus enabling me to check the section dealing with the Postscripts. I am grateful for salvation from more than one mistake to Mr A. F. Johnson of the British Museum, who kindly looked through the proofs of the portion dealing with the seventeenth century. The staff of the University Press have saved me from a number of literal errors. The index is by Mr J. S. Maywood.

Finally, I offer the Syndics of the University Press my thanks for the liberal scale upon which they have allowed the book to be illustrated.

S. M.

Cambridge
19 *April* 1932

THE ENGLISH NEWSPAPER
1622–1931

CHAPTER I

THE NEWS-PAMPHLETS, PREDECESSORS OF THE NEWSPAPERS

1622–1664

Introductory

§ 1 Corantos

§ 2 Diurnalls

§ 3 Passages

§ 4 Mercuries

§ 5 Intelligencers

§ 6 Posts

§ 7 Spies, Scouts, &c.

§ 8 The Official Intelligencer & News

type design, the tradition of typographical composition, disposition and arrangement, and changes of style parallel with or consequent upon spiritual or cultural movements. Quite apart from forming a chapter in a general and neutral history of 'taste', this knowledge can be used as a record of practice and style by printers. Also, apart from serving such ends, it is always worth while to know how things work, and, for that reason alone, it is good to trace cause and effect in the development of newspaper typography.

Moreover, even if we have no special interest in newspapers *qua* newspapers, the present enquiry may be of service if we are able to see printing in its correct perspective. There is a need for a sort of all-round attitude to printing if we are rightly to estimate the value of any department of it, and newspapers *qua* printing have been ignored by the historians of the craft. This is the more surprising, for if newspapers differ from books it is because the printing craft is a necessity of their existence.

Let me make myself clear. The superiority in speed, and advantage in textual accuracy, of printing over handwriting as a means of multiplication, were obvious gains; and the wisdom of avoiding even the slightest change in the alphabetical convention an obvious precaution. Printing did not change the book (it hasn't done so now—unless you exaggerate the invention and function of the title-page). But the invention did change the audience. Liturgy, Theology, Civil and Canon Law, History, Medicine, Rhetoric, were all on vellum before they were on paper. In spite of the fact that printing was a new invention, it did not produce a thing which looked 'new': it was content to extend the faculties of reading (the same old scripts in the same old lay-outs) and writing. In a word, it miraculously increased and multiplied, and hence cheapened, books. All this is familiar enough to us from half-a-dozen new or old histories of printing. But we are less accustomed to reflect that the great invention of the craft is the newspaper. Multiplication by printing is, first of all and last of all, an economy: for none can say that typography has any aesthetic advantage over calligraphy. We may debate whether or no printing is an Art, but we know it as a necessity to Trade and we know that in Trade, Time has to be paid for. Hence, I submit, as a final reason for our here undertaking some study of newspaper printing, that the fundamental economic character of printing became most explicit with the invention of the power press, constructed by a newspaper for a newspaper. Books there were in the Middle Ages, books there will always be because men who can write will write; but printing is a process optional to literature and to booksellers. On the other

INTRODUCTORY

To chronicle or to analyse the cause and effect of the changes in format through which the London dailies and weeklies passed in their progress from the seventeenth to the twentieth century is an intricate task; for me to undertake it, with any completeness, in the form of lectures would, it seems clear, be productive of more tedium than even bibliographers are trained to sustain. The mass of detail may, however, be of somewhat less aridity if I disengage such material as will be sufficient, fairly and justly, to illustrate at least the typical forms assumed, generation after generation, by our morning, evening and weekly journals.

It is proposed, therefore, to collect the main varieties of such publications, to note more especially such details as indicate or adumbrate tendencies which played a part in establishing conventions. From time to time we shall come across details of display long since dead but which, if isolated, will assist our understanding of certain survivals in *The Times* of this day and in the contemporary cheap newspaper press. We shall also notice developments in nomenclature, and the final emergence of titles regarded as appropriate for, or characteristic of, or even essential to newspapers, e.g. Gazette, Post, Chronicle, Journal, Mail, etc.

This, then, is the programme of this series of lectures. But, it may be asked, Why should bibliographers spend their time on newspapers? As it cannot be said that interest in the historical side of journalism is fashionable, some excuse may be in place before I plunge you into a general enquiry into the manifestations of the spirit which, after small beginnings, gives us our daily *Times*.

There is, I first submit, something to be said for examining the files of old newspapers, and endeavouring to make some sort of coherent story of their foundation, their youth, their coming of age, and their full development. There is a practical use in the organisation of knowledge of the history of hand, newspapers are the invention of the printer, and printing is absolutely essential to newspapers and newsvendors. The business of newspapers is to give the news of the moment at the moment. Hence their entire existence and progress depend upon speedy multiplication and transport. Inasmuch, then, as the fundamental economic character of printing is seen at its fullest in the history of newspapers, there is sufficient justification for our spending time in the endeavour to trace the chief points in their physical development.

English journalism, as to periodicity, started with weekly publication. It proceeded through the stages of twice weekly and thrice weekly to the every morning, to the morning and evening.

As to format, the successive early Corantos, some of which carried 'The Weekly News' (1622) as an overall catch-line, were eight pages quarto form, and so also were the Diurnalls and Mercuries which followed them. They were not books, but pamphlets. They were succeeded by the single-sheet, double-column, half-folio *London Gazette* (1665), later expanded to four pages (i.e. full folio folded once), which was also the format of the first 'morning'—*The Daily Courant* (1702). These two were neither books nor pamphlets; they were 'papers'—in fact, our first papers.

The changes in the size and number of pages; in the measure and depth and number of the columns; the size and design of the text and heading types; the methods of setting out the headings; the variations in style of titles, their decorations (if any), rules and other elements, were all infinitely various during the period of the development from the weekly to the daily, i.e. from the Coranto to *The Daily Courant*. But to the individualism of this early period there succeeded, in the first quarter of the eighteenth century, a measure of general consent as to make-up which finally crystallised into sharply defined conventions strong enough to govern the journals into recognisable categories corresponding to their several purposes as either news-sheets, essay papers, or advertisers. This was a slow process—*The London Gazette* is still what it was when it began in 1665, a standard late-seventeenth-century news-sheet; *Smith's Currant Intelligence* of 1681 died a pamphlet of the previous generation in news-sheet format, never having found its true level. *The Tatler*, a literary sheet, pure and simple, was an invention: it was right in format from the start. There had been already a flood of theological diatribes presented in news form, but *The Tatler* was a humanist essay paper, setting a typographical style for itself and its later imitators. The *Evening Posts* of the early eighteenth century followed the style of the daily press.

The *Weekly Journals* and tri-weeklies of 1715 developed a style different from the dailies, the evenings and the essay-weeklies. The mid-eighteenth-century 'weekly chronicle' and 'daily advertiser', in gradually defining their respective categories, ordered their contents and precised their formats. Both persisted well into the nineteenth century and then looked as 'old-fashioned' to the early Victorians as a pre-war *Times* looks to us today.

Cobbett's *Weekly Register* (1802) was a nineteenth-century invention, but his *Porcupine*, which he sold in the previous year, looked an eighteenth-century daily—like *The True Briton* with which it was ultimately merged. The true nineteenth-century daily was brought into existence when *The Times* came under the control of John Walter the Second.

In the meantime, many of the weekly newspapers had, after Cobbett's *Register*, become critical commentaries. The publication of week-end collections of news remained in the hands of Johnson's *Sunday Monitor* (an eighteenth-century paper later modernised) and *The Observer*. These were followed by a bare-faced copy of the latter entitled *The New Observer*, which became *The Sunday Times*; by *Bell's Weekly Messenger*, by *Bell's Weekly Dispatch* and by the *News of the World*.

All other dailies—and evenings—were more or less substantial shadows of that great paper, *The Times*. The original number of the *Daily Mail* was no exception to this rule. No. 1 of the *Evening News*, for all its being printed on Cambridge blue paper, might have been four pages of the *Daily News*. The papers were too exhausted with the struggle to collect and to digest news which came by telegraph, by cable and—huger novelty still—by telephone, to have time for typographical experiment. But with advertisements increasing in volume, and in display, the headlines had to be enlarged and displayed.

These are one or two of the main points which will stand out in our consideration of the physical development of English journalism. By 'journalism' I mean the printing of news; by 'physical development' I mean the shape, size and folding of the paper, the size and display of the type, the column arrangements and headings, and all the rest of the features which to the normal layman's eye contribute to the aspect of the paper.

The word 'journal' is vague in the extreme. Yet it is tantamount to an abuse to extend the term to the *Journal of Theological Studies*, a quarterly. The seventeenth-century 'Diurnalls', the eighteenth-century 'journals', were weekly chronicles of daily proceedings either in Parliament or abroad or at home. There is little movement in a week's theology! And, even as a quarterly, the *Journal of Theological Studies* is unpunctual. Clearly, as the periodicity of a paper is decelerated, its claim to the description 'journal' is reduced; and also, the claim of the writer of a quarterly to the term 'journalist'.

It is an essential condition of the journal that it should be issued with a certain frequency; and that frequency greater than once a year, or once a quarter, or once a month. These yearly, quarterly or monthly measures of frequency may constitute the Periodical, but publication more often than once a month is essential to a Journal. Fortnightly appearance seems not to have become, for any time, a workable term: the conventional measure of frequency within the month has always been the week. English journalism, as to periodicity, started with *weekly* publication. It proceeded through the stages of *twice weekly* and *thrice weekly* to the *daily* (Morning), to the *twice daily* (Morning and Evening). In tracing these stages it is necessary for us first to observe the most characteristic of the styles used by the printers of the news-pamphlets which preceded the newspapers.

§ 1 CORANTOS

THE development of the printed book from the incunable into the much more strictly governed production of the sixteenth century, with the gradual emergence of a consistent typographic aesthetic, is already well known to us. The familiarity of our Elizabethan and Jacobean forefathers with the latter formats inevitably prescribed a book style for 'The Relations'. The News-Books, Intelligencers, Proceedings, Diurnalls and Mercuries of the period from 1622 to 1665, like the earliest form of news relation, conformed to the style of the printed book, or pamphlet. Such a production had its normal text-page, its contents-page, and its title-page.

Thus '*Newes* concernynge the General Councell Holden at Trydent London Tho Raynalde, 1549,' may well be taken as an early predecessor of the news-book or pamphlet. A later production, dated London 1619, is headed: '*Newes out of* Holland: Concerning Barnevelt and his fellow-Prisoners,' etc. (cf. Fig. 1). There was published in 1621 (cf. Fig. 2) 'NEWES FROM FRANCE A true Relation . . . of fire in the Citie of Paris,'

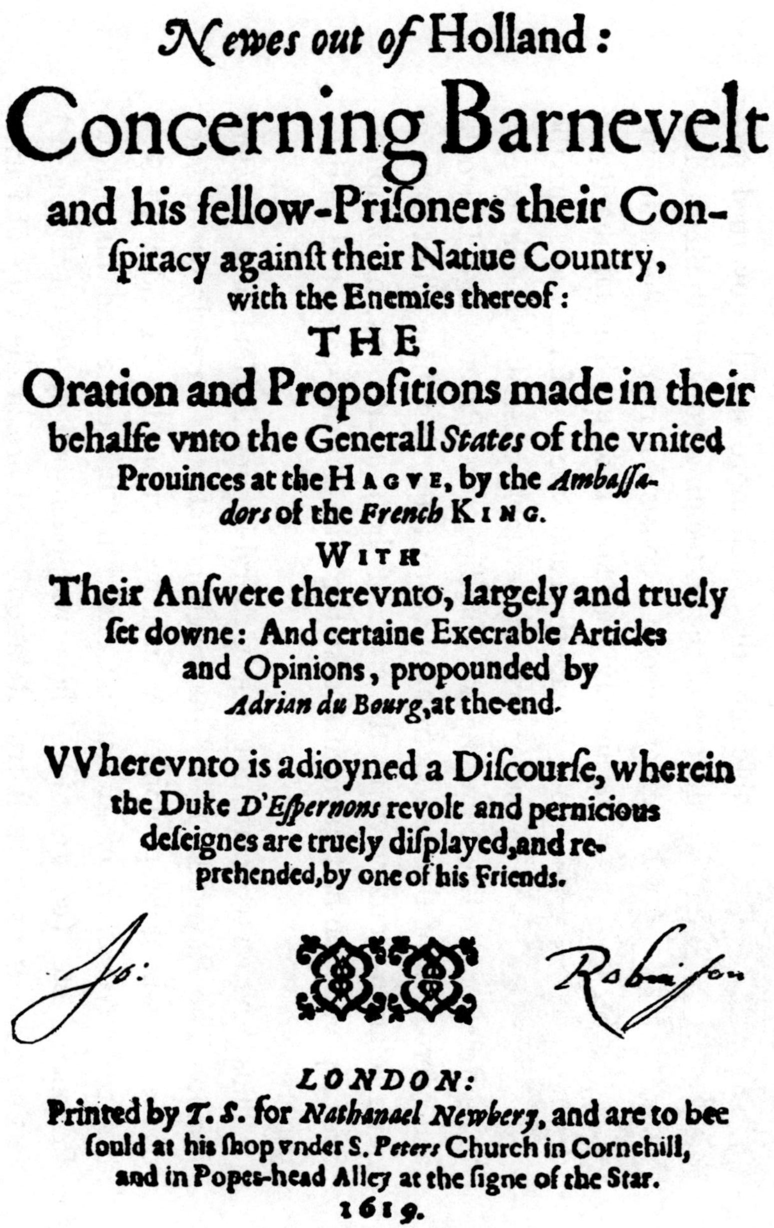

Newes out of Holland:

Concerning Barnevelt

and his fellow-Prisoners their Conspiracy against their Natiue Country, with the Enemies thereof:

THE

Oration and Propositions made in their behalfe vnto the Generall *States* of the vnited Prouinces at the HAGVE, by the *Ambassadors* of the *French* KING.

WITH

Their Answere thereunto, largely and truely set downe: And certaine Execrable Articles and Opinions, propounded by *Adrian du Bourg*, at the end.

VVhereunto is adioyned a Discourse, wherein the Duke *D'Espernons* revolt and pernicious deseignes are truely displayed, and reprehended, by one of his Friends.

Jo: Robinson

LONDON:

Printed by *T. S.* for *Nathanael Newbery*, and are to bee sould at his shop vnder S. *Peters* Church in Cornehill, and in Popes-head Alley at the signe of the Star. 1619.

Fig. 1. *A Relation*

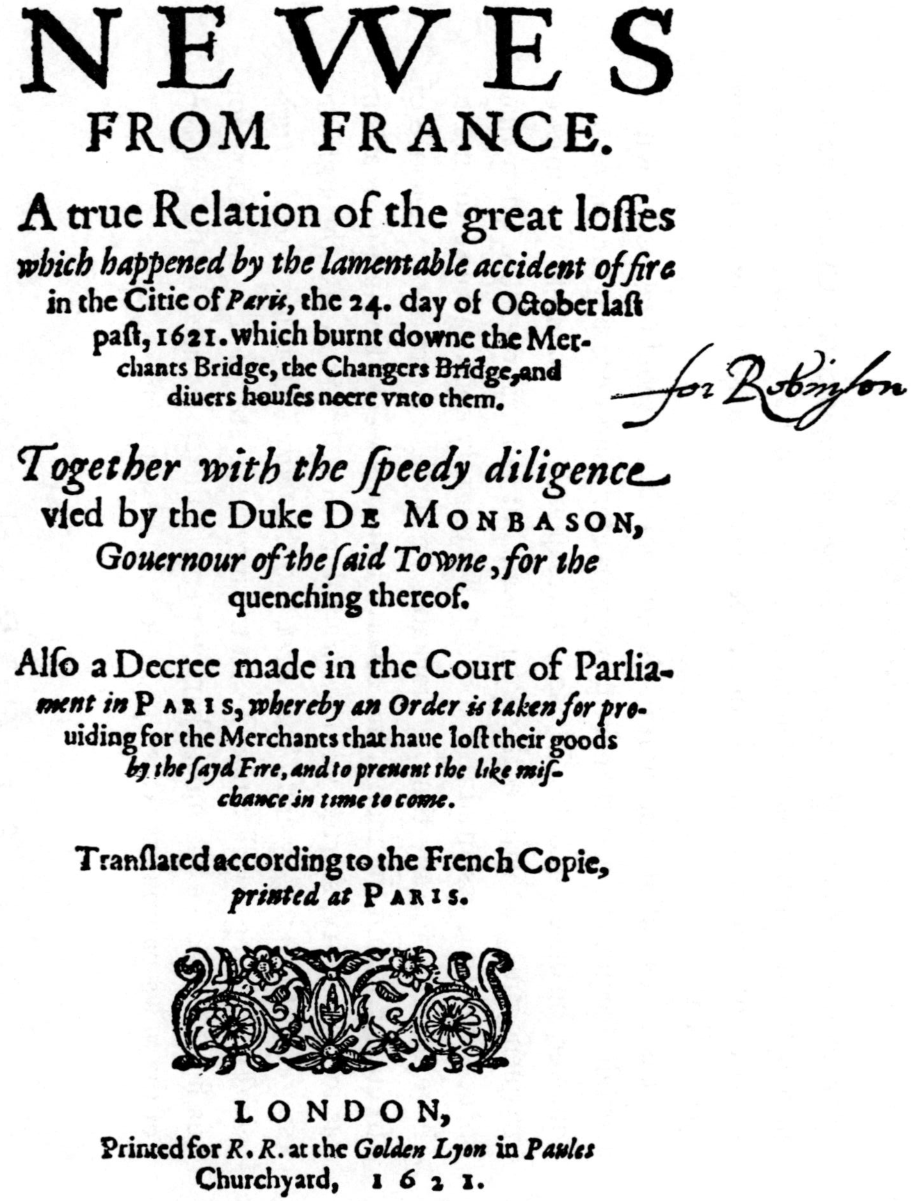

NEWES

FROM FRANCE.

A true Relation of the great losses *which happened by the lamentable accident of fire* in the Citie of *Paris*, the 24. day of October last past, 1621. which burnt downe the Merchants Bridge, the Changers Bridge, and diuers houses neere vnto them.

for Robinson

Together with the speedy diligence vsed by the Duke DE MONBASON, *Gouernour of the said Towne, for the* quenching thereof.

Also a Decree made in the Court of Parliament *in* PARIS, *whereby an Order is taken for prouiding* for the Merchants that haue lost their goods *by the sayd Fire, and to preuent the like mischance in time to come.*

Translated according to the French Copie, *printed at* PARIS.

LONDON,

Printed for *R. R.* at the *Golden Lyon* in *Paules* Churchyard, 1621.

Fig. 2. *A Relation*

etc. Each of these possesses a regular title-page, with year of publication below the imprint; a first page of text with folio at foot. Each sheet has its signature. There are catchwords to the pages, margins, decoration, head-pieces, vignettes, initials, borders and so on, all exactly according to book conventions. The presswork, sewing and publishing are equally normal in these productions which, though they used the word 'Newes', cannot be regarded as regular news-books, still less as journals. But in the year after the publication of the above-cited *Newes from France*, i.e. in 1622, comes

Weekly Newes from Italy, Germanie, Hungaria translated out of the Dutch copie London Printed by E. A. for Nicholas Bourne and Thomas Archer—

and it has the date, 'The 23 May',[1] over the top of the first word of the title. This production may be taken as a characteristic news-book of the first type entitled to be considered as an effort in journalism. Its construction differs from the 1549 pamphlet of 'Newes' concerning the Council of Trent, only in the setting of the title-page. Page 1 of the text of the Bourne and Archer pamphlet is a normal book page and the rest is according to form. Nevertheless, the nature of the two productions is radically different. The 1549 and similar publications were rather more in the nature of despatches analogous to the volumes on war and travel which today form a staple portion of the publisher's list. Such despatches, while giving news, gave it long after the occurrence, and their title-pages bore no more precise date of publication than the year of issue. They were as isolated and separate as any of the more solid works of the printing press, and they were not journalism in any sense. What was required was a continuum involving author, printer and public. Such a continuum developed out of common natural curiosity on the one hand and the convenience and cheapness of the pamphlets. The public liked these productions and wished for more. 'Custom', wrote the author of one of the Corantos, in justification for his issue of a series of these news-books or pamphlets at the rate of one a week,

is so predominant in everything that both the Reader and the Printer of these *Pamphlets* agree in their expectation of Weekly Newes, so that if the Printer have not wherewithall to afford satisfaction, yet will the Reader come and aske every day for new Newes; not out of curiosity or wantonness, but pretending a necessity either to please themselves or satisfie their

[1] Successors: May 30; June 18, I. D. for Nathaniel Newbery and Wm Sheffard (or Shefford); August 2, I. D. for Nathaniel Butter; August 13; August 23.

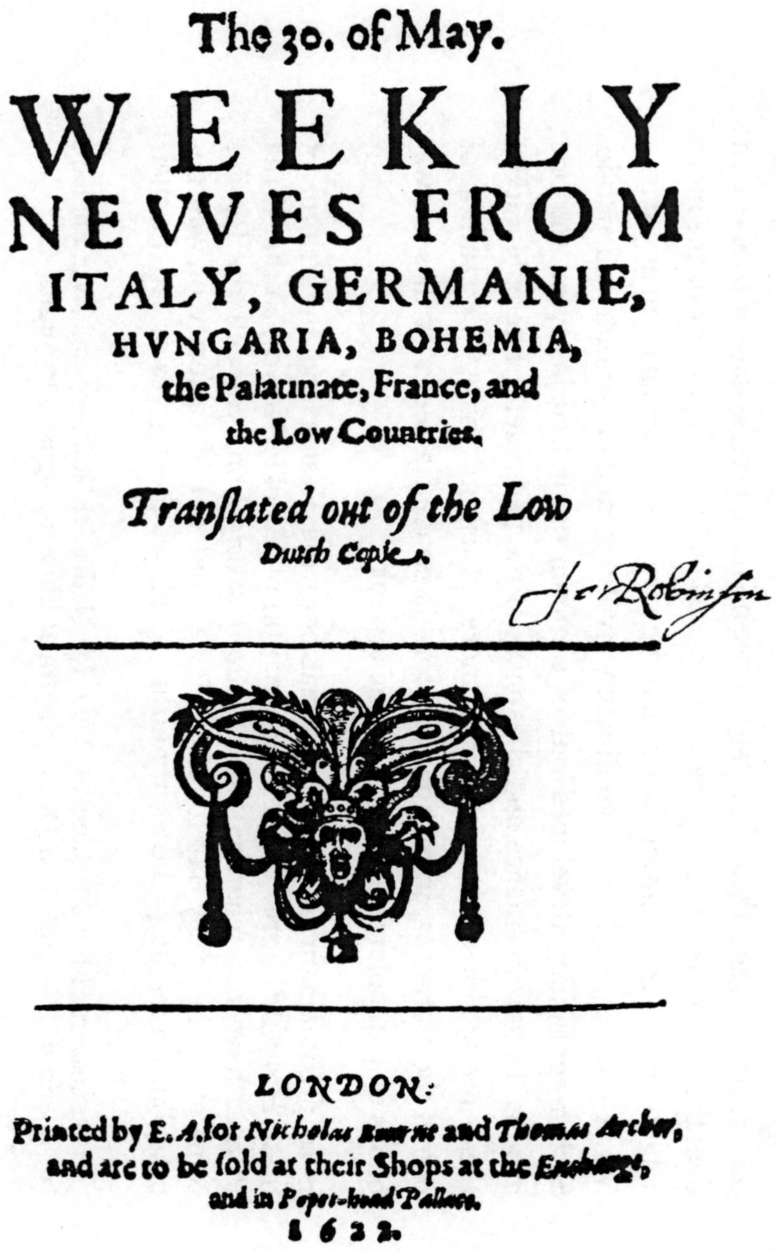

The 30. of May.

WEEKLY NEVVES FROM ITALY, GERMANIE, HVNGARIA, BOHEMIA, the Palatinate, France, and the Low Countries.

Translated out of the Low Dutch Copie.

LONDON:

Printed by E. A. for *Nicholas Bourne* and *Thomas Archer*, and are to be sold at their Shops at the *Exchange*, and in *Popes-head Pallace*.

1622.

Fig. 3. *An early dated News-Pamphlet*

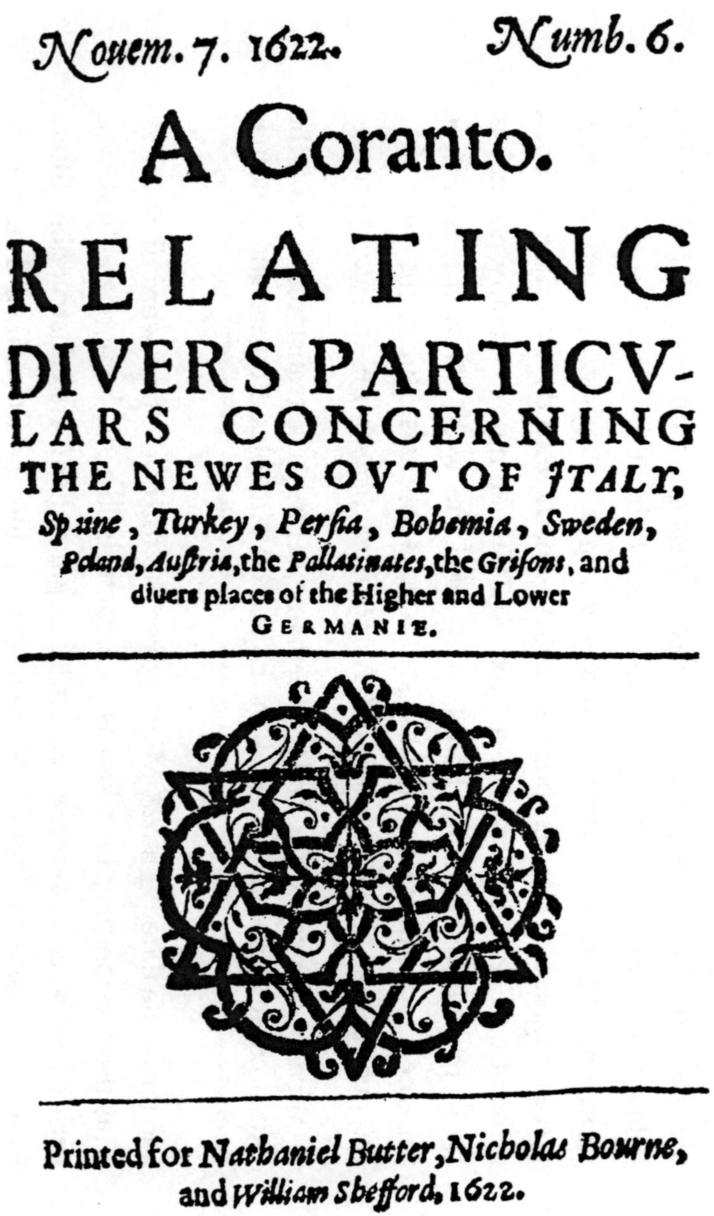

Nouem. 7. 1622. *Numb.* 6.

A Coranto.

RELATING DIVERS PARTICVLARS CONCERNING THE NEWES OVT OF *ITALY*, *Spaine*, *Turkey*, *Persia*, *Bohemia*, *Sweden*, *Poland*, *Austria*, the *Pallatinates*, the *Grisons*, and diuers places of the Higher and Lower GERMANIE.

Printed for *Nathaniel Butter*, *Nicholas Bourne*, and *William Sheffard*, 1622.

Fig. 4. *An early News-Pamphlet or 'Coranto', with date and serial number*

Customers. Therefore is the Printer, both with charge and paines taking, very careful to have his Friends abroad supply his wants at home with pertinent Letters, and acquaint him with the Printed copies beyond the Seas, that hee may acquaint you with such true intelligence as his fortune lights upon. So that according to the affaires published elsewhere, sometimes you may have two *Corantoes* in one Week. Which, seeing it is for your sake, and especially that you may make the country far off partake of our *London* Newes, be so far generous to acknowledge this his kindnesse, and doe not dishearten him in his endeavours, by asking impertinent questions and crossing his good interest, by making any doubt of the truth of his intelligence. For, to use a little protestation, I can assure you, there is not a line printed nor proposed to your view, but carries the credit of other Originalls, and justifies itself from honest and understanding authority; so that if they should faile there in true and exact discoveries, be not you too malignant against the Printer here, that is so far from any invention of his owne, that when he meets with improbability or absurdity, hee leaves it quite out rather than he will startle your patience, or draw you into suspition of the verity of the whole, because some one passage may be untrue, or reiterates the second time.

And so, if you be pleased with this his Apology, he proceeds in his businesse to afford you what contentment he can, beginning with foure several Letters from *Vienna* where the Imperiall Court lies.

Thus came into existence the continuous series of relations, in a word, 'Curranto', 'Courant' or, more usually, 'Coranto'.

A book-form title-page was prefixed to a pamphlet also printed for Nathaniel Butter, Nicholas Bourne and William Sheffard, 1622, carrying as its first line the italics '*Nouem.* 7. 1622. *Numb.* 6'. This serial number represents, therefore, a second notable detail conserved in every present-day periodical.[1] It is an important point, the first indication of divergence of the *periodical* from the *book*. Immediately below (cf. Fig. 4) the date and serial number is the line in canon upper- and lower-case

A Coranto.

In the same year, and dated equally conspicuously at the very head of the setting 'The 2. of September.', there was 'Printed by I. D. for Nicholas Bourne and Thomas Archer "An Account of two Great Battailes very lately Fought"'. In this issue, a skeleton summary of the actions is placed immediately below the title in the place normally occupied by the vignette, device

1 There were several periodicals in the eighteenth century which were not serially numbered, e.g. *The London Packet* of John Almon and several Sunday papers.

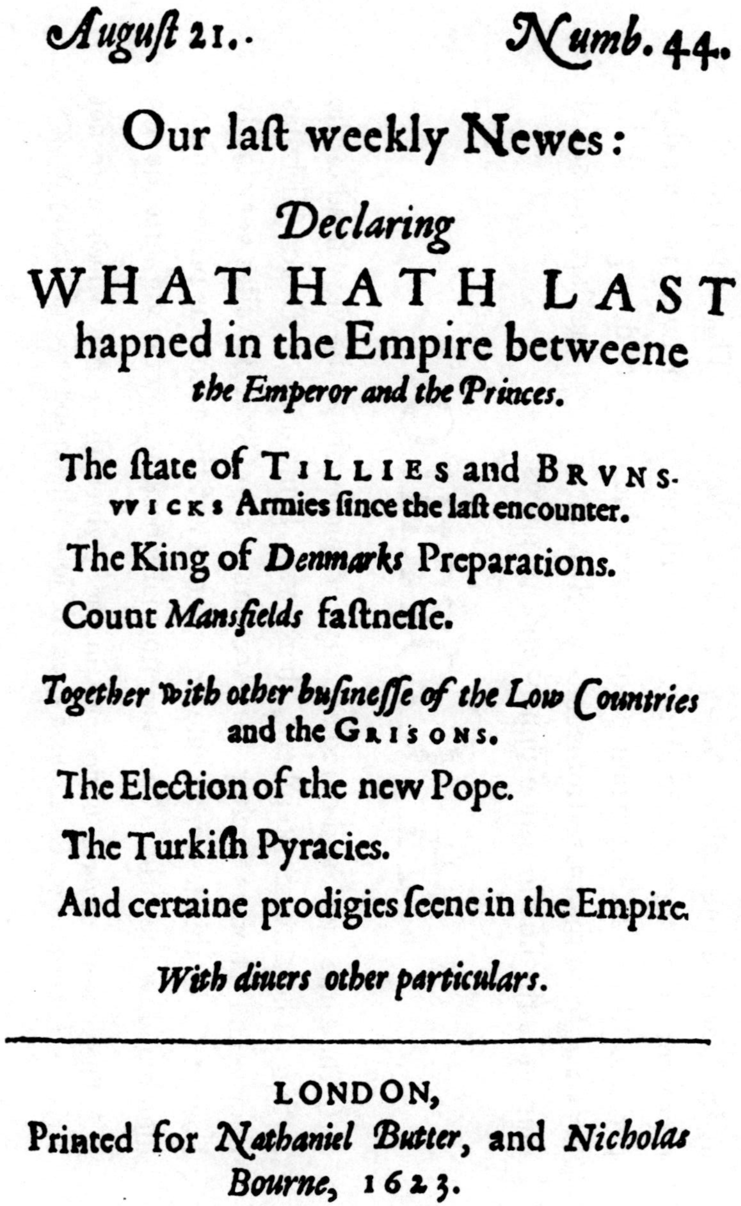

August 21.. *Numb.* 44.

Our laſt weekly Newes:

Declaring

WHAT HATH LAST

hapned in the Empire betweene

the Emperor and the Princes.

The ſtate of TILLIES and BRVNSWICKS Armies ſince the laſt encounter.

The King of *Denmarks* Preparations.

Count *Mansfields* faſtneſſe.

Together with other buſineſſe of the Low Countries and the GRISONS.

The Election of the new Pope.

The Turkiſh Pyracies.

And certaine prodigies ſeene in the Empire.

With diuers other particulars.

LONDON,

Printed for *Nathaniel Butter*, and *Nicholas Bourne*, 1623.

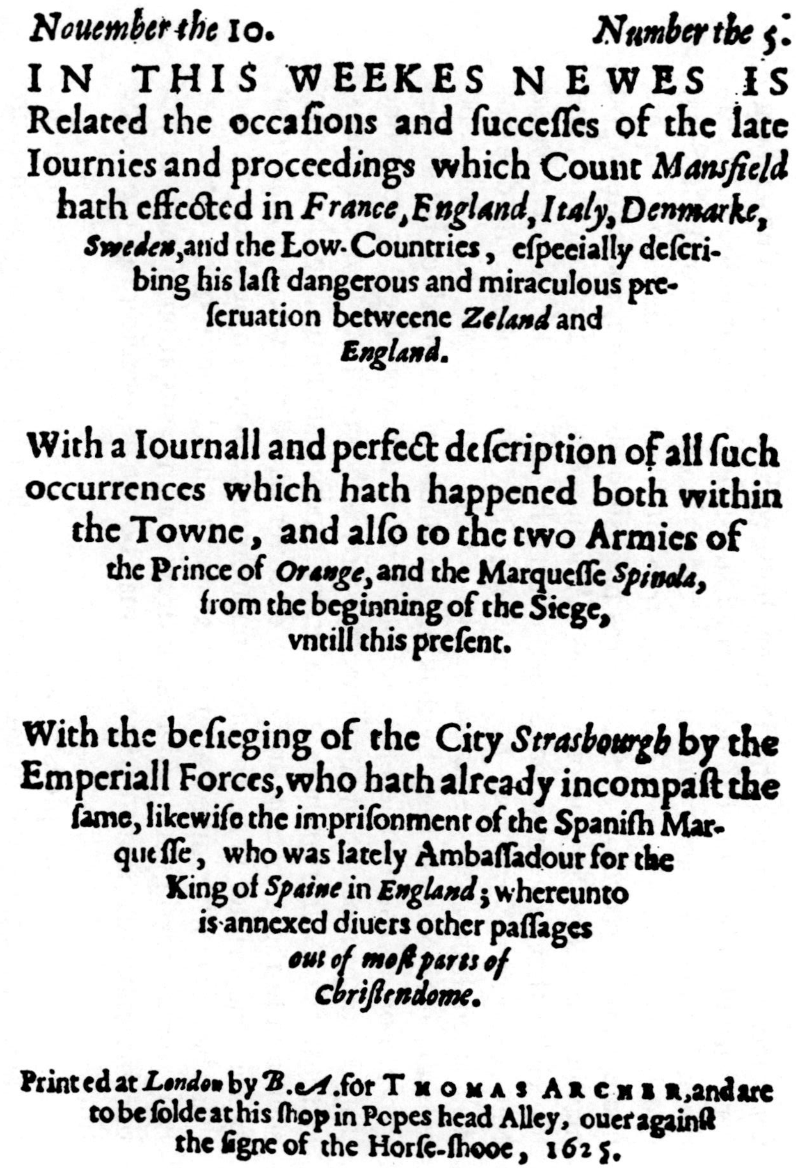

Nouember the 10. *Number the* 5.

IN THIS WEEKES NEWES IS

Related the occaſions and ſucceſſes of the late Iournies and proceedings which Count *Mansfield* hath effected in *France*, *England*, *Italy*, *Denmarke*, *Sweden*, and the Low-Countries, eſpecially deſcribing his laſt dangerous and miraculous preſeruation betweene *Zeland* and *England*.

With a Iournall and perfect deſcription of all ſuch occurrences which hath happened both within the Towne, and alſo to the two Armies of the Prince of *Orange*, and the Marqueſſe *Spinola*, from the beginning of the Siege, vntill this preſent.

With the beſieging of the City *Strasbowrgh* by the Emperiall Forces, who hath already incompaſt the ſame, likewiſe the impriſonment of the Spaniſh Marqueſſe, who was lately Ambaſſadour for the King of *Spaine* in *England*; whereunto is annexed diuers other paſſages *out of moſt parts of Chriſtendome.*

Printed at *London* by *B. A.* for THOMAS ARCHER, and are to be ſolde at his ſhop in Popes head Alley, ouer againſt the ſigne of the Horſe-ſhooe, 1625.

Figs. 5 and 6. *News-Pamphlets with date, serial number and contents in the body of the title-page* or other ornament, i.e. the title- and the contents-pages are amalgamated into one. The summary is not displayed but set out textually in paragraph form.

In the following year, the 'Numb. 31.' issued May 12 (1623) of 'The Newes of this Present Weeke' related several items. These items are not described on the title-page in paragraph form as in the 'Two Great Battailes' but are now *displayed*, i.e. expressed in summary form, centred on the title-page, and using an abundance of white for the purpose of throwing the entries more conspicuously into sight. There are specified as separate attractions, 'Reports of the death of the Pope and the Great Turk, with Divers other Memorable Occurrences from several Parts of the World'. Whatever the variations in the title, the first page of the text of these corantos is always (unless, by exception, there is not room for it) headed 'The Continuation of our Former Newes'. It is to be noted at this time that the periodicals issued by Nathaniel Butter and Nicholas Bourne, bearing the regular serial numbers, have widely varying titles. It would seem to have been the trade view that sales were more easily made if the coranto had a different title each week. Readers had to be given to understand that one week's news differed from another's; consequently, what was actually No. 36 of the 'Newes of this Present Week' is entitled 'The Affairs of the World for this Present Week', while No. 38 reads 'The Relation of our last Newes' and No. 44 (cf. Fig. 5) reads 'Our last weekly Newes'. Finally, No. 45 reads 'More Newes for this Present Week'. Therefore we must not say that the first English weekly periodical was entitled *The Weekly News*. The only invariable elements in the construction of the title-page are the date, which is almost always in the upper left-hand corner, and the serial number, generally in the upper right-hand corner. An important development of the typographical setting is the abandonment of the upper- and lower-case roman and italic for proper names in the early issues in favour of CAPS AND SMALLS. This use of caps and smalls for proper names in newspapers, a point to which we shall recur in a later lecture, is continued at the present day in all leading articles, and in the majority of Police Reports, Law Reports, etc. The amalgamation of the title-page and the contents-page, which we have noticed, continued to distinguish the news-books issued by Nathaniel Butter, or by Nathaniel Butter in combination with Nicholas Bourne throughout 1624. Thomas Archer, who engaged in partnership with Nicholas Bourne in the issue of 'Weekely Newes' dated 23 May 1622, produced news-books on his own responsibility in 1625. The issue for 'Nouember the 10.' [1625] is 'Number the 5'. Its title continues immediately under these two indications 'In this Weekes Newes is Related the occasions and successes ...', forming eight lines tapered off. Conversationally, as we have pointed out, these pamphlets were known as 'Corantos', a term indicating serial and not isolated publication; but it is clear that the notion of giving the periodical a short, easily memorable title and sticking to it, had not yet reached the printer, his editor, or the bookseller. We have noted that the date in the month is given; but there is not yet any indication of the day of the week. The imprint still remains in the form customary in books, with perhaps a more explicit address. Archer's corantos 'are to be solde at his shop in Popes head Alley, ouer against the signe of the Horse-shooe' (cf. Fig. 6).

It would be a reasonable guess that, if the lengthy titles of these newsbooks crystallised into some more convenient designation, such a term as 'Weekly Newes' would be acceptable. But the word 'Continuation' seems to have been equally regarded as a convenient catchword. It appears in the title of Bartholomew Downe's and Nathaniel Butter's publication of October 15, 1622, and also in the 'Continuation of our Weekly Newes from the 29 of March to the 7 of April', published by Thomas Archer with the serial number 16 of the year 1625. The title-page of this periodical shews, as a new development, the reduction of the table of contents into simpler draftsmanship and a more convenient and readable measure. The imprint now reads 'London, Printed for MERCURIUS BRITANNICUS. 1625'. The title 'MERCURIUS BRITANNICUS', printed in capitals and small capitals much more conspicuously than the 'contents', foreshadows the development with which the next generation was to be familiar.

§ 2 DIURNALLS

Such were the restrictions upon the Press that all these Continuations and Corantos dealt with foreign news and with foreign news only. In 1632 the Star Chamber—upon the complaint of the Spanish ambassador—put an end even to these, and for years there were no news-pamphlets. However, in December 1638, Letters Patent granted the monopoly of their revival to Butter and Bourne. Yet no domestic intelligence was printed in any periodical until the issue in 1641, under the Imprimatur of the Commons, of a pamphlet (drawn up by Samuel Pecke) described on its title-page as:

The Heads of Severall Proceedings in this Present Parliament from the 22 *of November to the* 29, 1641.

This production was published on November 29 by J. T(homas), a printer in Smithfield, and carried above the beginning of the text proper the convenient legend *Diurnall Occurrences in Parliament*. This is the first use of the term. Clearly the word 'Diurnall' is here used to describe a chronicle of daily proceedings; not a daily publication, but a daily recording for the purpose of weekly publication. This, our first English domestic news periodical, immediately (i.e. December 13–20, 1641) changed its front page title for the shorter legend of *Diurnall Occurrences or Heads*, etc., and there were other variations, alterations and precisions of title as identical publication progressed:

The Heads of Severall Proceedings in the Present Parliament, etc., November 22–29, 1641.
Diurnall Occurrences; or the Heads, etc., December 13–20, 1641.
Diurnall Occurrences in Parliament, January 2–10, 1641/2.
A Perfect Diurnall of the Passages in Parliament, January 24–31, 1641/2.
A Perfect Diurnall of the Passages in Parliament, June 13–20, 1642.
A Perfect Diurnall of the Passages in Parliament . . . More fully and exactly taken then by any other printed Copies (from September 5–12, 1642).

The word 'Passages' is given increased mention from the middle of 1642, and, moreover, although it is used in the same phrase with 'Diurnall' or 'Perfect Diurnall', typographical convention gave 'Passages' the largest type, as perhaps indicating that its diurnality was less important than the nature of the relation. The dozens of such Perfect Diurnalls which increasing competition brought into existence fall into distinct typographical categories. To the first type belongs such a booklet as that entitled *Heads*, etc., of November 1641, which possessed a title-page following the style of the Corantos. The second type is that in which the short legend over page 1 of the text itself alone performs the function of the title-page, the separate title-page being abandoned and the imprint either transferred to the last page, or placed between the legend and the first line of the text. In other words, type 1 led off with a title-page and type 2 with a front page.

William Cook or Cooke was a law publisher of Furnival's Inn, whose energy turned Samuel Pecke, the scrivener, into the first great English journalist. Cook and Pecke were the leading Diurnall publisher and writer respectively. The front page of their earliest publication, i.e. No. 1, January 24–31, 1641/2, was composed in the style which I refer to as type 2. But on September 19, 1642 (perhaps owing to William Cook's death—he is not heard of after the middle of 1642), Samuel Pecke's pamphlet came out from a new bookseller. Francis Coles gave *A Perfect Diurnall* a novel front page, heading it, for the first time in journalism, with an allusive device.

There had already been from time to time royal or other devices in official proclamations and in a very exceptional title-page to a coranto,[1] but Coles equipped Pecke's *Diurnall* with a lively illustration (cf. Fig. 8) of the *House of Commons* in session. It was a notable departure and it was quickly followed, imitated in fact; and imitated, not, of course, because it was thought handsome, but because its use by Pecke gave it a goodwill-value. The copying of devices, formats, and above all of titles, which was practised in the seventeenth century, and for that matter in our own time, has for its motive the desire of the new-comers to exploit an existing goodwill. Further to distinguish his (and Pecke's) product from counterfeits, Coles next added a fine factotum initial whose decorative elements, consisting of a packet-ship flying a jack, a triton, the sun, moon and stars, filled a space 2 in. × 2 in. deep. It was used for the first time, according to my searches, on the issue of *A Perfect Diurnall* dated December 26–January 2, 1642/3. The competing pamphlet under the same title had been using a factotum[2] whose area was filled with two facing griffins, but Coles's ship device was copied and adopted in its place in the same January, 1643. Others followed. Bernard Alsop took it for his *Weekly Account* (No. 44, June 26, 1644). It equally figures on Andrew Coe's *Perfect Occurrences of Parliament* (No. 16, June 21, 1644) and George Bishop's *London Post* (No. 5, September 10, 1644).[3] Coles's original *A Perfect Diurnall* began the new year of 1645 by recutting the ship design and imposing a well-drawn capital T upon the whole composition, thus restricting its use to words commencing with that letter. The plagiarists continued to use the original factotum until the end of 1648.

Coles, for the safeguarding of his own and his readers' interests, also warned readers in a shoulder note of his pamphlet to 'Take heede of a false and scandalous Diurnal which is this day printed & fashioned with such a modell like this, by a company of grub-street mercenary fellowes; let this note bee your informer to distinguish them hereafter by the Printers' names[4] and the Booke-seller which are here nominated'.[5]

[1] E.g. F. L. and G. T.'s *True Diurnall* (No. 3, January 24–31, 1642) which is framed with a fine border embodying a large royal device with supporters (Burney, 12*a*, no. 8). A wood-engraved coat-of-arms occurs in Butter's Coranto, September 25, 1622.

[2] A factotum is an initial letter whose centre is pierced for the accommodation of any capital letter required.

[3] See our p. 31 for particulars of this periodical.

[4] J. Okes and Fr. Leach.

[5] This appears December 26, 1642. The adversaries replied in a following

The 'Commons' headpiece does not seem to have maintained its position in either the genuine or the counterfeit *Perfect Diurnall* for more than a few months. Reasons of space would certainly make it difficult to perpetuate a block of such scale. In time, similar reasons told against the more spectacular form of factotum. In the 1650's, though types were worn and initials small, space was not wasted, but in the 40's, where we are at the moment, large initials are not rare. The *Perfect Occurrences of Parliament: And Chief Collections of Letters of severall Victories*, etc., No. 4, August 30–September 6, 1644, published by Jane Coe, is an interesting exception to several rules. Its size is larger than the average and advantage is taken to employ an enormous factotum (of twenty-one lines pica in depth) whose design (cf. Fig. 9) is plainly drawn from the heading of Coles's *A Perfect Diurnall.*

This is, admittedly, an exceptional setting. No. 1 of *A Perfect Diurnall of some Passages in Parliament*, etc., printed for Francis Coles and Laurence Blaikelock (June 26–July 3, 1643) is a good example of mature conventional setting. The measure of the type area is at its maximum, though the paper size is not increased, and there are italic shoulder headings serving to some extent the purpose of our headlines.

A highly important, though inconspicuous, detail of setting shews itself in the composition of the front page of Robert Williamson's *A Perfect Diurnall of the Passages in Parliament From the eleventh of July, to the eighteenth of the said Month*, 1642 (cf. Fig. 10). This title is followed by an indication, printed between two rules, that the publication is

---

Printed for *Robert Williamson. July* 18.

The value of these rules to the composition is that they emphasise the name of the publisher and the date of publication. They are single rules, not double and thick-and-thin, as they were to become later, and have since continued, as an essential detail of the newspaper heading of our own day. It is not too much to say that the double and thick-and-thin transverse rules are

issue of their pamphlet by adjuring that the 'Courteous reader, be pleased to notice that this is the most approved Copie that hath passed the Presse, and that not done by a company of grub-street mercenary fellowes under any false or counterfeit names: be pleased, therefore, to distinguish this from other false copies by the names of Walt Cooke and Rob. Wood'. It would, in fact, seem that the counterfeit was itself counterfeited. Walt. Cook is probably a kinsman of Wm Cook of Furnival's Inn who died, or at least ceased business, in the summer of 1642. Robert Wood often prints his name in caps and smalls—perhaps to distinguish himself from Ralph Wood, the printer of ballads and other London popular literature.

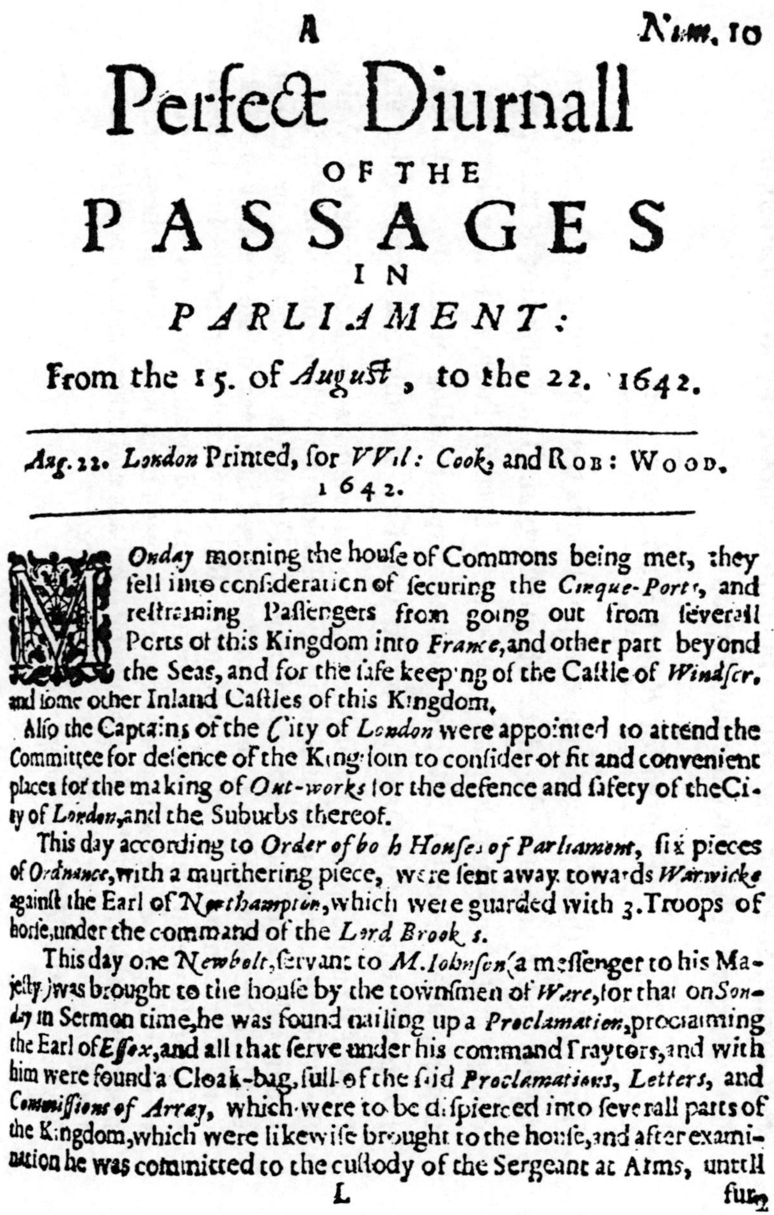

A Num. 10

Perfect Diurnall

OF THE

PASSAGES

IN

PARLIAMENT:

From the 15. of *Auguſt*, to the 22. 1642.

Aug. 22. *London* Printed, for *VVil: Cook*, and ROB: WOOD. 1642.

M*Onday* morning the houſe of Commons being met, they fell into conſideration of ſecuring the *Cinque-Ports*, and reſtraining Paſſengers from going out from ſeverall Ports of this Kingdom into *France*, and other part beyond the Seas, and for the ſafe keeping of the Caſtle of *Windſor*, and ſome other Inland Caſtles of this Kingdom,

Alſo the Captains of the City of *London* were appointed to attend the Committee for defence of the Kingdom to conſider of fit and convenient places for the making of *Out-works* for the defence and ſafety of the City of *London*, and the Suburbs thereof.

This day according to *Order of both Houſes of Parliament*, ſix pieces of *Ordnance*, with a murthering piece, were ſent away towards *Warwicke* againſt the Earl of *Northampton*, which were guarded with 3. Troops of horſe, under the command of the *Lord Brook's*.

This day one *Newbolt*, ſervant to *M. Iohnſon* (a meſſenger to his Majeſty) was brought to the houſe by the townſmen of *Ware*, for that on *Sonday* in Sermon time, he was found nailing up a *Proclamation*, proclaiming the Earl of *Eſſex*, and all that ſerve under his command Traytors, and with him were found a Cloak-bag, full of the ſaid *Proclamations*, *Letters*, and *Commiſſions of Array*, which were to be diſpierced into ſeverall parts of the Kingdom, which were likewiſe brought to the houſe, and after examination he was committed to the cuſtody of the Sergeant at Arms, untill

L fur-

Fig. 7. *Samuel Pecke's* Diurnall. (*For earlier examples of the use of rules for emphasis, cf. Figs.* 10–11)

Numb. 45

A PERFECT DIVRNALL OF THE PASSAGES IN PARLIAMENT.

From Munday the 17. of Aprill till Munday the 24. *Aprill.*

Collected by the ſame hand that formerly drew up the Copy for William Cooke *in Furnivals Inne. And now* Printed *by I. Okes and F. Leach and are to be ſold by* Francis Coles *in the Old Baily.*

Munday the 17. *of* Aprill 1643.

T He Lords and Commons taking into conſideration a late Proclamation dated at Oxford the firſt of this inſtant Aprill, for the holding and continuing of the Court of Chanchery and all proceedings herein the Receipt of his Majeſties Exchequer, and of the firſt fruits and tenthes, the Court of the Dutchies of Lancaſter, Court of wards, and Liveries, and Courts of Requeſts, at the City of Oxford for the whole Terme of Eaſter then next enſuing, and for the adjourning the Courts of Kings Bench, Common Pleas, and Exchequer from *Quindeva Paſche*, untill the returne of *Quinque Septianas Paſche*, next doe finde that it will much end to the prejudice of the Common-wealth to have the ſaid Courts and Receipts held and continued at Oxford where great part of an Army

Note that here is alſo a true and punctuall relation of the whole proceedings of the ſiedge at Reading for all the laſt weeke unto this preſent.

Fig. 8. *Later state of Samuel Pecke's* Diurnall

NUMB. 4

Perfect Occurrences

OF PARLIAMENT:

And Chief COLLEOTIONS of LETTERS of severall Victories; Obtained by

The Lord Generall.	Collonel *Sandys.*	Alisbury Forces.
Lieut. General *Middleton.*	Collonel *VVare.*	Cheshire Forces.
Major General *Whitbcot.*	Collonel *Gowre.*	Salisbury Forces.

The Kings Speech to Captain Blythe. *The Parliaments Message: A Copie of the* Palsgraves *speech to the* Lords *and* Commons. *The Queen sick again in* France, *and an Impost-hume broken under her right arm. A great victory at* Pomfret Castle, *obtained by* Collonel Sandys; *who hath kild a Lieutenant, and 4. others of quality, taken two of their chief Gunners, and other prisoners; wounded many, taken 100. sheep, and 40. oxen, and other perticulers thereof Also the Lord* Generall *relieved by Sea, and his beating of the Kings forces at* Blazey Bridge, *where were slain many of them; a* Collonel, 2. Captaines, *and others taken prisoners: and a Dam made to hinder the Enemy from relieving their forces at* Leslithcel *Castle. And new* Farthings *are not put down, but the abuse to be remedied.*

From Friday the 30. of *August*, to Friday the 6. of *September* 1644.

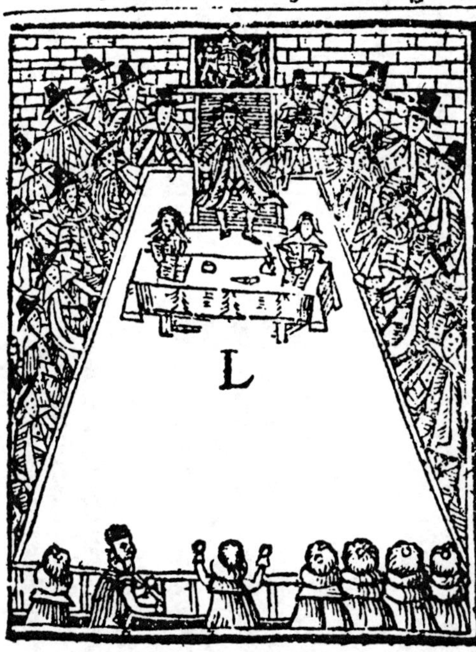

FRIDAY. August. 30.

Look about you brave spirits of London; if you go to Oxford, *Rupert* hath sent Colonel *Bu.rly* his Pastrey Cook thither, that hath trust up Citizens of London there for Spies, and hath sent his Nurse hither; I hope some these Spies will be found out here, it would vex you to have your throates cut, and to be Massacred on a suddain, when you dream not of it; well, for all the malice of the Enemy and all their plots and projects, I hope God will protect us.

For newes I finde in the collections in the first place, that the King was eight dayes before, for certain at the Lord *Mohuns* house in Cornwall, and that his forces are at the least 30000. but not half fitly armed to fight.

Captain *Blythe* came this day to town, who was taken at the Lady *Mohuns* house; and we are informed, that when he was brought before the King, his Majestie asked him, why hee would take up Arms against him? who answered his Majestie, that he did never take up Arms against his Majesties person: O! (said the King) *that is a mist ry you have.* But the truth of it is, that it is a mistery, and a misterie of iniquity, to pretend to settle the Protestant Religion, by the Priests, Jesuites, and Papists, that are in armes against the Parliament.

This Captain *Blythe*, is come up to see if he can be exchanged, and to labour the exchange of the Rest of the commanders that were taken with him. Judge *Mallet* is propounded to be exchanged, the very same man that was so violent in judgement against Master *Henry Walker*, for the Petition to the King of, *To your tents, O Israel, &c.* The Judges malignant faction, reported it to be because he was a Tub-preacher, as they called him; but the Judge knew well enough that false. Here followeth a true copie of Master *Walkers* Petition to the King, for which he suffered. D To

Fig. 9. *Jane Coe's* Perfect Occurrences

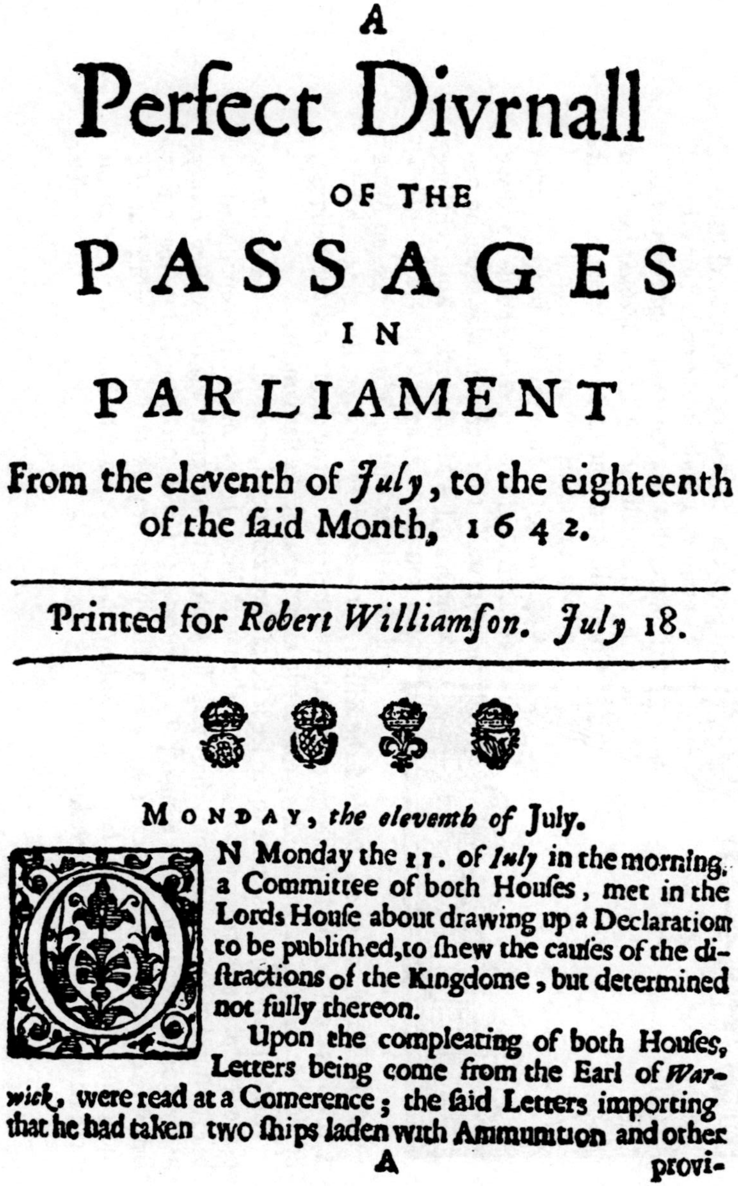

A

Perfect Divrnall

OF THE

PASSAGES

IN

PARLIAMENT

From the eleventh of *July*, to the eighteenth of the ſaid Month, 1642.

Printed for *Robert Williamſon*. *July* 18.

MONDAY, *the eleventh of* July.

ON Monday the 11. of *July* in the morning, a Committee of both Houſes, met in the Lords Houſe about drawing up a Declaration to be publiſhed, to ſhew the cauſes of the diſtractions of the Kingdome, but determined not fully thereon.

Upon the compleating of both Houſes, Letters being come from the Earl of *Warwick*, were read at a Conference; the ſaid Letters importing that he had taken two ſhips laden with Ammunition and other

A provi-

Fig. 10. *Shewing early use of rules to emphasize the proprietor's name*

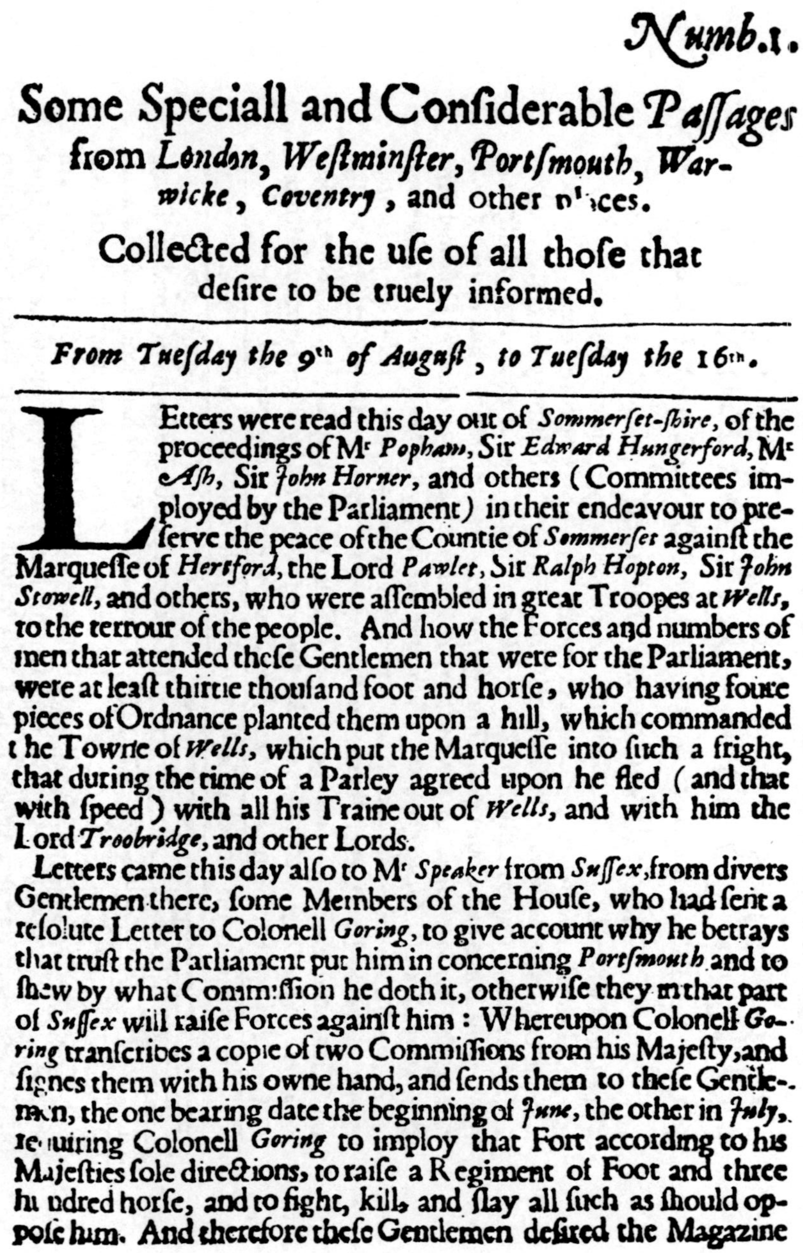

*Numb.*1.

Some Speciall and Conſiderable *Paſſages* from *London*, *Weſtminſter*, *Portſmouth*, *Warwicke*, *Coventry*, and other places.

Collected for the uſe of all thoſe that deſire to be truely informed.

From Tueſday the 9th of Auguſt, to Tueſday the 16th.

LEtters were read this day out of *Sommerſet-ſhire*, of the proceedings of Mr *Popham*, Sir *Edward Hungerford*, Mr *Aſh*, Sir *John Horner*, and others (Committees imployed by the Parliament) in their endeavour to preſerve the peace of the Countie of *Sommerſet* againſt the Marqueſſe of *Hertford*, the Lord *Pawlet*, Sir *Ralph Hopton*, Sir *John Stowell*, and others, who were aſſembled in great Troopes at *Wells*, to the terrour of the people. And how the Forces and numbers of men that attended theſe Gentlemen that were for the Parliament, were at leaſt thirtie thouſand foot and horſe, who having foure pieces of Ordnance planted them upon a hill, which commanded the Towne of *Wells*, which put the Marqueſſe into ſuch a fright, that during the time of a Parley agreed upon he fled (and that with ſpeed) with all his Traine out of *Wells*, and with him the Lord *Troobridge*, and other Lords.

Letters came this day alſo to Mr *Speaker* from *Suſſex*, from divers Gentlemen there, ſome Members of the Houſe, who had ſent a reſolute Letter to Colonell *Goring*, to give account why he betrays that truſt the Parliament put him in concerning *Portſmouth* and to ſhew by what Commiſſion he doth it, otherwiſe they in that part of *Suſſex* will raiſe Forces againſt him: Whereupon Colonell *Goring* tranſcribes a copie of two Commiſſions from his Majeſty, and ſignes them with his owne hand, and ſends them to theſe Gentlemen, the one bearing date the beginning of *June*, the other in *July*, requiring Colonell *Goring* to imploy that Fort according to his Majeſties ſole directions, to raiſe a Regiment of Foot and three hundred horſe, and to fight, kill, and ſlay all ſuch as ſhould oppoſe him. And therefore theſe Gentlemen deſired the Magazine

Fig. 11. *H. Blunden's 'Passages,' 1642 with rules used to emphasize the date* more characteristic of contemporary newspaper style than even the black-letter text of the title.

Hence the two rules on Robert Williamson's *Perfect Diurnall* are the earliest form of a convention which has never been since broken—though there have been variations, as we shall see in the course of this enquiry. Another interesting feature of the same front page is the inclusion of the badges of England, Scotland, Ireland and France—cast, it seems, upon type bodies of about canon size.

The term 'Diurnall' is little used after the middle of 1642, though there was an *Exact Diurnall* published in 1644. 'Passages', as we have noted, seemed a more convenient designation, and, as 'Diurnall' lapsed, 'Passages' abounded. Moreover, Parliamentary transactions, though the first permitted forms, were the least domestic. In 1638, Licensers of the Press were established to oversee the productions of the Press, and as these widened in interest, the word 'Diurnall' became unsuitable as being too closely identified with the records of purely Commons activities or debates.

But the Great Rebellion necessarily created a market for accounts of Battles or Passages, whether in or out of Parliament; and the provision, under licence, of secular news, gradually brought into existence a news-pamphlet offering accounts or 'passages' from outside London.

§ 3 PASSAGES

No. 1 of *Some Speciall and Considerable Passages*, published on August 16, 1642, by H. Blunden, collected, as the run-on of the title indicates, particulars 'from London, Westminster, Portsmouth, Warwicke, Coventry, and other places'. This front page (cf. Fig. 11) exhibits a simple economy of material and space. The date-line is enclosed between rules in Williamson's manner.

Today nobody would regard Hansard as a newspaper, nor would the *London Gazette* content an appetite formed by the perusal of even the least enterprising of our weekly journals. Consequently, every one of the Corantos, Diurnalls, Passages, Continuations, etc. which we have noted must be regarded as the immediate forerunners of journalism as we understand it, and certainly not as newspapers in the genuine sense of the word. And thus Blunden's *Some Speciall and Considerable Passages* (Fig. 11), though a notable step forward, is but a rudimentary news-book.

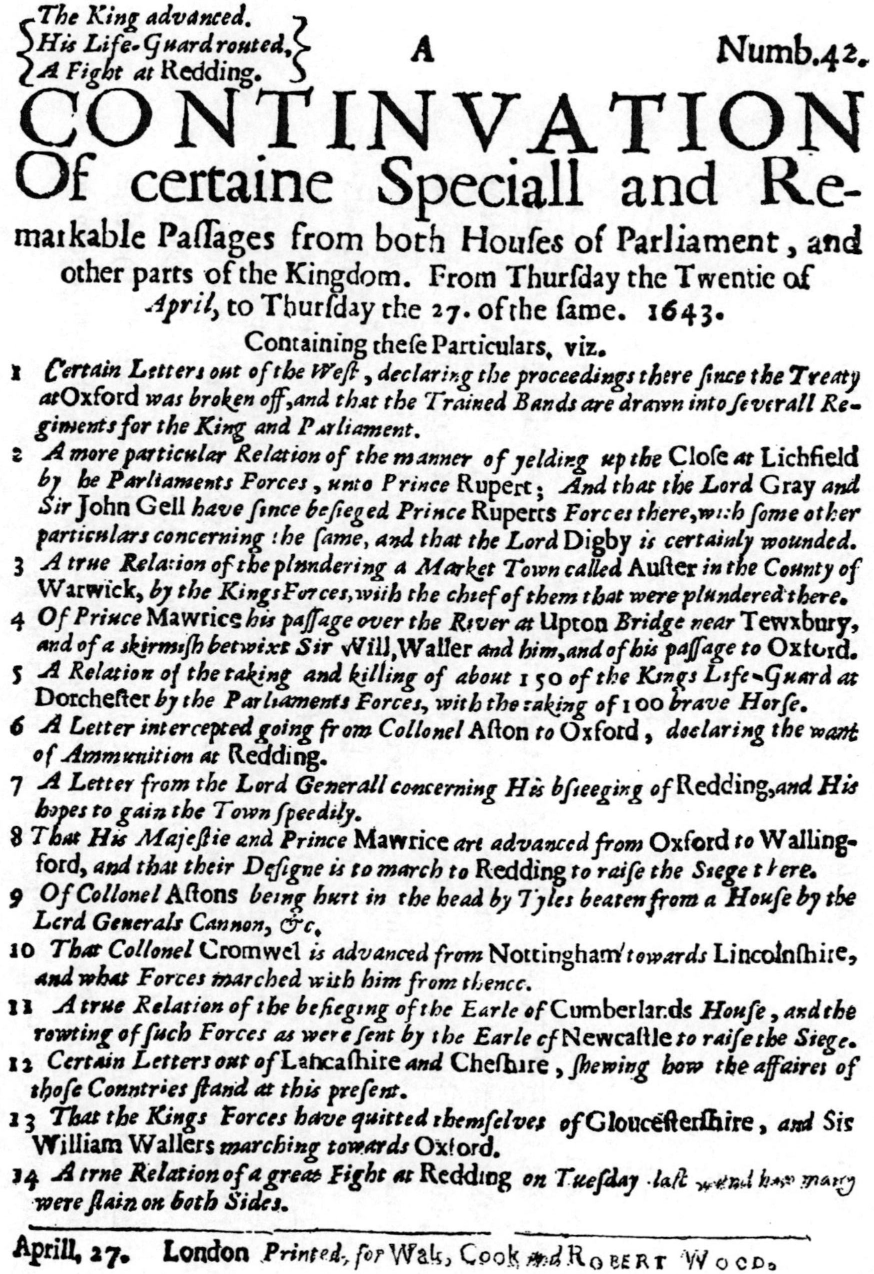

The King advanced.
His Life-Guard routed.
A Fight at Redding.

A

Numb.42.

CONTINVATION
Of certaine Speciall and Re-
markable Passages from both Houses of Parliament, and other parts of the Kingdom. From Thursday the Twentie of *April*, to Thursday the 27. of the same. 1643.

Containing these Particulars, viz.

1 *Certain Letters out of the West, declaring the proceedings there since the Treaty at* Oxford *was broken off, and that the Trained Bands are drawn into severall Regiments for the King and Parliament.*

2 *A more particular Relation of the manner of yelding up the* Close *at* Lichfield *by the Parliaments Forces, unto Prince* Rupert; *And that the Lord* Gray *and Sir* John Gell *have since besieged Prince* Ruperts *Forces there, with some other particulars concerning the same, and that the Lord* Digby *is certainly wounded.*

3 *A true Relation of the plundering a Market Town called* Auster *in the County of* Warwick, *by the Kings Forces, with the chief of them that were plundered there.*

4 *Of Prince* Mawrice *his passage over the River at* Upton Bridge *near* Tewxbury, *and of a skirmish betwixt Sir* Will. Waller *and him, and of his passage to* Oxford.

5 *A Relation of the taking and killing of about 150 of the Kings Life-Guard at* Dorchester *by the Parliaments Forces, with the taking of 100 brave Horse.*

6 *A Letter intercepted going from Collonel* Aston *to* Oxford, *declaring the want of Ammunition at* Redding.

7 *A Letter from the Lord Generall concerning His bsieeging of* Redding, *and His hopes to gain the Town speedily.*

8 *That His Majestie and Prince* Mawrice *are advanced from* Oxford *to* Wallingford, *and that their Designe is to march to* Redding *to raise the Siege there.*

9 *Of Collonel* Astons *being hurt in the head by Tyles beaten from a House by the Lord Generals Cannon, &c.*

10 *That Collonel* Cromwel *is advanced from* Nottingham *towards* Lincolnshire, *and what Forces marched with him from thence.*

11 *A true Relation of the besieging of the Earle of* Cumberlands *House, and the rowting of such Forces as were sent by the Earle of* Newcastle *to raise the Siege.*

12 *Certain Letters out of* Lancashire *and* Cheshire, *shewing how the affaires of those Countries stand at this present.*

13 *That the Kings Forces have quitted themselves of* Gloucestershire, *and Sir* William Wallers *marching towards* Oxford.

14 *A true Relation of a great Fight at* Redding *on Tuesday last* wh and how many *were slain on both Sides.*

April, 27. London *Printed, for* Wal. Cook *and* ROBERT WOOD.

Fig. 12. *Shewing news-ear in left-hand top corner, and summary in the body of the title-page*

OCTOB. 16. 1644.

Numb. 1.

Perfect Passages
OF
Each Dayes Proceedings
IN
PARLIAMENT:

From Wednesday Octob. 16. to Wednesday Octob. 23. 1644.

The particulars of the fight between the King and Sir W Waller *at Andover, certified by Letters from Sir* W. Waller, *and Sir* Arth. Hazzlerig. *The Kings Proclamation touching his coming to London. Articles about the surrender of Leverpool. A party of the Kings Horse defeated by the Garrison of Poole, many slaine, 11. Commanders, and 100. others taken. The enemies Garrison at Halton in Yorkeshire taken. Two defeats given the enemy, one at Belvoir, the other at Grantham. Col.* Masseyes *victory, certified in a Letter from dimself to M. Speaker. The great preparations to the great Battell, supposed to be fought this day.*

WEDNESDAY. *Octob.* 16.

A Letter came this day to London by the Post from Sir *William Wallers* Army, dated at Salisbury, certifying, that the King had commanded his men off from the sieges at Poole, Lyme, and Wareham, and other parts in the West, to march along with him in a full Body, and all together to march in a Battalia against Sir *William Waller*, expecting to gaine an opportunity to fall upon him before any strength come to him, and to rout and disperse him. Sir *William* hereupon set Scouts, and carefull Watches about his Quarters, to discover the approach of the Kings Forces, if they came.

By Letters from France it is certified, that *Wil. Crofts* the Queenes great Favourite his brother, upon some displeasure conceived against him by little *Jeffreys* the Queens Dwarfe, with her in France, was by him slaine, this brother being Captain of the Queens Life-guard, and Master of her horse.

A It

Fig. 13. *Printed by R. Austin with royal factotum. The initials C R were removed later*

The contents of Walter Cook and Robert Wood's *A Continuation of certaine Speciall and Remarkable Passages,* etc. may perhaps be counted as a closer approximation to the modern political newspaper, since its pages printed not only descriptions of sieges and battles, but letters and diplomatic happenings. The first page in No. 42, by listing no fewer than fourteen numbered headings, makes necessary a return to the title-page. A new feature (to use modern parlance) is the left-hand news-ear (cf. Fig. 12) of three italic lines enclosed in a pair of braces, so:

The King advanced.
His Life-Guard routed,
A Fight at Redding.

A weak feature in the composition is the burial of the day of the week of issue among the mass of upper- and lower-case concluding the long title and sub-title matter which still held an unchallenged position at the head of 'Passages' as it had of 'Diurnalls' and 'Corantos'. This masking of the date of issue seems to have been noted, for, a little laconically, 'Aprill, 27.' (without day of the week, or year) appears in front of the imprint below a rule at the foot of the title-page.

A less cumbrous title was printed on the front page of Bernard Alsop's periodical; while the sub-title retained the conventional lines describing the contents 'Certain Special and Remarkable Passages . . . Kingdome'. But, note well, the main heading was not 'Continuation' or 'Diurnall', but three simple and clear words, '*The* WEEKLY *Account, Containing,* etc.' There is at the head of No. 36 an ear of six lines of roman. The date, precisely stated with day of the week and the year, is in italics between single rules to the full measure of the page. The front page of a later number of *The Weekly Account,* No. 43, June 25, is of interest. The serial number and date are

The Weekly Account. Num. 43 / Iune. 25.

placed together but conspicuously in the upper right-hand corner, the three main items of news are summarised below the title, and the stolen factotum of Pecke's packet ship introduces the text. Alsop's management of this piece of typographical property was extremely careless, for almost every month he contrived to print the initial either upside down (No. 20, 1644) or sideways (December 11, 1644). I am not competent to indulge in deductions as to the order of printing from these accidents, but it is inconceivable that the occurrences of the beginning of the week would be hurriedly set, however urgent became the setting of delayed end-of-the-week news.

Another factotum was used elsewhere in 1644. No. 1 (October 23, 1644) of *Perfect Passages of Each Dayes Proceedings in Parliament* was a handsomely produced weekly issuing from the press of Robert Austin,[1] on Wednesdays. Its front page carried an italic summary in paragraph form immediately below a date line set between single rules to the full measure, and the text began with a wood engraving of the royal device of a rose, with centre pierced for the accommodation of a great primer initial. It is a finely designed, well-cut block. The provision of a lion and unicorn lend majesty to an ordered composition. The initials C R are cut out in the issue for October 8–15, 1645. The setting and printing of the text shew an improved standard of craftsmanship, and the display of the titular matter is as clear and as simple as the single sentence to which the name has at last been brought. Avoiding such clichés as 'Diurnall', 'Remarkable', 'Speciall', the complete title reads *Perfect Passages of Each Dayes Proceedings in Parliament* (cf. Fig. 13).

§ 4 MERCURIES

The titular—and very accurate—word 'Passages', whose significance must seem somewhat obscure to us at the present day, gave place to a symbolic description. The word 'Mercurius' occurs first in the imprint, but not in the name, of one of Archer's Corantos, i.e. for April 7, 1625. As a titular word it antedates the succinctly named *Weekly Account*. It figures for the first time in the Oxford-printed[2] royalist pamphlet dated January 8, 1643.

Aulicus avoided the set form of the puritan pamphlets by placing a strip of flowers over the top of the two simply set lines of the title. This, the most dignified of the Mercuries, was published on Sundays, doubtless for the purpose of registering its protest against the puritan sabbatarianising of that day. At first *Mercurius Aulicus* adhered to the strictest book-conventions, including the outside title-page, but in No. 3 the title-page was omitted. This first of all the Mercuries ceased publication with the issue of March 4, 1646.

[1] Austin, it will be recalled, was the printer of the counterfeit *Perfect Diurnall* issued by Walt. Cook and Robt. Wood, with the headpiece and factotum imitated from the true paper edited by Pecke, printed by Okes and Leach for Fr. Coles.

[2] *Mercurius Aulicus* also had a London edition.

The *Mercurius Academicus* (1645, cf. Fig. 14), political successor to *Mercurius Aulicus*, printed equally at Oxford, alone retains the strict book convention by having a line of flowers at its head and the two simple lines of its title over the text which begins with a six-line decorated initial.

A more interesting publication was the second in order of time. *Mercurius Civicus* was a Thursday publication and ran from May 1643 (No. 1, May 4–11) until December 10, 1646. Its complete title, under an ear (roman or italic), was *Mercurius Civicus.* | *Londons Intelligencer.* | *or,* | *Truth impartially related from thence to* | *the whole Kingdome, to prevent mis-information.* It carried a serial number in the extreme upper right-hand corner and a date between rules between the last line of title and the first of the text, which began with a plain three-line initial. The pagination, like that of most of the Mercuries, ran throughout the yearly volume. To return to *Mercurius Civicus*,[1] a unique feature of the setting of its front pages are the portraits. King Charles and Queen Henrietta Maria appear (cf. Fig. 16) on the front page of No. 8, July 13–20, 1643. No. 11 is headed with the portrait of the king only. It is an important issue, for on the fourth page (i.e. p. 84, as the pamphlet was folioed in continuation) there is a wood-cut illustration, *in the text*, below a paragraph describing weapons, of a useful stock, with an 'oval or round top, stuck full of iron spikes. The forme whereof for better satisfaction is here set down', and the block follows. This weapon is alleged to be a favourite with the Papists who call them 'Round-heads, for that with them they intended to bring the Roundheads into subjection'.[2]

The same Mercury gives a lively portrait of Prince Rupert on the front page of its forty-first number, and there are other subjects as publication progressed. The regularity of this feature entitles *Civicus* to rank as the earliest English illustrated news-pamphlet. It was also the first journal to use 'London' in its sub-title.

A battered block of King Charles, very similar to (if not identical with) that of No. 6 of *Civicus*, is printed at the side of an italic summary at the head of the front page of No. 38 (January 17, 1645/6) of '*The true Informer:* |

[1] Printed for John Wright and Thomas Bates, whose imprint is at the tail of the final page.

[2] This is not a little curious, for the identical block is used on the title-page of No. 6 of the same periodical where it certainly makes a very fine appearance flanking an ear whose first line reads 'The Papists Roundhead found is'. The text describes this pole 'or staffe' as '12 foot long with a round knob at the end of it stoven full of sharpe Pikes...which if they hit any way it is present death. This is the weapon with which the Papists would have set up the Protestant Religion by subduing the Protestants of the country' (p. 44, June 16, 1643 (cf. Fig. 15)).

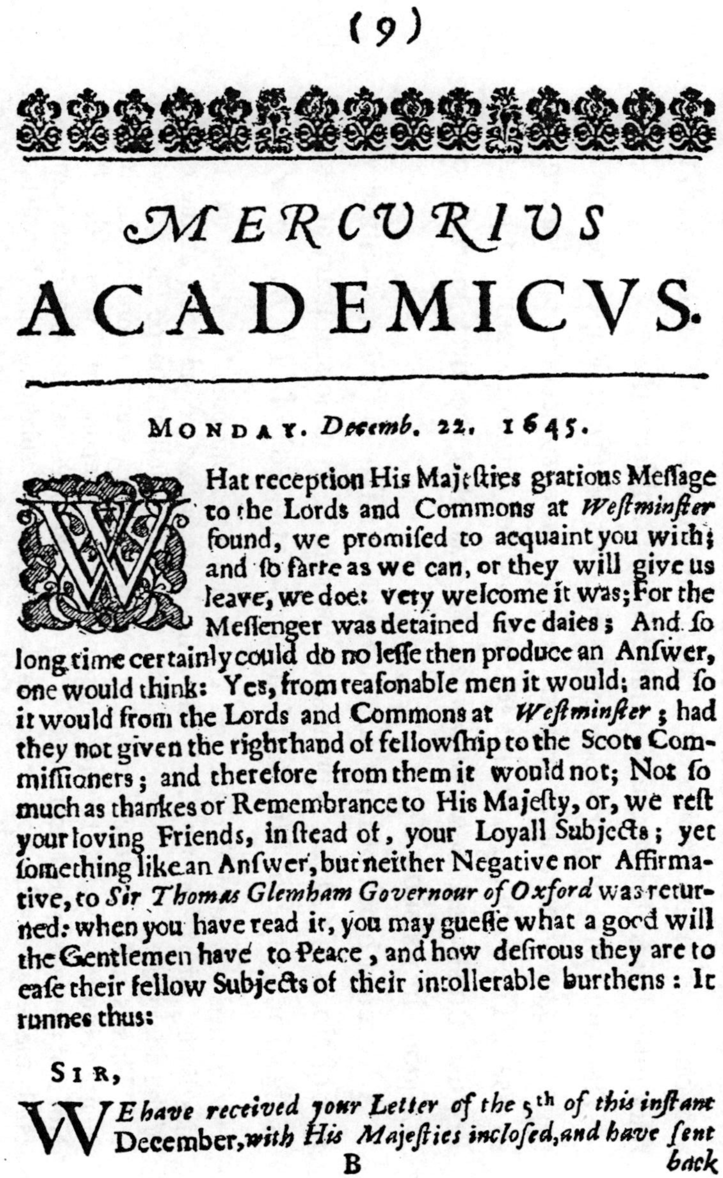

(9)

MERCURIUS
ACADEMICUS.

MONDAY. Decemb. 22. 1645.

WHat reception His Majesties gratious Message to the Lords and Commons at *Westminster* found, we promised to acquaint you with; and so farre as we can, or they will give us leave, we doe: very welcome it was; For the Messenger was detained five daies; And so long time certainly could do no lesse then produce an Answer, one would think: Yes, from reasonable men it would; and so it would from the Lords and Commons at *Westminster*; had they not given the righthand of fellowship to the Scots Commissioners; and therefore from them it would not; Not so much as thankes or Remembrance to His Majesty, or, we rest your loving Friends, in stead of, your Loyall Subjects; yet something like an Answer, but neither Negative nor Affirmative, to *Sir Thomas Glemham Governour of Oxford* was returned: when you have read it, you may guesse what a good will the Gentlemen have to Peace, and how desirous they are to ease their fellow Subjects of their intollerable burthens: It runnes thus:

SIR,

WE have received your Letter of the 5th of this instant December, *with His Majesties inclosed, and have sent back*

B

Fig. 14. *Front page of the (Oxford printed)* Merc. Academicus

(41)

The Papists Roundhead found is,
The Earle of *Antrim* taken is,
And *Wheatley* Bridge gained is,

Numb. 6.

Mercurius Civicus.

Londons Intelligencer.

OR,

Truth impartially related from thence to the whole Kingdome, to prevent mis-information.

From *Thursday, June* 8. to *Friday, June* 16. 1643.

1. IN my last weeks intelligence concerning *Oxford* occurents, I related the devices which many Carriers had to releeve the Cavaleers, and to convey things to them, which course it seemes is not yet stopped: on Thursday last, two carts full of severall commodities were carried to *Woodstocke*, which were brought from *London* by severall Carriers: Also divers packs with Paper (for *Mercurius Aulicus* to vent his falsities and querks in) came into *Oxford*, which were brought from *London* by long *Compton* Carrier. It is likewise observed that many who formerly had but two horses laden, go now with six into those parts, so that it

F

Fig. 15. *Front page of Thomas Bates's* Merc. Civicus

containing | A perfect Collection of the Proceedings in | Parliament, and true Information | from the Armies: |'. It was a Saturday publication[1] also from the press of Thomas Bates, printer of *Mercurius Civicus*. The date of *The true Informer* (cf. Fig. 17) is given between two full-measured rules as

For the whole Week past, ending Saturday Jan. 17. 1645.

When Bates started this, his second adventure, he gave its outside title-page a flower border. Unlike most of his fellows, Bates possessed a fine range of typographical material collected for the decoration and illustration of lampoons, ballads and the like which he formerly issued in partnership with John Wright.

The news-periodical most familiar to the public in the period 1643–7 was the Mercury. *Mercurius Britannicus*, *Mercurius Veridicus*, *Mercurius Pragmaticus* and the rest differ only in the display of the upper half of the first page. The style of the body of the Mercuries was that of the Diurnalls—plain, straightforward. The front pages, with the exceptions noted, lacked devices, decorative factotums or any relief to their puritanical aspect. The date line is invariably within rules, and the serial number is invariably in the upper right-hand corner. The placing of the title is invariable, but the founts of type used shew either a wide latitude of choice or that some printers only possessed small type. The title of *Mercurius Britannicus* represents a type to which *Mercurius Elencticus*, *Mercurius Politicus* (up to 1650) conform. The latin line is in upper- and lower-case italic about 16-point in size. *Mercurius Veridicus*, *Mercurius Publicus* and *Mercurius Politicus* (1659) enlarged this line and set it in roman. *Mercurius Pragmaticus* sets its name in two lines.

As a whole, the Mercuries must be rated a dull-looking lot. One is tempted to think that they were printed recklessly because they were bought recklessly, on the principle that one Mercury was no better than another. If the possession of distinguishing features was an advantage, the printer, for example, of *Mercurius Elencticus*, seems perversely to have ignored his opportunity to distinguish his product. *Mercurius Melancholicus*, an exception to the general rule, printed a verse at the beginning of its text; and, unlike *Mercurius Pragmaticus* which also carried verses, *Melancholicus* printed them on a crude title-page with blank verso.[2]

1 While *Civicus* was a Thursday.

2 *Melancholicus*, a royalist Mercury, was soon assailed by political enemies, *teste* the imprint to No. 3 which concludes: 'The Booke that came out yesterday under this Title is counterfeit'.

(57)

The KING *and* QUEENE *conjoyned,*
The Kentish news related,
Our Forces are united,
A publique Fast appointed.

Numb. 8

M R C R

Mercurius Civicus.

LONDONS

INTELLIGENCER.

OR,

Truth impartially related from thence to the whole Kingdome, to prevent mis-information.

From *Thursday, July* 13. to *Thursday. July* 20. 1643.

WHereas it is the generall expectation and desire of most people to be informed of the true state of the Army under the command of his Excellency the Parliaments Lord Generall; It will not therefore be amisse in the first place to impart something of the late intelligence from thence, which was informed by Letters from *Steny-stratford*, to this effect, That on Saturday last, being the 15 of

H *July*

Fig. 16. *Bates's* Merc. Civicus

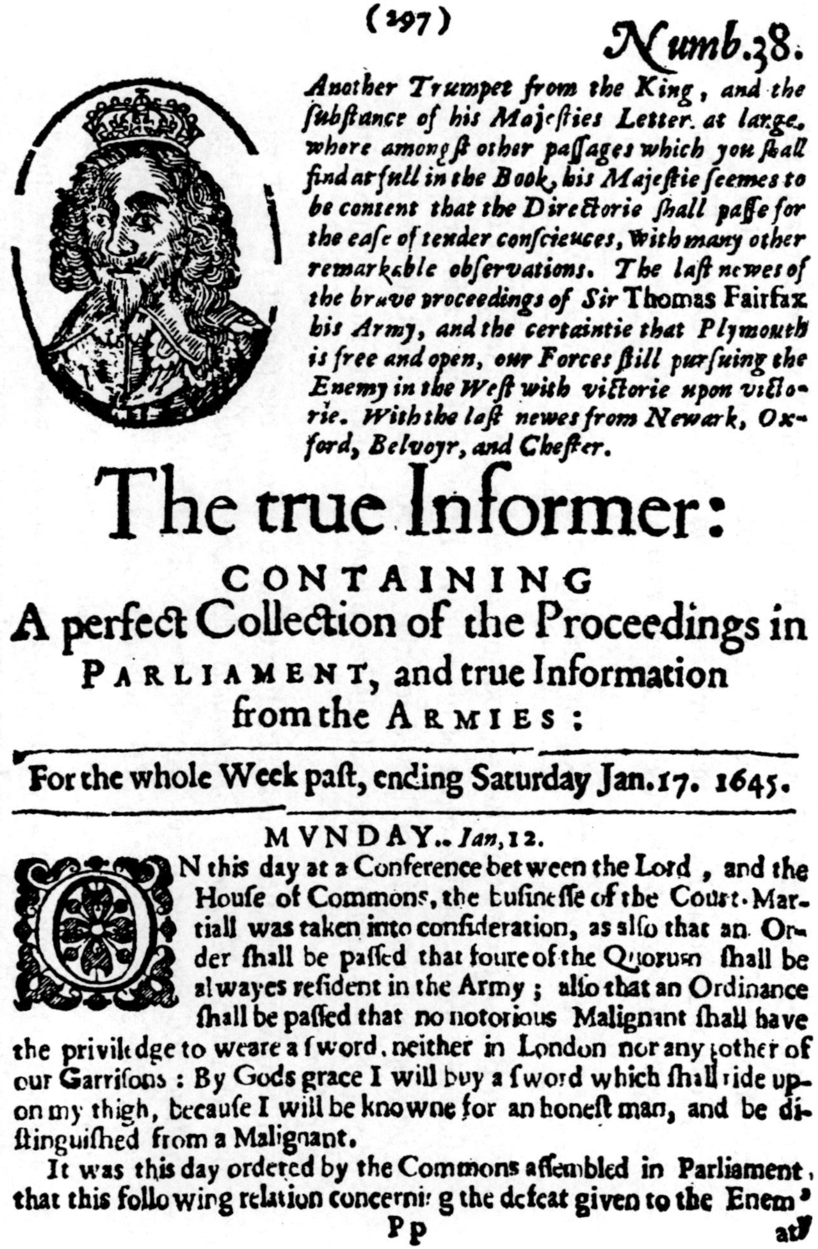

(297)

Numb. 38.

Another Trumpet from the King, and the substance of his Majesties Letter at large, where amongst other passages which you shall find at full in the Book, his Majestie seemes to be content that the Directorie shall passe for the ease of tender consciences, with many other remarkable observations. The last newes of the brave proceedings of Sir Thomas Fairfax *his Army, and the certaintie that Plymouth is free and open, our Forces still pursuing the Enemy in the West with victorie upon victorie. With the last newes from Newark, Oxford, Belvoyr, and Chester.*

The true Informer:

CONTAINING

A perfect Collection of the Proceedings in PARLIAMENT, and true Information from the ARMIES:

For the whole Week past, ending Saturday Jan. 17. 1645.

MVNDAY.. *Jan*, 12.

ON this day at a Conference between the Lord, and the House of Commons, the businesse of the Court-Martiall was taken into consideration, as also that an Order shall be passed that foure of the Quorum shall be alwayes resident in the Army; also that an Ordinance shall be passed that no notorious Malignant shall have the priviledge to weare a sword, neither in London nor any other of our Garrisons: By Gods grace I will buy a sword which shall ride upon my thigh, because I will be knowne for an honest man, and be distinguished from a Malignant.

It was this day ordered by the Commons assembled in Parliament, that this following relation concerning the defeat given to the Enem

Pp at

Fig. 17. *Bates's* True Informer

One or other of the Mercuries were published on every day of the week but Sunday (*Aulicus* and *Academicus* excepting). *Aulicus* ceased in 1645; *Academicus* ceased, apparently, at the end of 1646. From 1647 there were no Saturday journals.[1]

§ 5 INTELLIGENCERS

'Mercury' as a titular word had no great length of life. Its presence in the title of an indispensable literary monthly of the present day is due to a happy revival and not to any natural succession from the seventeenth century. It held a dominating position for some years, when it was menaced—at first in a sub-title. *Mercurius Civicus* uses the word in its secondary title 'or, Londons Intelligencer'. As a name in its own right, it occurs first in *The Kingdomes Weekly Intelligencer: sent abroad to prevent mis-information,* which is dated between two full-measure rules, December 27 (1642) to January 3 (1643), and has the imprint at the tail of the final page of G. Bishop and R. White (cf. Fig. 18).

The unlucky *Daily Intelligencer of Court, City and County,* January 30, 1643, cannot count as a daily since it only made one issue. *The Compleate Intelligencer and Resolver* (November 1643) was the next. Thereafter, 'Intelligence' appeared regularly in the descriptions of newly-established periodicals. Thus, Daniel Border's pamphlet printed for him by Bernard Alsop claimed to communicate the 'choisest and most Remarkable Intelligence from all parts of the Kingdome', etc. In 1645 there is a short-lived *Exchange Intelligencer,* secondly *The Moderate Intelligencer* which lived until October 4, 1649, and in 1647 a few numbers were issued of a *Moderne Intelligencer.* All these pamphlets were composed upon the typographical model of *The Kingdomes Weekly Intelligencer.* This pamphlet ceased in October 1649. Thus, at the beginning of 1650, the curious had still a Diurnall, a Mercury (Pragmaticus) and a Proceedings, but no Intelligencer. Then *Perfect Passages of Every Daies Intelligence* came out—at the beginning of July—and, perhaps somewhat encouraged by this, 'the hand which formerly drew up the

[1] The only publication which used a day of the week in its title was *A Tuesdaies Journall of Perfect Passages in Parliament* edited by Henry Walker and published by Robert Ibbitson (No. 1, July 23, 1649). It is a very handsome piece composed after a continental model with a well-designed circular commonwealth device at the head. It ran for two months. Walker earlier wrote a pamphlet with the title of *Perfect Occurrences of Every Daie Journall in Parliament,* etc., which used a specific factotum device. It ran until October 9, 1649 (cf. Fig. 21).

"Kingdomes Weekly Intelligencer"' began *The Weekly Intelligencer of the Commonwealth*, the printing of which was confided to R. Austin. Three other ill-starred Intelligencers were started in 1655. The original weekly ceased September 24, 1655, with the suppression of all the licensed presses by Cromwell. On October 8, Marchamont Needham brought out, under the supervision of John Thurlow, *The Publick Intelligencer. Communicating the chief Occurrences and Proceedings within the dominions of England, Scotland and Ireland. Together with an Account of the affaires from severall parts of Europe.* This work continued until April 9, 1660. It was an official publication made desirable by the suppression of the press in September 1655, and its publication was made on Mondays. The old-established *Mercurius Politicus*, a Thursday journal which made its first appearance on June 13, 1650, continued its career until April 12, 1660, as an official organ, surviving the Cromwellian decree of 1655. The intimate relations between the *Politicus* and *Intelligencer* made possible an exchange of text, so that the two pamphlets repeat each other. During 1656 and 1658 these were the only two news-pamphlets available to the public.

Cromwell died on September 3, 1658, and when in 1659 new foundations and old revivals appeared, there came a new *Weekly Intelligencer of the Commonwealth*, a new *Weekly Account*, and *Occurrences from Foreign Parts*. In 1660 many Mercuries were re-issued, and, in addition to these familiar titles, there came another revived series of pamphlets bearing a title, which, in one portion or combination, was destined to descend to our own day.

§ 6 POSTS

The history of the various pamphlets calling themselves "Posts" takes us back from the 1660's to the 40's. On November 9, 1643, John Hammond, printer, 'over against St Andrews Church in Holborne', printed the first number of *The Kingdomes weekly Post, with his packet of Letters, publishing his message to the City and Country.* Although this distinguished piece, bearing on its front page a decent 2¼ in. × 3 in. cut of a mounted postman blaring his horn, did not survive the following January (1643–4), the aptness of the title *Post* was too obvious to be missed. Bernard Alsop issued a *Flying Post*, in the May of that year, which also carried a block of a horsed postman blowing his horn. In August, John Rushworth wrote for George Bishop, *The*

London Post. This pamphlet existed until March 4, 1645; its early numbers carried a fine mounted post-boy with the towns of New Castle, Scarbourowe, Barwick, London and Edenburowe in the background of the cut. It was a large block, impossible to use when there was pressure of space. Hence No. 5 did not carry a 'Post', on horseback or otherwise, contenting itself with the old ship factotum invented by William Cook (cf. Fig. 19).

After the cessation of *The London Post,* George Bishop published *The Weekly Post Master* for a month (ceased May 6, 1645) and *The Parliament's Post* (May 13–October 6, 1645). At the turn of the year, there came, on Mondays, *The Citties weekly Post* (No. 1, December 15–22, 1645, until March 3, 1646), printed in ordinary Diurnall or Mercury style (cf. Fig. 20). At the end of 1646 *The London Post* was revived by Rushworth for some thirteen months. After this there came a spate of Mercuries and Intelligencers, but no more Posts until *The Faithful Post* of George Horton appeared in 1653. This much-metamorphosed journal became *Great Britain's Post, The Politique Post* and *The Grand Politique Post.* Finally, as *The Weekly Post,* it continued until January 19, 1655, but then there was a gap of more than two score years before a Post came back permanently into the list of English periodicals. *The Flying Post,* printed for John Salusbury at the Rising Sun, was not founded until 1695. Since then the 'Post' has never been absent from London journalism.

§ 7 SPIES, SCOUTS, &c.

To follow, here and now, the story of the successive Posts in the period after 1665 would be to anticipate. We have yet to notice one or two other types issued after 1644 in order to preserve a chronological understanding of the several groups of these news-pamphlets.

The Spie, communicating Intelligence from Oxford (January 30–June 25, 1644), whose title was also used in the eighteenth century, and *The Parliament Scout: communicating His Intelligence to the Kingdome,* a Thursday publication, of which the first number was dated June 20–27, 1643. *The Parliament Scout,* printed by George Bishop and R. White, flourished until January 30, 1645. *The Citie Scout,* with a bordered outside title (cf. Fig. 23), listing five items, lasted only for four months. In addition to Spie, Scout, several varieties of Messenger and Informer purveyed news to the kingdom. As, typographically, all were in the style and make-up of the Mercuries, they need not be studied here in detail—only their names are of interest.

(599)

Numb. 75.

A teſtimoniall of the valiant acts of the Plimouth *Regiment. The King moves not towards* Oxford. *Four Northern Counties entring into Aſſociation.* Crowland *Abby ſaid to be loſt. Two Popes of* Rome *choſen. The Archbiſhop of* Canterbury *to come to his laſt Triall. Propoſitions of Peace almoſt finiſhed. Colonell* Ware, *and Colonell* Urrey *two revolters, are come in againe to the Parliament with ſhame.*

THE KINGDOMES Weekly Intelligencer:

SENT ABROAD
To prevent miſ-information.

From *Tueſday* the 1. of *Octber*, to *Tueſday* the 8. of *October*, 1644.

THis week hath produced little matter of Action in our Armies, I ſhall therefore in the firſt place informe you, of ſomething done for the Armies, & concerning them.

1. The Parliament have voted (ſince my laſt) a Committee to go down to the Army, whoſe advice is to be taken by the Commander, or Commanders in chiefe; I think the like courſe is taken in *Holland*: There are ſome of the States of the United Provinces, that do accompany the P. of *Orenge*, whoſe concurrent advice he takes upon any deſigne, & he takes this for no deminution of his command; and how needfull this is in our Armies, the Kingdom is ſenſible of, conſidering what ill inſtruments have lately bin in the Army in the Weſt,

Gggg which

Fig. 18. *George Bishop's* The Kingdomes Weekly Intelligencer

THE Numb. 5.

LONDON POST:

Faithfully Communicating His
Intelligence of the Proceedings of Parliament, and many other Memorable Paſſages certified by Letters and Advertiſements,

From { Foy. Tichfield. Portſmouth. Plymouth. } { Briſtoll. Bathe. Wickwarr. Malmesbury. } { Bazing. Leverpoole. Latham. Banbury. } { Huntingdon. Saliſbury. Warcham. Poole. }

The true and perfect Copy of the Articles of Agreement made between his Highnes P. Maurice, *and his Excellence the Earl of* Brayncеford *and* Forth, *on the one part, and* Philip Skippon, *Serjeant Major Gen. on the other.* Sep-xemb. 1. *The Rendezvous of his Excellencie the Earle of* Eſſex *at* Portſmouth: *And the Ordinance of the Parliament, for a ſuddain ſupply for his Army with Armes, Cloathes, and Ammunition: The diviſion and weak condition of Prince* Ruperts *Army at* Briſtoll, *certified in a Letter from Colonell* Maſſey: *And the cheerfull Advance of the Northerne Armies towards the Weſt, certified in a Letter from the Earl of* Mancheſter.

Publiſhed by Authority: And Printed for G. Biſhop. Septem. 10. 1644.

HOw great a Plague the Queene hath been unto this Kingdome, the ſad Condition of this Land, in many bleeding Characters, doth abundantly declare. And now the Juſtice of God, which alwayes proportioneth the puniſhment to the ſinne, hath ſtrucken *her* in *France* (as we heare is credibly reported) with the Sickneſſe.

The Affaires and Actions of his Excellencies Army in the Weſt, in this enſuing Letter (directed to a Gentleman of Worth in *London*) are truly repreſented to your view, bearing date *Auguſt* the 28. 1644.

E *S I R*,

Fig. 19. *George Bishop's* The London Post

Besides the series of Diurnalls, Mercuries, Passages, Intelligencers, Posts, Spies and Scouts which we have grouped together, there are Occurrences, Accompts, etc., whose numerical importance does not entitle them to grouping by themselves. Several of them, however, are of typographical importance.

The front page of Henry Walker's *Perfect Occurrences of Every Daie iournall in Parliament* published in its issue (No. 127) of June 7, 1649, a curious factotum which deserves notice. The space for the initial is at the centre of a cross of St George which is encircled by a strip carrying the legend in roman capitals 'PERFECT OCCURRENCES'. The whole is set on a background, 2 in. square, strengthened with an outside beading and azured in the four spandrels. It is the first of two specific devices which I have come across. I have reproduced it in Fig. 21. The second, a copy, decorates *Perfect Passages of Every Daie's Intelligence from the Parliaments Army*, etc. (January 1650/1), reading within the circular band 'PERFECT PASSAGES'. An adaptation of the same invention occurs in an initial on the front page of *The Faithful Scout* (April 1651), in which an alert, armed and mounted scout is surmounted by a circular band upon which are engraved the letters 'THE FAITHFUL SCOUT'. A similar block (or perhaps the identical?), but without lettering, is used in *The Weekly Post* during 1654. No. 176 of this last is interesting for its woodcut illustrations of an eclipse of the sun, a portent alleged to have occurred as Queen Henrietta Maria left Paris.

An Exact Accompt of the daily proceedings in Parliament with occurrences from Foreign Parts, etc. (issued on Tuesdays and Fridays during 1659 and 1660, cf. Fig. 22) is a well-displayed piece in which individual use is made of plain rules. It has already been pointed out that this simplest of all typographical elements, the single rule, can be used to render conspicuous a name, a number or a date, and that, in 1642, Robert Williamson was the first to use it as an eye-catcher for his date-line. At no time during that century, as far as I am aware, was the rule doubled (so: ══════════) in the modern fashion. Often, in other news-pamphlets of the time, the rule was made up from short dashes (so: ——————) of about 2 picas long. *The Exact Accompt* adhered to the now-established convention of a date-line within rules—in this instance made up from short pieces—but, anxious to indicate its position as being 'Published by AUTHORITY',[1] it gave rules to these words also. The page, therefore, bears two pairs of such rules. They

[1] The earliest use of these rules in a news-pamphlet seems to be on the title-page of *A Continued Iournall....* (London, Thomas Walkley, 1627) in which the italic line *Publiſhed by Authoritie* is so emphasised.

The Num. 7.

Citties weekly

POST

Faithfully Communicating the Affaires of the Armies to the

KINGDOME.

From Tuesday the 27. of *January* to Tuesday the 3. of *February*.

The seven Propositions agreed upon by the House of Commons to bee sent to the King, and how far in each of them the King hath already assented to the Parliament, The great hopes of peace. A shippe taken coming from France, and letters intercepted of great and dangerous consequence concerning the Prince. Gorings *base recruits of* 10000. *men taken out of the prisons of France, and to be imbarked for England, The Earle of Bristole and divers Ladies escaped from* Excetter *with* 200 *horse: Sir* Thomas Fairfax *his summons unto* Excetter, *and Sir* Iohn Barkleys *refusall; Our forces quartered within a mile and a halfe of Exceter, and the great hopes of the speedy taking it: Divers gentlemen and commanders dayly coming in and submitting themselves to Sir* Thomas Fairfax *forces from Exceter and Cornwall. A Confident report of the taking* Belvoire *Castle with all the Armes and Ammunition in it.*

BEfore we begin with the proceedings of our Army in *England*, we will acquaint you with our successes in Wales and represent unto you what Mr. *Edward Vaughan* a well affected Gentleman hath performed for the service of the State, and for the honour of himselfe, who understanding that some who were active for the King, had raised about one

G hundred

Fig. 20. *F. Leach's* The Citties weekly Post, 1645–1646

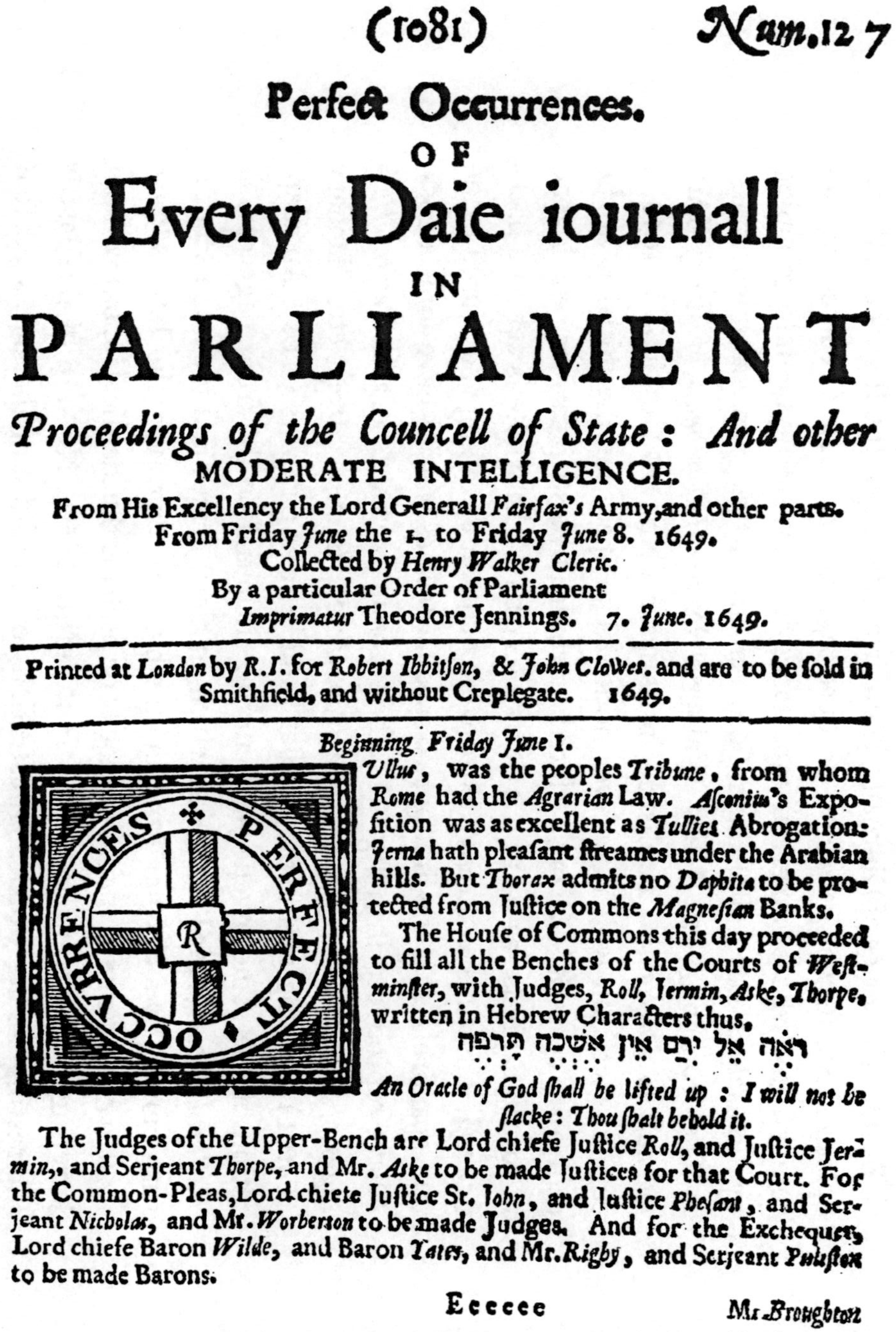

(1081) Num. 127

Perfect Occurrences.

OF

Every Daie iournall

IN

PARLIAMENT

Proceedings of the Councell of State: And other

MODERATE INTELLIGENCE.

From His Excellency the Lord Generall *Fairfax's* Army, and other parts.

From Friday *June* the 1. to Friday *June* 8. 1649.

Collected by *Henry Walker Cleric.*

By a particular Order of Parliament

Imprimatur Theodore Jennings. 7. *June*. 1649.

Printed at *London* by *R.I.* for *Robert Ibbitson*, & *John Clowes*. and are to be sold in Smithfield, and without Creplegate. 1649.

Beginning Friday June 1.

Ullus, was the peoples *Tribune*, from whom *Rome* had the *Agrarian* Law. *Asconius's* Exposition was as excellent as *Tullies* Abrogation: *Jerna* hath pleasant streames under the Arabian hills. But *Thorax* admits no *Daphita* to be protected from Justice on the *Magnesian* Banks.

The House of Commons this day proceeded to fill all the Benches of the Courts of *Westminster*, with Judges, *Roll*, *Iermin*, *Aske*, *Thorpe*, written in Hebrew Characters thus.

ראה אל ירם אין אשכה תרפה

An Oracle of God shall be lifted up: I will not be slacke: Thou shalt behold it.

The Judges of the Upper-Bench are Lord chiefe Justice *Roll*, and Justice *Jermin*, and Serjeant *Thorpe*, and Mr. *Aske* to be made Justices for that Court. For the Common-Pleas, Lord chiefe Justice St. *Iohn*, and Justice *Phesant*, and Serjeant *Nicholas*, and Mr. *Worberton* to be made Judges. And for the Exchequer, Lord chiefe Baron *Wilde*, and Baron *Tates*, and Mr. *Rigby*, and Serjeant *Puleston* to be made Barons.

Eeeeee Mr. Broughton

Fig. 21. *Henry Walker's* Perfect Occurrences *shewing specific factotum*

(649) Numb. 63

An Exact Accompt

Of the daily Proceedings in

PARLIAMENT.

WITH

OCCURRENCES

From Foreign Parts.

ALSO

ADVICE from the Office of INTELLIGENCE, Over against the Conduit near the Old Exchange in Cornhill.

Publiſhed by AUTHORITY.

From Friday *February* 3. *to* Friday *February* 10.

From Hamborough, 27 Jan.

IT ſeemeth that Count *Montecuculy* intendeth to take his winter quarters in the four Lordſhips about this City, he having demanded 100000 Rix-Dollers for thoſe quarters, which this City cannot agree to, but have ſent their Chiefe Secretary with one of the Councellors of this City unto the ſaid Count to confer with him about his demands, which if they cannot accommodate to let him take his courſe, there being not above 130 houſes in the ſaid Lordſhip ſo that all things will quickly be deſtroyed there. The chiefe Secretary of the City of *Lubeck* is here, to confer with Count *Ranſow* touching the new Oath which the Emperour would impoſe upon them, the which they are reſolved not to admit of. The Alliance of the Princes of *Germany* have been lately renewed at *Franckford*, unto which the Duke of *Wittenberg* hath condeſcended; the Deputies of the Elector of Tryer being daily expected there, to do the ſame. The Imperial Regiments which were marched paſt the City of *Franckford* (for the aſſiſtance of the Biſhop of *Munſter*) were endeavoured to be ſtopt by order of the Biſhop, who returned anſwer that they were ordered by the Emperour to march in-

Ppp

Fig. 22. *Oliver Williams'* Exact Accompt *shewing use of rules*

Sep. 30. | HEADS | Numb. 10.

OF SOME NOTES OF THE CITIE

SCOUT:

COMMUNICATING

The Affaires of the Army, to the Citie and Kingdome.

I. *Another mighty Victory obtained by Major Gen.* Pointz *in* Wales, *Major Generall* Gerrhard *killed,* Sir Thomas Glamham *taken priſoner, beſides* 800 *more killed and taken; With a Liſt of the Names of the chief of the Kings Officers, killed and taken,* 2000. *horſe taken,* 30. *Cullers, and* 1500. *priſoners taken, and* 3000. *Armes; and the King fled to* Bewmorris, *with* 8. *Lords, and his Life-guard, to take Boat to* Angleſey.

II. *How* Van Trump *is come to* Falmouth, *with a ſquad on of ſhips, and Prince* Charles *gone from* Exeter *thither to him.*

III. *The fight between* Greenvill *and the Club-men, near* Padſtow, *in the Weſt of* Cornwall, *and what loſſe; with other conſiderable newes from them, and the whole ſtrength of all the Forces in the Weſt, and where they quarter.*

IV. *How Collonel* Wagſtaffe, *Collonel* Arundell, *and Collonel* Pickel, *who is Leader of the* Iriſh *Rebels, have the command of* Gorings *forces, who is only with* 4. *Peeces of Ordnance at* Crediton.

V. Sir Brian Stapleton *ſlain, and Letters of great conſequence found in his Pocket.*

London printed, by R. A. and JANE COE. 1645.

Fig. 23

were retained when, in its Friday issue, e.g. No. 64, the title became *Occurrences from Foreign Parts, with An Exact Accompt of the daily Proceedings in Parliament*, etc. The same effect—of emphasising the regularity, legality and authority of the publication without detracting from the importance of the date—was secured with three rules by *London's Diurnal: communicating the most Remarkable Intelligence*, etc.... *Published according to ORDER* (No. 1, February 1–8, 1660).

§ 8 THE OFFICIAL INTELLIGENCER & NEWS

The Long Parliament came to its end on March 16, 1660. The executive Council of State under General Monck then governed, and under his authority the following paragraphs appeared in *The Parliamentary Intelligencer* for March 26–April 24, 1660:

ADVERTISEMENTS.

WHereas *Marchemont Nedham*, the Author of the Weekly News books, called *Mercurius Politicus*, and the *Publique Intelligencer*, is, by Order of the Council of State, difcharged from Writing or Publifhing any Publique Intelligence: The Reader is defired to take notice, that by Order of the faid Council, *Henry Muddiman*, and *Giles Dury*, are authorized henceforth to Write and Publifh the faid *Intelligence*, the one upon the *Monday*, and the other upon the *Thurfday*; which they do publifh under the Titles of the *Parliamentary Intelligencer*, and *Mercurius Publicus*.

At the Council of State at *VVhitehall.*

Ordered,

THat the Mafter and Wardens of the Stationers Company, London, be, and are hereby required to take care that no Books of Intelligence be printed and Publifhed on Mundayes or Thurfdayes weekly, other than fuch as are put forth by Mr. Henry Muddiman, and Mr. Giles Dury, who have an allowance in that behalf from the Council of State.

Signed by the Clerk of the Council.

Counterfeits of the two authorised pamphlets were short-lived, though the Council was far too occupied with negotiations to prosecute. At last Charles II landed at Dover on May 26. In a month the Commons enacted that 'no person whatsoever do presume at his peril to print any votes or proceedings of this House without the special leave and order of this House'. In effect, the press was now controlled by the Royal Prerogative. Fifth Monarchy Men, a sect violent as only the pious can be, used privy presses for their propaganda. Charles II determined to regulate the press. First, in May 1662, an Act for preventing 'abuses in printing, seditious, treasonable and unlicensed books and pamphlets' was passed; and in the following year, Roger L'Estrange was appointed Surveyor of the Press—a job which Thomas Dawks applied for. A Monday periodical entitled *The Intelligencer* (No. 1, August 31, 1663) and a Thursday entitled *The Newes* (No. 1, September 3, 1663) were established and, as L'Estrange's pamphlets retained the customary periodicity, they also retained the same form of textual composition. But, one important development took place: the titles at last were permanently shortened.[1]

L'Estrange made it clear in the first issue of *The Intelligencer* that he had no belief in the necessity or in the advisability of issuing any sort of 'Public Mercury...it makes the Multitude too familiar with the Actions and Counsels of their Superiors...and gives them not only an Itch but a Colourable Right to be Meddling with the Government'. But after this High Tory stuff he expresses his view that the 'prudent menage of a Gazett' may contribute to tranquillity. In sum, he considered a news-book pragmatically advisable. To quote him, with his own italics:

> for ought I can see yet *Once a week* may do the bus'ness (for I intend to utter my *Newes* by *Weight* and not by *Measure*). Yet if I shall find, when my *Hand* is *in*, and after the planting and securing of my correspondents, that the Matter will fairly furnish more without either incertainty repetition or impertinence, I shall keep myself free to double at pleasure. *One Book a Week* may be expected, however; to be published every *Thursday*, and *finished* upon the *Tuesday night*, leaving *Wednesday* entire for the *Printing it off*.
>
> The *Way* (as to the Vent) that has been found most *Beneficiall* to the *Master* of the *Book* has been to *Cry*, and *Expose* it about the Streets, by *Mercuries* and *Hawkers*; but whether *That Way* be advisable in some *other respects*, may be a *Question*; for under Countenance of that Imployment, is carried on the *Private Trade* of *Treasonous* and *Seditious Libels*, (nor, effectually, has anything considerable been dispersed, against either *Church*, or *State*, without the *Aid*, and *Privity* of this sort of *People*).

L'Estrange's measures for the discovery of unlawful printing, which he proceeds to catalogue, are important to us here only for their length. Four, and more, pages of Sir Roger's first number are given to the introduction. 'I have not', he says at page 5, 'spun my *Preamble* to this *Length*, but that *failing* of the News whereupon I principally *depended*, and being not very good at *Quoyning*, I chose rather to help out a sheet This way...'

[1] The last *Perfect Diurnall* published by Oliver Williams was actually a daily, but it contained only the daily votes of Parliament, and it existed only for three weeks from February to March, 1660.

These two news-books ran under L'Estrange's sole privilege for five years. Their bulk fluctuated from eight to sixteen pages, without change in

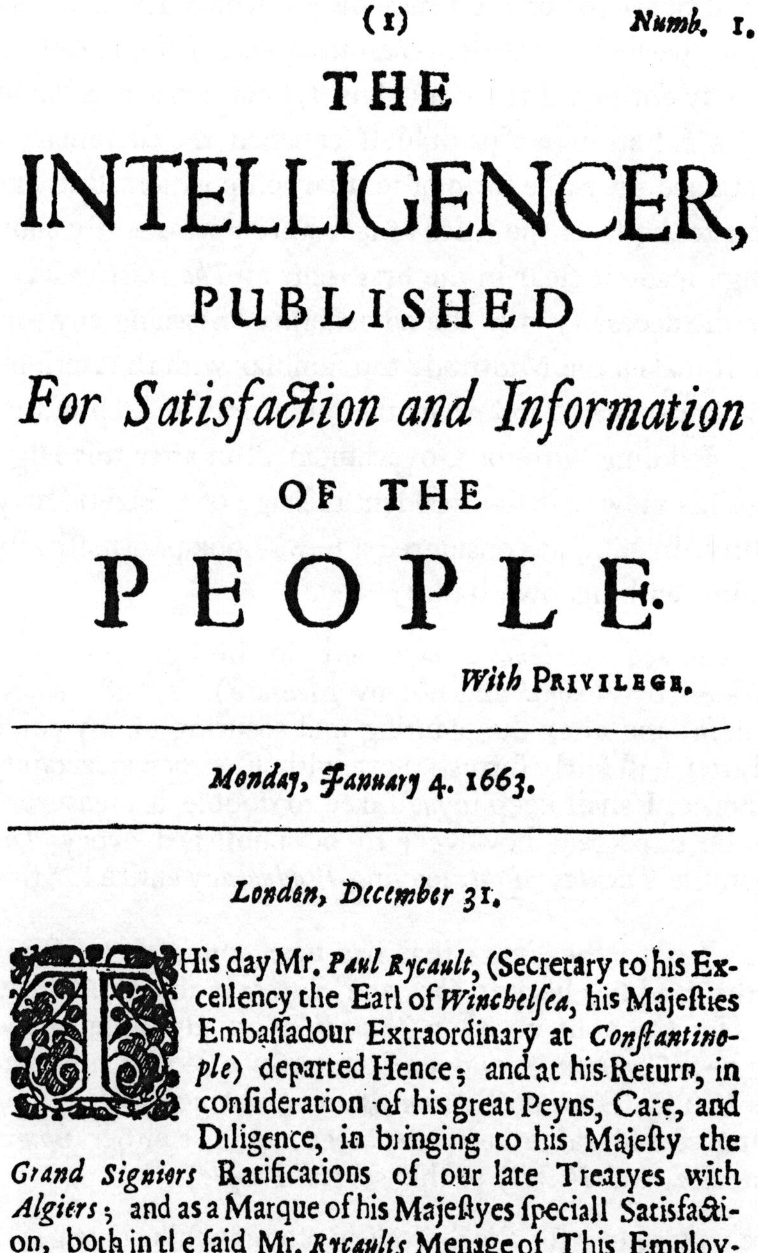

(1) Numb. 1.

THE INTELLIGENCER, PUBLISHED For Satisfaction and Information OF THE PEOPLE.

With PRIVILEGE.

Monday, January 4. 1663.

London, December 31.

THis day Mr. *Paul Rycault*, (Secretary to his Excellency the Earl of *Winchelſea*, his Majeſties Embaſſadour Extraordinary at *Conſtantinople*) departed Hence; and at his Return, in conſideration of his great Peyns, Care, and Diligence, in bringing to his Majeſty the *Grand Signiors* Ratifications of our late Treatyes with *Algiers*; and as a Marque of his Majeſtyes ſpeciall Satisfaction, both in the ſaid Mr. *Rycaults* Menage of This Employment, in the Meſſage he brought, and in the ſingular Diſ-

A eretion

Fig. 24. *Roger L'Estrange's* The Intelligencer. *The serial number is of the new volume for* 1663 (*i.e.* 1664)

the typography. When the Court was compelled to withdraw from London to Oxford on account of the plague, the Secretary of State permitted the issue, bi-weekly, of *The Oxford Gazette*, and there began a new chapter in the history of journalism and in the typography of news.

The typographical material used in the news-pamphlets we have just glanced at is, for the most part, either of foreign design and manufacture, or home manufacture from foreign matrices; very little of it is entirely designed and produced in this country. Where the large letters used for the titles of the Corantos, Diurnalls and Mercuries consist of extremely roughly cut characters, it may be conjectured that they emanated from one of the four typefounders licensed by the Court of Star Chamber. The better sort of Mercury (*Britannicus*, *Elencticus*) used Dutch founts as body-material, i.e. the pica, small pica, long primer, etc. of the text were cast in Holland, partly from Dutch material and partly from matrices struck from punches belonging to the Luther foundry in Frankfurt. To take one instance: the *Mercurius Politicus* of 1651 is set, for the most part, in a pica, roman and italic. These are identical with the 'romain cicero' of Garamond, and the 'cursive cicero' of Granjon, illustrated on the Berner-Luther (Frankfurt) specimen sheet of 1592. In other words, the text of *Mercurius Politicus* is set in what the Clarendon Press would call 'pica Fell'; this, again in other words, means that the *Politicus* was set in the roman and italic cut by French punch-cutters, from the hands of the great Garamond and Granjon respectively. The double pica roman, great primer and english, into which the title and sub-title of *Mercurius Politicus* tailed off, are coarsely-cut home imitations of the respective sizes shewn in the Frankfurt and Amsterdam specimen sheets. In May 1651, the *Politicus* used a fount of type which the Dutch would call brevier and the Frankfurt foundries gaillard. A very fine fount of great canon capitals designed by Guillaume Le Bé is used, for some time, for the word *Britaine* on the title-page of the *Britannicus* during and after 1643. The capitals may be seen in the word Parliament in Henry Walker's *Perfect Occurrences*, 1649 (see Fig. 21). What would appear to be the original superb upper- and lower-case canon first used by Robert Estienne (for his great bible of 1538) is used for the leading line of William Cook's *Perfect Diurnall.*

It would take us too deep into typographical technicalities if we were to proceed further with the examination of the founts used in the English journals, but it is important to realise that even though the Star Chamber and later authorities allowed typefounding at home, we depended upon foreign sources for the greater part of our material, and that although much of this continental material came to us from Holland it was cast from Frankfurt matrices.

The removal of press-restrictions in 1695 resulted, as one necessary consequence of the increase of journalism, in an extension of the type-founding trade in London. With the increase of technical accomplishment which increased business made possible, the engraving of home-designed founts improved, until, within the first thirty years of the next century, England produced in William Caslon a punch-cutter whose ability was second to none. His founts were used in the journals of the period from 1730 to 1780. Caslon's monopoly did not suffer from the competition of Fry (established 1764) for some time. From 1785 the newspapers bought more type from Fry who cut on the model of Baskerville. But this is to anticipate. The founts used in the period 1665–1695 which we are about to examine were a slight improvement upon those of 1622–1665 which we have been examining.

CHAPTER II

THE FIRST NEWSPAPERS

1665–1695

The London Gazette	1665
The Currant Intelligence, &c.	1681–
Dawks's News-Letter, &c.	1695–

Numb. 24.

The London Gazette.

Published by Authority.

From Thursday, *February* 1. to Monday, *February* 5. 1665.

Harwich, January 30.

THe Four Convoy ships from *Hamburgh*, (which were for some time missing) *viz.* The *Monke*, the *Amity*, the *Breda*, and the *Guift*, were discerned about Sunday noon, going to Anchor at *Oasley Bay*, where at present they remaine.

Dublin, Jan. 27. On Tuesday last the Court of *Claimes* sate, heard some motions, appointed daies of hearing several causes, and adjourned the Court till the 31 instant. Two *Gaboards* were sunck in this Harbour, and a Ship laden with Canary wines bulged, of which, it is feared, little can be recovered.

Kingsale, Jan. 23. On Saturday last here arrived 2 great Ships from the *Barbadoes*, the *Daniel* of *London*, Captain *Samuel Randall* Commander, of 12 Guns, and the *Adventure* of *London*, Capt. *Etherton* Commander, of 14 guns, the latter of which meeting with a *Flushinger*, killed and wounded 22 of them, as we are assured by several Vessels, and more particularly by that Ships Company, who (as you were lately told) regained their Vessels after they had been in the power of this *Flushinger*. Five other *Barbadoes* Ships were in fight with a *Flushinger* of 36 guns, one of which was taken, and 4 escaped. A Ship of *London* from *Bermudas*, Capt. *Bargrave* Commander, and a Ship from the *Maderas* came in this day.

Marseilles, Jan. 19. The St. *Malo* Ships are now at *Toulon*, attending Monsieur *de Beauforts* Order for their departure, whose Fleet being intended to carrene, it is thought they will be disappointed of their Convoy, in regard they cannot be ready in a Moneth, and what course they will then take, most conceive is yet unresolved.

This day came in a Ship of this Town from *Alexandria*, in 25 daies, who adviseth, that the Grand Signor has stopt several Ships for his service to carry Men and Provisions for *Candia*.

Legorne, Jan. 16. On the 12 instant the *Tunis* Merchant arrived here, coming from *Algier* in 11 daies, who adviseth that an *Algier* Ship had burnt the *Charity* of *Hamburgh*, bound hither from *Archangel*, with 106 packs of Hides, &c. He saies farther, that the *Algier* Men had sunck a *Dunkerke* Fregot with 300 Soldiers coming from *Spaine* and *Naples*, and several Dutch and French. The Peace which the French have concluded with *Tunis*, is reported here with much dishonour to the French ; and the Italians understand it so, the humor of *Tunis* being chiefly to follow Trade, in which they found themselves so much debarred, that they were in consultation to deliver up the French Captives gratis ; and indeed they might have been brought to any termes, had the French not been so forward to patch up a Peace with them. Since *Genoua* made their Agreement with the Grand Signor for Traffique, they are endeavouring to make all sorts of Cloth to send for *Smyrna* and *Constantinople*. The Grand Duke hath for some time been deteined by an Imposthume at *Florence*, from whence he is weekly expected, with the Court at *Pisa*.

Cleve, Jan. 26. *Monsieur Beverling* is arrived here, and Monsieur *Colbert* shortly expected, who brings with him a rich Furniture of a Chamber, as a present from the King of *France* to the Electress. *Beverling* has been offered as is reported, to be put into the States General for his life, and to be made Burgomaster of the Town of *Targo*, but excuses all upon pretence of his want of health to undergoe those employments ; though it is suspected he hath other reasons for not mixing in the present Government.

Hamburgh, Jan. 13. The Swedes are now in earnest upon their march over the *Elve*, and the Country people about us, though they have no cause for it, are so jealous of suffering from the Soldiery, that yesterday they sent into this City above 200 Waggons, laden with Houshouldstuff for security. Some would have it that *Bremen* is not yet fully agreed, but they cannot but see the necessity of falling into the Swedes hands, if they should offer to oppose them. Some further design, 'tis certain they have in hand, supposed to besiege *Embden*, and we have received from a very good hand, that the Swedes have sent to the Duke of *Lunenburgh* to consider well how he engages, or disposes of his Forces against the Prince of *Munster*, or in aid of the Hollanders. And surely there is something more then ordinary in it, at least, those of *Munster* apprehend it so ; for in the Prince of *Munster's* Court, in their general Healths, 'tis observed, that, next to that of His Majesties of *Great Britain*, they remember the King of *Sweden's*, and then Gen. *Wrangels*.

Warshaw, Jan. 7. We are now againe at a stand, to judge what will be the end of the Affair with *Lubomirski*, who instead of sending his Plenipotentiaries to the Treaty, according to his promise, on the 15 of *December*, has in his Letter sollicited that the High Marefchal, the Master of the Horse, and the Referendarius of the Crown, might be sent as Commissioners to the Frontiers of *Silesia* to Treat with him : This Proposition is not accepted by His Majesty, but referred to the Lord Bishop of *Cracaw*, who has all along treated with *Lubomirski*, to confer farther with him concerning it, according to the Declaration, published in *Rawa* and *Palczin*.

Rome, Jan. 16. In the Consistory held the 11 instant, his Holyness represented to the Cardinalls the great apprehensions he had, that Christendome would break out again into Warts, and desired the assistance of their Prayers for preventing them. The Cardinal *Corrado*, the Datary, took the Popes chiding, you heard of, so much to heart, that he is now reduced almost to the last gaspe. Here are come to this Town a company of Ordinary Players, who acted a play Entituled *Scaramuccia soldato a Gigiri controi Mori*, which reflecting upon the Frenches late disgrace there, Monsieur *de Burlemont*, who acts here for the French King, complained to the Popes Nephew of this designed insolence and Nationall dishonour, as he called it ; upon which the poor Players are laid by the heeles, which the Town takes very ill, as being in this time of Recreation denied the contentment of a peice of mirth, which was acted it seems at *Florence*, and other parts of *Italy*, with great applause. Here is in Town the Prince of *Baviere*, Brother to that Elector, the younger Brother of the Duke of *Longueville*, and a son of the Count of *Harcourt*, who came to see the curiosities of this City.

Durham, Jan. 27. Wednesday last was buried here Mr. *Anthony Pearson*, a man particularly noted in these parts, for having passed heretofore through all the degrees of Separation and Phanaticism, in all of which he was ever observed as a principal leader ; but having lived to see his Error sometime before his death, he himself, with his children and family, had received Episcopal confirmation, and did now at last upon his Deathbed very solemnly confess his former Errors, and the party that first seduced him into them, declaring that he now dyed a true Son of the Church of England.

Falmouth, Jan. 27. A Vessel of about 80 Tuns arrived here from *Dublin*, bound, with Tallow, Hides, and provision, for *Cadiz*, which proves so leaky, that she was forced to run ashoare here, and appears to be so unable to performe her voyage, that the Master will be obliged to sell Ship and Goods. Several of the Ministers, &c. of this County have made their subscriptions required by the late Act of Parliament.

Aa Smyrna,

Fig. 25. *The first issue of* The London Gazette (*Nos.* 1–23 *were headed* The Oxford Gazette)

CHAPTER II

THE FIRST NEWSPAPERS

1665–1695

THE official *Gazette* was first issued as a single leaf, printed both sides, identically in both its London and in its Oxford editions. The permanent London printer, Thomas Newcombe of the Savoy, exactly followed Leonard Lichfield of Oxford in format and typography. The composition of the body, unlike any Coranto, Diurnall, Mercury, Intelligence, Post or News, was in two columns divided by a rule. The title-line consisted of upper- and lower-case in canon size, to the full measure. The rubric

Published by Authority.

was set between two full rules at the position and in the style reserved for the date-line in the former Mercuries. In *The London Gazette* the date was inconspicuously centred immediately over both columns in the type of the body, which was, for the first years, a small pica. The royal device which we are accustomed to see in the present *Gazette* did not make its first appearance until 1785, but the title has always been set in upper- and lower-case. As for the date-line, at no time was it given the setting customary in the *Gazette* as in the later Mercuries. This breach of precedent in the case of the *Gazette* did not, however, mean a breach in the main tradition as far as the general run of the news-periodicals—we can now call them 'papers' since they are exactly that and nothing more—is concerned. The publications which made their first appearance during the succeeding score of years closely followed the example of *The London Gazette* in size and in setting, i.e. the headings were, for the most part, in upper- and lower-case, the text was in double column; but, although there were certain exceptions, the custom of setting the date of issue between two full-measured rules was generally respected.

The Currant Intelligence; or Impartiall Account of Transactions both Foreign and Domestic is a formidable-looking sheet which carries its somewhat top-heavy title in five lines, drafted, one is tempted to think, as some counter-balance to the general exiguity of the material. In comparison with *The London Gazette,* the column is 3½ picas narrower. The serial number of the sheet is printed in the extreme upper right-hand corner.

The great canon roman used for the title of *The Oxford Gazette* and *The London Gazette* was, in all probability, cut by Moxon.[1] It is an extremely interesting fount, masculine in design, and contrasting favourably as regards colour with the lighter French titlings to be seen in the Mercuries of the first half of the century. The blackletter in vogue for titles of the fourth quarter of the century probably comes from his hand. This also is a happy piece of designing and cutting, possessing considerable body.[2] The fount appears in the titles of news-sheets from 1679 onwards, being used for the very definite and utilitarian purpose of attracting attention. As yet, the newspaper publisher did not use blackletter in order to convey the impression of antiquity. The use of blackletter in the seventeenth century has no connexion with the use of a corrupt form of it by newspaper owners today. To the seventeenth-century printers, it was just the blackest letter they had in their cases, and was used as such. No founder then would have dreamt of cutting **a heavy BLOCK-letter** (as we should say, 'Sans serif') and, consequently, to use text was the only means of securing a bold title. Again, to choose a bold, i.e. a black-letter, for a title, was all the more natural when journals ran to lengthy names embracing one, if not two, sub-titles. Thus, the *Mercurius Civicus* of 1679/80—a new foundation,[3] not to be confused with the *Civicus* of Thomas Bates in 1643—set two out of its three main lines in blackletter. One or two other papers, such as *Mercurius Anglicus* (1680/1), used blackletter for its simple title; but, by the end of the seventeenth century, the blackletter was passing out of favour and the eighteenth opened with a daily whose heading, set in the canon roman of Moxon, firmly established that face in its position as a normal heading type for more than a generation.[4]

As it is within neither our purpose nor competence to tell in detail the story of the struggle between licensed and unlicensed presses, we have not attempted to decide disputes between any so-called original Diurnall, Passage, Post, Mercury or Intelligence and its alleged counterfeit; but such disputes will not be overlooked by the professed student of early newspapers. If we ourselves need to notice the existence of two competing, but unim-

[1] Moxon issued a specimen in 1669 which includes a 'Great Canon Romain.'

[2] It is used for the titles in Moxon's own book, set up, one supposes, about 1678.

[3] It 'shall not trouble the World but when it is furnished with New Intelligence, without repetition of other men's matter now so frequently practised. Wherefore, this Paper is not designed to come forth on any certain set Days, but as Posts arrive and new matter occurs worth imparting'. Printed by R E in Ave Mary Lane, it ceased May 6, 1680.

[4] This is not to say that there was no blackletter used.

portant papers, both entitled *Currant Intelligence*, it is because a change of title resulted. A paragraph from one of these warns us that:

> This *Intelligence*, having gained reputation as well by its truth as honesty, some persons have maliciously printed another with the very same title, which can be done with no other design than either to discredit ours by their falsities, or else in hopes to vend them under our Title; Therefore we think fit to give notice, that the Counterfeit *Currant Intelligence* is printed for Allen Banks[1] in Fetter Lane; but the true one for John Smith in great Queen Street, which for the future, to prevent mistakes, shall be called *Smith's Currant Intelligence*, etc.

The point for us to seize is that Mr John Smith of Great Queen Street, by printing his name immediately over the heading of his paper, initiated a custom which had its champion in *T. P.'s Weekly* and similarly named papers.

(John) *Smith's Currant Intelligence* ceased on May 4, 1680, to be revived the following year.

Another Smith, one Francis, though preferring the word 'Protestant' to 'Currant', also adopted blackletter. [Francis] Smith set his name in canon upper- and lower-case (cf. Fig. 27). Some two and twenty numbers of *Smith's Protestant Intelligence* were issued.

Such papers were, in their time, known as 'Intelligences'. Thus on April 26, 1681, John Smith of Great Queen Street, introducing himself at the top of column 1, claims that amongst the 'several Intelligences that have been published none hath gained greater Reputation, than that which went formerly by the name of *The Currant Intelligence*. At the persuasion of some friends the Author does now again resolve to serve the Publick by the same Title...' etc. His friends being, apparently, not numerous enough, the paper quickly dies—and finally. But the title *Currant Intelligence* did not disappear with Smith's Journal. 'Intelligence | *Domestick and Foreign*' was the title of a paper originated by Benjamin Harris, a stout enemy of Popery, and one that had been to America. Before he went to Massachusetts to found a paper there, he had had several adventures in London, including his *Intelligence*. He revived it, under the same concise title, on May 14, 1695, in the two-column standardised format of the 1690's. Harris thus maintained the continuity of the word 'Intelligence'. With No. 8 he added to the title the words: 'With the Flying Post Boy from the Camp in Flanders. Being an Historical Account of the Publick Transactions in Europe'.

The eighth number of *The Loyal London Mercury, or The Moderate Intelli-*

[1] Banks's *Courant* ran for four issues only.

Numb. 1.

THE

Currant Intelligence.

Tueſday, April 26th. 1681.

AMongſt the ſeveral Intelligences none hath gained greater Reputation, than that which went formerly by the name of *The Currant Intelligence.* At the perſuaſion of ſome friends the Author does now again reſolve to ſerve the Publick by the ſame Title, with ſuch paſſages of Foreign and Domeſtick Affairs, as may be uſeful as well as pleaſing to the Reader, without any reflections upon either perſons or things, giving only the bair matter of fact, as it ſhall from time to time occur to his Knowledge.

time paſt we have had great ſcarcity of Corn in this City, the beſt wheat being ſold for 30*s.* a Barrel, which is about 3 *l.* a Quarter; but there being great plenty in the Northern parts of this Kingdom, they begin to ſupply us from thence. Beſides ſeveral Veſſels from *France* laden with Corn, are already arrived here, and and many more are expected from *Holland*, ſo that there is already ſome abatement of this exceſſive rate.

Plymouth the 20. On the 16*th* about 40 or 50 Fire-Locks, together with ſeveral Blunderbuſſes, were ſeized in a Barn near this

Fig. 26. *Upper portion of* The Currant Intelligence *of John Smith*

Numb. 6.

Smith's, Proteſtant Intelligence: Domeſtick & Forein.

Publiſhed for the Information of all True Engliſh-men.

From Tueſday *February* 15. to Friday *February.* 18. 168$\frac{0}{1}$.

Weſtminſter, Febr. 16.

IN our laſt we told you, That the Grand Jury Sitting here, had found an Indictment of High Treaſon on *Saturday* laſt againſt Eight Perſons, for being concerned in the *Iriſh* Plot. And having ſince received a more particular Account of their Proceedings againſt them, we think it neceſſary to communicate it. . The Perſons mentioned

and in his way hither was met by as many more, as made up in all above three thouſand Horſe. Within half a mile of the Town, the Mayor, and Corporation received his Lordſhip; and after making their Complement, waited on his Lordſhip to the Seſſions-Houſe; where the Writ being open'd, they all unanimouſly Choſe again my Lord *Ruſſell*, and Sir *Humphrey Munnox*; though the latter could not perſonally appear

Fig. 27. *Upper portion of* [*Francis*] Smith's Protestant Intelligence *gencer*,[1] published by George Brome of Thames Street, substituted *Currant* for *Moderate*. The main title of this paper is notable as the first in which the lettering is engraved on wood and not set from type. The paper, however, did not have either a notable or an extensive career. The titles of *The Weekly News Letter* (No. 1, July 6, 1695), *The English Courant*[2] (No. 1, May 29, 1695) and *The London News Letter With Foreign and Domestic Occurrences* (No. 1, April 21, 1695, Fr. Leach, of Greyfriars, Newgate; revived by the same, No. 1, April 29, 1696)[3] are equally headed in roman upper- and lower-case with a body set in double-column of about small pica size.

The title *News-Letter* is restricted to a few papers, all of which were founded between 1695 and 1696. The restrictive measures which prohibited the printing of news did not destroy the scriveners' trade of gathering and circulating intelligence of foreign and domestic occurrences. The booksellers maintained scriveners whose written letters of news were sent on subscription to customers, mostly to country squires and parsons. When the restrictions were abolished in 1695, the news-letters continued side by side with the newspapers. Unfortunately Leach did not realise that in his time of transition there was not one public but two publics, corresponding to two habits of reading. The cheapness and despatch of the printer had brought into existence a fresh market for news, but there remained numbers of older readers who were used to the more personal tone of the written news-letters and they preferred them if they could get them at the cost and with the speed

[1] No. 1 (April 6, 1682) of *The London Mercury*, printed for T. Vile by Richard Baldwin, follows exactly the style of *The London Gazette*. Publication appears to have ceased on October 17, 1682. Another *London Mercury or Moderate Intelligencer* was started December 15, 1688, by G. C. at the Blue Bell, Thames Street. Another paper under this same title, but of a more literary character, was founded in 1671.

[2] *The English Courant*, printed for the author and published by John Whitlock 'To be published every Wednesday and Saturday, and to contain an Impartial... of Publick use and advantage, not only to the Curious and Speculative, but also to the Trading part of Mankind'.

[3] Frederick Leach's explanation, made on his going over from the written to the printed news-letter, is of interest as revealing that he accepted the help of the printer much against his will: 'The Trade of writing News, which has been my profession for several years, being now quite out of doors, I am forced against my own inclination to appear in Print, to recover, if I can, my former customers and preserve those few I have left, who, as they often told me, will rather read a printed paper than a written letter. And because there are already three papers published every Tuesday, Thursday and Saturday which have got some reputation, I have chosen to publish my paper on Monday, Wednesday and Friday. I shall take care, as I did in my Letters, to write Truth and give an impartial account of the most remarkable occurrences both at home and abroad'.

of the newspapers. Thus with these two traditions, there were two styles of news-writing. These distinctions were disregarded by the conductors of *The Weekly News-Letter*, or *The London News-Letter*, and the papers failed; partly, I am sure, because they looked unlike a news-letter and like *The London Gazette*—no pleasant object to any old-fashioned eye.

The same year, however, Edward Lloyd, the coffee-man in Lombard Street from whom the Underwriting Corporation takes its name, brought out a very distinguished single folio half-sheet with a heading 'Lloyd's News' set in a novel and pleasant manner. The text, printed in a large italic, though presenting to us a very distinguished appearance, may, at the time, have carried too personal a note. At any rate, it ran for a few months only. *Lloyd's News* was in the news-letter rather than in the newspaper tradition; and, as such, was more suited to country than to town appetites. But *Lloyd's News* also failed—dare we say because its form, for all its italics, was not close enough to the traditional hand-written news-sheet and too far from the newspaper style? That there was a market, even in London, for a news-letter which looked like a news-letter is proved by the successful career of Ichabod Dawks's publication. Dawks used a new scriptorial type cut for the purpose, and in other details took care to approximate the layout of news-letters.

These details are important, for, as soon as the public mind becomes habituated to certain arrangements of heading, type, column, margin, etc., it demands contents corresponding with these arrangements whenever and wherever these arrangements occur. As a corollary, when a certain type of journalism is associated in the public mind with a set typographical style, that same style will be adopted by newcomers aspiring to the public favour. In the 1620's, 30's and 40's, the typographical style was still so essentially bookish that the public mind could hardly have been able to distinguish news-books from books in general; and, without careful scrutiny, unable to distinguish one news-book or pamphlet or paper from another. It probably began to identify news-books with some rapidity only when the small devices, which we have noted, began to appear in the headings, e.g. of *Mercurius Civicus* or *The London Post*. But the manuscript news-letter had a very settled appearance, as settled and as formal as an Indenture. And, consequently, the news-letter had to look like a news-letter, whether it was printed or written. This 'looking-like' means that it had its individual format. There were news-letters which forgot this elementary truth. It was not enough that a news-letter should have its serial number, its date, its day of publica-

DAWKS's News-Letter.

Sr London

August 3. 699.

Laſt night we received an Holland Mail, with ſome of theſe particulars following.

Lemberg, July 11. The Baſſa Capigi, Treaſurer General to the Grand Seignior, arrived at Caminieck on the 6th. inſtant, and gave Orders to the Governour to prepare to March out with his Garriſon, and evacuate that Fortreſs to the Poles; whereupon the Turks have already begun to pack up their Baggage. The Hoſpodar of Walachia is alſo arrived upon the Frontiers, and is laying a Bridge over the Dnieſter, for the more convenient carrying of the Baggage. The Field Marshal of the Crown has ſent to acquaint the King herewith.

Warſaw, July 18. The Diet is now like to have a good Iſſue, the King having Declared that he will maintain the Liberties of the People; that his Saxon Troops were all on their March homewards; That he will keep no Regiments by his Perſon, but only a Guard of 1200 Men at his own Charge, all of them Poles and Lithuanians: That if the Saxons do not March out of the Kingdom within the time limited, or return again on any Pretence whatſoever, without conſent of the Republick, it shall be lawful for the Nobility to Aſſemble on Horſeback without his Order, and Treat them as Publick Enemies. And in return hereof the Diet have obliged themſelves to ſecure his Majeſties Perſon with their utmoſt Power; that they will Severely Punish all that Act or but Speak againſt him: That all Libels againſt him shall be Burnt by the Hand of the Hangman; and the Authors of them ſerv'd in the ſame manner, if they can be apprehended. His Majeſty will hold a Diet in Saxony in September; and its ſaid he will bring his Queen hither with him when he returns.

Hamburg, Auguſt 4. Dr. Meyer, the Miniſter having Printed his Latin Oration upon the Marriage of the King of the Romans, on Cloth of Silver and Gold, and edg'd every Leaf of it with Point of Venice, which altogether coſt this City 500 Crowns, he ſent the ſame to the Emperour and King of the Romans, who have thereupon made the Doctor a Palſgrave, and given him his Patent free.

Hague, Auguſt 8. They write from Nieuenheuſen in the County of Benthem, that 300 Neuburgers came to put the Countrey under Military Execution, for not ſubmitting to the Popish Count; but that a Body of Dutch Soldiers advancing, who were ſent by the States to ſupport the Proteſtant Count, put the Neuburgers to flight, having kill'd a Lieutenant and wounded three others. Letters from Hungary ſay, that General Nehm, who was impower'd to be preſent at adjuſting the Frontiers, falling into ſome Difference with the Baſſa of Temeſwaer, Struck him Dead from his Horſe; whereupon ſome other Turkish Officers taking up the Quarrel, there were 30 or 40 Men Killed on both ſides; however the Commiſſioners went on with adjuſting the Frontiers. Admiral Aylmer with his Squadron is Sail'd from Meſſina to Leghorn: The French Gallies shunn'd meeting him, becauſe they knew he would oblige them to Strike. A Million of Crowns has been collected at Rome by way of Alms, for the Irish Papiſts as is given out. The refreshing Rains we have had of late, have in ſome manner diſſipated the Fevers which raged in this Country, eſpecially at Amſterdam, where People ſuffered very

Fig. 28. *Ichabod Dawks's script type*

tion. The scriveners always began with '*London*' written in large characters followed by '*Sr*' in still larger script. Dawks reproduced all these details and with his script type successfully conveyed the personal character of the writer's style which was proper to a news-letter. Delivery of a Dawks's *Letter* was upon quarterly subscription and not upon a single-copy basis. Hence, *Dawks's News-Letter* represents a completely different tradition from that of the newspaper. Nor is there any evidence that it was sold by the

Fig. 29. *Dawks's blackletter heading*

Mercury women or other than by subscription to the printer. Interesting as Dawks's *Letter* is from one point of view or another—and it lived for more than a generation—it made no permanent contribution to the development of the English newspaper. Its final form was remarkably handsome. The splendour of its black-letter heading probably did something to keep alive the old tradition of gothic script and may conceivably have influenced its adoption as the titular lettering for the *London Chronicle* of 1757. The normal newspapers went on, notwithstanding Dawks's effort, on the lines of *The London Gazette*.[1]

[1] Another paper, *Jones's Evening News-Letter*, also printed in script type, is illustrated in Morison, *Ichabod Dawks and his News-Letter* (Cambridge, 1931).

When public support was first given to the official *Gazette*, it was given because the public had no alternative. As soon as the restrictions on the press were removed, sheets having an ambition similar to that of the *Gazette* expressed themselves in a typography similar to that with which *The London Gazette* had made the public familiar. *Dawks's*, having a different ambition, expressed itself in different style. But *Dawks's* was not the only innovation. The abolition of the restrictions upon the press brought forth a number of periodicals in which news, views and particulars of literary and religious controversy are all compounded. The typography, accordingly, changes, or rather fluctuates. A good example to take in is John Dunton's *Pegasus*. It is a vastly more agreeable piece of printing than any contemporary news-paper. It looked what it was, namely, as much a miscellany as a news-paper.

"The meaning of the word *Pegasus*", wrote Dunton in the first number, "being known to every Schoole boy, there is no great need of an explanation. But seeing the Instruments of conveyance as *Pacquet*, *Maile*, *Advice Boat* etc. are now become an usual figure to signifie the news convey'd by them, we think there is nothing to be urged against our *Winged Horse* why he may not be as good an Intelligencer as *Mahomet's Pigeon*. Then seeing the *Postmaster*, the *Post Man* and the *Post Boy* take the fatigue of serving the Publick with News, on Tuesdays, Thursdays and Saturdays, we thought that *Pegasus* would be able to keep pace with such nimble Courier as... *The Protestant Mercury* the *London News-Letter* and *Pacquit of Advice* etc. which assumes that province on the other three days.... Our design is a TRIPARTITE PAPER, NEWS, AN OBSERVATION and a JACOBITE COURANT by three distinct hands."

This, roughly, is also the composition of such journals of the next generation as *The Westminster Journal*, *Owen's Weekly Chronicle*, and the most famous of all, for which Johnson wrote 'The Idler' papers—*Payne's Universal Chronicle or Weekly Gazette* (1758).

By 'Observation' Dunton meant what the journalist of the next generation was to call the 'Essay' which is represented in the 'light leader' of *The Times*. A similar 'Essay' exists in such weeklies as the *New Statesman* side by side with the political leaders which also appeared in Owen's and Payne's journals. Our contemporary quality-weeklies, however, purport (and have done so for a hundred years) to supply not *news* but *views*. But to discuss this is to anticipate a future lecture. Dunton's *Pegasus* was not a purely literary or political chronicle: it chronicled as well as commented upon news, thus coming, with complete relevance, into our present consideration. It was a Monday, Wednesday and Friday publication, ceasing some time in the latter part of 1696. Physically, it is notable as possessing a fine head-piece of a postman mounted upon a flying pegasus. Such a device lies outside contemporary practice, for, notwithstanding the inclusion in the block of a postman, the convention of the day required a horse as familiar as the postman. Dunton, in giving his postman and his readers a mythical steed, took the

Fig. 30. *Heading device from Dunton's* Pegasus, 1696[1]

risk, in which no successor followed him, of provoking suspicion of the sources and character of his news. Notwithstanding Dunton, the real postman, the real post horse and the real packet became the insignia of two important types of Restoration newspaper, and continued thereafter for more than two generations—in all a century and a half after their introduction. And we shall now examine the development of this tradition.

[1] This first appeared in No. 10 in succession to a small and feeble pegasus cut. The original title, *Pegasus, with News, an Observator, and a Jacobite Courant,* became with Vol. 2, No. 1, *Pegasus, with an Observator on Publick Occurrences.*

CHAPTER III

THE THRICE-WEEKLY POSTS

1695–1702

The Post Boy

The Post Man

The Flying Post

& their Postscripts

CHAPTER III

THE THRICE-WEEKLY POSTS

1695–1702

THE most ubiquitous of all words in the narrow vocabulary of those responsible for drafting the titles of newspapers would seem to be 'Post'. First used by George Horton for his *Weekly Post* of 1653/4, it appears in one form or another in scores of titles between 1676 and 1776, and it exists today in *The Morning Post* founded in 1772. In typographical style, the English newspapers of the period 1702–25 may be roughly divided, first into modifications or adaptations of *The London Gazette*'s arrangement of heading and columns, and, secondly, some form or other of the heading of a periodical entitled *The Post Man*. *The London Gazette* style was plain, *The Post Man* style included two devices. There had been blocks in the *Mercurius Civicus* and other news-pamphlets, used by the publisher for the obvious purpose of distinguishing his product and so preventing substitution. A similar intention would naturally occur to the publishers of any generation. Blocks were inevitable, and the obvious and only possible positions for them then were in the heading and in the place of the initial letter to the text at the top of the extreme left-hand column. Such blocks would necessarily be symbolic of the collection or distribution of news, or, alternatively of a design specifically related either to the title or to the political or other purpose of the paper. Thus the blocks as a rule related to news in general or news in particular.

The relevance of a cut of a mounted postman is clear enough. A 'fame' with trumpet is not less so. The word 'Mercury' is equally clear in its relevance to news. A packet in full sail is another block which, relevant to news, would be irrelevant in the heading of a journal of literature, or a paper in which that sort of pabulum was the prime inducement to purchase. For such, headings composed of printers' flowers or some conventional engraved ornament, generally of a baroque tendency, were the most commonly employed. Essay papers and the like went in for decoration, but as these are foreign to our enquiry because they are not concerned with news, we shall ignore

(Numb. 1.)

The Old Post-Master.

WITH THE
Occurrences of GREAT BRITTAIN and IRELAND, and from Foreign Parts; Collected and Published.

From Saturday *June* the 20th. to Tuesday *June* the 23th. 1696.

THIS *Paper is intended constantly to be Publish'd Three Days in the Week, viz.* Tuesdays, Thursdays *and* Saturdays; *and to contain only matters of Fact, without Reflections on Persons or Things: As also such other matters as will be found Useful for the Trading part of Mankind, as well Merchants as Mechanicks, &c. So many News Papers (or so called) are daily Published, that it would seem needless to trouble the World with more; but the difference of this Paper from those others Published, is with all modesty submitted to the judgment of every Judicious and Impartial Reader.*

THE Advices from His Majesty's Camp, by the *Holland* Mail, which came in on *Saturday*, being in the Gazett and other Prints, I shall only add as follows, *viz.*

Paris June 21. We are extreamly surprized here, to hear of no action from any place, which makes News very bare; all our attention is on the side of *Piedmont*, being very impatient to see the issue of all our Negotiations with the Duke of *Savoy*: Couriers pass and repass the Mountains continually, and that which makes us the more uneasie, to know how the Affairs will be managed on that side, is, by reason of the Numerous Army that is kept there with so vast Expences and Charges, and great scarcity of Provisions, which cannot be sent to M. *de Catinat*'s Camp without excessive Costs; but it was absolutely necessary to be Superiour in Forces to the Duke of *Savoy*, to Intimidate him, and to oblige him to come to a composition, and in that case, to turn with those Troops the *Spaniards* and *Germans* out of his Dominions, which was the only obstacle lookt upon at Court, that could hinder His Royal Highness from accepting the Advantageous Proposals which would be offered him for a Separate Peace.— The last Letters from the Army are of the 16*th*, but bring no News; they say only, that M. *de Catinat*, before he enters upon action, stays for an answer from the Duke of *Savoy*, about the pressing Solicitations made him from the King and the Pope. His Majesty sent an Express yesterday with his last Resolutions, at the instances of the Duke of *Orleans*, and gives that Prince time, till the end of this month to declare himself; and if he continues to reject the Kings offers, the M. *de Catinat* will go on, either to Bombard *Turin*, or to ruine the Plain, which he can reduce to such a Deplorable Condition, that the damage will not be made good in 30 years, which would be the utter ruine of *Piedmont*; the more, by reason that its chief Commerce consists in Silk, and that the Plain is full of Mulberry-Trees; a few days will make us wise, and learn its destiny: The mean while they write from *Turin* of the 12*th*, that M. *de Catinat* observes at present a very strict discipline in his Army, and does not tolerate the least vexation, though the Scarcity of Provisions begins a new in his Camp; we cannot imagine the reason of it, they pretend that he stays for his Artillery; but we are perswaded that such a General as M. *de Catinat*, would cause his orders to be better observed than so, if there were not some very important reasons that hindred it hitherto, which are unknown to us: They that come from Court assure, that 'tis discoursed there, that all the Articles of Composition between His Majesty and the Duke of *Savoy*, are agreed on by his Royal Highness, that there remains no other difficulty, than to make good the damage sustained by that Prince, which will be easily composed by the Pope's means, who labours hard to procure a Peace to *Italy*. An Express is arrived from *Brest*, dispatched by M. *de Chateau Renaud*, to know his Majesty's last resolution concerning the Squadron of 12 Men of War, which he is to command; they say at Court, that he is designed for Cruising on the *Irish* Coast, to Sail thence for *Cape Finisterre*, to pass the *Streight*, and to joyn the *Mediterranean* Men of War and Galleys that are arming with a design to besieg *Barcelona* by Sea, whilst the Duke *de Vendome* shall Attack it by Land; the great quantity of Ammunition and Provision that are laying up in *Provence*, together with the Detachments that are to be sent from *Catinat*'s Army, after his Expedition in *Piedmont*, for *Catalonia*; confirm the opinion of the Sieg of that Important Place, after the great heats are over. 'Tis said that the Squadron of M. *Dandenne* is gone for the *East-Indies*; and that of Capt. *de Genes*, to cruise on the *English* and *Dutch* Colonies: and tho' some think that all our Naval Forces will act in several Squadrons; yet some are of opinion, that the Grand Fleet will put to Sea in *August* next, and that all the Privateers are to be called in, and ordered to come in Port by the end of *July*, in order to make use of their Equipages, as occasion shall require.

We have advice from *Stockholm*, that several Conferences have been held there with Count *d' Avaux*, about Peace, of which the King of *Suedeland* would fain be the only Mediator; and that the same might be Negociated in that Place; but that the said Count *d' Avaux* has declared, the King his Master not to be of that opinion; and that it will be convenient to regulate matters with *England* and the States of *Holland*, as to the quality King *William* must be treated with, before he enters upon any Negotiation.

Its wrote from *Collogne*, that the French have burnt *Treves*; but we hope it will need a confirmation.

Francfort June the 20*th*. The Allies on the upper *Rhine* have now finished their Line, which, when their Army passes that River, is to be guarded by 12 or 15000 of the Militia, to secure the Countrey of *Wirtemberg* from a French Invasion. The French continue to desert in great numbers, and their Army is still in the same

Fig. 31. *George Larkin's* The Old Post-Master

them—unless, as in the case of *The Tatler*, there is a peculiar reason for citation. News-papers, as such, went in for the familiar pictures of a postman or a packet.

The London Post is an early example of the use of a specific block. The paper was a venture by Benjamin Harris (whose *Intelligencer* we have already mentioned), *The London Post, with Intelligence Foreign and Domestick* (no relation to *The London Post* of 1647) was a thrice-weekly whose title was originally *The London Slip of News, Both Foreign and Domestick.* The title was changed with the second issue, June 6, 1699, and under that title the paper had, for its period, the considerable life of six years. It was a handsome-looking piece, the heading being some 2¼ in. deep. Its two columns were separated by a rule in the *London Gazette* manner. A feature of the composition in its second year was the use of a specific factotum cut for the purpose of identifying the paper. The block of the arms of the City of London, bearing the motto *Domine dirige nos*, was not pierced in the centre, but at a point above the shield. Over the top of the block was printed the line 'LONDON Arms'. Towards the end of its career, when the paper came under new proprietorship, the heading was brought into one single line of canon size, and the rest accommodated to the straightforward *London Gazette* style.[1]

The Old Post-Master (No. 1, June 20–23, 1696), i.e. earlier by three years than *The London Post*, is more important as being the forerunner of a style of which traces are to be found as late as 1820. *The Old Post-Master* did not, indeed, invent its style of heading but rather reverted to an idea—we can hardly refer to so restricted a use as a 'practice'—to be found in one of the Mercuries of half-a-century before. The heading, in three parts, possesses as its centre-piece a mounted postman blaring a horn from which issues the legend 'Great News'. The cut is strongly reminiscent of those on the front pages of *The Kingdomes Weekly Post* and *The London Post* of 1643 and 1644 respectively.

Although this is the first block of a flying post to be found in the Restoration period, *The Old Post-Master* was not the first paper to revive the use of the title *Post*. This old titular word was made popular by *The Post Boy, With Foreign and Domestick News*,[2] printed for A. Roper, E. Wilkinson and

[1] The number for April 6, 1705, carries on its back page the streamer (i.e. across the whole page) heading *Resolutions upon the present Postures and Affairs by TRUTH AND HONESTY.* This was a feature which had appeared in the paper since it had come under the management of Mr Bragg, when it appeared on Tuesdays and Fridays and not on Mondays, Wednesdays and Fridays as previously.

[2] For *The Flying-Post* (No. 1, May 17, 1695) see p. 69.

A N

ACCOUNT

OF THE

PUBLICK TRANSACTIONS in Christendom.

In a Letter to a Friend in the Country.

Saturday, August 11. 1694. LICENS'D.

SIR,

THE Gazette *and* News-Letters *being so common in your Country, I was not a little surprized to find that you should desire me to write to you once a Week what I hear concerning the* Publick Transactions *of the World, and what Reflections our Friends make on them. This, I am sure, is a harder Task than you imagined for me at first, and I think the Reasons I gave you in my last, in order to obtain your excuse, were very pertinent and sufficient; but seeing nothing can satisfy you, and that you are resolved to have a Letter of mine, I shall write to you as often as I shall have any Subject Matters; but as you must not always expect from me extraordinary things, so neither must you expect that I should take notice of all little Trifles; This is the Province of the most Common* News-Letters, *with whom I do not design in the least to interfere.*

We have been this Week in great impatience for want of News, and the *Holland* Mail we had on *Thursday*, has not yet quenched our thirst; for what we heard was not very material. The Letters from *Vienna* of the 31st of *July*, say, That the Imperial Forces were arrived at their *zette* says were arrived at *Belgrade*, it proves to be one of its ordinary wilful mistakes. Tho the Summer is so far spent, yet by these Preparations of the Imperialists, it seems that they design to do something; and if we may believe these Letters, the *Turks* are hardly in a Condition to oppose them. This backwardness of both Parties shews how much a Peace is necessary for them, and that they lie under a kind of impossibility to continue the War. I know that the *Turks* are sullen, as generally all Loosers are, and loth to quit the Play; but amongst other Reasons, if the *Arabian's* Insurrection continues, I am sure they will be glad to accept of Terms. Of these Commotions you have already an Account in one of our *Gazette's*, which is confirmed by the last Letters from *Transilvania* and *Venice*, with some other particulars. They write in short, That the *Czeriff* of *Arabia* having got a considerable Army together, had march'd towards *Mecca*, and defeated the Bassa of *Asia*, who intended to oppose him; that he possessed himself afterwards of that place, as well as of *Medina*, causing himself to be proclaimed Emperor; and that having seized on the Treasures of those Towns, he was marching into the *Up-*

Fig. 32. *Portion of Richard Baldwin's weekly. The title was altered to* An Historical Account etc. *with No. 2, and amalgamated with* The Post Boy *with No.* 15

R. Clavel, which was established in the previous year, on May 14, 1695.[1] Richard Baldwin was already the owner of *The Historical Account*. For reasons which will be immediately apparent, it is necessary that we should clearly understand the history of this merger—and subsequent de-merger.

[1] Frequent changes of printer: No. 10, *London*: Printed and Sold by John Whitlock near Stationers Hall, 1695; No. 13, *London*: Printed by J. Moxon and B. Beardwell for A. R. and E. W. in Fleet Street, 1695.

Baldwin's *The Historical Account* was called, in the first issue, *An Account of the Publick Transactions in Christendom*, and from the second, *An Historical Account of the Publick Transactions in Christendom In a Letter to a Friend in the Country*. Only a few issues were published of his paper. It was printed only for Richard Baldwin, and 'constantly published every Saturday morning...so that with the London Gazette of Mondays and Thursdays, and this Historical Account, you may with a very inconsiderable Expence be thoroughly acquainted with all the Publick Transactions in Christendom'. Baldwin, in accordance with what seems the latest salesmanship, seems to have sold the *Gazette* and *The Historical Account* on a combined subscription basis.[1] Robert Baldwin, shortly after, joined Abel Roper and *The Post Boy*, and decided to amalgamate his *Historical Account* with it. The amalgamation had lasted scarcely six months when Baldwin withdrew; and under the serial number of what should have been *The Historical Account*, there appeared the original issue of *The Post Man*, dated October 22–24, 1695. The last issue of *The Post Boy* printed by or for Baldwin was No. 70.[2] No. 71 appeared with the imprint of A. Roper and E. Wilkinson. Baldwin gave 'No. 72' to his new venture *The Post Man*, as if that paper had co-existed separately all the time. The continuity question seems not to have interested Baldwin; and, in any case, an important detail of his own practice was soon to be 'lifted' by the other side of the quarrel of *The Post Boy* v. *The Post Man*.

With No. 115 of *The Post Man*, two woodcuts, one of which is a postman on horseback blowing his horn (placed at the right of the title) and the other a packet in full sail (at the left), appear, the serial number being centred over the line *The Post Man* which remains in text. A note at the head of the first column reads:

Whereas I have for several Months published a News Paper called the Post Boy, and the Historical Account, I have now for some reasons, thought fit to continue my HISTORICAL ACCOUNT, by the same author, with the additional Title of the POSTMAN; and to give notice that what Advertisements shall be sent to me, shall be incerted in my News Paper as formerly.

Richard Baldwin.

[1] See No. 6, *The Historical Account*, May 4, 1695.

[2] The imprints to *The Post Boy* were: No. 15, *London*: Printed for R. Baldwyn, A. Roper and E. Wilkinson, 1695; No. 36, *London*: Printed for R. Baldwin, 1695; No. 37, *London*: Printed for R. Baldwin, near the Oxford Arms in Warwick Lane, 1695; No. 71, *London*: Printed for A. Roper and E. Wilkinson at the Black Boy in Fleet Street, 1695; No. 416, *London*: Printed by and for B. Beardwell in the Passage going into Swan yard, near Newgate; No. 1191, *London*: Printed by and for B. Beardwell next the Red Cross Tavern in Blackfriars. Later the paper is printed by L. Beardwell.

To this piece of enterprise *The Post Boy* at once replied in its issue No. 73, Thursday, October 24–Saturday, October 26, 1695:

Whereas R. Baldwin did on Thursday last publish a Paper called the *Post Man* where he would insinuate that the same was writ by the Author of the *Post Boy*. This is to give Notice that the same is altogether False, for that the author of the said *Post Man* and *Historical Account* is Monsieur *de Fonvive*, and that the *Post Boy* is, and always was, writ by me and no other. If any has occasion to insert Advertisements therein, they are desired to send them to *A. Roper*, at the *Black Boy* in *Fleet Street*; or J. Moxon and B. Beardwell at the Atlas in Warwick Lane.

The old sub-title of *The Post Boy*, i.e. *An Historical Account*, was, of course, dropped. That periodical proceeded under the title of *The Post Boy, With the Freshest Advices, Foreign and Domestick*, for some seven years. Finally, the title was stabilised as *The Post Boy* in 1711. Two cuts, one of a post boy and the other of a fame, were placed to the right and left respectively of the title with the issue of Tuesday, January 1, 1706. Both were arranged, in respect of the lettering, exactly to resemble the heading of *The Post Man* whose cuts had, by that time, been familiar to the public for more than a decade. Such an imitative form of flattery was hardly to the taste of Baldwin. Immediately after the issue of the newly-headed *Post Boy, The Post Man* (January 1–3, 1706) published this notice:

Whereas the persons concerned in the *Post Boy*, have thought fit, to put two cuts to their paper, one of which is like one of the *Post Man*, and the other is a fame sounding a trumpet; we think fit to acquaint our readers with it, and desire them to read the title of the newspapers that shall be offered them, which is the only means of preventing the mistakes that happen by reason of that alteration on Tuesday morning.

The journalist who had these cuts made for *The Post Boy* was 'one Boyer, a French dog', as Swift called him in a letter to Stella. Boyer's story is that he made several changes in the style of the text and in the title of *The Post Boy* when he first began to write for it in 1705, and afterwards that he added 'Two Cuts, one of a Post Boy on horseback, the other a Fame sounding her trumpet, with this motto "Viresque acquirit eundo"'. True, Baldwin's cuts were different in subject, but this did not prevent the appearance of two papers, *The Post Man* and *The Post Boy*, being so similar as to invite confusion. More confusion was to come, for Boyer, dismissed, he says, by Roper 'without any previous notice or a colourable reason being given', started his own *Post Boy*. The second *Post Boy* was 'Printed by A. Boyer'; it carried the serial number 2227, being that which followed the immediately preceding Roper number, dated August 23, 1709. Thus there were two *Post*

Numb. 6100

The Poſt-Man.

AND

The Hiſtorical Account, &c.

From Tueſday March 5, to Thurſday March 7, 1723.

LONDON.

THE following Speech, made by the Biſhop of Soiſſons to the King of France, the Day after his Majeſty's arrival at Soiſſons, has been made Publick at Paris, and 'tis thought a Tranſlation of it will be very grateful to the Curious.

'YOUR People in numerous Crowds flock to ſee your Majeſty paſs by, and at once ſatisfy their Curioſity, and their Love. Their

'Tis this, SIRE, that in our Prayers we continually beg of him; we beg it more than Succeſs and Proſperity; for to a wicked King, what would an Addition of Proſperity be, but a greater Addition of Pride, and a Courſe of unpuniſh'd Crimes? You are going to pray for it your ſelf in that ſolemn Day when you ſhall be anointed with holy Oil, and ſhall bind your ſelf more nearly to the Almighty by thoſe ſacred Oaths, on the Performance of which depends your Happineſs and Salvation,

'We will join our Vows to thoſe innocent Vows which you Heart will offer up. You may judge SIRE, of the Fervency of our Prayers, by our preſent Fears and Uneaſineſs, and by that Uneaſineſs meaſure our Reſpect and our Love for the Glory of your Majeſty.

Fig. 33. *The cuts in the headings of* The Post Man *were added in No.* 115, *Jan.* 30–*Feb.* 1, 1696. *The blocks were replaced in* 1699, 1700, 1701, *and at least every year thereafter, sometimes changing places from right to left.* The Post Boy *adopted similar cuts in Jan.* 1706. *The designs of* The Post Man, *shewn in this upper portion of the issue, are (including the factotum) engraved by Francis Hoffman*

Boys with identical cuts appearing together for a considerable period, and *The Post Man* with an almost identical heading. From this more or less unwilling consensus there arose a layout which became a tradition of the English newspaper trade. As time elapsed, these cuts on the Baldwin model became the common property of every newspaper printer. Their gradual development into necessary adjuncts of day-to-day journalism may be exactly traced. The three journals we have mentioned so firmly planted their simple layout in the consciousness of their readers that no later paper intended to serve the same market could afford to be 'different'.

Much of the controversial material exchanged between Boyer and Roper deserves quotation in any history of English journalism, but it cannot, unfortunately, be regarded as relevant to our enquiry. One point emerges for our consideration—Boyer admits he was paid extra for what he calls 'Postscripts'. We must describe these, for even until the close of the first quarter of the nineteenth century, London newspapers are still to be found heading their latest news with the word 'Postscript'. Thus [Mrs] *Johnson's British Gazette and Sunday Monitor*, the earliest established Sunday paper,

LLIL

Numb. 2398.

The Post Boy,

With the Freſheſt Advices, Foreign and Domeſtick.

From Saturday September 23. to Tueſday September 26 1710

Late on Friday *Night arriv'd One Mail from* Holland.

The following LETTER was written by an Engliſh Officer in the Queen's Royal Regiment of Dragoons.

Saragoſſa, Aug. 21. N.S.

YEſterday Morning at a Quarter after Eleven, we attack'd the Enemy, and by Four, had beat 'em entirely out of the Field. We have taken near 200 Colours, Standards, and Kettle-Drums, with all their Ammunition, and almoſt 4000 Priſoners; and have kill'd near as many. Their Foot are entirely ruin'd, and the Horſe are retiring, in the greateſt Confuſion, towards Navarre and Madrid. We have likewiſe taken 16 Pieces of Cannon, with ſeveral Priſoners of Diſtinction ... nance of our Courtiers. We ſee in their Faces a forc'd Gayety, which cannot, however, conceal their profound Thoughtfulneſs. The Duke d'Alba, who is a brave Gentleman, dares not ſpeak neither, but lets us know by his Shrugs, that the Affairs of Spain are come to a Criſis, which denotes an irremediable Danger. That Duke goes often to Verſailles, to ſolicite a numerous Succour of Troops. They promiſe him great Matters; but he frequently hints, that theſe are but Words. The Biſhop of Murcia, a firm Adherent to the Duke of Anjou, and conſequently, an inveterate Enemy to the Allies, no ſooner heard of the ill Succeſs of the Battle of Saragoſſa, but he rais'd Men at his own Charge, to reinforce the Garriſons of Alicant and Valencia; for which the Duke of Anjou wrote a Letter with his own hand, to thank him for his Zeal and

Fig. 34. *Upper portion of Roper's* The Post Boy *after the heading cuts had been added by A. Boyer in* 1706

IIII

Numb. 2664.

The Post Boy.

From Thurſday June 5. to Saturday June 7. 1712.

Yeſterday Morning came in the Mails due on Monday *from* Holland *and* Flanders, *with the following Advices.*

Rome, May 21. N S.

IN the laſt Conſiſtory, which was held on Wedneſday, upon the Subject of the Canonization, the Pope, at laſt, declared the Promotion of Eleven new Cardinals; two of whom, *viz.* the Fathers Tolomei and Tomaſi, did at firſt excuſe themſelves from accepting of that Dignity, and would not do it, but at the Pope's expreſs Command, *under the Pain of Sinning*; ſo that they took the Hat, with the others who were named, in the Publick Conſiſtory held this Morning, in order to their aſſiſting tomorrow at the Solemnity of the Canonization, for which all the neceſ... Duke de Vendoſme was ſtill at Tortoſa the 18th of May, where he was preparing an Artillery of 30 heavy Cannon; which makes us believe he deſigns to beſiege either Terragona or Montblanc; but as the Germans were already encamp'd, to the Number of 8 or 10000 Men, between Igualada and Santa Coloma, where they expected more Troops; many doubt whether either of thoſe Places can be attack'd with Succeſs. Letters from Court continue to aſſure, That Things go well with relation to the Peace. We are now told, the Spaniſh Plenipotentiaries will tarry here till the Queen of Spain is brought to bed, which we expect to hear of within a Fortnight at fartheſt.

Arras, June 6. N S. Two days ago, 22 of our Huſſars were hang'd up in the Mareſchal de Villars's Army, which continues in the ſame Situation along the Scheld, for committing Sacrilege and divers other Villanies in the Villages betwixt Cambray and Bapaume, under pretence of being Enemies. Yeſter-

Fig. 35. The Post Boy's *final title; the sub-title,* Freshest Advices, *etc.*, *was dropped in* 1711 which continued under the title of *The Sunday Monitor* until 1829, carried to its end a back-page column headed 'Postscript'.

The term 'Postscript' itself dates from the later seventeenth century, and Boyer's is the first direct reference to it which I have come across outside the sheets themselves. The term was applied to written additions of late news inserted in the margins of printed papers by the clerks of the booksellers through whom the subscribers received their copies. For instance, if the lately announced result of a law case at the Guildhall was considered of interest to a customer, the bookseller who supplied him would add it in MS. at the tail of the final page, and such an addition was a 'Postscript'. Dawks's *Letter*, amongst others, explicitly calculated for these additions and left space accordingly. The next step was the separate issue of printed single-sheet 'Postscripts'. The earliest forms of such prints are not clearly self-explanatory. They do not, for instance, label themselves as 'Postscripts'. Nor do they proclaim the title of their parent paper. Hence it is not easy to date these inchoate varieties; moreover, on account of their practical anonymity, due either to the imprint on surviving copies being omitted or shaved off in binding, their printers are unknown. The probability is that *The London Gazette* was first in the field with this innovation, and that upon perceiving its utility, as a side line, other journals followed. What was originally an emergency became a practice, and ultimately an abuse. As such it fell into disrepute and was abandoned, not to appear again until the late eighteenth century, when it reappears under the name of 'Extraordinary'. This we shall see in due time; at the moment, we have to return to the Postscript in its original form. It is a rough and obviously hurried piece of setting, printed, or rather shoved, on to an ordinary half-folio sheet, publishing a letter which had arrived after the issue of the parent journal. At first it did not itself bear any journal's name as its sponsor. Possibly this means that it was not delivered apart from the paper proper and only to customers who could be relied upon to pay an extra charge for it. It is also likely that, in the beginning, the regular writer of the journal was not responsible for the Postscripts. Perhaps he only came into possession of the originals as and when the Printer delivered them. Thus, if the Printer's 'Author' were absent, the Printer himself would, with the minimum of editing, rush a newly-arrived mail into type on his own account—if he knew the language, as men like Buckley and James did.

Leaving conjecture aside, it is well to base our observations upon the Postscripts in their comparatively mature form. The earliest complete sheet

I have come across is headed 'A | POSTSCRIPT | to the | **Post Boy**, in No. 23 | Wednesday, July 3, 1695', bearing the imprint 'Printed for R. Baldwin, A. Roper and E. Wilkinson, 1695'. It is a fairly well-arranged piece of type-setting. There is no device used, so that *The Post Boy*'s sheet is characteristic of the Postscript in its second stage.

Numb. 5221.

THE

Post-Boy.

From Saturday January 5. to Tuesday January 8. 1722.

On Saturday *arrived One Mail from* Holland; *as did the next day that due from* France.

Vienna, Dec. 26. N. S.

THE Emperor has taken a Reſolution to go with the Empreſs to Prague the Beginning of July next; and they are to continue there till May the next Year. They are both to be crown'd there; and then, according to the Conſtitutions of the Empire, the Empreſs will be entitled to a clear Revenue of 100,000 Crowns a Year for Life, if ſhe ſhould ſurvive the Emperor. ——Our laſt Letters from Conſtantinople ſay, it was reported there, that an Army werp, having obtain'd Leave to ſend a fourth Ship to the Eaſt Indies, the ſame will be ready to ſail in about a Fortnight's time from Oſtend; and they have appointed Capt. Hall their Captain and Supercargo.

Paris, Jan. 9. N. S. It is rumour'd, that the Marquiſſes de Levi, de Biron, and de la Valliere, who are Lieutenant-Generals, and the Prince of Talmont of the Houſe of Tremoille, will ſhortly be created Dukes and Peers; and that the Marquis d'Alegre, and the Counts de Medavi and du Bourg, Lieutenant-Generals, will be promoted to the Rank of Mareſchals of France.

Hague, Jan. 12. N. S. Mynheer Frederick Batavadurus Taets Van Amerongen is made Governor of Maeſtricht, in the room of Lieutenant-General de Villattes deceaſed; and Monſieur Henry de Monteze ſucceeds Mynheer Van Amerongen in the Government of Tournay.

Fig. 36. The Post-Boy *with heading cuts and factotum by Francis Hoffman*

Since, however, the development and commercialisation of the Postscript is in largest measure due to Richard Baldwin and to later proprietors of *The Post Man*, it will be more convenient if we take that journal, and not *The Post Boy*, as our field. In *The Post Man* of February 4–6, 1696, it is announced that:

This Paper having found a General acceptance, the Publisher has thought fit to add a Postscript on the 3d side of a whole sheet, which shall be done upon good Paper, and shall contain, all the most Remarkable occurrences if any Gentleman or News Writer[1] shall think fit to make use of them, etc.

By the 'third side of a whole sheet' it was probably meant that copies of *The Post Man*, being worked off upon a full, instead of the normal half-sheet, the first page of the second leaf (i.e. p. 3 of the entire sheet with a blank

[1] This inclusion seems to indicate that professional news-writers (attached to booksellers) purchased copies to use as the basis for their own despatches.

Numb. 1775.

Poſtſcript to the

Poſt-Boy.

London, Sept. 26.

BY Letters from Portſmouth, dated the 25th Inſtant, we have Advice, That that Morning arriv'd at Spithead her Majeſty's Ship the Fowey Pink, a Fifth Rate, of thirty two Guns, being ſent Expreſs from Sir John Leake, whoſe Squadron he left in Altea-Bay, homeward-bound. He reports, That the Caſtle of Alicant ſurrendred to her Majeſty's Forces, fourteen days after the taking of the Town; And, That Sir John Jennings in the Devonſhire, and about Eleven Men of War more, are Sail'd for the Weſt-Indies, in order to reinforce Admiral Whetſtone.

Brigadier Hamilton is come over in this Ship, which has been one and twenty days in her Paſſage.

The Chicheſter of Fourſcore Guns, and the Reſtoration and Elizabeth of Seventy Guns each, are ſuddenly to go to the Streights.

Printed for Abel Roper at the Black-Boy in Fleetſtreet.

Postscript to the Post-Boy, *September 26*, 1706, *from the original in the University Library, Cambridge*

verso) contained the lately arrived mail. It is likely that such lately arrived mails were not printed but written on the third side. The announcement proceeds to say that:

> They may have them at a very reasonable rate at the Publishers at the Oxford Arms in Warwick Lane,

and that

> there will be space left, for business or what other news they shall think proper to incert, they are designed to be publisht at 4 in the afternoon, every Post day and will begin next week....

From the Burney Collection it is evident that these Postscripts were also sold separately, i.e. in half-sheets. Evidently, too, the parent *Post Man* was issued in the mornings, as the announcement quoted makes it clear that the Publisher, when he thought circumstances were favourable, issued an evening edition with late news in time to catch the outgoing posts.

The matter in these printed postscripts was generally composed in larger type than the body of the paper and set to the full measure, not in double column. Printing the late news had its advantages, but it was obviously not always an economic desirability unless the number to print passed a certain point. Below that number, written postscripts were safer business. Yet experience demonstrated that written postscripts were open to abuse. First, bogus postscripts were written in and charged extra by certain of the more unscrupulous sort of bookseller and hawker; it then became necessary to answer the complaints of subscribers who found unsubstantiated news incorporated and palmed off upon them as written postscripts authorised by *The Post Man*, and to give the names and addresses of booksellers from whom authorised written postscripts could be secured. Thus, the number for April 15–18, 1704, announces that: 'A written postscript to this paper or news-letter, containing all the remarkable occurrences of the day and the chief heads of the foreign mails that came in after the printing of *The Post Man* is to be had of Mr Nye's...' and two booksellers are named, with their addresses. By this means, *The Post Man* was enabled to conduct a news service of items for which it was prepared to take responsibility.

An even more serious abuse then developed, by which the reputation of *The Post Man* was compromised by piratical or forged written and printed postscripts. The provision of a blank leaf was a great convenience to any subscriber, since he could write thereon any sort of message which, under existing circumstances, could be sent through the post at the newspaper rate. Such semi-blank issues of *The Post Man* invited abuse in an unscrupulous age. In No. 1223 of *The Post Man*, January 1, 1704, the publisher writes:

Whereas there is a considerable number of Post-Men with a Blank Leaf, for People to write their own News or Private business; now to prevent any mistake, the Author repeats here his former Advertisement, that he is neither directly nor indirectly concerned in any Written Postscript, or any other News but what is Printed in the Post-Man.

The important word here is 'Printed': *The Post Man* took responsibility only for printed postscripts. But finally, as a notice in *The Post Man* for December 1–4, 1705, warns us, printed postscripts were not more secure from the counterfeiter than the written ones:

Whereas a Sham News Paper was published on Saturday night, intituled, a Postscript to the Post-Man, we think fit to take notice of it here, not so much to undeceive the World, for 'tis hop'd nobody could fancy that it came from the Author of the Post-Man, but to give warning to the Persons concern'd, that they will find it in their Interest to give over their scandalous Practice, and that no body may be imposed upon, this is to give notice, that the Author of the Post-Man will never publish a Postscript[1] but when there is some extraordinary News, and never after Candle-light: the true Postscript shall have, as they always had, the same Cuts as the Post-Man.

The reference to the cuts as an identification of the true Postscript played into the hands of the enemy, as is revealed in *The Post Man*'s next notice, printed in the issue of April 11–13, 1706, and repeated in later numbers:

Whereas Sham Postscripts are frequently published with the Cuts and Title of the Post-Man, bating some small difference, whereby the Publick is notoriously imposed upon, as it happened on Tuesday night, when 2 or 3 pretended Postscripts to the Post-Man were published. We think fit to repeat what we have formerly declared, that in order to prevent such frauds, we have declined Printing any Postscripts; and therefore all Postscripts that shall come out with the Cuts or Title of the Post-Man are to be looked upon as Shams, and those who sell them as Cheats, and ought to be used as such.

[1] There is reason to believe that the written Postscript was an affair in which the Printer rather than the Author was interested. After 1700 *The Post Man* was 'Printed by Fr. Leach in Elliott's Court, Little Old Bailey', who is mentioned also in such notices as that 'The Author of this Paper having received new complaints about written Postscripts to his Paper, thinks fit to repeat once more that he is not concern'd therein, and knowing on the other hand, that the Postscript he has recommended, meets with a general approbation and good success. This is to give notice, That such who will have the same, may direct to Mr Leach, in the Little Old Bayly, and they shall be supply'd with whatever is worthy their information' (*The Post Man*, September 7–9, 1704).

A
Poſtſcript
TO THE
POST-MAN.

London, *Auguſt* 11. 1710.

This Day came in an Expreſs, with the welcome News of a Victory obtain'd by the King of Spain, *over the Forces of the Duke of* Anjou. *Which is in Subſtance as follows.*

THE Duke of Anjou being inform'd, That 5000 Palatines were on their March from Gironne, to join the King of Spain near Balaguer, reſolved to decamp the 26th of July from Ivars, and repaſs the Segra. Whereupon King Charles ordered General Stanhope with 14 Squadrons of Horſe and Dragoons, and a Detachment of Grenadiers, to march, and endeavour to fall on their Rear.

Accordingly General Stanhope advanc'd, though he had an Ague upon him, and attack'd the 27th their Rear, conſiſting of Twenty Six Squadrons, which were put into Diſorder; Whereupon the Duke of Anjou ſent all the Cavalry of his Army to ſupport them; and King Charles doing the like, the Engagement became general between the Horſe of both Armies. The Action laſted ſome Hours, but at laſt the Troops of the Duke of Anjou gave way. The General who commanded them, with ſeveral other Perſons of Note were taken Priſoners. The Slaughter was very great, both on the Field of Battel, and in the Purſuit. The Duke of Anjou retired with his Foot to Lerida. The Allies loſt ſome conſiderable Officers, and General Stanhope received a Contuſion in his Right Shoulder.

The Expreſs who brought this News to Prince Eugene and the Duke of Marlborough, went through Ghent in his way to the Army; and they have Printed there the following Account: Which perhaps in ſome Particulars is ſomewhat exaggerated.

Ghent, Aug. 18. Laſt Night an Expreſs arrived here from Milan, (from whence he ſet out the 8th Inſtant) in his way to the Army, with Diſpatches from the King of Spain for the Princes of Savoy and Marlborough. He reports, That the Army of his Catholick Majeſty has entirely defeated in Catalonia the Forces of King Philip. That on the Side of the Enemy, Two Lieutenants-General were killed, with Six Majors-General, Six Brigadiers, 20 Colonels, 24 Lieutenant-Colonels, and 7000 Private Men, beſides a great Number of Priſoners, amongſt whom are 700 Officers. They took from them 30 Pieces of Cannon, and ſeveral Standards and Colours. The Queen of Spain writ this News with her own Hand to her Father, the Duke of Wolfembuttel. The King of Spain was ſtill purſuing his Enemies, when the Expreſs came away.

Printed by *D. Leach* in *Elliot's Court*, in the *Little-Old Baily*, for the Author.

Postscript to the Post-Man (*August* 11, 1710), *showing watermark in the fore-edge of the sheet*

April 23–25, 1706:

There being a Sham Postscript published last night, with an Advertisement, intending to impose the same upon People as a Postscript to the *Post-Man.* We think fit to desire again our Readers to buy no Postscripts to the Post-Man, but from the Hawkers they know, as the only means to stop that Villainous practice; and when there is any material News, we shall take care to publish a Postscript, provided it be a Post-day and not too late.

Ultimately, *The Post Man*, unable to keep its threat to publish no more postscripts, devised, for the absolute safeguarding of its readers, water-marked paper which allowed the margin of each sheet to read 'The Post-Man' in fine large capital letters. It is to be noted that the written postscripts were still available from respectable booksellers, and that these, too, were written upon paper that had the same mark as *The Post Man*. The official notice deserves full quotation:

Since the counterfeiting of Papers under the Title of Postscripts etc. is so much in fashion, that People are not ashamed of that Villainy, the Author of the Post-Man has thought fit to have a particular sort of Paper made for his use having these Words THE POST MAN in the Margin, wrought in the making of the Paper, whereby his Postscripts may easily be distinguished from all others; for such where there is no such Mark are none of his. N.B. That the Post-Man and True Postscript shall be for the future printed on this new Paper; and 'tis hoped that the Paper-makers have not amongst them such scandalous People as to counterfeit this Mark, but if they do, they shall be prosecuted according to Law.[1]

The Postscript to *The Post Man*, in its full development, was often a good-looking sheet. A particularly fine example is the postscript to No. 1252 (March 14, 1704), of course, at this time, on the unmarked paper. A fine piece, setting forth an Express 'with the Welcome News of a Victory obtain'd by the King of Spain over the Forces of the Duke of Anjou', was issued on water-marked paper on August 11, 1710.

War and crisis being as much the fortune of news-men then as now, the forecast and the provisions of the Treaty of Utrecht were matter for several postscripts to Roper's *The Post Boy*. Also a number of issues of this journal during the spring of 1713 were headed, between the two devices of a post-

[1] See *The Post Man* for May 5, 1710. Written Postscripts continued, but, as the following notice proves (January 18–21, 1707), they were recognised, rather than guaranteed, by *The Post Man*: 'A Written Postscript to this Paper is to be had at Mr Mitchel's, at the Rainbow Coffee-house in St Martin's Lane, near Charing Cross, and at Mr Leach's in the Little Old Baily. Note, that it is written on a sheet of Paper that has the same mark as the Post-Man, tho the Author of the Post-Man is not directly nor indirectly concern'd therein'.

boy and a fame, *PAX, PAX, PAX, or a Pacifick Post Boy*, and the flysheets similarly: 'Pacifick Postscript to the Post Boy'.[1]

So much for Postscripts, over which we have perhaps been inclined to spend a little too much time—though with the excuse that no reference to them is made in any of the available histories of the trade.

A final word on them: false or true, they all bore a heading in text set between two cuts each about the size of a penny stamp. This spate of papers

Xx Numb. 3058.

THE Flying-Post: OR, THE POST-MASTER.

From Thursday April 26. to Saturday April 28. 1711.

Ratisbon, April 19.

ON the 15th Instant, the Dyet took into Consideration a Memorial they received the day before from the Chapter of Hildesheim, complaining of the Elector of Hanover's having taken Possession of the chief Towns in that Country, and that his Troops quartered there, have convey'd from thence a professed Enemy to his Native Country. M. Villars arrived Yesterday at Arras, where the Enemies Officers are getting ready their Equipage with great Expedition, because their Army will be formed in four or six Days at farthest. Yesterday a strong Detachment of Horse and Foot was sent by the Allies towards Diest, to secure, from Insults, a great number of Horses that are coming from Germany, to remount the Imperial Cavalry, upon Advice, that several French Parties are Abroad to intercept them, if possible. We hear from Lisle, that the 25th Instant, 80 Vessels arrived there, with Hay, Oats, Meal and other Provisions; and that 60 other Vessels, laden

Fig. 37. *The first heading-blocks of* The Flying-Post

so headed would be sufficient to create a style, but there was still another paper printed exactly in accordance with the *Post Man-Post Boy* formula, viz. *The Flying-Post*. This sheet, also a thrice-weekly (Tuesdays, Thursdays and Saturdays), originated in the same year as *The Post Boy* and it had its postscripts.[2] In 1710 *The Flying-Post* adopted two heading-blocks:

[1] See e.g. April 3, 1713, in which the express of the signing of the Peace was announced under the caption: *PAX, PAX, PAX, or a Pacifick Postscript to the*, etc.

[2] ☞ *The* Flying-Post *coming out early on* Tuesday, Thursday *and* Saturday *Mornings, there is added to it, and will be delivered at Six a Clock, for the future, the same Evenings, a* Postscript *printed, with all the* Domestick *Occurrences that happen, and the News of the* Foreign Mails *that arrive after the* Flying-Post *is published in the Morning. 'Tis done on a good Writing Paper, with Blanks so ordered, that any one may write of their Private Affairs into the Country.*

a fame whose trumpet bore a banner reading 'FAMA VOLAT' on the left, and a writing postmaster seated at a desk on the right. Its Postscripts were similarly headed and handsomely printed by William Hurt of Great Carter Lane. On Saturday, July 24, 1714, similar, but obviously newly engraved, cuts appeared in the heading, and, at the tail above the imprint, a notice that a new printer had been appointed.[1] Trouble with Hurt resulted. He complained that he had been laid off by a clique of writers in the absence

NUMB. 4582.

THE Flying-Post: OR, Post-Master.

From TUESDAY June 12, to THURSDAY June 14. 1722.

Yesterday arrived the Mails due from France *and* Holland.

Rome, May 30.

WHEN Cardinal Alberoni heard how the Congregation, or rather the *Secret Committee* of Cardinals had Sentenced him to Four Years Confinement to a Cloyster, and that the Pope had been so gracious as to change the Sentence to one Year only, his Eminency received the News with so much Resignation, and with such respectful Tokens of Gratitude to the Pope, that when his Innocency heard on't, it so affected him that he immediately shorten'd the Term of his Confinement to Five Months

Sunday last died *John Grigsby*, late Chief Accomptant to the South Sea Company.

Next Morning dyed the Honourable Charles William Vanhulse, Esq; a Member for Bramber, and late Clerk of the King's Robes. He was private Secretary to King *William* of Glorious Memory, and is said to have dy'd worth above 100000 *l.*

The Forces which were review'd by the King last Monday in Hide-park were only the 3 Regiments of Foot-Guards, the Horse being to be review'd another Time. His Majesty having rode round the 3 Regiments, the First of which was on the Right, the Second on the Left, (the Posts of Honour) and the Scots Regiment in the Center; his Majesty made a Stand afterwards near the Ring, the Prince at some small Distance from him, where all the Regiments passed by in Review, Earl Cadogan standing on his Right, and Gen. Withers on his Left, with each his Half-pike. His Majesty and his Royal Highness after having dined in

Fig. 38. The Flying-Post *with heading-cuts and factotum by Francis Hoffman*

beyond the seas of the 'true Author, and being unwilling to suffer any Person to deprive him of a Part of his Livelihood, has resolv'd to continue to print such a Paper'. Thus came out the schismatic *The Flying Post, and*

[1] 'The Proprietor of this Paper having thought fit to change his Printer: This is to acquaint the Publick that he has appointed R. Tookey to print it for the future, and to receive all the Correspondence thereto Belonging.'

Medley,[1] bearing, of course, the original cuts in its heading. The orthodox *Flying-Post* survived this challenge. In 1722 the paper, now printed by M. Jenour (a name we need to remember) of Giltspur Street, carried two superb cuts by Hoffman (signed) of a flying fame with trumpet and *fama volat* banner and two galloping postmen. There was also a fine factotum (twelve lines in depth) of two horsed postmen. But some time before 1727—the file is very incomplete, but 1725 is the indicated year—the paper abandoned its heading devices and cut the space to the minimum by setting its title in two lines of type, *The Flying-Post: or Post-Master*, until the close of its career.

The other two, and more widely circulated, papers of the period, *The Post Boy* and *The Post Man*, progressed with only the slightest changes of appearance. *The Post Boy* of 1711 cast off its sub-title, 'With the Freshest Advices, Foreign and Domestick'. Its devices were re-engraved from time to time. Slight variations appeared in the postscripts, e.g. *The Post Man* printed the word 'Postscript' in text and its name in roman, but it may be said with fair accuracy that before the year 1715 a newly founded newspaper published either on the mornings of alternate days, or twice weekly, or even weekly, would be printed in the format and style originated by Robert Baldwin for *The Post Man* of 1696. We now, however, have to turn back to 1702 and deal with the first English every-morning journal, *The Daily Courant*.

[1] The original *Flying-Post* replied on July 27–29, 1714, that 'whereas a Sham Paper was publish'd last Thursday with the Title of the *Flying Post and Medley*; These are to advertise, That the same was done without the Knowledge of the Proprietor and Authors of the *Flying-Post, or Post-Master*; and that this Original Paper, called the *Flying-Post, or Post-Master* will be carry'd on for the future by the same Hands as before, but with much more Advantage to the Publick than ever, the Proprietor having now enlarg'd his Correspondence both at home and abroad. It may perhaps be expected by some that we should here say something in Answer to the Preface of the first Sham *Flying-Post*, and that we should shew the Reasons why this Paper is taken from Mr Hurt: But tho we have a Copy of the Proprietor's Letter to Mr Hurt, and consequently are privy to his Reasons, and tho they are own'd by all who have seen them to be strictly just, yet as the Proprietor has hitherto thought fit to conceal them, we don't think it convenient for us to publish them, till we have his express Orders for so doing. In the mean time, how can Mr Hurt pretend, without Blushing to say, as he does in his Preface, *That he knows not the Reason of any real or pretended Difference betwixt him and the former Author*, (as he calls him) when he knows he had a Letter with the Reasons under the Proprietor's own Hand? After what has been advertis'd in This and our former Paper, 'tis hoped that Mr Hurt and his Publisher will be more Honourable to the Proprietor and just to themselves than to proceed in carrying on a Paper with another Man's Title'.

CHAPTER IV

THE FIRST DAILY NEWSPAPER AND THE DEVELOPMENT OF THE THRICE-WEEKLY EVENING POSTS

1702–1715

The Daily Courant

The Evening Post

The St James's Post

CHAPTER IV

THE FIRST DAILY PAPER AND THE EVENING POSTS

1702–1715

NOTWITHSTANDING the use of a uniform style for *The Post Boy*, *The Post Man*, *The Flying-Post*, their respective schismatic filiations and all their various true and sham Postscripts, the single line of text and the two small blocks never succeeded in establishing themselves as a normal heading in every-day, or every-evening, journalism. A curiously blind 'follow my leader' policy led *The Daily Courant* to model itself upon the typographical style of *The London Gazette*; and, as the several new evening journals based their settings upon *The Courant*, the *Gazette* style held the position of the leading alternative to that of *The Post Man* and *The Post Boy*. In 1715, however, the *Gazette* style was seriously menaced by *The St James's Post*, but between the beginning of the century and the foundation of the *St James's*, there were two styles, that of *The Courant*, that of *The Post Man*, with, of course, a separate style for essay papers.

The Daily Courant first appeared on Wednesday, March 11, 1702. The author, 'supposing other people to have sense enough to make reflections for themselves', promises news only, and that daily, because foreign prints and correspondences arrived continually and existing newspapers printed their contents as and when it was convenient. The writer of *The Daily Courant* confined his 'matter to half the compass, to save the public at least half the impertinences of ordinary newspapers'.[1] The first nine issues, printed one side only, bore the imprint 'London. Sold by E. Mallet, next door to the King's-Arms Tavern at Fleet-Bridge' placed below the rule at the foot of the two columns forming the body of the composition. The heading set its title, *The Daily Courant*, in Moxon's canon, added a serial number at the upper right-hand corner, and gave the date of issue between two rules. The matter led off with a five-line plain initial, the whole precisely in the format of *The London Gazette* except that the two columns were divided by

[1] By 'ordinary newspapers' the *Courant* author would appear to mean *The Post Man*, *The Post Boy* and the like. The 'impertinences', due to shortage of copy, consist, for the most part of 'observations,' and other random jottings with which these thrice-weekly sheets were supplemented.

a space only and not by a rule, and that the date of issue was placed between rules in the position occupied by the *Gazette*'s line 'Printed by Authority'. After these first nine, there followed some six unnumbered issues between April 22–30 with the imprint 'London. Printed and sold by Sam Buckley at The Dolphin in Little Britain'.

The paper progressed and, from time to time, under Buckley (who also published *The Spectator* from its commencement in 1711) it became a four-page sheet; even, from July 24th, 1710, occasionally becoming a six-page paper. It was always printed in double columns, and, though its dimensions were exceeded by later foundations, it may fairly claim to present the typical format of the first generation of English dailies. The author, a serious journalist, endeavoured to perform 'what he takes to be the proper and only business of a news-writer, to give news, to give it daily and to give it impartially'. He explained in the issue (No. 161) for Thursday, October 22 that he gave accounts which were well warranted rather than those of more doubtful authority;

therefore he makes more use of the Haarlem and Amsterdam Currants than the Gazettes in French that come from Holland; which are little else than Transcripts from the Dutch Prints, and if any thing seem rough, imperfect or obscure in those original accounts, commonly improve and refine them after the French Mode, to something beyond what they directly import. From things of greater moment, he descends to those of less importance, till he has given a thorough account of the Foreign Papers: preferring what is probable and easy to be believ'd, to what is more surprizing and unlikely or founded only on Rumour.

The paper was not dressed 'with an air of news, when there can be none'. When news was exceptionally plentiful, the heading was contracted, the main line being set in great primer. A feature of later issues is the signature conspicuously placed in the upper left-hand corner in order that binders might have the sequence of numbers made more obvious than the numerical notation would supply. The imprint continued at the foot of the first page, whether or no the back page was filled.[1] The custom of repeating the title in a somewhat contracted form at the head of the back page was initiated in 1710.

The circulation must have been reasonably good; or, at least, there is the possibility that the day's issue consisted of more editions than one. 'In some of yesterday's *Courants*' runs a note to No. 1838, 'the nineteenth line of the second column of the first page, for *favour* read *friendship*'—a note which

[1] The practice of printing the imprint under a rule at the foot of the front page continued until *circa* 1760.

Numb.

The Daily Courant.

Wednesday, March 11. 1702.

From the Harlem Courant, Dated March 18. N. S.

Naples, Feb. 22.

ON Wednesday last, our New Viceroy, the Duke of Escalona, arriv'd here with a Squadron of the Galleys of Sicily. He made his Entrance drest in a French habit; and to give us the greater Hopes of the King's coming hither, went to Lodge in one of the little Palaces, leaving the Royal one for his Majesty. The Marquis of Grigni is also arriv'd here with a Regiment of French.

Rome, Feb. 25. In a Military Congregation of State that was held here, it was Resolv'd to draw a Line from Ascoli to the Borders of the Ecclesiastical State, thereby to hinder the Incursions of the Transalpine Troops. Orders are sent to Civita Vecchia to fit out the Galleys, and to strengthen the Garrison of that Place. Signior Casali is made Governor of Perugia. The Marquis del Vasto, and the Prince de Caserta continue still in the Imperial Embassador's Palace; where his Excellency has a Guard of 50 Men every Night in Arms. The King of Portugal has desir'd the Arch-Bishoprick of Lisbon, vacant by the Death of Cardinal Sousa, for the Infante his second Son, who is about 11 Years old.

Vienna, Mar. 4. Orders are sent to the 4 Regiments of Foot, the 2 of Cuirassiers, and to that of Dragoons, which are broke up from Hungary, and are on their way to Italy, and which consist of about 14 or 15000 Men, to hasten their March thither with all Expedition. The 6 new Regiments of Hussars that are now raising, are in so great a forwardness, that they will be compleat, and in a Condition to march by the middle of May. Prince Lewis of Baden has written to Court, to excuse himself from coming thither, his Presence being so very necessary, and so much desir'd on the Upper-Rhine.

Francfort, Mar. 12. The Marquiss d' Uxelles is come to Strasburg, and is to draw together a Body of some Regiments of Horse and Foot from the Garisons of Alsace; but will not lessen those of Strasburg and Landau, which are already very weak. On the other hand, the Troops of His Imperial Majesty, and his Allies, are going to form a Body near Germeshein in the Palatinate, of which Place, as well as of the Lines at Spires, Prince Lewis of Baden is expected to take a View, in three or four days. The English and Dutch Ministers, the Count of Frise, and the Baron Vander Meer, and likewise the Imperial Envoy Count Lowenstein, are gone to Nordlingen, and it is hop'd that in a short time we shall hear from thence of some favourable Resolutions for the Security of the Empire.

Liege, Mar. 14. The French have taken the Cannon de Longie, who was Secretary to the Dean de Mean, out of our Castle, where he has been for some time a Prisoner, and have deliver'd him to the Provost of Maubeuge, who has carry'd him from hence, but we do not know whither.

Paris, Mar. 13. Our Letters from Italy say, That most of our Reinforcements were Landed there; that the Imperial and Ecclesiastical Troops seem to live very peaceably with one another in the Country of Parma, and that the Duke of Vendome, as he was visiting several Posts, was within 100 Paces of falling into the Hands of the Germans. The Duke of Chartres, the Prince of Conti, and several other Princes of the Blood, are to make the Campaign in Flanders under the Duke of Burgundy; and the Duke of Maine is to Command upon the Rhine.

From the Amsterdam Courant, Dated Mar. 18.

Rome, Feb. 25. We are taking here all possible Precautions for the Security of the Ecclesiastical State in this present Conjuncture, and have desir'd to raise 3000 Men in the Cantons of Switzerland. The Pope has appointed the Duke of Berwick to be his Lieutenant-General, and he is to Command 6000 Men on the Frontiers of Naples: He has also settled upon him a Pension of 6000 Crowns a year during Life.

From the Paris Gazette, Dated Mar. 18. 1702.

Naples, Febr. 17. 600 French Soldiers are arrived here, and are expected to be follow'd by 3400 more. A Courier that came hither on the 14th. has brought Letters by which we are assur'd that the King of Spain designs to be here towards the end of March; and accordingly Orders are given to make the necessary Preparations against his Arrival. The two Troops of Horse that were Commanded to the Abruzzo are posted at Pescara with a Body of Spanish Foot, and others in the Fort of Montorio.

Paris, March. 18. We have Advice from Toulon of the 5th instant, that the Wind having long stood favourable, 22000 Men were already sail'd for Italy, that 2500 more were Embarking, and that by the 15th it was hoped they might all get thither. The Count d' Estrees arriv'd there on the Third instant, and set all hands at work to fit out the Squadron of 9 Men of War and some Fregats, that are appointed to carry the King of Spain to Naples. His Catholick Majesty will go on Board the *Thunderer*, of 110 Guns.

We have Advice by an Express from Rome of the 18th of February, That notwithstanding the pressing Instances of the Imperial Embassadour, the Pope had Condemn'd the Marquis del Vasto to lose his Head and his Estate to be confiscated, for not appearing to Answer the Charge against him of Publickly Scandalizing Cardinal Janson.

ADVERTISEMENT.

IT will be found from the Foreign Prints, which from time to time, as Occasion offers, will be mention'd in this Paper, that the Author has taken Care to be duly furnish'd with all that comes from Abroad in any Language. And for an Assurance that he will not, under Pretence of having Private Intelligence, impose any Additions of feign'd Circumstances to an Action, but give his Extracts fairly and Impartially; at the beginning of each Article he will quote the Foreign Paper from whence 'tis taken, that the Publick, seeing from what Country a piece of News comes with the Allowance of that Government, may be better able to Judge of the Credibility and Fairness of the Relation: Nor will he take upon him to give any Comments or Conjectures of his own, but will relate only Matter of Fact; supposing other People to have Sense enough to make Reflections for themselves.

This Courant (as the Title shews) will be Publish'd Daily: being design'd to give all the Material News as soon as every Post arrives: and is confin'd to half the Compass, to save the Publick at least half the Impertinences, of ordinary News-Papers.

LONDON. Sold by *E. Mallet*, next Door to the *King's-Arms* Tavern at *Fleet-Bridge*.

Numb. [1] *of the first English daily newspaper, March* 11, 1702

must indicate that there was time to make the correction in some part of the edition.

In 1708 *The Daily Courant* followed *The Post Man*, *The Post Boy* and others in providing a Postscript giving the contents of mails which arrived after the publication of the morning's paper, and, presumably, this was published in the afternoon timed for the posts. *The Daily Courant* apparently ceased in June 1735—the last extant issue was numbered 6002—a splendid record for times which, if more settled than the Popish Plot period, can hardly be regarded as propitious. During the course of its career of a generation or more, *The Daily Courant* saw the foundation of more than one daily, several twice- or thrice-weeklies, weekly journals and a number of vigorous evening papers, one or two of which lived to serve an early nineteenth-century public.

The Evening Post, 'printed for the Author and published by John Morphew', is the first foundation in whose title the word 'Evening' is used. It was begun in August 1706—the earliest issue in the Burney Collection is No. 3, dated "*THURSDAY*, August 29 [Six at Night]" at its head, between the usual pair of rules. It is not, however, the first paper to be published in the evenings, for there were several publications—*Dawks's News-Letter* is the best known and most important—which came out on Tuesday, Thursday and Saturday. The day and time of publication were regulated by the Post Office. In the latter part of the seventeenth century six great roads to Holyhead, Bristol, Plymouth, Edinburgh, Yarmouth and Dover bore the mails, and with them the newspapers. As the date-line in the heading of *The Evening Post* explicitly says, the paper was published 'Six at Night'. The country carriers left London late at night on Tuesday, Thursday and Saturday. As there was no post between the various parts of London until 1680, a newspaper publisher had to effect delivery by his messenger. In consequence of these arrangements, the rule of evening thrice-weekly publication held until *The Daily Courant*.

In 1691 a daily post to Kent and the Downs was established—a great boon to a London daily.

It is not clear—so few are the copies that remain—when *The Evening Post, With an Historical Account*, etc., ceased publication. It always remained a single folio half-sheet. A second paper with the title of *The Evening Post* was brought out, in 4 pp. quarto, on September 6, 1709, by E. Berington and J. Morphew.[1] The prospectus printed in the first number claims that the

[1] The new serial numeration seems to prove it a separate foundation.

existing prints give little real news, and that in addition to this imposition "there must be £3 or £4 per annum paid by gentlemen that are out of town for written news which is so far generally from having any probability, of having any matter of fact in it, that it is frequently stuffed up with a *We hear etc.*, or *An Eminent Jew Merchant* has received a letter etc., being nothing more than downright fiction."[1]

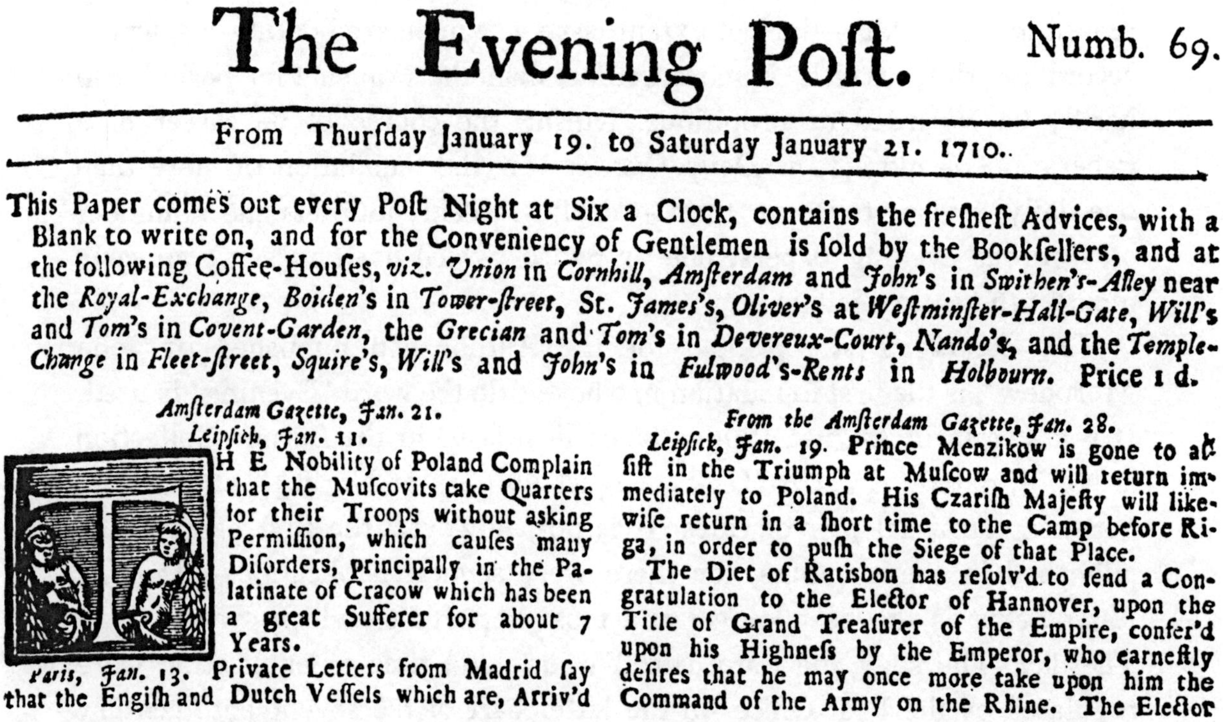

The Evening Poſt. Numb. 69.

From Thurſday January 19. to Saturday January 21. 1710.

This Paper comes out every Poſt Night at Six a Clock, contains the freſheſt Advices, with a Blank to write on, and for the Conveniency of Gentlemen is ſold by the Bookſellers, and at the following Coffee-Houſes, *viz. Union* in *Cornhill*, *Amſterdam* and *John*'s in *Swithen's-Alley* near the *Royal-Exchange*, *Boiden*'s in *Tower-ſtreet*, St. *James's*, *Oliver*'s at *Weſtminſter-Hall-Gate*, *Will*'s and *Tom*'s in *Covent-Garden*, the *Grecian* and *Tom*'s in *Devereux-Court*, *Nando's*, and the *Temple-Change* in *Fleet-ſtreet*, *Squire*'s, *Will*'s and *John*'s in *Fulwood*'s-*Rents* in *Holbourn*. Price 1 d.

Amſterdam Gazette, Jan. 21.

Leipſick, Jan. 11.

THE Nobility of Poland Complain that the Muſcovits take Quarters for their Troops without asking Permiſſion, which cauſes many Diſorders, principally in the Palatinate of Cracow which has been a great Sufferer for about 7 Years.

Paris, Jan. 13. Private Letters from Madrid ſay that the Engiſh and Dutch Veſſels which are, Arriv'd

From the Amſterdam Gazette, Jan. 28.

Leipſick, Jan. 19. Prince Menzikow is gone to aſſiſt in the Triumph at Muſcow and will return immediately to Poland. His Czariſh Majeſty will likewiſe return in a ſhort time to the Camp before Riga, in order to puſh the Siege of that Place.

The Diet of Ratisbon has reſolv'd to ſend a Congratulation to the Elector of Hannover, upon the Title of Grand Treaſurer of the Empire, confer'd upon his Highneſs by the Emperor, who earneſtly deſires that he may once more take upon him the Command of the Army on the Rhine. The Elector

Fig. 39. *Heading of E. Berington and J. Morphew's* Evening Post (4 *pp. quarto*)

There was a considerable town sale for the evening papers and copies were to be had all over town, as is proved by the naming of a string of fifteen coffee-houses in the streamer which *The Evening Post* carried under its heading.

Postscripts to *The Evening Post* were issued—one supposes primarily for town circulation, unless they came out well after six but before the closing of the posts. In the issue of *The Evening Post* for June 9–12, 1711, there is a postscript printed, not on a separate or separable sheet or page, but on the body of the paper, below the imprint. It was headed in large capitals, "POSTSCRIPT | London June 12 | This evening arrived 2 Mails from Flanders", etc. Throughout its career, the paper was headed with a simple line of upper- and lower-case roman, in its early days of a size equal to that of *The London Gazette*, and later of a size smaller.

In 1711 three new evening journals were started, *The Evening Courant*

[1] Timperley 594.

THE No. 14.

St. *JAMES*'s POST.

With the beſt Occurrences Foreign and Domeſtick.

From Wedneſday, February 23. to Friday, February 25. 1715.

Conſtantinople, Jan. 10.

THE Venetian Ambaſſador, having given freſh Aſſurances, that none of the Turkiſh Subjects, who were in the Dominions of Venice before the Declaration of War, ſhould be detained, but all ſuffered freely to depart, has been at length ſet at Liberty, with all his Family; but upon Condition, to depart this City within 24 Hours, and the Turkiſh Dominions in 20 Days, and he is accordingly ſail'd in a French Ship. The Warlike Preparations are carried on here, at Negropont, Lepanto, and throughout all Theſſaly; the Troops from the greater and leſſer Aſia are marching towards this City, and 40 Men of War are put out to Sea, to cruize on the Coaſts of the Morea. We hear from Smirna, That the Venetian Conſul there, who had withdrawn himſelf into the French Conſul's Houſe, for fear of being inſulted, is got away by Sea. The Turks in Barbary demand 50000 Pieces of Eight of the Engliſh, on Pretence, that by their Aſſiſtance a Ship of theirs was taken by the Malteſes.

Liſbon, Jan. 26. On the 22d in the Evening Mr. Vignory arrived here Poſt from Madrid, being commiſſion'd, as we are inform'd, by the King of Spain, to conclude the Peace between the two Crowns. Yeſterday he had a Conference with the Miniſters of our Court, and in the Afternoon an Audience of the King. This Day he has viſited the French Ambaſſador, which gives Uneaſineſs to ſome other Miniſters. We are aſſured, that the Difficulties which retarded the concluſion of the Peace, are removed, and that the next Expreſs from Utrecht will bring the Treaty ſign'd. 2 Men of War more are ſail'd out of this Port, to join the four others, which are cruizing upon the Salee Rovers, who every now and then take ſome Portugueſe Veſſels.

Madrid, Feb. 4. The King has appointed F. Francis Ami, a Jeſuit, Preceptor to the Prince of Aſturias. His Majeſty has ordered Monſ. Orri not to interfere any more in Martial Affairs.

Perpignan, Feb. 4. The 30 French Battalions which are in this Place and the adjacent Ports, have receiv'd Orders to be in a Readineſs to paſs the Mountains, and march to Girona, to remain in the Service of the King of Spain till the Reduction of Majorca, which is ſtill given out will be attack'd before the End of this Month.

Cleves, Feb. 23. All things hitherto ſeem to tend to a War on the Side of Pomerania. The Troops of Hannover have received Orders to be in a readineſs to march; as have alſo thoſe of Pruſſia, and the King's Regiment, which was to have march'd the 28th to Berlin, is countermanded. They write from Deux Ponts, that the Swedes are at a Stand how to convey the Troops they have raiſed there, into Pomerania.

Bruſſels, Feb. 21. Count Schonborn, Vice-chancellor of the Empire, arriv'd here 2 Days ago: The ſame Day the Pope's Nuncio gave an Entertainment to Count Coningſeck, and ſome

Fig. 40. *J. Baker's* The St James's Post, *shewing early use of royal device in newspaper heading*

(Tuesdays and Thursdays and Saturdays from July 17, 1711) and *The General Post* (on Thursdays and Saturdays from July 19, 1711). The former was a bare copy of *The Evening Post*. *The General Post*, in a streamer introduction running over two columns, claimed to give the substance of all the news scattered through the several existing papers. Little change was made in format. It was of the quarto size of *The Evening Post* and *The Evening Courant*. *The Night Post*, another thrice-weekly, founded in or about the same July 1711, used precisely the same conventions of size and display as its evening predecessors, namely the title in upper- and lower-case canon or two-line great primer; serial number in the upper right-hand corner in a small size of text; the day of the week and date between two rules of the full measure of the page; a plain or decorated initial letter to the first paragraph; the text in two columns, separated only by a space; the imprint on the final page. All such thrice-weekly Evening Posts, etc. were four pages of quarto, the thrice-weekly morning Post Boys, etc. were half-sheets in folio, or whole sheet (equals four pages) with Postscript. The newspapers were, therefore, plain as *The London Gazette* and *The Daily Courant* or decorated with blocks as *The Post Boy* or *The Post Man*. These two styles held good for the period 1702–14. But there was a change in 1715. A morning paper, *The St James's Post, With the best Occurrences Foreign and Domestick*, in four pages quarto, issued on Mondays, Wednesdays and Fridays from the January of that year by J. Baker, contributed an innovation to the arrangement of its title which had lasting consequences. From its earliest issue, the *St James's* carried a device centred between two blocks of the titling words.

This device, consisting of the royal bearings topped with a royal crown and imposed against a cope, is without precedent in English journalism. *The London Gazette* itself used no block of the royal arms until 1783, by which time the tradition begun by the *St James's* had secured the adhesion of half the newspapers of London. There does not appear to be any more authority for the use of the royal arms in the title of *The St James's Post* of 1715 than in the title of the *Daily Mail* of 1932, though the reason for its presence in an imperialist paper may be as evident as the reason for its absence in the heading of the *Daily Herald*.

So far as *The St James's Post* is concerned, the block is a permanency, i.e. until the demise of the paper in 1734. In the first state, as shewn in the earliest Burney number available (February 23–25, 1715), the cut is sensibly proportioned, although it does not part the two blocks of type any too happily. In No. 55 (May 30–June 1, 1715) a new cut appears in which the

[141] NUMB. 24.

The St. James's EVENING POST.

From Saturday, July 23. to Tuesday, July 26. 1715.

Hague, July 16.

WE expect with Impatience the next Letters from the North, as well to know whether any new Propositions of Peace have been made, as what Events of War have since pass'd; the Scituation of the Armies on both Sides giving great Grounds to believe that they cannot lie long without coming to some signal Action. The Marquis de Miraval, Ambassador of Spain, being arriv'd here, made his Visits on the 22d to the great Pensionary, and to the President for this Week of the Assembly of the States; and has deliver'd his Credentials.

Deal, July 24.

On Friday Afternoon last, Sir Geo. Bing arriv'd here in His Majesty's Yatcht Henrietta, and the next Day hoisted his Flag on Board the Windsor. This Day the Romney sail'd Westward, and the Deal-Castle for the Nore. Remain here, the Windsor Oxford, Pembroke, Antelope, Southampton, Strafford, and Faulkland.

St. James's July 20.

On Wednesday the 20th Instant, the Duke of Grafton and the Ld. Carteret, took the respective Oaths for their Employments; the first as Ld. Lieutenant of Suffolk; and the other as Bailiff of Jersey. On the 23d, the Earl of Suffolk and Bindon, took the Oaths as Ld. Lieutenant of Essex.

To the King's most Excellent Majesty.

The humble Address of the Archbishop, Bishops, and Clergy of the Province of Canterbury in Convocation assembled.

WE your Majesty's most dutiful and loyal Subjects the Archbishop, Bishops and Clergy of the Province of Canterbury, in Convocation assembled, do think our selves oblig'd in Duty and Gratitude to your Majesty, to make our most humble Acknowledgements for that gracious Message you were pleased to send to the House of Commons, recommending the Provision of a Maintenance for the Ministers who are to attend the Service of the 50 new Churches begun to be built in and about the Cities of London and Westminster, under the pious Encouragement of your Majesty's most excellent Predecessor of ever blessed Memory.

A Message so piously intended, and so well received, we trust cannot fail of its desir'd Effect to the Honour of the Church of England, and the Advancement of our Holy Religion.

After all the Declarations your Majesty has been pleased to make in Favour of our establish'd Church, and the real Proofs you have given of your Concern for its Interests, We hope that none will be found so unjust as to doubt of your Affection to it And we do most humbly assure Your Majesty, that we will take all Opportunities to instil into those who are under our Care, the same grateful Sense that we our selves have of your Majesty's Goodness, and that at this Time more especially, when the Quiet of our Realms is disturb'd by Insurrections at Home, and the Nation threatned with an Invasion from Abroad. We will put them in mind of those strict Obligations of Conscience whereby they are engag'd to defend and support your Majesty's Government, and will earnestly exhort them to exemplifie, by a suitable Practice, those Principles of Obedience and Loyalty which the Church of England hath always thought it her Duty to profess.

May the divine Providence defeat all wicked Designs that shall be form'd against our holy Faith, and your Majesty the Defender of it; and may that God who has put it into

(Price Three Halfpence.) Z to

Fig. 41. The St James's Evening Post *with royal device as printed by J. Baker of the Black Boy, Paternoster Row* coat-of-arms is given a flying cord. This design also appears, slightly reduced in size, on the earliest number I have been able to see (No. 24, July 23–26, 1715) of *The St James's Evening Post*, founded later in the same year by the same printer, J. Baker of the Black Boy, published on Tuesday, Thursday and Saturday nights. This, also a quarto in four pages, makes an even better appearance since its heading is relieved of the cumbrous cliché (descending from the Diurnalls and the Mercuries) 'Occurrences Foreign and Domestick'. By way of further adornment to No. 96 (January 7–10, 1715/6), the small (six-line) factotum initial which led off the text of the first column was superseded by a nine-liner in which the inserted capital is the centre-point of a shield whose supporters are a fine lion and true unicorn respectively. Obviously, in the absence of any official objections, it could

(*a*)

(*b*)

The first blocks of the Royal Arms (with supporters) in Newspapers. Factotum (a) from St James's Evening Post, *January* 10, 1715/6; *heading-block (b) from the same* Post, *September* 12, 1727

only be a matter of time before these supporters were transferred from the factotum to the shield in the heading. When this was effected, the design of the factotum was correspondingly altered. We can see this change in operation.

The earliest example, which the very imperfect Burney file provides, of a journal whose heading incorporates a full royal device is the issue of this same *St James's Evening Post* for September 9–12, 1727. The fine design of this heading-block of the royal arms is matched with a worthy twelve-line factotum of St George and the Dragon which occupies the place previously filled by a 'royal' factotum. By this time the measure of the sheet, increased from 14½ in. × 11¾ in. to about 16 in. × 10¾ in., enabled the width of the folded paper to accommodate a column 21½ picas wide in 1727 as against 13½ in 1715. From 1727 the *St James's* came from the office of James Read, printer of *Read's Weekly Journal*, a notable paper which we must now place in its true perspective.

CHAPTER V

THE WEEKLY JOURNALS, I

1713–1725

Mawson's	1713 (?)
Read's	1715
Mist's	1715, 1725
Applebee's	1713 (?)
The Shift Shifted	1716
The Charitable Mercury	1716

CHAPTER V

THE WEEKLY JOURNALS, I

1713–1725

THE title 'Weekly Journal', just mentioned in connection with Read, printer of *The St James's Evening Post*, is an addition to the roll of Courants, Posts and Gazettes. Read, however, did not invent the name. The story of the Weekly Journals involves a little bibliographical investigation, since the available books give no reliable guidance as to their origin. Cap. XIX of an Act passed in the tenth year of the reign of Queen Anne imposed a stamp duty of one half-penny sterling upon every pamphlet or paper contained in half a sheet or lesser piece of paper so printed, and one penny for every such pamphlet or paper being larger than a half-sheet, and not exceeding one whole sheet. The two shillings duty levied at the same time upon every pamphlet or paper 'being larger than a whole sheet' seems not to have been enforced; but, for the rest, the duties enacted (to be raised during a term of thirty-two years) were reckoned from August 1, 1712. Accordingly, the stamps may be seen gradually making their appearance in the margins of the newspapers.[1]

Now the result of this taxation, as Swift reports it, was that '*The Observator* is fallen; the *Medleys* are jumbled together in the *Flying Post*[2]; the *Examiner* is deadly sick; the *Spectator* keeps up and doubles its price'. But in fact the impost seems to have done but little serious harm to the newspaper press; for, from what we can ascertain from the Burney and Nichols collections, the number of periodicals and papers was not greatly diminished by the tax. *The General Postscript* for September 27, 1709 (i.e. three years before the tax), in animadverting upon the then existing papers, gave what purported to be a complete list which, arranged according to frequency of issue, comprises:

[1] The taxes at first proposed were 1*d.* and 2*d.* upon half-sheets and sheets respectively. The Honourable the House of Commons were memorialised severally by the Printers, the Stationers, and the Paper-makers. The Printers' case (see B.M. 8223 e. 82) submitted that after the said duty, 'of about twenty papers of half-sheets which come out every week, besides many other Occasional ones, there will not two be published by reason of this tax; which will advance every Penny paper to threepence'.

[2] From the issue of *The Flying Post*, August 26/28, 1712, *The Medley* is printed with it on the same half-sheet under a thirty-point titling.

NEWSPAPERS IN 1709

Daily

1 *The Daily Courant*

Monday, Wednesday and Friday

2 *The Supplement*
3 *The British Apollo*
4 *The General Remark*
5 *The Female Tatler*
6 *The General Postscript*

Wednesday

18 *The Observator*

Tuesday, Thursday and Saturday

7 *The London Gazette*
8 *The Post Man*
9 *The Post Boy*
10 *The Flying Post*
11 *The Review* 1712–1713
12 *The Tatler*
13 *The Rehearsal* revived
14 *The Evening Post*
15 *The Whisperer*
16 *The Post Boy junior*
17 *The City Intelligencer*

This total of eighteen publications regularly put out in the course of the week consists of one daily; four Monday, Wednesday and Friday; one Monday and Friday; one Wednesday; eleven Tuesday, Thursday and Saturday, papers. Of these, only *The Observator*, a literary weekly, seems to have come to grief as the direct result of the tax. *The British Apollo*, also a literary paper; *The General Remark*, a commercial paper, ceased separate existence twelve or more months before the Act came into operation; and *The General Postscript*, in which the list appeared, only published twenty numbers in all. *The Examiner*, mentioned by Swift as 'deadly sick', was his own paper; its opponent, *The Medley*, founded in August 1710 (since the above list was made), continued and discontinued irrespective of the tax. Benjamin Harris and Sarah Popping's paper, *The Protestant Post Boy*, ran for a year ending December 1711. *The Spectator* (No. 1, March 1, 1711) ran until 1714.

With these additions and omissions, the list in *The General Postscript* of the autumn of 1709 holds good for the autumn of 1712; and, tax or no tax, there was more general activity in journalism after 1712 than before. *The Weekly Packet*'s first issue came out in July 1712.

But if the direness of the effect of the tax upon the existence of the newspapers has been exaggerated, it nevertheless had serious consequences which changed their format and frequency. Before the Act, single half-sheet papers and whole-sheet, i.e. four-page papers, were the rule. After the Act, papers of one whole and a half-sheet, i.e. six-page papers, became the convention. The cause of this development seems to lie in the draftsmanship of the Act.

The incidence of the tax was thought to be clear and incontestable when all papers were affected whether they were *whole sheet* (i.e. four pages when once folded) or *half-sheet* (i.e. single leaf), any and every issue of such paper,

(1) N° 1.

The Charitable Mercury,

AND

Female Intelligence.

Being A

Weekly Collection

OF

All the Material NEWS, Foreign and Domeſtick:

With ſome NOTES on the ſame.

To be Publiſhed Every Saturday.

Saturday, April 7. 1716.

Chi biaſima i Grandi ſcorre pericolo ; chi li loda ſpeſſo dice la bugia.

IT is well enough known to the Publick, that I intended lately to entertain 'em with a Paper under another Title ; *and I need not tell by what means I am prevented from purſuing my Deſign. However, the ſame Reaſons ſtill prevailing with me to accept of that* Encouragement *the Publick then intended me, and ſome worthy Gentlemen generouſly offering their Aſſiſtance in carrying on a* Weekly Paper *for my Benefit, emboldens me to attempt this Publication, and I hope for better Succeſs with this than I had with my other Undertaking. Theſe Gentlemen bid*

Fig. 42. *Mrs Powell's* The Charitable Mercury

as also their postscripts. And as in 1712 the papers—i.e. the unique morning, *The Daily Courant*, and the tri-weeklies—were either whole or half-sheet in size, they all bear, from that date, the red tax stamp in one corner or the other. This was obviously the intention of the law, and the term of the Act was for 32 years. Nevertheless, in spite of the fact that, upon the passage of the law into operation, all the papers are to be found duly stamped, organised evasion seems to have been possible. Why, for instance, should Mrs Elizabeth Powell's *The Charitable Mercury*, with a 4½ in. deep heading, not bear a stamp; while *The Daily Courant*, as a mere single folio half-sheet, duly bears the stamp? *The Charitable Mercury* was a six-page paper, i.e. it was made up of a sheet and half a sheet. It can only be, I suggest, that the Crown did not prosecute Mrs Powell for stamp evasion—plain as the offence was—because a technicality stood in the way. In a word, whereas papers of half a sheet *or* a whole sheet were taxable, papers made up of a whole *and* a half went free because the law had not foreseen the development of papers of more than one whole sheet. In consequence, the extension of sheets to include six and eight pages in folio became a means, more or less 'recognised'.[1] There were stylistic consequences of this discovery by printers and publishers. *The Flying Post*, in order to fill six pages, went from small pica to english, and as a further necessary expedient the text was driven out to cover the increased space available.[2] Hence, the reason why Mrs Powell gave her *Charitable Mercury* a nine-line heading with two devices must be that the 4½ in. thus consumed proportionately helped to fill the space then not only abundant but superabundant. Obviously, too, the daily provision of news, whether 'foreign' or 'domestick', in small type, to full measure, for a daily[3] of two, four or six pages folio was a very serious task. It was not attempted. There were only one or two six-page issues and a four-page issue of *The Daily Courant* is a rarity. The fact is that news was always scarce. There was never enough of it, and, when found from abroad,

[1] Perhaps completely recognised, for *The London Gazette* itself of May 5/9, 1717, is a six-page unstamped, and the immediately previous issue a single half-sheet stamped.

[2] The clearest instance I have found of this means of tax evasion is in *The Reconciler*, a political paper printed for Jonas Browne and sold by John Morphew. No. I is dated Thursday, April 30, 1713, and it is a loose half-sheet with a halfpenny stamp. It so continued every Monday, Wednesday and Friday until No. IX, May 15, 1713. The next issue was a six-pager whose first page carried the serial indication, 'Numb X. XI', over the title of the paper in large capitals. Below there was printed in small canon upper- and lower-case an explanation that 'There will now henceforward be Published Two PAPERS together, for lessening the Price, and the satisfaction and convenience of the Readers, who cannot have matters driven to any satisfactory and convenient Point in single issues. N.B. *There will be about Sixty Lines more in the double Paper than in two single ones*'. There follows a rule, the imprint and 'Price Two Pence'. The verso of the title-page and of the last leaf are blanks. Neither this issue nor any other double number of the paper until its cessation with Nos. XXIV, XXV, June 19/22, 1713, is stamped.

Evasion also took place after the Act of 1725 tightened up the administration of the law. *The London Spy Revived. By Democritus Secundus of the Fleet* was a Monday, Wednesday and Friday quarto of four pages unstamped 'Printed for the Benefit of the Author and sold by those Persons that carry the News Papers'. From its first issue, dated August 6, 1736, until No. 88, February 16, 1736/7, it carried a three-line heading ruled off between the lines, the whole being 1½ in. deep. With No. 89 the place of the title was occupied by a 1-in. band of printers' flowers over the date line and was thus published thenceforth without title until March 1738.

[3] *The Evening Journal* (December 12, 1727), a four-page quarto, filled its front page with the ages of the sovereign princes of Europe.

costly in translation fees. These were serious charges to a daily, and also to a thrice-weekly half-sheet whose circulation naturally lost when the price was raised to include the tax. A weekly was in a better position from every point of view, since it could hope to fill six pages with the occurrences of seven days; also, at need, it could copy from the daily or 'alternate' papers, and, in addition, its immunity from the stamp was now equivalent to a bounty. Thus, the weekly of the decade 1715–25 was a fat three ha'porth, and there were many of them. The years after the imposition of the tax reveal among the new foundations an overwhelming majority of weeklies.

The structure of these new weeklies differs from that of their predecessors—and not only in dimension; their matter, by including essays, foreshadows the 'weekly review' as we should today understand the term.

We have ignored Steele's *The Tatler* (1709–11) as being, by profession, a vehicle of entertainment and not of information, of wit instead of news. But we need to point out that *The Tatler* had created a new class of reader which remained after the paper ceased. *The Tatler* was not a weekly, nor a newspaper, but it supplied more than one hint for journals which were both weeklies and newspapers.[1] 'The Journals',[2] as the new six-page inventions were called, gave pride of place to an essay on exact *Tatler* lines; next they printed Foreign Affairs, Home Affairs, London Intelligence, with late paragraphs and advertisements on the final page. This was the invariable order of make-up in the 'Journals'.

The moral dissertation and critical essay, so firmly established by Steele and Addison (and by nobody else) in the esteem of the many sceptics who cared little for faked news, became not only the staple but the sole material of many a tribe of imitators, periodicals which *ipso facto* were not newspapers, and which we must here ignore.

The tax of 1712 at first dealt more damage to these literary than to the news journals, but as the enlargement of the latter could only be made permanent by the inclusion of essay material, this feature was embodied in the weekly journals. Hence, the weekly journals established between 1715 and 1725 contain an essay, a letter, review, instruction or other article of considerable length. The subject of these articles, though frequently political,

[1] Dunton's *Pegasus* (1696) had, to some extent, anticipated *The Tatler* by providing what he termed 'An Observation', i.e. dissertation or serialised instruction on some moral, political or historical subject of greater or lesser topical interest.

[2] Only a periodical thus constituted is a 'Journal'. *The Weekly Packet* of 1714, a newspaper pure and simple, is *not* a journal because it has no essay.

varied between the highly moral and the scarcely decent. Party passions ran high, and the consequent division of the periodicals into opposite loyalties further inflamed Whig and Tory. The weekly journals were the predestined means of intrigue for or against the administration, for or against a minister, for or against a place-seeker. The dailies were left to invent occurrences when news was scarce and to do their best to fill up with advertisements.

Of the dailies founded in the same period, *The Daily Post* (printed by J. Roberts from the end of 1719) and *The Daily Journal* (J. Bickerton from January 23, 1720) were both similar productions to *The Daily Courant*, single half-sheets carrying stamps, and none was of any serious political importance. Later, when *The Daily Journal* went ahead of its rivals into four pages (a development to be chronicled in due order of time), its advance of format did not challenge the growing prestige of the weeklies. Since they, and they alone, were the organs of political groups, some account must be attempted of their gradual growth from *The Post Man* type of paper to *The Universal Chronicle*, in which Johnson regularly wrote.

To summarise: the tax was imposed in 1712, its most important consequence to our enquiry being the wholesale evasion rendered possible by increasing the extent of a paper to six pages—an increase which finally resulted in the obliteration of the formerly clear distinctions between the weekly essay-, and the weekly news-papers. Henceforth the space at their disposal threw upon each the necessity of filling up with the other's characteristic features. We shall see this merger gradually being accomplished.

First of all, taking advantage of the tacit understanding which permitted a six-page paper to be unstamped, one Robert Mawson established in January 1713[1] a paper which made a permanent contribution to the nomenclature of the newspaper. His venture was entitled *The Weekly Journal*, and as sub-title he continued the mid-seventeenth century phrase: *With Fresh Advices Foreign and Domestick*. Typographically, the paper followed the traditions of *The Post Man* in setting the first words of its title in text between two devices: in the case of *The Weekly Journal* a mounted postman (on the left) and the figure of a seated britannia (on the right). The date is placed

[1] *The Times Handlist* enters four periodicals entitled *Weekly Journal* of 1714, 1716, 1718, 1720 respectively. The first entry misprints 'Harrison' for 'Mawson' and gives its term as January 1, 1714–August 27, 1715 (*sc.* September 24, 1715). The paper was renumbered from 1 with the issue for January 8, 1714. January 1, 1714, is Part LIII, so that, unless this figure is bogus, the first *Weekly Journal* dates from the last week in 1712, or the first in 1713. Robert Mawson does not appear in *The Dictionary of National Biography*, Timperley's *Encyclopaedia*, or in Plomer's *Dictionary*.

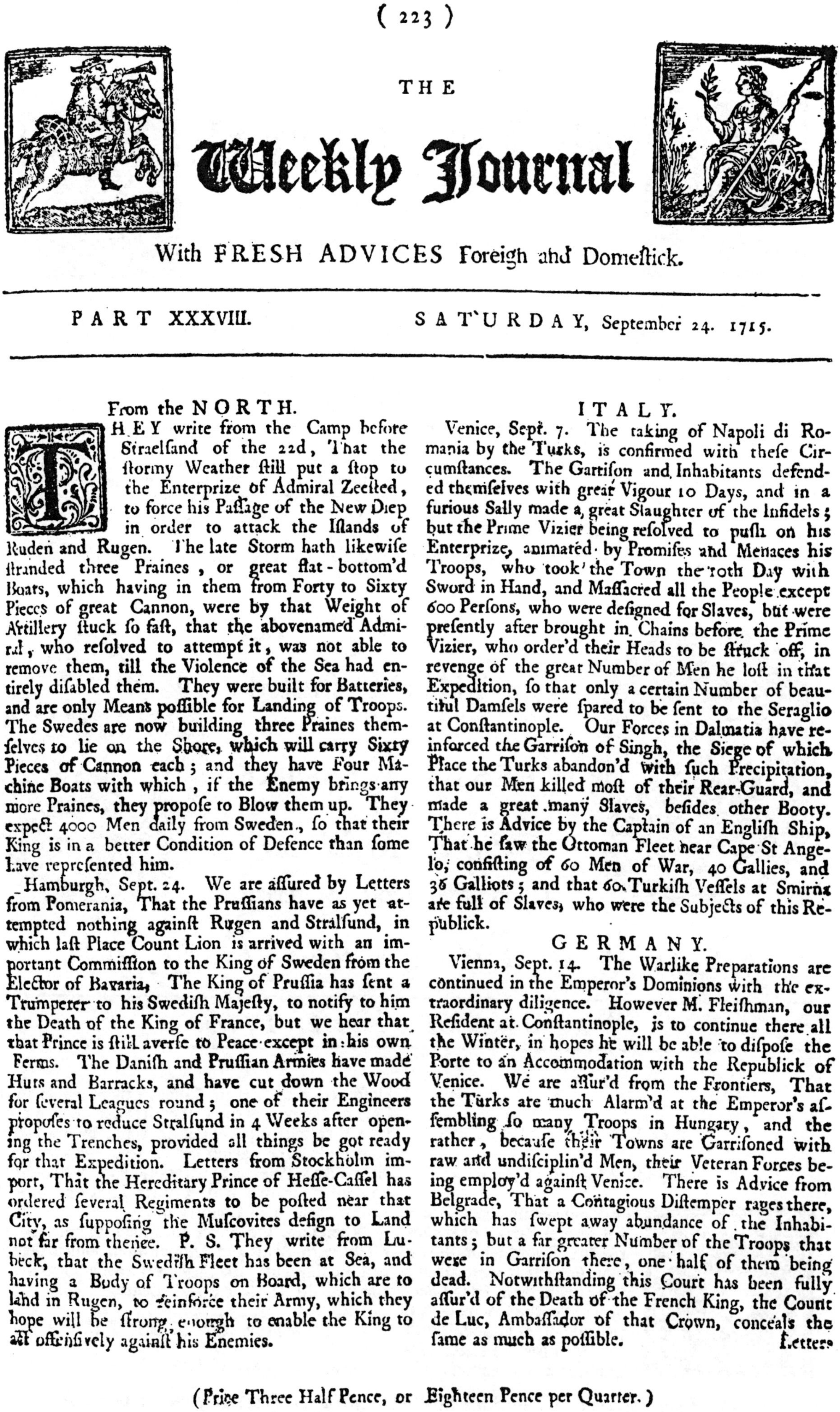

(223)

THE

Weekly Journal

With FRESH ADVICES Foreign and Domestick.

PART XXXVIII. SATURDAY, September 24. 1715.

From the NORTH.

THEY write from the Camp before Stralsund of the 22d, That the stormy Weather still put a stop to the Enterprize of Admiral Zeested, to force his Passage of the New Diep in order to attack the Islands of Ruden and Rugen. The late Storm hath likewise stranded three Praines, or great flat-bottom'd Boats, which having in them from Forty to Sixty Pieces of great Cannon, were by that Weight of Artillery stuck so fast, that the abovenamed Admiral, who resolved to attempt it, was not able to remove them, till the Violence of the Sea had entirely disabled them. They were built for Batteries, and are only Means possible for Landing of Troops. The Swedes are now building three Praines themselves to lie on the Shore, which will carry Sixty Pieces of Cannon each; and they have Four Machine Boats with which, if the Enemy brings any more Praines, they propose to Blow them up. They expect 4000 Men daily from Sweden, so that their King is in a better Condition of Defence than some have represented him.

Hamburgh, Sept. 24. We are assured by Letters from Pomerania, That the Prussians have as yet attempted nothing against Rugen and Stralsund, in which last Place Count Lion is arrived with an important Commission to the King of Sweden from the Elector of Bavaria. The King of Prussia has sent a Trumpeter to his Swedish Majesty, to notify to him the Death of the King of France, but we hear that that Prince is still averse to Peace except in his own Terms. The Danish and Prussian Armies have made Huts and Barracks, and have cut down the Wood for several Leagues round; one of their Engineers proposes to reduce Stralsund in 4 Weeks after opening the Trenches, provided all things be got ready for that Expedition. Letters from Stockholm import, That the Hereditary Prince of Hesse-Cassel has ordered several Regiments to be posted near that City, as supposing the Muscovites design to Land not far from thence. P. S. They write from Lubeck, that the Swedish Fleet has been at Sea, and having a Body of Troops on Board, which are to land in Rugen, to reinforce their Army, which they hope will be strong enough to enable the King to act offensively against his Enemies.

ITALY.

Venice, Sept. 7. The taking of Napoli di Romania by the Turks, is confirmed with these Circumstances. The Garrison and Inhabitants defended themselves with great Vigour 10 Days, and in a furious Sally made a great Slaughter of the Infidels; but the Prime Vizier being resolved to push on his Enterprize, animated by Promises and Menaces his Troops, who took the Town the 10th Day with Sword in Hand, and Massacred all the People except 600 Persons, who were designed for Slaves, but were presently after brought in Chains before the Prime Vizier, who order'd their Heads to be struck off, in revenge of the great Number of Men he lost in that Expedition, so that only a certain Number of beautiful Damsels were spared to be sent to the Seraglio at Constantinople. Our Forces in Dalmatia have reinforced the Garrison of Singh, the Siege of which Place the Turks abandon'd with such Precipitation, that our Men killed most of their Rear-Guard, and made a great many Slaves, besides other Booty. There is Advice by the Captain of an English Ship, That he saw the Ottoman Fleet near Cape St Angelo, consisting of 60 Men of War, 40 Gallies, and 36 Galliots; and that 60 Turkish Vessels at Smirna are full of Slaves, who were the Subjects of this Republick.

GERMANY.

Vienna, Sept. 14. The Warlike Preparations are continued in the Emperor's Dominions with the extraordinary diligence. However M. Fleishman, our Resident at Constantinople, is to continue there all the Winter, in hopes he will be able to dispose the Porte to an Accommodation with the Republick of Venice. We are assur'd from the Frontiers, That the Turks are much Alarm'd at the Emperor's assembling so many Troops in Hungary, and the rather, because their Towns are Garrisoned with raw and undisciplin'd Men, their Veteran Forces being employ'd against Venice. There is Advice from Belgrade, That a Contagious Distemper rages there, which has swept away abundance of the Inhabitants; but a far greater Number of the Troops that were in Garrison there, one half of them being dead. Notwithstanding this Court has been fully assur'd of the Death of the French King, the Count de Luc, Ambassador of that Crown, conceals the same as much as possible. Letters

(Price Three Half Pence, or Eighteen Pence per Quarter.)

Fig. 43. The Weekly Journal *printed by Robert Mawson of Ireland Yard*

No. 9. (49)

THE

Weekly-Journal: OR, Saturday's-Post.

With fresh Advices Foreign and Domestick.

SATURDAY, *February* 9. 1716.

Last Thursday arrived a Holland Mail.

From the NORTH.

was concluded; and from Praag, which is just over against Warsaw, on the other side the River, as London is to Southwark, that all was to pieces, and that a new Confederacy was formed.

Fig. 44. *Heading of an early number of Mist's* The Weekly Journal

No. 5. (25) Part. I.

The SHIFT shifted: OR, WEEKLY REMARKS AND *Political Reflections* Upon the most Material *NEWS Foreign and Domestick.*

SATURDAY, *June* 2. 1716.

POLAND.

Warsaw, May 15.

THE Confederates have lately put several Parties of Saxons to the Sword, but spar'd some Poles that were among 'em, upon their taking Service under the Confederates, to whom a Captain with 150 Men has deserted. 'Tis impossible to express the Flesh and Flood, their Country-men, would in this Case be themselves the first extirpated; which therefore they wisely prevented in time, by bravely turning their Faces against Foreigners, and against such vile wicked Poles as unnaturally sided with Foreigners, for their own little private Ends and Interests against their own Countrymen.

Wherefore, the Poles furnished themselves privately with Arms and Ammunition, which they hid past finding out, till they had an Opportunity to rise unitedly in their own Defence.

From the NORTH.

Hamburgh, May [illegible]

Fig. 45. *Upper portion of* The Shift Shifted *printed for Isaac Dalton, in Goswell Street* between two rules to the full measure and there is a pleasant factotum initial to the first paragraph of the left-hand column. The setting of the text, though more open, did not seriously depart from the standard two-column style initiated by *The London Gazette.* Mawson also published a supplement appointed to come out on Wednesdays, being the day following the arrival of the French and Dutch mails. The text of Mawson's statement in this connection is worth reading:

As it hath been the constant Endeavours of the Persons concern'd in the *Weekly-Journal* to entertain the Readers of that Paper with the Truest News, both Foreign and Domestick, which hath been hitherto Perform'd, so much to the Content and Satisfaction of the Publick: So, in the Present Hurry of Affairs, when News the most Expeditiously told, is the most Agreeable, they are Willing to Comply with the Desires of many that are their Customers; to Publish a Supplement thereunto, with which They will be for the Future supply'd, that they May not be at the Pains of Inquiring after any Other Paper.

And as for the Days, on which it will Come out; Wednesday's are the Days appointed: And it will be Sufficient to let the Curious Know, That as Tuesday is the likelyest Day for the Arrival of the French and Dutch Mails, on which they are Due; This Paper will have the Freshest and Fullest Account (of Any) without being any Impediment to the *Weekly Journal*: The Foreign News contained therein, Consisting, of All the Advices that Arrive between Wednesday and Saturday.

Moreover, by putting out this Supplement, We shall be enabled to entertain Our Readers with several other Things, which by Reason of the Fulness of News we cannot always find a Place for in our *Weekly Journal.*

Particularly, because we know, That there is nothing more Useful, nor more Acceptable to a great many Gentlemen, than to be inform'd of the Characters of all the Books and Pamphlets that are to be published here; both in our Own and Other Languages, we shall not fail from Time to Time, to give such an Account of all of Them, as will be agreeable to their Desires. And as for those Pamphlets in Latin, French, or other Languages that are Polite, we shall, where they are not very Voluminous, give an Abstract of them, and where they are short; deliver them in an Exact and Faithful Translation.

As for those of our Readers, who are Merchants, or concern'd in any Kind of Traffick: The first and the truest Notice shall be given of all Ships going out from, and coming in to the River; together, with a Compleat Account of most Commodities Exported from, and Imported into Great Britain.

By this Means I do not doubt but the Supplement will meet as favourable a Reception, from All its Readers, as our *Weekly Journal* doth, by intermingling in it all the best Accounts that will be agreeable to all Lovers of News in general. And to Tradesmen, Merchants, and other Gentlemen in particular, who are Delighted with the Works of Learning and Ingenuity.

THE

Shift's Laſt Shift: OR, Weekly-Journal

NUMB. I. SATURDAY, *February* 16. 1716.

From the NORTH.

Poland, February 2. 1717.

LETTERS from Warſaw of February 2. adviſe, That two Days before the Date of them, Marſhal Leduchowsky, made a very magnificent Entry into that Place, attended by many of the Grandees, and about 500 Gentlemen well mounted. He took his Quarters in the Cloiſter of St. Bernard, where the ſame Evening he received Viſits from moſt Perſons of Diſtinction. The Day following he went in Formality to the Palace, and was introduced into the Chamber of State, where he found the King ſitting on his Throne, attended by the Senatours. The Articles of the late Treaty were then read, in the manner they were reduced into the Form of a Conſtitution; which, with other neceſſary Ceremonies, took up near five Hours; at the Concluſion thereof, the Chief of the Confederates had the Honour to kiſs the King's Hand. Te Deum was afterwards ſung in the Great Church, at which moſt of the Senators aſſiſted; the Great Guns were alſo fir'd, and other uſual Demonſtrations of Joy were ſhewn. The Day after M. Leduchowsky had another Audidnce of his Majeſty, ſince which ſeveral of the Senators are retired to their Country Seats. The late report that ſome Companies were forming a new Confederacy, is entirely ſunk.

From the Amſterdam Gazette, Feb. 16.

Leopold, Jan. 2. Upon a refuſal of the Turks to releaſe ſome Priſoners which the Poliſh Commiſſaries had ranſom'd, the latter cauſed ſeveral Villages belonging to the Turks on the other Side of the Neſter to be plunder'd and burnt; on the other Hand, the Turks by way of Repriſal have made an Incurſion into Poland, ravag'd the Country as they march'd, and kill'd ſome of the Garriſon of Swanniek. The ſame Gazette acquaints us, That on Feb. 12th. the Baron Gersdorf the King of Poland's Miniſter, notified to their High Mightineſſes at the Hague, that on the 30th of the laſt Month, the Treaty of Pacification between his Poliſh Majeſty and the Confederates was ratified at Warſaw, and that the Diet is to Aſſemble forthwith: whereupon his Excellency has received the Compliment of Congratulation from their High Mightineſſes, and the Miniſters of Foreign Courts. Now theſe Troubles are concluded, it is generelly ſuppoſed a conſiderable Body of Saxon Troops will ſpeedily be tranſmitted into the Service of the Emperor. In the Dyet above-mentioned, the King, as well as all the Members of the Dyet took a reciprocal Oath to obſerve the Treaty inviolably: The particular Dyets of every Palatinate will be ſpeedily held, in order for a more fixed Eſtabliſhment of the Kingdom's Peace.

DENMARK.

From the Amſterdam Gazette, Dated Feb. 16.

Copenhagen, Feb. 6. We are now aſſured the Swedes have laid aſide their deſigned Invaſion of Norway, the greateſt Part of their Army being returned, and only 6000 Men left about Swinſund. We hear the King of Sweden marches the Bulk of his Horſes towards Gottenberg. Our Commodore Tordenſchild detached three Gallies into a Swediſh Port to burn three of our Ships that were driven thither by the late Storm, and a Swediſh Ship laden with Iron and Copper for Spain, which Orders they ſucceſsfully executed. We have Advice from Flaſtrand, that the Greyhound-Frigate has taken in the North-Sea, a large Dutch Merchant Ship coming from Holland, and bound for Sweden with a conſiderable Cargo, and 300000 Crowns in Specie, which was carried into Flaſtraud. The Court diverts it ſelf thrice a Week with Balls and Aſſemblies; a great Maſquerade is appointed on Monday

A next,

Price Three Half-Pence.

Fig. 46. *Isaac Dalton's* The Shift's Last Shift, 1716 (*i.e.* 1717)

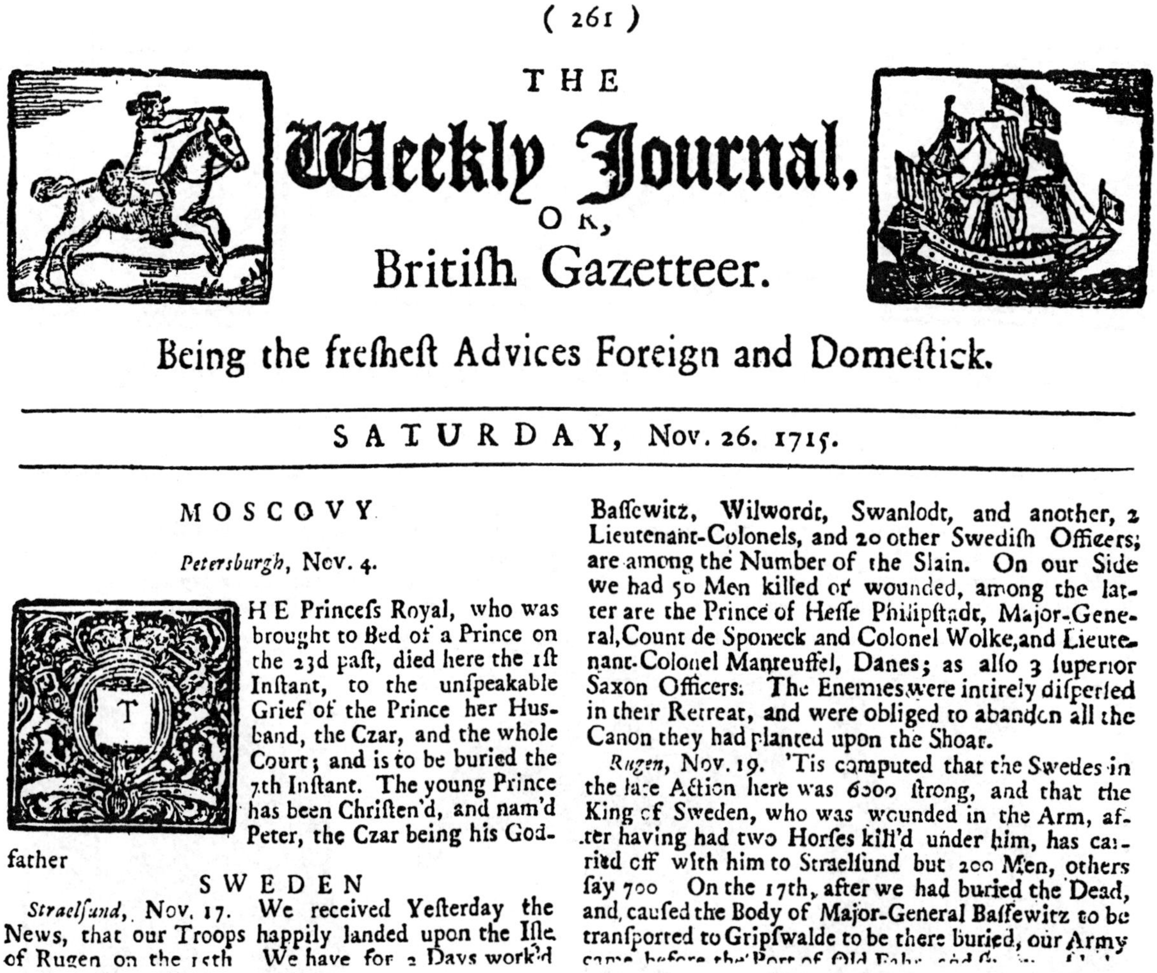
(261)

THE

Weekly Journal.

OR,

Britifh Gazetteer.

Being the frefheft Advices Foreign and Domeftick.

SATURDAY, Nov. 26. 1715.

MOSCOVY

Petersburgh, Nov. 4.

THE Princefs Royal, who was brought to Bed of a Prince on the 23d paft, died here the 1ft Inftant, to the unfpeakable Grief of the Prince her Husband, the Czar, and the whole Court; and is to be buried the 7th Inftant. The young Prince has been Chriften'd, and nam'd Peter, the Czar being his Godfather

SWEDEN

Straelfund, Nov. 17. We received Yefterday the News, that our Troops happily landed upon the Ifle of Rugen on the 15th We have for 2 Days work'd

Baffewitz, Wilwordt, Swanlodt, and another, 2 Lieutenant-Colonels, and 20 other Swedifh Officers; are among the Number of the Slain. On our Side we had 50 Men killed or wounded, among the latter are the Prince of Heffe Philipftadt, Major-General, Count de Sponeck and Colonel Wolke, and Lieutenant-Colonel Manteuffel, Danes; as alfo 3 fuperior Saxon Officers. The Enemies were intirely difperfed in their Retreat, and were obliged to abandon all the Canon they had planted upon the Shoar.

Rugen, Nov. 19. 'Tis computed that the Swedes in the late Action here was 6000 ftrong, and that the King of Sweden, who was wounded in the Arm, after having had two Horfes kill'd under him, has carried off with him to Straelfund but 200 Men, others fay 700 On the 17th, after we had buried the Dead, and caufed the Body of Major-General Baffewitz to be tranfported to Gripfwalde to be there buried, our Army

Fig. 47. *Heading of an early issue of Read's* The Weekly Journal

For no clear reason *The Weekly Journal* seems to have received considerable public support.[1] Or at least it is difficult otherwise to account for the immediate issue of two other journals of exactly the same textual and typographical character, preserving two similarly engraved blocks in precisely the same position. The two imitations were, respectively: *The Weekly Journal, or, British Gazetteer. Being the freshest Advices Foreign and Domestick*, founded some time before November 12, 1715,[2] by James Read of

[1] The last issue contained in the Burney Collection is Part XXXVIII, September 24. *The Supplement to the Weekly Journal*, printed by J. Dalton for Robert Mawson (Ireland Yard, as before), continued until December 1715 and perhaps later.

[2] Burney's first issue is dated November 12, 1715. It carries no serial number but is paged 144–51 (a final leaf, 152–3, is missing), which would comprise some twenty-four to twenty-five issues. This would indicate that Read's journal made its first appearance in June 1715. This is the more likely in view of the imprint to Mawson's journal: "Printed for Robert Mawson at the Bible and Star in Ireland Yard, next Fryer street in Black Friers where may be had the Weekly Journals from the first paper that ever was published under that title. And advertisements taken in'. According to Plomer, James Read was working as a printer in Whitefriars from 1709.

(1187)

THE

Weekly Journal.

OR,

Britiſh Gazetteer.

Being the freſheſt Advices Foreign and Domeſtick.

SATURDAY, NOVEMBER, 1. 1718.

AN HIEROGLYPHICK.

WILL *Fools* and *Knaves* their one Misfortune ſee,
And ponder on the *Tories* Villany?
Behold this *Hieroglyphick*, and admire
What *Loyalty* do's in true Souls inſpire!
Whate'er the *Figures* mean we ſhan't declare,
Becauſe the *Jacobites* will Curſe and Swear;
But if our *Readers* will this Piece explain,
Their *Explanation* we ſhall not diſdain.

SPAIN.

Madrid, October 6.

THE Court being return'd from Balſain to the Eſcurial. M de Nancre, Ambaſſador of France, is gone thither to Day, to receive the King's final Reſolution upon the Treaty propos'd to him.

Cadiz, Oct. 7. On the 4th Inſtant the Governour of this City communicated to the Britiſh Conſul, an Order from Court, for permitting all the Officers and Mariners of the Britiſh Ships ſeiz'd here, to to be tranſported, either to England or Portugal, upon giving Security for the Return of the Ships employ'd in that Tranſ[...] of France and Great-Britain, have been prevail'd with to continue there ſome time longer, in order to reſume the Conferences for accomodating the Differences between the Emperor and King Philip; but that Cardinal Alberoni will not agree to a Ceſſation of Arms, unleſs firſt Satisfaction be made for the Damage the Spaniſh Fleet receiv'd in the late Action with Admiral Byng: On the other hand, Col. Stanhope urg'd, that the Engliſh Merchants and their Ships ſeiz'd in the Harbours of Spain, muſt be releas'd, and due Reparation made for their Loſſes; but this being already complied with, 'tis thought a formal Treaty will be ſet on Foot in a ſhort time.

Paris, Oct. 25. 'Tis diſcours'd that ſeveral Regiments have receiv'd Orders to hold themſelves in a readineſs to March, and that if Spain refuſes to accept of the Terms of the Quadruple Alliance, an Army will be form'd in

Fig. 48. *Upper portion of James Read's* The Weekly Journal *with cartoon*

Whitefriars; and *The Weekly-Journal: or Saturday's-Post. With fresh Advices Foreign and Domestick,* which quickly came under the control of Mist. Further, the printer, Isaac Dalton, founder of *Robin's Last Shift* on February 18, 1716 (which became *The Shift Shifted* on May 5, 1716), brought out a paper with blocks identical with those in Mawson's *Weekly Journal,* using as his title *The Shift's Last Shift: or, Weekly-Journal.* The date of this last, No. 1, February 16, 1716, leads one to think that Mawson had died with his journal at the end of 1715, or at least permanently retired from the trade of bookselling and journalism.

There is another small point of interest in the relations of Mawson and Dalton with the newspaper trade. A weekly entitled *The News Letter* (No. 1, Saturday, January 7, 1716) was printed by Isaac Dalton for Nathaniel Storer at the Bible and Star in Ireland Yard, Blackfriars. Storer was the proprietor of *The News Letter*; the Bible and Star in Ireland Yard was the office of Mawson, and it would appear that there was some connection between the two proprietors. The first number of *The News Letter* carried at its head a notice signed by Robert Mawson to the effect that

> those gentlemen who have encouraged the *Weekly Journals* by subscription and their quarter's are not up until after Christmas are desired to pay them to Mr Nathaniel Storer the proprietor of this paper who will make up their quarters with his weekly *News Letters.* Those gentlemen who encourage it will find him a very fair dealer, and lay an infinite obligation upon their most humble servant R. M.

I have strictly no business to quote that interesting letter.

The relevant facts are that Mawson's *Weekly Journal,* begun in 1713, lasted for a couple of years or so, unexpired subscriptions being completed with issues of Storer's *News Letter.* The future of the title *Weekly Journal,* invented by Robert Mawson and in which we are interested, lay in the hands of his imitators; first, James Read of Whitefriars, and, secondly, Nathaniel Mist of Castle Lane. Read's journal, as I have pointed out, was probably founded in the June of 1715. Its format was almost identical with Mawson's itself based upon that of *The Post Man,* the only difference being in the character of the devices—their shape remained the same. Mawson's carried a seated figure of britannia in the place of *The Post Man*'s packet. Read returned to the packet, so that his heading-blocks were absolutely identical with those of *The Post Man.* There are signs that Read was a publisher of some enterprise. His printing was neat and above the ordinary when English standards were improving. His issue of November 26, 1715,

Fig. 49

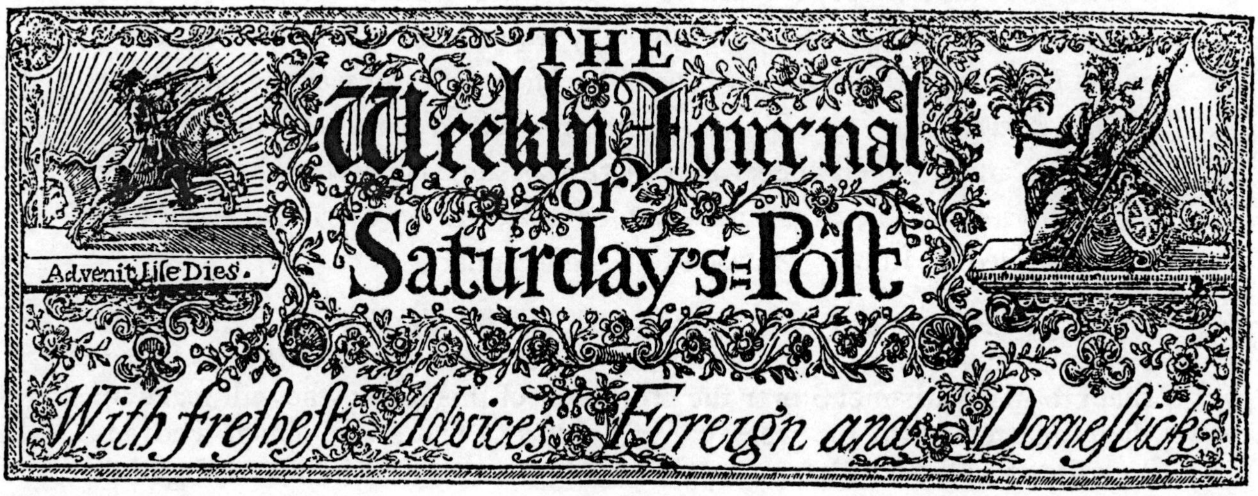

Fig. 50

Fig. 51

Figs. 49 *and* 50. *Headings of Mist's* The Weekly Journal *from* 1718–25
Fig. 51. *Heading of* The London Journal, 1719

states that 'Gentlemen and others, who are Encouragers of this Weekly Journal, making Collections thereof, they desire (*sic*) the same to be printed upon finer Paper; and, in compliance to their Request, it will for the future, but the Price will then be Three Half Pence'. On November 1, 1718, Read's gave its subscribers a political cartoon directed against the Jacobites. The block, a wood engraving, of course, in size 3 in. deep across two columns, is a very fine piece, making a striking front page. On another occasion, the same printer made his front page with a Poem 'on His Sacred Majesty King George I' which was headed with a well-designed cut $2\frac{1}{2}$ in. × $6\frac{1}{4}$ in. By this time, the devices in Read's heading had been re-designed, the mounted postman being signed 'J. Bell, fecit'[1]; the packet is also recut but not signed.

In the meantime, Nathaniel Mist had brought into prominence *The Weekly Journal or Saturday's-Post*[2] which he established at the end of 1715. Like Read's, it was in format, as in title, a copy of Mawson's, carrying devices of a postman and a britannia. With No. 97, for October 18, 1718, Mist's superseded the Mawson type of heading with a single block $2\frac{1}{4}$ in. deep running to the full measure. It is a striking headpiece, framing not only the redrawn postman and britannia which still kept their positions, but the title and sub-title in text and italic. The initial letters 'W(eekly)' and 'J(ournal)' were decorated after the fashion of the Dutch writing professors. The block is signed conspicuously 'F. HOFFMAN FECIT', an artist of whose origins we know nothing, but who seems to have specialised in working for newspapers. Amongst the designs performed by Hoffman, there are included several initial letters, many factotums, and several headings. He made a second heading-block for Mist's journal in which the floral were substituted for the calligraphic elements used in his first attempt. In the number for December 20, 1718, Mist uses a very fine factotum fame (thirteen lines small pica deep) blowing a trumpet, cut, one supposes, by Hoffman. A still more magnificent factotum, in which the artist's initials 'F. H. f.' are visible, was used from December 3, 1720.[3] The sun and the moon and

[1] Of whom there is no trace in the reference books.

[2] A six-page journal, *The Saturday's Post*, printed for W. Charlton, commenced publication on September 30, 1716. It seems to have had only a short career. Its heading was a single line of canon upper- and lower-case. Its only decorative feature was a seven-line factotum which turns up later in *The Entertainer* founded by N. Mist, November 6, 1717.

[3] In a re-designed form, used also in *The London Journal* from May 27, 1721, supplanting a set of floriated initials of about an inch square in size. This periodical, first entitled *The Thursday Journal*, started about 1719 as a rival to Mist and Applebee.

Numb. 2.

THE CHURCH-MAN's *LAST SHIFT*, OR, Loyalist's Weekly Journal.

SATURDAY, *June* 11.

T*HE Reader is not only desired to pass by the Mistakes in General, That thro' the Absence of the Author, who was call'd away by very urgent Business, escaped due Correction: but one in particular, which, with all the Respect due to the Known Worth and exalted Station of the Gentleman concerned therein, he hopes the whole Conduct of his Life will prove not to be wilful on his Side, and the Words subsequent to the Grounds of Cavil, which would be just without them, will clear him from. The Paragraph was unhappily Printed thus; which his excess of Joy for a certain Change, will no ways allow him to be Chargeable with,* viz. *One Sir* Robert Raymond *kiss'd the King's Hand,* &c. *Whereas, it should have been, On Sunday last Sir* Robert Raymond, *&c. This induces him in the Name of the Person left in Trust with the Correction thereof, humbly to ask Mr.* Attorney General's *Pardon, and not only to wish him the greatest Felicity possibly to be attain'd in this Life, through the whole Course of his Continuance in that Post, but as speedy a Transition to much greater Preferment, when his Majesty, who is the Fountain of all Honour and Dignity, shall be pleased to forward it.*

The Voyages of *Sinbad* the Sailor continued.

One Day I found in my way several dry Calabashes that had fallen from a Tree; I took up a large one, and after cleaning it, press'd into it some Juice of the Grapes which abounded in the Island having fill'd the Calabash, I set it in a Convenient Place, and coming thither again some days after, I took up the Calabash, and setting it to my Mouth, found the Wine to be so good, that it made me presently forget my Sorrow, so that I grew vigorous, and was so light hearted that I began to Sing and Dance as I walk'd along.

The old Man perceiving the Effect which this Drink had upon me, and that I carried him with more ease than before, made a sign to give him some of it. I gave him the Calabash, and the Liquor pleasing his Palate, he Drank it all off. There being enough of it to fuddle him, he became drunk immediately, and the Fumes getting up into his Head, he began to Sing after his manner and to Dance his Breech upon my Shoulders. His Jolting about made him Vomit, and losen'd his Legs about me by Degrees, so finding that he did not press me as before, I threw him upon the Ground, where he lay without Motion, and then I took up a great Stone, and crush'd his Head to Pieces.

I was extreamly rejoyced, to be freed thus for ever from this Cursed old Fellow, and walk'd upon the Bank of the Sea, where I met the Crew of a Ship that had Cast Anchor to take in Water and refresh themselves. They were extreamly surprized to see me, and to hear the Particulars of my Adventure. You fell say they into the Hands of the old Man of the Sea, and are the first that ever escap'd strangling by him. He never left those he had once made himself Master of till he destroy'd them, and hath made this Island Famous by the Number of Men he has slain, so that the Merchants and Mariners who landed upon it, dar'd not to advance into the Island but in Numbers together

After

Fig. 52. *Bickerton's Journal, June* 11 (1715), *shewing first state of heading* several constellations of stars in the background of this block are rayed—perhaps in counter allusion to the proprietor's name, now well known.

The journal itself became notorious—Mist was fined and pilloried twice in 1720, and later the House of Commons voted his *Weekly Journal* 'a false, malicious, scandalous, infamous and traitorous libel', on which Mist was committed to Newgate with his printers. This is not the place for a narration of the action taken by the Commons against any newspaper which reported what the House was doing, or more could be said on the way the journals were harried and still managed to come out. At least there was no reaction in their typographical style. The heading devices and factotums cut for Mist's set a high standard in design and engraving, and ultimately prevailed over other styles of display for weekly journals. There was a limited vogue for the use of circular or vignetted devices. The two oval blocks of an orpheus and a mercury, both wreathed in laurels, used in Isaac Dalton's *The Shift Shifted* were copied, line for line, in *The Weekly Journal* published by one Heathcote, who also owned *The Original London Post.*

In 1719, the heading to *The Weekly Medley, or The Gentleman's Recreation, containing An Historical Account of all News Foreign and Domestick...* (founded 1719), $6\frac{1}{2}$ in. above the date line, exhibited a circular device $3\frac{5}{8}$ in. in diameter. The paper, in ceasing publication with its issue for January 16–23, 1720, took its farewell in 'A Letter from the Author of the Medley to his Readers' printed on the back page. Readers are asked to transfer their custom to another paper in these words:

> There is one Mrs Powell, of the Printing Trade who is fallen unluckily under the Displeasure of the Government, and is (according to Report and all Probability) fled to France, for what occasion I don't exactly know. In her house that was are two pretty Children whose Father has been lately buried and whose Mother is now dead to them, so that they remain helpless Orphans and in this House, the Sign of which is the Prince of Wales's Arms in Blackfryers, is printed a Paper called the ORPHAN: It is a Journal of all the News Foreign and Domestick; it is perfecter and better than any of the others; and besides, the Writer of it does, what no other Journalist does. He forms pretty tracts upon Religion and Morality, and attacks those Enemies of both, the Dissenters, with a great deal of Spirit and Vigour. I desire, therefore, that now the Medley is deceased, the Orphan may live in the Esteem of all my Readers, and that my Readers will be Executors of this my Last Will and Testament.

I have no information of the author's name. He seems to have conducted the paper with fair success on a singularly broad basis, for, apart from 'occurrences foreign and domestick', 'The State of Europe' was impartially considered, the whole, 'Embellish'd and Intermixed with Observations, Historical, Political and Philosophical', was concluded with the 'Tea-Table Tatler or the Ladies Delight'. A heading of this kind was inevitably expensive of space, but it was more expensive to pay the Stamp duty. *The Orphan Reviv'd* presented a spectacular appearance, for, in addition to this lengthy title, there was, over all, a circular cut of $3\frac{1}{2}$ in. in diameter, and, further, it was provided with a very fair factotum twelve lines deep. The text remained in the standard double column arrangement. *The Orphan* cannot be traced after February 1719/1720.[1]

On June 4, 1715, Thomas Bickerton of Paternoster Row brought out a six-page folio entitled *The Church-Man's Last Shift, or, Loyalist's Weekly Journal*, the heading to which carried a circular device with the text *Contra Audentior Ito*. The twelve-line factotum is a variation of that used on *The Flying Post* (see April 9/11, 1719) which is signed 'F. H.' It is a handsome setting but was apparently considered to carry the wrong connotation, for with its twenty-third number it adopted a heading-block $2\frac{3}{16}$ in. deep across two columns in the style of Mist's *Weekly Journal*. From this time, it is apparent that Mist's was the dominating weekly, and was, by its example, setting the style for any competitors. This becomes notably clear in the instance of one of the several rivals to Mist's.

A *Weekly Journal* established and printed by John Applebee of Blackfriars in 1714 (Mawson's was started in 1713, it will be recollected) exchanged its old heading of two separate devices of a postman and a britannia for a single block, signed J. Bell, in Hoffman's style. This change in Applebee's occurred in 1721. *The Original London Post or Heathcote's Intelligence* (June 12, 1723), though not using the word 'Journal' in its title, was headed with a conventional $2–2\frac{1}{2}$ in. double-column block. Doctor Gaylard, upon whose head, when he was helping Mist, a thousand pounds had been set, used a block of these dimensions. A cut-down tree, a new branch and other specific emblems took the place of the now conventional britannia and postman, and the block

[1] With No. XVI the title was shortened to *The Orphan Reviv'd; | or | Powell's Weekly Journal | Containing | all Remarkable Occurrences Foreign and Domestick | together | with a Tatler* and with No. XXIII to *The Orphan Reviv'd | or | Powell's Weekly Journal*. No. XXIII uses a fine factotum by Hoffman of three infants being mothered against a background of St Paul's. Mrs P. returned at the end of 1719. The imprint to the last-known issue is 'Printed and Sold by Eliz. Powell, at Mr Clifton's, in the Old Baily'. Her *Charitable Mercury* is shewn on p. 85 ante.

omitted the barock italic calligraphy of the characteristic Hoffman head-piece. His title *The Loyal Observator Revived; or Gaylard's Journal* was in roman only but gave a note of distinction to his paper which was increased by his thirteen-line factotum. The Burney collection preserves an odd number of *The Gentleman's Journal and Tradesman's Companion* for April 15, 1721, headed with a handsome double-column block in which the title on a barock frame is supported by two amorini each flourishing a newspaper. A curious feature of this paper is its possession of the factotum designed for Mist's by Hoffman. If the block in *The Gentleman's Journal* is a copy, the engraver has not scrupled to reproduce the signature 'F. H. f.' The Burney copy is imperfect, the final page with printer's imprint being missing.

John Trenchard, described by a contemporary as 'a man of severe principles with regard to Liberty', founded, in 1719, *The Thursday Journal*, but changing its publication day to Saturday, and title, with its second issue, to *The London Journal*, also carried a deep double-column heading. The design, in the style of Bell, though unsigned, is composed of allegorical figures of Isis and Thames flanking a view of London from south of the river; overhead is the simple title in roman—there is no sub-title—between the royal device and the Arms of the City of London. An almost precisely similar cut —the sole difference is that a seated britannia is used in the place of *The London Journal*'s royal device—figures at the head of *The London Mercury or Great Britain's Weekly Journal With the Freshest Advices Foreign and Domestick*. Unfortunately, No. 23, April 1, 1721, single copy in the Burney collection is imperfect, lacking the final sheet with imprint of the imitator. According to Timperley, this paper began with *The Penny Weekly Journal, or Saturday's Entertainment* (No. 1, October 19, 1720) for title, becoming *The London Mercury* (a title which had had no representative since a sheet so named, founded in 1719, had ceased) with No. 15.

The London Journal, at first printed by Roberts of Warwick Lane and subsequently by J. Peele and William Wilkins, underwent no change in heading for four years, other than that the block was re-engraved from time to time. The Hoffman factotum of a fame with sun, moon and stars, originally designed for Mist, except that here it lacks its bordering of a thick and thin rule, is first used in *The London Journal* of May 27, 1721.

Throughout this period Read's *Weekly Journal, or, British Gazetteer*, founded in 1715, retained its original appearance modelled upon the format of *The Post Man* of 1696. At the beginning of 1725 it was the only weekly journal preserving a device at the right and left of a title set in black-letter.

MIST's *WEEKLY JOURNAL*. [NUMB. I.]

SATURDAY, MAY I. 1725.

——— *Quantum mutatus ab illo.* ———

AS all Men, who have any Thing to do with the Publick, should render a strict Account of their Actions, I therefore, in my last, gave the Reasons why I was obliged to alter the Form and Price of my Journal. Since therefore it has pleased the Wisdom of the Legislature to think, that a considerable Sum of Money may be raised towards paying the Debts of the Nation, by this Paper; I, as a true *Briton*, and good Protestant, being desirous to ease my Fellow-Subjects of the Burden of some of their Taxes, by these my Labours, am resolved, henceforth, to exert my self in a more than ordinary Manner, towards making this Paper more diverting, as well as instructive, than heretofore, that, by the Sale it may answer all the Purposes design'd, that no Deficiencies may be hereafter found in the Supplies granted for the Year seventeen hundred twenty five; and that, at next Sessions of Parliament, the Tax on Soap, Candles, Leather, or some other Manufacture, which deserves Encouragement more than the Paper Trade, may be taken off, to the great Ease of the middling and poorer Sort of People.

Yet I can't help observing, that while I look on my self in this new Dress, the Gracefulness of my Figure seems to suffer some Diminution from the Change: Methinks I look like some veteran Soldier, who, by the Misfortunes of War, had lost a Leg and an Arm in the Service of his Country. —— Yet I comfort my self with this Reflection, that tho' this Mutilation impairs the Beauty of such, they are look'd upon with the more Respect. Upon which Consideration I am resolved, that if, for the Good of my Country, it should be resolved, by any future Act, to cut me off another Limb, and oblige me to appear in half the Quantity of Paper in which I am now seen, I shall not quit the Field; nay, tho' I should be reduced at last, like the valiant *Widdrington* of old, to fight upon my Stumps.

I flatter my self upon the whole, that my Readers will not suffer in their Diversions, by this new Regulation; for in my initial Essays, I shall now lie under a Necessity of avoiding Prolixity, a Fault which has spoil'd the best Productions of the Pen, and which we are warn'd by the Criticks, above all others, to beware of.—Nay, it is observ'd by Philosophers, as well as Criticks, that all Things which are small, whether Animals or Vegetables, are more perfect in their Kinds, than those of a larger Growth; and the Reason they are pleased to give for it is, that the latter require a greater Quantity of Spirits to animate and give them due Vigour, than Nature allows to one Body.———And the same Rule, they tell us, often holds in Respect to the human Species; and, indeed, we sometimes see the largest Bodies and Heads have very little in them.—— Nay, there is a Characteristick of Dullness fix'd upon particular Nations; that of the *Germans* is grown proverbial every where, and if they are more stupid, their Breed of Men, as well as *Women*, is also larger than that of other Countries.————From all the aforesaid Considerations my Readers may expect that I shall be smarter than before.

As to the historical Part of my Works, or what relates to News, I am sensible it will bear no Abridgment; for I have observ'd, that Abridgments of Matters of Fact ever render Works imperfect; I therefore resolve, that whatever Relations fall within my Province, as a weekly Historian, to omit no material Circumstance which may serve to elucidate or clear up the Truth, or illustrate the Story, whether the Point of History be a Robbery, or some barbarous and bloody Murder, a Rape, or a Marriage, the Tryal of a ——— at *Westminster*, or of a Felon at the *Old Baily*. —— But when I come to treat of the more profound and secret Matters of State, as Frauds, Hocus-Pocus, Legerdemain, Plots, &c. I shall take Care to make my self well understood.

I also think fit to assure my Readers, that if the Princes of *Europe* should hereafter go together by the Ears, and a War should happen to break out, that when they come to Action, I will not shorten a Battle; I know the material Humour of my Countrymen too well for that, and have observ'd, with what just Disdain they look on those who fight a Cheat, and hurry over the Weapons, either at *Figg*'s Amphitheatre, or that of *Hockley in the Hole*: I therefore promise, that whenever there is a Battle, to give my Readers fair play for their Money, and to go quite thro' the Fight to their entire Satisfaction.

Perhaps it may be objected, that tho' I may have Room for a Skirmish, I shall never be able to draw up a great Army, and fight a pitch'd Battle within the Compass of this small Paper, but much may be done in a little by Discipline and good Conduct; for by frequenting the Play-House, and observing with how much Suppleness and Dexterity of Limbs, *Scaramouch*, who is a clean well shap'd Fellow, contracts himself, and lessens his Appearance to half what he really is, I have borrow'd a Hint, which may prove of singular Use to me under my present Circumstances; whereas by drawing my Lines a little closer, and some other Arts, tho' I may look something less to the Eye, yet when you come to examine me close, you will find my Matter and Substance to be much the same.

I will not pretend to take to my self the Invention of this ingenious Contrivance; it is well known, that a famous Artist inserted the whole Book of Psalms in the Hair and Beard of a Picture of King *Charles* the First, which Picture is still to be seen at *Oxford*. I do not intend to draw my Lines altogether as close as that ingenious Gentleman has done; for, I consider, that the finest Eyes in Great Britain are sometimes employ'd in perusing this Paper, and as I intend to dedicate some of my Labours particularly to the Ladies, I shall take Care not to hurt their Sight; I therefore promise to inlarge my Quantity of Paper, every now and then, as I find Matter increase upon my Hands.

Upon the whole, as I know it is in the Nature of Man to be greedy of Knowledge, I shall conceal nothing from my Readers, which by good Intelligence comes to my Hands, so that if I shou'd at any Time be obliged to abridge my weekly Labour, it shall be the Essay, by which, as I observed before, I conceive the Diversion of my Readers will be rather improved than lessen'd. ——For all Productions of Wit have something in them of the Nature of bottel'd Ale, that is a Kind of Froth or Scum, which being thrown away, renders the Liquor which remains more palatable as well as wholesome.

To conclude, I can't help confessing, that this Act has render'd me a little vain; as it has made me a Person of more Consequence to my Country, than many Thousands who make a greater Figure in the World; before I was useful in employing the Poor, and now I shall every Week add something to the Riches of the Commonwealth. ——— Besides, I am considering what a considerable Figure we the Writers of this Age shall hereafter make in History, when it shall be said of us, ——— *That about the Beginning of the eighteenth Century, the Wits were look'd upon to be so wealthy a Body, that they were obliged to pay a considerable Sum towards discharging a heavy Debt, under which the Nation at that Time labour'd.* —— And all that I'm in Pain about, is, least it should not be believ'd.

P. S. Our last Advices from the polite End of the Town, concerning the Affairs of Gallantry, tell us, that Mother *N*———*m*, and Mother *J*———*y* are broke, and gone off; ——— but that Mother *Heyd*——*ger* still carries on a good comfortable Trade, she having had a *Ballam Rankum* on Thursday Night last, at which most of her former Customers were present, except such as were a little out of Order since her last *Passa-Tempo*. ——— And, it is said, the good old Gentlewoman, out of a tender Regard to her Children, as also for the Encouragement of *Basket-making*, intends to set up an Office of Insurance on Noses.

Price Two-Pence.

Fig. 53

Mist's, Applebee's, and all the rest were, as we have seen, headed with a single double-column block either 2 or 2½ in. deep, designed after the Hoffman heading engraved for Mist's in 1720. The style was brought to an abrupt termination in the spring of 1725 by an enactment precising the Stamp Act of 1712. The law now insisted upon the use of stamped paper for any kind of news-sheet, mercury or paper, as to one penny for a sheet and one halfpenny for a half-sheet. The journals, priced at three halfpence, were compelled to pass on the tax to the customer and at the same time reduce their extent. The standard journal size: the six pages, of a type area measuring approximately 6¼ in. × 11 in., which had obtained for more than a decade, now came down to four pages of 8¼ in. × 10¾ in.—i.e. from six-page folio to four-page quarto. The column width, formerly 18 ems, became 24. Mist's paragraph preparing his readers for the change appeared in the issue of April 24, 1725, the last of the three-halfpenny folios. As a postscript to the political essay on his front page, he wrote:

> Whereas by an Act of the present Sessions of Parliament, this Paper is made liable to pay a Stamp Duty of a half Penny every half sheet it shall contain, which Act takes place immediately after the present 25th of April; the Proprietor thinks fit to let his Readers know, that in order to make it as easy as possible to them, he will contrive in such a Manner, that it may be sold for Two pence, being persuaded, that they will not think the half Penny advanced for it any Hardship, since it is a Matter of Necessity, and not done to grasp any unreasonable Profit to himself.—In order to this, he will be oblig'd, for the future, to publish it under another Form; but he thinks fit to promise and assure the Publick, that though it may suffer some Diminution in Quantity of Paper, yet it shall be as copious in Matter, and as entertaining and useful, in all Respects, as at any Time since its first Publication.

The new form duly appeared on Saturday, May 1, 1725, and Mist, under the caption *Quantum mutatus ab illo*, confessed to feeling that 'while I look upon my self in this new Dress, the Gracefulness of my Figure seems to suffer some Diminution from the Change: Methinks I look like some veteran Soldier, who, by the Misfortunes of War, had lost a Leg and an Arm'.

The paper does, indeed, look changed. The Hoffman factotum of the fame with sun, moon and stars, now considered too expensive of space, is sacrificed. But the most conspicuous of all changes is the abandonment of the deep wood-engraved heading in favour of the narrow titling 'MIST'S WEEKLY JOURNAL' in two-line english capitals, roman for Mist's name and italic for the title. The date line is run in between single rules to the full measure. Thus, *per saltum*, the paper returns to the formula established by

The London Gazette in 1665 with the difference that the title is not in canon upper- and lower-case, but in capitals. For a reason which is not clear, Mist's and Read's journals were renumbered from this first issue in the new format. Applebee's *The London Journal* and *The British Journal* continued their respective series of numeration, but with compressed headings conformably with Mist's model. Read's was an exception in one important economic respect, which had consequences in the typography; the journal was printed upon a distinctly inferior paper and the price—for some time—remained at $1\frac{1}{2}$*d.* Its typographical character was preserved in its quarto size. The title of the new series is still in text and the packet and postman devices keep

Fig. 54. *Heading-blocks from Read's journal*, 1727

their positions. The handsome factotum of the royal arms with supporters, some twelve lines small pica in depth, is still used at the beginning of the first column.[1] The heading-blocks are sufficiently distinguished to justify reproduction in their original size. The one serious difference between the old and new series, other than the change in the size of the paper, was in its quality. 'Readers', said a note at the head of column 1, page 1 of the No. 1 for Saturday, May 1, 1725,

> are desired to excuse the coarseness of the Paper for the present, and better shall be provided with all possible Expedition to shew the earnest Desire we have to oblige our customers, we shall continue to entertain them with the same Variety of Intelligence, contriv'd so, that, tho' compriz'd in a less Compass, it shall be equal in Quantity, in as fair a Print, and at the same Price as heretofore, as we hope the courteous reader will find in what follows to his entire Satisfaction.

In 1727 Read's altered its make-up to three columns of $15\frac{1}{2}$ picas in measure, the depth remaining the same. The factotum was reduced in area. A normal issue for this year consists first of a long epistle addressed to the conductor

[1] This is the factotum used at the heading of Chapter IV

on an urgent domestic or foreign topic; an instructive article on the history of this or that monarch; a chronicle of foreign affairs; a page of London news (generally the whole of page 3) and a final page of miscellaneous information with the third column containing advertisements. Applebee, Mist and others equally adopted the three-column arrangement. The news-reading public had been familiarised with this make-up by *The Daily Journal*, a paper established in 1720 as a single folio half-sheet in double column. With its heading in canon upper- and lower-case, *The Daily Journal* was composed precisely in the style of *The Daily Courant* and *The Daily Post*. *The Daily Journal* went to three $14\frac{1}{2}$ pica columns in January 1727. Not only so, but on January 19, 1728, the same paper carried on its front page an interesting notice which must be quoted:

> That we may not omit any Material Part of our Intelligence etc. for the future, or lessen the Use and Value of our Paper in the Opinion of ANY of our Readers, we shall, whenever press'd for Room, print the same, as at present, on larger Paper, in four columns, without raising the Price to the Public, notwithstanding the extraordinary Expense to ourselves.

After two such issues (of type area 15 in. × $9\frac{4}{5}$ in.) the paper returned to three columns (on the smaller sheet) but ran to the larger format on several days in the month. On February 1st, 1728, however, *The Daily Journal*, in returning permanently to three columns, admitted that 'the Method of Four Columns, in which we have of late been often obliged to print this Paper', had been found 'inconvenient by many of our Readers'. The statement adds that the method is 'also too expensive to be continued at the same Price'. For the future, subscribers were told that *The Daily Journal* will be 'printed in the same Manner as This Day, and on the like good Paper'. The size was four pages of quarto which continued for a few weeks. In April 1728 the paper was again in folio with three columns.

The weekly journals remained in double-column for some time. Caleb D'Anvers' paper *The Craftsman* was the first to follow Read's example given in his *Weekly Journal*. Read also reconstructed his *St James's Evening Post*, setting it in three columns on a large quarto sheet—and retaining the royal device. None of the weekly journals of the period from 1725 to 1742 carried a device of any kind. As the next chapter will indicate, the weekly journals became increasingly political in tendency as statesmen saw the advantage of spending money on the press.

[illegible]

CHAPTER VI

THE WEEKLY JOURNALS, II

1727–1742

The Craftsman	1727
The Grub-street Journal	1730
The Weekly Miscellany	1732
The Westminster Journal	1742

NUMB. I.

The Grub-ſtreet Journal.

To be continued Weekly.

Thurſday, JANUARY 8. 1730.

The INTRODUCTION.

Dullneſs! whoſe good old cauſe I yet defend,
With whom my Muſe began, with whom ſhall end!
For thee I dim theſe eyes and ſtuff this head
With all ſuch reading as was never read. Dunciad. B. I.

Grub-ſtreet, Jan. 7. 1730.

T*HE beſt Things here below are liable to be corrupted, and the better Things are in their own Natures, the more miſchievous are they if corrupted* †. Books are on all hands allowed to be of the greateſt Benefit to Mankind: whence I infer, that a bad Book muſt be one of the greateſt of Evils. Our Society has been always compoſed of ſuch learned and worthy Members, as have produced the beſt of Books themſelves, and done what in them lay to ſuppreſs the bad. This Procedure has drawn on them the Oppoſition of ſome Men, whoſe Malice infinitely ſurpaſſes their Ability: but after all the Pains they have taken, they have proved nothing, but that they themſelves have *neither the reaſoning of Men of Senſe, nor the Style of polite Men, nor the ſincerity of honeſt Men, nor the humanity of Gentlemen, or Men of Letters* †. Theſe Men (if I may ſo call them) whenever they have been deſirous to run down any Book, as low, trivial, and contemptible, have beſtowed on it the Epithet of *Grub-ſtreet*, as if it was a ſufficient Note of Infamy to ſuppoſe it to come from this Place. But this Paper will abundantly convince the Publick of what Dignity, Excellence, and Uſe our Society is; and how mean and deſpicable our Adverſaries are. The Reaſons already laid down ſeem ſufficient to ſhew, why this Paper ought now to be publiſhed: it will perhaps be more difficult to ſatisfy the Publick why ſomething of this kind never came out before.

It is true indeed, that altho' this Society has ſubſiſted many Years, yet they have never before publiſhed any thing as a Society. But if this be an Objection, it muſt hold as ſtrong againſt other Societies of Men of Letters. The *Royal Academy of Sciences* at *Paris* never publiſhed any of their Memoirs till thirty Years ago; and the *Royal Society* of *London* have not publiſhed any Hiſtory of themſelves, except what was done by Dr. *Sprat* ſoon after their Inſtitution. But that nothing be wanting, a learned Member is preparing an Account of the Antiquities of *Grub-ſtreet*, with it's Hiſtory, continued down to the preſent Time So that our Account in this Paper may begin at this Inſtant; and we may continue to give the Publick a weekly Hiſtory of the moſt important of their Tranſactions.

In the purſuit of this Deſign, we ſhall relate their admiſſions of new Members, which are very frequent. For no ſooner does any learned Gentleman publiſh a Work, which they approve of, but they immediately give him a Place among them. We ſhall alſo communicate an Account of ſuch Books, as ſhall receive their Approbation. It may be objected perhaps, that this is already done in the *New Memoirs of Literature.* I anſwer; That Author, tho' he gives an Account of the Works of ſeveral of our Members, and is indeed one of them himſelf, yet omits a great Number of excellent Books; the deſign of his Undertaking being chiefly to recommend thoſe which are publiſhed for one Bookſeller only. We ſhall alſo publiſh Diſſertations, as the Society and the Compoſers of them ſhall give leave; and ſometimes relate the learned Debates which happen among our Members on a great variety of Subjects. And as political Diſſertations have been always the peculiar Province of this Society, care will be taken that their Journal may never be deficient in this particular. This Branch is committed to Mr. *Quidnunc*, a worthy old Citizen, who has ſacrificed his own Advantage to that of the publick. This great Scholiaſt has undertaken to collect all the material Articles of News from the other Papers; to digeſt them into a proper Method, and illuſtrate them with critical Obſervations. He has likewiſe ingaged to publiſh ſeveral occaſional Papers, relating to Murders, Apparitions, Prodigies, &c.

Mr. *Quidnunc*'s conſtant Employment in the Service of the Society, obliges him to reſide in their Houſe; that he may always be in a readineſs to make the moſt proper Uſe of any Intelligence which may be communicated. He is accompany'd, in his Reſidence, by Mr. *Poppy*, an excellent Poet; who will not only frequently entertain the Town with ſome of his Poems in this Paper; but is likewiſe ready to compoſe Panegyricks or Satyrs, Anagrams or Acroſticks, Copies of Verſes from Friends of Authors, or annual Salutations from City Bell-men to their worthy Maſters and Miſtreſſes, at reaſonable Rates.

I muſt not omit the mention of one very conſiderable Member, who bears the Title of Hiſtorian to the Society, *Gyles Blunderbuſs*, Eſq; The other Officers receive Salaries from the Society; but Squire *Blunderbuſs* has generouſly declin'd the receiving of any of the publick Money; *ſomebody having left him ſomething to live on.* We ſhall ſometimes oblige the Publick with the Characters drawn by him of our deceaſed Members.

As for my ſelf, the Care of publiſhing this Paper will lie on me. And tho' I ſhall have ſufficient Matter from the Journals of the Society, to continue the Publication of it weekly; yet if any learned Perſons will favour me with their Correſpondence, their ingenious Communications ſhall be honourably taken notice of, by their Faithful Friend and Humble Servant,

BAVIUS.

† *Theſe Words are borrow'd from Mr.* Dennis, *in his Preface to* The uſefulneſs of the Stage.

Fig. 55

CHAPTER VI

THE WEEKLY JOURNALS, II

1727–1742

THE next development in weekly journalism came from a Whig hack writer, Nicholas Amhurst, who, under the name of 'Caleb d'Anvers', was responsible for *The Craftsman*. At first (No. VI is the earliest issue in the British Museum) the paper was a single sheet, published Monday and Friday and printed in english-size type (14-point), double column, containing no news, and having the air of a late seventeenth-century paper. With No. 45 the paper became a quarto of four pages in the modern standard three-column journal manner (May 13, 1727). The title (see Fig. 57) reads *The Country Journal: or, The Craftsman,* and there follows between single rules the line 'To be continued every Saturday'; next, the line 'By Caleb d'Anvers, of Gray's-Inn, Esq'; a third rule and the date. With No. 46 a fourth rule under the date was added; all which rules, being extended to the full measure, presented a highly conspicuous feature in a heading without being expensive of space. This arrangement of rules is not original to Amhurst's paper. We have seen it in the Commonwealth Mercuries, in one or more of Dunton's journals, and they were much used by all printers for the title-pages of tracts, pamphlets and books. In periodicals their most familiar use had been in the heading of *The Tatler* which ruled off the title, the name of Isaac Bickerstaff, Esq., and the motto *Quicquid agunt*, etc., i.e. the paper's heading contained three transverse rules. The date was not ruled.

Clearly, then, it was Amhurst's intention to give his paper the 'Tatler' connotation. Years before *The Freeholder's Journal* (a six-page folio, published Wednesdays from January 31, 1722) and *The Universal Journal*, a literary paper, in the main, also published on Wednesdays, from January 1723, attempting the same thing, employed a deep title, amply spaced with ornamental rules, for ten months. On October 10, 1722, a 2-in. deep barock headpiece was placed over the title which remained, as before, in canon upper- and lower-case. A fine factotum signed by Hoffman had first appeared on October 3.[1] Such headings indicated that the papers were not weekly

[1] Used occasionally also in *The True Briton* from No. 7, June 17, 1723, also printed by T. Payne, a political paper published on Mondays and Fridays in single half-sheet form.

Numb. X.

The Craftſman.

Et tenuit noſtras numeroſus HORATIUS *aures.* Ovid.

By CALEB D'ANVERS, *of* Gray's-Inn, *Eſq;*

From MONDAY, January 2. to FRIDAY, January 6. 1727.

I ſhall always have the greateſt reſpect for the family of the *Shallows*, whom I have reaſon to look upon as *riſing* men, ſeveral of them having already diſtinguiſh'd themſelves as the greateſt *Ornaments* and *Supports* of their country, both in *Church* and *State*; for which reaſon I cannot poſtpone the following Letter; eſpecially ſince I am reſolved to preſerve the utmoſt impartiality in this undertaking, and was unwarily impoſed on by a former Letter, which I am inclined to believe, upon maturer thoughts, to be very diſingenuous, and heartily wiſh that it had not obtained a place in this Paper; but I hope the *learned Divine*, who may be prejudiced thereby, will accept of this apology and have the candor to excuſe the inadvertency of an old Man, who is ready to make him all the reparation in his power, by publiſhing the following Letter in his defence.

To CALEB D'ANVERS *Eſq;*

SIR,

AS you have publiſhed a Letter containing ſome account of the Life of HORACE, ſaid to be delivered by the famous Mr. *H*——*y* in his academical oration on *Wedneſday* the 21ſt of laſt Month, I hope you will pay the ſame regard to this, which comes from one of his conſtant *Hearers*, and is deſign'd to vindicate our *Modern Orator* from the imputation of ſeveral paſſages, which ſeem very injurious to his character, as well as to the memory of that *ancient Poet*.

Your correſpondent begins with a juſt commendation of that *ingenious Divine*, whoſe inſtitution he allows to be an *uſeful* undertaking; but from the manner, in which he has repreſented that learned entertainment, I cannot help concluding, and muſt take the freedom to declare, that either the *Letter-writer* entirely miſunderſtood Mr. *H*——*y*, or that he had ſome ſecret ill intention of prejudicing the Town againſt his *Orations*.

This writer, *in* his character of *Horace*, obſerves that he calls himſelf *Epicuri de grege Porcum*, i. e. litterally tranſlated, *a Swine of Epicurus's herd*; from whence he makes Mr. *H*——*y* infer, that he was ſomewhat *fat*, and very *dirty*; whereas this is only a *metaphorical* expreſſion; and in the uſe of *Metaphors* an author is not obliged to include all the properties of the thing, from whence he takes it as it would be eaſy to prove from numberleſs inſtances out of the beſt Writers, ancient and modern. That *Horace* was *fat*, we have his own word, and the confirmation of ſeveral writers; but that he was *dirty*, is not any where confeſſed by himſelf, nor charged againſt him by others; nor did Mr. *H*——*y* mention any ſuch thing. This expreſſion therefore ought to be underſtood ſo, as to denote the *fatneſs* only, and not the *filthineſs* of the *Swine*.

The charge of *Horace's dirtineſs* is farther urged from this paſſage,

—— *Non ego paucis*
Offendar Maculis —

which every School-boy knows to be alſo a *Metaphorical* expreſſion, and that it alludes to *inaccuracies* of Stile, and not to any want of delicacy in *dreſs*; yet your correſpondent makes Mr. *H*——*y* affirm, *that from theſe two paſſages it is manifeſt that* Horace *was little better than a* Sloven; whereas I muſt inſiſt on it that he ſaid no ſuch thing, as indeed he ſeems to have no manner of foundation to do, ſince in the line immediately before that quoted to prove him a *Sloven*, he deſcribes himſelf in the figure of a BEAU.

Me pinguem et nitidum, *bene* curata cute, *viſes.*

I am ready to grant that *Horace's* fortune was originally very *ſmall*, and that he had encreaſed it conſiderably, as Mr. *H*——*y* obſerved and proved, not only from the paſſage quoted by this writer, but alſo from the following one.

— Natum et *in tenui Re*
Majores pennas nido extendiſſe loqueris.

Tho' my paternal eſtate was very inconſiderable, yet by a laudable ambition I have made very great additions to it.

But Mr. *H*——*y* did HORACE the Juſtice to obſerve, that what he wanted by *inheritance*, he made up in *Virtue*.

Ut quantum generi *demas, virtutibus* addas

Which this Letter-writer has, I am afraid, *purpoſely* omitted.

I muſt likewiſe agree with him, that *Horace* was very *cholerick*, as he acknowledges himſelf; but with this alleviation, that he was *eaſy* to be *reconciled*; of which likewiſe your correſpondent takes no notice

Iraſci celerem, tamen ut *placabilis* eſſem.

But I am perfectly aſtoniſhed at this writer's aſſertion, that *Horace* married a woman of *Lombardy*, which he fathere

Fig. 56. *First title of D'Anvers' journal*

journals in the Saturday sense. They were rather boulevard journals comparable with *Cyrano, Aux Ecoutes* or *Le Cri de Paris*. They retailed gossip from Child's, the Smyrna, the St James's and other coffee-houses. No space is given to stock quotations or the prices of the funds. Amhurst, besides following Steele's use of an obvious pseudonym, added 'Esq of Gray's Inn', in which innovation he was himself followed by many imitators. The new layout, then, was intended to prepare readers for a paper in which the 'Tatler' quality should be more distinctly conveyed than it had been in Mist's, Applebee's and other weekly journals. Yet it had to conform to the standard construction of the normal weekly journal. Consequently, when with No. 45 Amhurst revised its name, so that it became *The Country Journal: or, The Craftsman*, instead of *The Craftsman*, he also expanded its contents to include news under the conventional rubrics, 'Foreign Affairs', 'Home Affairs', 'London', and a mass of advertisements. Finally he, or his backers, appointed a new printer who brought it out on Saturdays instead of Mondays and Fridays (cf. Fig. 57). *The Craftsman* affords, therefore, an excellent instance of the strength of the weekly tradition.

There was one noticeable idiosyncrasy in the setting of the text of the paper in its new form, i.e. exaggerated use of italics and small capitals. Other journals employed the same methods of emphasis in the main political article on their front pages. *The Craftsman* exploited the italics still further, and multiplied small capitals in its essay; and it extended the practice to 'Foreign Affairs'. This habit was, by degrees, so copied that, elsewhere ultimately, the smart journals were a mosaic of italics. This elementary exercise in the art of typographical ingenuity, as far as italics are concerned, had been discovered, in a crude form, by the Elizabethan printers. They enjoyed lengthy titles and headings set in lines of roman and italic—a piece of faddishness which I have never seen explained. I hazard the guess that it descends from the blackletter title-pages whose lines were set alternately in red and black. This, however, is to digress.

The Civil War or Commonwealth Mercuries used italics for names of persons, ships, inns and places, whether native or foreign; occasionally they were used for purposes of emphasis and citation. The Intelligencers at the end of the seventeenth century and *The Post Man* and *The Post Boy* were, as genuine seventeenth-century foundations, governed by the same principles.

But *The Daily Courant*, as a genuine eighteenth-century paper, reduced italics to the barest minimum. The Evening Posts followed the *Courant* in using italics only for the places of foreign origin of despatches. The weekly journals took the place of origin from its old position at the very beginning of the first line of the despatches and centred it over the top of the paragraph. At the same time, they set it in spaced roman capitals of the body size—and not in italic upper- and lower-case. Mawson introduced this usage; Read and the rest followed. Mist gave a sprinkling of italic for proper names and place names. *The Craftsman*, the essential Whig paper, squandered them. As it made money,[1] and was consequently imitated, its format became identified in the public mind of 1730 with a specific kind of weekly journal of opinion.

The other journals, e.g. *The London* and *The British*, gave more general news. Mist's came into serious trouble in 1729, being abandoned in favour of an immediate successor under the instantly recognisable name of *Fog's Weekly Journal*. This paper, in precisely the same format, fared little better, the printers and publishers being arrested for defaming the memory of King William. But the journal, though hardly in the same strength as before, managed to maintain itself until the death of Mist in 1737. This left the task of carrying on the old weekly tradition, created by Robert Mawson, to *Read's Weekly Journal*.

Read was merely a printer, and as such represented a tradition older than Mawson; as old, in fact, as the Corantos. He was in the succession to Arthur Buckley and the rest of the printers who were newspaper owners, whereas Mist was a seaman turned journalist, and Amhurst was a scholar turned hack. When politicians found the money for the weeklies, printers were unable to compete. When, later, booksellers found the capital for the dailies, the printer thought himself lucky if he secured a proprietor's share—and this he forfeited if the paper was taken away from his office. In the 1730's an entirely new set of economic factors began to affect the trade. Amhurst was the first of a new type of journalist, and he gave newly founded journals an example which they closely followed.

The British Journal, or The Censor, 'By Roger Manley, Lincoln's Inn, Esq' (which came out on January 20, 1727/8), was the first, and *The Universal Spectator, and Weekly Journal*, 'By Henry Stonecastle of Northumberland Esq' (*circa* 1729), the second new weekly inspired by *The Craftsman*.[2]

[1] 'Largely', says an anonymous writer of the time, 'owing to the articles of Daniel Poultney, he being at that time the living Oracle of the Party, it was no wonder if whatever was supposed to come from his Pen was received as so many sacred responses.' Cf. *An Historical View of the Principles, Characters, Persons etc. of the Political Writers in Great Britain* (London: Printed for W. Webb, 1740).

[2] In 1737 one 'Mooney, an Irish Roman Catholic, and likewise a Nonjuring Counsellor at Law', who had conducted *Fog's Weekly Journal* while Mist was

There followed a third foundation, as a novelty for 1730, the first number of *The Grub-street Journal | To be continued Weekly | Thursday, January* 8. 1730. The head added an introductory verse from the *Dunciad*, ruled off in the same fashion as the title-line and the date-line, making, in all, four such lines across the full measure over two wide columns, the first of which began with a nine-line initial. *The Grub-street Journal* was a literary paper run by a number of smart alecks who answered the prejudices of others with vigorous enunciation of their own. As a literary journal the *Grub-street* does not concern us, but, although it never ceased to be preoccupied with matters dramatic and literary, it did, for a period, find regular space for news items, attacks on the rest of the political sheets, upon booksellers and upon the newspapers. We need to notice it because, having paragraphs of domestic news, it was a sort of newspaper, carrying further the plan of *The Craftsman*. The final successors to the Mawson-Read-Mist-Applebee weekly journals were the weekly chronicles of the next generation. *The Craftsman* and *The Grub-street Journal* were the productions in a transitional period in which men of some formal education no longer disdained connection with the newspaper press. Steele and Addison were essayists, their papers were essay papers. Boyer and Ridpath were news-writers, and in the estimation of many, at the best, mere overgrown booksellers' clerks who had scratched together a fortuitous list of ignorant correspondents. In the transition to the weekly chronicles, with which we shall deal in a later chapter, *The Grub-street Journal* took a notable part.

In its two-column format, the *Journal* made a neat piece of composition (cf. Fig. 55). The sections which constituted the paper were marked off with a row of small ornamental flowers run between two rules cut to the column measure. An average issue contained an epistolary dissertation introduced with a small factotum; a set of verses, a quip or a riddle; a page of domestic news compiled from *The Daily Courant*, *The Post Boy*, *Daily Post*, *Daily Journal*, *Daily Advertiser*, *St James's Evening Post*, *Whitehall Evening Post*, *London Evening Post*, each being keyed with an initial C, P, D, E, etc.; miscellaneous verses headed 'From the Pegasus in Grub Street'; a column or more of Foreign News and a fourth page of advertisements by booksellers. The paper ceased in 1737, but was revived in February 1738 as the *Literary*

hiding in France, brought out a paper with the title *Commonsense*, which met with some success. A rival paper, begun under the same title by some disaffected members of Mooney's staff, published but a few numbers. Both were political journals on *The Craftsman* model, but paying less attention to general news.

The COUNTRY JOURNAL: OR, THE CRAFTSMAN.

N° 45.

To be continued every SATURDAY.

By CALEB D'ANVERS, *of* GRAY'S-INN, *Esq*;

——*Alter et Idem.*

SATURDAY, MAY 13. 1727.

ALL Proposals, which seem really calculated for the Good of the People, either by promoting any valuable Branch of Trade or easing them of any burthensome Tax, being generally received by them in a grateful manner, and the only Design of this Paper having been to discourage all *unnecessary Expences*, as well as to detect every Species of Corruption, it is not to be doubted that my Readers will be highly pleased to see my practice conformable to my Doctrine, and that I am resolved, upon all occasions, to contribute my utmost assistance, towards reducing the *national Expences*, at this *chargeable* Season, by publishing my Paper but once a Week; especially, since I hope that I shall lighten the burthen of the *Subject*, without diminishing the Revenues of the *Crown*. For tho' I can, with great Truth and Pleasure, reflect that I find no alteration in the opinion of the Town concerning my Writings, as far as I can form any Judgment by common discourse, or the sale of them; though, with equal concern, I must observe that I can foresee no probability of my wanting sufficient matter to continue them as often as I have hitherto done; and though I am firmly resolved not to slacken my Zeal in the Interest of my Country and the Cause which I have undertaken; yet I have been induced, by several Reasons, to appear in this manner; especially for the remaining part of the Summer; at the End of which, I may resume my former method.

In the first Place, as I must expect that the Recess of Parliament will carry a great number of my Readers out of Town into different and distant parts of the Country; so I am not unacquainted with the *Difficulties* and *Inconveniencies*, which they will meet with, in having my Papers regularly convey'd to them, from time to time, as they have been hitherto publish'd; whereas they will easily find their way, *once a Week*, into most parts of *Great-Britain*, in the same manner that other *Journals* and *News-Papers* do.

For this Reason I have thought fit, by and with the advice of my *Bookseller*, *Printer*, and *Publishers*, to convert the *Craftsman* into a *Weekly Journal*, and subjoin to my usual Dissertations, which shall be continued in the *same* manner, a faithful account of all occurrences *foreign* and *domestick*; for tho', during the *Session* of *Parliament*, which detains the greatest part of the Nobility and Gentry, in Town, where they are themselves at the Fountain-head of all Intelligence (which it is to be presumed they are as capable of obtaining as any common News-writer whatsoever) there did not seem to be any great necessity for me to trouble either them or my self with such Narrations; yet being determin'd to continue my *political* and *moral* Essays, I thought it proper at the same time to accommodate my Readers, whilst in the Country, with all Transactions both publick and private, at home and abroad; which I doubt not will be kindly received on many accounts, and particularly, as it will save those, who take in this Paper, the expence of some *others*, in which they can expect to find nothing but the most *abject*, *ill-tim'd Flattery*, *mercenary Falshoods* and *political Legerdemain*.

Indeed I have been often tempted to something of this nature before, by observing the shameless and abandon'd manner, in which several Writers have garbled the publick accounts, in order to serve certain, private Ends, which can be no secrets to the World; and the only Reason, which has hitherto dissuaded me from it, hath been the gross, palpable and bare-fac'd method of their doing it, which I apprehended could not impose on any Man of common sense and understanding.

But being, at length, determin'd to this undertaking, for the Reasons before-mention'd, I have chosen to distinguish it from other Papers of the same kind by the name of THE COUNTRY JOURNAL; in which the Reader may depend on the most faithful, genuine and authentick account of all Occurrences, whether our fate be *Peace* or *War*, without any disguise, misrepresentation or party-view whatsoever: For as the only rational end of such a Paper is to set every thing that passes in the World, in a true light, I conceive it would be much better for the World to receive no account at all of these matters, than to have them related in such a *false*, *partial* and *Sophisticated* manner.

But, though my design be to adhere strictly to Truth my self, as well as to correct the mistakes and expose the falshoods of others, yet I cannot pretend to be *infallible*; for as I shall be often obliged to mention current Reports, and the opinions of Mankind concerning things, which are in agitation, as well as to relate what shall have actually happen'd; as there are several artful Rumours and fictitious Articles of Intelligence trumpt up, almost every Day, by *Stock-jobbers* and *others*, in order to carry on private views, and as several *foreign News-Papers* may be reasonably suspected, as well as *some* of ours, of being written under *Influence* and *Direction*, so it will be absolutely impossible for me to preserve my self, at all times, free from wrong Surmises, Errours and Impositions.

All therefore that I can either promise or propose is, to make the strictest scrutiny into the Truth of what I hear and what I read; to assert nothing for *Fact*, but what I certainly know or firmly believe to be so; to mention *Rumours*, only as *Rumours*; to form *Conjectures*, only by way of *Conjectures*; and to relate every thing, according to the best Information I can receive, without *Hopes* or *Fears* from any man, as becomes an impartial Lover of Truth and his Country.

In *foreign Affairs*, either with regard to the operations of the *Field* or the intrigues of the *Cabinet*, I shall not only consult all the publick Prints both at home and abroad, but likewise compare them with those *private Intelligences*, with which I have taken care to be constantly supplied; and extract, from both these, such materials, for this Paper, as shall seem most agreeable to Truth, Reason or Probability.

In matters of a *domestick* nature my Boo[k]seller hath provided a Person who, I hope, will have the same regard to veracity; tho' he may sometimes treat them in a different and more diverting manner than others; and will now and then, in a dearth of News, entertain the Publick with such little pieces of wit and humour, either in Verse or Prose, as may be occasionally handed about the Town, or with which our Correspondents shall, at any time, oblige us.

As I have always paid the utmost regard to the *fair Sex*, and am resolved to let slip no opportunities of entertaining them, in the most agreeable manner, consistent with that good breeding which is due to them, and that decency which becomes a man of my years, I cannot in the least doubt of their good opinion and candid acceptance of my writings.

In short, nothing shall escape my notice, that falls within the *Province*, which I have now undertaken; nor will I spare any endeavours to recommend my self to the favour of all Persons, of both Sexes, and of every Party, except *Those*, whom I shall esteem it no dishonour to disoblige.

It may, perhaps, raise the wonder of some People, that a Man of my Age, Character and Fortune should condescend so far as to Prostitute his Name at the Head of a *common News-Paper*; to which I reply, that since I have been provok'd and, in a manner, call'd up to this undertaking by the unexpected Conduct of *some Men*, I think my self obliged to go thro' with it, and wear out the Remains of my Life in any manner, that I apprehend will be serviceable to my Country. Besides, I cannot help observing, that however mean or contemptible the business of a *Journalist* may have formerly been; yet, of late Years, it seems to have been a Post of great *Credit* and *Honour*; nor can I possibly see any Reason why I may not, without any Disreputation, hold the Property of a JOURNAL, *in Commendam*, as well as another.

This Day is Published,

The fourth *Collection* of the *CRAFTSMA*[N] By CALEB D'ANVERS of Gray's-Inn, Esq; P[rinted] for *R. Francklin* in *Covent-Garden*, price 1 *s.*

N. B. *The fifth* Collection, *which compleat[s the] first Volume, is in the Press; and no more will b[e pub]lished in* Pamphlets *for the future.*

[Price Two Pence.]

Fig. 57. *Second and permanent title of D'Anvers' weekly journal*

Courier of Grub-street in small quarto size. By the wit and vehemence of their criticism, the Grub Street writers worked to improve the style of writing in the newspapers, and raised the standard of reporting. Their campaign was largely a successful one. If Johnson could write a regular column for one of the journals, it is largely owing to the efforts of *The Grub-street Journal.* By bringing a critical public into existence, the paper prepared the way for the ably conducted weeklies of the next generation. *The Grub-street Journal* also had its effect upon the dailies. These had increased in number—and perhaps importance—by the end of 1737 when the *Grub-street* was discontinued.

'*The Miscellany:* giving an account of the Religion, Morality, and Learning of the Present Time. With Occurrences Foreign and Domestick. By Richard Hooker, of the Temple, Esq:' fairly prepares us for a journal in which scholarship and literature shall be combined with news and views. The antique phrase 'Occurrences Foreign and Domestick' was justified by the inclusion of Foreign Affairs, Country news and London Intelligences. A new feature of this three-column folio of four pages (price 2*d.*), No. 1, December 16, 1732, is a list of books published in Great Britain which depended for its contents upon the booksellers' information supplied in the form of advertisements in the same paper. The list presages the regular reviewing of new books which the chronicles, successors of the miscellanies, made a considerable feature.

The main article, devoted more to common than to political matters, was, however, not so humanist as *The Tatler.*

The Miscellany is, in fact, an excellent example of the growing control exerted by the booksellers upon the journals. It was a leisurely paper written by those accustomed to deal with books, and calculated to increase the circulation of the booksellers' wares. The epistle addressed to the author (or, on occasion, to 'Good Mr Hooker') was introduced with a pleasant barock factotum of a size which was convenient for the purpose and no greater. 'As you have formerly obliged me with the Publication of a short Epistle', wrote one of these scribes, 'I am encouraged to ask the Favour of you to insert, when the length of your *Initial Letters* will leave room for it, the following Account of a Piece of Conversation,' etc.

With No. 3 the paper became *The Weekly Miscellany*, printed by C. Jephson for J. Roberts, of Warwick Lane. *The Weekly Miscellany* had the respectable life of some nine years. Its reputation is witnessed to by the fact that in 1734 Jonathan Swift's foundation chose the *New Miscellany* for its title. On the demise, on June 27, 1741, of the original 'edited by Richard Hooker, of the Temple, Esq', *The New Weekly Miscellany* was brought out and lived for less than six months from July 18, 1741.

The next paper which we have to consider—and in some detail since its career was long and curious—is indicated by its sub-title, but the first half of its title should be noted as it uses the word 'Journal'. *The | Westminster Journal: | Or, New Weekly Miscellany. | By Thomas Touchit, of Spring-Gardens, Esq; | Saturday* (cf. Fig. 58) is constructed as a normal weekly journal,

THE N° 48.

WESTMINSTER JOURNAL:

Or, New Weekly Miſcellany.

By THOMAS TOUCHIT, *of* Spring-Gardens, *Eſq*;

SATURDAY, October 23, 1742.

From my own Apartment in Spring-Gardens.

A DIALOGUE *between* Bob *and* Will, *with the Remainder of their* Hiſtory, *being the* Sequel *of the two preceding Papers.*

Scene the Court of ———, *without the Veſtry.*

Will.

WHAT my *old Particular*?—Give me thy Hand Man.

Bob. Umph!———

[*Turns ſullenly away.*

Will. Nay, nay! but why ſo *ſhy*? What have I done to affront thee?——Is it becauſe———

Bob. Inſulting Wretch! [*Aſide.*

Will. Becauſe I have *kept my Word* with thee? hah! Did I not ſay I would *never leave* thee, till I had got 'tis not a Thing that a Man would *greatly covet*: But if People will be *Rogues*, they muſt take what follows: Who can help it?

Bob. Nobody, if they are *fairly* and *fully convicted*. ——But I remember the Time, *Will*, when you were not ſo *plaguy honeſt* yourſelf, nor ſo eager to procure *Juſtice* to the Pariſh.——Tell me then, is it *Principle* you now act upon, or only *Enmity* to me? If the firſt, I muſt make the beſt *Defence* in my Power: If the latter, have you not your *Ends*? Have you not *conquer'd*? Do I not *quit* the Field, and demand *Quarter*? Think then, might not this be *made up* between us? Your own Friends come *in* next; and too much Severity to me will be but a *ſcurvy Precedent* againſt them, whenever the *Tables*, as no doubt they will, come to *turn again*.

Will. What! *compound Felony*, and *drop the Intereſt* I have ſo warmly eſpouſed!

Bob. Why not? 'Tis not the firſt Time. We have they have *run down* their Prey? By their Obſtinacy, they ſhould be a *different* Race of Mortals from any I have before met with: Otherwiſe, I think, I ſhould have known how to *ſilence* at leaſt ſome of the loudeſt.

Will. Leave that to me; they are of my own *breaking*. I am a true Sportſman, and can bring them *off* as well as I brought them *on*. The ſame Offers they *refuſed* from you, never doubt they will *accept* from me. A *Coalition of our Friends* will ſecure us both, and be better for his Lordſhip's Servants than a *Coalition of Parties* throughout the Pariſh. The latter indeed are *fine Words* to harangue on in the Veſtry; but between Friends, who know the World, and one another, they mean *nothing*.

Bob. Openly and honeſtly ſpoken.——Give me thy Hand again, Boy.——The ſame *Will Trimmer* ſtill; and the ſame *Bob Monopoly*, after a Difference of near twenty Years.

Will. I never thought, in the Main, that we *differ'd*

Fig. 58. *Upper portion (reduced) of the first title of* The Westminster Journal

but its title is ruled off above, between and below the author's name and the date in the style of a Miscellany and not of a Journal. A small factotum introduced the text of column 1 of the front page; a row of small flowers between rules was used as a mid-column cut-off in the manner first sponsored by *The Grub-street Journal*. The layout, therefore, is exactly normal, i.e. what one would expect from a paper using in its title and sub-title the words 'Journal' and 'Miscellany'. *The Westminster Journal: Or, New Weekly Miscellany* represents the transitional stage of the weekly between *The Grub-street Journal* and *The Universal Chronicle*.

In this account of the main tendencies of journalistic typography and make-up *The Westminster Journal* must be studied, for it was one of the few weeklies of that time which lasted out the century. Of course it changed a great deal. The *Journal* continued to be printed by one family for more than a generation, so that there was little change in the first decade or two.

In 1745 one James Hinton[1] of St Paul's Churchyard brought out the first number of *The London Courant*,[2] a single sheet full folio (of which the verso was advertising) whose large canon upper- and lower-case heading was ranged between a packet ship and a mounted postman framed in a floral border. This must have seemed a slightly archaic performance to the readers

THE
WESTMINSTER JOURNAL
And OLD BRITISH SPY.

No. 2368.] From SATURDAY, August 31, to SATURDAY, September 7, 1805. [Price Six-Pence.

THE ONLY LOTTERY

BANKRUPTS to surrender at GUILDHALL.

THE DUKE OF GLOUCESTER.

AGRICULTURE, &c. MONTHLY REPORT FOR AUGUST.

Fig. 59. *Upper portion (reduced) of the last title of* The Westminster Journal, 1805

of that day, since such blocks had completely disappeared as a result of the 1725 Stamp Act. But a few years later, perhaps fired by Hinton's example, the printer of *The Westminster Journal*, Redmayne, added two blocks to his heading, i.e. a flying fame and a packet ship—both of which, now rare enough, had been considered essential to the heading of all the weekly

[1] Formerly of Covent Garden. In 1739 he brought out a paper 'intitled the *Craftsman*' which drew a disclaimer from Cal. d'Anvers and an assurance that 'the Gentlemen who have written and conducted that paper for above Twelve Years past have no manner of concern in it; and that the *original Craftsman* is now printed by H. Goreham in Fleet st.' The piracy brought H. Goreham's name to the top of the front page where it was ruled off below the date line.

[2] *The London Courant* was a Monday, Wednesday and Friday publication. It came into the hands of the bookseller, John Almon, who continued it until 1780 (and perhaps later) with a heading distinguished by two armorial blocks of London and Westminster respectively. Later, *The London Courant* came out daily. At its cessation in 1782 it bore the title *The London Courant, Westminster Chronicle and Daily Advertiser*.

journals in the period of 1713–25. The *Westminster*, however, did not reproduce any of the earlier designs, but, by vignetting instead of bordering them with a frame, effected a slight modernisation.

Without any public announcement that I have come across, the *Westminster* was absorbed in January 1760 by *The Universal Chronicle*, begun by Payne and at that date resigned into the hands of William Faden.

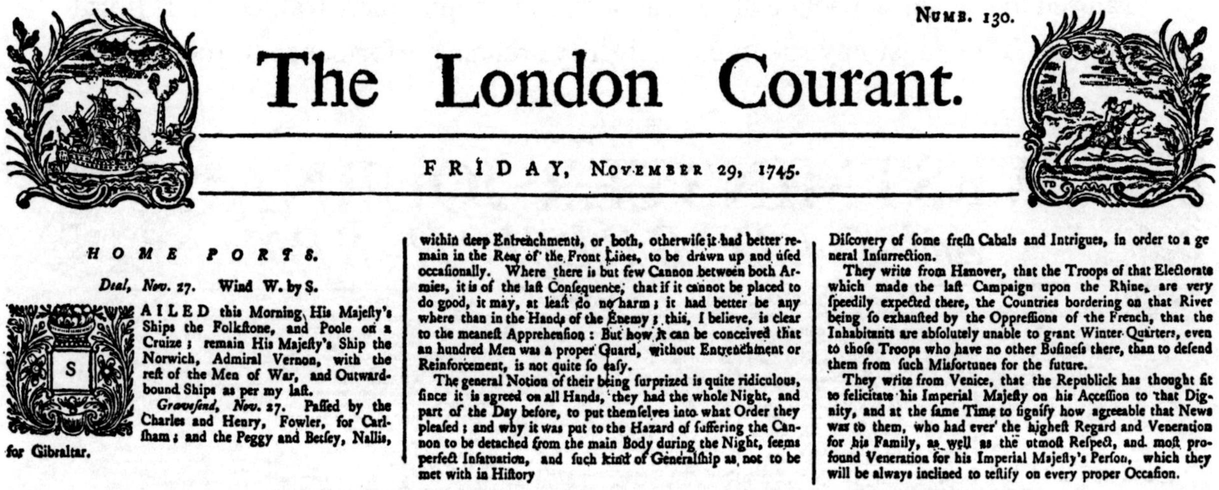

NUMB. 130.

The London Courant.

FRIDAY, NOVEMBER 29, 1745.

HOME PORTS.

Deal, Nov. 27. Wind W. by S.

SAILED this Morning His Majesty's Ships the Folkstone, and Poole on a Cruize; remain His Majesty's Ship the Norwich, Admiral Vernon, with the rest of the Men of War, and Outward-bound Ships as per my last.

Gravesend, Nov. 27. Passed by the Charles and Henry, Fowler, for Carlsham; and the Peggy and Betsey, Nallis, for Gibraltar.

within deep Entrenchments, or both, otherwise it had better remain in the Rear of the Front Lines, to be drawn up and used occasionally. Where there is but few Cannon between both Armies, it is of the last Consequence, that if it cannot be placed to do good, it may, at least do no harm; it had better be any where than in the Hands of the Enemy; this, I believe, is clear to the meanest Apprehension: But how it can be conceived that an hundred Men was a proper Guard, without Entrenchment or Reinforcement, is not quite so easy.

The general Notion of their being surprized is quite ridiculous, since it is agreed on all Hands, they had the whole Night, and part of the Day before, to put themselves into what Order they pleased; and why it was put to the Hazard of suffering the Cannon to be detached from the main Body during the Night, seems perfect Infatuation, and such kind of Generalship as not to be met with in History

Discovery of some fresh Cabals and Intrigues, in order to a general Insurrection.

They write from Hanover, that the Troops of that Electorate which made the last Campaign upon the Rhine, are very speedily expected there, the Countries bordering on that River being so exhausted by the Oppressions of the French, that the Inhabitants are absolutely unable to grant Winter Quarters, even to those Troops who have no other Business there, than to defend them from such Misfortunes for the future.

They write from Venice, that the Republick has thought fit to felicitate his Imperial Majesty on his Accession to that Dignity, and at the same Time to signify how agreeable that News was to them, who had ever the highest Regard and Veneration for his Family, as well as the utmost Respect, and most profound Veneration for his Imperial Majesty's Person, which they will be always inclined to testify on every proper Occasion.

Fig. 60. *Title (reduced) of James Hinton's* The London Courant

In 1763, when its separate existence was again determined, the paper was headed with its original two cuts at the right and left respectively of the title which read: '*The Royal Westminster Journal and London Political Miscellany*, By Simon Gentletouch of Pall Mall Esq, author of the old Westminster Journal, by the name of Thomas Touchit of Spring-Gardens Esq: and of Mitchell's Political Miscellany'. The original title was reverted to in the following year as '*The Westminster Journal*, etc.... by Simon Gentletouch[1]... etc.' The title remained in this exact form, with the original cuts, until 1794 when, on the absorption of another property, the sub-title became *And Old British Spy*, and so remained until 1810 (cf. Fig. 59). *The Westminster Journal*, always and until the end a Saturday journal, perpetuated the flying fame and ship-packet devices derived ultimately from 'Baldwin's *Post Man*' of 1696. Read's, the only other weekly journal carrying a device in its heading, cannot be traced after 1761.

[1] The reference to Simon Gentletouch was suppressed in 1769 and restored in 1771. In 1794 the author's name was permanently suppressed in favour of a notice giving the name and address of the printer (A. West, 9 Creed Lane, successor at the same address to G. Redmayne). The paper at last came into the hands of Draper Brewman and ceased, still a Saturday paper, with the issue of December 29, 1810.

CHAPTER VII

DAILY JOURNALS POSTS & ADVERTISERS &c.

1719–1741

The Daily Post	1719
Parker's London Post	1719
The Daily Journal	1720
Parker's Penny Post	1725
The Daily Advertiser	1730
The London Daily Post	1741

CHAPTER VII

DAILY JOURNALS, POSTS & ADVERTISERS &c.

1719–1741

DURING the generation which had seen the foundation of Mawson's *Weekly Journal* and its imitators in 1715, there had been several noteworthy developments in the rest of the periodical press. First as to dailies, *The Daily Post* began in October 1719 as a proud single sheet in the conventional style of a daily, i.e. in double column with a type-set heading like *The Daily Courant* or *The London Gazette*. It was printed by H. Meere in Blackfriars for the bookseller Boreham of Paternoster Row. The author, considering that it was the 'misfortune of the Town to have much News; but little Intelligence', counselled any writers or proprietors of other papers 'concern'd in our setting up this *Daily Post*' that they 'forbear to envy and strive to excel'—a somewhat self-righteous admonition in view of the new paper's lack of enviable innovation or excellence in direction. But later *The Daily Post* set forth its matter in three columns. The typographical differences between the dailies and the weeklies, striking enough when the journals were all equipped with spectacular headings and factotums, had almost disappeared as a result of the revised Stamp Act of 1725. Thus, in 1724, each of the three dailies—*The Daily Courant*, printed by Buckley, Amen Corner; *The Daily Post*, printed by Meere, Old Bailey; *The Daily Journal*, printed by Applebee, Fleet Ditch—possessed titles which were in upper- and lower-case; while, in 1725, as we have already noted, the weekly journals of Mist, Read and Applebee (printed by those named) and *The London Journal*[1] printed by Wilkins, Little Britain, were each given a new title in capital letters, either roman or italic. Both dailies and weeklies were in triple column make-up. George Parker's penny (Monday, Wednesday and Friday) paper (it began early in 1719 as *Parker's London News or The Impartial Intelligencer...Foreign and Domestick*) was

[1] And perhaps *The Freeholder's Journal* (Sharp, Ivy Lane), *The British Spy* and *The Whitehall Journal* (Wilkins) which I have not been able to see. *The British Journal* was headed in upper- and lower-case.

The Daily Advertiſer.

Numb. 21.

FRIDAY, February 26, 1730.

THIS PAPER *will be Printed every Day,* Sundays *excepted, and deliver'd to any Perſon within the Bills of Mortality at One Penny* per *ſingle Paper, or Six Shillings* per *Quarter. It is requeſted of all Perſons who will pleaſe to take in this Paper, that they Book the ſame, as they uſually do other Papers. All Advertiſements of moderate Length will be taken in at Two Shillings each, and the moſt eaſy Advance for thoſe of a greater Length. And the Publick is hereby aſſur'd, that neither the Paper, (although the ſame ſhould amount to one or more Sheets) or Advertiſing therein, will ever be raiſed in Price, on any Account whatſoever, except in the manner before mention'd. This Paper will conſiſt wholly of Advertiſements, together with the Prices of Stocks, Courſe of Exchange, and Names and Deſcriptions of Perſons becoming Bankrupts; as alſo in an Alphabetical Manner a Daily Account of the ſeveral Species and Quantities of Goods Imported into the Port of* London, *as alſo of ſuch Goods as are Exported from thence, not being of the Growth, Product, or Manufacture of* Great Britain. *And whereas it frequently happens, that Letters, as well Inland as Foreign, are directed to Perſons Unknown, and for want of proper Deſcriptions remain undelivered, to the Prejudice of his Majeſty's Revenue of Poſtage, and Injury of ſuch Perſons to whom they belong; to prevent which Inconveniences for the future as far as may be, authentick Liſts of ſuch Letters will be Daily Printed in this Paper, to the end thoſe whom it ſhall concern may apply at the* General Poſt-Office *in* Lombard-Street *for the ſame. And whereas by reaſon of the great Number of News-Papers daily Printed, and that few Perſons Advertiſe in more than ſome one of them, and that none except the moſt eminent Coffee-Houſes take in all the Daily Printed Papers, and that few Gentlemen or Others who frequent thoſe Houſes, read every Paper there taken in, the Advertiſement remains unknown to great Numbers of Perſons, to the Prejudice and Inconvenience of the Advertiſer. It is apprehended that the Publication made by this Paper will be very general and uſeful, all the Advertiſements being collected together, every Perſon may readily find out whatever can properly fall under the Denomination of an Advertiſement, without having recourſe to any other Paper And in order to make the Publication as known and general as poſſible, ſeveral Copies of this Paper will be every Day fix'd up AT and WITHIN the* Royal Exchange, *the* Poſt-Office, *the* Cuſtom-Houſe, Exciſe-Office, Bank of England, Eaſt-India-Houſe, South-Sea-Houſe, Temple-Bar, Weſtminſter-Hall, *and in ALL other the moſt publick Places of the Town. The Extenſiveneſs of the Publication, which is of the laſt Importance, being ſufficiently proved, it is hop'd that the Reaſonableneſs of the Expence, as well to thoſe who Advertiſe, as to ſuch as ſhall Take it in, will give it a Preference, with both, to any other Paper yet extant. Any Perſon deſirous to Advertiſe in the ſaid Paper, (or to have any ſingle Advertiſement Printed and diſpers'd at any time of the Day) may apply to the Printer hereof.*

February 23.

IMPORTED.

Cocos	32	C
Holland	342	Ells
Indico	3600	lb.
Olives	10	Ton
Ditto	309	Gals.
Pimento	12650	lb.
Pipe & Hhd Staves	1400	
Platt	500	lb.
Rice	236	C.
Rum	800	Gals.
Silk raw	250	lb.
Skins, Bear	3	
Beaver	272	
Ditto Pelts	60	
Cat	10	
Deer	500	lb.
Fiſher	9	
Fox	36	
Goat	623	Doz.
Martin	300	
Mink	140	
Otter	100	
Raccoon	12	
Sugar	290	Casks
Tobacco	262	Hhds.
Tortoiſhell	750	lb.
Wall-nut tree Planks	20	
Wine, Spaniſh & Port	236	Casks
Ditto Canary	30	Casks
Ditto French	6	Casks

EXPORTED.

Alkermes, Syrup	2	lb.
Almonds	3	C.
Balauſtins	2	lb.
Bejutapauts	50	
Brawls	98	
Buckram	438	Yds.
Byrampauts	[illegible]0	
Callicoes	1121	
Cambricks	70	
Cantharidees	6	lb.
Canvas	215	Ells
Carmenia Wool	780	lb.
Caſſia Lignea	30	lb.
Caſtorum	6	lb.
Chillaes	44	
Chints	80	
Cinnamon	12	lb.
Coffee	453	C.
Contra Yerva	1	lb.
Coral	155	lb.
Coopees	60	
Cotton Wool	3050	lb.
Crabs Eyes	4	lb.
Cuttanees	20	
Damasks	4	
Ditto	24	Yds.
Drugs	4	C
German Linnen	9900	Ells
Gurrahs	20	
Hemp	4	Ton
Holland	541	Ells
Jallop	3	lb.
Jamwars	9	
Incle	4	lb.
Lawns	115	
Linnen-Yarn	30	lb.
Long Cloths	30	
Lunges	10	
Manna	30	lb
Metal prepar'd	1	C.
Muſlin	31	Yds.
Myrrh	8	lb.
Neganepauts	30	
Oil, Anniſeed	2	lb.
Juniper	4	lb.
Spike	4	lb.
Oppoponax	1	lb.
Paper	21	Ream
Pepper	318	lb
Photaes	30	
Pipeſtaves	3000	
Quick-ſilver	6	lb.
Rhubarb	26	lb.
Romals	101	
Saccus Liquoritia	6	lb.
Saffron	4	lb.
Sail Cloth	4700	Ells
Scamony	3	lb.
Seerſuckers	13	
Senna	48	lb.
Siſters Thread	12	lb.
Soap	1	C.
Spice	65	lb.
Stock-fiſh	3	C.
Stuffs	15	
Taffa de Folas	11	Pcs.
Taffaties	6	
Tobacco	49008	lb.
Twiſt	1	Doz.
Whale-fins	3	C.
Wine	188	Gals.

The Courſe of the EXCHANGE.

Amſterdam	34 10
Ditto at Sight	34 8
Rotterdam	35 a 34 11
Antwerp	35 8
Hamburgh	33 5
Paris at 1 Day's Date	32 a 1 $\frac{7}{8}$
Bourdeaux at $\frac{1}{2}$ Uſance	31 $\frac{1}{2}$
Cadiz	42
Madrid	42
Bilboa	41 $\frac{5}{8}$
Leghorn	50 $\frac{3}{4}$
Genoua	53 $\frac{3}{4}$
Venice	48 $\frac{1}{2}$
Lisbon	5s. 5d. $\frac{5}{8}$ a $\frac{7}{8}$
Porto	5s. 5d. $\frac{3}{4}$
Dublin	11 $\frac{7}{8}$ a 12

Colcheſt. Bays, 6 Seals, Red Liſt, 13 d. per Ell, and 8 s. per Pc.

Gold in Coin, 3l. 18s.
Gold in Bars, 3l. 18s.
Pillar Pcs of Eight, 5s. 5d. $\frac{3}{4}$
ditto Mexico, 5s. 5d.
Silver in Bars Standard, 5s. 5d.
} per Ounce.

Thurſday Night, February 25.

Bank Stock	144 $\frac{3}{4}$
Eaſt-India	191 $\frac{3}{4}$
South-Sea	101
Ditto Annuity	107
3 per Ct.	94
Million Bank	109
Equivalent	105
African	54
York Buildings	25 $\frac{3}{4}$
Roy. Aſſ. 100l. pd. in	94 $\frac{3}{4}$
Lond. Aſſ. 13l. pd. in	12 $\frac{1}{8}$
Bank Circulation	$\frac{5}{8}$ præ:

Intereſt *per Cent.* — BONDS, *&c.*

4	India	5l. 7s.	præ
4	South-ſea	5l. 3s.	præ
3	Nevis & St. Chriſtop. Deb. at 7 per Ct. Diſc.		

ANNUITIES, *viz.*

14l. per Cent, at — 24 $\frac{1}{2}$
1704 to 1708 incluſive, — 25 $\frac{3}{4}$
9l. per Cent. *Anno* 1710, — 9
Priz. 1710 for 12 Yrs. from Mich. laſt 8 $\frac{3}{4}$ a 9
} Years Purch.

Blanks ditto for 12 Years from Michaelmas laſt, 6l. 3s. per Sett.

Fig. 61. *Earliest make-up of* The Daily Advertiser

an exceptional undertaking,[1] printed on cheap paper with the news set to the full measure and not in columns. Its serialised 'Story of the Pyrates, or Arabian night's entertainments'[2] used as fill-up matter, though printed in the forepart of the paper, was set double column. Its first heading, nearly 5 in. above the date line, was reduced to 1 in. after the passing of the Act of 1725. The text of its title was then contracted to *Parker's Penny Post* in a single line of upper- and lower-case, and the paper into the size of a small four-page quarto.

To complete a rough survey of the London press[3] in 1729, it is necessary to name the old thrice-weekly papers: *The Post Man*, then printed by Dryden Leach, Old Bailey; *The Post Boy*, printed by James, Little Britain; *The Flying Post*, printed by Jenour, Giltspur Street.

On Wednesday, February 3, 1730, occurred an event of the highest importance in the history of English journalism. This day saw published No. 1 of *The Daily Advertiser*, a paper at first 'given gratis to all Coffee Houses four days successively and afterwards printed every day, Sunday excepted, and delivered to any person within the bills of mortality at one penny per single paper', and soon enlarged to carry news as well as advertisements of the day. *The Daily Advertiser*, headed in the same manner as *The Daily Courant* and *The Daily Journal* with a leading line in canon and a date between rules, began as a single half folio, of a sheet larger than *The London Gazette*. It copied *The Daily Journal*'s three-column make-up and was printed by Matthew Jenour in Queen's Head Court, Giltspur Street near West Smithfield. During the first year, the paper made several changes in size of sheet before it found its permanent level. The first issues contain nothing but advertisements, but in three weeks it was announced in a streamer and over all three columns that 'the best and freshest accounts of all occurrences foreign and domestick will be published, as well as the account of goods imported and exported'. In the same notice it was intimated that the paper 'will be left gratis for some days at most of the houses of the nobility and gentry and the Coffee Houses and such who are pleased to approve thereof, are humbly desired to signify the same to the person who leaves it'. The thirtieth number of the paper is a four-pager in which the heading was repeated at the tops of pages 2, 3 and 4. Shortage of news and advertisements brought

[1] The issue for May 11, 1724, included a magnificent half-page cut of the phases of an eclipse.

[2] It lasted for nearly three years and was followed by an extensive relation of a lady's voyage into Spain.

[3] I.e. leaving out of account all the essay papers.

The Daily Advertiſer.

Numb. 23.

SATURDAY, February 27, 1730.

IT *being intended to render this* Paper *equally* Uſeful *and* Acceptable; *As well to entertain our* Readers, *as to ſerve thoſe who* Advertiſe *in it*; At *the earneſt Importunity of* Both, *we deſign for the future to publiſh* Daily *the beſt and freſheſt Accounts of all Occurrences* Foreign *and* Domeſtick. *The Account of* Goods Imported *and* Exported *to be inſerted in the* Papers *of* Tueſday *and* Friday, *and the* Courſe of Exchange *on* Wedneſdays *and* Saturdays. *The* Advertiſements *to be taken in at Two Shillings each, and to be paſted up at the ſeveral Publick Parts of the Town in the Uſual Manner. And for the better Diſperſing and Publiſhing the Uſefulneſs of this Undertaking, This* Paper *will be left* Gratis *for ſome Days at moſt of the Houſes of the Nobility and Gentry, and the* Coffee-Houſes; *and ſuch who are pleaſed to approve thereof, are humbly deſired to ſignify the ſame to the Perſon who leaves it.*

eſterday arriv'd a Mail from HOLLAND.

GERMANY.

VIENNA, *Feb.* 21. N. S. The Emperor was hunting the Day before Yeſterday about Laa, and at his Return to the Palace admitted to Audience ſeveral Perſons of divers Ranks. The Duke de Liria, late Ambaſſador from Spain at the Ruſſian Court, is to ſtay here till the Return of an Expreſs he ſent lately to Seville, to know the Reſolutions of his Court touching the Death of the Duke of Parma, in order to regulate his Conduct conformable to his Catholick Majeſty's Intentions: That Duke in the mean time confers now and then with the Imperial Miniſters of State, and 'tis given out that he is making ſome Propoſitions of Accommodation between his Sovereign and his Imperial Majeſty, which however is very much doubted here among the Publick, the Miniſters of State keeping a profound Silence concerning this momentous Affair: We have however ſtronger Reaſons to induce us to believe that the aforeſaid Accommodation is conducting by ſome other Powers, and that in the mean time it was reſolv'd in Yeſterday's Council of State, holden in the Preſence of the Emperor, to ſtop the March of more Troops to Italy, and other Warlike Preparations, till the Event of the ſaid Negociations now upon the Anvil, determine it one way or other. Since the Declaration made by this Court to the Pope's Nuncio, Cardinal Grimaldi, not to concern himſelf any further relating to the pacifick Negociations between the Imperial and Spaniſh Courts, his Eminency is entirely ſilent upon that Subject, and prepares every thing for his Departure for Rome, unleſs freſh Orders from thence ſhou'd command him to tarry longer at this Court.

The Imperial Commiſſary of War ſent ſome Weeks ago to the Palatine and Bavarian Courts, is returned from thence, and made his Report to Prince Eugene of Savoy, that the Auxiliary Forces ſtipulated for the Emperor's Service were fully compleat, and in a Readineſs to march upon the firſt Warning.

The Velt-Mareſchal Count de Harrach is return'd from Breſlau, where he executed a Commiſſion of great Importance at the Court of the Elector of *Mentz*.

The Ruſſian Miniſter had ſome Days paſt a private Audience of his Imperial Majeſty, and afterwards a long Conference with Prince Eugene; ſince which a Courier de Cabinet was diſpatch'd to Moſcow; and 'tis ſaid that proper Meaſures are taken by both Courts to oppoſe the Ottoman Port, if they ſhou'd attempt any Hoſtilities againſt the Emperor or the Ruſſian Monarchy.

Some Recruits have paſs'd by this City, purſuing their March to Tranſilvania; and we hear that ſome new Levies will be made in Hungary to ſtrengthen the Imperial Forces there at all Events.

Hamburg, Feb. 27 N. S. We learn from Peterſbourg, that the Admiralty there receiv'd Orders from Moſcow to equip ten Frigates from 30 to 40 Guns, in Order to go to the Ports of France, Spain and Portugal, and that their Lading is to conſiſt of all Sorts of Materials and Utenſils fit for the Building of Ships, which are to be drawn out of the Czarina's Magazines for the Service of the aforeſaid three Potentates.

'Tis written from Stockholm, that the States of that Kingdom aſſembled in Diet proceed unanimouſly in their Deliberations for the Good of the Swediſh Nation, and the Service of their Sovereign; and as they come to any Reſolution they impart it to his Swediſh Majeſty by Deputies, as is cuſtomary on the like Occaſions.

SPAIN.

Seville, Feb 9. N. S. The Court receiv'd the 4th Inſtant ſeveral Expreſſes from Italy, with the ſudden News and Confirmation of the Demiſe of his moſt ſerene Highneſs Antony Duke of Parma, Uncle to her Catholick Majeſty, who died the 20th paſt at his Reſidence in the City of Parma after a ſhort Illneſs; whereupon ſeveral Conferences were held in the Preſence of their Catholick Majeſties, and an Expreſs was afterwards ſent to the Marquiſs de Caſtellar, our Ambaſſador at the Court of France, with Inſtructions ſuitable to that unexpected Event. Soon after the Departure of that Expreſs there arriv'd another from Placentia, with Diſpatches from the Dutcheſs Dowager our Queen's Mother, which occaſion'd freſh Conferences, and the ſending away a ſecond Expreſs to the Spaniſh Ambaſſador at Paris, relating to the Death of the aforeſaid Prince.

Her Catholick Majeſty is intirely recover'd from her laſt Indiſpoſition, and their Majeſties with the Royal Family and the whole Court are preparing to go into Mourning for 4 Months, but the Infant Don Carlos is to wear the ſame two Monts longer than the reſt of the Royal Family.

This Day arriv'd another Expreſs from Parma, with Advice, that the Imperial Troops have taken Poſſeſſion of the Dutchies of Parma and Placentia.

New Levies are making with great Application throughout the whole Kingdom: and 'tis ſaid that the Court receiv'd Advice that the Engliſh South-Sea-Company's Ship going to Porto Bello, was loſt at a ſmall Diſtance from that Port.

FLANDERS.

Bruſſels, March 1. N. S. The Archdutcheſs our Governeſs has declar'd her Intention to keep her Reſidence at the Palace of Orange; and the Count de Viſconti, Great Maſter of her moſt ſerene Highneſs's Houſhold, goes from that Palace to that of the Count de Maſtin, to live there.

HOLLAND.

Hague, March, 6. N. S. The Sieur de Marſhs, Envoy Extraordinary of the King of Pruſſia, was on the 4th Inſtant in Conference with ſome Lords of our Regency, as were alſo ſome Miniſters from other Foreign Powers.

We hear from Caſſel, that the Troops of that Name in the Britiſh Pay will be review'd and muſter'd by a Britiſh Commiſſary in the enſuing Month of May.

An Expreſs from London paſs'd thro' this Place for Vienna, from whence we expect the Return of one lately ſent to the Imperial Court with Diſpatches of great moment.

LONDON, *Feb.* 27.

The Lord Marquis of Blandford honoured the Clergymens Sons with his Company at their Feaſt; and to ſhew his Concern for the unhappy Offſpring of the Church of England, his Lordſhip gave very Liberally to the Baſon.

Several Merchants are arrived from Briſtol and Liverpool, to Petition the Parliament for Relief againſt the illegal Captures and Depredations of the Spaniards, who have lately plundered and taken many of their Ships, and uſed their Men very Barbarouſly. And,

We hear this Affair will be taken into Conſideration by the Houſe of Commons on Tueſday next, when it is not doubted but they will be reliev'd.

Yeſterday the 2d Reading of the Penſion Bill in the Houſe of Peers was deferr'd till next Tueſday, upon account of the Lord Faulconbridge's Cauſe coming on before, which was ſeveral Hours depending.

The great Number of Tragedies performed this Year at the Theatres Royal with ſuch indifferent Succeſs, makes a farther Attempt that Way almoſt Hopeleſs; notwithſtanding which we are well aſſured, that the Tragedy of Merope, which is to be performed this Evening at the Theatre Royal in Lincoln's-Inn Fields, wants no Encomiums for its Introduction, but is ſaid in general to be a fine and well wrote Piece, and may be truely aſſerted to be the Spirit of Dramatic Poetry, whatever its Succeſs may be.

This Day his Royal Highneſs the Prince of Wales, intends to take the Diverſion of Hunting in Richmond-Park, if the Weather permits.

Yeſterday the Commiſſioners concern'd for the Affairs of Chelſea-College, ſat at their Chamber at the Horſe-Guards, and examin'd ſuch invalid Soldiers that had been recommended to the Penſion of the ſaid Hoſpital, in order to be admitted the next Board-Day.

Laſt Night a Committee of Council was held at the Cockpit Whitehall, on ſome Affairs relating to the Iſland of Jerſey.

—— Jacomb, Eſq; Deputy Pay-Maſter General to his Majeſty's Forces, lies at the point of Death at his Houſe at Whitehall.

Laſt Night the Corpſe of Mrs. Charwood, a Widow Lady, who died a few Days ſince at her Lodgings in Covent-Garden, was interr'd with great Funeral Solemnity at Uxbridge.

Feb. 27. *N.S.* 'Tis written from Utrecht, that their New Lottery being quite full, the Directors have reſolv'd to begin Drawing the firſt Claſs on Monday the 22d of March next, or to make double Reſtitution to the Adventurers, as is confirm'd by the Dutch Prints at Bridges's Coffee-Houſe in Cornhill, where the Tickets may be procured, renewed, regiſtred, or examined, and the Prizes diſcounted.

On Wedneſday the 3d of March, the Millers, Coopers, Bakers, Labourers, &c. employ'd in the Victualling Service of his Majeſty's Navy for the Port of London, will be paih half a Year's Wages due at Midſummer 1730.

Laſt Night the Coroner's Inqueſt ſat upon the Body of Mr. Delicate, who cut his Throat at his Brother's Houſe in Spittle-fields on Wedneſday laſt, and brought in their Verdict Lunacy.

Yeſterday both Houſes of Parliament adjourn'd themſelves till Tueſday next.

Yeſterday Morning Mr. Clark, a Wholeſale China Man in King-ſtreet near Guild-hall, was married to Miſs Ann Rickard, youngeſt Daughter to Mr. Pickard of Tibbald's in Hertfordſhire, a young Gentlewoman of great Merit and ample Fortune. The ſame Day Mr. Palmer, an eminent Grocer in Broad-ſtreet, and Partner with Mr. Richard Cope, was married to Miſs Pickard, Siſter to the aboveſaid Lady, with whom he has a Fortune of 3000l. the Ceremony was perform'd by the Rev. Mr. Biſcoe, at the Pariſh Church of St. Martin's Outwich.

The ſame Day the Captains of the outward-bound Ships in the India Company's Service now at Graveſend, took their Leaves of the Court of Directors, in order to proceed on their Reſpective Voyages.

We hear that the Beginning of the next Week ſeveral of his Majeſty's Ships of War will be put into Commiſſion for the Mediterranean Service.

February 23.

IMPORTED.

Cotton	15	Bags
Carpets	19	
Cambrick	1	
Cotton Stripes	400	
Cork	70	C.
Cocoa Nuts	145	C.
Elephants Teeth	10	C.
Fuſtick	20	Ton
Guiney Grain	1	C.
Indico	1432	lb.
Juniper Oil	48	lb.
Linnen Holland	58	Ells
Oranges	45000	
Palm Oil	20	Gals.
Pepper	8808	lb.
Piemento	3600	lb.
Rum	1116	Gals.
Rice	100	C.
Scaleboard	40	C.
Silk thrown	872	lb.
Ditto wrought	45	lb.
Ditto raw	250	lb.
Skins Deer	1200	
Sugar	199	Casks
Tobacco	33	Hhds.
Wool Nicorago	30	Ton
Water Citron	1	Gal.
Wine French	12	Casks
Ditto Port	327	Casks
	200	Gals.

Fig. 62. *Second make-up of* The Daily Advertiser *with news on front page (arranged in orthodox sequence, with foreign news first)*

the paper back to the early format in folio. It was not until 1750 that *The Daily Advertiser* was able to come out in four pages full folio. The four pages quarto had been a possibility only upon a few days in 1730, and it was twenty years before the paper reached its maximum size and extent. In the year 1754, the paper, still printed by 'Matthew Jenour, opposite St Dunstan's Church in Fleet Street' ('JENOUR over the door'), appeared in the format which was to be the standard for the English newspaper until *The Times* added a fifth column in 1808. Hence *The Daily Advertiser* may be fairly regarded as the first modern newspaper. It is satisfactory that it succeeded in maintaining separate existence, until the year 1807, and that for much of this period it ranked, not only as a good newspaper, but as an institution. Its early policy of printing advertisements only, with a modicum of such commercial intelligence as stock and exchange prices, gave the paper a hold on the commercial classes which it never lost when the policy was changed. Towards the end of the century, the surviving member of the family, James Jenour of 33 Fleet Street (the street was now numbered, but this was the same office opposite St Dunstan's), published a Sunday edition of the paper 'in order that the public may be accommodated with an early report of Saturday's State trials'.[1] The heading, in upper- and lower-case, with the date line between two rules of the full measure, was maintained absolutely without change until publication was relinquished. But we must make it convenient to postpone further treatment of the details of the composition of *The Daily Advertiser* in the days of its prime until we are abreast of the contemporary tendencies expressed in other foundations. It is important at the moment to note, first, that *The Daily Advertiser*, from the date of its foundation, adopted the three-column disposition which had been originated and standardised, until its demise in 1742,[2] by *The Daily Journal*. Secondly, it should be noted that Jenour's paper gave permanent establishment to the word 'Advertiser' in the titular vocabulary of English newspapers, as witness *The Morning Advertiser*, still published daily. After *The Daily Advertiser* came, first, *The London Daily Post and General Advertiser*, managed by a certain Theophilus Cibber, which had, as a shareholder, Henry Sampson Woodfall[3], founder of the famous dynasty of printer-journalists of that name whose policies and properties will later call for frequent mention. In March 1743–4 *The London Daily Post and General Advertiser* became *The*

[1] The State trial referred to was that of Thomas Hardy.

[2] But for a few weeks of four-column make-up, the three-column arrangement was followed in weeklies; by *Read's Journal* in 1727 and later by the rest.

[3] Not in 1726, as Fox Bourne says, but in 1736.

General Advertiser. In 1752 the title was changed to *The Public Advertiser*, the journal in which the *Letters of Junius* were to appear in 1767 when Henry Sampson Woodfall was the manager, publisher and printer.

Another notable foundation of this period was *The Daily Gazetteer* (No. 1, June 30, 1735), a paper to which we shall have to make many references when we enter the second half of the eighteenth century. Incidentally reviving an old Mercury title, *The Daily Gazetteer* was responsible for giving the words 'Gazette' and 'Gazetteer' a new lease of secular life (of course *The London Gazette* still remained and remains) which not only carried the word 'Gazette' over the turn of the century, but, in fact, to the evening papers of the last generation.

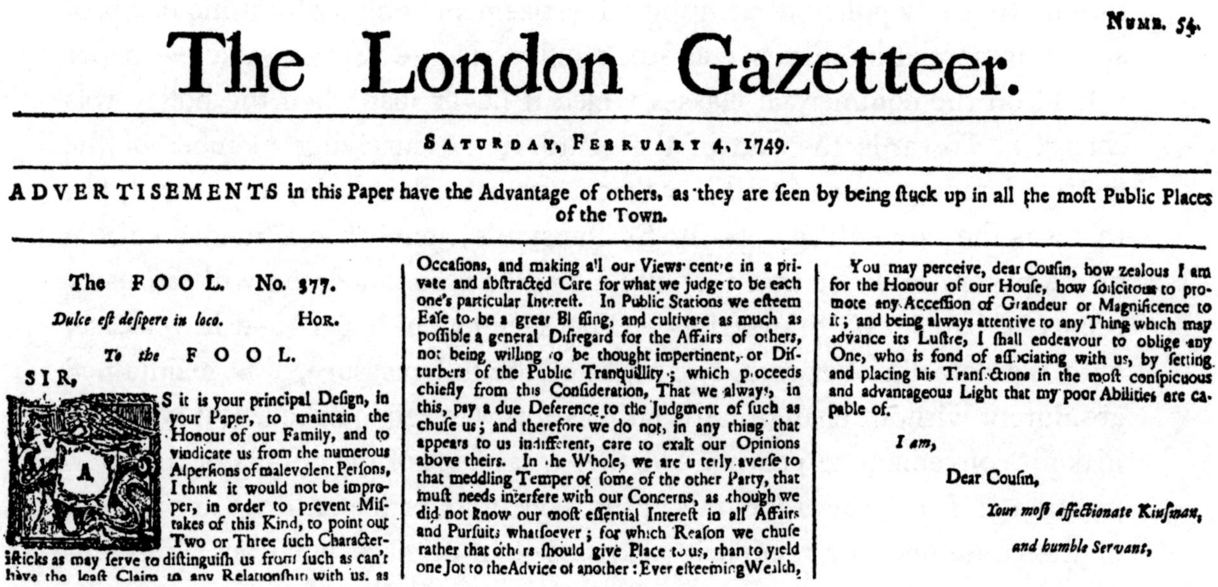

NUMB. 54.

The London Gazetteer.

SATURDAY, FEBRUARY 4, 1749.

ADVERTISEMENTS in this Paper have the Advantage of others, as they are ſeen by being ſtuck up in all the moſt Public Places of the Town.

The FOOL. No. 377.

Dulce eſt deſipere in loco. HOR.

To the FOOL.

SIR,

AS it is your principal Deſign, in your Paper, to maintain the Honour of our Family, and to vindicate us from the numerous Aſperſions of malevolent Perſons, I think it would not be improper, in order to prevent Miſtakes of this Kind, to point out Two or Three ſuch Characteriſticks as may ſerve to diſtinguiſh us from ſuch as can't have the leaſt Claim to any Relationſhip with us, as

Occaſions, and making all our Views centre in a private and abſtracted Care for what we judge to be each one's particular Intereſt. In Public Stations we eſteem Eaſe to be a great Bleſſing, and cultivate as much as poſſible a general Diſregard for the Affairs of others, not being willing to be thought impertinent, or Diſturbers of the Public Tranquillity; which proceeds chiefly from this Conſideration, That we always, in this, pay a due Deference to the Judgment of ſuch as chuſe us; and therefore we do not, in any thing that appears to us indifferent, care to exalt our Opinions above theirs. In the Whole, we are utterly averſe to that meddling Temper of ſome of the other Party, that muſt needs interfere with our Concerns, as though we did not know our moſt eſſential Intereſt in all Affairs and Purſuits whatſoever; for which Reaſon we chuſe rather that others ſhould give Place to us, than to yield one Jot to the Advice of another: Ever eſteeming Wealth,

You may perceive, dear Couſin, how zealous I am for the Honour of our Houſe, how ſolicitous to promote any Acceſſion of Grandeur or Magnificence to it; and being always attentive to any Thing which may advance its Luſtre, I ſhall endeavour to oblige any One, who is fond of aſſociating with us, by ſetting and placing his Tranſactions in the moſt conſpicuous and advantageous Light that my poor Abilities are capable of.

I am,

Dear Couſin,

Your moſt affectionate Kinſman,

and humble Servant,

Fig. 63

The initial copies of *The London Gazetteer*, printed for J. Griffiths, are fair, three-column single-sheet small folio papers, with a flying fame factotum to grace the first paragraph of an essay contributed (by Sir John Hill) under the heading 'THE FOOL'. This column and a half of copy is followed by a letter addressed to the same pseudonymous contributor. Single rule cut-offs separate Foreign, Home and London items of intelligence. It is not an important paper at this time, but it became a valuable property, as we shall see in a later lecture.

The London Morning Advertiser, *The Generous London Morning Advertiser* and Rayner's *Universal London Morning Advertiser* were all short-lived, cheap, competitive rags of the years 1741, 1742 and 1743 respectively. Another *General Advertiser* was founded in 1766 (?).

The Penny London Post; or, the Morning Advertiser (1745)—a title changed to *London Morning Penny Post* in 1751—a twice-weekly, deserves mention for one reason. In January 1749 it published on its front page a large wood-engraving, about 6 in. × 10 in., of the fireworks with which the public were regaled on the occasion of the Peace of Aix-la-Chapelle. In style the paper was four pages folio in three columns, headed in two blocks of roman type with a 2½ in. × 2 in. cut of the royal arms with supporters. It was a deep heading. One suspects that the use of it and of the block of fireworks indicates a poverty-stricken news-service due to lack of capital, as a small man's property. The paper had no serious career. The commercialisation of journalism by the joint-stock partnership method was proceeding and was soon to supersede the old traditional individualistic journalism.

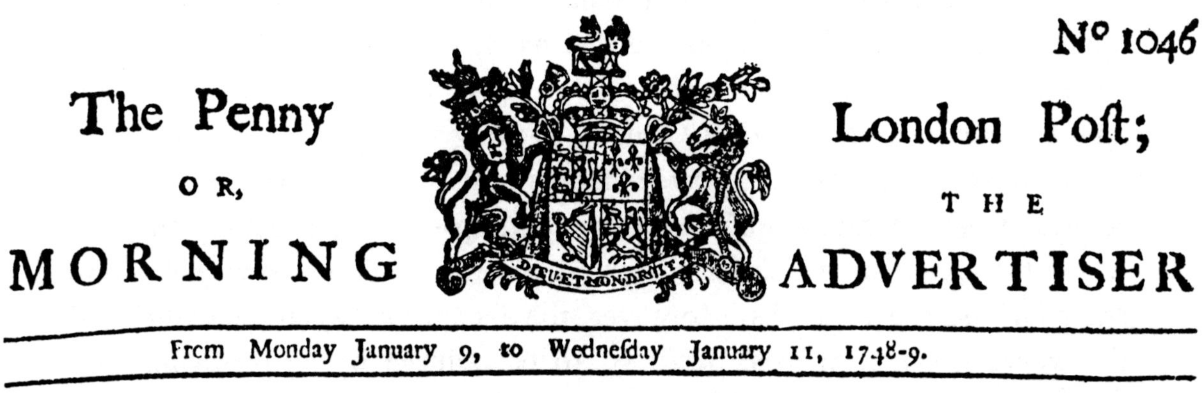
Nº 1046

The Penny London Poſt;
OR, THE
MORNING ADVERTISER

From Monday January 9, to Wedneſday January 11, 1748-9.

Fig. 64

Commercial intelligence which, in the case of the early *Daily Advertiser*, formed not merely an essential part, but the entire contents of the early issues, speedily took its important place as one normal constituent of a morning paper. By the end of ten years, from the foundation of *The Daily Advertiser*, all the mornings gave commercial intelligence, and advertising, relative and regular space. Thus the course of the Exchange, the quotations of the public funds and market news become firm features by 1740. Indeed it is at this period that the morning paper first becomes comparable with the morning paper as we have it. Parliamentary Reports, over which the press was to struggle in the next decade, were still forbidden fruit; but the increase of advertising, the energetic patronage of booksellers, the general economic recovery of the country after the disaster of the South Sea Bubble, the growing importance of the theatre, were all factors which gave the dailies of 1750 an opportunity of adapting themselves to the more intelligent and more critical public, encouraged, at first slowly, by the literary genius of *The Tatler* and, later, more rapidly by the satirical genius of *The Grub-street Journal.*

More important than all these, however, was the reorganisation of the postal services of the country by Ralph Allen, the original of 'Squire Allworthy' in Fielding's *Tom Jones.* The farming of the posts was renewed to him in 1741 on the understanding that he arranged for six a week, instead of three a week, posts from London to Cambridge, Lynn, Norwich and Great Yarmouth, and from London to Bath, Bristol, Gloucester and intermediately.

With these facilities of transport, daily papers—at first little more than modest advertising sheets for circulation to, and reading in, the coffee-houses of the metropolis—were stimulated to a considerable advance, e.g. upon the old *Daily Courant* on the one hand, or *The Post Boy, The Post Man, The Flying Post* among the tri-weeklies, or *The St James's Gazette* and *The Whitehall Evening Post* among evening journals.

The development of daily posts between London and the Home Counties could not but extend the influence of the daily press in the country and also widen the area from which some newspapers were able to draw their news and advertising paragraphs. Moreover, the distance between the dailies and the weeklies came, at least partially, to be reduced by writers who contributed to both categories of journalism. The morning paper had come of age by 1750.

CHAPTER VIII

EVENING JOURNALS

1739–1758

The Champion	1739
The Evening Advertiser	1754
The London Chronicle	1757
Lloyd's Evening Post	1757
The Universal Chronicle (Payne)	1758
The New Weekly Chronicle (Owen)	1758

CHAPTER VIII

EVENING JOURNALS

1739–1758

THE evening journals were less affected by these influences, but before long a fresh impulse made itself felt in this department. *The Evening Post* (founded 1706, discontinued 1740) had seen the invention and more or less immediate demise of *The Evening Courant*, *The General Post* and *The Night Post*. All started and gave up in the same year, 1711. *The St James's Evening Post*, founded 1715, died in 1734. *The Whitehall Evening Post* (1716), *The General Evening Post* (f. 1733), *The London Evening Post* (f. 1737)[1] all lived until the nineteenth-century railway made rapid the delivery (with consequent easy hiring) of dailies. They were strong papers, and withstood for some time the competition of dailies and weeklies. In the eighteenth century the country welcomed the evening papers. The history of *The Champion* proves that the evening public was becoming commercially more important.

The Champion represented a bold attempt to provide a thrice-weekly in the journal style, i.e. printing a political essay and a collection of articles of intelligence, both foreign and domestic. It carried on its front page a long article in the form of a letter addressed to the author 'Capt Hercules Vinegar of Pall Mall' (a *Craftsman* touch), letters from abroad headed 'Foreign Affairs', followed by domestic paragraphs entitled 'Home News' and the usual advertisements. The paper was printed by the Quaker Huggonson in excellent style. The heading had as centre-piece an admirable cut of Hercules slaying the hydra. This is the first device to appear after the removal, as a result of the Stamp Act of 1725, of all the flying fames, post boys and post men. '*The Champion*', says the anonymous writer I have more than once quoted, 'was at first published three times a week in the mornings, but, not

[1] I omit *The Evening Journal* which published only forty-three numbers from December 1, 1727, since 'three Nights of the Week no Paper appeared to the Publick, though the Entertainment was as Proper...as on the Post Days, when there are rather too many'. *The Evening Journal* hoped to 'supply that Chasm'. As it failed, though no worse conducted than the *Whitehall* or the *St James's*, we may guess that the custom of country readers was an important economic consideration and thus such subscribers would not take an Evening Journal published a day in advance of the Posts.

THE NUMB. 327.

White-hall Evening-Post.

From Saturday, October 15. to Tuesday, October 18. 1720.

Since our last came in 1 Mail from Holland, and 1 from France,

Extract of a Letter from Marseilles, dated Sept. 13.

SIR,

'AS I flatter my self the melancholly Condition this City is in gives you some Uneasiness on Account of me and my Family, it were but just that I should ease you of that Trouble by acquainting you, that, altho' we have been and still are surrounded with the Dead and Dying, we are (Thanks to the Almighty) hitherto preserv'd from the cruel Distemper which reigns here, and are at present in perfect Health. After satisfying you in the Point most concerns me, be pleas'd to let me have the Honour of satisfying you in a few Words of all that has pass'd in this miserable Conjuncture.

'The dreadful Distemper wherewith this City has been visited these 10 Weeks, was unhappily brought us by a Ship from Sidon, which came into our Road the 15th of June. The Fair of Beaucaire being at hand, the Owners of her Cargo procur'd Delivery of her too soon, and the Merchandize, which was reposited in the Infirmaries. The Porters first employ'd on this Occasion were immediately seiz'd with violent Pains of the Head, Reaching to Vomit, and a general Faintness, accompanied with (Buboes or) Plague Sores, and died thereof in 3 Days. Those who succeeded them in this Work were taken in the same Manner, and died likewise. Hereupon some Surgeons were sent to examine into the Nature of this Distemper, who reported that it was really the Plague: But proper Care was not immediately taken; the Effects were only remov'd to a desert Isle call'd Jarre, about 6 Miles off, where all those who went to air the Goods died suddenly of the same Distemper. Nevertheless some Officers of the Ship were permitted to come into the City, and many of the Sailors brought in Goods privately; upon which a considerable Mortality ensu'd in that Part of the Town where they lodg'd. Several Physicians who visited them, publickly declar'd, that the Plague began to spread, and acquainted the Magistrates with it; but they slightly regarded it, as believing it to be only a putrid Fever, which was rife only among the poorer Sort, who had liv'd much upon Fruit. Thus it continu'd neglected throughout the Month of July. Our Merchants went to the Fair of Beaucaire as usual, being persuaded there was nothing in it, and return'd in the same Opinion, except some few who proceeded into Languedoc, and elsewhere.

'About the Beginning of August the Commander, Intentendant and General Officers of the Gallies hearing every Day various Reports of this Distemper, and perceiving the Mortality to encrease, sent a Physician and Surgeon of their own, together with some of the Town, to visit the Sick in different Quarters. These reported, that from the Inspections they had made, that it was undoubtedly a pestilential and very contagious Distemper, and that they could not take too much Caution to prevent its fatal Consequences. Hereupon our Gallies, which usually lie on the Town-side, pass'd over to the Arsenal, a Palisade was made to cut off all Communication with the Town, and only the principal Officers suffer'd to go out. Hitherto we were safe in our Hospitals and Gallies, but the Distemper began now to attack us in our Trenches. The Hospital des Equipages behind the Citadel was appointed for the Infected, whither they were carried in great Numbers in small Boats, all having Buboes or Carbuncles, and some both. In the mean time, the Distemper spread so fast in the City, that the Magistrates were oblig'd to send the Infected of both Sexes promiscuously into their Infirmaries and Hospitals clear'd for that Purpose. The Physicians and Surgeons, with their Servants, who attended the Sick, died after some time, and the Chaplains did not escape; so that the Sick lay in the Streets, and at their Doors, without Help, till they perish'd. M Chicoineau, Chancellor of the University of Montpellier, and M. Verny, a Physician of the same Place, arriv'd here the 13th of August, by express Order of his Royal Highness the Regent, to take particular Information of this fatal Distemper. Having for this End visited and examin'd several sick Persons both in the Town and Hospitals, and caus'd some of the Dead to be dissected in their Presence, by a Chirurgeon they brought with 'em, they soon satisfied themselves, and were surpriz'd at the Progress of the Disease, and at the Havock they apprehended it would make, without any Hope of stopping it presently. They sent their Report to Court, and set out the 20th for Montpellier, without giving us the least Advice what to do in this dreadful Distemper, which was very amazing to most People.

'Since their Departure, the Infection is spread into all Parts of the Town, and when it gets into a Family, it runs immediately from one to another, till it has gone thro' it; so that 20 lie often dead at once in an House. The worst of all is, that they cannot be buried, but lie in the Houses or Streets many Days, the Carts appointed to carry them out not being sufficient. The Magistrates have been assisted several times with 500 Galley Slaves for this Work, yet there are still above 3000 Bodies in the Streets unburied, which cause an intolerable Stench. 'Tis computed, that between 20 or 22000 are already dead of the Plague, two Thirds of which are observ'd to be Women, most of 'em with Child, who died after Miscarriages or Lying in, for Want of Help.

'In short, the Calamity is so bad, that the Poor can hardly get Water, because few or none will go near them. The rich and able are gone into the Country with all Manner of Provision, and there is not a Shop left open. So that we who were but 3 Months ago in so flourishing a Condition, are now overwhelm'd with Consternation and Amazement, and this City is become a Place of Desolation. Here is but little Butcher's Meat, and that is extreme dear; but if that should fail us, we should still be more miserable. Bread, Wine, and other Necessaries are very scarce, and consequently as dear; so that People of the best Conditions, have enough to do to subsist.

'Our Physicians have omitted nothing in this Case, that they thought proper, whether Cordials, Sudorificks, Cathartics, or Emeticks, but had no Success in the latter, proving fatal, as well as bleeding, after which not one recover'd; indeed it was past their Skill, for they die as well with [illegible] without. The Buboes or Plague Sores can har[illegible] to suppurate. To conclude this Distemper [illegible] carried off the infected in a few Hours, beg[illegible] Point of Time, many living 6 or 7 Days, an[illegible]

SEMPER EADEM

HALFPENNY

125

Fig. 65. *The first title* (*original size*) *of* The Whitehall Evening Post being able to hold up its head in that form, it was changed into an evening paper, in which shape it has had some success and gained over the lower class of Readers'. This author, who, it will be observed, was certainly no Whig, proceeds to lament that the 'peculiar strain of humour' enlivening the paper 'takes exceedingly with the lower kind of Readers' and adds that other journals are imitating *The Champion*. Fielding brought it to an end in 1742.

The Evening Post, after a career of thirty years or more, had come to an end in 1740, leaving the post nights with the burden of delivering the three most vigorous general newspapers for news-readers namely *The Whitehall*, *The General Evening* and *The London Evening Posts*. With *The Champion* out of the way, these Posts, all foundations of the period between 1716 and 1734,

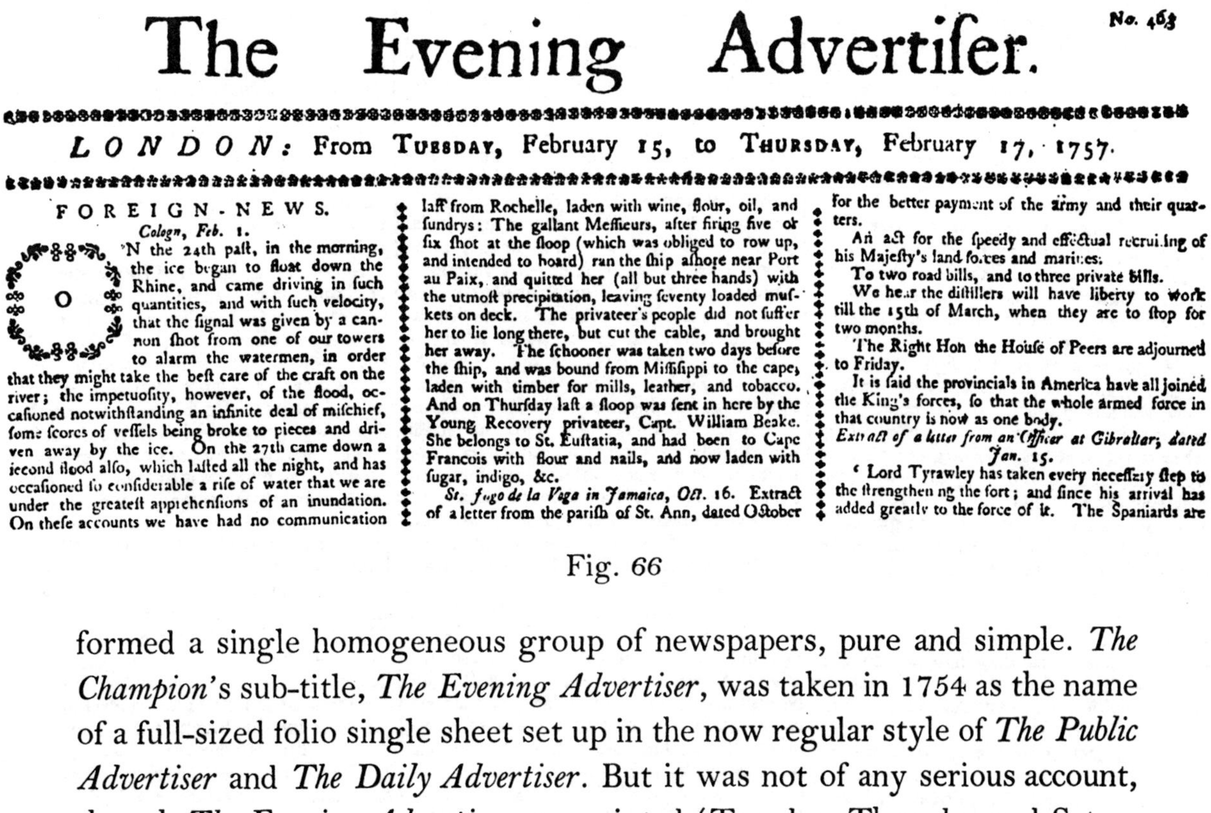

The Evening Advertiſer. No. 463

LONDON: From TUESDAY, February 15, to THURSDAY, February 17, 1757.

FOREIGN-NEWS.

Cologn, Feb. 1.

ON the 24th paſt, in the morning, the ice began to float down the Rhine, and came driving in ſuch quantities, and with ſuch velocity, that the ſignal was given by a cannon ſhot from one of our towers to alarm the watermen, in order that they might take the beſt care of the craft on the river; the impetuoſity, however, of the flood, occaſioned notwithſtanding an infinite deal of miſchief, ſome ſcores of veſſels being broke to pieces and driven away by the ice. On the 27th came down a ſecond flood alſo, which laſted all the night, and has occaſioned ſo conſiderable a riſe of water that we are under the greateſt apprehenſions of an inundation. On theſe accounts we have had no communication

laſt from Rochelle, laden with wine, flour, oil, and ſundrys: The gallant Meſſieurs, after firing five or ſix ſhot at the ſloop (which was obliged to row up, and intended to board) ran the ſhip aſhore near Port au Paix, and quitted her (all but three hands) with the utmoſt precipitation, leaving ſeventy loaded muſkets on deck. The privateer's people did not ſuffer her to lie long there, but cut the cable, and brought her away. The ſchooner was taken two days before the ſhip, and was bound from Miſſiſippi to the cape, laden with timber for mills, leather, and tobacco. And on Thurſday laſt a ſloop was ſent in here by the Young Recovery privateer, Capt. William Beake. She belongs to St. Euſtatia, and had been to Cape Francois with flour and nails, and now laden with ſugar, indigo, &c.

St. Jago de la Vega in Jamaica, Oct. 16. Extract of a letter from the pariſh of St. Ann, dated October

for the better payment of the army and their quarters.

An act for the ſpeedy and effectual recruiting of his Majeſty's land forces and marines.

To two road bills, and to three private bills.

We hear the diſtillers will have liberty to work till the 15th of March, when they are to ſtop for two months.

The Right Hon the Houſe of Peers are adjourned to Friday.

It is ſaid the provincials in America have all joined the King's forces, ſo that the whole armed force in that country is now as one body.

Extract of a letter from an Officer at Gibraltar, dated Jan. 15.

' Lord Tyrawley has taken every neceſſary ſtep to the ſtrengthening the fort; and ſince his arrival has added greatly to the force of it. The Spaniards are

Fig. 66

formed a single homogeneous group of newspapers, pure and simple. *The Champion*'s sub-title, *The Evening Advertiser*, was taken in 1754 as the name of a full-sized folio single sheet set up in the now regular style of *The Public Advertiser* and *The Daily Advertiser*. But it was not of any serious account, though *The Evening Advertiser* was printed (Tuesday, Thursday and Saturday) 'by T. Moore of Bartholomew Lane (for J. Payne at the Pope's Head in Paternoster Row)' in fine style. Its transverse 'rules' above and below the date line and separating the three columns of text were composed of a small and very simple form of the printers' flower. The factotum at the head of the first column was composed of four pairs of two types of large flowers. The heading was in the traditional style, canon upper- and lower-case.

Great as was the prestige of the word 'Advertiser', it was less apt for evening journals which were now expected to yield entertainment and in-

The London Chronicle: N° 1

OR,

UNIVERSAL EVENING POST.

To be continued every TUESDAY, THURSDAY, and SATURDAY.

SATURDAY, JANUARY 1, 1757.

IT has been always lamented, that of the little Time allotted to Man, much must be spent upon Superfluities. Every Prospect has its Obstructions, which we must break to enlarge our View: Every Step of our Progress finds Impediments, which, however eager to go forward, we must stop to remove. Even those who profess to teach the Way to Happiness have multiplied our Incumbrances, and the Author of almost every Book retards his Instructions by a Preface.

The Writers of the *Chronicle* hope to be easily forgiven, though they should not be free from an Infection that has seized the whole Fraternity; and, instead of falling immediately to their Subjects, should detain the Reader for a Time with an Account of the Importance of their Design, the Extent of their Plan, and the Accuracy of the Method which they intend to prosecute. Such Premonitions, though not always necessary when the Reader has the Book complete in his Hand, and may find by his own Eyes whatever can be found in it, yet may be more easily allowed to Works published gradually in successive Parts; of which the Scheme can only be so far known as the Author shall think fit to discover it.

The Paper which we now invite the Publick to add to the Papers with which it is already rather wearied than satisfied, consists of many Parts; some of which it has in common with other periodical Sheets, and some peculiar to itself.

The first Demand made by the Reader of a Journal is, that he should find an accurate Account of foreign Transactions and domestick Incidents. This is always expected; but this is very rarely performed. Of those Writers who have taken upon themselves the Task of Intelligence, some have given, and others have sold their Abilities, whether small or great, to one or other of the Parties that divide us; and without a Wish for Truth, or Thought of Decency, without Care of any other Reputation than that of a stubborn Adherence to their Abettors, carry on the same Tenor of Representation through all the Vicissitudes of Right and Wrong, neither depressed by Detection, nor abashed by Confutation; proud of the hourly Encrease of Infamy, and ready to boast of all the Contumelies that Falsehood and Slander may bring upon them, as new Proofs of their Zeal and Fidelity.

With these Heroes we have no Ambition to be numbered; we leave to the Confessors of Faction the Merit of their Sufferings, and are desirous to shelter ourselves under the Protection of Truth. That all our Facts will be authentick, or all our Remarks just, we dare not venture to promise: We can relate but what we hear, we can point out but what we see. Of remote Transactions the first Accounts are always confused, and commonly exaggerated; and in domestick Affairs, if the Power to conceal is less, the Interest to misrepresent is often greater; and what is sufficiently vexatious, Truth seems to fly from Curiosity; and as many Enquirers produce many Narratives, whatever engages the public Attention is immediately disguised by the Embellishments of Fiction. We pretend to no peculiar Power of disentangling Contradiction, or denuding Forgery. We have no settled Correspondence with the Antipodes, nor maintain any Spies in the Cabinets of Princes. But as we shall always be conscious that our Mistakes are involuntary, we shall watch the gradual Discoveries of Time, and retract whatever we have hastily and erroneously advanced.

In the Narratives of the daily Writers every Reader perceives somewhat of Neatness and Purity wanting, which at the first View it seems easy to supply: But it must be considered, that those Passages must be written in Haste, and that there is often no other Choice, but that they must want either Novelty or Accuracy; and that as Life is very uniform, the Affairs of one Week are so like those of another, that, by any Attempt after Variety of Expression, Invention would soon be wearied, and Language exhausted. Some Improvements however we hope to make; and for the rest we think, that when we commit only common Faults, we shall not be excluded from common Indulgence.

The Accounts of Prices of Corn and Stocks, are to most of our Readers of more Importance than Narratives of greater Sound, and as Exactness is here within the Reach of Diligence, our Readers may justly require it from us.

Memorials of a private and personal Kind, which relate Deaths, Marriages, and Preferments, must always be imperfect by Omission, and often erroneous by Misinformation; but, even in these, there shall not be wanting Care to avoid Mistakes, or to rectify them whenever they shall be found.

That Part of our Work by which it is distinguished from all others, is the *Literary Journal*, or Account of the Labours and Productions of the *Learned*. This was, for a long Time, among the Deficiencies of English Literature, but as the Caprice of Man is always starting from too little to too much, we have now, amongst other Disturbers of human Quiet, a numerous Body of *Reviewers* and *Remarkers*.

Every Art is improved by the Emulation of Competitors; those who make no Advances towards Excellence, may stand as Warnings against Faults. We shall endeavour to avoid that Petulance which treats with Contempt whatever has hitherto been reputed sacred. We shall repress that Elation of Malignity, which wantons in the Cruelties of Criticism, and not only murders Reputation, but murders it by Torture. Whenever we feel ourselves ignorant, we shall, at least, be modest. Our Intention is not to preoccupy Judgment by Praise or Censure, but to gratify Curiosity by early Intelligence, and to tell rather what our Authors have attempted, than what they have performed. The Titles of Books are necessarily short, and therefore disclose but imperfectly the Contents; they are sometimes fraudulent, and intended to raise false Expectations. In our Account this Brevity will be extended, and these Frauds, whenever they are detected, will be exposed; for though we write without Intention to injure, we shall not suffer ourselves to be made Parties to Deceit.

If any Author shall transmit a Summary of his Work, we shall willingly receive it; if any literary Anecdote, or curious Observation, shall be communicated to us, we will carefully insert it. Many Facts are known and forgotten; many Observations are made and suppressed; and Entertainment and Instruction are frequently lost, for Want of a Repository in which they may be conveniently preserved.

No Man can modestly promise what he cannot ascertain. We hope for the Praise of Knowledge and Discernment, but we claim only that of Diligence and Candour.

[Price Two Pence.]

Fig. 67. The London Chronicle *as set up by William Strahan* telligence rather than commercial data. *The Evening Advertiser*, too, seems to have erred in its conduct: its personalities were not too vigorous or too strong, they were only indiscriminate. And a fine piece of typography failed.

Conveniently for the sole new journalistic enterprise of the year 1757, the first of the year was a Saturday. There came out from the house of J. Wilkie of The Bible, St Paul's Churchyard, *The London Chronicle: or, Universal Evening Post*. The plan of the paper was a complete one: it gave impartial and accurate accounts of 'Foreign Transactions' and 'Domestick' incidents, and a survey of contemporary literature. There was no claim to possess 'settled correspondence with the Antipodes, nor to maintain spies in the Cabinets of Princes', as Johnson wrote in the introduction.[1] The paper was at least free from the worst sort of scurrility, and it had no ambition to be of political importance.[2] *The London Chronicle* was, in fact, a family paper.

It was printed by W. Strahan[3] in the best style. There were two sheets, each bearing a half-penny stamp, so that the price of 2½*d.* (at first only 2*d.*) was a very reasonable one. There were three columns to the page. The type was smaller than that usually seen in newspapers, but it was clear and gained from the good presswork normally given to it. The front page was usually given either to 'Foreign Mails' or, in their absence, to an extract from a serious work recently published. Overleaf, at the top of page 2, the previous Gazette was habitually summarised, and followed by a short section headed 'Country News'. In accordance with the make-up familiar to readers of the old weekly journals, 'London News' followed, and never preceded, both the foreign and the country sections. This arrangement was retained for each of the two days of the week covered by the respective issues, and each section headed with the day and date, *The London Chronicle* being a Tuesday, Thursday and Saturday publication. The sections were cut off with a line of small printers' flowers. The only other decorative element in the production was the small factotum of the barock sort which led off the beginning of column 1, page 1. The main heading words, *The London Chronicle*, were in black-letter, printed, so far as one can see, from a wood block and not from type. It so remained until 1804 or so when Austin's open fake-gothic type was substituted. At that time *The London Chronicle* was still published by one

[1] Boswell says Johnson was paid a guinea by Robert Dodsley for writing this introduction.

[2] But it soon lapsed into personal invective and Dodsley withdrew from the venture, selling his share. Cf. Straus, *Robert Dodsley*, London, 1910 (pp. 96 *et seq.*). Yet Boswell reports that *The London Chronicle* was the one paper which Johnson always made a point of seeing.

[3] His imprint does not appear, but Dodsley's memoirs reveal the fact.

THE NUMB. 1.

UNIVERSAL CHRONICLE, OR WEEKLY GAZETTE.

To be Publiſhed every SATURDAY, Price TWO-PENCE HALF-PENNY.

SATURDAY, APRIL 8, 1758.

THE number of News-Papers already publiſhed is ſo great, that there appears, at the firſt view, very little need of another; but the Truth is, that this great number makes another neceſſary.

The different Compilers of the Papers now circulated round the Nation endeavour, according to their various Opportunities of Information, and Tracks of Correſpondence, to excel in different kinds of Intelligence: it is therefore proper to unite weekly in ſome ſingle Paper the different Accounts of different Tranſactions, which are now ſo widely ſcattered, that many uſeful Hints may paſs unregarded for want of Leiſure to peruſe all the Papers, and for want of Knowledge where to enquire.

It is well known to all thoſe whoſe curioſity haſtens them to the earlieſt Intelligence, that the ſame Event is every week affirmed and denied; that the Papers of the ſame day contradict each other; and that the Mind is confuſed by oppoſite Relations, or tortured with Narrations of the ſame Tranſactions tranſmitted, or pretended to be tranſmitted, from different places. Whoever has felt theſe inconveniencies will naturally wiſh for a Writer who ſhall once a week collect the Evidence, decide upon its probability, reject thoſe Reports which, being raiſed only to ſerve the day, are naturally refuted before the end of the week, and enable the Reader to judge of the true State of Foreign and Domeſtic Affairs.

By ſuch a method of Intelligence, that Knowledge, which, in times of Commotion, every man's Intereſt or Curioſity makes neceſſary or pleaſing, will be obtained at leſs Expence both of money and time; many fooliſh Triumphs and needleſs Terrors will be prevented or ſuppreſſed, the Hiſtory of the laſt week will be clearly known, and the gradual progreſs of Affairs be diſtinctly traced in the memory.

This CHRONICLE, beſides a judicious Collection of News, will contain a variety of ſuch other matter as may be thought either uſeful or entertaining. A part whereof will be compoſed of Letters on intereſting Subjects, which we expect to receive, nay, which we are aſſured will be communicated, by Perſons of Eminence in the Literary World, who are friends to this Deſign; a Deſign, not haſtily conceived, and imperfectly formed, but which has, for near twelve months paſt, been under the inſpection of thoſe who are able to promote the Undertaking.

A Portion of our Paper will be aſſigned to ſome of thoſe Productions of Genius or Learning which daily receive their birth from the Preſs, and occaſional Extracts or Specimens of Books and Pamphlets will be exhibited, with ſuch candid remarks, as may contribute either to the Inſtruction or Entertainment of the Reader; and in this laſt caſe if we err at all, we hope it will be on the ſide of Good-nature: we ſhall not attempt (as many have baſely done) to clip the wings of Genius, but to plume and direct its flight.

This Paper, which will be made as uſeful as poſſible to Readers of every denomination, may be ſent in a frank to any part of Great Britain or Ireland; and may be had from *the Secretary of States Office*, or *General Poſt Office*, by thoſe Gentlemen, Ladies, and Others, who will pleaſe to leave their orders with the Poſtmaſter in their neighbourhood, or ſend to the Publiſher, Mr. PAYNE, in *Pater-noſter-Row*. It may alſo be had of the News-Carriers in Town and Country. And as it is intended to be bound in volumes, a General Title and complete Index to all the Literary articles will be given *gratis* at the end of the year; ſo that thoſe who preſerve their Papers will have, not only a Political Hiſtory, but alſo an uſeful Body of Literary Compoſitions, of more value than the original price of the Papers.

Of the Duty of a JOURNALIST.

IT is an unpleaſing conſideration that Virtue cannot be inferred from Knowledge; that many can teach others thoſe Duties which they never practiſe themſelves; yet, tho' there may be ſpeculative Knowledge without actual Performance, there can be no Performance without Knowledge; and the preſent ſtate of many of our Papers is ſuch, that it may be doubted not only whether the Compilers know their Duty, but whether they have endeavoured or wiſhed to know it.

A Journaliſt is an Hiſtorian, not indeed of the higheſt Claſs, nor of the number of thoſe whoſe works beſtow immortality upon others or themſelves; yet, like other Hiſtorians, he diſtributes for a time Reputation or Infamy, regulates the opinion of the week, raiſes hopes and terrors, inflames or allays the violence of the people. He ought therefore to conſider himſelf as ſubject at leaſt to the firſt law of Hiſtory, the Obligation to tell Truth. The Journaliſt, indeed, however honeſt, will frequently deceive, becauſe he will frequently be deceived himſelf. He is obliged to tranſmit the earlieſt intelligence before he knows how far it may be credited; he relates tranſactions yet fluctuating in uncertainty; he delivers reports of which he knows not the Authors. It cannot be expected that he ſhould know more than he is told, or that he ſhould not ſometimes be hurried down the current of a popular clamour. All that he can do is to conſider attentively, and determine impartially, to admit no falſehoods by deſign, and to retract thoſe which he ſhall have adopted by miſtake.

This is not much to be required, and yet this is more than the Writers of News ſeem to exact from themſelves. It muſt ſurely ſometimes raiſe indignation to obſerve with what ſerenity of confidence they relate on one day, what they know not to be true, becauſe they hope that it will pleaſe; and with what ſhameleſs tranquillity they contradict it on the next day, when they find that it will pleaſe no longer. How readily they receive any report that will diſgrace our enemies, and how eagerly they accumulate praiſes upon a name which caprice or accident has made a Favourite. They know, by experience, however deſtitute of reaſon, that what is deſired will be credited without nice examination: they do not therefore always limit their narratives by poſſibility, but ſlaughter armies without battles, and conquer countries without invaſions.

There are other violations of truth admitted only to gratify idle curioſity, which yet are miſchievous in their conſequences, and hateful in their contrivance. Accounts are ſometimes publiſhed of robberies and murders which never were committed, mens minds are terrified with fictitious dangers, the publick indignation is raiſed, and the Government of our country depreciated and contemned. Theſe Scriblers, who give falſe alarms, ought to be taught, by ſome public animadverſion, that to relate crimes is to teach them, and that as moſt men are content to follow the herd, and to be like their neighbours, nothing contributes more to the frequency of wickedneſs, than the repreſentation of it as already frequent.

There is another practice, of which the injurious neſs is more apparent, and which, if the law could ſuccour the Poor, is now puniſhable by law. The Advertiſements of Apprentices who have left their Maſters, and who are often driven away by cruelty or hunger; the minute deſcriptions of men whom the law has not conſidered as criminal, and the inſinuations often publiſhed in ſuch a manner, that, though obſcure to the publick, they are well underſtood, where they can do moſt miſchief; and many other practices by which particular intereſts are injured, are to be diligently avoided by an honeſt Journaliſt, whoſe buſineſs is only to tell tranſactions of general importance, or uncontested notoriety, or

[This firſt Paper is given gratis.]

Fig. 68. [*John Payne's*] The Universal Chronicle

G. Wilkie of Paternoster Row, where, as was indicated in the imprint to the very first number, 'Persons who chuse to be regularly served with this Paper are desired to apply'. There was, indeed, remarkably little change in the style, the format, or the content of *The London Chronicle*. The factotum remained at the head of column 1, page 1, for fifty years, though the sub-title *Universal Evening Post* was dropped after a decade. Clearly, the paper was a success, and, as such, had its influence upon the minds of the newspaper trade. For one thing, we hear of no more Journals; but, during the following decade or so, several Chronicles make their appearance. *Lloyd's Evening Post and British Chronicle* confessed that its general plan was the same as that of *The London Chronicle*, and in format it was a careful copy except that there was no gothic in the title. This paper first appeared in the July of the same year, 1757, but instead of appearing on the Tuesday, Thursday and Saturday of *The London Chronicle*, the *Lloyd's Evening Post* came out on Monday, Wednesday and Friday—and did so for over sixty years.

The success attending these journals, published in the evenings of alternate days, inevitably reacted upon the rest of the periodical press, and, as we have indicated, Chronicles were now the vogue. At the end of 1757, evening journalism consisted of *The Whitehall Evening Post*, *The London Evening Post* and *The General Evening Post* and the two newcomers.

In the April of 1758, a new weekly was started on the model of *The London Chronicle*, with the title *The Universal Chronicle, or Weekly Gazette*. The initiator and publisher was John Payne, whose friend, Samuel Johnson, contributed the 'Idler' papers from the second number. The first number contained a prospectus of the paper's objects. These do not appear to differ from those of other weekly papers, certainly not from those of *The London Chronicle*; but the claim is more explicitly made that this 'Universal' will have the benefit of communications from 'Persons of Eminence in the Literary World'. No doubt 'The Idler' is here forecast. That series of papers made a great stir,[1] and there were other features which must have impressed the public. With No. 5 the paper's title became *Payne's Universal Chronicle* and appearances seem to indicate that Payne was very energetic in his attempts to please readers. There was a fine woodcut illustration 4¼ in. × 2¾ in. to an article on Bridges in No. 19 (p. 151), and in No. 22 there was a full-page copperplate map of the Island of Cape Breton. These laudable endeavours,

[1] The manifesto by the *Universal* against the piracy of this feature by many in the trade is well known to be Johnson's own composition. It appeared as a streamer in No. 42 for January 13–20, 1759.

Vol. I. **OWEN's Weekly Chronicle.** Numb. 19.

OR,

UNIVERSAL JOURNAL.

From SATURDAY, August 5, to SATURDAY, August 12, 1758.

☞ *The favourable* Reception *this* Paper *hath met with from the* Public, *gives great Uneasiness, it seems, to some of the Printers of the Country Journals. They are angry to see a* new *Weekly Paper giving better Intelligence than themselves. But we do assure our Readers, that their Anger shall not in the least abate our best Endeavours to merit their Attention. And though we cannot, by our* Authentic Intelligence, *give Accounts of* Battles never fought, Victories never obtained, *or* Skirmishes that never happened; *yet, we will venture to say, that in general, we* have *and* shall *give* more Authentic Intelligence *than any Country Journal whatsoever. They cannot possibly know any Thing of* Foreign Affairs, *but what they collect from the* London *News Papers, whose Advices are only taken from the* Foreign Prints; *and how much they are to be* credited, *we leave the World to judge. Of this the Authors of the* London *News Papers are so sensible, that they now all* feed *upon our* Authentic Intelligence. *And we will venture to say further, that as we are the* first, *so we are the* only *Weekly News Paper in* England, *that ever gave* constant Food *to the* London *Daily and Evening Papers; although we cannot say the* latter *do by us as they would be done by, for some of them take the* Substance *of the* Extracts *we publish on* Saturday *Morning, and others the* Whole, *and put them into their* Postscripts *the same Night, without saying from whence they took them, by which Means they have the Credit of being quoted for them in the Country Journals instead of this Paper, of which ungenerous Treatment we can give numberless Instances.*

The HISTORY of EUROPE, For this Week.

RUSSIA.

THE Czarina has long entertained a personal resentment against the King of Prussia; and the court of Petersburgh has been long aiming to get a footing in Germany. It is not three years since that they negociated to march an army to cover Hanover from the French: that treaty was cancelled at Petersburgh as soon as it was signed at London; and the Russian army, after taking possession of his Prussian Majesty's dominions in Poland, is now making an invasion upon his dominions in Germany. The vacant throne of Courland is a proof that *Take and hold* is the standing maxim in the Russian cabinet. If they hold Ducal Prussia, perhaps, they may have the ambitious views of extending their conquests through the Upper and Lower Saxony, as far as Holstein; so that when the Czarina's nephew succeeds to her throne, he may find nothing to disunite his imperial and ducal dominions. If this should be attempted, it may be thought a bold and dangerous project: but it is no more than what was accomplished by the Czar Peter, when he conquered and held the Swedish provinces, which made him formidable in the Baltic. — They write from Petersburgh, that the combined fleets of Russia and Sweden are intended to execute a scheme of very great importance, chiefly for the benefit of the latter of these two powers; and it is thought that an Imperial manifesto will be quickly published, to explain and justify that design; though some are still of opinion that nothing further is intended than to exercise the seamen.

POLAND.

Count Dohna, the Prussian General, on his entering the territory of Poland, to seek the Russians, published a manifesto, setting forth the ravages, murders, rapes, and other violences committed by the Russians in several places in Pomerania and the New Marche; which unprecedented and scandalous behaviour could be no otherwise considered than as the work of a gang of banditti, who by such cruelties dishonour the name of soldier. That the Prussians were obliged to clear the country of such villainous men, and to enter Poland, where they would observe the strictest discipline, and desired to be treated as good neighbours and friends. — The last letters from Count Dohna's army advise, that its vanguard was arrived at Francfort on the Oder; but these letters make no mention of any farther enterprize of the Russians against the Prussian territories. On the other hand we learn, that his Prussian Majesty, in order to defeat their projects, has detached ten battalions from the towns in Silesia to reinforce Count Dohna's army. — The Russians are followed by Count Dohna, and may be met by the King of Prussia: so that they seem to be put between two fires; and we may soon see how far these barbarians can act in the capacity of soldiers, when their brutality is opposed by bravery.

[*Price Two-pence Half-penny.*]

BRANDENBURGH-PRUSSIA, and POMERANIA.

Letters from the Swedish camp, say that their army consisted of 15,000 men, exclusive of several regiments of horse and foot that had not joined it. But they add, that they have heard nothing farther about the Russians who were to have seconded their operations in Prussian Pomerania. — They write from Hamburgh, July 28, that a considerable detachment of Swedish troops has entered Rostock, the capital of the dutchy of Mecklenbourg, and disarmed the burghers. The same thing, it is said, has happened at Custrow. And they have penetrated into the Uckrane Marche, where they have exacted great Contributions. — The Russians have again entered the New Marche with a considerable body of forces, and have taken the town of Driesen by assault.

SWEDEN and DENMARK.

They write from Stockholm, July 23, that the convention by which the crowns of Sweden and Russia, for jointly fitting out a fleet in case the English should send a squadron to the Baltic, was ratified on the 20th. The treaty of Friendship and alliance between the two crowns has been lately renewed, on the same footing for 12 years.

It is said, that the combined fleet of Russia and Sweden has 14000 troops on board; and on the 21st past these ships appeared off the island of Amagh, where a body of Danish troops were cantoned. But we hear from Copenhagen, of the 28th, that those troops embarked that

Fig. 69. [*William*] Owen's Weekly Chronicle

however, do not seem to have succeeded in establishing the paper. The name of Payne is dropped from the title in No. 92, December 29–January 5, 1760, and the paper is printed for 'W. Faden, Wine Office Court, Fleet Street'. Faden was a business associate of Newbery's. The full title of the paper at the same time became *The Universal Chronicle and Westminster Journal*. There is no explicit mention of the deal, but it is clear that *The Westminster Journal*, founded in 1742 and conducted by 'Thomas Touchit, of Spring-Gardens, Esq', was temporarily absorbed, as I reported earlier when tracing the general career of *The Westminster Journal*. During its period of inclusion in *The Universal Chronicle*, Thomas Touchit's feature was headed with a sectional title which preserved *The Westminster Journal*'s separate identity. In the absence of any published reason for the merger, we are left to speculation. It can hardly be regarded as otherwise than probable that the vogue for Chronicles had something to do with it. As we have seen, the *Westminster* was a combination of the old Journal fashionable in 1713–30 and the Miscellany fashionable in the 1740's, when the *Westminster* first appeared. *The London Chronicle* so impressed the public with its liberal news and literary plan that a new situation now confronted the publishers, more particularly the publishers of weeklies. Its first weekly imitator, *The Universal Chronicle or Weekly Gazette* of Payne and thereafter of Faden, was followed by *The New Weekly Chronicle or Universal Journal* initiated by the bookseller, Owen, of Temple Bar, whose name was prefixed to the title from the fourth number. The original issue (April 8, 1758) which, in accordance with custom, announced that 'This first Paper is given gratis' indicated the intention of the conductors as being the 'furnishing private families and public houses throughout the whole Kingdom with a larger quantity of foreign and domestic intelligence interspersed with curious extracts from the best literary performances at a much cheaper rate than has been done'. There was, of course, no more originality in the programme than in the title of *The New Weekly Chronicle or Universal Journal*. The really important phrase in the long effusion from which partial quotation has been made, is that in which the new Chronicle was described as intended for circulation 'throughout the whole Kingdom'—a plan which could have had little success before the recent completion of the communication system with a network of cross-road posts; and none, if the provinces were supplied with either daily, alternate or weekly newspapers comparable with those of the metropolis. *Owen's Chronicle* appears, perhaps on account of superior circulation efforts, to have had more success than Payne's. At least, the transfer, in January 1767, of

'Thomas Touchit's' *Westminster Journal* from the columns of *The Universal* to *The Weekly Chronicle* is a curious incident. 'Thomas Touchit's' main feature, obviously suggested by 'The Idler', was entitled 'The Babler'. Physically, Owen's strongly resembled *The London Chronicle*. The letters 'Weekly Chronicle' of the title were in text. The one difference, a noteworthy one, was Owen's provision of a headpiece in the journal manner, but with an element of novelty. Between the packet at the left and the mounted postman at the right there was centred a view of St James's Street with the Palace in the background. The type of the heading was set below the headpiece, in accordance with the old weekly convention, not between the packet and the post—to which convention *The Westminster Journal* returned on resuming separate publication.

CHAPTER IX

THE MID-EIGHTEENTH-CENTURY PAPERS

1748–1770

The Gazetteer	1748
The St James's Chronicle & other Evening Posts	1761
The Public Ledger	1769
The Independent Chronicle	1769
The Middlesex Journal	1770

CHAPTER IX

THE MID-EIGHTEENTH-CENTURY PAPERS

1748–1770

ECONOMIC and political factors—e.g. the persistent growth of English commerce following the stabilisation of the new Guelph dynasty under George I and II, the recovery after the bursting of the South Sea Bubble, and the final extinction of Stuart ambitions in the '45—all combined to render the content, size and circulation of newspapers published at the end of the period 1730–60 notably superior to those of the preceding generation. They differed in scale, they also differed in ownership. Naturally, the four-page full-folio required the backing of greater capital than a single half-sheet. Also the emergence of advertising as a dominant economic factor expanded the financing of the papers favoured by the buying and selling public. Advertising announcements, mere incidental paragraphs in the Mercuries and Diurnalls of the seventeenth century, and but little more in the Courants and Post Boys of the early eighteenth century, became the staple element of the appropriately named 'Advertisers' which came into vogue in the generation after 1730, the year of the foundation of *The Daily Advertiser*. There is no evidence that advertising revenue was the prime—though it was assuredly calculated for—object of any paper founded before 1730. Everything points to the probability that for the first hundred years of their history, newspaper production appealed to printers who were already living on books and pamphlets and whose necessity then, as now, was to keep their plant regularly occupied. In those days the printer was the responsible head of the paper, whether he retained the services of a conductor or not; and whether he admitted anybody else to a share of the profits, the printer desired proprietary control, otherwise he might see the paper transferred to a rival office after he had invested in extra plant. Printer-control was also supported by statutes which made him personally responsible for any contravention of the licensing, libel or stamp laws. But the discovery of advertising was bound, sooner or later, to divide his control. In spite of the fact that correspondence is invariably addressed 'To the Printer' as late as 1790, his authority had, for a long time, been shrinking into the merely executive. It is difficult to point to the beginnings of the development by which newspapers came under the control of a score of proprietors. Many such proprietors were given a share on the understanding that they would accord their advertising support, a co-operative scheme responsible for the foundation of our oldest existing daily, *The Morning Post*, in 1772.

At the year 1760 the daily press was flourishing. The public could choose between three morning advertisers, and, in addition, a new paper, *The Public Ledger*, which we shall mention immediately. *The Gazetteer* affords an interesting example of development. It originated in 1735 as *The Daily Gazetteer or London Advertiser*.[1] In December 1748, according to a surviving copy[2] of the Articles of Agreement, the 'Property of the said Paper shall be divided into Twenty shares of which each subscribing Party shall only be entituled to one'. Article Five reads 'that any of the said subscribing and contracting Parties[3] who shall be concerned as a Proprietor in any other Daily Paper, are hereby agreed and declared to forfeit all their Right, Title and Interest in these Articles, or in the said Paper which they are intended to establish'. It was agreed sixthly 'that no Person...shall be entituled to interfere in the Conduct or Management of the said Paper unless first admitted with the consent of the majority of the remaining subscribers at a general quarterly meeting and the same entered in the Book of Orders and signed by the majority so consenting'. The ninth article requires that 'each Proprietor, at the time of signing these Presents, shall pay into the Hands of the Treasurer Ten guineas as a Fund, or Joint Stock towards carrying on and supporting the said Paper'. Exception was made in respect to 'several Persons, subscribing Parties hereto...concerned in another Daily Paper entituled the *Daily Gazetteer or London Advertiser* and which, for the better carrying on of the said *London Gazetteer*, they have agreed to lay down' and they were to be reimbursed such sums as they were out of purse in carrying on 'the said now declined Paper'. Mr Robert Wilson, stationer, was elected treasurer and Mr John Griffith, Green Arbour Court, Little Old Bailey, printer and publisher 'so long as a majority of the Parties subscribing and continuing shall think proper'.

[1] As we reported at page 126.

[2] B.M. MSS. Add. 38729 d 5 Dec. 1748. Unfortunately the copy reproduces only the ten articles of agreement and not the signatures.

[3] This rigorous exclusion seems to be singular. John Newbery, famous as a publisher of children's books, who died in 1767, mentions, in his will, an interest in: *The London Chronicle*, *Lloyd's Evening Post*, *The Public Ledger*, *Owen's Chronicle*, *The Westminster Journal*, and the *Sherborne and Yeovil Mercury*.

This is the first direct documentary evidence I have come across of the application of the joint stock principle to the establishment and control of a newspaper, including control over the printer. Thereafter cases are frequent in which the printer is appointed by the proprietors. The proprietors of the new thrice-a-week *London Packet* resolved on January 12, 1770, that 'Mr Thomas Spilsbury of Cooke's Court, Lincoln's Inn, should be the future Printer of the said Paper'.[1] A memorandum dated July 2, 1771, now in the British Museum,[2] reveals that a dispute occurred between the printer Charles Say and the proprietors of *The General Evening Post*. The memorandum proposes that 'The Partners shall reinstate him' (C. Say) 'as Printer in The General Evening Post, and not dismiss him without a Special meeting for that purpose and agreed to by two-thirds of the Partners'. Thus the newspapers came into the hands of groups of shareholders who appointed a printer and dismissed him on a majority vote. Spilsbury, of *The London Packet*, did not last long. That addition to thrice-a-week papers had five printers in three years. Edward Say printed *The General Evening Post* until his death in 1769, and his son's name is found on the imprint of copies of 1785. Charles Say was a partner in *The London Packet* in 1770, but, though a specialist in newspaper printing, was never a printer to that paper. *The London Gazetteer*, which arose, as we have seen, from the ashes of *The Daily Gazetteer*, became *The Gazetteer and London Daily Advertiser* in 1755. The very explicit imprint to the issue for January 1, 1756, reads as follows:

> Advertisements of all Sorts and Letters of Intelligence post paid are received by C. Say at his Printing Office in Newgate street; where Gentlemen, either in the Law, Physic, Merchants, Brokers, Shopkeepers etc. etc. may have anything in the Printing Business executed as elegant and reasonable as anywhere in England, he having a very great variety of curious New Types, all cut by Mr Caslon.

In the light of the articles of agreement respecting *The General Evening Post*, the text of this imprint must not be taken to mean that Charles Say was more than the printer authorised by his partners. The paper, at first a single sheet set in three 19-em columns, was re-arranged in four columns of 14 ems in 1762. In 1764 the paper's sub-title was changed from 'London' to 'New Daily Advertiser' and the perpendicular rules dividing the columns, with the horizontal rules indicating the date in the heading, were changed from single to double. The heading itself was set in 24-point Caslon upper- and lower-case: 'The Gazetteer' in roman and 'New Daily Advertiser' in italic. The

[1] B.M. MS. Addl. 38728. [2] MS. Addl. 38729.

text of the paper began with letters from pseudonymous correspondents addressed 'To the PRINTER' and consisting of three columns more or less. The first letter is introduced with a factotum initial made up from Caslon's flowers. This correspondence occupied the second, third and fourth columns, the first and a portion of the second column being reserved for advertisements. On a day that the space-seller would regard as 'good', advertisements covered the inside pair of pages. The fourth page was available for news.

In this wise, advertisements and letters occupied the first page, foreign, provincial and London news the fourth page, and advertisements the two centre pages. The placing of advertisements on the front page was characteristic of any Advertiser. It was never attempted before the foundation of *The Daily Advertiser* which, of course, had no alternative, consisting, as it did, entirely of advertising.

The Daily Advertiser seems to have concentrated upon purely commercial advertising, auctions, shipping, etc. *The Gazetteer* endeavoured to make itself welcome in the West End as well as in the City. As an instance, there appears at the head of column 1 of some issues in the early part of the year 1769, the following notice:

The Plays and Entertainments of the Theatres Royal of Drury-Lane and Covent-Garden: the Operas and the Oratorios: are advertised in this Paper
By Direction of the respective Managers.

The theatre advertising is henceforth a regular, and conspicuous, feature of the London newspapers. The conditions of its inclusion differed radically from those governing ordinary commercial advertising. Today, as everybody knows, the rates for space in the national dailies vary in accordance with the nature of the services or commodities advertised; that estate-agents and publishers, for example, pay less for their space than company promoters, issuing houses or motor-car dealers. So today, theatres pay less for preferential position. Who, or what, else could be accorded free advertising on the most important and jealously watched page in the entire present-day newspaper world, viz. the main news-page of *The Times*? Why indeed is the main news-page, facing the leader-page, in the centre of *The Times* known in Printing House Square as the 'Bill' page? The answer to these questions is to be found in the preferential treatment given to the theatres from the very beginning of their appearance in the advertising columns of the papers. First, certain newspapers contracted with the theatres for details of the casts in advance. Such newspapers paid the theatres for this exclusive and authoritative information. Hence, the notice reproduced above from *The Gazetteer* indicates that that paper had paid the managers of the theatres mentioned.[1] Secondly, other newspapers copied these authorised announcements. Hence the theatres were either paid for their advertisements, or at least were advertised gratis. Moreover, the theatrical announcements required special positions, or at least convenient positions, since they were often arranged at the last minute. A note in *The Gazetteer* of January 15, 1772 (col. 1, p. 2), reads as follows:

We should be glad to intimate to our advertising customers that the inner part of this paper is now regularly put to press at a very early time in the evening; by which alone we find ourselves enabled to supply the demand of the morning. By this new regulation it will often happen that the *London News* (which, with the Play bills, usually come late to hand) must necessarily appear on the *first* and *last* pages; which going latest to press will give us the opportunity of inserting many occurrences, that otherwise would be omitted.

For continuation of This Day's News see last Page.

When *The Daily Advertiser*, owing to a dearth of advertising, found it convenient to include news-paragraphs, such advertising as there was necessarily took precedence over the somewhat perfunctorily gathered items of general intelligence. In this way the public were gradually accustomed to papers which did not fear to place advertising on their front page. Hence *The Morning Post* and *The Times* (and the *Daily Mail* which closely followed *The Times*) appear to this very day with advertisements on the first page. *The Weekly Dispatch* and *The News of the World* have never done so, as these are, in theory and in origin, weekly budgets of matter giving a whole week's news intended to last for more than one day. Such weekly journals depended upon wide circulation, and wide circulation depended upon maximum reading matter excluding advertisements. Accordingly, such space as was sold was taken from the back, and never from the front, of the paper.

To return to the eighteenth century, the other papers comparable with *The Daily Advertiser*, i.e. *The Public Advertiser*, *The Gazetteer*, though

[1] 'The printers of the *Gazetteer* and *Public Advertiser*, besides paying 200 *l.* a season to the managers for having the play-bills in their papers, discharge the stamp-duty on the bills, and all the Green room puffs and paragraphs,' *The Monitor*, vol. 4, 1767, p. 4. *The Monitor*, voicing the grievances of the players against the managers, complained that no word of criticism of the managers was ever allowed in the *St James's*, *Public Advertiser*, or *Gazetteer*. Henry Woodfall of *The Public Advertiser* paid Playhouses £100, Drury Lane £64. 8*s.* 6*d.*, Covent Garden £66. 11*s.*, in one year. The description 'playbill' instead of 'programme' was used at least until the end of the eighteen-seventies. *The Play*, a chronicle of the London Stage, founded October 20, 1881, gives full casts at all the theatres under the heading 'Play Bills'.

following its example by printing advertisements on their front pages, made essays, correspondence, articles of intelligence and news-paragraphs a prime inducement to the reader. *The Daily Advertiser* never became a first-class newspaper, and a notice in *The Gazetteer* seems so justly descriptive of the respective aims of the two papers that quotation is desirable. There appeared an italic paragraph immediately below the heading 'London' on the back page of *The Gazetteer* for Monday, January 2, 1769:

A printed paper having been industriously circulated by some of the venders of the newspapers complaining of the hardships of not being supplied with The Gazetteer, at so early an hour as with the Daily Advertiser; We beg leave by way of apology, to remind the friends of this paper, that the Daily Advertiser, from the uniformity of its contents, being enabled to keep its stated hour of going to press in the evening, is, in consequence, published with great regularity, very early in the morning. Whilst the Gazetteer, being open to political and other discussions, which so frequently come to hand at night, and being also connected with the Theatres, the Police, and other Public offices, has not, it must be confessed, the advantage of the favourable circumstances above mentioned; to say nothing of its superiority in point of number, which is very considerably encreased this winter, and must therefore proportionably encrease the number of hours in which it is working off. Gratefully sensible, however, that nothing can insure a continuance of this success but a readiness to oblige, it shall be our study to accommodate both the purchasers and the venders to the utmost of our power.

The typography and make-up of *The Public Advertiser* and of *The Gazetteer* were virtually identical in 1769, the year in which the former carried the most famous of the letters of Junius. *The Gazetteer* had more advertisements than *The Public Advertiser* and fewer than *The Daily Advertiser*.

The layout of the Evening Posts of the period (1760–1770) followed what may now be termed the 'old' traditions of English journalism, i.e. the customs of the first quarter of the eighteenth century. The order of printing gave first place to 'Foreign Affairs', or, in the absence of any new mails, an abstract of *The London Gazette*, or that failing, particulars of 'Ship News'; and 'Country News' followed immediately, preceding 'London Intelligence'. The position of 'Correspondence' was variable. In many papers the layout always provided the front page with some 'Letters to the Printer', or 'Letters to the Author'; while others grouped these in the centre of the sheet. Light verses were grouped at the upper extreme left of the back page under some such title as 'The Poet's Corner'. Finally, the 'Postscript' of a column (or a column and a half or so), being late news, completed the back page.

The factotum and the title device were persistent features of front pages of the Evening Posts. *The General*, though using a severely plain title throughout its big career, carried a fine factotum of a sailing packet and a horsed postman until the close of the eighteenth century; the *Whitehall* began with a britannia (see Fig. 65), later adopted a packet and flying post, and to them added a woodcut of Whitehall with St James's Palace in the background as a title-device—which, though changing its form very considerably, never vanished even when the *Post* was amalgamated in the nineteenth century

THE WHITEHALL EVENING-POST.

PRICE TWO-PENCE HALFPENNY.] From TUESDAY, October 16, to THURSDAY, October 18, 1770. [N°. 3802.

To the Printer of the Whitehall-Evening-Post.

SIR,

THOUGH I am not one of the faculty, nor have any peculiar friend that is, yet having a numerous acquaintance belonging to the Royal Navy, and seeing *lately* orders from the Navy-office, for the surgeons, and surgeons mates, to repair forthwith, or the former will be struck off the list; I could not help taking notice of it, and reflecting on the great hardships and grievances those gentlemen have long laboured under: And as I have the good of the nation only at heart, and no interested views, or private ends to answer, I now beg leave, through the channel of your useful paper, to communicate my thoughts to the public, if you think them worthy of a place. As on the health of our fleets and armies all our victories both by sea and land entirely depend, and to the care of those medical gentlemen, the lives of our brave fellows when sick, or wounded, are wholly entrusted; we cannot be too circumspect in the choice of skilful surgeons, whose judgment and expe-

would have the surgeons (as well as the Lieutenants) warrants now be called commissions (though, in fact, none is a commission, but under the King's sign Manual) be issued from the Admiralty also, and in future, share prize-money with the Lieutenant. But the surgeons mates should still be warranted from the Navy-office, only instead of sharing prize-money with the petty officers, they should now share with the warrant officers, as the masters mates do.

These regulations would be a great encouragement, as it would render the medical gentlemen of still greater consequence in their department; more respected on board his Majesty's ships, than they are in general at present; and what is more than all, the great advantages they would gain (if their ship or ships were fortunate) in sharing much more prize money than the share at present established for them.

In peace, let every surgeon that is hereafter paid off at the conclusion of a war, be allowed two shillings a day, while unemployed; and a provision be made for their widows, in case of death; then the government could compel them to go, whenever the

discharged to seek their bread; when perhaps, the best of their days are gone, their constitution shattered, and their pristine health and vigour (the greatest comfort in this life,) become totally irrecoverable.

All these things considered, I now most heartily wish, for the honour of his Majesty, the good of his service, and consequently that of the nation in general; that some effectual method may speedily be taken, amply to reward, and induce, those medical gentlemen (who are of far greater importance than is commonly imagined) again to serve their King and country, otherwise, our fleets and armies will become useless; and should it be a war, (which seems to be unavoidable) we shall unhappily find neither surgeons nor surgeons mates sufficient for the ships, unless the same arbitrary and inhuman method is used to procure them, as is most cruelly imposed on the public to get common seamen.

Rangbiarr and Browmuilly.

WEDNESDAY, Oct. 10.

FOREIGN AFFAIRS.

Constantinople, Sept. 3. The Russians have taken the isle of Lemnos, in which there is

The report of the Court of Spain having declared war publicly in the city of Madrid against the Crown of Great Britain, is wholly groundless.

The account of the Spaniards having a design on the island of Jamaica must be a mistake; that island is able to muster at least fifteen thousand white people, who have been regularly trained to arms, and have, for many years, been mustered and exercised once a month: they have at present two regiments of regular troops from Britain, and they can arm from fifty to a hundred thousand negroes, if there should be occasion. The whole inhabitants of Jamaica are reckoned fifty thousand whites, and a hundred and fifty thousand negroes; it is not therefore likely that the Spaniards can raise a force in the West-Indies or America, even with the assistance of troops from Old Spain, that could make a conquest of this important island.

The report of an intended augmentation of the army is entirely groundless.

His Majesty has promoted Lord John Murray to the rank of General of his forces.

The Lords of the Admiralty have appointed Lieuts. William Osborne and James Williams Lieutenants of his Majesty's ship

Fig. 70

with *The London Chronicle*. The early *London Evening Post* employed a factotum of the Arms of the City of London; but when, later, it admitted advertisements in the first columns of its front page, and was consequently forced to abandon its use, an elongated title-block of the Arms of the City was placed between the words 'The London' and 'Evening Post'—and so continued until late in the century. Thus the *St James's* was in the tradition when it adopted a title-device. But a novelty in the heading of *The St James's Chronicle* is the inclusion of the legend 'Price Two-pence Half-penny' at the left of the date which, with the serial number on the right, is enclosed between two single rules. Hitherto, the particulars of the price of the paper had, as a rule, been placed at the bottom of the centre column of the older

Posts. This, obviously, became a difficulty when the make-up was altered from three to four columns—in the latter case there was no centre column. Also, in a large number of instances, the price was never printed upon the paper at all, in the heading, at the foot of the centre column, or even on the back page. But after *The St James's Chronicle* it became the rule to place particulars of the price at the extreme left of the date line.

The *St James's* made no change in the relative position of the 'London Intelligence'. It is a point to be noted, as upon it depends our understanding of the later make-up practice of the London journals, for inasmuch as it seems to be evident that, whatever the position of the 'London Intelligence', it was the vital point of the paper—the point to which readers' attention was inevitably given. It followed that when the conductor of *The St James's Chronicle* desired to give his readers notice of any change in the conditions of subscription, notice of the advantages of advertising, warning against the malpractices of competitors, or advice in dealing with delinquent news-agents, he set the respective italic lines immediately between the heading 'London' and the first line of 'London News'.

The St James's Chronicle possesses one other detail of interest to us, namely, the triple-line cut-offs used between the important sections of the paper, i.e. between 'Correspondence' and 'Advertising'; between 'The Poet's Corner' and the 'Correspondence'; between the 'Correspondence' and the 'Postscripts'. This triple rule (≡≡≡≡≡), in which the centre strip is twice the thickness of the two outside strips, is a feature of English evening newspaper make-up which soon found a place in all the important dailies of the next decade, e.g. *The Morning Chronicle*, *The Morning Post* and *The Morning Herald*. It is a type of rule unknown before 1750, and the first indication I have met of the influence of an evening paper's technique upon that of a 'morning'. *The St James's Chronicle* is, for all practical purposes, the model for the early numbers of *The Morning Chronicle*. The style, indeed, of all newspapers—whether daily, or thrice-weekly, or, in a few years, even the Sunday journals—becomes, in the period from 1770 to 1785, so standardised as to display only such minor differentiae as the type display, size and the design of the heading, and points of typographical usage as the use of italic in text and in advertising, the employment of leading between the paragraphs, and the insertion of rules across the columns. In these details, the influence of the *St James's* was considerable, primarily, no doubt, owing to its having started at full folio. It can usefully be contrasted with a new morning paper, *The Public Ledger*.

The Public Ledger is the first daily newspaper which set out with a large solid blackletter heading printed from a block. The immediate precedent is, of course, *The London Chronicle*, founded three years previously. The resemblance is curious: both are roughly cut on wood from originals neither of which reflects any credit upon the clerk who wrote the model. It is the sort of writing which figured in the openings of accounts in City offices, and hence was considered appropriate. *The Public Ledger* (the first issue of which states: 'This issue is given GRATIS, and the future Numbers will be Sold at Two-Pence Half Penny each') had in view, as its sub-title 'The Daily Register of Commerce and Intelligence' indicates, a commercial audience. It was designed to promote the interests of those buyers and sellers of all sorts of articles who were inscribed in the membership of an institution entitled

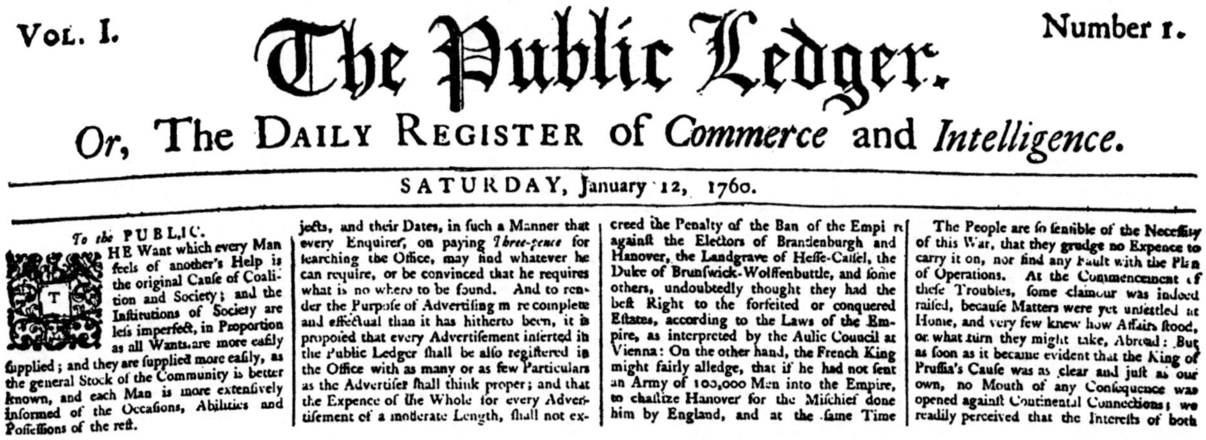

VOL. I. The Public Ledger. Number 1.

Or, The DAILY REGISTER of *Commerce* and *Intelligence*.

SATURDAY, January 12, 1760.

To the PUBLIC.

THE Want which every Man feels of another's Help is the original Cause of Coalition and Society; and the Institutions of Society are less imperfect, in Proportion as all Wants are more easily supplied; and they are supplied more easily, as the general Stock of the Community is better known, and each Man is more extensively informed of the Occasions, Abilities and Possessions of the rest.

jects, and their Dates, in such a Manner that every Enquirer, on paying *Three-pence* for searching the Office, may find whatever he can require, or be convinced that he requires what is no where to be found. And to render the Purpose of Advertising more complete and effectual than it has hitherto been, it is proposed that every Advertisement inserted in the Public Ledger shall be also registered in the Office with as many or as few Particulars as the Advertiser shall think proper; and that the Expence of the Whole for every Advertisement of a moderate Length, shall not ex-

creed the Penalty of the Ban of the Empire against the Electors of Brandenburgh and Hanover, the Landgrave of Hesse-Cassel, the Duke of Brunswick-Wolffenbuttle, and some others, undoubtedly thought they had the best Right to the forfeited or conquered Estates, according to the Laws of the Empire, as interpreted by the Aulic Council at Vienna: On the other hand, the French King might fairly alledge, that if he had not sent an Army of 100,000 Men into the Empire, to chastize Hanover for the Mischief done him by England, and at the same Time

The People are so sensible of the Necessity of this War, that they grudge no Expence to carry it on, nor find any Fault with the Plan of Operations. At the Commencement of these Troubles, some clamour was indeed raised, because Matters were yet unsettled at Home, and very few knew how Affairs stood, or what turn they might take, Abroad: But as soon as it became evident that the King of Prussia's Cause was as clear and just as our own, no Mouth of any Consequence was opened against Continental Connections; we readily perceived that the Interests of both

Fig. 71

'Public Register' in St Paul's Church Yard. The scheme was proposed, or at least sponsored, by Francis Newbery, and provided that 'every Advertisement inserted in the Public Ledger shall also be registered in the office...so that by advertising in this paper he that desires to conceal any part of his proposal from the public eye may insert a short hint in the paper'. In spite of its primary concern with commerce, a portion of *The Ledger* was set aside for 'public occurrences, both Foreign and Domestick, in which if we do not excel any other daily paper, we shall take care not to fall short of any'. The news was placed on the front page in the early years of the paper but was later ousted by advertising, the theatres being given the preferential position at the top of the first column.

The *St James's*, on the other hand, like the other evening journals, made it a point to keep the front page clear of advertising. They all retained a specific factotum (i.e. an individual block, not a substitute made up from

The *St. James's* CHRONICLE,

OR, *BRITISH* EVENING-POST

Price TWO-PENCE HALF-PENNY.] From TUESDAY, SEPTEMBER 17, to THURSDAY SEPTEMBER 19, 1771. No. 1649.

WEDNESDAY, Sept. 18.

FOREIGN AFFAIRS.

Warsaw, August 31.

FROM Wilkoursk in Lithuania we have received an Account, that the Confederates had taken Lieut. Gen. Grabowski from his Country Seat there; but fearing they should not be able to overcome the Russian Detachment which was sent after them, they gave Gen. Grabowski two dangerous Cuts in the Head, and left him in that State. We are not yet certain whether the said General can recover. his advanced Age makes us rather in fear of his Life.

SHIP NEWS.

Deal, Sept. 16. Wind S. by W. Came down and remain with the Ships as per last, the Prosper, Hall, for Bristol. Arrived and sailed for the River, the George, Trenham, from Jamaica; and Crook, Duffield, from St. Vincent's.

Arrived.

At Ayr, Hero, Johnson, from Antigua.
At Jamaica, Maredith, Peacock, from London.
At Maryland, Hope, Hooper, from London.
At Leith, Minerva, Alexander, from South Carolina.
At Dover, Nancy Graham, Lynch, from Maryland; and, Kitty, Wood, from St. Kitt's.
At Dover, Alexander, Reed, from the Grenades.
At Virginia, Hansford, Wilson, from the West Indies.
At Jersey, Triton, Collas, from Honduras.
At Philadelphia, Globe, Gartiques, from Cork.

LONDON.

St. James's, Sept. 17. His Majesty has been pleased to grant unto Lewis Bagot, M. A. the Canonry or Prebend in the Cathedral of Christ Church, in the University of Oxford, void by the Resignation of Dr. John Moore.

Lord Chatham speaking of the Struggle likely to be in the City for the Office of Lord Mayor, declared, that Mr. Wilkes acted very imprudently to make his Designs so public: "He is so eager (said this great Man) to engross all the Employments to his own Circle, that his true Motives cannot remain long concealed; and the Moment the Livery discover that he is only labouring to make himself their Master, they will see their Independency as much in Danger from him, as it is from an abandoned Administration."

The new Excise Office in Broad-Street, is to be opened on Tuesday the 24th inst. for the Transacting of Business there.

[illegible]cart Taylor, Esq. is appointed Captain-Lieutenant in the 2d Regiment of Dragoon Guards.

Francis Hugonin, Gent. is appointed Lieutenant in the 4th Regiment of Dragoons.

Lieut. Geo. Petrie, Gent. is appointed Adjutant to the 31st Regiment of Foot.

The General Howard, Huntrio, from North-Carolina to Bristol, sprang a Leak lately, was obliged to put back, and is condemned.

A Letter from India mentions the Death of Capt. Cooke, of the Earl of Elgin East-Indiaman.

We hear that Mademoiselle Clairon, the celebrated French Actress, is just put into Prison, on Account of some disrespectful Words she let drop against the Government. This Lady has been addicted to a Slightness for some Time, very near bordering on Insanity.

The Rev. Mr. Johnson was a few Days since presented to the Vicarage of Playstone, in the County of Wilts and Diocese of Salisbury, void by the Cession of the late Incumbent.

On Monday Night as Robert Bentham, Esq. of St. James's Street, was returning to Town from Kensington, he was attacked in Hyde Park by two Footpads, who robbed him of his Watch, a Diamond Ring, and about 4l.

Yesterday Edward Burch and Matthew Martin were tried at the Old Bailey, on an Indictment for feloniously publishing, as true, a certain Hand-Writing purporting to be the last Will and Testament of Sir Andrew Chadwick, knowing the same to be forged with Intent to defraud the Heirs at Law of the said Sir Andrew, when they were both found guilty.—The Trial lasted from about half an Hour past Nine in the Morning, till near Twelve at Night, after which the Jury were out about half an Hour.

The Business of the Court was stopt some Time on Account of the Will, produced in Evidence against them, being mislaid; it was handed about to different Persons in Court, and by some Accident dropped on the Ground.

The forged Will bore Date in 1764, and a wholesale Paper-Maker, who was very instrumental in convicting the above Men, swore by the Stamp, or Mark, that was upon the Paper, that he made the said Paper in 1768, four Years after the Will was dated, which Circumstance had great Weight with the Court.

Sir Andrew Chadwick's Estate was about 7000l. per Ann. and 14,000l. in the Stocks, which is now possessed (except the Cash) by James Taylor, Esq. of Carter-Place, in Lancashire, who married Miss Lowes, second Cousin to Sir Andrew.

The Cross Roads in Scotland, it is said, are to be farmed out in the Manner those of England were some Years ago by the late Ralph Allen, Esq.

At Monmouth Races on Tuesday the 50l. Weight for Age, was won by Sir Richard Phillipps's Horse, Le Brun, beating the Duke of Beaufort's Old Lad. Mr. Ward's Careless broke down on Sunday in his Exercise.

Wednesday the Give-and-Take Plate was won by Dr. Kinneir's Twinger, at three Heats, beating Mr. Dutton's Windrush, which won the first Heat, and Sir Richard Phillipps's Macaroni. There was good Sport this Day. The first Heat was hard run between Windrush and Macaroni, and Twinger just saved his Distance. The Odds were now greatly on the Side of Windrush: but the next heat Twinger went off at Score and maintained it throughout, beating Windrush by two Lengths. The third Heat Macaroni was drawn, and Twinger won it hollow.

On Thursday there was no Race for want of Horses.

DERBY RACES.

Tuesday the 3d inst. the Purse of 50l. was run for by five Horses, &c. and won by Mr. Malkin's bay Colt, Rowland.

Wednesday the 4th three started for the Purse of 50l. which was won by Mr. Morgan's grey Mare, Damsel.

Married.] Yesterday Mr. Lisle, Apothecary, in Newgate-Street, to Mrs. Beauchamp, of South Ockingdon, in Essex.—Yesterday James Maxwell, Esq. of David-Street, Grosvenor-Square, to Miss Elizabeth Playdell of Marlborough-Street.

Died.] A few Days ago John Harvey, Esq. at his Seat at Ickwelburg, in Bedfordshire.—Monday at his House at Bow, Capt. James Harvey, formerly in the Virginia Trade.—A few Days ago at Dunkirk, Mr. Wilson, Grocer, in Carey-Street.—Saturday at Reading, in Berkshire, Mrs. Harrison, Mother of Mr. Thomas Harrison, Printer of the London Gazette.—Thursday last Mr. Gilbert Hearne, a great Antiquarian, of the City of Hereford.—Monday at his House at Kensington Gore, aged 92, the Rev. Mr. Fleming, a nonjuring Clergyman.—Monday at his Country House at Hillingdon, near Uxbridge, ——— Bell, Esq.

For The St. James's Chronicle.

Extracts from celebrated Authors, concerning imposed Subscriptions to human Explications of the Scripture.

[*Continued from No.* 1633.]

THERE is nothing more ridiculous than for a Man, or Company of Men, to assume the Title of Orthodoxy to their own Set of Opinions, as if Infallibility were annexed to their Systems, and those were to be the standing Measures of Truth to all the World; from whence they erect to themselves a Power to censure and condemn others for differing at all from the Tenets they have pitched upon. The Consideration of human Frailty ought to check this Vanity; but since it does not, but that with a Sort of Allowance it shows itself almost in all religious Societies, the playing the Trick round sufficiently turns it into Ridicule: For each Society having an equal Right to a good Opinion of themselves, a Man, by passing but a River or a Hill, loses that Orthodoxy in one Company, which puffed him up with such Assurance and Insolence in another, and is there, with equal Justice, himself exposed to the like Censure of Error and Heresy, which he was so forward to lay on others at home. When it shall appear, that Infallibility is intailed upon any one Set of Men of any Denomination, or that Truth is confined to any Spot of Ground, the Name and Use of Orthodoxy, as it now is in Fashion every where, will in that one Place be reasonable. Till then, this ridiculous Cant will be a Foundation too weak to sustain that Usurpation raised upon it.—*Locke's second Vind. of the Reas. of Christianity.*

Christianity is a Religion suited to vulgar Capacities, and the State of Mankind in this World, destined to Labour and Travail. The Writers and Wranglers in Religion fill it with Niceties, and dress it up with Notions, which they make necessary and fundamental Parts of it; as if there were no Way into the Church but through the Academy, or Lyceum.—*Locke, on the Reas. of Christianity.*

If you consider their (the Papists) ecclesiastical State and System in general, as a Body Politic, and as a spiritual Power, it is certainly calculated to keep the Commonalty in Ignorance, and in an implicit Faith, and a blind Submission to human Authority; and, under the plausible Pretence of Unity and external Peace, to discourage Liberty of Conscience, and free and rational Examination. But, to say the Truth, there has been too much of the determining and domineering Spirit in most Christian Societies of every Denomination. I wish I could except one!—*Jortin's Serm. V. 1. P.* 13.

Men will compel others, not to think with them, for that is impossible, but to say they do, upon which they obtain full Leave not to think or reason at all; and this is called Unity, which is somewhat like the Behaviour of the Romans, as it is described by a brave Countryman of our's in Tacitus—*ubi solitudinem faciunt, pacem appellant.*—*Jortin's Remarks on Eccl. Hist Pref.*

Scripture, say the Protestants, is the only Rule of Faith; and they say well. There is no other Christianity than this; no other Test of Doctrines than this; no other Centre of Union than this. Whatsoever is not clearly delivered there, may be true, but cannot be important. *Hæc mea est sententia, neque me ex ea ulius unquam aut docti aut indocti movebit oratio.*—*Jortin's Remarks on Eccl. Hist.*

To the Printer of the S. J. CHRONICLE.

SIR

HAVING read, in your last Saturday's Paper, an Extract from a Pamphlet entitled, "Advice from a Bishop," in a Series of Letters to a young Clergyman," it brings fresh to my Remembrance a remarkable Circumstance of a real and well known Matter of Fact, which is as follows. In the Month of September, many Years ago, upon Occasion of a publick Ordination in a certain Diocese, there came many Candidates for Holy Orders from both our Universities, who acquitted themselves exceedingly well in the several Parts of their Examination, to the Approbation of the Bishop and other neighbouring Divines then present; indeed one young Student from Cambridge, much celebrated for his shining Talents, which, however, it seems he exercised more for the Theatre than the Pulpit, was found altogether deficient, to the great Astonishment of all, as will appear to your Readers. The first Question asked him was; how do you prove the Existence of God? He was instantly struck as with a Convulsion, continuing in profound Silence, rolling his Eyes upward and downward by turns for some Time, then toward the Window on his Right Hand, and lastly to the Door on his Left, as if he wanted to make his Escape, still without uttering a Syllable. The Arch-Deacon then hinted to him, that surely the Objects he had seen, and the Sense of his own Existence, might have furnished him with a full and proper Answer. Soon after a second Question was proposed, viz. How many Natures has our Lord and Saviour? but he remained stupid and dumb as before. After some considerable Pause the third Question was; What meanest thou by the Word Sacrament? To which no Answer being made, the Arch-Deacon remitted him to his College with peremptory Orders to learn his Catechism before he pursued any other Studies, especially Theological. Here the Bishop interposed, and desired the young Gentleman to follow him into another Room; but the Arch-Deacon prevented, assuring his Lordship, that he neither would, nor conscientiously could recommend him as fit for Ordination. Upon this the Candidate retired, hastened to the Inn, mounted his Horse, and rode Post to his Alma-Mater, for a restorative Draught to raise his Spirits, &c. &c. &c.

Now, Sir, if you choose, and think it will be agreeable or edifying to any of your Readers, intended for the sacred Function, I will willingly, through the Channel of your Paper, communicate the Advice, Directions, and Injunctions, both of a late Arch-Bishop and Metropolitan also to their Candidates for Holy Orders, how to prepare themselves duely for Examination.

Your's, &c.

VERAX.

ON Monday, October the 7th, G. FORDYCE, M. D. Physician to St. Thomas's Hospital, will begin his Lectures, viz.

On the Practice of Physick and Materia Medica, at Eight in the Morning.

On Chemistry, at Nine, at his House in Henrietta Street, Covent Garden, where Proposals may be had.

IN Soho Square, the Corner of Charles Street, is to be Sold by public Auction, or private Contract, on or before the 5th Day of October next,

All the fashionable, genuine, rich, and elegant FURNITURE of a House situate as above, the Property of a Gentleman gone abread, consisting of blue and crimson Silk Damasks, Chintz, Moreens, &c. &c. together with all the Fixtures, &c. The Whole remaining as when occupied, quite complete for the immediate Use of a Family, for whose Reception the House, with a Coach House, and Stabling for six Horses, with Room to make an Enlargement thereto adjoining, may be taken on Lease. And as the late Possessor spared no Pains to render the Premisses thoroughly commodious, and finished in the present Taste, makes it beyond a Doubt that the same, with the Furniture, will be singularly advantageous to any Family of Fashion, desirous of being directly settled without any Trouble.

For further Particulars, enquire for S. S. at the Bar of the Antigallican Coffee House, behind the Royal Exchange; or of Mr. Noble, Appraiser, in Long Acre.

TO be Sold by Auction, by Mr. Pond, at Newmarket, on Thursday October the 3d, which is in the next Newmarket Meeting,

The entire Stud of Brood Mares, Colts, and Fillies, which did belong to Richard Croftes, Esq. deceased

To be viewed till Thursday, September the 26th, at West Harling, in the County of Norfolk, and on Monday, the 30th, at Newmarket, till the Sale, which will be about two Hours before the Races begin.

☞ West Harding is twenty five Miles from Newmarket, and six from Thetford.

Catalogues to be had of Mr Pond, in Bridges Street, near Russel Court Covent Garden.

TO be Sold by Auction by Mr. POND, on Friday the 4th, and Saturday the 5th of October, Several valuable Brood Mares, Colts, and Fillies; Goldfinder (who to all Appearance is now perfectly sound) Petruchio, Khalen, Maga Arabian, and six Grey new Hampshire Forresters, which did belong to JENNISON SHAFTO, Esq. deceased. To be viewed at Wratting Park, eight measured Miles from Bourne Bridge, and nine from Newmarket, and at Newmarket on the Day of Sale, which will begin about two Hours before the Races.

Catalogues to be had at Mr. Pond's, in Bridges Street, near Russel Court, Covent Garden.

Navy Office, Sept. 16, 1771.

THE principal Officers and Commissioners of his Majesty's Navy give Notice, that on Tuesday the 24th Inst. at Noon, they will be ready to treat with such Persons as are willing to supply his Majesty's several Yards with dryed Bullocks Hydes with the Hair on, on a standing Contract.

TO be Lett, from Michaelmas next, for one, two, or three Years, furnished with all useful necessary Furniture,

A very commodious DWELLING HOUSE, with every Convenience, fit to receive a large Family. Good Stabling for twenty Horses, and a large Coach House; walled and other Gardens, on an excellent Soil, and a very pleasant Shrubbery and Terras Walk, with about thirty Acres of fine Pasture Ground, and Orchard. It is situate in the Western Part of the County of Somerset; about one Mile from a good Market and Post Town, and the same Distance from the great Turnpike Road, leading from Exeter to Bath and Bristol.

For further Particulars, enquire of Mr. Prockter Thomas, Attorney at Law, in Wellington, Somerset; Messrs. Popham and Santer, at New Inn, London; or Mr. Blake, Apothecary, on the South Parade, Bath.

TO be Lett for a short Term, to enter upon immediately,

A Capital MANSION-HOUSE, ready furnished, situate in the West Riding of Yorkshire, within six Miles of the Town of Leeds: There are six Rooms on a Floor with Closets; the Offices are large and commodious, consisting of a Brew-house, Laundry, and a Coach-house, Dove Cote, Barn, Stabling for upwards of twenty Horses, and many other Conveniencies. The Garden, in which there are Stoves and Hot Walls, is well planted and very fruitful, and Part of it is laid out in Pleasure Ground. There is a large Paddock before the House with Deer in it, which will be either let with the House or not, as agreeable to the Tenant, and any other Quantity of Land not exceeding thirty Acres. The Manor is well stocked with Game, which the Tenant will have Leave to kill.

Further Particulars may be had by applying to Mr. Dyneley, at his Chambers in Gray's Inn, or of Mr Shipley, Attorney, in Leeds

---

TO be Sold, on Friday the 11th of October next, at Twelve o'Clock at Noon, at Lloyd's Coffee House, in Lombard-street,

Several Freehold and Leasehold Messuages or Dwelling Houses, well situated near and adjoining to the General Post Office in Lombard Street, and now in the Occupation of Messrs. Bloxam, Griffith, Hanbury, and Co. Moffatt, Lawrence, and Knight, at several yearly Rents, amounting in the whole to 459l. 10s. per Annum. A very small Part of the Premisses is Leasehold, and the Remainder is Freehold, and the same will be sold in five distinct Lots.

For further Particulars apply to Mr. Reade, No. 6 in Copthall Court, London; or to Mr. Kinder, etc. in Ipswich.

TO be Sold by Auction, on Tuesday the 8th Day of October, between the Hours of Four and Seven in the Afternoon, at the White Hart Inn at Thrapston in the County of Northampton, subject to such Conditions of Sale as shall be then and there produced.

A FREEHOLD ESATE, situate in the Parish of Brighton, within five Miles of Kimbolten, six of Thrapston, and about seven of Oundle, consisting of a good Farm-House, Barn, Stables [illegible] with 48 A. 3 R. 35 P. of inclosed Pasture and Meadow Land; 19 A. 2 R. 7 P. of common Field Pasture, 4 A. 1 R. 35 P. of inclosed Arable Land and 144 A. 4 P. of common Field Arable Land. The above Farm is now in the Occupation of the Widow Maynard. The Estate is well wooded and watered, the common Fields lie very contiguous to the Town, and the Premisses are in good Repair.

For further Particulars enquire of Mr Thomas Botcher, at Copie, near Bedford; or the Widow Maynard, who will shew the Premisses.

Land to be Sold by Auction.

TO be Sold by Auction, on Tuesday the 1st of October, 1771, at Three o'Clock in the Afternoon, at the Swan, in Atherstone, Warwickshire, if not sold before by private Sale,

A FREEHOLD ESTATE, lying in the Parish of Witherly, in Leicestershire, within about three Quarters of a Mile of Atherstone, in Warwickshire, now in the Tenure of Thomas Slack, at the annual Rent of 80l. The Premisses consist of about 63 Acres and an Half of good Pasture and Meadow Land, well watered, have a good Fold Yard, a large Barn, and three Brick Stables, and a Brick Kiln thereon erected.

Also a Quantity of Clay Dug for making Brick and Tyle: At the same Time and Place will be sold two Houses, and Land, in Atherstone, with their Rights of Common, now in Tenure of Joseph Smith and Charles Beal.

For further Particulars, enquire of Mr. William Ebotral, Attorney, at Law; or of Mr. John Willday, both of Atherstone

---

To the Nobility and Gentry travelling the Kent Road from London to Dover.

THOMAS TEMPLEMAN, at the Red Lion and Post Office, at Sittingbourn, takes this Method to acquaint the Publick, that he has provided the best Four-wheeled Post Chaises, with able Horses, which he intends to run at Nine-pence per Mile: And as he will be ever studious to merit the Encouragement of those who please to favour him with their Company, he keeps a professed Cook, has the genteelest Attendance, and best Accommodations. And as he has been well assured, that the Inn Keepers of Rochester and Canterbury have endeavoured to injure him, by preventing Company coming to his House, he hopes their Malevolence and Ill Nature will prove ineffectual, as he has no other Wish, but by a strict Attention to his Business, to prove himself the Publick's most grateful,

And obliged humble Servant,

T. TEMPLEMAN.

Canal Navigation from Chesterfield to the River Trent, Sept. 5, 1771.

IN pursuance of an Order made at the General Assembly of the Company of Proprietors of the said Navigation, held at Retford this Day, all and every the said Proprietors are required to pay into the Hands of Mr George Pipewell, in Retford; Mr. Allwood Wilkinson, in Chesterfield, the Treasurers to the said Company; or to Messrs. Smith, Wright, and Gray, Bankers, Lombard Street London, on the 25th Day of December next, such Sum of Money as together with what already paid by each Proprietor, will make the Sum of Ten Pounds for each, and every Share, which the said Proprietors are respectively possessed of, or entitled to in the said Navigation.

☞ A Penalty of Five Pounds per Share is, by the Act inflicted upon every Person who shall neglect to pay his Calls, on or before the Day appointed for Payment of the same.

ANTH. LAX,

Clerk to the said Company.

Fig. 72

flowers in *The Gazetteer*'s style or a barock fixture in the style of *The Public Ledger*) of, e.g., a britannia for the initial paragraph of their first column. Any advertisements which these evening journals admitted on the front page were of an official or personal nature and they were placed in the fourth column. Only after 1790 did such papers fall into line with the dailies and fill their front page with advertising, and thus use it as a sort of 'cover'. Notwithstanding, theatrical advertising never appears in the evening papers—I suggest because their circulation was in the main a country one and the evening papers could only arrive, in many parts of the country, first thing the following morning.

The St James's Chronicle at no time surrendered its first column to the advertiser, although nearly a third of its space was sold. The printer, Henry Baldwin,[1] 'at the Britannia Printing office, White-Friars, Fleet street'—probably a relative of Richard Baldwin of *The Post Man*—was Strahan's predecessor as printer of *The London Packet.* A factotum of a britannia seated in her chariot graces the top of the first column for more than half a century, without interruption, after August 6, 1751.[2] Nor was there any serious change in the heading. The cipher GR monogram, crowned, varied first in scale and later in design—a sword, sceptre and other trophies were added by Charles Baldwin at the beginning of the nineteenth century, and the subtitle 'British' was changed to 'London Evening Post', and again to 'The General Evening Post'. The britannia remained, just as the name of the office remained when it was removed to New Bridge Street. We shall in due time return to the later issues of the *St James's.* For the present, it must be enough to take it as an evening newspaper which—unlike its competitors, the *Whitehall*, or the *General*, for instance—began at full scale. Whereas the *Whitehall* began as a four-page quarto in two columns, the *St James's* began as a four-page folio in four columns[3].

In 1769 there appeared the first issue of a thrice-weekly evening journal

[1] 'The Genius', a weekly series of Idlerish papers 'duly entered at Stationers' Hall of which this Notice is given that no Person presume to reprint or abridge the same, as they will thereby subject themselves to a Prosecution' began in No. 39, 'but genius' good Friend, Mr H. Baldwin... fairly tells me to my Face that though *the* GENIUS were to stand in the Front of his Paper three times a week the public Attention would flag without great Incidents and alarming paragraphs' (No. 53, July 14, 1761).

[2] Britannia was enclosed first upon a square and later (1771) upon an oblong ground.

[3] *The London Evening Post* was already in four columns, but *The Whitehall Evening Post* and *The General Evening Post* remained in three for several years. Of the morning papers, *The Daily Advertiser* was in three columns and remained so. *The Public Advertiser* was four columns and *The Gazetteer* four.

entitled *The Independent Chronicle; or Freeholder's Evening Post* (with britannia device centred in the heading), initiated by one William Bingley, who should be commemorated in the *D.N.B.* Bingley was a Radical, suffered much for the cause, and died unappreciated even by his own side after adventuring his all in the newspaper trade. Bingley's imprisonment was hardly compatible with running a newspaper. With the ninth issue, the paper passed into the hands of Messrs Robinson and Roberts, 25 Paternoster Row, who, having removed the britannia device, and the sub-title, ran it for the remaining six or seven months of its existence. *Bingley's Journal; or the Universal Gazette* was a 'weekly political and commercial paper' (*sic*) issued from Saturday, June 9, 1770, by W. B. now 'utterly incapable of adhering to the plan I had laid down for the continuance of the *Independent Chronicle* on its usual days of publication'. The type-set (Caslon) heading of the first number gave way in No. 2 to a blackletter title with a central device of a britannia, with a staff exhibiting a cap of liberty, reclining on a seat inscribed 'Magna Charta' in the exact style of *The Middlesex Journal* founded shortly before *Bingley's Journal*.

The bookseller, Isaac Fell of Paternoster Row, who published *The Middlesex Journal*, made himself personally responsible for the secrecy of all communications made to it—in view of the prosecutions of Baldwin, Woodfall and Almon, a necessary protection for any critic or even reporter of the doings of George III's administration. *The Middlesex Journal* was a Tuesday, Thursday and Saturday publication. It owed its existence to William Beckford, Lord Mayor of London, and a notorious supporter of Wilkes who was standing for the county of Middlesex in April 1769, when the first issue appeared, to champion Liberty.[1] As a piece of printing, with its bold roman heading in large sizes of the now familiar Caslon capitals, *The Middlesex Journal* was a success. At first the transverse and column rules were double, in the style of *The Gazetteer*. The rules were single from October 1769 until the end of the year, and double again in January 1770. There was a text from Cato, apostrophising Liberty, set in the heading over the date line and below the liberty device. In its entirety the heading, from top to bottom of the date line, was 3 in. The nine-line small-pica factotum in the first column of the front page was exclusive to the paper, bearing in a circular band the motto '*Libertas Pretiosior Auro*'. In January 1770 there was a change of printer and owner. Lord Mayor Beckford died suddenly—but the paper's politics were still advanced. Its circulation appears

[1] Chatterton, on more than one occasion, wrote for the *Middlesex Journal*.

to have increased in 1770 to the point at which advertisements were numerous. For instance, John Bell advertises some novels and there is an increasing number of trade announcements.

With the issue for June 5, 1770, there was another change, and *The Middlesex Journal* was published by the same John Wheble, at 20 Paternoster Row 'where letters to the Editor' are received, whom we shall find associated with *The Morning Post*. In 1771 Wheble was arrested for his activities with *The Middlesex Journal*, taken to the Guildhall and rescued by

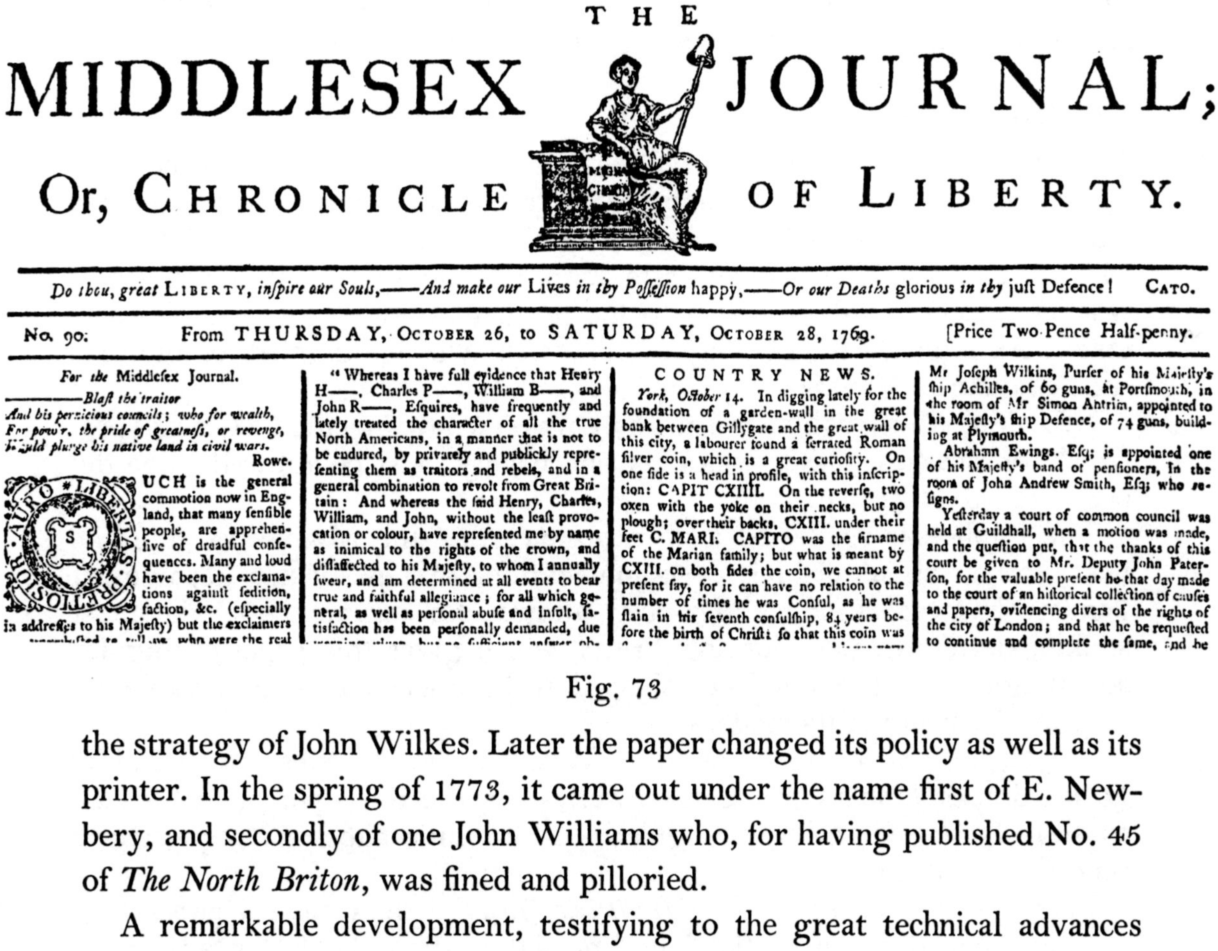

THE MIDDLESEX JOURNAL; Or, CHRONICLE OF LIBERTY.

Do thou, great LIBERTY, *inspire our Souls,——And make our* Lives *in thy Possession* happy,——*Or our Deaths* glorious *in thy* just Defence! CATO.

No. 90. From THURSDAY, OCTOBER 26, to SATURDAY, OCTOBER 28, 1769. [Price Two Pence Half-penny.

For the Middlesex Journal.

——————*Blast the traitor*
And his pernicious councils; who for wealth,
For pow'r, the pride of greatness, or revenge,
Would plunge his native land in civil wars.
Rowe.

[S]UCH is the general commotion now in England, that many sensible people, are apprehensive of dreadful consequences. Many and loud have been the exclamations against sedition, faction, &c. (especially in addresses to his Majesty) but the exclaimers

"Whereas I have full evidence that Henry H——, Charles P——, William B——, and John R——, Esquires, have frequently and lately treated the character of all the true North Americans, in a manner that is not to be endured, by privately and publickly representing them as traitors and rebels, and in a general combination to revolt from Great Britain: And whereas the said Henry, Charles, William, and John, without the least provocation or colour, have represented me by name as inimical to the rights of the crown, and disaffected to his Majesty, to whom I annually swear, and am determined at all events to bear true and faithful allegiance; for all which general, as well as personal abuse and insult, satisfaction has been personally demanded, due

COUNTRY NEWS.

York, October 14. In digging lately for the foundation of a garden-wall in the great bank between Gillygate and the great wall of this city, a labourer found a serrated Roman silver coin, which is a great curiosity. On one side is a head in profile, with this inscription: CAPIT CXIIII. On the reverse, two oxen with the yoke on their necks, but no plough; over their backs, CXIII. under their feet C. MARI. CAPITO was the sirname of the Marian family; but what is meant by CXIII. on both sides the coin, we cannot at present say, for it can have no relation to the number of times he was Consul, as he was slain in his seventh consulship, 84 years before the birth of Christ: so that this coin was

Mr Joseph Wilkins, Purser of his Majesty's ship Achilles, of 60 guns, at Portsmouth, in the room of Mr Simon Antrim, appointed to his Majesty's ship Defence, of 74 guns, building at Plymouth.

Abraham Ewings. Esq; is appointed one of his Majesty's band of pensioners, In the room of John Andrew Smith, Esq; who resigns.

Yesterday a court of common council was held at Guildhall, when a motion was made, and the question put, that the thanks of this court be given to Mr. Deputy John Paterson, for the valuable present he that day made to the court of an historical collection of causes and papers, evidencing divers of the rights of the city of London; and that he be requested to continue and complete the same, and he

Fig. 73

the strategy of John Wilkes. Later the paper changed its policy as well as its printer. In the spring of 1773, it came out under the name first of E. Newbery, and secondly of one John Williams who, for having published No. 45 of *The North Briton*, was fined and pilloried.

A remarkable development, testifying to the great technical advances which English engraving and typefounding had made since the advent of William Caslon in 1726, is to be seen in *The Middlesex Journal* during April 1773. For a short time after the temporary disappearance of Wheble, 'E. Newbery of St Paul's Church Yard' was the printer and publisher of the paper. On the back page of the journal for January 12, 1773, there appeared under the heading 'Postscript' (in 24-point Caslon) a paragraph set in 18-point italic, thus:

On Thursday next, and in future regularly every Tuesday, Thursday and Saturday at Five o'clock the MIDDLESEX JOURNAL will be published by

J. WILLIAMS at No. 39 opposite Fetter Lane in Fleet-street, to whom all letters are requested to be sent.

The paper under Newbery's direction had become somewhat broader in its outline. The 'Choisest' essays from *The Gazetteer*, *The Public Advertiser* and *The Morning Chronicle* were reprinted, and the securing of publisher's advertising gave the paper a certain literary importance, or at least convenience. In the issue of April 9, 1773, in the space between the transverse rules below the date line on the front page, the following paragraph appeared in the same back-page position and set in 14-point roman:

☞ To the Public:

THE Proprietors of the MIDDLESEX JOURNAL studious to render it peculiarly entertaining to the Public, propose to give therein, for the future, at least once a week a PIECE OF MUSIC consisting either of a SONG, CATCH-GLEE, or MINUET etc. etc. (Never before attempted in a newspaper) in the choice of which great care will be taken to merit their attention and gratify their tastes. Accordingly on Tuesday evening next will be inserted for the first time a favourite NEW SONG.

N.B. The Music will be printed by Falkner's new-invented Music Types, which for clearness, ease, symmetry and beauty must be allowed to be the best hitherto projected.

The Public are requested also to observe that the MIDDLESEX JOURNAL has another distinguishing recommendation, viz. particular department (under the head, *Literary Chronicle*) allotted for extracts from the most striking letters in the Morning Prints, which gives this paper a singular advantage over others and occasions it to be preserved as a valuable repository by many of its readers.

Advts, Letters etc. are taken in (J. WILLIAMS No. 39 Fleet-street and by D. Bond at St John's Gate, Clerkenwell; to whom those persons who shall chuse to be served with this singularly entertaining paper are requested to send their orders).

Whoever advertises in the *Middlesex Journal* shall have a paper containing such Advt sent gratis if residing within the bills of Mortality. Any other Advt of a moderate length brought by Eleven o'clock on the morning of publication, shall be inserted without fail.

In the following issue a conspicuous notice reads that *The Middlesex Journal* is 'The Only NEWS-PAPER upon the Plan, containing Once a Week, either a Song set to MUSIC, CATCH, GLEE OR MINUET etc.' A Song entitled *The Sun Gone Down* filled more than half of the second page of the paper. The music type is a very remarkable fount, well cast and composed with good alignment. The fount does not appear to be Caslon's, though obviously the work of an expert engraver. It was apparently an expensive feature. Alcock's two-part song, *Take Those Lips Away*, appeared on April 20, and thereafter there were songs twice a week, the notice at the head being changed accordingly. *The Fields are Green*, by T. Dale, appeared on the 29th of the month and was the last piece so printed. On May 6, the notice at the head was altered to read: 'The only newspaper upon the plan allotting a Department for extracts from the choisest Letters in all the Daily Prints'.

At this time, Williams was also publisher of *The Morning Post*, to be described in the next lecture .There were duplications of text—race-meeting reports, for example, being common to both papers. There was also some assimilation in the layout of *The Middlesex Journal* with *The Morning Post*, the details of which we must postpone until we are able to deal chrono-

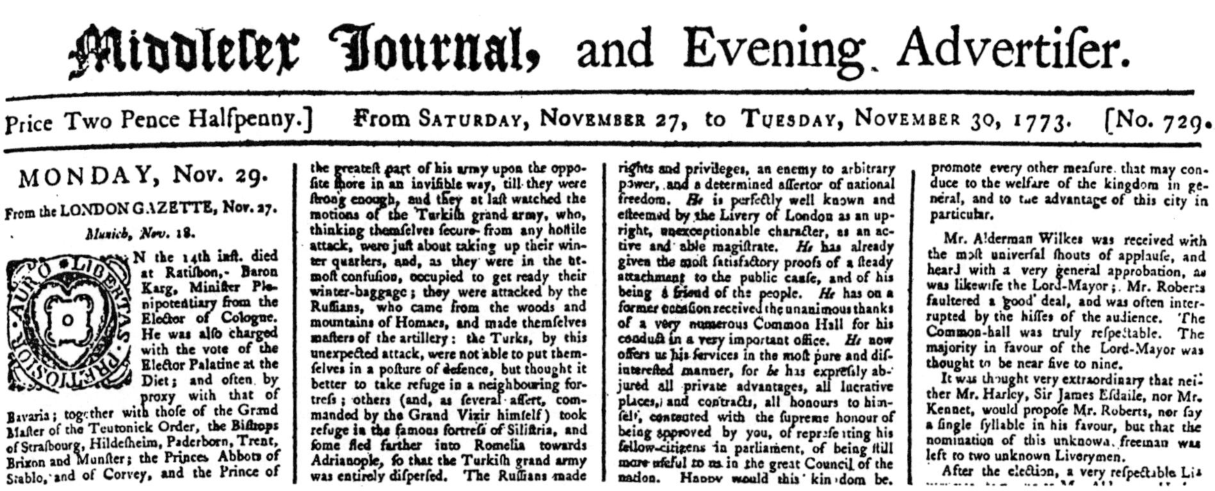

Middlesex Journal, and Evening Advertiser.

Price Two Pence Halfpenny.] From SATURDAY, NOVEMBER 27, to TUESDAY, NOVEMBER 30, 1773. [No. 729.

MONDAY, Nov. 29.

From the LONDON GAZETTE, Nov. 27.

Munich, Nov. 18.

ON the 14th inst. died at Ratisbon, Baron Karg, Minister Plenipotentiary from the Elector of Cologne. He was also charged with the vote of the Elector Palatine at the Diet; and often by proxy with that of Bavaria; together with those of the Grand Master of the Teutonick Order, the Bishops of Strasbourg, Hildesheim, Paderborn, Trent, Brixon and Munster; the Princes Abbots of Stablo, and of Corvey, and the Prince of

the greatest part of his army upon the opposite shore in an invisible way, till they were strong enough, and they at last watched the motions of the Turkish grand army, who, thinking themselves secure from any hostile attack, were just about taking up their winter quarters, and, as they were in the utmost confusion, occupied to get ready their winter-baggage; they were attacked by the Russians, who came from the woods and mountains of Homaes, and made themselves masters of the artillery: the Turks, by this unexpected attack, were not able to put themselves in a posture of defence, but thought it better to take refuge in a neighbouring fortress; others (and, as several assert, commanded by the Grand Vizir himself) took refuge in the famous fortress of Silistria, and some fled farther into Romelia towards Adrianople, so that the Turkish grand army was entirely dispersed. The Russians made

rights and privileges, an enemy to arbitrary power, and a determined assertor of national freedom. *He* is perfectly well known and esteemed by the Livery of London as an upright, unexceptionable character, as an active and able magistrate. *He* has already given the most satisfactory proofs of a steady attachment to the public cause, and of his being a friend of the people. *He* has on a former occasion received the unanimous thanks of a very numerous Common Hall for his conduct in a very important office. *He* now offers us his services in the most pure and disinterested manner, for *he* has expressly abjured all private advantages, all lucrative places, and contracts, all honours to himself, contented with the supreme honour of being approved by you, of representing his fellow-citizens in parliament, of being still more useful to us in the great Council of the nation. Happy would this kingdom be,

promote every other measure that may conduce to the welfare of the kingdom in general, and to the advantage of this city in particular.

Mr. Alderman Wilkes was received with the most universal shouts of applause, and heard with a very general approbation, as was likewise the Lord-Mayor; Mr. Roberts faultered a good deal, and was often interrupted by the hisses of the audience. The Common-hall was truly respectable. The majority in favour of the Lord-Mayor was thought to be near five to nine.

It was thought very extraordinary that neither Mr. Harley, Sir James Esdaile, nor Mr. Kennet, would propose Mr. Roberts, nor say a single syllable in his favour, but that the nomination of this unknown freeman was left to two unknown Liverymen.

After the election, a very respectable Li...

Fig. 74

logically with *The Morning Post*. There also appeared in *The Middlesex Journal* the advertisements of a bookseller begging leave to 'acquaint the public who have impatiently waited for *Trusler's Chronology*' that he had ready an edition of 10,000 copies. The printing of the paper came into the hands of one William Griffin, a bookseller of 6 Catherine Street, towards the end of 1773. The news-men were 'desired to take notice that on Tuesday next the *Middlesex Journal* will be published by William Griffin of 6 Catherine street', the date being December 21, 1773. The setting of the title had now been altered into exact accordance with *The Morning Post* and the sub-title to *Evening Advertiser*. The factotum device with the text '*Libertas Pretiosior Auro*' is the single feature which remained from the original paper. The paper, which cannot be traced after September 1776, does not appear to have altered its format, now the standardised typography of most of the

London newspaper press. It has been of some importance to trace the career of *The Middlesex Journal*, because that paper began with a voluminous title in the manner of *The St James's Chronicle* and found it convenient to abandon it in favour of a single-line title and sub-title, of which the title proper was in blackletter and the sub-title in roman. In effect, *The Middlesex Journal* looked like a London daily. It did not have the aspect of an Evening Post nor that of an Advertiser, since no front-page space was sold. For the rest, the normal structure was kept, namely, first the Gazette, then Foreign Affairs, then London Intelligence, Advertisements, Correspondence, Post-script, etc.

CHAPTER X

THE MATURE EIGHTEENTH-CENTURY NEWSPAPER, § 1

1770–1781

The Morning Chronicle	1770
The Morning Post	1772
The English Chronicle	1779
The Morning Herald	1780
Aurora	1781
Noon Gazette	1781

CHAPTER X

THE MATURE EIGHTEENTH-CENTURY NEWSPAPER, § 1

1770–1781

T*he Morning Chronicle*, destined to be the most formidable competitor of *The Times* until a series of misfortunes brought it to an untimely end a few days before the Christmas of 1862, was in typographical appearance and history similar to *The Middlesex Journal. The Morning Chronicle* began with a main title in 42-point upper- and lower-case Caslon, with sub-title, in 24-point capitals, grouped to allow a central position to the device of a lion trampling a griffin and brandishing the text 'Invidia fortitudine superatur'. The whole heading, to the date line, was some 2 in. deep. In the Burney Collection, No. 493 (December 29, 1770) has a front page of advertising: theatrical advertisements in the first column, concerts, Mayor's notices in column 2, publishers' advertisements, a newly invented portable printing press, etc. On the second page, a flower factotum introduced an epistle addressed 'For the Morning Chronicle'. The entire page was full of political and personal matter in epistolary form, each letter being introduced with a two-line plain initial. The 'Foreign Intelligence', beginning at the top of p. 3, is followed by 'London Intelligence', from which it is distinguished by a triple rule cut-off in the style of *The St James's Chronicle.*

Immediately below this triple rule, on the third page, there is a novelty of which it is important to take clear and accurate notice. This novelty consists of the place-name 'London' and the date printed, below the triple rule cut-off, '*December 29*' in italics; immediately below these two lines there occurs a notice which we transcribe in full:

The reputation and esteem we are so happy as to possess having equally increased the sale of the *Morning Chronicle* and the number of advertisements daily sent us, we are under the necessity of lessening the *Title* of our Paper and contracting it into a smaller space that we may have more room to insert the advertisements on the First Page. We therefore think it necessary to inform our Friends and Customers that we shall make this alteration on Tuesday next the First of January, and continue it all the Winter, by which

The Morning Chronicle, and *London Advertiſer*.

[No. 6259.] FRIDAY, *MAY* 29, 1789. [Price Three-Pence.]

DRURY-LANE.

(Laſt Time of performing till the Holidays.)

AT the Theatre-Royal, in Drury-Lane,
THIS EVENING,
The CONSTANT COUPLE;
Or, A TRIP TO THE JUBILEE.
Sir Harry Wildair, Mrs. JORDAN;
Beau Clincher, Mr. BANNISTER, jun.
Clincher, jun. Mr. SUETT;
Alderman Smuggler, Mr. PARSONS.
And Lady Lurewell, Mrs. WARD.

To which will be added,
The DEVIL TO PAY.
Or, The WIVES METAMORPHOSED.
Sir John Lovgrule, Mr. DIGNUM;
And Jobſon, Mr. MOODY.
Lady Loverule, Mrs. WARD;
And Nell, Mrs. JORDAN.

COVENT-GARDEN.

AT the Theatre-Royal, in Covent-Garden,
THIS EVENING,
Will be preſented SHAKESPEARE's
COMEDY OF ERRORS.
Antipholus of Syracuſe, Mr. LEWIS;
Antipholus of Epheſus, Mr. BERNARD;
Angelo, Mr. [illegible]; Dr. Pinch, Mr. WEWITZER;
Ægeon, Mr. HULL; Duke, Mr. GARDNER;
Dromio of Syracuſe, Mr. EDWIN;
And Dromio of Epheſus, Mr. QUICK.
The Abbeſs, Mrs. INCHBALD;
Luciana, Mrs. MOUNTAIN;
And Adriana, Mrs. BERNARD.

End of the Comedy, a MUSICAL OLIO; or,
The FEAST OF ANACREON.
The principal parts by Mr. Johnſtone, Mr. Blanchard, Mr. Davies, Mr. Darley, Mr. Cubitt, and Mr. Edwin.
Preſident, Mr. DAVIES;
The Anacreontic Song by Mr. DARLEY.
GLEE—"Come, come, all Noble Souls."
GLEE—"How ſhall we Mortals ſpend our Hours?"
CATCH—"Poor Thomas Day," by Mr. EDWIN, Mr. BLANCHARD, and Mr. DARLEY.
GLEE—"Sing Old Roſe and burn the Bellows."
Full Chorus "GOD SAVE THE KING."

After which will be preſented a Farce, in One Act, called
The CHEATS OF SCAPIN.
Scapin, Mr. RYDER;
Gripe, Mr. WEWITZER; Leander, Mr. DAVIES;
Thrifty, Mr. THOMPSON; Octavian, Mr. MACREADY;
Lucia, Miſs BRANGIN;
And Clara, Miſs ROWSON.

To which will be added, the Burletta of
TOM THUMB.
Grizzle, Mr. EDWIN; Arthur, Mr. QUICK;
Huncumunca, Mrs. MOUNTAIN;
And Dollalolla, Mrs. MARTYR.

SADLER'S WELLS

THIS and the FOLLOWING EVENINGS, great Variety of Entertainments, particularly
A favourite Muſical Piece, called
The MISCHANCE.
A Comic Intermezzo of Singing and Dancing, called
The QUAKER's WEDDING.
In the courſe of the Performances will be preſented a New Hiſtorical Romance, called
The RIVAL CAVALIERS;
Or, BERTRAND and MATILDA.
Characters:
Clifford, Monſ. Duranci; Sir Elvin, Mr. Brouguier; Bertrand, Monſ. Boi-Maiſon; Pandolph, Mr. Dubois; King, Sig. Bologna; and Matilda, Mrs. Harlowe.
To conclude with
A GRAND TOURNAMENT.
In which will be exhibited, Combats with the Mace d'Arme, Poignard, Small Sword, Sabre, and Javeline, according to the Cuſtom of the Ancient Chivalry.
Extraordinary Exhibitions and Performances on the
SLACK WIRE,
By SIGNOR BOLOGNA.
Who alſo, in a moſt whimſical manner, will entertain the Spectators with Two Drums, and ſeveral curious Equilibres with a Peacock's Feather.
For the firſt time, a New Grand Spectacle, in Commemoration of the King's Happy Recovery, called
BRITANNIA's RELIEF;
Or, The GIFT of HYGEIA.
In which will be introduced a complete and exact Repreſentation of
The ROYAL PROCESSION to St. PAUL's,
On the Twenty-third of April, as it moved on between Temple-bar and Ludgate-hill.
The Scenery, Dreſſes, and Decorations entirely new.
TIGHT-ROPE DANCING,
By the LITTLE DEVIL, Madame LA ROMAINE, and LA BELLE ESPAGNOLE.
The whole to conclude with a favourite Entertainment, called
The WITCH of the LAKES;
Or, HARLEQUIN in the HEBRIDES.
The Scenes deſigned by Mr. Greenwood. The Muſic compoſed and compiled by Mr. Taylor.
Boxes, 3s. 6d.—Pit, 2s.—Gallery, 1s.
Places for the Boxes to be taken at the Wells, from ten till two.
The Doors to be opened at half paſt five o'clock, and begin at half paſt ſix preciſely.
A new Muſical Piece, called "The Two Little Savoyards," taken from the French, will be brought out in a few days.

This Day is publiſhed, in 12mo. price 3s. ſewed.

THE CASTLES of ATHLIN and DUNBAYNE, a Highland Story.
——For juſtice bares the arm of God.
And the graſp'd vengeance only waits his nod.
CAWTH.
EMMA DORVILL,
By a LADY,
12mo, price 2s. 6d. ſewed.
FASHIONABLE INFIDELITY;
Or, the TRIUMPH of PATIENCE,
Three vols. 9s. ſewed.
Printed by T. Hookham, New Bond-ſtreet.
Juſt publiſhed,
LEITH HILL. A POEM.
Quarto, price 2s. 6d.

RANELAGH

IS THIS DAY opened with the uſual Entertainments of
VOCAL and INSTRUMENTAL MUSIC.
Admittance 2s. 6d. each perſon, Coffee and Tea included.
N. B. It will NOT be opened on Monday next, on account of the preparations for the GRAND FETE to be given by the SPANISH AMBASSADOR on TUESDAY.

VAUXHALL GARDENS

WILL open TO-MORROW, the 30th Inſtant, with the much admired Decorations of the late GALA, conſiderably augumented and improved.
Admittance FIVE SHILLINGS.
Tea, Coffee, Lemonade, and Capillaire included, from the opening of the Doors till the laſt Act of the CONCERT.
Should the weather prove unfavourable the CONCERT will be in the
IMPERIAL EASTERN TENT
The Doors open at half paſt Seven, and the CONCERT to begin at half paſt Eight o'Clock.
The temporary decorations will be removed after Saturday, and the GARDENS will be open on TUESDAY next, the 3d of June, for the Seaſon.

HANOVER-SQUARE.

For the Benefit Mr. RAIMONDI.
On WEDNESDAY next, the 3d of June, 1789,
WILL BE
A GRAND CONCERT
Of VOCAL and INSTRUMENTAL MUSIC
FIRST ACT.
Symphony (M. S.), RAIMONDI. ——Song, Signora GIULIANI.—Solo, Violin, Mr. RAIMONDI.——Song, Signor MARCHESI.—Sonata, Piano-Forte, Mr. CLEMENTI.—New Symphony, the concluding part intended to repreſent a ſtorm at ſea, RAIMONDI.
SECOND ACT.
Concerto, Pedal Harp, Madame KRUMPHOLDTZ.—Song, Signora GIULIANI.—New Duet for a Violin and Violoncello (by Meſſrs. RAIMONDI and CERVETTO) RAIMONDI.——Duetto, Signora GIULIANI and Signor MARCHESI.—The Battle, RAIMONDI.
The doors will be opened at Seven o'Clock, and the Concert begin at Eight.
Tickets, Half-a-Guinea each, to be had of Mr. RAIMONDI, No. 7, Oxendon-ſtreet, Hay-market; and at Meſſrs. Longman and Broderip's muſic ſhops.

EAST-INDIA HOUSE,
28th May, 1789.

THE Committee of Shipping of the United Company of Merchants of England trading to the Eaſt Indies, do hereby give notice, that the Committee will be ready to receive propoſals in writing, ſealed up, on WEDNESDAY the 10th of next month, for ſupplying the Company with COPPER.

And ſuch perſons who chooſe to deliver in tenders, are deſired to expreſs therein the loweſt prices, as they will have no opportunity of making any abatement.

The conditions of the contract may be ſeen by applying to Mr. Coggan, Clerk to the ſaid Committee, with whom the tenders muſt be left before twelve o'clock at noon on the above day, as none will be received after that hour.

This Day is publiſhed, in 12mo.
Price Three Shillings, ſewed,
VOLUME FOURTH of
THE SCOTCH PREACHER;
Or, A COLLECTION of SERMONS,
By ſome of the moſt eminent CLERGYMEN of the Church of Scotland.
Printed for C. Elliot and T. Kay, No. 332, Strand, London; and J. Dickſon, Edinburgh.
Of whom may be had,
Complete Sets, in 4 vols. price 12s. ſewed, or 14s. bound.
Alſo, All the New Sermons lately publiſhed.

This Day is publiſhed, Price 6d.
A COMMENT on Dr. WATTS's DIVINE SONGS for Children; with Queſtions; deſigned to illuſtrate the Doctrines and Precepts to which they refer; and induce a proper application of them as inſtruments of early piety.
By Mrs. TRIMMER.
London: Printed for J. Buckland; J. F. and C. Rivington; T. Longman; T. Field; and C. Dilly.
N. B. This Comment was written to agree with Dr. Watts's Divine Songs in their original ſtate, as publiſhed by Buckland, &c. and will not accord with any altered edition.

IRISH SENATE.

The decided part which has been taken by the Iriſh Parliament, on the late buſineſs of the REGENCY, ſo momentous to both Kingdoms, has made the individuals of whom it is compoſed, the object of much and of curious enquiry.—We ſhall, therefore, occaſionally dedicate a column of the MORNING CHRONICLE to this ſubject, and give ſome ſketches of the characters moſt prominent, in a manner which, without any comment, ſhall evince its own impartiality.

Sir BOYLE ROCHE, Bart.

TO ſpeak with eaſe and elegance his native language has ever been deemed one of the moſt indiſpenſable requiſites in the public declaimer, without which ability was fruitleſs, and underſtanding obſcured: and ſome of the moſt celebrated orators of antiquity, ſuch as the Grachi and Julius Cæſar, derived no ſmall ſhare of their fame from their ſuperior excellence in that reſpect, due to the early cares of a venerable parent, and are ſaid to have been educated *non tam in gremio quam in ſermone matris*. Whether Sir Boyle aſpires to emulate ſuch noted names in the region of eloquence we preſume not to determine: but aſſuredly, if he does, he has as much to unlearn as he has to acquire. Indeed in that character which he obviouſly ſeems to wiſh to ſupport, the character (now almoſt exploded) of a blunt blundering Iriſh ſoldier and true old Mileſian, oratory formed not an eſſential part; for they were wont to excel, not in words but in action. Yet as the Knight has frequently diſplayed his abilities as a public ſpeaker, as ſuch we ſhall endeavour to ſketch his portrait.

His voice is clear and diſtinct enough, but diſagreeable and grating to the ear; without harmony or ſweetneſs, it has a wirey tone offenſive to the ſenſe: and his pronunciation is diſgraced by the moſt glaring fault a gentleman's can have. It is not a provincial accent, it is not an affected liſp, it is not a broad vulgarity—but it is what an eminent and worthy divine (now no more) with ſpirit and humour, was wont to call, 'a ſneering of the brogue.' His language is neither ſimple, correct, nor pure; ſeemingly the ſpontaneous production of the moment, though conceived with eaſe, yet delivered with difficulty: in a high degree quaint, and plentifully *ornamented* with that flower of rhetoric which our Engliſh friends have denominated a Bull.

His action, which aims not at grace, has indeed ſometimes force and ſtrength; and his manner is ſpirited, warm and vehement, with much of the eager partizan and little of the deliberating ſenator; and it is well known that his fire evaporates not in ſmoke, as he is undoubtedly a man of approved courage. In reaſoning he exhibits much dry humour blended with ſome archneſs, and is not deſtitute of point, nor of keen and ſarcaſtical alluſion, but we cannot ſay that we have been much ſtruck with the power of his arguments or the energy of his deductions; and in them we fruitleſsly ſeek for that luminous order and methodical diſpoſition that add weight to truth, and force to ſentiment. Deſultory in the extreme, they are embarraſſed and involved in inexplicable confuſion; they are a chaos over which no brooding ſpirit has ſpread its wings to reduce the maſs into order.

His matter is of that obvious and common ſort that occurs at once, requiring no deep thought or laboured ſearch to find it, but floats on the ſurface to bleſs the firſt occupant, but is ſometimes marked by ſenſe, and ſometimes by obſervation; or to borrow the words of the elegant poet—

"His matter, now to ſenſe, now nonſenſe leaning,
"Means not, but blunders round about a meaning."

—Yet we muſt allow it to poſſeſs ſome *extraordinary* merit, for no member is more attended to than Sir Boyle—but that, perhaps, may ariſe from his never offending and always *entertaining* the Houſe. Graced with a title by the court, and holding a place there, he ſtrenuouſly contends for every meaſure that adminiſtration chooſes to ſupport.

Parliamentary Intelligence.

HOUSE OF LORDS.

THURSDAY, *May* 28.

Read a third time, and paſſed, ſeveral Private Bills, and directed two Maſters in Chancery to take a meſſage to the Commons, acquainting them therewith.—Adjourned to Monday the 8th of June next.

HOUSE OF COMMONS.

THURSDAY, *May* 28.

GARDENERS.

After the ſecond reading of the Bill to explain and amend an Act paſſed in the 6th year of the reign of his preſent MAJESTY, intituled, "An Act for the Protection of Trees, Plants, Shrubs, &c."

Mr. MAINWARING moved, "that this Bill be committed."

Mr. WINDHAM oppoſed this motion, on the ground which he had oppoſed the motion for leave to bring in the Bill, viz. that of wiſhing to reſiſt the idea of increaſing the penal laws, which were already much too numerous.

The ATTORNEY GENERAL was of opinion, that the preſent Bill was neceſſary, in order to protect property which was at preſent liable to dangerous depredation; trees and ſhrubs had often been taken away in the day-time, which, as the law now ſtands, was deemed only a treſpaſs; he knew of many actions brought for treſpaſs in which the utmoſt extent the jury could go, was found very inadequate to the loſs of the perſon ſeeking redreſs; nothing, in his opinion, would tend effectually to afford neceſſary protection to property thus ſituated, but the making of the offence complained of, a felony.

Mr. BURKE ſaid he had not the happineſs of concurring with the Attorney General as to the propriety of making the offence of which complaint is now made, a felony; our ſtatute laws were already much too numerous and much too ſevere upon points of what are called *criminal offences*, he was much more inclined to allow redreſs by *civil* than *criminal* procedure; indeed, if this ſanguinary inclination of increaſing the criminal law was to be much further indulged, the moſt trivial offences committed by the moſt ignorant individuals, would become liable to criminal proſecution; *cellery, ſpinnage*, and other inſignificant vegetables would, and might as well become the objects of the penal ſtatutes as thoſe now in queſtion; in ſhort, it was impoſſible to know where this rage for criminal proceeding would end, he therefore ſhould decidedly oppoſe the preſent Motion.

Mr. MAINWARING, in reply, urged the neceſſity of this Bill.

The Houſe divided,

For the Commitment,	41
Againſt it, ——	11
Majority	30

BUDGET.

Mr. PITT obſerved, that ſeveral papers relative to the Revenue were now upon the table for the peruſal of the Members of the Houſe. There was one paper, which was a very material one, which he had not yet been enabled to produce, it not being yet ready, but he truſted it would be ready on Friday the fifth of June; but as it might require ſome ſhort time to peruſe it, and as he wiſhed the opening of the Budget ſhould take place before as many Members as could conveniently attend, he was convinced it would be proper to bring forward that buſineſs at a time as near as poſſible to the Call of the Houſe.—He therefore gave notice, that inſtead of Friday the fifth he ſhould on Monday the eighth of June, open the Budget.

SUPPLY.

Mr. GILBERT brought up the Report of the Committee of Supply on the Extraordinaries of the Army, &c.

The reſolutions were read, and all agreed to *nem. con.*

SLAVE TRADE.

Mr. TIERNEY gave notice he ſhould, on Friday the 5th of June, move, "That the queſtion of the *Policy* of the Slave Trade ſhould be decided previous to the entering on the propoſitions now before the Houſe." All of theſe propoſitions were reducible to two points, viz. *Policy* and *Humanity*. Upon the former, difference of opinion may ariſe—upon the latter, none; if, therefore, the policy were decided againſt the trade, all other reſolutions would be needleſs; he wiſhed it to be underſtood he had not converſed with any perſons intereſted on either ſide; what he now hinted was from the pure impulſe of his own feelings.

Mr. PITT hoped, that although the intended motion could not tend ultimately to the prejudice of the reſolutions propoſed by Mr. Wilberforce, yet as it might tend to derange the ſyſtem already formed, by thoſe who oppoſe the reſolutions, he hoped Mr. Tierney would not perſiſt in his motion.

Mr. WILBERFORCE wiſhed that this motion ſhould not be brought forward on Friday the 5th of June, becauſe it would call Members to town ſooner than it was now underſtood there would be an abſolute neceſſity for their attendance.

Mr. TIERNEY ſaid, he would judge of the propriety of the motion by the attendance on that day.

The Houſe then reſolved itſelf into a Committee upon the Slave Trade.

Sir WILLIAM DOLBEN took the Chair.

The Committee heard Evidence, after which the Houſe adjourned to Friday the 5th of June.

TO CORRESPONDENTS.

The Editor *has to acknowledge the receipt of an anonymous letter, in which it is ſtated that the* Mrs. FARRER, *who died at* Brompton, *was not the perſon deſcribed in the* MORNING CHRONICLE, *and that the latter is actually married to the Gentleman whoſe name ſhe bears.—Without profeſſing to doubt theſe facts, we ſhall only ſay, that the other parts of the letter cannot be inſerted, unleſs the writer will give his name and authority.*

Simplex *would have cauſe to deem us* ſimple *indeed, if we were to inſert a chargeable article, on an anonymous promiſe of payment!*

Dicky Quid *is an unfair attack on a worthy and valuable member of ſociety.*

Spitfire *to the* Duke *of* RICHMOND, *is certainly miſ-directed.*

Harry Hearty *has ſome* joviality, *which we apprehend he has miſtaken for* wit.

MORNING CHRONICLE.

LONDON, MAY 29, 1789.

A Privy Council is to be held this day at Kew, and to-morrow their Majeſties and the Princeſſes return to Windſor Lodge.

Yeſterday the Prince of Wales and his brothers viſited the Royal Family at Kew Palace.

Yeſterday the Lord Chancellor held the firſt Seal after Eaſter Term, at Lincoln's Inn Hall; after which his Lordſhip went to the Houſe of Peers. The ſecond Seal will be on Tueſday the ninth of June.

Yeſterday the Lord Biſhop of Rocheſter held a confirmation at St. Margaret's church, Weſtminſter.

This day, being the Anniverſary of the Reſtoration, there will be no buſineſs done on Change, and all the Public Offices will be ſhut up.

Yeſterday the anniverſary meeting of the charity children was held at St. Paul's Cathedral. The Counteſs Fitzwilliam, and a few other nobility were preſent; but the company were not numerous.

The new Commander in Chief for the North American ſtation, is Sir R. Hughes, ſenior Rear Admiral of the Red Squadron. The Adamant of 50 guns, Captain David Knox, now at Sheerneſs, is the flag ſhip.

The promotions now in contemplation in the church, and in the naval, military, and civil eſtabliſhments will take place immediately after the King's birth day.

The Eaſt India Company will have occaſion to take up more ſhips in Auguſt for the ſeaſon 1789, than they have ever yet had occaſion to employ in any former ſail. The laſt liſt contained thirty-two ſhips; the enſuing will be little under forty, and the ſhips lately arrived are going into dock for repair on that account.

Yeſterday arrived a mail from the Leeward Iſlands, brought to Falmouth by the Antelope packet, in 21 days

Fig. 75. *The second setting of the title of* The Morning Chronicle means we hope no Person will be disappointed of having their Advertisements inserted on the very day on which they were ordered, unless they are uncommonly long and sent to the Printing Office too late to be composed.

This explicit statement of the reason for the contraction of the title becomes the more convincing when it is borne in mind that advertisements on the front page were charged extra. The importance of the inclusion of the name of the paper, the place-name and the date of publication immediately above the official pronouncement by the proprietor is an extension of a practice which we have already noticed in *The St James's Chronicle*. That paper, however, contented itself with inserting its paragraph in that portion of the paper

The Morning Chronicle;
And LONDON ADVERTISER.

NUMB. 493.] SATURDAY, DECEMBER 29, 1770. Price Two-pence Half-Penny

HAY-MARKET.
By PARTICULAR DESIRE.
AT the KING's THEATRE, in the HAY MARKET,
THIS DAY, the 29th of December,
Will be performed
The favourite COMIC Opera, called
La BUONA FIGLIUOLA.

ALMACK's.
Messrs. BACH and ABEL
Take the Liberty to acquaint the NOBILITY and GENTRY,
Subscribers to their Concerts,
THAT Attendance will be given at their house in King-square-court, Soho, This Day, and every morning following, from Ten 'till Two o'clock

Removed from Coventry-street,
RICHARD WARREN,
PERFUMER,
Humbly begs Leave to acquaint the Nobility and Gentry, his Friends, and the Public in general,
THAT he is removed back to MARY-LE-BONNE Street, Golden square; where he has laid in an elegant Stock of ITALIAN

In the Press, and speedily will be published,
Price Two Shillings and Six-pence,
Dedicated to Sir JOHN FIELDING, Knt.
THE CASE of HENRY FREDERICK,
Publisher of the
BUTTON-MAKER's JESTS.

This Day is published, in 4to.
The SECOND Edition,

Fig. 76. *First setting*

which was most likely to be read, and which was indeed most certain to be read first. The vital portion of either paper, therefore, is not, as one might reasonably expect, the top of the first column of the first page. Whether or no the first page was let to advertisers, the 'London Intelligence' seldom appeared there. As a consequence, the heart of the mature eighteenth-century paper lay in a position which varied between the middle of page 2, page 3 or, often enough, even on the final page itself. With certain exceptions, which we shall in due time notice, the practice of *The Morning Chronicle* in this respect determined, for the rest of the journals of its own generation, the position in which official announcements by the publisher, conductor or printer of the paper would address the reader. *The Morning Chronicle* is the first paper to use its own name, the place-name (London) and date over a manifesto. The leading article developed out of the manifesto and inevitably occupied its position. This is the reason for the printing, in all our present day papers, of the leaders in the middle of the paper.

The front page of the *Chronicle* was sold as far as possible. When this was not done, news would be included in the available space according to practically invariable rules: first a political letter, secondly the foreign mails, thirdly the 'London Gazette'. The extracts from the 'Gazette' were dated—and in the absence of the 'Gazette' or any announcement by the proprietor—the 'London Intelligence' was headed 'MORNING CHRONICLE' in full capitals; followed by a number of paragraphs, extracts and miscellaneous information, including sporting, theatrical, and other varieties of fashionable intelligence. With the recollection that the heart of the paper was not on the first page but more or less in the centre, we may, for the moment, leave *The Morning Chronicle*.

In view of the difficulties of continuing this enquiry on strictly chronological lines, it is better for the avoidance of confusion if we now discuss *The Morning Post* whose foundation dates from November 2, 1772. Its early fortunes are better described before we compare, as we shall need to do, its mature format with that of *The Morning Chronicle* and that of *The Daily Universal Register* of 1785.

It is necessary, therefore, for us to go back to 1771 when *The Middlesex Journal* and *The Morning Chronicle* were both new foundations and the Advertisers completed the daily journals of the town. These were the constituents of the London newspaper press when *The Morning Post*, now our oldest surviving daily, made its *début*.

The Morning Post, founded by a syndicate of tradesmen,[1] made its first appearance on November 2, 1772, from the press of Edward Cox and George Bigg, 405 Strand. It was published by Wilkes's friend, John Wheble, formerly of Paternoster Row and of *The Middlesex Journal*, and in 1772 a bookseller in Fleet Street. The first thirteen numbers issued were, though printed on the same single sheet as *The Morning Chronicle*, by an extra fold, half the expanse and double the number of pages, i.e. eight pages instead of four (cf. Fig. 77). The sub-title for these first thirteen numbers was 'And Daily Advertising Pamphlet', and, as is implied, advertisements were a speciality of the paper. 'None to be omitted that are brought before Ten at night on any pretence;—as an additional sheet will be given gratis, should necessity require it'. The price, 1½*d*., instead of the usual 2½*d*., was a possibility so long as the Stamp Office remained under the impression that *The Morning Post* was not a 'paper'

[1] As the advertisements of Christie, the auctioneer, and John Bell, bookseller, appear in the earliest extant number (No. 5, Friday, November 6, 1772) kindly lent me by the manager of *The Morning Post*, it is likely that they were among the founders. Their names (together with those of Skinner, auctioneer, the Rev. Dr John Trusler; Tattersall, the horse dealer and others) figure in a list of the proprietors issued by *The Morning Post* in 1776: cf. Morison, *John Bell*, 1745–1831 (Cambridge, 1930).

because it was in eight pages and its sub-title affirmed it was a pamphlet. The proprietors, having visited the Stamp Office before the first issue was published, left with an assurance that the authorities held the new undertaking to be tax-free—and so it was for a fortnight. On November 17, 1772, the paper came out with a statement explaining that as the authorities now insisted, *The Morning Post; or, Cheap Daily Advertiser* (as its sub-title now became) was printed upon stamped paper in the now common format (cf. Fig. 78) for daily newspapers. The price became twopence, but there was no change in the typography or the layout of the matter, except that the heading was run-on in one line according to the model of *The Morning Chronicle*. Obviously, from the use in the *Post*'s title of the word 'Morning'—never used before the *Chronicle*—other resemblances are to be found; thus, the *Post* used the triple line cut-offs. The name of the paper (in 18-point roman upper- and lower-case) was set in the body of the paper in the style of *The Morning Chronicle*. But there was an important difference: whereas the *Chronicle* set its name over the 'London Intelligence',[1] the *Post* chose the space over the 'Foreign Intelligence'. On the numerous occasions when no mails had arrived, the practice of the two papers was identical, and long remained so. The conspicuous difference between the two front pages was in the setting of the titles **The Morning Post**, and Daily Advertiser; The Morning Chronicle, and *London Advertiser*. The papers themselves, however, were very different in character. *The Morning Chronicle* was the property of William, younger brother of Henry Sampson Woodfall of *The Public Advertiser*. Owing to his possession of a rare faculty, 'Memory' Woodfall, as the *Chronicle* proprietor was called, used to sit in the House of Commons gallery, leaning, hour after hour, on a stick, with his eyes closed and then, without taking a single note, return to the office to write sixteen columns of word-for-word report. As, with the summer of 1771, he could now afford to do so with impunity, William Woodfall specialised in parliamentary news, and on a scale which John Almon of the regular *London Evening Post*, the initiator of Commons reporting, never attempted.[2] *The*

[1] On days when there was no 'Gazette'. Later, when Woodfall reported Parliament he headed that section with the legend 'Morning Chronicle'. This feature was often found in the first page when space was available.

[2] John Almon, bookseller and proprietor of *The London Evening Post*, relates the circumstances which led to the relaxation and final abandonment of the claims of Parliament to prohibit any form of newspaper reporting of the proceedings of either house. Cf. Almon, *Bibliographical ...Anecdotes*, London, 1797, III, 403 ff. The last prosecutions were attempted in February 1771, when Thompson, printer of *The Gazetteer*, and Wheble, of *The Middlesex Journal*, ignored a summons to

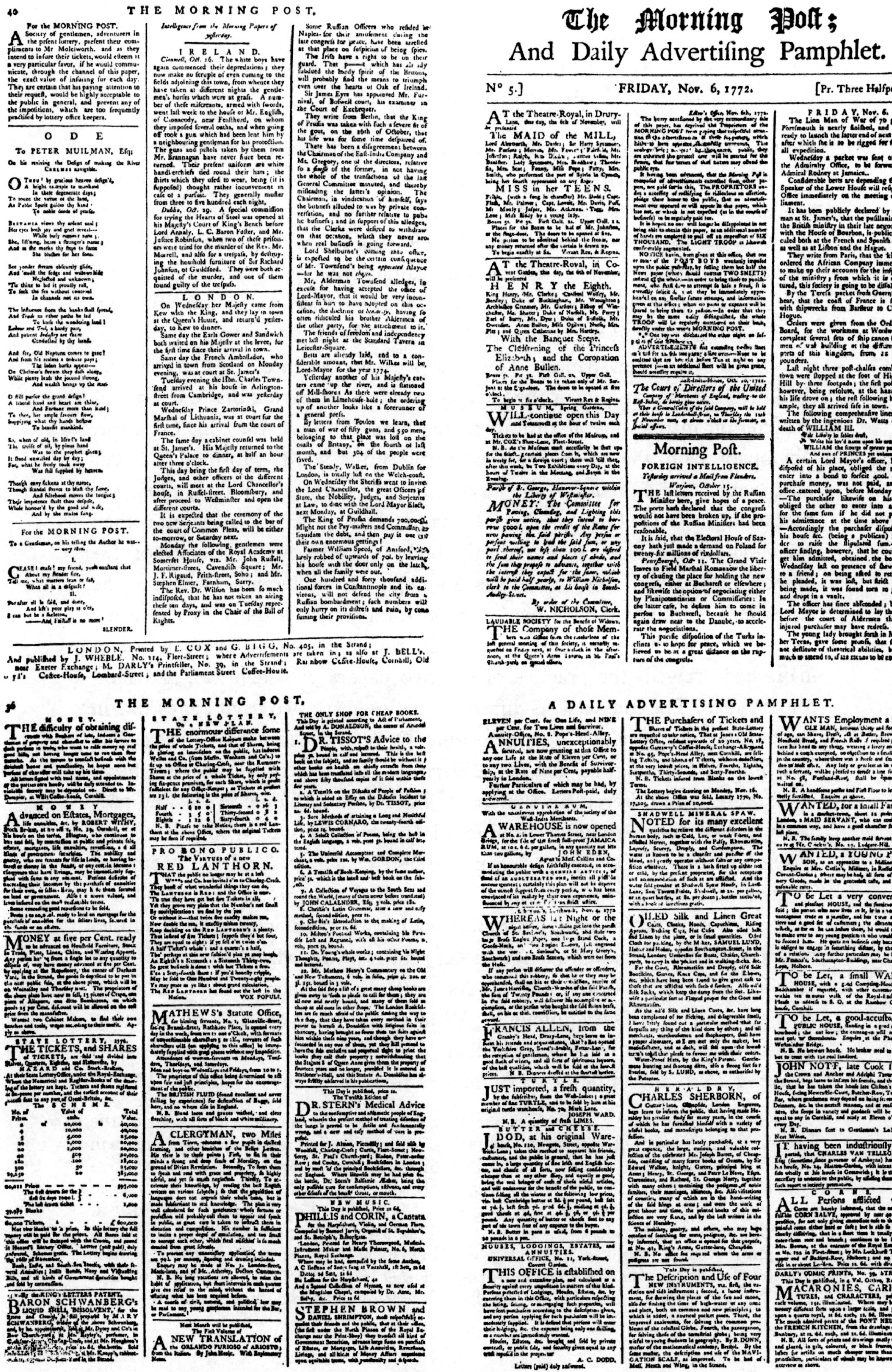
40 THE MORNING POST,

The Morning Post; And Daily Advertising Pamphlet.

N° 5.] FRIDAY, Nov. 6, 1772. [Pr. Three Halfpence

Morning Post.

FOREIGN INTELLIGENCE.

36 THE MORNING POST,

A DAILY ADVERTISING PAMPHLET. 37

LONDON, Printed by E. COX and G. BIGG, No. 405, in the Strand; And published by J. WHEBLE. No. 114, Fleet-Street; where Advertisements are taken in; as also at J. BELL's, near Exeter Exchange; M. DARLY's Printseller, No. 39, in the Strand; Rainbow Coffee-House, Cornhill; Old Lloyd's Coffee-House, Lombard-Street; and the Parliament Street Coffee-House.

Fig. 77. *Four pages of the original eight-page format (reduced) of* The Morning Post

Morning Chronicle consequently developed into London's leading political journal. The 'Parliamentary Intelligence', as the main feature, was headed accordingly in a clear type larger than the body fount. In the course of time, the subject-matter of the debate was indicated by the inclusion of sub-headings.

Moreover, while the House was in session, the title of the paper and the day's date were taken from their old position over 'London' and placed at the head of the 'Parliamentary Intelligence'. *The Morning Herald* quickly followed Woodfall's example, and by the year 1788 other morning papers were giving space and display to columns headed invariably 'Parliamentary Intelligence'. The accuracy and completeness of the paper's reporting, the provision of the sub-heads to the reports and the manner of their display, all alike the inventions of Woodfall, entitle *The Morning Chronicle* to rank as the most influential foundation of the period, 1775–89. *The Times* (1785) was nothing more than an estimable second-rate paper—and not always that—until the succession of the second John Walter. *The Morning Post*, having failed as a cheap advertiser, succeeded as a fashionable Gazette. The Reverend Mr Bate, who apostatised from the *Post* in 1780, followed the lead of Woodfall and attempted, with some success, to establish a serious paper in *The Morning Herald*. John Bell, who retired from *The Morning Post* to found *The World*, whose example changed the typography and display of all the newspapers of town and country, specialised in racing, boxing, the stage and west-end gossip. But the lighter side of journalism is the most ephemeral, and Woodfall's serious *Morning Chronicle* was the most stable, and *The Morning Herald* only less so. The last quarter of the eighteenth century, in the development of newspapers, does not close until 1808, when the second John Walter brought out *The Times* with five columns to the page. But to take a century, as it were, literally, there is more history, typographical and other, between 1775 and 1800 than we can afford time to notice.

the bar of the House of Commons. In the March of 1771 William Woodfall (*The Morning Chronicle*), T. Evans (*The London Packet*), Henry Baldwin (*The St James's Chronicle*), Thomas Wright (*The Whitehall Evening Post*), John Miller (*The London Evening Post*), and John Bladon (*The General Evening Post*) surrendered. Wheble resisted, but on the advice of Wilkes got himself arrested by his own 'devil', was brought to the Guildhall on a day when Wilkes was sitting magistrate, who discharged Wheble and sent the 'devil' to the Treasury to claim the £50 reward which the royal proclamation offered for the apprehension of his employer. Cf. Bleackley, *John Wilkes*, London, 1917, p. 260. After July 1771 no consistent attempt was made to prevent the publication of parliamentary reports in any of the newspapers.

The Morning Post; or, Cheap Daily Advertiser.

N° 14.] TUESDAY, November 17, 1772. [Price Two Pence.

AT the Theatre-Royal, in Drury-Lane, this day, the 19th of November, will be presented

AS YOU LIKE IT.

Touchstone, Mr. KING.
Orlando, Mr. BRERETON.
Jaques, Mr. LOVE.
Amiens, (with Songs) Mr. VERNON.
Adam, Mr. MOODY.
Sylvius, Mr. WHEELER.
Corin, Mr. HARTRY.
Oliver, Mr. PACKER.
Duke Frederick, Mr. HURST.
Celia, (with Songs) Miss MANSEL.
Audrey, Mrs. BRADSHAW.
Phoebe, Miss AMBROSSE.
Rosalind, Mrs. BARRY.
To which will be added

HARLEQUIN's INVASION.

Harlequin, Mr. WRIGHT.
Corporal Bounce, Mr. BRANSBY.
Gasconade, Mr. BADDELEY.
Snip, Mr. PARSONS.
Abram, Mr. WESTON.
Justice, Mr. Hartry. | Constable, Mr. Ackman.
Mercury, Mr. DAVIES.
Forge, Mr. GRIFFITHS.
Welshman, Mr. Waldron. | Irishman, Mr. Messink.
Old Woman, Mr. DODD.
Mrs. Snip, Mrs. BRADSHAW.
Sukey Chitterlin, Mrs. DAVIES.
Dolly Snip, Miss POPE.
To conclude with a GRAND CHORUS.

Boxes 5s. Pit 3s. Gall. 2s. Upper Gall. 1s.
The doors to be opened at five o'clock, to begin exactly at six.

AT the Theatre-Royal, in Covent Garden, this day, the 17th of November will be presented

The BEGGARS OPERA.

Captain Macheath, Mr. MATTOCKS.
Peachum, Mr. SHUTER.
Lockit, Mr. DUNSTAL.
Filch, Mr. HOLTOM.
Mr. Peachum, Mrs. VINCENT.
Lucy, Mrs. MATTOCKS.
Diana Trapes, Mrs. PITT.
Mrs. Slammekin, Mrs. GREEN.
Polly, Miss CATLEY.
The HORNPIPE by Miss TWIST.
To which will be added

The Deuce is in Him.

Col. Tamper, Mr. WROUGHTON.
Major Belford, Mr. DU-BELLAMY.
Prattle, Mr. LEWIS.
Bell, Mrs. BULKLEY.
Mad. Florival, Mrs. LESSINGHAM.
Emily, Mrs. MATTOCKS.
The doors to be opened at five o'clock, to begin exactly at six.
Boxes 5s. Pit 3s. Gall. 2s. Upper Gall. 1s.
Vivant Rex & Regina.

MUSEUM, Spring Gardens,

UNTIL the Removal of the several pieces about to be selected, there will be two Exhibitions every Day, at the hours of Twelve in the Morning, and Seven in the Evening.

Tickets to be had at the Office, and at Mr. Cox's, Shoe-Lane. Those for the morning at 5s. 3d. for the evenining at 7s.

N. B. None of the pieces have yet been removed since the first opening.

GENUINE RUM.
With the unanimous approbation of the society of the West-India Merchants,

A WAREHOUSE is now opened at No. 2. in Lower Thames Street, near London Bridge, for the sale of the finest full-proof JAMAICA RUM, at 10 s. 6 d. per gallon, in any quantity not less than two gallons, by

JOHN EDEN,
Agent to Mess. Collins and Co.

If an honourable design, formed and executed *under the immediate sanction of the most eminent West-India planters and merchants*, of accommodating the public with GENUINE RUM, of the *finest quality* that can possibly be procured, instead of the *adulterated mixtures* which have been generally sold for it, merits the encouragement of the public !---certainly this plan, *being the only one of its kind* will naturally excite their attention and support ;---Every person will, *upon trial of its strength*, find it to be not only the wholsomest, but even the cheapest spirituous liquor that can be drank in this country.---And, as no artifice is made use of to abuse the public confidence in this undertaking, punctual regard is paid to written, as well as to personal orders.

GENUINE RUM WAREHUSE at No. 16. facing the South-Sea-House, in Bishopsgate-Street.

TO expose the imposition of a plan invented by a person incognito, whose *alluring pretences to a consequential and exclusive sanction from the society of West-India merchants*, is refuted by their own publication in the news-papers, in June last ; and whose invective and atrocious calumny against every other dealer in Rum, has been circulated under the signature of "John Eden, agent to Messrs. Collins and Co. at No. 2. in Lower Thames-Street," *where, in fact, no such principals now do, nor ever did exist* : I will engage, under any penalty that may be proposed by the most sanguine advocate for the new plan, to deliver the finest genuine full proof Jamaica Rum that can be procured, at 9s. 6d. per gallon, exactly the same in purity, and strength, as that specified to be sold under the boasted plan, at the exorbitant price of 10s. and 6d. per gallon. The attention that has been shewn to my objections against a scheme evidently calculated *to abuse the public confidence*, and to decry many men of strict honor and integrity in their dealings, has far exceeded my expectation. And as every species of imposture and circumvention should be strenuously opposed and defeated, especially when the interest of the public, and the reputation of a respectable class of the mercantile and commercial part of that public, are so basely attacked, I have the greatest reason to depend upon the farther countenance and support of rational and discerning persons.

THO. BROUGHTON.

ANNUITY-OFFICE,
No. 10, Birchin-lane, or 'Change alley, London,
Eleven per Cent. for One Life, or Ten for Two.

AT this office five or six capital annuities are now granting, uncommonly well secured, on landed estates, from 50l. per ann. to 1000l. per ann. such as seldom offer, and punctually paid at a banker's in London. The purchaser or purchasers to be at liberty to put in any life or lives they please. Principals only will be treated with, by applying at this office from ten to three.

To be SOLD, a lot of land on the island of Dominica, situate in a fine bottom, near Commissioner's-Bay, in the Parish of St. Andrew's, in quantity about 200 acres. A plan of the estate may be seen at the Office.

EUROPEAN LODGE of BUCKS.

THE Brethren of this ancient and honourable Order are requested to dine with the most noble Grand, &c. on Friday, the 20th inst. (being the day fixt for holding the anniversary) at the

as much ardor as you have done his former insinuations. Mr. Wilkes, the man to whom you are indebted for your right honorable post, has been the object of your malice ever since the canonical apostate missed the aim of his pursuit, by endeavouring to stab the vitals of liberty, by the ignominious hand of dissimulation: the intent, happy for our constitution ! was discovered e'er confusion wholly assumed her anarchy ; but not without the elopement of several revolting patriots, who had digested his pernicious seeds of discord. Your right honorable self, Mr. Sawbridge, and Mr. Oliver, were the material principles of this undermining machine: with subtilty he drew ye forth by his persuasive eloquence, clapped a doubtful mist before your eyes, and fixed his *insignia* in your hearts.—*Pro sibi non Patria.*

This contagion met repulse from men of principle; and when he found he had lost access to the rest, he, the herald and pedagogue of your behaviour, in your names, and with your complying condescension to his superiority in judgment, levelled war against those who stood inflexible to the man, to whom you now, and the rest of your fugitive adherents, owe all the honors a candid city could have bestowed on the prostituted friends of freedom.

Little did your friends imagine of your present conduct, when you launched into the political world ! when you pledged your integrity to the man you now basely disown, in a vociferous harangue at Brentford, that futurity should prove you a renagadé to the cause, to make Mr. Wilkes the ladder of your policy, to climb up thereby to honor's summit, which, when gained, you pushed from under you ; to make the sacred birthright of a Briton an ambush to aim at interest ; to prove the tool of a vain priest, who fell, like Satan, when he bid defiance to the Omnipotent in the dreary cave of oblivion, with damnation to his memory.

You have sated your thirsty appetite of ambition (which ever burned predominant in your breast sufficient to consume the qualms of conscience, should they rise in defence of martyred equity) by filling the first office the city can bestow on real worth.

You may enjoy your success, tho' attained by hypocrisy and the sole aid of the unprincipled impostor, which title you have deservedly adopted since the scurrilous invective was darted at the victor of adversity, your butt for calumny : your criterion is approached, when you may rescue fidelity from the rapacious jaws of ingratitude, and by an absolution of your errors, reinstate that wonted praise your once laudable actions inherited from a truly discerning people.

Abuse and malevolence are familiar to your elocution, or why did you fix so uncharitable ...

ANECDOTE
Of the TRADING SHADWELL JUSTICE.

FOrtunately for GREAT-BRITAIN, the hero of this *Anecdote* was ever trained up for its defence. He formerly defended it by ARMS—as affectually, as now by—the STATUTES.—Allowing it honorable, yet his former station had the stamp of meanness and inferiority, as now it has, in the *trading* execution of his office. The following will throw a light upon the whole.—

He was an officer of marines on board the ********* privateer, and by some dirty compliances, paved his way to the captain's table and his friendship.—Nature had furnished him with an unblushing set of features !—a heart secure from the approach of feeling !—and that low penetrating kind of understanding, which is usually her first present, to equip a complete villain !—A fortune thus gained in the estimation of mankind, is alarming to the individual, and the public ; and often drives the former to injure the latter, contrary to his wishes.—It was well known, that fortune for some time did not attend the above-mentioned privateer, and the crew continued at sea a considerable while, prizeless, and inactive.—Revolving this hopeless situation in his mind, the faithful officer of marines concluded, that in this instance at least, "*Necessity had no law.*" —Accordingly he intimated to his friend, who commanded the ship, that it was better to avail themselves of a favorable opportunity of disposing of the ship, cargo, stores, &c. by running into—*Cadiz*, than to lie log-like upon the watry element; eating inglorious salt beef, and stale biscuit.—The captain, as a man of honor, despised the proposal; but could not totally reject the sycophant, who had too closely twined himself round his bosom.——Repeated, and pressing solicitations from the *marine*, worked imperceptibly on the commander, and would most assuredly have sapped his honor, had not the interposition of Providence prevented such an insult being offered to the British flag. —A French privateer espying this sail, came up with, and by an honorable, though easy conquest, seized what was going to be treacherously, and villainously bartered away.

A matchless superintendant over the actions of others, who has wantonly trampled on those laws, he is now deputed to protect from violation !

Morning Post.

FOREIGN INTELLIGENCE.

Extract of a letter from Warsaw, Nov. 7.

THIS unfortunate city, the capital of a more unfortunate kingdom, is likely to be torn in pieces by intestine divisions.

Fig. 78. *The second title of* The Morning Post

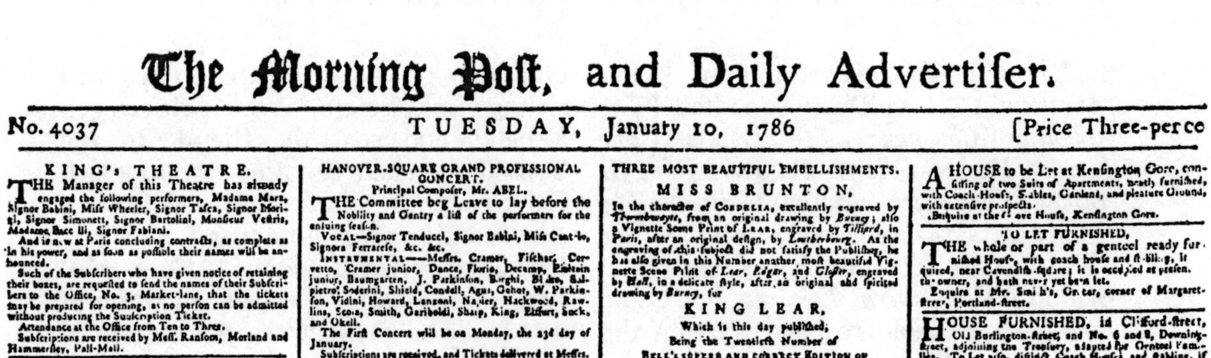

The Morning Post, and Daily Advertiser.

No. 4037 TUESDAY, January 10, 1786 [Price Three-pence

KING's THEATRE.

THE Manager of this Theatre has already engaged the following performers, Madame Mara, Signor Babini, Miss Wheeler, Signor Tasca, Signor Morigi, Signor Simonett, Signor Bartolini, Monsieur Vestris, Madame Baccelli, Signor Fabiani.

And is now at Paris concluding contracts, as complete as in his power, and as soon as possible their names will be announced.

Such of the Subscribers who have given notice of retaining their boxes, are requested to send the names of their Subscribers to the Office, No. 3, Market-lane, that the tickets may be prepared for opening, as no person can be admitted without producing the Subscription Ticket.

Attendance at the Office from Ten to Three.

Subscriptions are received by Mess. Ransom, Morland and Hammersley, Pall-Mall.

THEATRE-ROYAL, DRURY-LANE.

HANOVER-SQUARE GRAND PROFESSIONAL CONCERT.
Principal Composer, Mr. ABEL.

THE Committee beg Leave to lay before the Nobility and Gentry a list of the performers for the ensuing season.

VOCAL—Signor Tenducci, Signor Babini, Miss Cantelo, Signora Ferrarese, &c. &c.

INSTRUMENTAL——Messrs. Cramer, Fischer, Cervetto, Cramer junior, Dance, Florio, Decamp, Eichstein junior, Baumgarten, J. Parkinson, Borghi, Blake, Salpietro, Soderini, Shield, Condell, Agus, Gehot, W. Parkinson, Vidini, Howard, Lanzoni, Napier, Hackwood, Rawlins, Scola, Smith, Gariboldi, Sharp, King, Eiffert, Sock, and Okell.

The First Concert will be on Monday, the 23d day of January.

Subscriptions are received, and Tickets delivered at Messrs. Ransom, Morland, and Hammersley's, No. 57, Pall-mall.

THREE MOST BEAUTIFUL EMBELLISHMENTS.

MISS BRUNTON,

In the character of CORDELIA, excellently engraved by *Thornthwayte*, from an original drawing by *Burney*; also a Vignette Scene Print of LEAR, engraved by *Tilliard*, in *Paris*, after an original design, by *Loutherbourg*. As the engraving of this subject did not satisfy the Publisher, he has also given in this Number another most beautiful Vignette Scene Print of *Lear*, *Edgar*, and *Gloster*, engraved by *Hall*, in a delicate style, after an original and spirited drawing by *Burney*, for

KING LEAR,

Which is this day published;
Being the Twentieth Number of
BELL'S SUPERB AND CORRECT EDITION OF

A HOUSE to be Let at Kensington Gore, consisting of two Suits of Apartments, neatly furnished, with Coach-House, Stables, Garden, and pleasure Ground, with extensive prospects.

Enquire at the Grove House, Kensington Gore.

TO LET FURNISHED,

THE whole or part of a genteel ready furnished House, with coach house and stabling, if required, near Cavendish-square; it is occupied at present by the owner, and hath never yet been let.

Enquire at Mr. Smith's, Grocer, corner of Margaret-street, Portland-street.

HOUSE FURNISHED, in Clifford-street, Old Burlington-street, and No. 6 and 8, Downing-street, adjoining the Treasury, adapted for Genteel Families. To Let also, distinct Coach Houses and stabling, if required.

Fig. 79. *The third title of* The Morning Post

The prominent names of the period are John Almon, John Bell, Henry Bate, Edward Topham, the Woodfalls, Charles Say, John Walter, Daniel Stuart. *The Morning Herald, The World* (1787), *The Oracle* (1789) and *The Times* (1785) are the prominent new every-morning papers founded after *The Morning Post; The Star* (1788) and *The Courier* (1792) are the prominent every-evening papers; *The British Gazette, and Sunday Monitor* (1779), *The Sunday London Gazette* (1783), *The Observer* (1791) are the prominent Sunday papers got up in the general style of the dailies, and the compendious *Bell's Weekly Messenger* (1796) also a Sunday paper but giving a week's, rather than a day's, 'occurrences foreign and domestick'.[1]

The new developments in the daily field occurred following the successful establishment of *The Morning Chronicle* and *The Morning Post.* In 1775 the latter came into the editorship of the Rev. Henry Bate, who afterwards added Dudley to his surname. Bate was the town *beau* who made a national reputation as a result of his duel with Captain Crofts and his boxing with Captain Miles.[2] *The Morning Post,* under Bate's hand, was a notorious success, and made good profits. But there were quarrels. Bate left to found a new paper, *The Morning Herald.*

There were failures as well as successes in this period. Two we may notice, since their style was fresh. In January 1781 a sheet entitled *The Aurora,* of distinguished appearance, came out under the auspices of the fashionable hotel-keepers and the landlords of the principal taverns and inns in the West End. The paper looked like a very superior *Morning Post.* Its heading was new, being set in 60-point of Fry's very handsome capitals and lower-case, the sub-title 'Universal Advertiser' being in italic. The triple rule and the french rule were used with discretion. William Jerdan, the editor, recalls in his *Memoirs* that 'the paper was of superior quality, creamy and clear, the typography was unimpeachable, and the whole performance such as to justify the congratulations which everybody concerned showered upon everybody else'.

[1] For some account of (? Mrs) *E. Johnson's British Gazette and Sunday Monitor* and other Sunday papers see Chapter XIII *infra.*

[2] For an account see *The Vauxhall Affray* (London, J. Williams, 39 Fleet street, 1773). There was a counterfeit set up by discharged printers with the title *The Morning Post* from Nov. 4, 1776 and *The New Morning Post* from Nov. 14, 1776. The Revd. Bate and his colleague the Revd. Trusler were attacked by their former printers as 'two reverend parsonical banditti who, with all the chicane of sacerdotal hypocrisy, had not only insidiously wormed themselves into the knowledge of the customary emoluments of printing and publishing in general...' etc. The new *Post* ceased in February 1777 (cf. Morison, *John Bell,* 1745–1831).

The Noon Gazette, and Daily Spy.

Publiſhed at Twelve o'Clock, and contains all the actual News of the Nine Morning Papers.

MONDAY, DECEMBER 10, 1781. [Price Three-Pence

The above is a VIEW of the Town, Bay, and Rock of GIBRALTAR, with the Spaniſh Gun Boats firing at the Town. The Gun Boats generally take the advantage of a dark night, having deſtroyed great part of the Town and out-buildings.—In a few days will be given a GROUND PLAN of GIBRALTAR BAY and preſent SPANISH INCAMPMENTS.—The Print given in our Paper ſome time ago, repreſenting the Straights of Gibraltar, together with this and the one intended, will ſufficiently ſhow the whole of that important Fortreſs.

(Eleventh Night.)

By His MAJESTY's COMPANY.

AT the THEATRE-ROYAL, DRURY-LANE, THIS EVENING will be preſented
A New Tragedy, called

The FAIR CIRCASSIAN,

The Principal Characters by
Mr. SMITH,
Mr. BENSLEY,
Mr. PACKER,
Mr. R. PALMER,
Mr. WRIGHTEN,
And Mr. PALMER,
Miſs SIMSON,
And Miſs FARREN.
In Act III. An EPITHALAMIUM.
The Prologue to be ſpoken by Mr. Banniſter, jun.
And the Epilogue by Miſs Farren.
With New Scenes, Dreſſes, and Decorations.
The ſcenery deſigned by Mr. De Loutherbourg, and executed under his direction.

To which will be added the laſt new Pantomime Entertainment, in Two Acts, called

ROBINSON CRUSOE;
Or, HARLEQUIN FRIDAY.

The Principal Characters by
Mr. WRIGHT,
Mr. GRIMALDI,
Mr. DELPINI,
And Miſs COLLETT.
To conclude with a Dance by Miſs Armſtrong, the Miſs Stageldoirs, &c.
The Scenery deſigned by Mr. DE LOUTHERBOURG, and executed under his Direction.

☞ *The laſt new Tragedy of the* Fair Circaſſian *will be performed, for the 11th time, this evening, to which will added the pantomime entertainment of* Robinſon Cruſoe, *or* Harlequin Friday. *To-morrow, by particular deſire, for the 7th time, the dramatic piece of* King Arthur, *with* Catherine and Petruchio. *The public are reſpectfully acquainted that the 12th night of the* Fair Circaſſian *will be on Wedneſday next, with the 2nd time of the Paſtoral Opera of the* Gentle Shepherd, *after which both thoſe pieces muſt be laid aſide for ſome time, on account of the new Comic Opera of the* Carnival of Venice, *which will certainly be performed (for the 1ſt time) on Thurſday next. The principal characters by Mr. Palmer, Mr. Bannister, Mr. Parſons, Mr. Du Bellamy, Mr. Banniſter, jun. Mr. Burton, and Mr. Dodd; Mrs. Cargill, Mrs. Wrighten, Miſs Phillips, and Miſs Pope; with entirely new muſic, and a new overture, compoſed by Mr. Linley, and new ſcenes, dreſſes, dances, and decorations; the ſcenery deſigned by Mr. De Loutherbourg, and executed under his direction.*

Not acted this Seaſon.

AT the THEATRE-ROYAL, COVENT-GARDEN, This EVENING will be preſented, a Tragedy, called

JANE SHORE,

Haſtings, Mr. LEWIS,
Ratcliffe, Mr. Robſon, Gloſter, Mr. Clarke,
Cateſby, Mr. L'Eſtrange, Belmour, Mr. Hull,
Derby, Mr. Thompſon, And Dumont, Mr Wroughton;
Alicia, Miſs YOUNGE,
And Jane Shore, Mrs. YATES.
After which will be performed (for the 63d Time)
a Pantomime, called

HARLEQUIN FREE MASON.

To conclude with a PROCESSION of the principal GRAND MASTERS, from the Creation to the preſent Century, dreſſed in the HABITS of their reſpective AGES and COUNTRIES.
With New MUSIC, SCENES, DRESSES, PAGEANTS, and DECORATIONS.

The Paintings by Meſſrs. Richards, Carver, and Hodgings,
The Pantomime by Mr. Meſſink.
Books of the Songs, with an Explanation of the Pageants, to be had at the Theatre.

☞ *To-morrow (not acted this ſeaſon) the 1ſt part of* King Henry IV. *Falſtaff Mr. Henderſon, Prince of Wales Mr. Lewis, and Hotſpur Mr. Wroughton, with (for the 4th time here)* The Son in Law. *Ladies and gentlemen, pleaſe to obſerve that Farce will be performed only twice more at this Theatre. On Wedneſday (the 9th time) Mr. Macklin's comedy called the* Man of the World. *The new Comic Opera called* The Banditti, *being withdrawn by the Author, in order to undergo a total alteration cannot be produced again till after the Holidays. The new Pantomime, which has been long in preparation, called* The Choice of Harlequin, *will be preſented next week, with entire new ſcenes, muſic, dreſſes, decorations, and machinery. The ſcenery deſigned and executed by Meſſrs.* Richards, Carver, Hodgins, Mr. Cipriani, Mr. Catton, *and others. The muſic compoſed by Mr. Michael Arne.*

To the EDITOR of the NOON GAZETTE.

SIR,

IT appears from an extract from Blackſtone, in your Paper of this day, that annexing new fees to *old offices*, is a tax upon the ſubject which cannot be impoſed but by Act of Parliament. See Blackſtone's Commentaries, vol. I. page 272.

Our Miniſter thinks, and has acted very differently. For within theſe ſix months he has augmented the ſalaries of the eighteen Commiſſioners of Exciſe and Cuſtoms, TWO HUNDRED POUNDS each. This ſum of THREE THOUSAND SIX HUNDRED POUNDS muſt lay a TAX on the PUBLIC, without the CONSENT of PARLIAMENT. If a Treaſury Order is ſufficient to admit the Commiſſioners to pay themſelves an annual Penſion out of their Duties *on Stationary Wares*, why may not the ſame Order hereafter be iſſued to pay what other Bounties a Gracious Miniſter may be pleaſed to allow? If the Commiſſioners merit an enlarged Salary, it ſhould be done by PARLIAMENT. The Mode it is now done in flies in the Face of it, by evading its own Acts, which have laid the LAND TAX AND OTHER DUTIES ON PLACES.

Your's,

Dec. 6, 1781. AN OBSERVER.

A letter addreſſed to the PRINTER *of the* LONDON COURANT.

I Yeſterday accidentally dined with a very large and reſpectable body of the real friends of this country; men, Mr. Miller, who are the determined enemies of miniſterial perſecution, in whatever way it may be exerciſed. You will not, therefore, wonder, that your ſufferings ſhould very naturally become a general ſubject of their converſation, nor that it ſhould have ended in a reſolution to ſubſcribe towards your relief. Several plans were immediately ſuggeſted as beſt ſuited to ſerve you in this particular inſtance, but upon the intimation of a certain member, that the matter had been taken into conſideration more by a popular ſet of men, nothing farther of it was mentioned than that every member preſent would conſider your caſe, which, I doubt not, they will do with that liberality, which ever has, and ever will continue to adorn and fertilize the breaſt of an Engliſhman.

As one of the above mentioned body, I am ready to contribute my mite towards your relief, whenever it ſhall be called for; and I ſhould be ſorry, indeed, if I could for a moment heſitate in thinking, that there are not many hundreds more in this great metropolis, ready to come forward on the occaſion with the ſame chearfulneſs.

Our boaſted Freedom, the pride of our anceſtors, and the bleſſings of poſterity, lives but in the Liberty of the Preſs. Take that away and the foundation is gone. The noble fabric, raiſed by the bravery of our forefathers, and cemented by their beſt blood, in the words of an immortal Bard, will preſently diſſolve, and leave not a wreck behind. The preſervation of this invaluable privilege, ſo eſſentially neceſſary to our exiſtence as a free people, is no longer to be expected, than men can be found to ſtand forth as the avowed and reſponſible conductors of our public Prints in the hour of TYRANNY and PERSECUTION.

You have every claim upon the public as A CONSTITUTIONAL PRINTER, who after FOURTEEN YEARS ſervices in that line, is now immured within the walls of a priſon. Be aſſured, Mr. Miller, it is not in the nature of Engliſhmen, to ſuffer you, with A WIFE and SEVEN CHILDREN, to remain unaſſiſted. Thank God, this is yet a Land of Humanity, and the open hand of charity ſtill expands, in proportion to the oppreſſion, or diſtreſs, that invites its aid.

Dec. 8, 1781. A BRITON.

In anſwer to the above letter, Mr. Miller moſt reſpectfully begs the Writer of it will pleaſe to accept of his grateful acknowledgments, and will only preſume to obtrude himſelf ſo far on the Public, as to inform him, that he has been given to underſtand that his Caſe has been conſidered in a very popular and reſpectable Society, in which a zeal for the Public Good is not more the diſtinguiſhing characteriſtic, than a ſympathetic feeling for private ſufferings. Mr. Miller entreats this may likewiſe be conſidered as an anſwer to all thoſe who have been pleaſed, either by letter or meſſage, to think of him in his preſent ſtate of confinement. Mr. Miller is conſcious how much is to be expected from the humanity of the Public, and truſts he may at leaſt be conſidered as an old and faithful Servant. From the confidence he *repoſes* in it, his ſpirits will never forſake him under his impriſonment, nor a dread of the Fine and Expences attending it. He will add nothing more at preſent, than to entreat that he may be permitted to throw himſelf upon the Conſideration of the Public, in the ſervice of which he hopes he ſhall always be found to act with Gratitude, Firmneſs, and Reſpect.

*** VIRGILIUS VINEGAR—*and* A BLACK LETTER MAN—*are unavoidably poſtponed till tomorrow.*

For the NOON GAZETT,

SIR,

I Hear a great number of the Guards, as well as Conſtables, and others, are to be employed to-day to intimidate the People from meeting together in Weſtminſter-Hall, *under pretence of preſerving the public peace.*

I don't know the intention of my Fellow-Citizens; but if any man, whether in the name of a MAGISTRATE, a CONSTABLE, or SOLDIER, ſhall dare to ſtop me from going into the Hall, or interrupt me from expreſſing my ſentiments when in it, on the preſent alarming criſis of Public Affairs, I hereby ſolemnly pledge myſelf, for one, that I WILL RESIST ANY THING OF THE KIND, and will come PROPERLY ARMED for THAT PURPOSE.

NOW OR NEVER!

Bow-ſtreet, Dec. 8.

To the INHABITANTS *of* WESTMINSTER.

Fellow Citizens, and Fellow Sufferers!

THE preſent alarming criſis of affairs, demands both your attention, and aſſiſtance. The multiplied expenditures in fruitleſs attempts, and theſe terminating in national diſgrace, call aloud for remedy: Review with attention what

Fig. 80. *Vincent Trehearn's* The Noon Gazette, 1781

The Aurora, as befitted a paper published in the interests of hotel-keepers, was given a handsome send-off before a grand muster at the Imperial Hotel, Covent Garden, then kept by Mr Kinsey, the leading proprietor. Only forty-two numbers of this precursor of *The Morning Advertiser*, the present licensed victuallers' organ, were published.

The same year saw the issue of another unsuccessful effort which, as far as typography and other features of make-up are concerned, deserved success—*The Noon Gazette, and Daily Spy*, 'Published at Twelve o'Clock, and contains

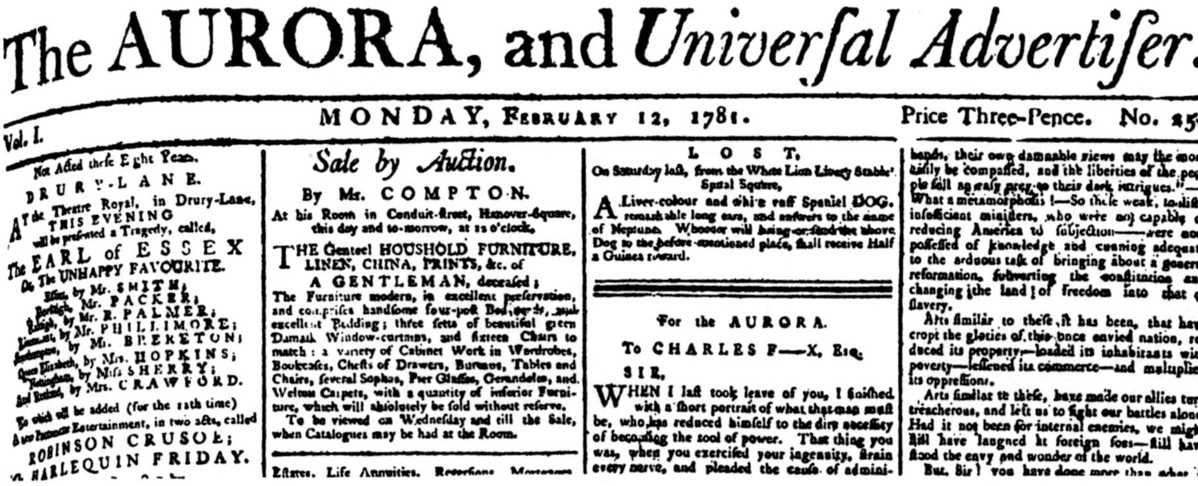

The AURORA, and *Univerſal Advertiſer.*

Vol. I. MONDAY, February 12, 1781. Price Three-Pence. No. 25.

Not Acted these Eight Years.
DRURY-LANE.
At the Theatre Royal, in Drury-Lane, THIS EVENING will be presented a Tragedy, called,
The EARL of ESSEX
Or, The UNHAPPY FAVOURITE.
Essex, by Mr. SMITH;
Southampton, by Mr. PACKER;
Burleigh, by Mr. R. PALMER;
Raleigh, by Mr. PHILLIMORE;
Lieutenant, by Mr. BRERETON;
Southampton, by Mrs. HOPKINS;
Queen Elizabeth, by Mrs. HOPKINS;
Nottingham, by Miss SHERRY;
And Rutland, by Mrs. CRAWFORD.
To which will be added (for the 12th time) A new Pantomime Entertainment, in two acts, called
ROBINSON CRUSOE;
Or, HARLEQUIN FRIDAY.

Sale by Auction.
By Mr. COMPTON.
At his Room in Conduit-street, Hanover-square, this day and to-morrow, at 12 o'clock,
THE Genteel HOUSHOLD FURNITURE, LINEN, CHINA, PRINTS, &c. of
A GENTLEMAN, deceased;
The Furniture modern, in excellent preservation, and comprises handsome four-post Bedsteads, and excellent Bedding; three setts of beautiful green Damask Window-curtains, and sixteen Chairs to match: a variety of Cabinet Work in Wardrobes, Bookcases, Chests of Drawers, Bureaus, Tables and Chairs, several Sophas, Pier Glasses, Gerandoles, and Welton Carpets, with a quantity of inferior Furniture, which will absolutely be sold without reserve.
To be viewed on Wednesday and till the Sale, when Catalogues may be had at the Room.
Estates, Life Annuities, Reversions, Mortgages

LOST,
On Saturday last, from the White Lion Livery Stable, Spital Square,
A Liver-colour and white rough Spaniel DOG, remarkable long ears, and answers to the name of Neptune. Whoever will bring or send the above Dog to the before-mentioned place, shall receive Half a Guinea reward.

For the AURORA.
To CHARLES F—X, Esq.
SIR,
WHEN I last took leave of you, I finished with a short portrait of what that man must be, who has reduced himself to the dire necessity of becoming the tool of power. That thing you was, when you exercised your ingenuity, strain every nerve, and pleaded the cause of admini-

hands, their own damnable views may the more easily be compassed, and the liberties of the people fall an easy prey to their dark intrigues."—What a metamorphosis!—So these weak, foolish, insufficient ministers, who were not capable of reducing America to subjection—were now possessed of knowledge and cunning adequate to the arduous task of bringing about a general reformation, subverting the constitution and changing the land of freedom into that of slavery.
Arts similar to these, it has been, that have cropt the glories of this once envied nation, reduced its property,—loaded its inhabitants with poverty—lessened its commerce—and multiplied its oppressions.
Arts similar to these, have made our allies turn treacherous, and left us to fight our battles alone. Had it not been for internal enemies, we might still have laughed at foreign foes—still have stood the envy and wonder of the world.
But, Sir! you have done more than [illegible]

Fig. 81

all the actual News of the Nine Morning Papers'. Only two sheets, dated December 10 and 26, 1781, remain. There is a record that in the July of 1781 'the printer was fined a hundred pounds and imprisoned for twelve months, and, for an aggravated paragraph, a second hundred pounds and sentenced to a further six months'.[1] As this printer was no doubt in gaol in December, the imprint to the extant copies, December 10 and 26, Vincent Trehearn, jun., is probably that of a nominee. Neither of the surviving issues bears a serial number. The issue of December 10 is a remarkably interesting achievement. Typographically, its merits entitle it to the respect which elsewhere we have given to Bell. The matter is well leaded, and, although there are no such practical innovations as the laying aside of the long ſ, the increased legibility due to leading alone makes it a very distinguished production. Another feature, as agreeable as it is conspicuous, is the remarkably fine block 11 in. × $4\frac{5}{8}$ in. deep of the Rock of Gibraltar in the background, with seven Spanish gun-boats in the foreground bombarding

[1] *Gentleman's Magazine*, August 1781.

the town. The block is a spirited and technically admirable piece of work, cut apparently in two, if not three sections, and follows a 'Print given in our Paper some time ago, representing the Straights of Gibraltar'. In view of the fact that only two numbers remain, it is not possible to carry further the account of this singularly interesting paper.

CHAPTER XI

THE MATURE EIGHTEENTH-CENTURY NEWSPAPER, § 2

1786–1789

The English Chronicle	1786
The World	1787
The Daily Universal Register: The Times	1785: 1788
The Star	1788
The Oracle	1789
Woodfall's Diary	1789

CHAPTER XI

THE MATURE EIGHTEENTH-CENTURY NEWSPAPER, § 2

1786–1789

FOLLOWING the secession of Bate, *The Morning Post* lost Bell, in 1785. With John Wheble[1] he engaged in a thrice-weekly evening paper entitled at its foundation (1779) *The English Chronicle*,[2] and later (July 1781) *The English Chronicle; Or, Universal Evening-Post.* With No. 1082, for January 28, 1786, the paper announced that new proprietors had entrusted the management of the paper to persons 'from whose judgment, ability, activity, and independence, they are most confident of success'. This pronouncement, in the inflated English of John Bell,[3] recalls the introductions written for the Chronicles published by Payne and Owen for the previous generation. The typographical style of *The English Chronicle* under the new proprietors underwent some change. The heading was again reconstructed: the main legend was set in large (60-point) caps and smalls, and the sub-title in text. The device was a finely engraved royal arms into the base of which there was set, in small type, the lines 'John Bell, Bookseller to His Royal Highness the Prince of Wales'. At the head of the first column of the front page, introducing 'Foreign Intelligence', is an eight-line factotum of the Prince's Star with text '*Honi soit*', etc. The 'Postscript' in the back page was headed with a handsome block of the Prince's 'feathers' and

[1] Wheble was succeeded as publisher in 1773 by J. Williams, former publisher of *The North Briton*; by R. Haswell, 1775; by J. Burd and R. Bell, 1776. In November 1776, George Corrall, bookseller, published a false *Morning Post* on behalf of the two dismissed printers, Bigg and Cox. The format was identical (see S. Morison, *John Bell*, pp. 6ff.).

[2] I am ignorant of the original founder. The earliest issue in the British Museum is No. 191, March 21, 1780, which carries a fine, large, britannia device in the centre of the heading (in 60-point Caslon), a flower factotum at the top of col. 1, p. 1, and triple-rule cut-offs. The imprint is: 'London, Printed by J. S. Barr, at the Paper Warehouse, opposite Catherine street, Strand'. With No. 400, July 21, 1781, the paper supplanted britannia by a scriptorial cypher G.R. device, and was published by 'R. Haswell, 283 Strand'. Both Barr and Haswell were, at one time or other, publishers of *The Morning Post*.

[3] I was unaware of the existence of *The English Chronicle* when I recently published the *Memoir of John Bell.*

The ENGLISH CHRONICLE; Or, Universal Evening-Post.

J. Bell, Bookseller to his Royal Highness the Prince of Wales.

No. 1082] From THURSDAY, January 26, to SATURDAY, January 28, 1786. [Price Threepence.

ENGLISH CHRONICLE OFFICE,
opposite NORFOLK-STREET, STRAND.

THE Proprietors, who have lately purchased THE ENGLISH CHRONICLE, have now assumed their right, and entrusted the management of it to persons, from whose judgment, abilities, activity, and independence, they are most confident of success. They will not pledge themselves for a pertinacious adherence to any politics, party, or subject, longer than circumstances, in their own opinion, will warrant, and yet they hope to act judiciously, and with spirit, whatever cause they may chuse to espouse; but they will promise, for the satisfaction of private families, that not a sentence, *even by Advertisement*, shall be admitted into their print, which may wound the ear of modesty. They will endeavour to render THE ENGLISH CHRONICLE a valuable Miscellany, of Commercial Intelligence, of Useful and Entertaining Information; and they are persuaded it will be looked up to in future as the Political Beacon, which is erected to point out the *real* dangers that may threaten the welfare of the State. These are the sentiments, and resolutions, which have met with the approbation and promises of support from many persons of taste, and others highly distinguished for their eminence in Literature; nevertheless the correspondence of the ingenious and well informed, in general, is solicited, which will ever meet with the most respectful attention.

If any difficulties should arise in obtaining THE ENGLISH CHRONICLE every TUESDAY, THURSDAY, and SATURDAY Evenings, the Publisher will obviate the inconvenience, on receiving a message or line for that purpose.

Foreign Intelligence.

NAPLES, *January* 4.

A LETTER from on board the Andromache frigate, Captain O'Hara, says, "After a stay of two days at Marseilles, whither we had been sent by the Commodore's order, to accommodate their Royal Highnesses the Duke and Duchess of Cumberland and their suite, who are now making a tour to all the ports of Italy, we sailed on New Year's day morning, and are just arrived safe in this bay, where our visitors are landed, under a discharge of cannon from the Neapolitan Admiral, who has his yellow flag on board a very fine ship, La Reine, of 66 guns. There are also four other Neapolitans, two Dutch, and one French man of war here. Our stay is very uncertain, as we are to attend the Duke till he shall think fit to discharge Captain O'Hara and the ship from further services. Our crew have lived most excellently since we have been on this business. There is a talk that that the Court of Naples will be entertained on board before we sail; but this is not yet certain. Our next place we expect to be Venice, to see the Doge's annual wedding of the Adriatic (one of the finest aquatic shews in the world) and from thence we shall probably be back to Gibraltar in June.

Ireland.

DUBLIN, *Jan.* 21. In the House of Peers yesterday, Lord Tyrone reported the Address to his Majesty, which was opposed by Lord Mountgarret, and supported by the Lord Chancellor and Lord Earlsfort; it afterwards passed in the affirmative—The Earl of Port Arlington reported the Address to the Lord Lieutenant, which was also agreed to.—The Lord Chancellor gave notice, that his Grace the Lord Lieutenant would receive the Address at three o'clock this day.

The Lord Lieutenant's Speech is certainly a master stroke in politics; it promises nothing, and leaves room for every thing—so that if it is objected, that no Commercial Negociation ought to take place between the two kingdoms, the answer is, look to the Speech; Is there any thing there warranting a supposition, that the measure is intended? If it is said a negociation ought to take place—look to the Speech: Is it said to be relinquished? No:—And so, throughout the whole, save the common place of charter-schools and agriculture, it appears like the response of an oracle, containing a double meaning, and leaving every body to construe it according to their inclination.

It is surprising that when the accumulation of debt is so injurious to the nation, the 140,000l. should not be applied to a Sinking Fund, in order to pay off our old debt—but perhaps, tho' it may correspond very well with the situation of some gentlemen not to *borrow* more, it would not be quite so congenial to their feelings to *pay* off what they already *owe*—men of delicate feelings must certainly not be hurt.

How happy is it for Ireland, that notwithstanding our obstinacy in refusing British offers, that virtuous sister is too forgiving to resent this refusal. She still *generously* pours in her manufactures upon us; and even the new stores at the Parliament House, are monuments of her affection. The word *London* stands conspicuous to the eye, and proves, that though we could not manufacture a grate fit to warm the toe of a footman, England kindly supplies the defect, and sends over patent stoves for the use of the party coloured gentry.

General Post-Office, Nov. 5, 1785.

MR. PALMER *having engaged to accomplish his plan for the conveyance of his Majesty's Mails to all parts of the kingdom as soon as possible, the Letters for every part of Great Britain and Ireland, must be put into the Receiving Houses before Five o'clock in the evening, and into this Office before Seven, in order to prevent the inconveniencies which have arisen to the Public from two deliveries in London on the same day, and the sending out the mails at different hours in the same evening.*

The letters are intended to be sent out regularly from hence between the hours of Nine and Ten in the morning, so as to reach the most distant parts of the town by twelve at noon.

It is necessary that all Newspapers should be put into this Office before Six o'clock, otherwise they cannot be certain of an immediate conveyance.

By command of the Postmaster-General,
ANTHONY TODD, *Sec.*

The following (exclusive of those on the Cross Post Roads) are the Mail Coaches already established.

To BATH and BRISTOL, from the Swan with Two Necks, Lad-lane, and the Gloucester Coffee-house, Piccadilly.

To NORWICH and YARMOUTH, through Newmarket and Thetford, from the White Horse, Fetter-lane.

To NORWICH, through Colchester and Ipswich from the same place.

To NOTTINGHAM and LEEDS, from the Bull and Mouth, in Bull and Mouth-street.

To MANCHESTER, through Derby, from the Swan with Two Necks, Lad-lane.

To LIVERPOOL, through Coventry and Litchfield, from the same place.

To PORTSMOUTH, from the Angel behind St. Clement's Church.

To SOUTHAMPTON and POOLE, from the Bell and Crown, Holborn, and the Gloucester Coffee-house, Piccadilly.

To GLOUCESTER, SWANSEA, and CAERMARTHEN, from the Angel, behind St. Clement's Church, and the Gloucester Coffee-house, Piccadilly.

To HEREFORD, BRECKNOCK, CAERMARTHEN, and MILFORD HAVEN, from the Angel behind St. Clement's Church, and the Gloucester Coffee-house, Piccadilly.

To WORCESTER and LUDLOW, from the George and Blue Boar, Holborn, and the Gloucester Coffee-house, Piccadilly.

To BATH and BRISTOL, through Andover and Devizes, from the Swan with Two Necks, Lad-lane, and the Gloucester Coffee-house, Piccadilly.

To SHREWSBURY and to BIRMINGHAM, KIDDERMINSTER and BEWDLEY, from the Bull and Mouth, Bull and Mouth-street.

To OXFORD, and to CIRENCESTER, TEDBURY, and STROUD, from the George and Blue Boar, and also from the Bell and Crown, Holborn.

To WINDSOR, from the Three Cups, Bread-street, and the Gloucester Coffee-house, Piccadilly.

To CHESTER and HOLYHEAD, from the Swan with Two Necks, Lad-lane.

To CARLISLE, by way of Manchester, from the Swan with Two Necks, Lad-lane.

To DOVER, from the George and Blue Boar, Holborn, and the Gloucester Coffee-house, Piccadilly, to York-House, Dover.

To EXETER, through Salisbury, Blandford, and Dorchester, from the Swan with Two Necks, Lad-lane, and the Gloucester Coffee-house, Piccadilly.

And to EXETER, by the way of Wells, Bridgewater, and Taunton, from the Swan with Two Necks, Lad-lane, and the Gloucester Coffee-house, Piccadilly.

General Post Office, Jan. 28, 1786.

THE *Owners of a Bank Note of Ten Pounds, and of two Promissory Notes of the Lincoln Bank for Ten Pounds each, sent in the mail that was robbed near Hull on the 2d instant, are desired to apply immediately at this Office.*

By command of the Postmaster General,
ANTHONY TODD, *Secretary.*

East India House, 20th Jan. 1786.

THE *Court of Directors of the United Company of Merchants of England trading to the East Indies, do hereby give notice,*

That they are ready to receive proposals in writing, at any time on or before the 3d of February next, from any persons, on what terms, and conditions, they are willing to let their ships to China, and all parts of the East Indies, for one or more voyages, to be chartered at builders contract tonage, and the kintlage to be considered as part thereof; and that the same be severally sealed up, and left with the Secretary, in order to be laid before this Court.

THOMAS MORTON, *Secretary.*

YORKSHIRE.

WANTED to purchase in the county of York, a CAPITAL MANSION, with a demesne and estate contiguous, well watered and wooded, having a large command and royalty annexed to it, and being in every respect fit for a Nobleman with a large family.

Proposals to be sent to Mess. Kilvington and Lowndes, in Lincoln's Inn, London.

This day is published, price 2s. 6d.

THE Present POLITICS of IRELAND: Consisting of, I. The Right Hon. Mr. Hutchinson's Letter to his Constituents at Cork. II. Parliamentary Discussions of the Irish Arrangements; by

Messrs. Connolly,	Fitzgibbon,
Grattan,	Mason,
and	Foster,
Flood,	Hutchinson,
Against them.	For them.

III. Mr. Ledan's Observations on the relative situation of Great Britain and Ireland; with Notes thereon by an English Editor.

Printed for John Stockdale, opposite Burlington-house, Piccadilly; Scatcherd and Whitaker, Ave-maria-lane; and W. Richardson, Royal Exchange.

CRITICK

WILL Cover this Season at Boroughbridge, at Three Guineas a Mare, and Five Shillings the Groom.

CRITICK's PEDIGREE.

"Critick was got by Match'em, brother to Jemmy; was out of Miss Stamford, a grey mare I bought of Dick Stamford; she was got by Whitenose, his dam by Lord Portman's Spinner; her grand dam by his Lordship's Old Crab; his great grand dam by Darley's Arabian, his gt gt grand dam called Fustian, bred by old Squire Thomson, of Marston, in Yorkshire, out of his Old Mil-key, a noted good runner; she was bred by old Mr. Leeds, of North Milford.

"Charles-street—taken from my stud book.

"P. BLAKE.

For the USE of SCHOOLS.

This day is published, price 3s. 6d. bound,

A New Edition of the SPEAKER; or MISCELLANEOUS PIECES, selected from the best English Writers, and disposed under proper Heads, with a view to facilitate the improvement of youth in reading and speaking, as well as to lead young persons into some acquaintance with the most valuable writers, and impress upon their minds the sentiments of honour and virtue. To which is prefixed, an Essay on Elocution. By W. Enfeld, LL.D.

Printed for J. Johnson, in St. Paul's Church-yard, where may had Exercises in Elocution, being a sequel to the Speaker. Price 3s. 6d. Also elegant editions, in 8vo. with Copper-plates, price 5s. each, in boards.

This Day are published, in 2 vols. (small 8vo. price 8s. sewed, or 10s. bound.

SERMONS on the Efficacy of Prayer and Intercession; on the Articles of the Christian Faith; on the Ten Commandments; and on the Lord's Supper.

By SAMUEL OGDEN, D.D.

Late Woodwardian Professor in the University of Cambridge.

To which is prefixed an Account of the Author's Life.

By Dr. H. HALIFAX, Bishop of Gloucester.

Cambridge: printed by J. Archdeacon, Printer to the University; for J. Johnson, in St. Paul's Church-yard, London.

To LADIES that wear FALSE HAIR.

W. VICKERY, from Paris, respectfully assures the Ladies, that his transparent Toupees are the most natural, elegant, and convenient Tetes ever made. They sit firm to the head, suit every Lady's hair, whether short or thin; as well as those that by choice or necessity wear whole Tetes. Mr. Vickery is emboldened to say farther for their reputation, and that he does from the astonishing number he daily sells, and the approbation they meet with from Ladies of the highest rank, as also from the generality of Ladies that now wear them; that they are of all others the most easy, light, and best suited to the present mode of dress, but well dress in any future fashion. Ladies sending a pattern, and saying whether for elderly, middle-aged, or young Ladies, suited from 16s. to 1l. 1s. each.

N.B. For the satisfaction of Ladies that have not made trial of them, they will be exchanged or altered without any other charge.—Braids from 10s. 6d. to 10l. 10s. each. Le Chignon a la Figaro, at 10s. 6d. each. Ringlets and Curls, 2s. a pair.—No. 119, BISHOPSGATE-STREET, near CORNHILL.

THE BEST NEWCASTLE LARGE COALS, at 36s. a Chaldron, of 13 Sacks, containing 39 Bushels, are delivered, cartage free, at any part of the town at the above price for ready money, and 1s. a chaldron for each mile off the stones, and the tolls paid.

Orders in writing, by post, or otherwise, directed to the Proprietors of the Coal Merchants Office, No. 8, Mermaid-court, Charing-cross, will be carefully executed.

N.B. Please to observe, the best Coals are at the above price; inferior at one or two shillings lower.

That the purchasers may be sure of having fair measure with all Coals sent from this office, the Real Meters Tickets, signed by the principal and deputy Meters, are sent, and any purchaser may see them measured.

Country carts immediately supplied at 34s. a chaldron, by applying at the office.

To the LADIES.

WINTER CLOAKS, MUFFS, and FUR TRIMMINGS.

MESSRS. SMITH and Co. at the Three Pigeons and Sceptre, No. 173, Fleet-street, opposite Serjeant's Inn, beg leave to inform their friends, that they have now made by them, of the most fashionable winter patterns, an assortment of blue, white, pink, and brown Sattin Cloaks, trimmed with white, red, and blue Fox, price with white trimmings from 50s. to 5l. 5s. each. In red and blue, from 4l. 4s. to 10l. 10s. each. Also Alamode Cloaks trimmed with Gauze and Laces, from 16s. to 5l. 5s. each. Black Pelese, from 36s. to 5l. 5s. each. Ell-wide Lawn Handkerchiefs, from 2s. to 3s. 6d. Ell-wide Tiffany dittos from 2s. 6d. to 4s. 6d. each. Crape Gauze, from 10d. per yard upwards; other Gauzes in proportion. Beautiful ell-wide Lawn Gauze, from 2s. to 3s. per yard. Ditto ell-wide Tiffany, at 2s. 6d. and upwards. Three-quarter wide Tiffany, from 12d. to 16d. Yard-wide Tiffany, from 18d. to 3s. per yard. Some curious black Book Muslin, or uncrimped Crape, at 2s. and 2s. 6d. usually sold at 4s. and 4s. 6d. per yard. White and coloured half-ell Persians, from 16d. to 2s. per yard. Narrow Black and White Real Crape, from 12d. to 18d. per yard. Yard-wide Black Real Crape, from 2s. 6d. to 4s. 6d. per yard.

Our Alamodes for Cloaks, we are convinced, are not to be equalled in town for colour and wear; and notwithstanding the great advance on Silk, are sold at the reduced prices: Rich white and coloured three-quarter figured and plain Satin, for Cloaks and Gowns, from 6s. to 8s. 6d. per yard. Our friends, who chuse to make their Cloaks, will have them cut out gratis.

Some curious Buff Shawls, from 3. to 12s. each, and which are preferred to most others for warmth and wear, and have that valuable quality of not changing. Red and white Fox Muffs, from 10s. 6d. to 2l. 2s. and 3l. 3s. each; but of the real blue Fox, it is proper to remark, that at least a week's notice must be given, either for a Muff or Trimming.

N.B. Ladies who have orders for Ribbands in quantities, either for abroad, or home consumption, will have 12 and a half per cent. or 2s. 6d. in the pound allowed, in order to save them the trouble of applying to the warehouses.—Sixpenny colour'd Sattin Ribbands, at 4½d. and Tenpenny colour'd ditto, at 6d. and 7d. per yard.

HIGHFLYER

WILL Cover Mares at Ely, in Cambridgeshire, at Fifteen Guineas a Mare, and Half a Guinea the Groom.

*** Highflyer is a most certain foal-getter, and gets more colts than fillies.

There will be good grass, hay, corn, &c.

Ely is 13 miles from Newmarket, 17 from Cambridge, and 22 from Huntingdon. No mares will be delivered till paid for, or an order in writing from Mr. Tattersall.

Highflyer was got by Herod; his dam (Marc Anthony's dam) by Blank; grand dam by Regulus, a daughter of Soreheels, which mare was the dam of Matchless, South, and Danby Cade), a daughter of Makeless, and was Sir Ralph Milbank's famous black mare, the dam of Hartley's Blind Horse. At Newmarket Second October Meeting, 1777, Highflyer won a sweepstakes of 900gs. for three years olds, colts 8st. fillies 7st. 11lb. D. I. beating Justice, Bourdeaux, Sweetmarjoram, &c. In the second Spring Meeting, 1778, Highflyer won a sweepstakes of 2500gs. for four year olds, colts 8st. fillies 7st. 11lb. B.C. beating Il'mio, Thunderbolt, Jupiter, Chesfield, Fulmine, and four others. In the July Meeting, Highflyer won a sweepstakes of 600gs. colts 8st. 7lb. fillies 8st. 4lb. B.C. beating Stormer, Statellite, and Dragoon. In the first October Meeting, he won the renewed 1400gs. colts 8st. 10lb. fillies 8st. 7lb. B.C. beating Il'mio, Firm, and Jupiter; he also won the weights and scales plate of 100gs. wt. for age, B.C. beating Pearl, Vestal, and Tremamondo. In the second October meeting he received 400gs. forfeit in a post sweepstakes. In the Houghton meeting Highflyer at 8st. beat Lord Clermont's Dictator, five years old, 8st. 7lb B.C. 500gs. In the first Spring meeting, 1779, Highflyer at 8st. 3lb. won a sweepstakes of 750gs. B.C. beating Mr. Stapleton's Magog, 8st. 7lb. In the second Spring meeting, he won a sweepstakes of 700gs. 8st. 7lb. each, B.C. beating Dorimant, aged, and Dictator, six years old. He afterwards walked over for a subscription of 280gs. at Nottingham, and the great subscription of 295l. at York; he also won the great subscription of 295l. for six year olds and aged horses, at York. He likewise won the King's plate at Litchfield, beating at two heats (though lame) Lord Grosvenor's bay mare, by Dux, and Mr. Smallman's Chesfield. Highflyer was never beat, nor ever paid a forfeit, and was undoubtedly the best horse of his time in England. The sums he won and received amounts to 8920gs. though he never started after five years old. HIGHFLYER is sire of his Royal Highness the Prince of Wales's ROCKINGHAM, (late Camden) who has proved himself to be much superior in point of running, to any other horse in England; he is also sire of Lord Derby's Lady Teazle, Mr. Bullock's Miss Blancoard, Mr. Coates's Omphale, Mr. Goodrick's Dexter, Mr. Hutchinson's Fairy, Sir Frank Standish's Delpini, Mr. Bullock's Balloon, &c.

N.B. Highflyer gave Dorimant two years, and beat him easy.

TANDEM

WILL cover Mares at Brumton near Catterick and Richmond, in Yorkshire, at Three Guineas a Mare, and a Crown the Groom.

TANDEM, the property of the late ROBERT SHAFTO, Esq. was bred by him, and got by Syphon; his dam by Regulus; grandam by Snip; great grandam by Cottingham, (son of Hartley's Blind Horse); gt gt grandam, called the Warlock Galloway, (and was the dam of Mr. Routh's Cub and Blackeyes, and grandam of Judgment and Apollo) by Lister's Snake, a daughter of the Bald Galloway, a daughter of the Carlisle Turk, (sire of the Carlisle Gelding's dam) and out of a daughter of the Pulleine Old Arabian. At Newmarket in July 1777, Tandem, (then four years old) at 8st. 13lb. beat Lord Abingdon's Oxonian, 6yrs old, 8st. two miles of B.C. 50gs. In the second October Meeting, Tandem at 8st. 3lb. won a sweepstakes of 600gs. B.C. beat Lord Clermont's Mistly, 8st. and Mr. Vernon's Warwick, 8st. 6lb. In the first Spring Meeting, 1778, Tandem at 8st. 4lb. won a sweepstakes of 1050gs. B.C. beating Dictator 8st. 9lb. and Vengeance, 7st. In the second Spring Meeting, Tandem at 8st. 8lb. beat Laburnum, 7st. 11lb. B.C. 300gs. and received 200gs. from Mr. C. Pigott's Hottentot. About this time, Mr. Shafto refused 1800gs. for Tandem. He was sent to York to run for the great subscription against Magog, &c. but unfortunately broke down in his exercise about a week before the race, and was never sound after. On Mr. Shafto's demise, Tandem became the property of Mr. Wastell, and at Newmarket July Meeting, 1780, he won (though lame) the 60gs. plate, wt. for age, D.I. beating Fame, Cordial, Wickham, Bridget, Nabob Zadee, and Rocket. This was the last time of Tandem's running.

N.B. Tandem gave Oxonian two years and 13lb. and won easy.

GLASS's MAGNESIA,

APPROVED and recommended by the most eminent of the faculty, is sold by W. Jackson, Printer, in Oxford, in Guinea, Half Guinea, Six Shilling, and Three Shilling boxes, with directions.

*** This preparation, which for purity and goodness far exceeds every other, is well known to be the most powerful corrector of acid in the stomach and bowels; and is therefore particularly efficacious in childrens disorders, and may be safely given to them in their earliest infancy. It is equally serviceable to persons of more advanced years, of delicate constitutions, and to those whose powers of digestion are naturally weak, or impaired.—The heart-burn it constantly cures, and is an effectual remedy for habitual costiveness. It is also the most gentle purgative yet discovered, operates without sickness or griping, requires no confinement, or regimen of diet, and is entirely without smell or taste.

It is appointed to be sold in London by M. Davis, bookseller, in Piccadilly; W. Nicoll, and F. Newbery, in St. Paul's Church-yard, (with usual allowances) and by a dealer in most of the principal towns in England.

Dr. LOCKYER's PILLS

So well known for their great Cures both at home and abroad,

FORMERLY sold in Racquet-court, Fleet-street, are now sold only at W. Nicoll's, No. 51. St. Paul's, Church-yard, Bookseller, wholesale and retail, with good allowance to merchants, captains, and country dealers.

These pills are made up in tin boxes, fifty in the box, price 2s. and sealed at one end with the arms of T. Fyge, the Doctor's nephew, and the Doctor's coat of arms as usual.

N.B. The Proprietors having discovered that all these marks and seals are counterfeited by artful and designing men, for the purpose of selling a base and counterfeited medicine, in order to prevent the pernicious consequence of such spurious sort being obtruded on the public, each one will be now signed on the outside by M. Watson, one of the Proprietors.

Fig. 82. The English Chronicle *as published by John Bell*

the word 'Postscript' set in type in the ribbon at the base. In other respects the details of the paper shewed the hand of a typographic artist and enthusiast who can only be Mr Bell. There are sectional headings in a small size of text. The french rule (———) first introduced into *The Morning Post* during 1772, and only sparingly used there, or elsewhere, was employed to separate the several sections of *The English Chronicle.* The text is set throughout with the short round *s*, a novelty in the newspaper trade which had only been introduced into the regular printing of books in the previous year. In the first volume of his admirable set of Shakespeare,[1] Bell wrote that

in the mode of printing, too, he hath ventured to depart from the common mode by rejecting the long ſ in favour of the round one, as being less liable to error from the occasional imperfection of the letter *f*, and the frequent substitution of it for the long ſ; the regularity of the print is by that means very much promoted, the lines having the effect of being more open, without greatly adding additional distance.

The 'rejecting the long ſ in favour of the round one' applied to both the roman and the italic founts, and to every column of *The English Chronicle* of the date cited—Saturday, January 28, 1786—which is the unique surviving copy in any public library known to me. The single ſ in the composition occurs in the word 'Poſt' of the sub-title, allowed, one imagines, by oversight or perhaps because the old form of this familiar word was considered too well established for revision to be desirable. The natural conservatism of every class of reader had to be given consideration, and it may have been that the word 'Engliſh' in the old title was altered to 'ENGLISH' as having, for its generation, a more familiar aspect than 'English'. However, the plan of rejecting the long ſ was not approved, for the number dated September 30 of the same year, 1786, is printed throughout with the long ſ though published by the same Wheble at the same address.[2] It is more than probable that Bell had, by this date, withdrawn from partnership in *The English Chronicle,* for in the June of the same year, Captain Topham, late of the University of Cambridge, a young gentleman of means, was negotiating with him for the foundation of a new daily. Under the general editorial direction of Topham, *The World* made its *début* on January 1, 1787. It was

[1] Dedicated to H.R.H. the Prince of Wales.

[2] The heading device omits the name of Bell and includes in its place the notice 'Published TUESDAYS, THURSDAYS, AND SATURDAYS' for which room had to be made by cutting a larger base for fitting to the old royal device.

The World,
FASHIONABLE ADVERTISER.

NUMBER 1] MONDAY, JANUARY 1, 1787. [PRICE 3d.]

OPERA.

TO-MORROW, at the *King's Theatre*, in the HAY-MARKET, will be performed, A SERIOUS OPERA, in Two Acts, called,

ALCESTE.

The Music entirely new, by Monsieur GRESNICH.

THE PRINCIPAL CHARACTERS BY

Signor RUBINELLI,	Signor CREMONINI,
Signor CALVESI,	Signora SCHINOTTI,
Signor FABELLI,	And Madame MARA.

Leader of the Band, Mr. CRAMER.
Ballet-master, Mons. HUS.

End of ACT I. A DIVERTISSEMENT.
By Mademoiselle Mozon, Mons. L'Aborie, Mons. Henry, Monsieur Gricourt, Mad. Bithmer, Mad. Delsevre, and Madame JERVET PERIGNON,
Being her third appearance in England.

End of the Opera, the Ballet

LA CHERCHEUSE D'ESPRIT.

THE PRINCIPAL CHARACTERS BY
Mons. GOJON,
Being his third appearance in England.
Mons. Laborie, Mademoiselle Mozon, Mons. Henry, Mons. Gricourt, Mad. Delsevre, Mad. Bethmer, and Madame Jervet Perignon.
Painter and Machinist, Signor Gaeteno Marinari.
Taylor, Signor Luppino.

By Their MAJESTIES COMMAND, no Person can be admitted behind the Scenes.

Pit 10s. 6d.—First Gallery 5s.—Second Gallery 3s.

The Doors to be opened at *Half past Six*, and begin exactly at *Half past Seven o'Clock.*

Vivant Rex & Regina.

SUBSCRIPTIONS are received at Mess. *Ransom, Morland,* and *Hammersley's*, Bankers, No. 57, Pall-Mall, who will deliver the Subscription Tickets.

The Nobility and Gentry, Subscribers to the Opera-House, are respectfully entreated to send for them, in order to prevent future Mistakes, as nobody can be admitted without producing a Ticket.

N. B. To prevent inconvenience to the Nobility and Gentry in getting to their Carriages, they are most respectfully intreated to give positive orders to their Servants, *to set down and take up with the Horses Heads towards Pall-Mall. The Doors in Market-lane for Chairs only.*

GENERAL POST OFFICE.

December 30, 1786.

BANK NOTE for 15l. No. 513, dated 2d November, 1786.

THE PERSON in possession of the above BANK NOTE, or any through whose Hands it may have passed since the 16th of November, are requested to give immediate information at this Office.

By Command of the Postmaster-General,
ANTHONY TODD, *Secretary.*

FLOOR CLOTHS.

BULMER, FLOOR-CLOTH MANUFACTURER, to his MAJESTY, at No. 284, Strand, opposite Norfolk-street; and at his Manufactory, South side of St. James's Park, begs leave respectfully to acquaint Noblemen, Gentlemen, and the Public in general, that he has made, upon an entire new principle, without seams, a large quantity of dry and well-seasoned Floor and Passage Cloths, from small to very large dimensions, of the best quality, in great variety of new and elegant patterns, which he is now selling, wholesale and retail, upon the very lowest terms.

Merchants, Captains, and Shop-keepers, who take a quantity to sell again, will be allowed a Discount.

Old Cloths repaired, and painted to look as well as new.

JONES, JEWELLER, ST. JAMES'S-STREET,

BEGS Leave to acquaint the NOBILITY and GENTRY, That he is going to *quit Business*, and is now selling off his *valuable Stock*, consisting of fine articles in the Jewelling and Goldsmith branch. Dresden Porcelaine, and fine old China. Shells for Grottos, &c. &c.

N. B. The Shop to Let.

FOREIGN FRUITS.

Just imported from FRANCE, SPAIN, *and the* WEST-INDIES.

SPANISH Potatoes,	*Aman de Suede Pear,*
Malaga Grapes,	*Cashew-nuts, Hickery and Ground Nuts,*
Pomegranates,	*Cocoa-nuts and Yams,*
Boncbretien Pears,	*Water and Musk Melons.*
Colmar Pears,	

Which, with a variety of other scarce Fruits, may constantly be had in their respective Seasons, at the Old Fruit Shop, No. 4, facing the Mansion-House.

TO MR. J. P. DUBOURG,

NOTARY PUBLIC,
No. 5, Grocer's Alley, POULTRY.

SIR,

STUPIDITY is but a misfortune---but impudence and calumny are vices—which betray the baseness of the heart. I am told you spread a rumour in town, of my not having been admitted a Notary Public, *and what are your motives, I let every honest man determine. The proof of your asserting a most impudent* lye, *may easily be shewn to any one who will take the trouble to see the* Register of Doctors' Commons; *where I was duly admitted, on the 14th of Nov. 1783, through the medium of* CHARLES BISH, Esq; Proctor of that Court. *As to your being the only* French Notary, *who has a right to making instruments for France, it is another falsehood; and the protection of the* Courier de l'Europe, *is too paltry that you should be allowed such a degree of brazen-faced impudence.*

PETER GUEDON, NOTARY PUBLIC.
No. 5, James-street, Golden-square.

FENCING ACADEMY,

Bell-Yard, Carey-Street, Lincoln's-Inn.

MR. OLIVIER's PUBLIC DAYS are on MONDAYS, WEDNESDAYS, and FRIDAYS, from Twelve o'Clock till Three; and on the other days, attends Gentlemen at their own houses. Likewise private attendance at home at any hour appointed.

N.B. Mr. Olivier's new edition, intitled, FENCING FAMILIARIZED, dedicated by permission to the Right Hon. the Earl of Harrington, with AN ORIGINAL SET OF PLATES, Is sold at Mr. Bell's, the British Library in the Strand, or at Mr. Olivier's, Bell-Yard, Temple-Bar.

LA COIFFEURE DE NINA.

STUARTS, MILLINERS, No. 8, GERRARD STREET, SOHO, beg leave to inform the LADIES, that they have lately received from PARIS,

THE NINA CAP,

now so universally admired there. They have also received some other CAPS, of the present PARISIAN FASHION.

STUARTS having now established a Correspondence with one of the first MILLINERS of PARIS, to interchange, *monthly*, the Fashions of both Capitals, they flatter themselves, that they will always be enabled to afford their customers a new and elegant *Variety of Caps, Hats, and Handkerchiefs.*

A HEALTHY PERSON, with a good BREAST of MILK, whose child is six weeks old, would be glad to engage herself as WET-NURSE. Can have an undeniable character, and recommendation.

Please to enquire or direct for E. B. at the China-Shop, No. 105, in Oxford-street; or at Mr. Shelborn's, Fruiterer, near the Mount Coffee-house, Lower Grosvenor-street.

THE PLAY-HOUSE.

DRURY-LANE.

THIS EVENING will be performed, the COMEDY of

SHE WOU'D AND SHE WOU'D NOT.

Trappanti, Mr. KING;	Diego, Mr. SUETT;
Don Philip, Mr. BENSLEY;	Don Manuel, Mr. PARSONS;
Don Octavio, Mr. BARRYMORE;	Violetta, Miss POPE;
Soto, Mr. BADDELEY;	Hippolita, Mrs. JORDAN.

To which will be added (the 5th time these five years) the PANTOMIME ENTERTAINMENT of

HARLEQUIN's INVASION.

With ALTERATIONS and RESTORATIONS,

Particularly the admired SHADES and TRANSPARENCIES, representing the Amusements of HARLEQUIN, and the Destruction of the PANTOMIMICAL FLEET.

Boxes 5s. Pit 3s. First Gallery 2s. Upper Gallery 1s.

Places for the Boxes to be taken of Mr. FOSBROOK at the Theatre.

The Doors will be opened this evening at a *quarter past five*, and the performance begin at a *quarter after six o'Clock*, and so continue till further notice.

Vivant Rex et Regina.

To-morrow the *Grecian Daughter*, with the *Virgin Unmasked*; and on Wednesday, the Comedy of *Love for Love*, with (22d Time) the favourite Historical Romance of *Richard Cœur de Lion*. The *Persian Tale of Selima and Azor*, will be revived in a few Days, and due Notice given.

THE FINE ARTS, &c.

NEW PRINTS.

Speedily will be Published,

TWO ENGRAVINGS by BARTOLOZZI, after very capital Drawings by the late Mr. CIPRIANI, being the last finished works of that inimitable Artist. The subjects from the History of England; OLIVER CROMWELL detecting his Chaplain making Court to his Daughter, whom he thereupon obliged to marry her Maid; and LORD DARNLEY, husband of MARY QUEEN OF SCOTS, discovering his jealousy at finding her entertained by DAVID RIZZIO; price in red, One Guinea, and in colours, Three Guineas the pair. To be had of MRS. BRYER, No. 5, Poland-street, Soho,

Where may also be had,
King Henry II. Rosamond, Jane Shore, and Edward VI. by the same eminent Artists.

NEW PRINTS.

J. R. SMITH, begs leave to inform his Friends and the Public, *That he is removing to No. 31, King-street, Covent-Garden*, where the following PRINTS will be Published in the course of the next month: Proofs in their present state to be seen, and orders received at No. 83, Oxford-street, viz.

Nine SUBJECTS from CHAUCER, after MORTIMER, by Sherwin, Sharp, Hogg, &c.

The MORNING VISIT, after J. R. Smith, by W. Nutter.

CHANTERS, after the REV. MR. PETERS, R. A. by J. R. Smith.

SHEPHERDESS and WOOD NYMPH, after S. Woodford.

Portrait of MRS. MILLS, after G. Englehart, by J. R. Smith.

AMOROUS SPORTSMAN, after Wheatly, by C. H. Hodges.

The FINDING of MOSES, after Pelham, by W. Ward.

STUDYING a COUNTENANCE; and a RIDICULOUS LETTER, after J. R. Smith, by P. Simon.

Two SUBJECTS from Marmontel, after Wheatly, by W. Ward.

COLLEGE SCENE, after Rowlandson.

VICAR'S FIRE-SIDE, after Wigstead.

A YOUNG LADY, after Opie, by J. R. Smith.

VIEWS OF LONDON.

MR. MOLTON begs leave to acquaint his Subscribers, That the FIFTH PAIR of his VIEWS of LONDON, ST. GEORGE's, Hanover-square; and ST. PAUL's, Covent-Garden, are compleated, and will be published in a few days, Price 10s. 6d.

The Sixth Pair are in great forwardness, CHARING-CROSS, and ST. DUSTAN's, Fleet-street: Also the last set of his Views of Bath, containing the Crescent, the New Banks, the front of the New Bridge, and the west front of the Abbey. Any of the former Views to be had at his house, No. 6, Conduit-street, Hanover-square.

MR. MOLTON continues to give Lessons in Landscape Drawing, and Perspective.

Wanted an ingenious Youth as an Apprentice.

Dedicated by Permission to HER MAJESTY.

Just published,

TWO PRINTS of the DOWAGER QUEEN of EDWARD the IVth, parting with the DUKE of YORK, by Order of the Council of RICHARD the IIId. and the DUKES of NORTHUMBERLAND and SUFFOLK praying LADY JANE GRAY to accept the CROWN—from DRAWINGS by the late Mr. CIPRIANI, and Engraved by Mr. BARTOLOZZI.

The Nobility and Gentry are most respectfully informed, that Names are set down for the Two Companion Prints to the above, viz. JOHN, King of France, and his SON, brought Prisoners before EDWARD the IIId. by EDWARD PRINCE OF WALES.—And VORTIGERN and ROWENA—the first settling of the SAXONS in BRITAIN. From Paintings by Mr. RIGAUD, R. A. and Engraved by Mr. BARTOLOZZI, R. A.

N. B. No Money to be taken until the delivery of the Prints, which will be in the course of Six Months.—Prints in a forward state may be seen at the Proprietor's, W. PALMER, No. 165, opposite the New Church, Strand, London.

TO MERCHANTS, WHOLESALE DEALERS, &c.

A PERSON wishes to treat with the Firm of some respectable HOUSE of credit, to act either in the Counting House, as a Rider, or some other respectable and active part. Is under 27 years of age; of character, family and connections. Has been used to business, and possesses personal Property of his own, near 1000l. Would be agreeable to employ a principal part of the same, after being well acquainted with the House, and well secured.

Address A. B. C. Holyland's Coffee-House, near Somerset-House, Strand. Only Principals will be attended to, with real names. The strictest honour may be depended on.

CONVEYANCING IN GENERAL.

At No. 46, Devonshire-street, Red Lion Square, Holborn.

LEASES made for One Guinea and a Half a pair, Articles of Copartnership, Marriage Settlements, Indentures of Apprenticeship, and Covenant Servants, Mortgage and Annuity Deeds, Assignments, Bills of Sale, Deeds of Separation, Bonds and Warrants of Attorney, Letters of License, and Deeds of Composition, Agreements, Letters of Attorney, Bargain and Sale, Deeds of Gift, Wills, Bonds, Petitions, and every branch of Conveyancing, drawn with precision, accuracy, secrecy, and dispatch, on the most reasonable terms, by PHILLIPS and Company.

*** Money ready to advance on Mortgage, of eligible Security, in Middlesex; and advice on moderate terms to those who are withheld from their Estates, Legacies, Money, or Effects, or who are in embarassed circumstances.

THE PLAY-HOUSE.

COVENT-GARDEN.

THIS EVENING will be performed, a COMEDY, called

THE PROVOK'D WIFE.

Sir John Brute, Mr. RYDER;	Lady Brute, Mrs. BATES;
Heartfree, Mr. AICKIN;	Belinda, Mrs. WELLS;
Constant, Mr. FARREN;	Lady Fanciful, Mrs. POPE;

Mademoiselle, Mrs. MATTOCKS.

To which will be added, for the SIXTH TIME, a NEW PANTOMINE, intermixed with DIALOGUE and SONGS, called

THE ENCHANTED CASTLE.

With NEW MUSIC, SCENES, MACHINERY, DRESSES, and DECORATIONS.
A few of the AIRS compiled from
PURCELL, TRAVERS, SACCHINI, &c.
The rest of the MUSIC composed by Mr. SHIELDS.
The SCENERY and MACHINERY designed by
Mr. RICHARDS and Mr. CARVER,
And executed by them,
Mr. HODGINS, and MANY ASSISTANTS.

To conclude with the REPRESENTATION of the INSIDE of

A NABOB's PALACE.

Books of the Songs to be had at the Theatre.
Nothing under full price will be taken.

Boxes 5s. Pit 3s. First Gallery 2s. Upper Gallery 1s.

Places for the Boxes to be taken of Mr. BRANDON, at the Stage Door.

The Doors will be opened at a *Quarter after Five.*
To begin at a *Quarter after Six.*

Vivant Rex & Regina.

On Saturday the Comedy of the *Wonder*, and the *new Pantomime*, were received with unbounded applause, from a most splendid and overflowing Theatre: From the very extraordinary demand for places, the Pantomime will be repeated every night till further notice. To-morrow, Mr. *Ryder* will perform *Colonel Feignwell*, (for the first time) in the revived Comedy of a *Bold Stroke for a Wife*. On Wednesday, the Comic Opera of *Love in a Village*. On Thursday, (not acted this season) the *Beaux Stratagem*. On Friday, the Comedy of the *Funeral*. And on Saturday, Mr. *Leoni*, who is engaged for a few nights, will appear in the character of *Arbaces*, in the Serious Opera of *Artaxerxes*—the part of *Mandane* by Mrs. *Billington*. Ladies and Gentlemen who have places for the succeeding nights of the new Comedy of *He Would be a Soldier*, are informed it is obliged to be postponed on account of Mr. *Edwin's* illness. A new Opera, in three acts, called the *Prophet*, is in rehearsal.

POLITE LITERATURE.

This Day is published,
Price One Shilling,
DEDICATED TO HER MAJESTY.

RICHARD CŒUR DE LION; A COMIC OPERA, performed at the Theatre Royal, Covent Garden:

Partly taken from the French Comedy of the same name, By Monsieur SEDAINE, and partly written by Mr. MACNALLY.

Printed for T. CADELL, in the Strand.

This day are published, in octavo, price 3s. 6d. in boards,

THE POEMS OF MR. GRAY. With NOTES, BY GILBERT WAKEFIELD, B. A. Late Fellow of Jesus College, Cambridge.

Ingenium cui sit, cui mens divinior, atque os
Magna sonaturum, des nominis hujus honorem.
HORAT.

Printed for G. Kearsley, at Johnson's Head, No. 46, Fleet-street.

VOLTAIRE's last Production, printed at Bern, in Switzerland, translated into English by J. KNIGHT, and imported and sold by G. KEARSLEY, at Johnson's Head, No. 46, in Fleet-street, Price 2s. 6d.

THE EARS OF LORD CHESTERFIELD and PARSON GOODMAN.

*** *This Piece was suppressed at Paris and Brussels, but was afterwards published at Geneva and Bern.*

This Day is Published, Price 3s. 6d. bound.

RECUEIL Choisi de Traits Historiques et de Contes Moraux avec la Signification des Mots en Anglois au Bas de chaque page. A l'Usage des jeunes Gens, de l'un et de l'autre Sexe, qui veulent apprendre le François.

Par M. WANOSTROCHT.

Second Edition Revue, Corrigée, et Augmenté.

Printed for JOHN BOOSEY, King-Street, Cheapside; Where may be had, by the same Author, a PRACTICAL GRAMMAR OF THE FRENCH LANGUAGE, and second Edition of A CLASSICAL VOCABULARY, *French and English.*

With a List of his Works, and the different Characters he performed, arranged in chronological Order: Also a short account of his Life, and the Monody on his Death, written by MR. SHERIDAN, *and spoken by* MRS. YATES, *of Drury-lane Theatre.*

This Day are published,
In Two Volumes, Price 7s. in boards,

THE POETICAL WORKS of *DAVID GARRICK*, Esq.

Now first collected, with explanatory notes.

Printed for J. Debrett, in Piccadilly; G. Kearsley, at Johnson's Head, No. 46, in Fleet-street; and J. Sewell, in Cornhill.

Of whom may be had,
Price 2s. 6d. sewed, (never before collected)
The Poetical Works of Doctor Samuel Johnson.

This Day was Published, in Quarto,
Price One Pound Seven Shillings in Boards,
VOL. I. Of

A COLLECTION of TRACTS relative to the LAW of ENGLAND, from Manuscripts never before published; with a Preface,

By FRANCIS HARGRAVE, Esq. Barrister at Law.
Sold by E. BROOKE, in Bell-Yard, Temple-Bar.

CONTENTS OF THE VOLUME.

1. Lord Hale on the Ports and Customs; with various Incidental Subjects.
2. Lord Hale on the Amendment or Alteration of the Law.
3. Treatise on the Office of Master in Chancery.
4. Two Treatises on the Chancery Jurisdiction; one of them being by the Author of the Doctor and Student.
5. Lord Hale on the Disputes between the King's Bench and Common Pleas, whilst he was Chief Baron of the Exchequer.
6. Discourse against the Jurisdiction of the King's Bench over Wales, by Process of Latitat.
7. Mr. Norbury on the Abuses and Remedies of Chancery, written soon after Lord Bacon's Removal.
8. On the Effect of Matrimonial Sentences, when pleaded, or offered in Evidence in the Courts Temporal; by the Editor.
9. Mr. Justice Blackstone's Argument in Perryn and Blake; from the Original in his own Hand-writing.
10. Argument by the Editor before the House of Lords on an Appeal, in which it was material to consider the Doctrine of Executory Devises, and the Distinctions between the Distribution of personal Estate per Stirpes, and that per Capita.
11. Observations by the Editor on the Rule in Shelley's Case.

LONDON, DEC. 1, 1786.

SHAKSPEARE.

MESS. ALDERMAN BOYDELL, JOSIAH BOYDELL, AND GEORGE NICOL,

Propose to PUBLISH by SUBSCRIPTION
A most Magnificent and Accurate EDITION
OF THE

PLAYS OF SHAKSPEARE, IN EIGHT VOLUMES

Of the largest QUARTO SIZE, on the finest Royal ATLAS PAPER, to be fabricated for that purpose by Mr. WHATMAN.

The LETTER-PRESS will be executed by Mr. HUGHS, with a Set of New TYPES cast by Mr. CASLON.

The TEXT to be regulated, and the LITERARY PART of the Undertaking conducted,

By GEORGE STEEVENS, Esq.

To accompany this Work

MESSIEURS BOYDELL

Intend to PUBLISH by SUBSCRIPTION

A series of LARGE and CAPITAL PRINTS,

After Pictures to be immediately painted by the following ARTISTS, from the most striking Scenes in the same Author:

SIR JOSHUA REYNOLDS,
Principal Painter to his MAJESTY, *and President of the Royal Academy.*

ANGELICA KAUFFMAN, R. A.	Mr. NORTHCOTE.
	Mr. OPIE.
Mr. BARRY, R. A. *Professor of Painting to the Royal Academy.*	Rev. Mr. PETERS, R. A.
	Mr. RIGAUD, R. A.
	Mr. ROMNEY.
Mr. COPLEY, R. A.	Mr. WEST, R. A. *History-Painter to his Majesty.*
Mr. FUSELI.	
Mr. MILLER.	Mr. WRIGHT, &c. &c. &c.

To be Engraved by

Miss CAROLINE WATSON.	Mr. HALL.
Mr. BARTOLOZZI, *Historical Engraver to his Majesty.*	Mr. HAWARD, A. R.
	Mr. HEATH.
Mr. COLLIER.	Mr. LEGATT.
Mr. FARLOM.	Mr. MICHEL.
Mess. FACIUS.	Mr. RYDER.
Mr. FITTLER, *Marine Engraver to his Majesty.*	Mr. SHARPE, &c. &c. &c.

The PICTURES will be of various SIZES, chiefly as large as Life.

As soon as they have all been engraved, they will be hung up in a Gallery built on purpose, and called

THE GALLERY OF SHAKSPEARE.

CONDITIONS.

I. Seventy-two Scenes will be painted, being two appropriated to each of the PLAYS of SHAKSPEARE. As, however, some of them exhibit more interesting Subjects than others, the Plates will be given without regard to any certain Number for each Drama. For instance; HAMLET, KING LEAR, ROMEO and JULIET, MACBETH, OTHELLO, and the two Parts of HENRY IV. may furnish three apiece, while the MIDSUMMER NIGHT'S DREAM, the COMEDY OF ERRORS, the TWO GENTLEMEN OF VERONA, LOVE'S LABOUR'S LOST, ALL'S WELL THAT ENDS WELL, TROILUS and CRESSIDA, and TITUS ANDRONICUS, may each contribute only one.

II. The whole to be published in Numbers, each containing at least Four CAPITAL PRINTS. The size of the largest to be about 19 inches by 24 long. The largest of the upright ones about 16 inches by 24 high. The other Sizes in proportion to the Subjects.

III. The Plates to be finished in the highest manner possible, at the Price of THREE GUINEAS each Number.

IV. On account of the unprecedented Expence attending this Work, the Subscription will be Two GUINEAS at the time of subscribing, and the remaining Guinea on the delivery of each Number, containing Four Prints.

V. That on delivery of each Number, Two GUINEAS more are to be advanced by the Subscribers, for the Number immediately following.

VI. That One Number, at least, shall be published annually. The Proprietors hope, nay are confident, they shall be enabled to produce Two Numbers within the course of every Year; but do not chuse to promise absolutely what they may not with certainty perform.

VII. A HEAD OF SHAKSPEARE, accurately delineated from the BUST on his MONUMENT, at Stratford upon Avon, engraved by BARTOLOZZI, and designed as a Frontispiece to the First Volume of the PLAYS, will be delivered gratis with the last Number of them; as also the Prefaces of POPE and JOHNSON; Title Pages, &c. &c.

IT is likewise designed to publish, from the same Pictures, a smaller Collection of PRINTS, four at least in each Number. These will be delivered at the same time with the larger ones, and are to be engraved in the most elegant and finished manner, by Mr. HEATH, as Embellishments to the Eight Volumes in Quarto, already described.

The Price of the Letter-Press and Quarto Plates, to Subscribers, will be Two Guineas; one half of the Money to be paid at the time of subscribing, and the remainder on delivery of each Number, which will consist of Two Plays, and at least four Large Quarto Prints.

The Plays will be printed singly, each beginning with page 1, so that the whole Number may be bound up according to the arrangement of former Editors, with regard to general Chronology, where it can be ascertained, or the order of time in which these celebrated Dramas are supposed to have been written.

This undertaking, being planned on an extensive scale, will be executed in a manner not less liberal on the side of its Proprietors. They will furnish more rather than fewer Plates than they promise; and hope to attain exactness, even as to their stated periods of Publication. Yet, let it be remembered, that correct and characteristic Representations of SHAKSPEARE's SCENES cannot on a sudden be compleated, nor Engravings worthy of such Productions be precipitately finished. And though, in great attempts, delays are less injurious than haste, the former need only to be apprehended during the infancy of the present Scheme, as its nice dependencies cannot at once be adjusted, nor its various difficulties be effectually surmounted, till the Work is advanced beyond the delivery of its first Number. From that time, its progress will be regular; and in case of unforeseen accidents among the numerous Artists employed, one series of Plates, &c. shall always be in readiness, to supply the failure of any other which may chance to be retarded, after it had been announced.

It may be necessary to subjoin, that the Plates, when printed off, will most scrupulously be delivered in the order they are subscribed for; so that priority of Subscriptions will necessarily include Superiority of Impressions.

As the foregoing Work is undertaken in honour of SHAKSPEARE, with a view to encourage and improve the Arts of Painting and Engraving in this Kingdom; and at the same time cannot fail to be attended with the Expence of 50,000l. or more, it is hoped the Public will be forward in their Subscriptions, and thereby incite the various Artists engaged in the present arduous design, to exert their utmost abilities in the execution of it.

The ROYAL PATRONAGE and Munificence having been extended in a peculiar manner to this Undertaking, it will be inscribed, as the joint Solicitations of Respect and Gratitude, TO HIS MOST SACRED MAJESTY KING GEORGE THE THIRD.

COUNTRY NEWSPAPERS.

ADVERTISEMENTS for all the COUNTRY PAPERS in the KINGDOM, are taken in by W. TAYLOR, at his Office, No. 5, Warwick-Court, Newgate-Street, to whom the Papers are all regularly sent up every Week by the respective Printers, and where every Paper is distinctly and separately filed and kept PERFECT, for the convenience and inspection of those Persons who bring Advertisements. An Alphabetical List of the Country Papers, denoting the Days on which they are published (very useful to those who have occasion to advertise), is printed and given gratis at the Office abovementioned.

Fig. 83. The World, *edited by Edward Topham, printed and published by John Bell at the British Library, Strand. The sub-title was quickly dropped* a brilliant piece of typography, 'Printed', said the imprint on the last page, 'under the Direction of J. BELL at the British Library in the Strand'—and without a single ſ from beginning to end. The first important novelty in the setting of *The World* is the leading between the paragraphs. The value of this innovation will be seen by placing *The Morning Chronicle* and *The World* in parallel columns:

MORNING CHRONICLE.

LONDON, AUGUST 30, 1781.

Yeſterday there was a levee at St James's. His Majeſty, with the Right Hon. the Lord Chancellor, Lords Mansfield, Stormont, Mountſtuart; the foreign Miniſters, with divers of the Nobility were preſent. After the levee there was a Council to receive the Recorder's report of the priſoners now under ſentence of death in Newgate; and about half paſt four his Majeſty returned to Windſor.

Yeſterday Lord Robert Bertie came into waiting as Lord of the Bedchamber to the King, in the room of Lord Onſlow.

Yeſterday Lord Mountſtuart was at the levee at St. James's, and took leave of the King, in order to return to Vienna.

Yeſterday Admiral Marlow was at the levee at St. James's, for the firſt time for ſeveral months.

Yeſterday his Excellency the Portugueſe Embaſſador was at the levee at St. James's, and introduced to his Majeſty.

This day there is to be a drawing room at St. James's, and in the evening the Royal Family is to go to the Theatre in the Haymarket.

Yeſterday General Conway was at the levee at St. James's, for the firſt time, ſince his return from the Iſland of Jersey, and laid before the King a ſtate of the defence of that place.

THE WORLD[1]

LONDON, NOVEMBER 6.

It is with extreme concern, that we communicate any alteration for the worse in His MAJESTY's health; but it may not be improper to state the facts—that on Tuesday evening, the KING found himself very much indisposed; by the advice of his Physician, he was cupped three times; and yesterday morning, Dr. *Heberden* was sent for express to attend a consultation with Sir *George Baker*. Notice was sent last night of the Drawing-room being postponed; but at the same time giving the pleasing intelligence of His MAJESTY being much better than he was in the morning.

Nothing can more fully evince the superiority of Mr. PITT's financial abilities over his predecessors in Office, than the very great INCREASE in the REVENUE, which has taken place since the commencement of his Administration.

Venal eulogium may attempt to pourtray a Minister with abilities he does not possess, and give him credit for obtaining national advantages which never subsisted.

The Minister whose measures need such a support, will have recourse to it. With GREAT BRITAIN's present Minister, it is different; venal Panegyrists would but injure his reputation—HIS BEST PRAISE IS OBTAINED BY AN APPEAL TO FACTS.

It is obvious that the new setting is more lucid. Another novelty was the use of capitals and small capitals for proper names in his paragraphs. The use of italics is also new—though, some might reasonably consider, overdone. Whether this be so or not, the rest of the newspaper press quickly followed. The principle of leading which John Bell sponsored was an immediate and a permanent advantage to the newspaper reader. *The Morning Chronicle* saw the benefit of it at once. The abolition of the long ſ was also permanent, but slower in making its way—the long ſ was used in journals published as late as 1810. A third innovation, also permanent in its effect, and much less creditable to Bell's taste, was the front page. The heading *The World, and Fashionable Advertiser* was new. First, the lettering of the main title

[1] From the issue of November 6, 1788.

THE Universal DAILY Register,

Printed Logographically — By His Majesty's Patent.

DIEU ET MON DROIT

NUMB. 1.] SATURDAY, JANUARY 1, 1785. [Price Two-pence Halfpenny.

The SIXTH NIGHT.
By His MAJESTY's Company

AT the THEATRE ROYAL in DRURY-LANE, this present SATURDAY, will be performed

A New COMEDY, called
The NATURAL SON.

The characters by Mr. King, Mr. Parsons, Mr. Bensley, Mr. Moody, Mr. Baddeley, Mr. Wrighten, and Mr. Palmer. Miss Pope, Miss Tidswell, and Miss Farren.
With new Scenes and Dresses.
The Prologue to be spoken by Mr. Bannister, jun.
And the Epilogue by Miss Farren.
After which will be performed the last New Pantomime Entertainment, in two Parts, called
HARLEQUIN JUNIOR;
Or, The MAGIC CESTUS.
The Characters of the Pantomime, by
Mr. Wright, Mr. Williamson, Mr. Burton, Mr. Staunton, Mr. Williames, Mr. Palmer, Mr. Waldron, Mr. Fawcett, Mr. Chapin, Mr. Phillimore, Mr. Wilson, Mr. Alfred, Mr. Spencer, Mr. Chapman, and Mr. Grimaldi. Mrs. Burnet, Miss Burnett, Miss Tidswell, Miss Barnes, Miss Cranford, and Miss Stageldoir.
To conclude with the Repulse of the Spaniards before
The ROCK of GIBRALTAR.

To-morrow, by particular desire, (for the 4th time) the revived Comedy of the DOUBLE DEALER, with the favorite Masque of ARTHUR and EMMELINE.
On Tuesday the Tragedy of VENICE PRESERVED: Jaffier by Mr. Brereton, Pierre by Mr. Bensley, and Belvidera, by Mrs. Siddons; And on Friday the Carmelite. Massinger's Play of the MAID of HONOUR, (with alterations and Additions) is in Rehearsal and will soon be produced.

NINTH NIGHT. FOR THE AUTHOR.

AT the THEATRE-ROYAL, COVENT-GARDEN, this present SATURDAY, January 1, 1785, will be performed, a New Comedy, called
The FOLLIES of a DAY,
Or, The Marriage of Figaro.
With new Dresses, Decorations, &c.
The principal characters by Mr. Lewis, Mr. Quick, Mr. Edwin, Mr. Wilson, Mr. Wewitzer, Mr. Bonnor, Mr. Thompson, and Mrs. Martyr; Mrs. Bates, Mrs. Webb, Miss Wewitzer, and Miss Younge.
With a new Prologue, to be spoken by Mr. Davies.
To which will be added, for the the sixth time,
A new Pantomime, called,
The MAGIC CAVERN,
Or, VIRTUE's TRIUMPH.
With new Scenery, Machinery, Music, Dresses, and Decorations.
The Scenes chiefly designed by Mr. Richards, and executed by him, Mr. Carver, Mr. Hodgins, and Assistants.
The Overture, Songs, Chorusses, and the Music of the new Pantomime, and composed by Mr. Shield.
Nothing under full Price will be taken.
The Words of the Songs, &c. to be had at the Theatre.

MR. WALTER returns his thanks to his Friends and the Public for the great encouragement and generous support he has already received from them to his new improvement in Printing, by the readiness with which they have subscribed to his intended publication of the works of some eminent Authors; and whilst he solicits a continuance of their favours, begs leave to acquaint them that by
The middle of January will be published,
In One Volume 12mo,
MISCELLANIES IN VERSE AND PROSE,
Intended as a Specimen of his Printing Types at the Logographic Office, Printing-House Square, Blackfriars.—And by the beginning of February, his first volume, containing Watts's Improvement of the Mind, with an Introduction written on the occasion, will be ready to be delivered to the subscribers.

This Day is published, Price 6d.

PLAN of the CHAMBER of COMMERCE, King's-Arms Buildings, Cornhill, London; which is open every day, for Consultation, Opinion, and Advice (verbal or in Writing) Mediation, Assistance, Arbitration, &c. in all *Commercial*, *Maritime*, and *Insurance* Affairs, and matters of *Trade* in general; and the *Laws* and *Usages* relating thereto.——The Address is, To the Director of the Chamber of Commerce, as above.
To be had of Richardson and Urquhart, Royal Exchange; J. Sewell, Cornhill; T. Whieldon, Fleet-street; W. Flexney, Holborn; and at the aforesaid Chamber.
Where may also be had, in one Volume Folio,
Mr. Weskett's COMPLETE DIGEST of the THEORY, LAWS and PRACTICE of INSURANCE; an entire new and comprehensive work, including all the adjudged Cases extant, with several never before printed; Extracts from the Statutes, foreign Ordinances, and marine Treaties; accounts of all the Insurance Companies the MaritimeCourts, the commercial and maritime Laws, the Law of Nations, &c. the whole forming (alphabetically) a new *Lex Mercatoria*.
☞ "This Work has been compiled with great Care and Industry, by one who is evidently a Master of the Subject. It abounds with Proofs of extensive Reading, as well as mature Reflection, and judicious Remarks; and if the completest System of Insurance that has hitherto been composed be entitled to Praise, the present useful Digest must meet with the Approbation of the commercial World." Crit. Rev. Vol. 52, p. 443.—All the other Literary Journals speak in similar Terms of this Book; which had already been translated abroad.

This Day is published, in 3 Vols. Price 9s. sewed.
By the LITERARY SOCIETY,

MODERN TIMES: or The ADVENTURES of GABRIEL OUTCAST. A Novel, in Imitation of Gil Blas.
"Qui capit ille facit."
Printed for the Author, and sold by J. Walter, Printing-house Square, Black-friars; where may be had, gratis, the Plan of this Society, associated for the Encouragement of Literature, who propose to print and publish at their own Risk and Expence such original Works as they may approve of, and give their Authors all Profits arising from the same.

MRS. KING begs leave to acquaint her Friends she opens her SCHOOL at CHIGWELL in ESSEX, on Monday, the 10th of January, for the EDUCATION of YOUNG LADIES: as she has always been accustomed to watch and improve the opening mind, hopes to give satisfaction to those who trust her with so important a charge.
Till the 10th of January Mrs. King may be spoke with at Mr. Kerr's, Bitt-maker to his Majesty, in the Mews, Charing-cross.
N. B. Wanted an Apprentice and Half-boarder.

SHIP-PING ADVER-TISEMENTS

For NICE, GENOA, and LEGHORN,
(With Liberty to touch at One Port in the Channel,)
The NANCY.
THOMAS WHITE, Commander,

BURTHEN 160 Tons; Guns and Men answerable. Lying off the Tower, and will absolutely depart on Saturday the 8th instant.
The said Commander to be spoken with every morning at Sam's Coffee-house, near the Custom-house; at Will's Coffee-house, in Cornhill; and at Exchange hours on the French and Italian Walk, or
WILLIAM ELYARD, for the said Commander,
No. 16, Savage-Gardens.

Direct for LISBON,
The NANCY.
JOHN RACKHAM, Commander,

BURTHEN 300 Tons, Men answerable. Lying off Horslydown Chain; Seven-eighths of her Cargo absolutely engaged, and is obliged by Charter-party to depart on Saturday the 8th instant.
The said Commander to be spoken with every morning at Sam's Coffee-house, near the Custom-house; at Will's Coffee-house, in Cornhill; and in Exchange hours in the French and Italian Walk; or
WILLIAM ELYARD, for the said Commander,
No. 16, Savage-Gardens.

For NICE, GENOA, and LEGHORN.
(With Liberty to Touch at One Port in the Channel.)
The LIVELY,
ROBERT BRINE, Commander,

BURTHEN 209 Tons, Guns and Men answerable. Lying off Iron Gate.
The said Commander to be spoke with every Morning at Sam's Coffee-house, near the Custom-house; at Will's Coffee-house in Cornhill; and in Exchange Hours in the French and Italian Walk; or
WILLIAM ELYARD, for the said Commander,
No. 16, Savage-Gardens.

For CONSTANTINOPLE and SMYRNA, or SMYRNA and CONSTANTINOPLE,
(With Liberty to Touch at One Port in the Channel,)
The BETSEY,
ROBERT LANCASTER, Commander,

BURTHEN 200 Tons, Men answerable. Lying at Iron-Gate. Two-thirds of her Cargo engaged, and is obliged to depart by Charterparty, in all the present Month of January.
The said Commander to be spoke with every Morning at Sam's Coffee-house, near the Custom-house; at Will's Coffee-house in Cornhill; and in Exchange Hours in the French and Italian Walk; or
WILLIAM ELYARD, for the said Commender,
No. 16, Savage-Gardens.
N. B. No Goods to be taken on Board the Vessel without an Order from the Broker.

NEW NOVELS.
This Day are published, (in two Volumes, price 5s. sewed,)

THE YOUNG WIDOW; or, the HISTORY of Mrs. LEDWICH.
The HISTORY of Lord BELFORD and Miss SOPHIA WOODLEY, 3 vol. 9s. bound.
Printed for the Editor, and sold by F. Noble, in Holborn;
Where may be had lately published,
St. Ruthin's Abbey, a Novel, 3 vols. 9s. bound.
The Woman of Letters; or, History of Fanny Belton, 2 vol. 7s. bound.
A Lesson for Lovers; or, History of Col. Melville and Lady Richly, 2 vols. 7s. bound.
Literary Amusements; or, Evening Entertainer, 2 vol. 7s. bound.
Adventures of a Cavalier, by Daniel Defoe, 3 vols. 9s bound.

T. RICKABY, PRINTER,
No. 15, Duke's Court, Drury Lane;

RESpectfully informs his Friends and the Public in general, that the Partnership between him and Mr. Moore being entirely dissolved, he now intends to carry on every branch of the PRINTING BUSINESS upon his own account;—and having purchased a complete assortment of the neatest and best materials, is determined to pursue a Mode of Printing which he hopes will meet with the approbation of his employers.
N.B. Cards, Hand-Bills, Circular Letters, and all articles of the kind, accurately printed at a few hours notice. in a manner particularly neat, and at the lowest prices.
*** An Apprentice wanted.

To the Readers of the London Medical Journal.
This day is first published, price 1s.

SYMPATHY DEFENDED; or, the State MEDICAL CRITICISM in London; written to improve the Principles and Manners of the Editor of the London Medical Journal: To which are added the Contents of the Treatise on Medical Sympathy, and a Postscript, on account of a premature Review in a late Number of the London Medical Journal.
By a Society of Faculties;
Friends to the Public and Enemies to Imposition.
"Cum tua non edas, carpis mea carmina, Laeli,
"Carpere vel noli nostra, edo tua."
MART. Epig.
This pamphlet has been hitherto distributed gratuitously. The repeated applications for them, particularly from the country, have become so numerous, that the Society feel themselves under the necessity of putting them into the hands of a publisher.
Sold by J. Murray, Bookseller, Fleet-street.

Nondum lingua silet dextra, peregit opus.
MART.

SHORT-HAND, on the latest and most approved Principles taught by J. LARKHAM, No 11, Rose Alley, Bishopsgate Street.
It would exceed the limits of an advertisement merely to mention the various errors either in the *plan* or the *execution* of the different schemes of Short-hand hitherto made public, or to point out the peculiarities and excellencies of the present: Mr. L. therefore only begs leave to observe, that the approbation of many gentlemen well known in the literary world, and well versed in the *Theory* and *Practice* of Short-hand, expressed in stronger terms than delicacy will permit him to repeat, warrants him in saying *his* will be found a system of short and swift writing, more *easy* to acquire and retain, more *expeditiously*, more *legible* and more *regular* than any ever yet offered to the Public.
The terms of teaching *one* Guinea, the *usual* time of learning *seven* lessons.

To the Public.

TO bring out a New Paper at the present day, when so many others are already established and confirmed in the public opinion, is certainly an arduous undertaking; and no one can be more fully aware of its difficulties than I am: I, nevertheless, entertain very sanguine hopes, that the nature of the plan on which this paper will be conducted, will ensure it a moderate share at least of public favour; but my pretensions to encouragement, however strong they may appear in my own eyes, must be tried before a tribunal not liable to be blinded by *self-opinion*: to that tribunal I shall now, as I am bound to do, submit these pretensions with deference, and the public will judge whether they are well or ill founded.

It is very far from my intention to detract from the acknowledged merit of the Daily Papers now in existence; it is sufficient that they please the class of readers whose approbation their conductors are ambitious to deserve; nevertheless it is certain some of the best, some of the most respectable, and some of the most useful members of the community, have frequently complained (and the causes of their complaints still exist) that by radical defects in the plans of the present established papers, they were deprived of many advantages, which ought naturally to result from daily publications. Of these some build their fame on the length and accuracy of parliamentary reports, which unquestionably are given with great ability, and with a laudable zeal to please those, who can spare time to read ten or twelve columns of debates. Others are principally attentive to the politics of the day, and make it their study to give satisfaction to the numerous class of politicians, who, blessed with easy circumstances, have nothing better to do, than to amuse themselves with watching the motions of ministers both at home and abroad; and endeavouring to find out the secret springs that set in motion the great machine of government in every state and empire in the world. There is one paper which in no degree interferes with the pursuits of its cotemporaries; it looks upon parliamentary debates as sacred mysteries, that cannot be submitted to vulgar eyes without profanation; political investigations it apprehends to be little short of treason, and therefore *loyally* abstains from them; it deals almost solely in advertisements; and consequently, though a very useful, it is by no means an entertaining paper. Thus it would seem that every News-Paper published in London is calculated for a particular set of readers only; so that if each set were to change its favourite publication for another, the commutation would produce disgust, and dissatisfaction to all; the politician would then find nothing to amuse him but long accounts of petty squabbles about trifles in Parliament, or panegyrics on the men and measures that he most disliked; or libels on those whom he most revered. The person to whom parliamentary debates afford unspeakable delight, would find himself bored with political speculations about the measures that the different courts in Europe might probably adopt; or disgusted with whole pages of advertisements, in which he felt no concern;—whilst the plain shop-keeper who wanted to find a convenient house for his business, and the servant who purchased his paper in hopes of seeing in it an advertisement directing where he might find a place to suit him, would have their labour for their pains, in perusing publications, filled with senatorial debates, or political essays and remarks, which would direct them to nothing less than the house or place they wanted.—A News-Paper, conducted on the true and natural principles of such a publication, ought to be the Register of the times, and faithful recorder of every species of intelligence; it ought not to be engrossed by any particular object; but, like a well covered table, it should contain something suited to every palate: observations on the dispositions of our own and of foreign courts should be provided for the political reader; debates should be reported for the amusement or information of those who may be particularly fond of them: and a due attention should be paid to the interests of trade, which are so greatly promoted by advertisements.—A paper that should blend all these advantages, and by steering clear of extremes, hit the happy medium, has long been expected by the public.—Such, it is intended, shall be the UNIVERSAL REGISTER, the great objects of which will be to facilitate the *commercial* intercourse between the different parts of the community, through the channel of *Advertisements*; to record the principal occurrences of the times; and to abridge the account of debates during the sitting of Parliament.

It is no less the interest of the proprietors of News-Papers, than of the public, that every encouragement should be given to advertising correspondents; yet this private interest of the proprietors is frequently sacrificed to the rage for parliamentary debates, to the great injury of trade; for the extreme length of these debates so greatly retards the publication of the New-Papers which are noted for detailed accounts of them, that the advantages arising from this species of intelligence, though highly acceptable in itself, are frequently over-balanced by the inconveniences occasioned to people in business by the delay. These inconveniences are great and many; it generally happens, that when either House of Parliament has been engaged in the discussion of an important question till after midnight, the papers in which the speeches of the Members are reported at large, cannot be published before noon; nay, they sometimes are not even sent to press so soon; consequently parties interested in *sales* are essentially injured, as the advertisements, inviting the public to attend them at *ten* or *twelve* o'clock, do not appear, on account of a late publication, till some hours after.—From the same source flows another inconvenience; it is sometimes found necessary to *defer* sales, after they have been advertised for a particular day; but the notice of putting them off not appearing early enough, on account of the late hour at which the papers containing it are published, numbers of people, acting under the impression of former advertisements, are unnecessarily put to the trouble of attending.—It will be the object of the *Universal Register* to guard against these great inconveniences, without depriving its readers of the pleasure of learning what passes in Parliament.—It is intended, then, that the debates shall be regularly reported in it; but on the other hand, that the publication may not be delayed to the prejudice of people in trade, the speeches will not be given on a large scale; the *substance* shall be faithfully preserved; but all the uninteresting parts will be omitted. I shall thus be enabled to publish this paper at an early hour; and I propose to bring it out *regularly* every morning at *six* o'clock. The *Universal Register* will therefore have this advantage over the *Daily Advertiser*, that, though published as early, it will contain a substantial account of the proceedings in Parliament the preceding night, which is never to be found in that paper; and compared with the other morning papers it will be found to have the merit of containing in substance, what they give in long detail (which men in business cannot well spare time to read) and, nevertheless, of being published much sooner. These circumstances, it is hoped, will give the *Universal Register* at least an *equal* claim to public favour with the parliamentary papers, and the *trading* part of the metropolis, it is presumed, will find it their advantage to give it the preference.

An essential part of the plan of this new paper is, that, for the convenience of advertising correspondents, their favours shall, *to a certainty*, be inserted on the very day that they shall direct; provided they deliver them at the office in due time. For the *strict* observance of this rule, the credit of the paper shall stand pledged; and its pretensions to public countenance will be renounced, if this fundamental principle in its institution shall ever be violated, except in cases of absolute necessity, which human prudence cannot prevent.—And here I beg it may be understood that I do not make use of the word *necessity* as a reserve, under colour of which, I may, whenever I think fit, be released from my engagements; I mean by that word a necessity arising from accidents that sometimes happen in the printing business, and from which, the most careful man cannot, at all times, be secure. But so far from wishing to shrink from my engagements, I intend, whenever the length of the Gazette, Parliamentary Debates, &c. shall render it impossible for me to insert all the advertisements promised for the day, in *one* sheet, to print an additional half sheet, and publish it with the ordinary paper without any additional charge to my customers.—From the difficulty that people experience in procuring the insertion of their advertisements even in the *Daily Advertiser*; and particularly from the impossibility of obtaining an *early* insertion at some periods of the year, it may be presumed that this regulation will greatly recommend the UNIVERSAL REGISTER to public notice, and procure it support.

These, though in my opinion good, are not the *only* grounds on which I build my hopes of success. I flatter myself, I have some claim to public encouragement, on account of a great improvement which I have made in the art of printing. The inconveniences attending the old and tedious mode of composing with letters taken up *singly*, first suggested the idea of devising some more expeditious method. The cementing of several letters together, so as that the type of a *whole word* might be taken up in as short a time as that of a *single letter*, was the result of much reflection on that subject. But the bare idea of cementing was merely the opening, not the accomplishment or perfection of the improvement. The fount consisting of types of words, and not of letters, was to be so arranged, as that a compositor should be able to find the former with as much facility as he can the latter. This was a work of inconceivable difficulty. I undertook it however, and was fortunate enough, after an infinite number of experiments, and great labour, to bring it to a happy conclusion. The whole English language is now methodically and systematically arranged at my fount: so that printing can now be performed with greater dispatch, and at less expence, than according to the mode hitherto in use.

In bringing this work to perfection, I had not my own advantage solely in view; I wished to be useful to the community; and it is with pleasure I see that the public will derive considerable benefit from my industry; for I have resolved to sell the REGISTER *One halfpenny* UNDER the price paid for seven out of eight of the morning

Fig. 84. The Daily Universal Register, *printed at the Logographic Press* was not set from type but cut on wood, secondly it was of a design of blackletter entirely without precedent. The heading-type of *The World* is 'old-world'; or rather 'Ye olde Tudor Tea-Shoppe' in connotation. The old solid blackletter type had been used for the words 'Morning Post', the only daily carrying a title in text. *The London Chronicle*, still, of course, an evening journal, was headed in text. But these were straightforward pieces in which the blackletter was obviously used as a bold type to distinguish the main from the sub-title. Bell's mock-antique was tricked out with a white line drawn or 'tooled' upon every letter—thus making a namby-pamby, artificial affair of it. The mannerism was consistent with, if not inspired by, Strawberry Hill. Unfortunately, *The World* became an immediate vogue—a rage, in fact—it was copied, everywhere, in every detail, leading, italics, small capitals, Strawberry Hill gothic and all. By 1800 all the daily papers in London had altered their make-up and headings into accordance with that of *The World*. The writing and reporting style, frivolous, up-to-date, and very personal, was also widely copied; a notably sedulous imitator being *The Times*, which, as *The Daily Universal Register*, started its career in 1785. The early years of *The Times*, in fact, form the best example of the effects of Bell and Topham's success. The future Thunderer grew out of a printing experiment into a copy of *The World*, before it came of age, and independence, under John Walter II.

About the year 1778, one Henry Johnson, intending to publish a lottery list, found that the work of composition could not be completed, as he desired, on the evening of each day's drawing. He devised a method of expediting the composition by soldering together types of two, three, four or five figures in advance. The success of these castings gave Johnson the idea of experimenting with affixes, suffixes and other language particles, and a royal patent was secured to protect the invention. Nothing was done, however, in any practical way, until John Walter, who had, owing to severe business reverses, failed as a coal-factor, resolved to undertake its commercial exploitation. Under the title of 'The Logographic Press', the former King's Printing House, Blackfriars, was refitted, during 1784, for the purpose of 'carrying on the printing business in general', and work was begun on Dr Watts's *Improvement of the Human Mind* as the first of a series of reprints of English classics. But books were a slow method of propaganda. For the better advertisement of the logographic method, and its claim to be more expeditious and economic than any other, the proprietor, counselled by friends, determined to print and publish a daily newspaper. There was issued on January 1, 1785, No. 1 of *The Daily Universal Register*, four pages in the now standardised full-folio. In most respects the appearance of the first paper resembled *The Morning Chronicle*, using the triple rule between different sections, and the french rule to mark distinctions between relatively similar sections. But the plan was alleged to be new. The front page of the *Universal Register* (see Fig. 84) gave two columns of preamble (concluding with a third overleaf) in which John Walter reasoned his justification for starting his paper.

"Some of the best, some of the most respectable, and some of the most useful members of the community, have frequently complained that by radical defects in the plans of the present established papers, they were deprived of many advantages, which ought naturally to result from daily publications", and, wrote John Walter, "it would seem that every News-Paper published in London is calculated for a particular set of readers only."

In the writer's judgment

A News-Paper, conducted on the true and natural principles of such a publication, ought to be the Register of the times, and faithful recorder of every species of intelligence; it ought not to be engrossed by any particular object; but, like a well-covered table, it should contain something suited to every palate...Such, it is intended, shall be the UNIVERSAL REGISTER, the great objects of which will be to facilitate the *commercial* intercourse between the different parts of the community, through the channel of *Advertisements*; to record the principal occurrences of the times; and to abridge the account of debates during the sitting of Parliament.

So far, the expressed purposes of *The Universal Register* differ only slightly from those of *The Morning Chronicle*. But it is otherwise when Walter, in proceeding, says that advertisements will not be 'sacrificed to the rage for parliamentary debates'. We need not consider the two points of view, but Walter should be quoted when he says that the 'extreme length of these debates so greatly retards the publication of the News-Papers which are noted for detailed accounts of them, that the advantages arising...are frequently over-balanced by the inconveniences occasioned to people in business by the delay'. The papers containing the completest reports are even published at noon—'nay, they sometimes are not even sent to press so soon; consequently parties interested in *sales* are essentially injured, as the advertisements, inviting the public to attend them at *ten* or *twelve* o'clock, do not appear, on account of a late publication, till some hours after'. As a protection to his advertisers, *The Universal Register* was promised at six o'clock every morning—'and, so great is the economy of the logographic method, at one halfpenny under the price paid for seven out of eight of the morning papers'.[1] As a policy *The Universal Register* was to be of no party and to be made up of articles of intelligence, parliamentary, summary and accounts of all remarkable trials at law, particularly those 'in which the mercantile world may be most interested'. The title of the newspaper was impressive in size and design, being printed from three wood blocks, viz. a centre royal device and two lettering pieces with flourishes. The whole has its precedent rather in provincial, than in metropolitan, journalism. Flourishes were common enough in the country. *The Berkshire Chronicle* (founded 1771), *The Kentish Gazette* (1770), and *The Chelmsford Chronicle* (1777) all display singularly fine flourished blackletter headings, and the *Daily Universal Register* heading is as good as any of them—and larger in scale, being 2½ in. deep. *The London Packet* was the only town journal with a calligraphically flourished heading and this, like the country specimens mentioned, was in blackletter.[2] The word 'Register', a novelty in the newspaper titling, is perhaps an equivalent of 'Advertiser' to which Walter felt himself driven by the existence of several papers using this name, and by the necessity for finding a new and suitably distinctive variation. Had John Walter worked in the printing industry for any length of time, it is probable that a title more orthodox in design, and less clumsy in phrasing, would have been chosen. Orthodoxy, however, was not John Walter's, any more than it was John Bell's, natural tendency. Walter believed in experiment, mechanical and other. A curious instance is indicated in the following paragraph which appeared in *The Daily Universal Register* for June 29, 1785:

☞ As many persons, particularly those in the commercial line, have experienced great inconvenience from not knowing those holidays usually called RED LETTER DAYS, when no business is transacted at the Public

[1] The extra halfpenny was added after a few months.

[2] John Almon, in association with William Woodfall and others, secured *The London Packet, or New Evening Post* (the sub-title was changed to *The New Lloyds Evening Post*, April 17, 1772), which had been founded as a thrice-weekly in 1771. It was often prosecuted, but maintained itself as an influential paper by reason of Almon's and Woodfall's attention to Parliamentary debates. In form the paper followed *The Morning Chronicle* except in the heading which was a singularly fine piece of flourished fraktur, equalled only by the later style of *Dawks's News-Letter*. There was a factotum in the first column which varied between the barock and the built-up printers' flowers type which contributed to the old-fashioned appearance of the paper. In 1870 Woodfall withdrew from the undertaking and the paper was printed with a simpler heading in the original *Morning Chronicle* style. The paper carried a 'Postscript' on the final page until the end of the century. The career of *The London Packet* ended in 1803, when it was absorbed by *The St James's Chronicle*.

Offices, the head of the UNIVERSAL REGISTER will in future be printed in red on such days which will, of course, prevent the trouble of referring to other publications.

The legend, in spaced capitals, 'THIS DAY IS A HOLIDAY AT ALL THE PUBLIC OFFICES' appeared immediately below the date line. This singular practice of red-printing was continued for two years, Lammas Day (August 1), 1787, being the first 'holiday' number to be in one colour.

A new heading-block of the same dimensions, but with bolder lettering, was substituted on December 13, 1786. It continued in use during the whole of 1787, memorable as the first year of *The World, and Fashionable Advertiser*. On January 1, 1788, *The Universal Register* 'added to its original name, that of the TIMES' which 'being a monosyllable, bids defiance to corrupters and mutilators of the language', and was, withal, free from risk, in the minds of coffee-house waiters and boys, who 'universally omitted the word "Universal"', of confusion with *The Annual Register* or *Harris's Register*, etc. The column and a half announcement of the change concluded with a paragraph affirming that

the alteration we have made in our *head* is not without precedents. *The World*[1] has parted with half its Caput Mortuum, and a moiety of its brains. *The Herald*[2] has cut off half its head and has lost its original humour. *The Post*, it is true, retains its old head and its old features, and, as to the other public prints, they appear as having neither *heads* nor *tails*.

The style of the typography of the first issue of *The Times* at last revealed some understanding of the fundamental problem of newspaper display: to order the material for rapid reading. Newspapers had been set by book-printers since their foundation, and, in consequence, the composition of both newspapers and books was solid. The founts of type were the same for both categories of printing, and, until *The World*, the methods of setting were identical. Bell had made *The English Chronicle* the most elegant sheet of its time, but its setting remained as bookish as the rest. *The World* was no less elegant in appearance, but in setting was more consistent with its purpose than any of its predecessors. Both Bell and Walter were book-printers to begin with. They knew already that the book is composed on the understanding that it will be read attentively, but they did not for a long time realise that the newspaper must be set-up on the understanding that it will

[1] *The World* dropped its sub-title 'And Fashionable Advertiser' on November 27, 1787. The 'AND' being within the centre of the device, a new block was necessary.

[2] *The Morning Herald* for some time after its foundation carried as sub-title the words 'And Daily Advertiser'.

be read inattentively. Moreover, a book is composed for consecutive, a newspaper for inconsecutive, reading; the nature of the book-page is homogeneous, of the newspaper, heterogeneous. It follows that news-paragraphs relating occurrences of the most diverse character demand a different setting from the consecutive paragraphs of a book, whatever its subject. That this lesson had to be learnt all over again by journalists of 1855 and even 1905, was due to the oppressive Stamp Acts which, rising to 4*d.* a copy, crushed every atom of spacing and leading out of the paper. All newspapers had set their news-paragraphs exactly as if they were the constituent paragraphs of a book page—until the first number of *The World* in 1787—and again, after 1815 until the first number of *The Daily Telegraph and Courier* in 1855.

Typographically, the first number of *The Times* (cf. Fig. 86) is a duplicate of *The World*, except the heading, an unprecedented piece, $5\frac{1}{8}$ in. × $2\frac{1}{4}$ in. deep, engraved in all probability by Richard Austin. The policy of the paper

Fig. 85. *John Walter's heading for* The Times, *March* 18, 1788, *copied from the lettering of* The World

had changed. During 1787 less interest was taken in the City and more in the West End, less in 'trade' and more in 'life'. Ungratefully enough, the approximation in typography and policy was accompanied by a stream of attacks on Bell and Topham's paper. *The Daily Universal Register*, on the eve of changing name, modestly allowed that 'it would savour too much of the vanity of *The World* to publish a panegyric on ourselves' and, in its issue for January 3, 1788, *The Times* pointed out 'What a very unaccountable thing it is, and yet it is as true as unaccountable, that the *best of Times* and a *trifling* World actually exist at the same moment...'. This was kindly, and not typical of the later acid paragraphs written by *The Times'* staff against 'Don Whiskerandos Tip-Top' and the 'Bell, which was hollow indeed'. Its typography and make-up prove its complete dependence upon the model of *The World*, except that John Walter clung to the long ſ with all its combinations until 1799. On March 18, 1788, the lettering of *The World* (it had dropped its sub-title) was copied, and a new royal device—of the same

THE TIMES
OR DAILY UNIVERSAL REGISTER
PRINTED LOGOGRAPHICALLY

NUMB. 940. TUESDAY, JANUARY 1, 1788. (Price Three-pence.)

Theatre-Royal, Drury-Lane.
By his MAJESTY's COMPANY,
THIS EVENING,
Will be presented the Tragedy of
JULIA:
OR, THE ITALIAN LOVER.
The principal Characters by
Mr. KEMBLE, and Mrs. SIDDONS.
The Prologue to be spoken by Mr. Kemble;
And the Epilogue, by Mrs. Siddons.
With new Dresses, Decorations, &c.
To which will be added
The DESERTER.
Henry, Mr. KELLY; Skirmish, Mr. BANNISTER, jun.
And Louisa, by Mrs. CROUCH.
Tomorrow, (by Desire) The Wonder, with, the 6th Time, Harlequin, jun. On Thursday the Tragedy of Percy; Elwina, Mrs. Siddons.

BY COMMAND OF HIS MAJESTY,
And under the same DIRECTORS as the CONCERT of ANTIENT MUSIC,

THE Oratorios of SOLOMON, ALEXANDER's FEAST with the CHOICE of HERCULES, JOSEPH, ACIS and GALATEA, with DRYDEN's ODE, ESTHER, and MESSIAH, will be performed on the Six FRIDAYS in LENT, at the CONCERT ROOM in TOTTENHAM-STREET.

Subscriptions taken at Messrs. Longman and Broderi 's Music Shops, in the Haymarket and Cheapside; and at Mr. Ashley's, No. 4, Pimlico; at Three Guineas each, the Tickets NOT transferable.

ROYALTY THEATRE,
WELL-STREET, NEAR GOODMAN's FIELDS.
THIS EVENING
An OCCASIONAL ADDRESS,
By Mr. PALMER,
In the Character of Christmas.
A Musical Entertainment, called
THOMAS and SUSAN Or,
The GENEROUS TAR.
For the 3d Time, a New Pantomimic Entertainment, called,
The DESERTER of NAPLES:
Or, ROYAL CLEMENCY.
Under the Direction of Mr. DELPINI.
The Airs, Duets and Choruses, composed by Mr. REEVE,
The DESERTER by Mr. PALMER.
The other Characters by
Mr. W. Palmer, Mr. Cooper, Mr. L'Estrange, Mr. Hudson, and Mr. DELPINI.
Mrs. Delpini, Modems. Bitthemer, and Mrs. GIBBS.
End of the first Part, a Grand Representation of MOUNT VESUVIUS at the Time of Eruption, with the Flowing of the Lava.
The Dances by Mr. Holland, Mad. Bitthemer, and Mad. Constance; composed by M MALTER.
A SONG by Master BRAHAM.
The Whole to conclude with (37th time) a new Pantomimic Entertainment, called
HARLEQUIN MUNGO;
Or, A PEEP INTO THE TOWER.
Harlequin, Mr. RAYNER, jun.
Mungo Harlequin, Mr. BOURKE;
Pantaloon, Mr. FOLLETT, sen.
Keeper of Wild Beasts and Warder of the Tower, (with a Chaunt) Mr. GRACE.
Captain, Sailor, and first Waterman (with Songs), Mr. ARROWSMITH;
Clown, Mr. FOLLET, jun.
Planter's Wife, Mrs. BURNETT;
And Columbine, Mrs. GIBBS.
In Part First, a Dance of Slaves, by Messrs. Holland, Bourke, Menage, &c.
To conclude with a grand Ballet,
By Mons. Malter, Mr. Holland, Mad. Bithemer, and Mademoiselle Constance.
Boxes 5s. Pit 3s. First Gall. 2s. Second Gall. 1s.
Places for the Boxes to be taken of Mr. Clark, at the Stage Door of the Theatre.
The Doors to be opened for the future at Half past Five, and to begin precisely at Half past Six o Clock.
*** No Money will be returned after the Curtain is drawn up; nor will any Person be admitted behind the Scenes. Vivant Rex & Regina.
N. B. Nothing under 3s will be taken.

TO BE LETT OR SOLD,
EXTENSIVE Premises in the Neighbourhood of Cheapside.
Apply at No. 9, Cheapside.

A CAUTION to prevent IMPOSITION.
SHARP's CONCAVE RAZORS
ARE made of the very best Steel that can be possibly procured in this or any other country, tempered and finished with the greatest nicety and circumspection. Their superior excellence above all others, has made them more esteemed, than any Razor now in use; the consequence of which is, that some persons have offered, and still do offer, an inferior article under their name.

C. SHARP, Perfumer and Razor-Maker to his Royal Highness the Prince of Wales, at No. 131, Fleet-street; and No. 57, Cornhill,

Most respectfully intreats the public to observe, that his Concave Razors are not sold at any other places in London, but at his shops as above, Sharp stamped on the blade of the Razors; all others are counterfeits.

Sharp's Metalic Razor Strops, which keep the Razor in good order, without the use of a Hone or grinding, are not to be equalled; but the above articles are too well esteemed to need any thing being said in their behalf.— His Alpine Soap for shaving, is by far the best adapted for that purpose of any yet invented; it never causes the least smarting sensation, but is perfectly soft, sweet and pleasing. Likewise, his curious Cyprian Wash-balls. Great variety of shaving cases and pouches, that hold all the implements necessary for shaving, dressing, &c.

Sharp's sweet, hard, and soft pomatums, are remarkable for keeping good in any climate, longer than any other. His Lavender Water drawn from the flowers, his warranted Tooth Brushes, and the Prince of Wales's Tooth Powder, are articles worthy the attention of the public.

Combs, soaps, wash-balls, and every article in the Perfumery branch, wholesale, retail, and for exportation.

N. B. Families, &c. who take any of Sharp's articles by the dozen, save considerably.

A complete Dressing-case, fitted up with razors, combs, &c. for 10s. 6d.

KING's THEATRE, Haymarket.
By PARTICULAR DESIRE, on Thursday next, January 3, 1788.
WILL BE PRESENTED THE SERIO-COMIC OPERA, called
IL RE TEODORO in VENEZIA,
Or, THEODORE, KING OF CORSICA, AT VENI
The Principal Characters by
Sig. MORELLI, Sig. MORIGI,
Sig. BALELI, Sig. CALVESI,
And Sig. FINESCHI,
Signora SESTINI, and Signora STORACE.
The Music composed in his best stile, by the celebrated Mr. PAESIELO,
Under the Direction of
Sig. MAZZINGHI.
And Leader of the Orchestra, Mr. CRAMER.
Painter and Machinist, Sig. GAETANO MARINARI.
Inventor and Maker of the Dresses, Sig. LUPINO.
The Doors to be opened at Six, and begin precisely at Half past Seven o'Clock.
Pit 10s. 6d. First Gallery 5s. Upper Gallery 3s.
Tickets to be had, and Subscriptions paid, as usual, at Messrs. Ransom, Moreland, and Hammersley's, Bankers, No. 57, Pall-Mall.

End of Act I. a New DIVERTISSEMENT, composed by Mons. CHEVALIER, and performed by
Mons VESTRIS, Mons. COULON,
And Mons. CHEVALIER;
The two Miss SIMONETS, Signora BEDINI,
And Mad. COULON.
End of the Opera, a New BALLET, composed by Mons. NOVERRE, called,
LES OFFRANDES A L'AMOUR.
And performed by
Mons. VESTRIS, Mons. COULON,
And Mons. DIDELOT,
Miss HILLESBERG, Mad VEDIE,
And Mad. COULON.
The other Characters by
Messrs. SAUNLIER, COULON, HENRY, SALA,
Madomoiselles GRENIER, &c. &c.
And MEZIERRES.
N. B. For the better accommodation of the Subscribers, the office is removed back to Union-court, Haymarket.
The Nobility and Gentry are requested to take notice, that the first Masqued Ball will be given at this place, on Monday, the 4th of February, 1788.

NEW MUSIC.
This day is published,
By *LONGMAN* AND *BRODERIP*,
Music Sellers, and Musical Instrument Makers to his Royal Highness the PRINCE of WALES,
No. 26, Cheapside, and No. 13, Haymarket,

Authors		£	s	d
J. Haydn,	THREE SYMPHONIES for a Grand Orchestra, dedicated to his Royal Highness the Prince of Wales, Op. 51.	0	10	6
Ditto,	A Set of QUARTETTS for two Violins, Tenor and Violoncello expressive of the Passion of our Saviour, Op. 48.	0	8	0
Mozart,	Two SYMPHONIES for a Grand Orchestra, Op. 8 and 9, each	0	6	0
Ditto,	Six QUARTETTS, dedicated to Mr. Haydn, Op. 10.	0	15	0
Ditto,	QUARTETT for the Harpsichord	0	3	0
Storace,	CARE DONNE CHE BRAMATE, sung by Signora Storace, in Il Re Teodore in Venezia	0	2	6
Pleyel,	Two SONATAS for the Harpsichord, with an Accompaniment for a Violin, Op. 7.	0	4	0
Ditto,	TRIOS for a Violin, Tenor, and Violoncello, Op. 11.	0	6	0
Giordani,	Three GRAND DUETS for the Harpsichord, from the works of Haydn	0	7	6
Chalon,	Three DUETTS for the Harpsichord, Op. 7.	0	7	6
Barthelemon.	COMPLETE INSTRUCTIONS for the Pedal Harp, with Airs, Arpegios and Sonatas, and an easy method for tuning	0	10	6
Percy,	Six ITALIAN ARIETTAS in the Venetian style, for the Voice and Piano Forte, Op. 5.	9	5	0
Starkel,	Three SONATAS for the Harpsichord, with Accompaniments, Op. 22.	0	7	6
Millico,	A Fourth Set of Six ITALIAN CANZONETS, dedicated to Lady Louisa Hervey.	0	5	0
Bishop,	Six MINUETS, and Twelve COUNTRY DANCES, for the year 1788.	0	2	6
Jones,	Ditto, ditto, ditto.	0	2	6
Shield,	The FARMER, a Comic Opera, for the Voice and Harpsichord.	0	6	0

NEW MUSIC.
This Day are published,
By J. BLAND, No. 45, Holborn,
THE SONGS in Robin Hood, of "Charming Clorinda," and "When generous Wine," sung by Mr. Bowden, 1s. each. "When ruddy Aurora," and "The Trump of Fame," each 6d. Aurora, a ballad, 1s. He vow'd to love me, Goodwin, cantata; O thou wert born to please me, a duet; Ye woods and ye mountains, an elegy; each 6d. Bland's 13th and 14th ladies glees, each 1s. 6d. Ditto, first vol. of ditto, bound, 18s. Periodical Ital. song, No. 35. 2s. 6d; ditto No. 36, 2s. 6d. Pleyl's Sonatas composed for the harpsichord, op. 7. 4s. C. I. L. T. Sonatinas, dedicated to Dr. Burney, 5s., Mozart's Terzelte, 2s. 6d Bland's Harpsichord Collection, No. 1. to 6, each 5s. Hoffmeister s Duets, violin and violoncello, op. 6. or 13. 4s. Ditto Flute Trios; 6s. Ditto Flute Quartets, 10s. 6d. and a variety of new publications.

OIL AND LAMP WAREHOUSE.
No. 5, New-street, Covent-Garden.
GEORGE DOWNING, Oil Merchant, proprietor of the above Warehouse, begs leave to offer the most proper tender of his grateful acknowledgments to the Nobility, Gentry, and public in general, for the repeated favours conferred on him, the respectfully informs his friends, that the OIL and LAMP TRADE continues to be transacted on the same liberal terms, that first recommended him to their particular attention.
N. B. Orders for town and country executed with punctuality.
New-street, Covent Garden, Jan. 1, 1788.

CALEDONIAN MACABAU SNUFF.
JOHN YOUNG, Manufacturer and Vender of the Hibernian high dried or Lundy Foot's Snuff, presents his respects to the Nobility, Gentry, &c. with his Caledonian Macabau Snuff, which upon trial he is convinced will be found deserving the estimation his Irish Snuff has so justly acquired. Orders sent to his Snuff Manufactory, No. 73, in Drury-Lane, near Russel Court, will be attended to with the highest respect and gratitude.
N. B. Snuffs and Tobacco in the highest perfection.

STATIONARY.
ADAM THOMPSON, at his Paper Manufacturers Warehouse, Hand-Court, Upper Thames-street, begs leave to return his Friends sincere thanks for all past favours; and as he is now well stocked with a general and choice Assortment of Writing, Printing, Wrapping, Sugar and Blue Papers, summer made, shall be happy to receive their farther orders, which shall be duly attended to on the most moderate terms. Notes and Bills taken in payment, at one, two, and three months.
N. B. Has also about fifty reams French Mezzotinto Bay, to be sold 20 per cent. below current price.

NEW MUSIC.
This Day is published,
By LONGMAN and BRODERIP, No. 26, Cheapside, No. 13, Haymarket; and at their Manufactory in Tottenham Court Road.
MUSICAL INSTRUMENT MAKERS, AND SELLERS, TO HIS ROYAL HIGHNESS THE PRINCE OF WALES;
THE New Comic Opera, now performing at Covent-Garden Theatre with great applause, called the Farmer, composed and compiled by Mr. Shield, 6s. Pleyel's two grand Sonatas, op. 7. for the Piano Forte, 4s. Pleyel's three Trios Concertante op. 11. for a violin, tenor, and violincello 6s.; Percy's Italian Arietts, op. 5th, 5s.; Mozart's Harpsichord Quartett, 2s. 6d.; complete Instructions for Pedal Harp, with a Selection of favourite Songs and Sonatas, by Mr. Barthelemon, 10s 6d. Stockel's three Sonatas, op. 22, with accompanyments 7s. 6d; Thomas and Susan, or the Fortunate Tar, performed at the Royalty Theatre, 3s 6d.; Chalon's three Duets for the piano forte, op. 7th, 7s. 6d.; Mozart's Airs, with Variations for the piano forte, each 2s.; Breval's hasy Solos for the violincello, op 18th, 7s. 6d.; Clementi's Sonata, op. 20, 3s.—Lately imported from the Continent, great variety of Harp Music, by the most eminent masters; together with the most distinguished new works of the following authors, consisting of Simphonie, Concertos, Quartetts, Trios, Duets, Solos, and Harpsichord Sonatas, by Haydn, Preyel, Kozeluch, Mozart, Breval, Trickler, Fodor, Devieme, Vanhal, Stirkel, Viotti, &c.—Also the Overture and Songs of Tarare, and select Collections of the most favourite Songs from the latest French operas, for the Harpsichord.—Where may be seen, their new-improved grand and small Piano Fortes, and Mr. Corri's new-invented Harpsichord Desk, with a Dictionary of Musical Terms, Examples, &c.—Also, his new-invented Piano Forte Board, with Dictionary, &c. Each one Guinea.

THE OPERA FANS.
To the Subscribers and Frequentors of the
KING's THEATRE,
Last Saturday were published, according to Act of Parlament.
THE delivery, however, was put off till the re-opening of the Opera House, next week, for the purpose of presenting them in the best state of improvement.
These FANS, calculated to present, at one view, both the number of boxes, including the additional ones, names of Subscribers, &c. have been carefully compared with the plan of the House, as kept at the Office, and will be sold only by the Proprietors,
Mrs. H. M. No. 81, Hay-Market,
Where she will receive, with respectful gratitude, any commands from the ladies, and wait on them if required

HANDEL's SUBSCRIPTION.
Dedicated by Permission to His MAJESTY,
This day is published,
THE ELEVENTH NUMBER of HANDEL's WORKS. The Four First Numbers, comprehending the compleat Score of the Oratorio of Athalia; the four following the whole of Theodora, and the remainder a large portion of the Messiah. The elegant Apothesis of Handel will be delivered to subscribers only, with the Twelth Number.
Subscriptions are received by Dr. Arnold, No. 480, Strand; Messrs. Longman and Broderip, No. 13, Haymarket; and Birchall and Co. New Bond-street.

This day is published,
Price 2s. 6d separately, or 4s. 6d. together,
AN ABRIDGMENT of the MEMORIAL addressed to the KING of FRANCE.
By M. DE CALONNE,
Minister of State.
In FRENCH and ENGLISH.
TRANSLATED from the French by W. WALTER
Printed at the *Logographic Press*, by J. WALTER, Printing House Square, Blackfriars; and sold by Messrs. Robson and Clarke, and T. Hookham, New Bond Street; P. Elmsley, Strand; Messrs. Egertons, Charing-Cross; and W. Richardson, Royal Exchange.

This day is published,
Price One Shilling,
CRAZY KATE; A FAVOURITE BALLAD;
Taken from Cowper's Task,
Set to Music, with Accompaniments,
By JOHN MOULDS
THE FEAST OF APOLLO, No. IV.
Price One Shilling,
Containing a Favourite Overture for the Piano Forte,
"Sans Vous Ma Chere," a Favourite Song.
"The Sailor he fears not the Roar of the Seas," ditto.
London: Printed for G. Goulding, Haydn's Head, No. 6, James-street, Covent Garden.
Where may be had,
LA FEVRE,
Taken from STERNE,
A Favourite SONG, set to Music by HAYDN,
Price only Sixpence.
"The Sailor he fears not the Roar of the Seas."
A Favourite SONG, set to Music with Accompanyments by RELFE, Price One Shilling.
SANS VOUS MA CHERE,
A Favourite SONG, sung by Mr. INCLEDON at Bath.
Composed by MOULDS. Price Sixpence.

Theatre-Royal, Covent-Garden.
THIS EVENING,
Will be presented the revived Tragedy of
The ROMAN FATHER
Horatius, Mr. Farren; Tullus Hostilius, Mr. Alckin Valerius, Mr. Davies; and Publius, Mr. Pope. Valeria Mrs. Morton; and Horatia, Miss Brunton.
In Act V. will be introduced a Roman Ovation.
To which will be added, (6th time) a New Pantomime called
THE DUMB CAKE;
Or, the REGIONS OF FANCY.
With new Music, Scenery, Dresses, Machinery, and Decorations.
N. B. Nothing under full price will be taken
To-morrow, (not acted this Season) The Suspicious Husband; Ranger, Mr. LEWIS, and Clarinda, Mrs. ABINGTON.

PROPAGATION OF A LIE.
W DICKINSON, Bond-Street, has this Day published a Print from an original Drawing, by H. Bunbury, Esq. representing the Propagation of a Lie. being a companion to the much admired print of the Long Minuet.
Likewise just published,
An Academy for grown Horsemen, containing the compleatest instructions for

Walking,	Galloping,
Trotting,	Stumbling, and
Cantering,	Tumbling.

Illustrated with Copper-plates, and adorned with a Portrait of the Author, by Geoffry Gambado, Esq. Riding-master, Master of the Horse, Grand Equerry to the Doge of Venice.
Where likewise is published all Mr. Bunbury's elegant and caricature Prints.

FESTIVAL OF ANACREON.
This day is published, price 3s. 6d.
A New Edition, of
THE FESTIVAL of ANACREON: Containing the Songs of Capt. Morris, Mr. Hewerdine and other Lyric Writers, as sung at the Anacreontic Society, the Beef-Steak, and Humbug Clubs.
Published by William Holland, No. 50. Oxford-street, near Berner's-street, removed from No. 66, Drury-Lane.
Of whom may be had, just published,
A Portrait of Kitty Cut-a-Dash; a Dilly setting out from King's Place with a Guard; History of Modern Flagellants, in seven distinct works, each of which may be had separate; Comtesse de Barre's Whim; the Pretty Nursery Maid; My Aunt; Hal's Looking Glass; and a large Collection of Books, Pamphlets, Paintings, Drawings, and Prints, for the Cabinets of the Moralist, the Politician, and the Bon Vivant.
☞ Pæans of Pleasure, and Memoirs of Kitty Cut-a-Dash, will be speedily published.

This day is published,
Price Six Shillings in Boards,
MEDICAL COMMENTARIES for the Year 1787, exhibiting a concise View of the latest and most important Discoveries in Medicine and Medical Philosophy; collected and published by
ANDREW DUNCAN, M. D. F. R. & A. S. Edin. &c.
Decade Second. Volume Second.
Printed for C. Elliot, T. Kay, and Co. opposite Somerset-Place, Strand, London; and C. Elliot, Edinburgh.
Of whom may be had,
Complete SETS of DECADE FIRST, from 1773 to 1785, inclusive. Ten vols. 8vo. price 3l. in boards, and 3l. 10s bound.
ALSO,—Vols. 8, for 1781-2, Vol. 9, for 1783-4, Vol. 10, for 1785, and Vol. 1. Decade II. for 1786, at Six Shillings each in boards.
N. B. As above may be had gratis,—C. Elliot, T. Kay, and Co.'s Catalogue of Books in all the different branches of Medicine for 1788, with the lowest prices affixed.

This Day are published,
Printed in One Volume Octavo, on a superfine Medium Paper, price 6s. in Boards,
I.
FAMILIAR and FRIENDLY CORRESPONDENCE of FREDERICK the SECOND, KING of PRUSSIA, with U. F. DE SUHM, Counsellor to the Elector of Saxony.
II.
Handsomely printed in 2 vols. large Octavo, on a Superfine medium Paper, price 12s. in Boards,
A SELECTION from the WORKS of FRANCIS LORD BACON, Viscount St. Alban; consisting of his ESSAYS on Civil, Moral, Literary, and Political Subjects; the Advancement of Learning, System of Moral Philosophy, Theology, &c. and his celebrated History of Life and Death; together with his own Life, by Dr. WILLYMOTT.
III.
In 2 Vols. 8vo. on a superfine Medium Paper, Price 12s in Boards, illustrated with Copper-plates,
A new and elegant Edition of
DR. DERHAM's PHYSICO and ASTRO-THEOLOGY; the first contains a Demonstration of the Being and Attributes of God, from his Works of the Creation; the second, a General Survey of the Heavens; with considerable Notes, and many curious Observations.
IV.
In Three Volumes, price 9s. sewed,
The MINIATURE PICTURE;
OR,
PLATONIC MARRIAGE.
A NEW NOVEL.
By Mrs. CARTWRIGHT.
This Lady displays, throughout the work, a perfect knowledge of the human passions, and the characters are pourtrayed in the most chaste and elegant language.
V.
Elegantly printed in a small Pocket Volume, on superfine Writing Paper, Price 1s. 6d. sewed in Marble Paper,
A New Edition, being the Third, of
LETTERS which passed between an ILLUSTRIOUS PERSONAGE, and a LADY of HONOUR at Brighton.
London: Printed at the *Logographic Press*, by J. Walter Printing-House-Square, Blackfriars; and sold by T. Longman, Paternoster-row; Robson and Clarke, New-Bond-street, and W. Richardson, under the Royal Exchange.

Fig. 86. The Times (*i.e. No.* 940 *of* The Daily Universal Register) dimensions as *The World*'s badge—adopted. Thus *The Times*, abandoning its roman lettering, came into possession of the shadowed mock-gothic which Bell had introduced into English journalism in January 1787. The Walter lettering is so similar to Bell's that it is hardly possible to doubt that it was engraved by the same artist, Richard Austin, who had cut the punches for Bell's set of new types, slowly being prepared at his foundry.[1] *The Times*, then ambitious to become 'an amusing and instructive Companion for the Breakfast-table',[2] as yet gave no sign that it was destined to achieve such a paramount position that the story of nineteenth-century development in journalism is little more than an account of Printing House Square enterprise.

The World continued as the first fashionable paper. In May 1789, the separation of Topham and Bell, after a quarrel, led to the foundation of a new morning paper which, disregarding all the precedents of Advertisers, Posts, Registers, Chronicles, Heralds, etc., called itself *The Oracle; Bell's New World*. The first number of this appeared on June 1, 1789, and was advertised to be 'novel, interesting and useful'. Six columns of the first number were devoted to a recital of Bell's charges against Topham—exciting indeed to the many business rivals of the former partners, and to the smart set to whom the witty Topham's sartorial extravagances and matrimonial adjustments were of prime curiosity. Bell, however hard he pursued his vendetta in *The Oracle*, later proved himself a generous forgiver; but the early issues of the paper shew that the fortnight which had elapsed between the withdrawal of *The World* from his office, and the issue of No. 1 of *The Oracle*, was insufficient for the due organisation of a news service. Hence it consisted of personal letters, attacks and sallies, news from Vauxhall and Ranelagh, and abuse of the old *World*. Topham persevered with his paper, now printed by R. Bostock of 335 Strand, but the break with Bell robbed *The World* of an indefatigable manager—and *The Oracle* as much needed Topham's direction. In this situation, the other papers regained a little of the public esteem which they had lost during the brilliance of *The World* when jointly controlled by Bell and Topham. John Walter's venture was being consolidated, but the more slowly for his obstinate adhesion to the logographic principle, long a proved failure.[3] *The Public Advertiser*'s position

[1] For an account of Bell's British Letter Foundry, see Morison on *John Bell*. For Richard Austin, see appendix, p. 137.

[2] The leaflet addressed 'To the Readers of News-Papers', B.M. P.B. 823 c. 1, is a lengthy statement of the reasons for the change of name and is worth reading.

[3] See Bell's attack on the patent in *The Morning Post*, February 15, 1785. Walter had printed Bellamy's Memoirs for him.

The Star
VESPERO SURGENTE.
AND
EVENING ADVERTISER.
ICH DIEN

NUMBER 1.] SATURDAY, MAY 3, 1788. [PRICE

PUBLIC AMUSEMENTS.

ING's THEATRE.—THIS EVENING, will be presented the favourite Serious Opera of
GIUDIO SABINO.
The Music composed by Signor SARTI,
Under the directions of MAZZINGHI.
The principal Characters by
Signor MARCHESI,
Signor BALLELI, Signor CALVESI,
And Signor PORLIVESI.
Signora SCHINOTTI,
And Signora GIULIANI.
Leader of the Orchestra, Mr. CRAMER.
End of the First Act an entire New Ballad, Serious and mi-characteristic, composed by Monf. NOVERRE, and formed by Monf. GARDEL, Mad. COULON, Miss LLIGSBERG, Monf. DIDELOT, Monf. CHEVALIR, Monf. HENRY, the two Miss SIMONETS, Miss RVEY, and Monf. VESTRIS.
End of the Opera a New Ballad,
Composed by Monf. NOVERRE, called
LES FETES DE TEMPE.
The principal characters by Miss Hilligsberg, Mad. alon, Monf. Didelot, Monf. Vestris, Monf. Henry, the Miss Simonets, and Monf. Coulon.
ainter and Machinist, Sig. GARTANO MARINARI; Inventor and Maker of the Dresses, Sig. LUPINO.
The doors to be opened at half past Six, and begin precisely half past Seven o'clock.
Vivant Rex et Regina.

FOR THE BENEFIT OF
Mr. FEARON.
OVENT-GARDEN.—On WEDNESDAY next, May 7, will be presented, the last New Play, called
SUCH THINGS ARE.
The PRINCIPAL CHARACTERS by
Mr. LEWIS, Mr. QUICK, Mr. POPE,
Mr. FARREN, Mr. MACREADY, Mr. DAVIES,
Mr. FEARON,
Mr. BOOTH, Mr. THOMPSON.
Mrs. MATTOCKS, Mrs. MOUNTAIN,
And Mrs. POPE.
To which will be added, the Burletta of
POOR VULCAN!
Vulcan, Mr. QUICK;
The Squire, Mr. JOHNSTONE;
Joe, Mr. DAVIES;
Bacchus, Mr. BONVILLE; Apollo, Mr. BROWN;
Mercury, Mr. BLURTON; Serjeant, Mr. DARLEY;
Grace, Mrs. BROWN,
And Maudlin, Mrs. MARTYR.
Tickets to be had of Mr. Fearon, No. 1, Broad Court; of Mr. Brandon, at the Theatre; where places for the es may be taken.

FOR THE BENEFIT OF
Mrs. WEBB.
OVENT-GARDEN.—On THURSDAY, May 8, will be performed the favourite Comic era of
FONTAINBLEAU;
Or, OUR WAY IN FRANCE.
Lackland, Mr. LEWIS,
Lepoche, Mr. QUICK,
Squire Tally-ho, Mr. EDWIN,
Sir John Bull, Mr. BOOTH,
Lord Winlove, Mr. DAVIES,
Colonel Epaulette, Mr. WEWITZER,
And Henry, Mr. JOHNSTONE.
Mrs. Casey, Mrs. KENNEDY,
Celia, Mrs. MARTYR,
Rosa (first time), Mrs. MOUNTAIN,
Lady Bull, Mrs. WEBB,
Nanette, Mrs. MORTON,
And Miss Dolly Bull, Mrs. MATTOCKS.
WITH
ENTERTAINMENTS.
Tickets to be had of Mrs. Webb, No. 38, King-street, Covent-Garden; and of Mr. Brandon at the Theatre, where places for the Boxes may be taken.

FOR THE BENEFIT OF
Mr. WILD.
OVENT-GARDEN.——On MONDAY, May 12, will be performed for the first time at this Theatre, and with permission of G. COLMAN, Esq. a Comedy in three acts, called
TIT FOR TAT.
Villamour, Mr. FARREN
(Being his first appearance in that character);
Old Meanwell, Mr. BOOTH;
Young Meanwell, Mr. MACREADY;
And Skipwell, Mr. RYDER
(Being the first time of his performing that character in England).
Letty, Mrs. MATTOCKS,
And Florinda, Mrs. WELLS
(Being their first appearance in those characters).
End of Act II. A description of the Curiosities in the Tower, By Mr. EDWIN.
After which a FAVOURITE PIECE in Two Acts.
To which will be added, the revived Pantomime of
THE ROYAL CHACE;
Or, HARLEQUIN SKELETON.
Harlequin, by a GENTLEMAN
(Being his first appearance on any stage);
Pantaloon, Mr. THOMPSON;
Old Woman, Mr. STEVENS;
Pierrot, Mr. BLANCHARD;
And Columbine, Mrs. WATTS.
Tickets and places for the boxes to be had of Mr. Wild, No. 7, Catharine-street, Strand; and of Mr. Brandon, at the Stage door.

CORNISH's REFINED LIQUORICE,
COUGHS, COLDS, and HOARSENESS,
THE ORIGINAL PREPARER, in Boxes, at 1s. or 6d. each, at his Drug and Chemical Warehouse, No. 403, opposite Salisbury-street, Strand, and the Warehouse for D. Ingram's Medicines.
N. B. Great allowance made to those who buy to sell again.

PUBLIC AMUSEMENTS.

ROYAL SOCIETY OF MUSICANS, under the PATRONAGE of THEIR MAJESTIES, and under the Direction of
The Earl of UXBRIDGE, Honorary President.
The Marquis of CAERMARTHEN,
The Earl of EXETER,
The Earl of SANDWICH,
Lord Viscount DUDLEY and WARD,
Lord Viscount FITZWILLIAM,
Lord GREY DE WILTON,
Sir WATKIN WILLIAMS WYNN, Bart.
JOAH BATES, Esq.
Honorery Vice Presidents.
Will be performed in the PANTHEON,
On FRIDAY, the 16th of MAY,
A SELECTION OF MUSIC,
From the Works of HANDEL.
Act I. Overture and Marchs (Scipio.)—Chorus. The many rend the Skies. (Alexander's Feast.)—Song. Pleasure my former ways resigning. (Time and Truth.) Mr. Harrison.—Second Grand Concerto.—Long. Caro vieni a me, (Richard the First.) Signora Storace.—Air. Tyrants would in impious throngs. Madame Mara. Athalia.—Chorus. Tyrants would in vain conspire. Athalia.—Song. Dal 'ondoso periglio. (Julius Cæsar). Signor Marchesi.—Chorus. No more to Ammon's God and King. (Jephtha.)
Act II. From harmony, from heavenly harmony. (Dryden's Ode.)—Song. Angels ever bright and fair. (Theodora.) Madame Mara.—The Passions. (Solomon.) Air and Recitatives. Mr. Harrison.—Eleventh Grand Concerto.—Song. O Caro Parolette. (Orlando.) Signora Storace.—Chorus. May no rash intruder. (Solomon.)—Song. Doppo l'Ottore. (Otho.) Signor Marchesi.—Recitative. But bright Cecilia raised the wonder higher. Madame Mara.—Air and Grand Chorus. As from the power of sacred lays. (Dryden's Ode.)
The following is a list of the principal Vocal Performers, who have generously offered their assistance at this performance:—Madame Mara, Signora Storace, Mr. Harrison, Signor Marchesi, Mr. Parry, Mr. Sale, Mr. Knyvett, Mr. Champness, Mr. Dyne, Mr. Hindle, Osmand, &c. &c.
In the list of Instrumental Performers are:—Mess. Cramer, Crosdill, Mara, Parke, William Parke, Borghi, Ashley, Baumgarten, Hogg, Lyon, Holmes, Foster, Blake, Dance, Soderini, Giarboldi, Billington, Hackwood, Scola, Phillips, Waterhouse, Napier, Shield, Gresbach, Sharp, Neibour, Sarjant, Patri, Kellner, Cantelo, Fitzgerald, Aibridge, &c. &c.
The Tickets for this Musical Festival in the Pantheon, are now delivering at One Guinea each, at the Office at St. Alban's Tavern, at Longman and Broderip's Music-shops, in Cheapside and the Hay-market.
The doors to be opened at Six o'Clock, and begin at Eight precisely.

PANTHEON.
A GENERAL REHEARSAL OF THE MUSIC selected for the Grand Performance of the ROYAL SOCIETY OF MUSICIANS, on THURSDAY the 15th of May.
The doors to be opened on that occasion at Ten o'Clock, to begin at Twelve o'Clock exactly.
Admittance HALF-A-GUINEA.
By Order of the Directors,
JOHN ASHLEY.
Books of this performance (including a correct list of the Benefactors, Honorary Subscribers, Professional Members of the Royal Society of Musicians; also an Alphabetical List of the Band, are to be had at the Pantheon only. Those which may be sold in the streets, or elsewhere, will be spurious and imperfect.

May 2, 1788.
ROYAL CIRCUS.—THIS and EVERY EVENING, till further Notice,
Will be presented the following Entertainments:
A NEW COMIC BALLET DANCE,
Composed by Mr. SIMONET.
The Principal Characters by Monf. Sauhnier, Monf. Bedotti, Madame Julien, Miss Granier, and the two Miss Simonets.
HORSEMANSHIP,
In various Parts,
By Mr. HUGHES and PUPILS
A new Humorous Burlesque Entertainment, called
THE HUBBUBBINARIANS;
Or, THE SHOREDITCH SCAVOIR VIVRE.
The Principal Characters by Mr. Davidson, Mr. Grove, Mr. Colvill, Mr. Page, and Others.
With new Scenery, Dresses, and Decorations,
Under the Direction of Mr. DELPINI, Acting Manager.
A new Comic Divertissement, called
A DUTCH TEA-GARDEN,
Composed and directed by Mr. DELPINI, Acting Manager, With new Music, Scenery, Dresses, and Decorations.
THE NEW FOUR AND TWENTY FIDLERS,
By Mr. WILLIAM PALMER,
As sung by him at the Royalty Theatre with the greatest Applause.
To conclude with a Musical, Comic, Pantomimic Entertainment, called
THE VICISSITUDES OF HARLEQUIN.
Box 3s. Pit 2s. Gallery 1s.
Places for the Boxes to be taken of Mr. Read, at the Stage Door.
N. B. A variety of Entertainments are in preparation, and will be produced as speedily as possible.

MR. WELCH, No. 102, near Beaufort Buildings, Strand, respectfully acquaints his Senior Friends, and such Ladies and Gentlemen as wish to be initiated or improved in private Lessons, that his ACADEMY for DANCING, continued upwards of twenty-one years, is now open, where address and every requisite accomplishment in the line of Dancing are taught. There are evenings appropriated for such Scholars as choose to join for their improvement in Country Dances, Cotillons, &c.
In order to prevent unnecessary application, this Academy is to be considered as a place of decorum, where no promiscuous Company are admitted; and circumspection is paid to the character and respectability of those who apply, except introduced or recommended.
N. B. The Academy is attended on Thursdays and Saturdays afternoon, from three till five o'clock, for young Ladies.

PUBLIC AMUSEMENTS, &c.

PANTON-STREET, HAY-MARKET.
ON MONDAY NEXT, for the Seventeenth Time, at the Great Exhibition Room, No. 6, will be presented,
COLLINS's EVENING BRUSH.
With the
ANNALS of the GREEN-ROOM, A-LA-SCARRON:
INTERSPERSED WITH
ORIGINAL SONGS.
Particularly,
THE STAGE-PLAY OF LIFE, DATE OBULUM BELISARIO, THE SPORTS OF THE TOWN, and THE DAYS OF QUEEN BESS.
To begin precisely at Eight.—Doors open at Seven.
Admittance—Three Shillings.
N. B. As this Exhibition, which the Public have so highly honoured with its approbation, will be very shortly published by the Author, together with all the Songs, and a copious collection of others never yet in print, for which he has already near three thousand subscribers; he earnestly requests his patrons and friends to pay no regard to any spurious catchpennies which may possibly anticipate the said publication.
Mr. COLLINS's constant nights are Mondays and Fridays.

MONEY on BOND, or otherwise.
THE Nobility, Gentry, Ladies possessed of DOWERS, SETTLEMENTS, or JOINTURES; CLERGY, OFFICERS of the GUARDS, ARTILLERY, ENGINEERS, INVALIDS, or the LINE on HALF-PAY; MARINES in FULL or HALF-PAY; PLACEMEN, PENSIONERS, or any persons possessed of FREEHOLD, COPYHOLD, or LEASEHOLD ESTATES, or INCOMES for LIFE, of any description whatever, may be accommodated with MONEY, from 100l. to any amount, on applying by letters, (post paid) or personally, to Mr. TEASDALE, facing the ADMIRALTY, Whitehall.
N. B. From 500l. to any amount always ready to be lent on MORTGAGES, at four and a half and five per cent. and from SIX to FIFTEEN YEARS PURCHASE, given to GRANTORS of WELL-SECURED ANNUITIES, according to the nature of the security.
All ANNUITIES granted here are covenanted in the deed, to be paid off at the pleasure of the Grantor.

No. 107, Corner of Savoy-steps, Strand.
A SAUCE FOR COLD MEATS.
BURGESS having been applied to by a Number of Families, for a SAUCE to eat with all kinds of COLD MEATS, has now prepared one, which he flatters himself will be found a most useful and agreeable article.
SAUCE ROYAL.
BURGESS's NEW-INVENTED SAUCE ROYAL, which he can offer to the Nobility, Gentry, and Families in general, as one of the highest-finished and most convenient articles ever used, for dressing all kinds of stewed Carp, Tench, Barble, Pyke, Eels, and for making of Matlets with a very small expence, and without any trouble, as it only requires the fish to be stewed gently in a little broth or gravy, and when done sufficiently, let it be taken out and put on the dish it is to be served on, then add a small quantity of the Sauce Royal to the liquor that remains, and thicken it with a little butter and flour, pour it over your fish, and it will be found superior to the extravagant methods that are used in preparing those kinds of dishes. It is likewise an excellent sauce for the sideboard, with plain butter; it is proper for all kinds of fish. Burgess warrants it to keep years in any climate.
ESSENCE OF ANCHOVIES.
BURGESS's GENUINE ESSENCE of ANCHOVIES, which makes in a moment the richest and best Anchovy Sauce that is possible to be made, and will keep for years in any climate. Families returning to their country residence, going to watering places, Captains of ships, and every person who travels, will find great use and satisfaction in providing themselves with Burgess's Essence of Anchovies, which he has made for these thirteen years past with credit to himself, and great satisfaction to families in general; it is proved to be an excellent article, and what can be relied upon. Also for Hashes, Beef-steaks, Fish, &c. viz. Devonshire sauce, Camp Vinegar, Zoobdity Match, Quin's sauce, Cherokee sauce, Walnut Ketchup, Bengal Currie Powder, with a receipt how to use it.
New Bologna Sausages, German ditto, with and without Garlic, Dutch Herrings, Dutch Beef, best Gorgona Anchovies, fine Capot Capers, New Morells and Truffles, New French and Spanish Olives, Vermicelli and Maccaroni, Green and Yellow India Mangoes, Hambro' Beef in ribbs, and Roots for grating; Parmesan Cheese, true Durham Mustard, exceeding fine Piccalillie, Girkins, large French Walnuts, Rein Deer Tongues, and very fine Red Herrings.
Curious Tongues in Pickle, always ready without soaking; dried Tongues, Mutton Hams, Venison Hams, Westphalia and Portugal Hams, Superfine Sallad Oil; Genuine Cayenne Pepper, Cayenne Vinegar, Elder, Tarragon and Garlick Vinegars; Red and White French Vinegar, and French Soup Strainers.
ESSENCE of LIME.
Genuine American Spruce, and Spruce Beer, at 4s. per dozen, sent to any part of the Town.

TO THE LADIES.
SPRING AND SUMMER CLOAKS.
AT HARTSHORN's, No. 44, Wigmore-street, Cavendish-square, great variety of Muslin and Lawn Cloaks, trimmed, at 18s. each, equal in goodness to what are charged a guinea at other houses: Likewise Black Mole Cloaks, of materials warranted equal in beauty and durability to the most esteemed French manufacture, at 16s. ditto, trimmed with lace, from one to twelve guineas; Bonnets, Aprons, and every other article of Millinery; Straw Petticoats at 10s. 6d.; Wove Hair Coats at 1l. 3s. and 1l. 8s. each; a superior stock of rich Tiffany, Gauze, and Crapes, in various colours, for Dresses; Artificial Flowers, Fancy Feathers, Ribbons, White and Coloured Gloves, Silk and Cotton Hose, Fans, Black, Blond, and Thread Laces, Muslins, Lawns, &c. &c. on terms that cannot fail being approved. The following is a list of a *few* of the Articles much under Market Prices: Full yard wide Italian Tiffany, 2s. 3d. per yard, or 2s. by the piece; ell wide ditto, 3s. 9d. or 3s. 3d. by the piece; one-half ell, real Crape, from 1s. to 1s. 6d. per yard; yard wide ditto, at 3s. 6d. and 4s. 6d.; ell wide ditto, 6s. and 6s. 6d. per yard, full width; Crape Gauze, from 10d. to 2s. per yard, with a large quantity of other Black and White Gauzes, great bargains; the best ell wide Tiffany Handkerchiefs, 3s. 6d. and 4s. 6d. each; Italian Tiffany Aprons, from 5s. to 8s. each.
N. B. A quantity of fine Chip Hats, remarkably White, from 4s. to 18s.

MISCELLANEOUS.

MILLINERY.
STUARTS,
No. 4, GERARD-STREET, Soho,
WISH to inform the LADIES, that they have lately received, from PARIS, some of the most fashionable CAPS, HATS, and BONNETS, now worn there.

LADIES BEAVER HAT WAREHOUSE,
No. 91, Oxford-street.
W. WIGLEY begs leave to inform the Ladies, that he has completed a large assortment of Ladies Beaver Hats, elegantly trimmed in the first fashion; and humbly solicits a continuance of their favours.
W. W. thinks it requisite to observe, that owing to the very great demand for the article of Ladies Beaver Hats, he is enabled to keep a superior variety for choice to any other shop, consequently empowered to sell on terms more moderate.
Ladies are requested to be very particular in their directions to No. 91,—and to observe, each Hat sold at the above Warehouse, is stamp'd, "WIGLEY, No. 91, Oxford-street." Some Ladies having experienced a deception, makes this caution necessary.

SEA-COAL COMPANY,
No. 8, UPPER THAMES-STREET,
BY POOL MEASURE.
THE great advantages of this admeasurement not being generally known, or clearly understood, RICHARD MILES and JACOB BIRD presume to inform the Public, that they have undertaken the Agency and Management of this Office, pursuant to a Deed of Settlement enrolled in the High Court of Chancery, for the sale of Coals by Pool Measure only; a capital fund, for that purpose, having been subscribed by a number of respectable and opulent citizens, which will enable them to furnish the Public with Coals at the Billingsgate Price; and they do pledge themselves to sell, without fraud or deceit, whatever sort of Coals is ordered, Six-pence per Chaldron only being added as a small commission; by which, with the advantage of prompt Payment, the Proprietors will be enabled most essentially to benefit the Public in this expensive article.

PATENT BEDSTEADS,
Of every Description, upon a New, Permanent, and Elastic Construction, which, for Use and Ornament, claim the greatest attention.
THEY prevent even the possibility of Bugs harbouring in them, are not liable to be out of order, and are put up and taken down with the greatest ease by any person in a few minutes.
The Bed-furniture is made in a correspondent and tasteful style, to fix without tacks or studs.
The objections to Bedsteads upon the common principle, are in these, from their peculiar construction, entirely obviated, and being free from any receptacle to retain Bugs, render the use of chemical preparations to destroy them unnecessary.
These Bedsteads will prove highly acceptable to the inhabitants of foreign countries, particularly the East and West Indies. Made and sold only by THOMAS WALDRON, the Patentee, at his Cabinet and Upholstery Manufactory, No. 11, Catherine-street, Strand.

SILVER PENS IMPROVED.
THE Construction of these PENS is simple, neat, and convenient; and the extraordinary pains that have been taken to mould the points exact, perfect, and of that hardness and well-tempered elasticity as to give the finest hair-strokes in a style so extremely commanding and pleasant, renders them now unrivalled in this kingdom, by their smoothness, ease, freedom, and their superiority, in fine Writing and Drawing, to all other pens whatever.
The utility of this article is so obvious and interesting to every writer, that they save a considerable portion of time and trouble, and are so well and usefully contrived, that new points may be fitted in at pleasure, and to write any kind of hand at the will of the writer, and by these means will write for several years without repairing. They are particularly recommended to Ladies for Letter-writing; Gentlemen of the Law; SHORTHAND WRITERS, &c. and are very ready, portable, and the best contrivance ever invented for travelling.
Made and Sold by *E.* and *T. Williams*, No. 13, Strand.
Portable FOUNTAIN PENS, to carry ink, and made upon a new, convenient, and safe construction, warranted to write well, and remain in perfect order.
The very great success that the Inventors of this article have met with in the sale thereof, has induced many persons to procure them from Birmingham and other places, and made of an inferior quality, who sell them under the feigned name of WILLIAM's SILVER PENS. The public are therefore respectfully informed, that their Pens are sold no where but at their House, as above.

SCORBUTIC INFLAMMATION OF THE EYES, AND LOSS OF SIGHT.
IN the Beginning of the Year 1787, William Lewis, Son of Samuel Lewis, had a violent inflammation in the eyes, and a considerable eruption about the mouth. On taking him to St. George's Hospital, the attending Surgeons apprehended the loss of one eye, if not both. Being only four years old, he was made an out-patient, and a blister ordered behind the right ear; this produced no good effect, and the eruption spread over his head; discharging the most offensive matter in considerable quantities. In three months the disease had proceeded in its ravages, wholly deprived him of sight in one eye, and daily threatened the loss of the other, and he could take very little food; when his danger and misery drew the attention of William Pulteney, Esq. M. P. who recommended him to Mr. Swainson, in the March of the same year. Mr. Swainson ordered the Vegetable Syrup of D. Velno's in small quantities, on account of the reduced condition of the patient. In a fortnight he was sufficiently improved in health to take two table spoonfuls night and morning. The medicine, as usual, augmented the diseased discharge, restored the natural secretions; and the child proceeded rapidly in his recovery; his sight is perfectly restored, his health re-established, and he has no eruption on any part of his body.
Mr. Swainson has the permission of Mr. Pulteney to add his testimony and sanction to the account of this interesting case.
The genuine medicine is sold at the Proprietor's house, No. 21, Frith-street, Soho, at 11s. 6d. per bottle; and by his appointment, at Mr. Atkinson's, Chemist and Druggist, No. 196, Bishopsgate-street Without, and at Mr. Ridgway's, York-street, St. James's-square.
April 21, 1788.

Fig. 87. *Peter Stuart's* The Star, *printed in association with William Lane of the Minerva Press* was weakening. Matthew Jenour's *Daily Advertiser* still flourished in what was now almost a primitive make-up. *The Morning Chronicle* continued as the most complete parliamentary report, but *The Morning Herald* also specialised in parliamentary and political intelligence. On January 1, 1789, the latter paper celebrated the new year with a physical change thus announced:

> We gladly embrace the opportunity offered us on the return of a New Year, gratefully to acknowledge the liberal and increasing patronage which has been bestowed on the *Morning Herald*, a patronage which we can only return by our exertions to preserve its distinguished simplicity...An entire *New Type*, and a superior *Paper* are proofs that our assiduity is unabated and our ambition tenacious to attain the utmost height of public approbation.

The detail of the typography approximated the Bell style; the roman heading was redesigned in accordance with the model of *The World*; but no device was introduced. The change was one more indication of Bell's prestige.

Peter Stuart, brother of Daniel Stuart (manager of *The Morning Post* from 1788), made his first entry into evening journalism with *The Star*. The paper, as the first every-evening journal, was something of a sensation. Palmer's Improved Mail Coach Plan,[1] which made a vital difference in the despatch and carriage of letters and newspapers, also made an every-day evening paper possible. Peter Stuart was the first to take advantage of the new invention. It is not so easy to be certain that Stuart's paper was the first under this title. Mrs Elizabeth Johnson, of Ludgate Place, who had been publishing *The Sunday Monitor* for ten or fifteen years—the date of its foundation is uncertain—brought out on April 1, 1788, a 'new, moral, commercial and entertaining paper' under the title of *The Evening Star, And Grand Weekly Advertiser*. Mrs Johnson's handsomely produced sheet[2] of the usual dimensions had as its economic justification an advertising revenue; an insufficient justification in the circumstances, for there seem only to have

[1] John Palmer was the inventor of the Mail Coach, which was first tried, by the order of Pitt, on the Bath Road, August 2, 1784. In 1785 Palmer created a 'newspaper office' which dealt with these, separately from letters. Evening newspapers were required to be delivered to Palmer's agents not later than 6 p.m. The coaches undertook the responsibility of delivering newspapers all over the town.

[2] The title-page was in roman capitals for the main title and in upper- and lower-case for the sub-title of 'And Grand Weekly Advertiser'. The first column of the front page contained a manifesto which claimed that the paper was on the plan of *The Tatler, Spectator* and *Guardian*. This column was introduced by a handsome factotum in the form of the accompanying reproduction.

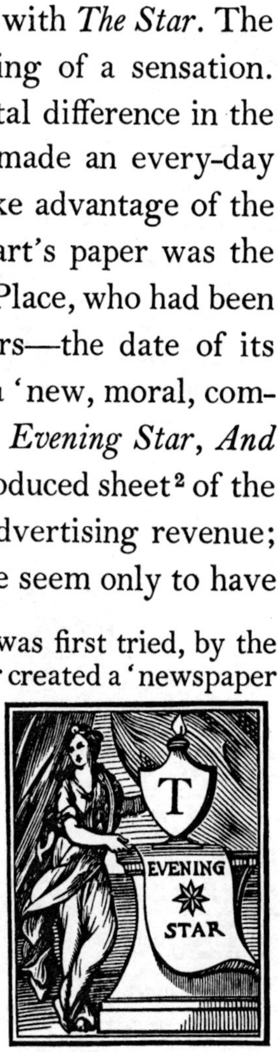

The Star

EVENING ADVERTISER

VESPERO SURGENTE

NUMBER 187.] SATURDAY, DECEMBER 6, 1788. [PRICE 3D.

DRURY-LANE.

AT the Theatre-Royal, in DRURY-LANE, THIS EVENING, KING HENRY THE EIGHTH.

(*Written by* SHAKESPEARE.)

With new Scenes, Dresses, and Decorations.

King Henry, —— Mr. PALMER;
Duke of Buckingham, —— Mr. WROUGHTON;
Cranmer, —— Mr. AICKIN;
Duke of Norfolk, —— Mr. WHITFIELD;
Duke of Suffolk, —— Mr. WILLIAMES;
Lord Surry, —— Mr. BARRYMORE;
Lord Chamberlain, —— Mr. R. PALMER;
Cromwell, —— Mr. KEMBLE;
Lord Sands, —— Mr. BADDELEY;
Winchester, —— Mr. SUETT;
Cardinal Campeius, —— Mr. PACKER;
Sir Henry Guilford, —— Mr. LAMASH;
Sir Thomas Lovel, —— Mr. FAWCETT;
Doctor Butts, —— Mr. WALDRON;
Surveyor, —— Mr. BENSON;
And Cardinal Wolsey, —— Mr. BENSLEY.
Anne Bullen, —— Mrs. FARMER;
Lady, —— Mrs. LOVE;
And Queen Catherine, —— Mrs. SIDDONS.

In Act IV. a song by Mrs. CROUCH.

THE POLYGRAPHIC EXHIBITION OF PICTURES COPIED IN OIL-COLOURS By a CHYMICAL and MECHANICAL PROCESS, The Invention of *Mr. JOSEPH BOOTH,* With the ORIGINALS from which they have been taken, Will continue open At the POLYGRAPHIC ROOMS, *Opposite* BEAUFORT BUILDINGS, *Strand,* EVERY DAY, (Sundays excepted,) Till about the middle of the present month, when the Proprietors intend to close it for this season, to give them an opportunity of executing the orders they are honoured with.

Admittance ONE SHILLING.

From TEN in the Morning to Four in the Afternoon.

N. B. A Catalogue, mentioning the Price and Conditions of Sale to Subscribers, gratis.

☞ Good Fires will be constantly kept in the Rooms.

MILITARY AND NAVY LINEN WAREHOUSE.

MRS. MACKENZIE begs leave to return

To the GENTLEMEN, CLERGY, and FREEHOLDERS of the COUNTY of HUNTINGDON.

GENTLEMEN,

I TAKE the Liberty to solicit your Votes and Interest to be one of your REPRESENTATIVES in PARLIAMENT at the next GENERAL ELECTION.

I am sensible that the station to which I aspire, is as difficult, as it is important and honorable; and I am induced to be a candidate for it, not by a rash confidence in my own abilities, nor by the partiality of my friends, but by a sense of my duty as a citizen of this free State, the energy and vigour of which must result from the exertions of individuals. It belongs to you, GENTLEMEN, to determine whether I am possessed of those qualities which may enable me to be of service to the PUBLIC. On my part, I can only promise the utmost diligence and attention in the execution of so great a trust, and the warmest ZEAL for the PROSPERITY and GLORY of my COUNTRY.

I am,

With great Respect,

EAST-INDIA HOUSE.

DECEMBER 2, 1788.

THE COURT *of* DIRECTORS *of the* UNITED COMPANY *of* MERCHANTS *of* ENGLAND *trading to the East-Indies, do hereby give Notice—*

That a GENERAL COURT *of the said* COMPANY *will be held at their House in Leadenhall-street, on Tuesday the 16th Instant, (December) from Nine o'Clock in the Morning, until Six in the Evening, for the* ELECTION *of a* DIRECTOR *of the said* COMPANY, *in the room of* JOHN MICHIE, *Esq. deceased.*

EAST-INDIA HOUSE,

DECEMBER 3, 1788.

THE COURT *of* DIRECTORS *of the* UNITED COMPANY *of* MERCHANTS *of* ENGLAND, *trading to the East-Indies, do hereby give notice,*

That at the QUARTERLY GENERAL COURT *of the said* COMPANY, *appointed to be held at their House in Leadenhall-street, on Wednesday, the 17th instant, at Eleven o'clock*

Fig. 88. *Peter Stuart's* The Star, *second heading before the break with William Lane*

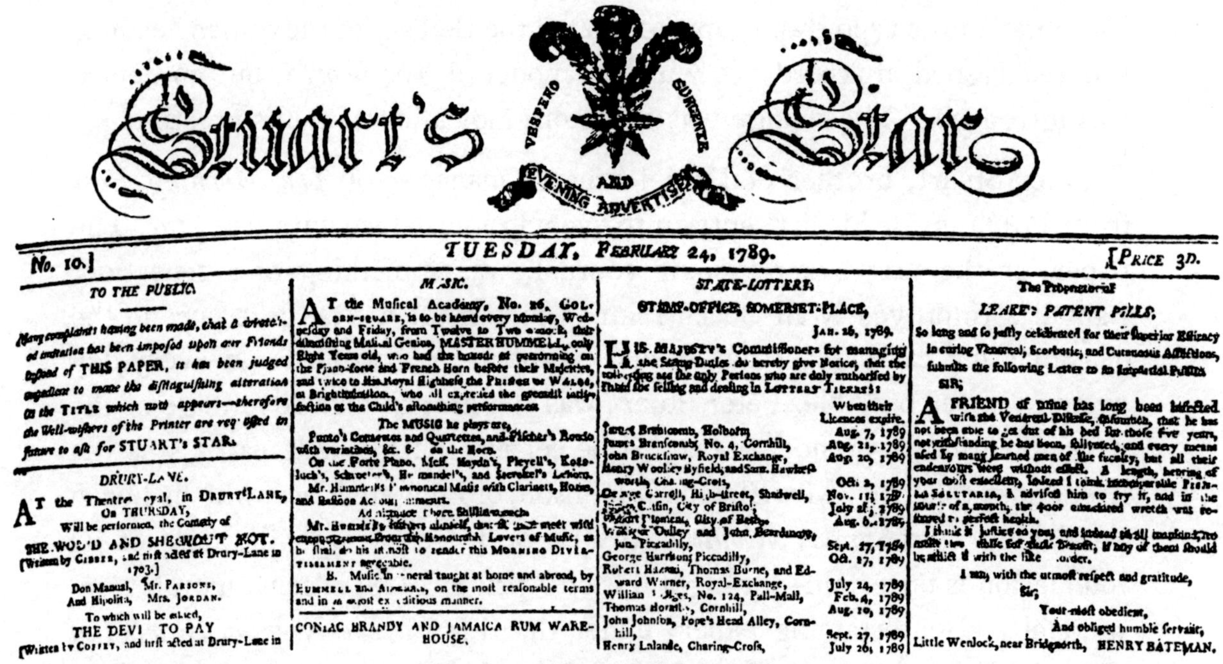

Stuart's Star

VESPERO SURGENTE AND EVENING ADVERTISER

[No. 10.] TUESDAY, FEBRUARY 24, 1789. [PRICE 3D.

TO THE PUBLIC.

Many complaints having been made, that a wretched imitation has been imposed upon our Friends instead of THIS PAPER, *it has been judged expedient to make the distinguishing alteration in the* TITLE *which now appears—therefore the Well-wishers of the Printer are requested in future to ask for* STUART'S STAR.

DRURY-LANE.

AT the Theatre-Royal, in DRURY-LANE, On THURSDAY, Will be performed, the Comedy of THE WORLD AND SHE WOULD NOT. (Written by CIBBER, and first acted at Drury-Lane in 1703.)

Don Manuel, Mr. PARSONS,
And Hipolita, Mrs. JORDAN.

To which will be added,
THE DEVIL TO PAY
(Written by COFFEY, and first acted at Drury-Lane in

MUSIC.

AT the Musical Academy, No. 26, GOLDEN-SQUARE, is to be heard every Monday, Wednesday and Friday, from Twelve to Two o'clock, that astonishing Musical Genius, MASTER HUMMELL, only Eight Years old, who had the honour of performing on the Piano-forte and French Horn before their Majesties, and twice to His Royal Highness the PRINCE OF WALES, at Brighthelmston, who all expressed the greatest satisfaction at the Child's astonishing performances.

The MUSIC he plays are,

Parto's Concertos and Quartettos, and Fischer's Rondo with variations, &c. & on the Horn.

On the Forte Piano, Mess. Haydn's, Pleyell's, Kozeluch's, Schroeter's, Handel's, and Steibelt's Lessons.

Mr. Hummell's Harmonical Music with Clarinets, Horns, and Bassoon Accompaniment.

Admittance Three Shillings each.

Mr. HUMMELL, . . . Lovers of Music, . . . MORNING DIVERTISEMENT agreeable.

B. Music in general taught at home and abroad, by HUMMELL and ASSOCIATES, on the most reasonable terms and in the most expeditious manner.

CONIAC BRANDY AND JAMAICA RUM WAREHOUSE.

STATE-LOTTERY.

STAMP-OFFICE, SOMERSET-PLACE,

JAN. 26, 1789.

HIS MAJESTY's Commissioners for managing the Stamp Duties do hereby give Notice, that the following are the only Persons who are duly authorized by Patent for selling and dealing in LOTTERY TICKETS:

	When their Licences expire.
James Branscomb, Holborn	Aug. 7, 1789
James Branscomb, No. 4, Cornhill,	Aug. 21, 1789
John Brucklaw, Royal Exchange,	Aug. 20, 1789
Henry Woolley Byfield, and Sam. Hawkesworth, Charing-Cross,	
George Carroll, High-street, Shadwell,	Oct. 2, 1789
Joseph Catin, City of Bristol,	Nov. 11, 1789
Robert Cotton, City of Bath,	July 28, 1789
Walter Dalley and John Beardmore, Jun. Piccadilly,	Aug. 6, 1789
George Harrison, Piccadilly,	Sept. 27, 1789
Robert Harman, Thomas Burne, and Edward Warner, Royal-Exchange,	Oct. 17, 1789
William Hodges, No. 124, Pall-Mall,	July 24, 1789
Thomas Horatio, Cornhill,	Feb. 4, 1789
John Johnson, Pope's Head Alley, Cornhill,	Aug. 10, 1789
Henry Lalande, Charing-Cross,	Sept. 27, 1789
	July 26, 1789

The Proprietors of LEAKE's PATENT PILLS, So long and so justly celebrated for their superior Efficacy in curing Venereal, Scorbutic, and Cutaneous Afflictions, subjoin the following Letter to an impartial Public.

SIR,

A FRIEND of mine has long been afflicted with the Venereal Disease, and, that he has not been able to get out of his bed for those five years, notwithstanding he has been salivated, and every means used by many learned men of the faculty; but all their endeavours were without effect. A length, hearing of your most excellent, indeed I think incomparable PILULA SALUTARIS, I advised him to try it, and in the course of a month, the poor emaciated wretch was restored to perfect health.

I think it justice to you, and indeed to all mankind, to make this public for their benefit, if any of them should be afflicted with the like disorder.

I am, with the utmost respect and gratitude,

Sir,

Your most obedient,

And obliged humble servant,

Little Wenlock, near Bridgnorth, HENRY BATEMAN.

Fig. 89. [*Peter*] Stuart's Star

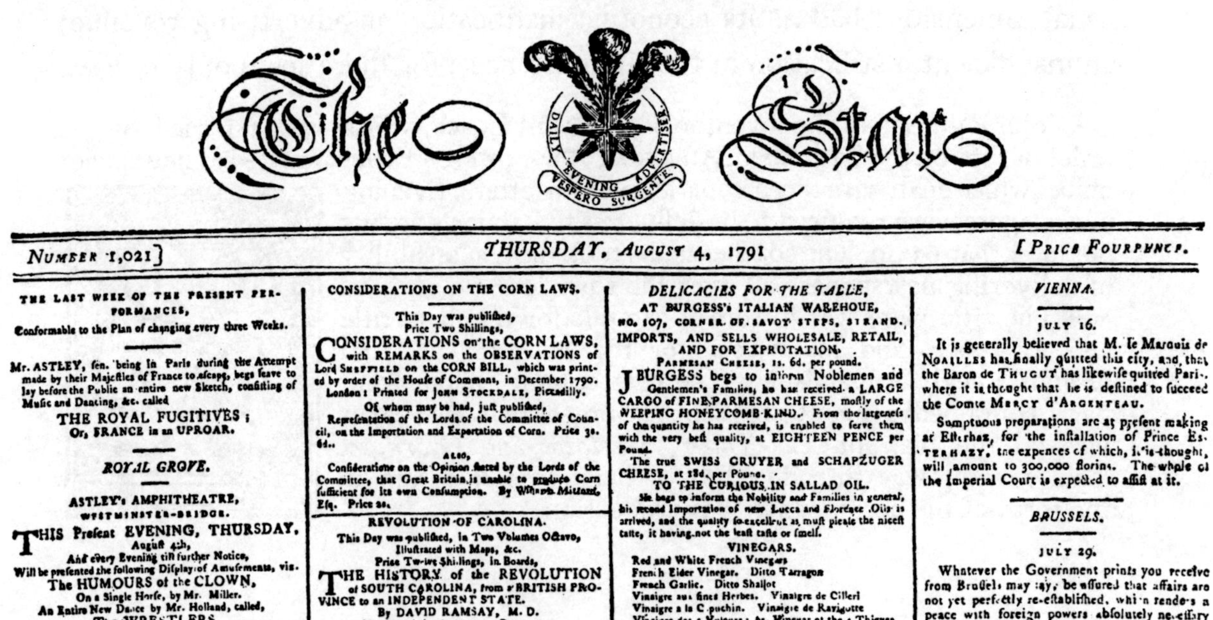

The Star

DAILY EVENING ADVERTISER

VESPERO SURGENTE

NUMBER 1,021] THURSDAY, AUGUST 4, 1791 [PRICE FOURPENCE.

THE LAST WEEK OF THE PRESENT PERFORMANCES,

Conformable to the Plan of changing every three Weeks.

Mr. ASTLEY, sen. being in Paris during the Attempt made by their Majesties of France to escape, begs leave to lay before the Public an entire new Sketch, consisting of Music and Dancing, &c. called

THE ROYAL FUGITIVES; Or, FRANCE in an UPROAR.

ROYAL GROVE.

ASTLEY's AMPHITHEATRE, WESTMINSTER-BRIDGE.

THIS Present EVENING, THURSDAY, August 4th, And every Evening till further Notice, Will be presented the following Display of Amusements, viz. The HUMOURS of the CLOWN, On a Single Horse, by Mr. Miller. An Entire New Dance by Mr. Holland, called, The WRESTLERS

The principal Characters by Messrs. Holland, Marqui, and Miss Smith

CONSIDERATIONS ON THE CORN LAWS.

This Day was published, Price Two Shillings,

CONSIDERATIONS on the CORN LAWS, with REMARKS on the OBSERVATIONS of Lord SHEFFIELD on the CORN BILL, which was printed by order of the House of Commons, in December 1790. London: Printed for JOHN STOCKDALE, Piccadilly.

Of whom may be had, just published,

Representation of the Lords of the Committee of Council, on the Importation and Exportation of Corn. Price 3s. 6d.

ALSO,

Considerations on the Opinion stated by the Lords of the Committee, that Great Britain is unable to produce Corn sufficient for its own Consumption. By William Mitford, Esq. Price 2s.

REVOLUTION OF CAROLINA.

This Day was published, In Two Volumes Octavo, Illustrated with Maps, &c.

Price Twelve Shillings, in Boards,

THE HISTORY of the REVOLUTION of SOUTH CAROLINA, from a BRITISH PROVINCE to an INDEPENDENT STATE.

By DAVID RAMSAY, M. D.

Member of the AMERICAN CONGRESS.

London: Printed for JOHN STOCKDALE, Piccadilly.

DELICACIES FOR THE TABLE,

AT BURGESS's ITALIAN WAREHOUSE, NO. 107, CORNER OF SAVOY STEPS, STRAND. IMPORTS, AND SELLS WHOLESALE, RETAIL, AND FOR EXPORTATION.

PARMESAN CHEESE, 1s. 6d. per pound.

J. BURGESS begs to inform Noblemen and Gentlemen's Families, he has received a LARGE CARGO of FINE PARMESAN CHEESE, mostly of the WEEPING HONEYCOMB KIND. From the largeness of the quantity he has received, is enabled to serve them with the very best quality, at EIGHTEEN PENCE per Pound.

The true SWISS GRUYER and SCHAPZUGER CHEESE, at 18d. per Pound.

TO THE CURIOUS IN SALLAD OIL.

He begs to inform the Nobility and Families in general, his second Importation of new Lucca and Florence Oils is arrived, and the quality so excellent as must please the nicest taste, it having not the least taste or smell.

VINEGARS.

Red and White French Vinegar
French Elder Vinegar. Ditto Tarragon
French Garlic. Ditto Shalot
Vinaigre aux fines Herbes. Vinaigre de Cileri
Vinaigre a la Capuchin. Vinaigre de Ravigotte
Vinaigre des 4 Voleurs; or, Vinegar of the 4 Thieves
Vinaigre a l'Estragon
French Soup-strainers

VIENNA.

JULY 16.

It is generally believed that M. le Marquis de NOAILLES has finally quitted this city, and that the Baron de THUGUT has likewise quitted Paris, where it is thought that he is destined to succeed the Comte MERCY d'ARGENTEAU.

Sumptuous preparations are at present making at Esterhas, for the installation of Prince ESTERHAZY, the expences of which, it is thought, will amount to 300,000 florins. The whole of the Imperial Court is expected to assist at it.

BRUSSELS.

JULY 29.

Whatever the Government prints you receive from Brussels may say, be assured that affairs are not yet perfectly re-established, which renders a peace with foreign powers absolutely necessary for some time.

Fig. 90. *William Lane's* The Star

been printed a few numbers. On May 3, 1788, the first number of *The Star and Evening Advertiser* was produced. Mrs Johnson answered with a change in the title of her own paper to *The Original Star*, while Stuart alleged that the other paper was not started until news of his venture had been published. Among the backers of *The Star* was Mr William Lane of the Minerva Press, a bookseller famous for his circulating library and gothic novels. He was a printer of some taste, faithfully formed on the example of Bell, and *The Star*'s appearance was eminently elegant and Bell-ish. It had a fine heading; indeed, too fine a heading. The title *The Star*, a gothic piece, was tricked out with large command-of-hand flourishes cut on the wood, plus a device of a star with regency feathers. The engraving was signed by Lee, the whole piece being three inches deep (cf. Fig. 87). The programme of the paper was new. Mrs Johnson's *Star* was a weekly, Stuart's an every-evening paper, published at three o'clock in the afternoon. It was claimed that 'the news received by the Post cannot be inserted in the other papers until the *next day*; whereas the intelligence received by the proprietors of *The Star* will be published on the *day it arrives*'. The long pronouncement in the first issue made a particular address to advertisers. It deserves to be quoted, since it indicates the growing importance of this factor in newspaper production, and Stuart's determination to secure it by offering what news-men of today would call a 'copy service'.

"The Proprietors of this Paper", said Stuart, "formed their first idea of establishing it from the many abuses and inconveniences they sustained by the neglect and inattention of other Papers—Many of their Advertisements were not inserted properly, others not at all, and others not till the procrastination rendered them of no use; this being the grievance of which they themselves have had reason to complain, it will not only be their duty, but their inclination to redress it in the present instance; in addition to which advantage, those who apply in time may have their advertisements drawn up *gratis*, by a gentleman properly qualified for the undertaking."

The Star was a success, and the demand for the space on its front page had the inevitable result of restricting the area available for the heading. This was contracted into 1⅝ in. depth before the end of 1788. The new year was hardly a few weeks old before a political quarrel resulted in the immediate termination of Stuart's agreement with his partners. Two columns headed 'P. Stuart's Reasons for Abandoning the Exeter Street Star' (February 13, 1789) claimed among other things that he had raised the circulation of *The Star* to above 2000 daily, but that the new political line required by his partners had 'sunk the sale of the paper between 2/300 today'. Mr Lane had apparently instructed Stuart that 'he must support Mr Pitt through thick and thin'. The imprint to this paper remains as before 'Printed by P. Stuart, No. 9 Feathers-Court, Drury Lane'. The serial number, which should have been 246, was omitted, and again on the following day. On Monday, February 16, 1789, there appeared the first number of *Stuart's Star and Evening Advertiser* in which the Prince of Wales's feathers and the device were joined to lettering of a character precisely similar to that of the original paper, Stuart's public also being regaled with attacks on Lane's 'Dog' *Star*—

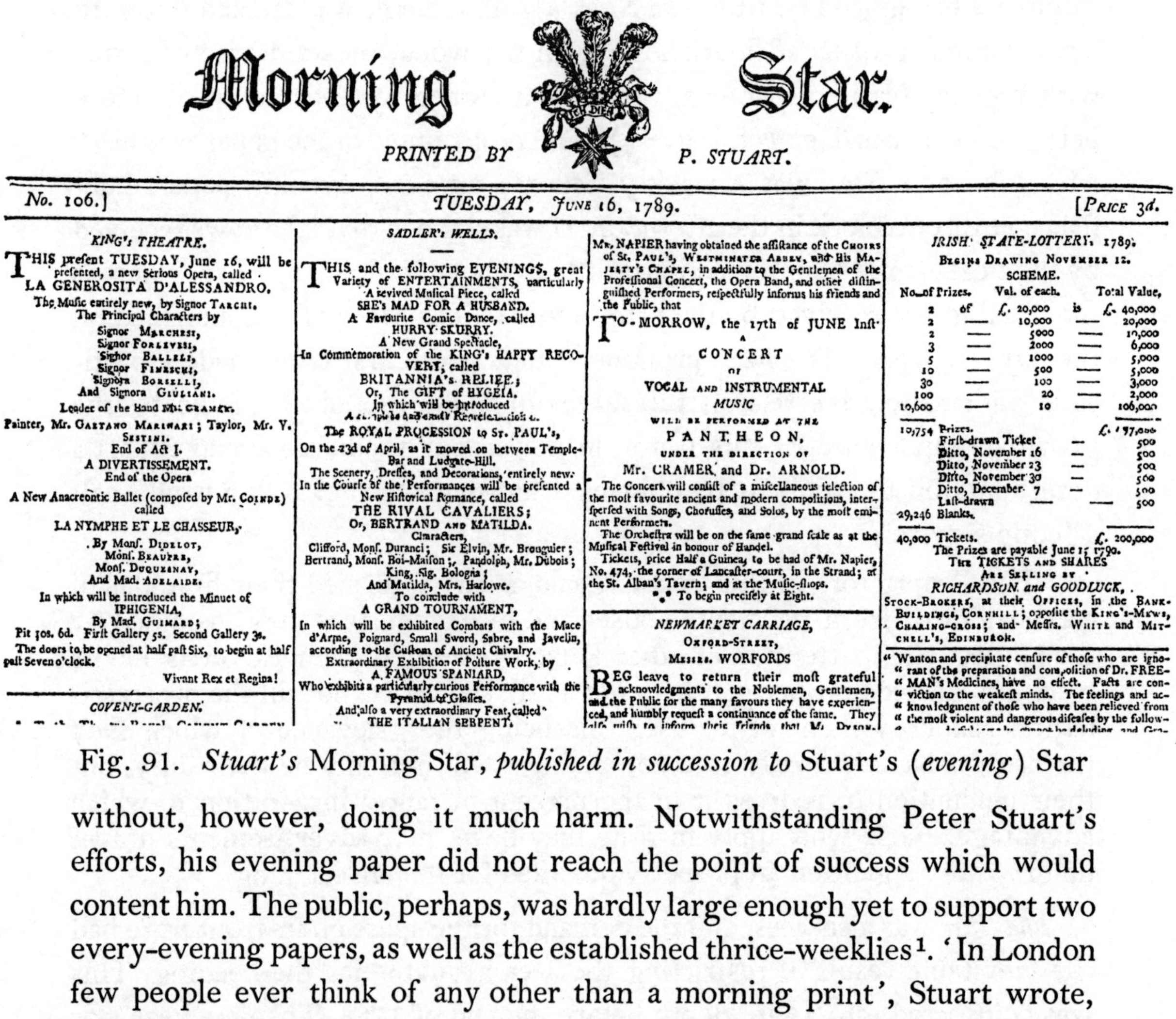

Morning Star.

PRINTED BY P. STUART.

No. 106.] TUESDAY, JUNE 16, 1789. [PRICE 3d.

KING's THEATRE.

THIS present TUESDAY, June 16, will be presented, a new Serious Opera, called LA GENEROSITA D'ALESSANDRO. The Music entirely new, by Signor TARCHI. The Principal Characters by Signor MARCHESI, Signor FORLIVESI, Signor BALLELI, Signor FINASCHI, Signora BORSELLI, And Signora GIULIANI. Leader of the Band Mr. CRAMER. Painter, Mr. GAETANO MARINARI; Taylor, Mr. V. SESTINI. End of Act I. A DIVERTISSEMENT. End of the Opera A New Anacreontic Ballet (composed by Mr. COINDE) called LA NYMPHE ET LE CHASSEUR, By Monf. DIDELOT, Monf. BEAUPRE, Monf. DUQUESNAY, And Mad. ADELAIDE. In which will be introduced the Minuet of IPHIGENIA, By Mad. GUIMARD; Pit 10s. 6d. First Gallery 5s. Second Gallery 3s. The doors to be opened at half past Six, to begin at half past Seven o'clock.

Vivant Rex et Regina!

COVENT-GARDEN.

SADLER's WELLS.

THIS and the following EVENINGS, great Variety of ENTERTAINMENTS, particularly A revived Musical Piece, called SHE's MAD FOR A HUSBAND. A Favourite Comic Dance, called HURRY-SKURRY. A New Grand Spectacle, In Commemoration of the KING's HAPPY RECOVERY, called BRITANNIA's RELIEF; Or, The GIFT of HYGEIA. In which will be introduced [illegible] The ROYAL PROCESSION to ST. PAUL's, On the 23d of April, as it moved on between Temple-Bar and Ludgate-Hill. The Scenery, Dresses, and Decorations, entirely new. In the Course of the Performances will be presented a New Historical Romance, called THE RIVAL CAVALIERS; Or, BERTRAND AND MATILDA. Characters, Clifford, Monf. Duranci; Sir Elvin, Mr. Brouguier; Bertrand, Monf. Boi-Maison; Pandolph, Mr. Dubois; King, Sig. Bologna; And Matilda, Mrs. Harlowe. To conclude with A GRAND TOURNAMENT, In which will be exhibited Combats with the Mace d'Arme, Poignard, Small Sword, Sabre, and Javelin, according to the Custom of Ancient Chivalry. Extraordinary Exhibition of Posture Work, by A FAMOUS SPANIARD, Who exhibits a particularly curious Performance with the Pyramid of Glasses. And also a very extraordinary Feat, called THE ITALIAN SERPENT.

MR. NAPIER having obtained the assistance of the CHOIRS of ST. PAUL'S, WESTMINSTER ABBEY, and His MAJESTY'S CHAPEL, in addition to the Gentlemen of the Professional Concert, the Opera Band, and other distinguished Performers, respectfully informs his friends and the Public, that

TO-MORROW, the 17th of JUNE Inst. A CONCERT OF VOCAL AND INSTRUMENTAL MUSIC WILL BE PERFORMED AT THE PANTHEON, UNDER THE DIRECTION OF Mr. CRAMER and Dr. ARNOLD.

The Concert will consist of a miscellaneous selection of the most favourite ancient and modern compositions, interspersed with Songs, Choruses, and Solos, by the most eminent Performers.

The Orchestra will be on the same grand scale as at the Musical Festival in honour of Handel.

Tickets, price Half a Guinea, to be had of Mr. Napier, No. 474, the corner of Lancaster-court, in the Strand; at the St. Alban's Tavern; and at the Music-shops.

*** To begin precisely at Eight.

NEWMARKET CARRIAGE, OXFORD-STREET, MESSRS. WORFORDS

BEG leave to return their most grateful acknowledgments to the Noblemen, Gentlemen, and the Public for the many favours they have experienced, and humbly request a continuance of the same. They

IRISH STATE-LOTTERY, 1789. BEGINS DRAWING NOVEMBER 12. SCHEME.

No. of Prizes.		Val. of each.		Total Value,
2	of	£. 20,000	is	£. 40,000
2	—	10,000	—	20,000
2	—	5000	—	10,000
3	—	2000	—	6,000
5	—	1000	—	5,000
10	—	500	—	5,000
30	—	100	—	3,000
100	—	20	—	2,000
10,600	—	10	—	106,000
10,754	Prizes.			£. 197,000
	First-drawn Ticket		—	500
	Ditto, November 16		—	500
	Ditto, November 23		—	500
	Ditto, November 30		—	500
	Ditto, December 7		—	500
	Last-drawn	—	—	500
29,246	Blanks.			
40,000	Tickets.			£. 200,000

The Prizes are payable June 1, 1790. THE TICKETS AND SHARES ARE SELLING BY RICHARDSON and GOODLUCK, STOCK-BROKERS, at their OFFICES, in the BANK-BUILDINGS, CORNHILL; opposite the KING's-MEWS, CHARING-CROSS; and Messrs. WHITE and MITCHELL's, EDINBURGH.

"Wanton and precipitate censure of those who are ignorant of the preparation and composition of Dr. FREEMAN's Medicines, have no effect. Facts are conviction to the weakest minds. The feelings and acknowledgment of those who have been relieved from the most violent and dangerous diseases by the follow-

Fig. 91. *Stuart's* Morning Star, *published in succession to* Stuart's (*evening*) Star

without, however, doing it much harm. Notwithstanding Peter Stuart's efforts, his evening paper did not reach the point of success which would content him. The public, perhaps, was hardly large enough yet to support two every-evening papers, as well as the established thrice-weeklies[1]. 'In London few people ever think of any other than a morning print', Stuart wrote, and in consequence determined 'to render the papers of more importance

[1] John Walter's *The Evening Mail* (1789) was a Monday, Wednesday and Friday publication. A handsome-looking sheet, with a heading of shaded Chancery-lane gothic and a good royal device. *The Evening Mail* carried a 'Postscript' on the back page. No advertisements appear during the first ten years of the paper's life. The title was altered to *The Mail* in 1868 and published on alternate days. More recently *The Mail* was incorporated with *The Times Weekly Edition* which was founded in 1877.

both to the advertiser and to the reader by an alteration in the time of publication'. Thus No. 65 of *Stuart's Star* became the *Morning Star*. The typography of *Stuart's Star* and of Lane's *Star* had throughout been modelled closely on the Bell example except in the headings. The *Morning Star*, from the first, by redressing its heading, established a still closer stylistic approximation. Yet Lane had the satisfaction of witnessing the early end of the *Morning Star* while his own foundation remained strongly established—and continued until 1831 when it was absorbed by *The Albion*.

At this time, there were changes in the fortune, constitution, the management and in the typography of William Woodfall's *Morning Chronicle*. Some twenty proprietors were interested in it at the foundation in 1769. In 1789 James Perry—an Aberdonian and one of the first of a clan of Scots who made their mark on London newspapers—with one Gray, and money advanced by Bellamy, keeper of the refreshment rooms of the House of Commons, purchased the paper. Perry had formerly been a reporter on *The General Advertiser*, a writer on *The London Evening Post*, initiator and editor of *The European Magazine*, and immediately before going to *The Morning Chronicle* was editor of *The Gazetteer*. Perry brought *The Gazetteer* into the front rank of serious journals by employing several reporters responsible for the debates in Parliament, whereas the rest of the press employed only one reporter each, and printed the reports days after the event. The result was fatal to *The Morning Chronicle*. Woodfall sold, and, starting his unsuccessful *Diary or Woodfall's Register*, looked on while Perry next made the *Chronicle* not only successful but the greatest of the Whig journals.[1] Perry began by revising the typography of *The Morning Chronicle*, changing the roman head in favour of Bell's up-to-date gothic and resetting the text in accordance with the new style. Woodfall's *Diary*, similarly dressed (from the earliest number available in the Burney collection[2]), ran only for three years, the *Chronicle* for nearly eighty, from 1790.

In the meantime, Bell's paper, *The Oracle*, well in its stride from the circulation standpoint, made a signal contribution to typographical history

[1] There is an excellent obituary of Perry in *Bell's Weekly Messenger*, December 7, 1821.

[2] No. 239, January 1, 1790, has a heading rather in the style of an open German fraktur than in Bell's. Woodfall was curiously irregular in his use of headings. He changed the open fraktur to an obviously sedulous copy of Bell's lettering on March 31, 1790. This has the serial number 315. Thursday, April 1, 1790, reverted to the original design and this issue was also numbered 315. The error was repaired. No. 318 is Saturday and carries the new device. Monday, April 5—old device and until the end of 1790.

THE ORACLE.
BELL's NEW WORLD.

NUMBER 2.] *TUESDAY, JUNE 2, 1789.* [PRICE 3D.

KING's THEATRE.
AT THE KING's THEATRE, HAY-MARKET, THIS EVENING, June 2, 1789, Will be performed, a new serious Opera (never performed), called
LA GENEROSITA D'ALESSANDRO.
The Music entirely by Signor TARCHI.
The Principal Characters by
Signor MARCHESI,
Signor Forlevesi, Signor Balleli, Signor Finacchi, Signora Borselli, and Signora GIULIANI.
End of Act I. a new Anacreontic Ballet, composed by Mr. COINDE, called
LA NYMPHE ET LE CHASSEUR.
By Mons. DIDELOT,
Mad. Emilie Colombe, Mons. Beaupre, Mr. Duquesnay, And Mad. ADELAIDE.
End of the Opera, an entire new Ballet, called
LES CAPRICES DE GALATEE,
Composed on purpose, in Paris, for Mad. GUIMARD, By Mons. NOVERRE,
In which Mad. Guimard will perform GALATEE.

VAUXHALL GARDENS
WILL OPEN THIS EVENING, TUESDAY, 2d June, for the Season.
Admittance ONE SHILLING.
The Doors open at Seven o'Clock, and the CONCERT will begin at Eight.
TEA and COFFEE at Side Boards on the same Terms as last Season, till the End of the First Act.

FRANCE AND IRELAND.
Law and Agency Office, Gough-Square, Fleet-street, London.
A MESSENGER will set out EXPRESS from this Office on Wednesday the 10th instant, for the City of PARIS and another for DUBLIN. The First will return in 31 days, and the Second in 21 days, from the time of their departure, weather permitting. Such persons as have deeds, papers, or parcels to send, or business to transact in either of those cities, are requested to send their instructions to the Office in Gough-Square before Six o'clock in the evening of Tuesday the 9th instant.

THIS, AND EVERY EVENING THIS WEEK.
ROYAL CIRCUS.
THE MANAGERS of this Theatre have, at a very great expence, for the Entertainment of the Public, engaged the Two Wonderful BROTHERS, called
ALBINOS.
Just arrived from the Glaciers, in the Grand Mountains of the Alps.
They have had the honour to be presented to Sir JOSEPH BANKS, who pronounced them a perfect and new Variety of MEN, and the Greatest and most Pleasing NATURAL CURIOSITY ever seen in England.
HUGHES, and his inimitable PUPILS, will perform several
NEW FEATS OF HORSEMANSHIP.
A New Ballette (composed by Mr. HOLLAND) called
THE MORRIS DANCERS;
Or, The HUMOURS of MAY-DAY.
The Principal Dancers, Mr. HOLLAND, Mons. FERRERE, Madame FERRERE, Mademoiselle FOUZI.
An EQUESTRIAN STATUE, by four Horses; and various other NEW FEATS, never performed.

For LOSS of APPETITE, LOWNESS of SPIRITS, and NERVOUS DISORDERS.
DR. HUXHAM's TINCTURE of PERUVIAN BARK, Improved and Prepared by F. C. WALSH, Chemist to His Royal Highness the Duke of York, No. 100, Strand, five doors from Beaufort-Buildings; and sold by him in Bottles, at 8s. and 2s. 6d. each.
The Properties of this Medicine are so generally known, that any particular specification is almost needless; in weakness of the Stomach, Lowness of Spirits, or Loss of Appetite, it is singularly beneficial. In nervous and debilitated constitutions, whether proceeding from nature, or from what is generally termed hard drinking, it will always afford relief. A Table Spoonful taken in a Wine Glass of Water, or of Wine, an hour or two before dinner, will, beside removing these complaints, create an appetite, and promote digestion. In short, it is a medicine particularly calculated for all nervous and stomachic disorders, and to convalescents, after long fevers. But perhaps the most forcible encomium that can be stamped on it, is, that the Royal College of Physicians have admitted it into their late edition of the Pharmacopœia Londinensis.

Fig. 92. The Oracle, *published by John Bell after the break with Edward Topham*

THE ORACLE.

NUMBER 875] *FRIDAY, MARCH 16, 1792.* [PRICE FOUR PENCE.

THEATRE-ROYAL, HAY-MARKET
TO-MORROW, SATURDAY, March 17, 1792, will be performed, the favourite Comic Opera, called
LA LOCANDA.
Composed by the celebrated PAESIELLO.
Under the direction of Signor MAZZINGHI.
Principal Performers,
Signora CASENTINI, Signor LAZZARINI, Signor AGOSTINO LIPPARINI, Signor CIPRIANI, Signora CALVESI, Signora SCHINOTTI.
End of the First Act, a Pastoral Ballet, called
LE FETE VILLAGEOISE.
End of the Opera, a New Pantomimic Ballet, in One Act, called
LE VOLAGE FIXE.
Composed by Mons. D'AUBERVAL.
The Ballet will end with a Pas de Cinq; entirely new, called,
LE MENUET DU VOLAGE.
Leader of the Band, Mr CRAMER;

READINGS.
LISLE-STREET, LEICESTER-FIELDS.
THIS EVENING, FRIDAY the 16th inst. by particular desire, will be repeated, for the Seventh Time, the new favourite Comedy, called
LES DEUX FIGAROS.
In Five Acts.
After which it will be laid aside for some time on account of many demands of the Subscribers.
On Monday next, the 19th instant, will be repeated the same Reading which succeeded so much the last Night, (the New Play,) called
LE DESESPOIR DE JOERISSE.
In Two Acts.
And MOLIERE's favourite Play, called
LES PRECIEUSES RIDICULES.
An entire New Comedy, written by a Lady, as much distinguished by her rank and high situation in life, as by her rare talents and superior genius. This Play is called
NOURJAD,
In Three Acts,
Will be read as soon as possible.

SANS SOUCI.
TO-MORROW EVENING, SATURDAY, March 17,
Will be presented to the Public,
At SANS SOUCI, opposite Beaufort-Buildings, in the Strand,
AN ENTERTAINMENT, consisting of the most admired Songs and Recitation in the WAGS and ODDITIES, called
THE COALITION.
Among a variety of other Characters will be pourtrayed, A Half-pay Brigadier, A Patron, A Yellow Admiral, A Ballad Singer, A Shatterbrain Irishman, A Negro, A Jester, A Mulatto, An Indian, A Dealer in Mysteries, A Chronicle of the Times, A Raireeshew Man, and several others—all either Wags or Oddities.
The Songs will come in the following Succession.
Part I. The Camp of Pleasure, Death or Victory, Peggy Perkins, Ben Backstay, the Joys of the Country, the Virtue of Drunkenness, Sly Old Hodge, and the Flowing Can.
Part II. The Greenwich Pensioner, the Soldier's Adieu, the Pleasures of the Chase, Poor Tom, Irish

Under the DIRECTION of Mr. LINLEY.
ORATORIOS,
At PLAY-HOUSE PRICES.
AT the KING's THEATRE, HAY-MARKET, THIS EVENING, March 16, 1792, will be performed, the Sacred Oratorio of
REDEMPTION.
Selected from the Works of HANDEL;
By Dr. ARNOLD.
PART I.
Overture to the Occasional Oratorio.
Chorus, "O First Created Beam."—Samson.
Air, Mr. REINHOLD, "He layeth the Beams."—Eatius.
Chorus, "When his loud Voice."—Jephtha.
Air, Mrs. CROUCH, "Lord, what is Man?"—Semele.
Chorus, "How excellent thy Name."—Saul.
Air, Mr. KELLY, "Speak ye who best can tell."—Ptolomy.
Air, Mrs. BLAND, "Abraham, enough."—Susannah.
Air, Miss HAGLEY, "Jehovah is my Shield."—Occasional Oratorio

Fig. 93. *Second heading of John Bell's* The Oracle

THE ORACLE, AND PUBLIC ADVERTISER.

NUMBER 19,221.] *WEDNESDAY, JANUARY 20, 1796.* [PRICE FOUR PENCE HALFPENNY.

GREAT ROOM, KING'S THEATRE.
January 8, 1796.
THE NOBILITY and GENTRY, Subscribers to the OPERA CONCERT last Season, and the PUBLIC are most respectfully acquainted, that the same Concert will be continued in future under the name and title of
THE ACADEMY OF MUSIC.
The Terms of the Subscription are FOUR GUINEAS for Ten Concerts, to be given on the Monday Evenings of

February	1	April	4
——	8	——	18
——	22	May	2
March	7	——	16
——	14	——	30

The Vocal Performers for the next Season are

SHAKSPEARE GALLERY, PALL-MALL.
MESSRS. BOYDELLS and NICOL beg leave to acquaint the Subscribers to the SHAKSPEARE, that the NINTH NUMBER of that Work is now ready for delivery.
The SECOND VOLUME of the MILTON, uniform with the Shakspeare, is also published.
The Gallery is open to the Subscribers and the Public as usual.

TO THE OFFICERS
OF
THE ARMY.
CHARLES BIGGAR, Master of the SPRING GARDEN COFFEE-HOUSE, encouraged by the many favours he has received from Gentlemen in the Army, has thought it his duty, from respect and gratitude, to compile a MANUSCRIPT LIST, shewing, in one

WALTER'S
NEW INVENTED BRITISH POWDER,
Manufactured at his Warehouse only, No. 210, Oxford-street.
WALTER begs to inform the Nobility, and Ladies in general, that, owing to the high price of Powder, he has invented a very beautiful fragrant Powder, as much for the accommodation of his Customers as any little emolument he may obtain. The Ladies who use this incomparable Powder will save the expence of the high priced Marechall, as no Powder can be more pleasant, or have a more beautiful effect on the hair.
N. B. The price is Fourteen Shillings per dozen, or One Shilling and Three-pence per pound.

TO MONIED PERSONS.
ANY Gentleman or Lady having a Sum of Money at command, from 500l. up to any amount,

room without assistance; my lungs were so loaded with phlegm, that I breathed with great difficulty, and my Cough so extremely violent, that I hourly looked for my dissolution.
Being frequently advised to try the efficacy of your remedy by a number of my friends, and my Apothecary discovering that I was determined to take no more of his preparations, requested me to try some of your improved Balsam of Honey; before I had taken one Bottle, found my breathing very much relieved, I expectorated a great quantity of phlegm, which has eased me of one of the most violent Coughs that ever a man had. I have taken it regularly ever since, and now find myself completely recovered and shall certainly, for the benefit received, recommend it as far as I can, believing it to be a most efficacious Medicine in the above complaints. I remain, with the greatest respect,
Your highly obliged humble servant,
Islington, July 2, 1795. CHARLES HARRIS.
☞ CAUTION.—The very great advantages this

Fig. 94

The Oracle,

PUBLIC ADVERTISER.

NUMBER 19,412.] MONDAY, AUGUST 29, 1796. [PRICE FOUR PENCE HALFPENNY.

THEATRE-ROYAL, HAY-MARKET,
THIS PRESENT EVENING, August 29, will be presented (by permission of the Proprietors of the Theatre Royal Drury-Lane,) a Play in three acts, called
THE IRON CHEST.
Previous to the Play, will be performed a Farce, called
THE DEAF LOVER.
Boxes 5s. Pit 3s. First Gall. 2s. Second Gall. 1s.
The Doors to be opened at Six o'Clock, and to begin at Seven.
Places for the Boxes to be had of Mr. Rice, at the Theatre.
To-morrow, The School of Shakespeare, or Humours and Passions; with the Son-in-Law.

VAUXHALL.
LAST GALA THIS SEASON.
TO-MORROW, TUESDAY, August 30, will be
A GRAND GALA,
In the same SUPERB STILE as that given by Desire of their Excellencies the TURKISH and TUNISIAN AMBASSODORS.
In the Crescent, adjoining the Rotunda, will be exhibited the GRAND CAR of APOLLO, beautifully ILLUMINATED, in which His Royal Highness the Duke of York's Band (by Permission in full Uniform,) will perform Martial Music, at the End of the First Act.
The TRANSPARENT ARCHES, with EMBLEMATICAL DEVICES, will be exhibited in one of the principal Walks.

BRITISH THEATRE, at HALF PRICE, consisting of NINETY of the most esteemed ENGLISH PLAYS.
Royal Edition, originally sold at 22l. 10s. now may be had for 11l. 5s.
Fine Edition, originally sold at 6l. 15s. now may be had for 3l. 7s. 6d.
Common Edition, originally sold at 2l. 5s. now may be had for 1l. 10s.
N. B. If not sold in Complete Sets the Price as under:
Royal, originally sold in single Plays at 5s. now may be had at 3s.
Fine, originally sold in single Plays at 1s. 6d. now may be had at 1s.
Common, originally sold in single Plays at 6d. now may be had at 4½d.

per ones, in a manner as simple as ingenious. A Mechanism equally as simple joins the parts of Sets to the Natural Teeth which remain; and single, double, or treble Teeth, fit with the greatest facility, because M. De Chemant has found means of boring his Paste, so as to place pins in them, and to make any slides he pleases.
"His manner of taking measure of the Teeth, which he means to replace, adds greatly to the merit of his invention. His process is such, that each piece is moulded, as it were, for the place which it is to fill; and as for the whole sets, half sets, or any other portion whatsoever, their base receives and surrounds the edges of the gums, on the parts on which they are applied, so as to render their position very solid, and to prevent the painful pressure they may otherwise occasion. By this

Fig. 95

The Oracle, AND THE DAILY ADVERTISER.

No. 22,232.] THURSDAY, FEBRUARY 27, 1800. [PRICE SIX PENCE.

THEATRE-ROYAL, DRURY-LANE.
THIS PRESENT EVENING, Feb. 27, Their Majesties Servants will act a Tragedy, called
PIZARRO.
Ataliba, Mr. Powell; Rolla, Mr. Kemble; Alonzo, Mr. C. Kemble; Pizarro, Mr. Barrymore; Valverde, Mr. Palmer; Las-Casas, Mr. Packer; Orozembo, Mr. Dowton; Blind Man, Mr. Cory; Centinel, Mr. Holland; Cora, Miss Biggs; and Elvira, Mrs. Siddons.
To which will be added, a New Musical Farce, in Two Acts, called
OF AGE TO-MORROW.
On Saturday, a New Comic Opera, in Three Acts, called The Egyptian Festival.

BY COMMAND OF THEIR MAJESTIES.
THEATRE-ROYAL, COVENT-GARDEN.
THIS PRESENT EVENING, Feb. 27, Will be performed a New Comedy, called

This Day is published, Price 2s.
FORETHOUGHTS on the GENERAL PACIFICATION of EUROPE.
Printed for J. Wright, No. 169, Piccadilly, and J. Hatchard, Bookseller to the Queen, No. 173, Piccadilly.

This Day is published, the Third Volume, in Octavo, Price 7s. in Boards,
CANTERBURY TALES. By SOPHIA and HARRIET LEE.
Printed for G. G. and J. Robinson, Pater-noster-row.
Of whom may be had, Price 7s. each in Boards, the Second Editions of the First and Second Volumes.

Saturday, March 15, will be published, in Nine Volumes Octavo,
A SUMMARY of UNIVERSAL HISTORY. Exhibiting the Rise, Decline, and Revolutions of the different Nations of the World, from the Creation to the present Time. Translated from the French of

TO THE LIVERY OF LONDON, WELL-AFFECTED TO OUR GLORIOUS CONSTITUTION OF KING, LORDS, AND COMMONS.
THE COMMITTEE of the CONSTITUTIONAL LIVERY think proper to inform you, that the COUNTER-PETITION is intended to be presented to the Honourable HOUSE of COMMONS, TO-MORROW, the 28th inst. and will remain for Signature, from Ten to Four o'Clock, THIS DAY, and from Ten to Three o'Clock, TO-MORROW, at the following Houses only:
The Antwerp Tavern, Threadneedle-street; Lloyd's Coffee-house; the London Tavern, Bishopsgate-street; and the London Coffee-house, Ludgate-hill.
Signed by Order of the Committee,
EDWARD KEMBLE, Chairman.
Thursday, Feb. 27, 1800.
N. B. The Committee will meet at the Antwerp Tavern this Evening, from Seven till Ten o'Clock, to receive the Signatures of their Brother Liverymen.

BY ACT OF PARLIAMENT.
The DRAWING of the present STATE LOTTERY will begin on MONDAY NEXT.
GRAND SCHEME.

No. of Prizes		Value of each.		Total Value.
2	of	£30,000	of	£60,000
3	—	20,000	—	60,000
3	—	10,000	—	30,000
4	—	5,000	—	20,000
5	—	2,000	—	10,000
10	—	1,000	—	10,000
10	—	500	—	5,000
26	—	100	—	2,600
54	—	50	—	2,700
16,650	—	18	—	299,700
16,767 Prizes				£500,000
38,233 Blanks				
55,000				

Fig. 96

Figs. 94 to 96. *Successive headings of John Bell's* The Oracle. (*In* 1803 *the paper incorporates* The True Briton)

by appearing in a new type-face, the first English 'modern'. The details of type designing are subtle enough to make a discussion of serif-construction unprofitable in this place. It is sufficient to say that the cutting of type had undergone a change in France; and that when Bell started a type foundry of his own in 1788, he perfected by slow degrees a new design, to some extent in the new French fashion, in various sizes.[1] After trying it in pamphlets and books,[2]

[1] The pages of the present volume are set in a reproduction of the english (14-point) size of Bell's design, cut by the Monotype Corporation for machine setting from the original material kindly furnished by Messrs Stephenson, Blake & Co., whose foundry, the richest in England, inherited the punches and matrices of the British Letter Foundry.

[2] The capitals of the size used in this book are to be found in *The World*, 1788.

he brought out *The Oracle*, composed entirely in several sizes of the new fount, on Wednesday, March 21, 1792. The heading, in Fry's shadowed capitals, was new and set a fashion followed later by *The Sun* and other new foundations. The centre-piece of the title of *The Oracle* was a really distinguished piece of engraving, suitably introducing the new type. The letters themselves, a little more condensed than any of its predecessors, were perhaps more suitable for newspaper than for book composition. There was, of course, no long ſ, the only ligature being the ct.

The paper makes an undeniably handsome appearance; it was an improvement upon all Bell's previous attempts to combine rationalism and elegance. Nor has any similar degree of intelligence and conscientiousness been lavished on the newspaper since *The Oracle*. And Bell himself, deserting daily for weekly newspaper effort, produced in his *Messenger* (1796) a purely efficient layout, lacking any hint of the *Oracle*'s elegance. The fact seems to have been that misfortune cured him of aesthetic enthusiasms. He overtaxed his financial powers, was bankrupted in 1793, but struggled to maintain *The Oracle*. Friends stood by him, and on behalf of the paper John Bell went to Flanders in 1794 for the purpose of reporting the war between the British and the French. Bell described the actions of the British at Ypres and marched with the army from Courtrai to Tournai, sending regular despatches to his paper. In this capacity as the first of the English war correspondents Bell once more proved himself a pioneer. Yet Bell's control over the paper rapidly lessened. An amalgamation with the old and enfeebled *Public Advertiser* seems not to have been of any benefit. In 1795 the paper was bought by Peter Stuart, loose from the defunct *Morning Star*. The heading of *The Oracle* was brought into accord with the style followed by the majority of the town morning papers, namely, that of *The World*. Stuart continued to print *The Oracle* in the Bell style until 1810. Although the composition was diluted with supplementary orders of Fry's or Wilson's founts, the Bell fount was used for headings for some time. None of those responsible for the developments between 1788 and 1800 had been bold enough to follow Bell's example in abolishing the long ſ, nor did their successors, even in the newly invented papers of the early 1800's, hasten that salutary reform.

The principal morning and evening newspapers of the year 1790, given in Dr Trusler's *London Advertiser and Guide*[1] as appealing to the visitors from the provinces, are:

[1] Second edition 1790, pp. 135–7. This is the same Trusler of *The Morning Post* 1772– (cf. p. 169).

Every Morning[1]

The Daily Advertiser	*Woodfall's Diary*	*The Gazetteer*
The Morning Chronicle	*The Morning Post*	*The Patriot*
The Herald	*The Ledger*	*The World*
The Argus	*The Times*	*The Public Advertiser*
The Oracle		

Every Evening *The Star*

Tuesday, Thursday and Saturday Evenings[2]

The General Evening (Post)	*The Evening Mail*
The St James's Chronicle	*The Middlesex Journal*
The English Chronicle	*The London Packet*
The London Chronicle	*Lloyd's Evening Post*
The London Evening Post	

On January 2, 1792, a very handsome production under a title, in shaded blackletter, reading *The Cabinet*, issued its first number. It was set throughout in the Bell types, with extraordinary care, and with intelligent leading. The effect is a little over-conscious for a newspaper, and we can well believe the notice that 'The Newsmen are not to be blamed for the late delivery'. Whether this irritated the 'more polished and enlightened of our Countrymen' in whose interest this handsome daily was published, we doubt; and whether the promise made in the next paragraph that 'Tomorrow and To-morrow—and Tomorrow—the Paper will be out precisely as the HORSE GUARDS STRIKES FIVE!' was kept, we do not know. Its elegance is its only interest, for its life, pathetically brief, was hardly longer than a month. An innovation was its running headline—over a rule. This new feature, however, was long in coming into general newspaper use. *The Times* did not accept the suggestion until 1825. *The Cabinet* paper also set its title in slightly different form; the serial number and the date were set in italic right and left of the title, instead of between rules. The paper's column rules were single in the first issue and double in the second. A somewhat similar journal, set, with double rules[3], in Bell's types from the British Letter Foundry (which

[1] Stuart's *Morning Star* should have been included in this list. I have found no trace of a daily *Patriot* until 1792. Trusler writes: 'Of the morning papers, those most in circulation are *Daily Advertiser*, *Gazetteer*, *Ledger* in the city and the *Herald*, *Morning Post*, and *World* in the west end. The *Daily* is best calculated for advertisements being taken in chiefly on that account, the news, of course, is much confined'.

[2] 'The Evening Papers are circulated chiefly in the country, and those most in circulation are the *General Evening* and *St James's Chronicle*', reports Trusler.

[3] The double rules were changed to single, June 17, 1795.

had an advertisement on the front page), was *The Telegraph* whose first issue was published on the curiously unsuitable date, Tuesday, December 30, 1794. Looks, however, could not save it. *The Telegraph* was quietly bought up by Daniel Stuart of *The Morning Post*. We mention it because it is well to note the extension of Bell's typographical influence.[1] Even where, as in the instance of *The True Briton* (1793), the type was not Bell's, the style of composition and display was his. *The Express and Evening Chronicle*, a thrice-weekly (Tuesday, Thursday and Saturday) founded in 1794, contained a good deal of Bell's type set in the master's fashion. *The Courier*, founded by John Parry in 1792, was the longest lived of any of the finely printed papers issued in the immediate range of Bell's influence. The paper, established in the autumn of 1792, was printed without apology in the style of *The Cabinet*. *The Courier* maintained the exactly similar shaded gothic title, running head-lines, double rules and Bell founts of type, for six years or so. In 1796 Parry sold to Daniel, the brother of Peter Stuart, but the style of the paper was not interfered with, little change being observable until the next century was well advanced.

The Morning Advertiser—set in the conventional, i.e. the Bell, style—was founded to achieve the position which *The Aurora* of 1781 had sought in vain. With its centre device of a Regency star and open gothic lettering, the first number of *The Morning Advertiser*, February 8, 1794, is a fair example of the normal good style of the period. There was some hesitation in respect to the heading. In No. 2 the centre device was altered and in No. 20 the gothic lettering was abandoned in favour of a large size of Fry's titling capitals, reading in two lines 'THE PUBLICANS | MORNING ADVERTISER'. In the following year, the old heading was reinstated with a large star, and so continued until the nineteenth century was well advanced.

The printer of *The Sun*, Buchanan Millan, formerly printer of *The Oracle*, closely followed the Bell style and brought out one of the most dignified and readable papers in a half century responsible for a round dozen of handsomely produced journals. While Bell's efforts were never surpassed, he was closely imitated by worthy disciples such as Bostock and Millan. *The Sun* was established to support Pitt. From the first number (October 1, 1792) it was enterprising in the matter of news. A fine wood-engraved map of Valenciennes was 'procured at considerable expense' and printed in the issue for July 6

[1] *The Telegraph* was printed in 1795 by R. Bostock, formerly printer of *The World*. Bostock shaded the lettering of the title and re-dressed the date-line, making a truly delicate piece.

of that year. Illustrations were still sparse in either dailies or weeklies. The splendid example given by *The Noon Gazette* in 1781 had not been followed up by wealthier contemporaries. On September 8, 1794, the 'Conductor' of *The Oracle and Public Advertiser* printed a dissertation upon 'The Telegraph' whose mysteries were elucidated by two small cuts. This niggardliness may be due to the rising costs of production—compositors, for example, were agitating for a rise because of increased cost of living. Yet *The Oracle* in 1796, perceiving maps elsewhere, bestirred itself to keep the reputation for news which the personal foreign service of John Bell had created:

> It may not be unworthy of observation that the Proprietors of *The Oracle* were the first[1] who introduced Maps in any Newspaper, and they flatter themselves that their new and singular design, announced for Wednesday, will add another to the many proofs which they have already given of their undoubted claim to a superiority of information.

The paper for October 6, 1796, accordingly published on its second page a map of the theatre of war on the Continent 'Drawn for *The Oracle*'. There were two novelties. First, the lettering was type-set and not engraved, the type-bodies being let into two cuttings on the face of the block. This expedient had two virtues; of saving much time in engraving and of allowing the use of smaller lettering. *The Oracle*'s block is lettered in Bell's roman capitals, lower-case roman and italic in three sizes. The past and present strategical advances and retreats, etc. were indicated by a second block printed—unique performance to my knowledge—in red.

In the beginning of 1794 the London dailies were compelled to increase their prices to the public in order to cover new taxes. The cost of living was rising and the wages of printers were increased. *The Oracle* for April 21, 1794, gives a consequently succinct account of the circumstances. It is so admirably set out with John Bell's characteristic and unique mastery of typographical display, that I cannot refrain from reproducing the column in type-facsimile (see p. 200).

The cost to *The Times* was £100 a year 'more than ever before'. The price of that paper was raised to 4½*d.* per copy; but, 'as a grateful return on our part for the patronage we receive', a new type was promised in *The Times* of April 19, 1794. In spite of the fulfilment of this promise, complaints were made that no new types had yet been seen in *The Times*. The proprietors

[1] Unless this is interpreted to mean 'the first (in our time)' the claim cannot be substantiated. There were maps in Read's *Weekly Journal* during the 1720's.

THE NEW DUTY ON PAPER,

THE ENCREASED PRICE OF

PRINTING MATERIALS,

AND THE ADVANCE OF

JOURNEYMEN'S WAGES,

Within the last twelve months, have augmented the expences of Printing a Morning Newspaper, at least Twenty-five per Cent.

This leads to a declaration, that the Proprietors of the ORACLE AND PUBLIC ADVERTISER must, with the Printers of *well conducted Newspapers* in general, be under the disagreeable necessity of raising the price of their Paper, in future, to FOURPENCE HALFPENNY each; and for the clearest of reasons, viz. that they cannot continue their publication at a less price, without a very material and manifest loss to themselves. To prove this, it need only be stated, that the average sale of London Morning Newspapers, may be fairly taken at 1500 per day.

COST THEREOF.	£.	s.	d.	PRODUCE.	£.	s.	d.
3 Reams of Paper for 1,500, at One Guinea per ream, with the new duty,	3	3	0	1,500 of these Papers are sold by the Proprietors to the newsmen at 28s. for every 104, which amount to	20	3	11
1,500 stamps pay to Government	12	10	0				
Not less than 20 persons are constantly employed, almost day and night, in the Printing Department alone of a Morning Paper, whose wages amount on an average to	6	6	8				
	21	19	8				

Thus it appears evident that there is an absolute loss of 1l. 15s. 9d. per day, on the sale of 1500 Papers, exclusive of the expences attending the PARLIAMENTARY REPORTS—LITERARY COMMUNICATIONS—COMMERCIAL ARRANGEMENTS—and FOREIGN INTELLIGENCE.—*These last Articles* amounting altogether to little less than THIRTY POUNDS per WEEK, which must be indemnified by the profit on Advertisements alone, before the PROPRIETORS of the NEWSPAPER can derive one farthing advantage, in recompence of their great speculation and unremitting exertions.

After this fair representation, the PROPRIETORS of the ORACLE and PUBLIC ADVERTISER will not entertain a fear of losing even one Friend by the present NECESSARY advanced price of their Paper.

ON THE CONTRARY,

They will look forward, in full confidence of experiencing a most liberal reward, from a candid and discerning PUBLIC, for their future exertions—which they mean to be distinguished by a zeal, vigilance, activity, and abilities, that shall entitle the ORACLE and PUBLIC ADVERTISER to a most decided preference as a DAILY PRINT.

FOR THIS PURPOSE,

MR. BELL,

OF THE BRITISH LIBRARY,

INTENDS IMMEDIATELY TO MAKE

THE TOUR OF THE SEAT OF WAR

IN

FLANDERS;

AND TO SCOUR ALONG THE FRENCH FRONTIERS, AS NEARLY AS POSSIBLE,

IN ORDER TO ESTABLISH

A CHAIN OF REGULAR CORRESPONDENCE

WITH EVERY PART OF

THE ALLIED ARMY;

AND TO TAKE EVERY POSSIBLE METHOD OF OBTAINING

THE FRENCH PAPERS

WITH MORE REGULARITY AND DISPATCH THAN HAS HITHERTO BEEN PRACTICABLE.

SUCH IS THE PRESENT PLAN for improving this Property, and of being grateful for whatever patronage

THE ORACLE

AND

PUBLIC ADVERTISER

May be honoured with.

Mr. BELL purposes to set off on this expedition on THURSDAY NEXT. The PUBLIC may therefore afterwards look for a daily instance of his attention and success.

THE ORACLE,

AND

PUBLIC ADVERTISER.

LONDON, APRIL 21.

There will be no business done at St. James's till Wednesday se'nnight, when the KING will hold a Levee.

Yesterday at noon THEIR MAJESTIES, accompanied by the PRINCESSES ROYAL, AUGUSTA, and ELIZABETH, came from Buckingham-house to the Garden-gate, St. James's Palace, from thence they went to the QUEEN'S apartments on the east wing of the Palace, where they, joined by their retinue, the Heralds, &c. proceeded in state to the Chapel Royal. They then attended divine service, and heard a sermon preached by the Rev. Dr. VINCENT, Sub-almoner. After divine Service the ROYAL FAMILY came down and proceeded to the altar, where they received the Sacrament, which was administered to them by the LORD BISHOP of LONDON, as Dean of the Chapel.

At three they returned to Buckingham-house, and at four set off for Windsor Lodge, where THEIR MAJESTIES and the SIX PRINCESSES will reside till Wednesday se'nnight.

answered with a statement that Mrs Elizabeth Caslon had indeed furnished the new type and that it had been in use since January 1, 1795. There were readers, evidently, who expected something more up-to-date than the old face which Mrs Caslon supplied. The modern face used first in *The Oracle* in 1789, and elsewhere since, was taken up in several parts of the country, and had attracted the attention of such book printers as William Bulmer, who, on arriving in London from Newcastle, was given work by John Bell. When Bulmer set William Martin in charge of the foundry attached to his office a memorable work was initiated. The Martin fount had a deep influence upon subsequent typefounding, whether for books or newspapers. William Martin's type was itself scarcely a true 'modern', being fundamentally, and finally, a variation on the Baskerville theme. But when the same design was taken as a basis by a punch-cutter who worked upon it according to the methods of Richard Austin, and added an infusion of Bodoni, the result was a true 'modern'. And this, roughly speaking, is the way in which Bulmer came to use a definitely condensed, rigid and well-coloured 'modern face' for Dibdin and other esteemed authors of the period.

These developments took place between 1792 and the end of the century. It is only to be expected that some such face would make its appearance in newspapers. On November 9, 1799, *The Times* announced that the issue for the day was 'printed in an entire new and beautiful type from the foundry of Mrs Caslon which we hope will meet with the public approbation'. The new type was such as we have described. It was heavier than the other—and earlier—modern of Bell. This was a practical change, for its additional weight gave the type more legibility by artificial light, and, in view of the rapidly expanding circulation of the paper, helped the pressman a little, since under-inked copies were more readable in the new than in the old fount. A final advantage was the extra degree of condensation permitted by the new design. In view of the rising price of paper and the increased stamp duties, *The Times* exerted itself to give readers the maximum quantity of reading matter. The new type was a help to the realisation of this aim, and so obviously that the fount, in one cutting or another, established itself in every newspaper in London, and holds the same position to this day.

The fount which *The Times* uses today is closely related to the same early fount. The rest of the London newspapers use the same root-design in one or another corrupt version[1]. This final typographical innovation of the

[1] The *Daily Herald* excepted. In this journal 'Ionic', a recently-made revival of one of Messrs Miller and Richard's founts, first cut in 1821, is used for the

eighteenth century took place, as we have seen, in the year 1799. The old-face steadily declined as the new century progressed; and not until the foundation of *The Pall Mall Gazette* (1865) and *The Westminster Gazette* (1893) was old-face used after its complete abandonment by the year 1820.

text. The differences between the 'old face' and the 'modern face' are illustrated in the article on Newspaper Types in the Printing Number of *The Times* (October 29, 1929). The point, though a simple one, is too technical to justify treatment in these lectures; it is amply illustrated and discussed (in connexion with the printing of *books*) in Updike, *Printing Types* (Harvard, 1922), McKerrow, *Introduction to Bibliography* (Oxford, 1928), and Morison, *Type Designs of the Past and Present* (London, 1926).

CHAPTER XII

THE NINETEENTH-CENTURY DAILY

1803–1846

The Times (*continued*)

The Standard 1827

The Daily News 1846

CHAPTER XII

THE NINETEENTH-CENTURY DAILY

1803–1846

THE close of the eighteenth century was not signalised by any sudden development in the size of newspapers. Apart from the relatively inconspicuous change of type from old-face to modern, the nineteenth-century daily newspaper cannot be said to have begun until the year 1819, when five columns were permanently established as the measure of the pages of *The Times*, and the heavy gothic lettering was introduced. *The Morning Post*, *The Morning Herald* and *The Morning Chronicle* followed in course of time. Although there were new papers, like *The Day* (later incorporated with *The New Times*, started by Dr Stoddart) and two or three others of shorter life, the new century does not become really famous[1] for any new foundations in daily journalism until *The Daily News* (No. 1, January 21, 1846).

There was a high rate of mortality, too, in the evenings. *The Globe* persisted, successively absorbing *The Traveller*, *The Statesman*, *The Evening Chronicle*, *The Argus* and *The Nation*. We have *The Evening Standard* from 1827 (No. 1, May 21), which absorbed *The Albion* and *The Star*, then an ultra-Protestant paper. *The Express*, an evening paper, in connection with *The Daily News*, ran between 1846 and 1869. *The St James's Chronicle* (which out-lived by half a century the other tri-weeklies, such as *The London Chronicle*, and the several *General*, or *Lloyd's*, *Evening Posts*), debilitated at last by the monotony of its protestantism, ceased separate publication in 1866.

The outstanding newspaper achievements of the century, therefore, are not to be found in new establishments but in developments of the old. From the invention of the Koenig Press[2] in *The Times* office, 1814, which, by first bringing power into the service of printing, increased, almost to infinity, the economic character of Gutenberg's invention, *The Times* became the

[1] *The Standard* (f. 1827), with its heavy gothic heading, was always a dreary paper until the '70's. It was started by Charles Baldwin to uphold the banner of protestantism. Baldwin already owned *The St James's Chronicle* and *Baldwin's London Weekly Journal*. The former he had turned from a newspaper into a serial anti-popery tract. Liquor advertisements were accepted in both papers.

[2] The first power-press used—instead of the Stanhope—was employed for the production of the issue dated November 24, 1814, printing one side only.

classic nineteenth-century morning paper. Nevertheless, if it is the fact that no *new* morning paper, until *The Daily News*, was of any consequence, there was one other nineteenth-century development of such importance that a separate lecture must be devoted to it. This development was the Sunday paper.

The Sunday paper, as invented and continued in the eighteenth century, was an utterly negligible affair. In the hands of John Bell, Robert Bell and John Browne Bell, it became an enormous engine. We must postpone consideration of their three Sunday papers—*Bell's Weekly Messenger* (1796), *Bell's Weekly Dispatch* (1801) and *The News of the World* (1843)—but they must be kept in mind as we turn over the files of *The Times* between the end of the eighteenth and the middle of the nineteenth centuries.

The purely typographical changes in the London dailies, in the years from 1799 to 1836, were in the uniform direction of smaller front-page titles, and over all, a completely flat and unrelieved massing of tiny body types all closely set, with headings of the same fount-sized capitals. In the advertising, all 'display', i.e. the centring of lines, was avoided in favour of running them on. By these means, there was no 'waste' of space, every available fraction was printed on; all white space was crowded out, and the inviting, open, airy Bell style was succeeded by a setting which was as solid and as forbidding as a fourteenth-century codex of canon law. The dead weight of taxation upon paper, upon advertisements, and an extra $3\frac{1}{2}d.$ upon each and every sheet, made the newspaper an expensive possession. It was taken up in a spirit of duty and read religiously. The levity of the eighteenth-century *Times* evaporated when the practice of leading was perforce abandoned. The legibility of the graceful old-faces of Caslon and Fry depended upon their being set with adequate space between the lines and headings; the modern-faces of Thorne and Steele, set as close as possible, were not provided with anything like adequate white space and could only achieve legibility by a process of thickening. Inevitably, the newspapers became progressively blacker in appearance as taxes were increased and space became more and more valuable. The physical history of the London newspaper, morning and evening, of the early nineteenth century, yields no novelty of setting of the text, or change in the display of the front-page heading. The journals were almost alike to the eye; and necessarily, since all had the identical needs to serve in the same identical circumstances.

The lead which *The Times* gave at the end of 1799 pre-figured the changes which were to come as soon as the new century was well started. *The*

Morning Post adopted modern type in 1802 and, like *The Times*, has never since abandoned it. If *The Times* had chosen to revert to old-face, it may be taken as certain that the rest of the press would have followed.

The supremacy of Printing House Square dated from the appointment of John Walter II as 'joint proprietor and exclusive manager' in 1803. In 1802, the year before John Walter II succeeded his father in the management of *The Times*, the paper was still hardly more than a fair, witty 'west-endish' sheet with good political news, parliamentary reports and foreign intelligence. *The Morning Chronicle*, under Perry, was regarded as of greater importance, and it remained the greatest rival to Printing House Square until a series of unfortunate speculations brought it to an end in 1862. The power—material, mechanical and editorial—of *The Times* became such that two generations of fine journalists, on *The Morning Chronicle* and on *The* (evening) *Courier*, were unable effectively to challenge its supremacy. It was the first journal to print by power instead of by hand, thereby introducing the greatest improvement to the art of printing since its foundation; it was the first journal to engage specially rapid foreign news services. Until the 'sixties were over, no paper surpassed it in independence, circulation, bulk or enterprise. As in journalism nothing succeeds like success, it was inevitable, first that the example of *The Times* should be taken as a typographical model by the printers and publishers of other newspapers; and secondly that the appearance of the journals of the first half of the century should lack variety. This monotony of journalistic style has at least the merit of simplifying our task, since, in the circumstances, we may concentrate our attention chiefly upon *The Times*.

When John Walter II came to Printing House Square, he found *The Times* a mature eighteenth-century newspaper. He, and his editor Thomas Barnes of Pembroke College in the University of Cambridge, made it a modern newspaper in every sense of the word. If Walter II's sense of typographical display was inferior to Bell's, he was justified by the ever-increasing demand upon space, and the unremitting demands of the Inland Revenue which taxed the paper before it was printed, and again when it was printed.[1]

The year 1804 witnessed the first printing in *The Times* of three head-pieces of which two survived a month or less, while the remaining one has come down to our own day. This is perhaps a better symbol of *The Times*, its personality and its authority, than any other device that has been or could

[1] Stamped paper was so valuable that I have seen a sheet of *Bell's Weekly Messenger* patched in two places before printing in order to prevent waste. No allowance was made for spoiled stamps.

be invented, namely, the Clock device, with the timepiece bearing the time of 6.6 a.m.[1]

This block first appeared in the paper of January 2, 1804. It was followed by two others heading the columns respectively of 'Fashion'[2] (February 1,

Fig. 97. *Column heading-blocks of* The Times, 1804

1804) and 'Naval Register' (January 2, 1804). The Clock device now heads the Table of Contents, which is placed immediately over the summary. In 1804 the leader had not yet become fully developed, being still a somewhat tedious expansion of an item of important or late news. By 1804 a paragraph, which later grew into a column or more, was given to discursive reflections upon a more or less important military or political occurrence. In 1804 the Clock and this early form of leader were separated by the theatrical announcements which formerly appeared on the front page.

The new position seems strangely authoritative. Theatrical advertising had always been important to a proprietor, for readers referred to newspapers then, as now, for particulars of the plays and casts. The time-honoured place for these advertisements was in the first two columns of the front page, pride of place being given to the Theatres Royal: Drury Lane, Hay Market, Covent Garden. The bills of the Theatres Royal were transferred on March 31, 1794, to a position between the end of the Parliamentary intelligence and the beginning of the London intelligence. In time, notices of entertainments

[1] The time represents the average hour of completing publication. To state the time was an important method of preventing substitution by newsmen of e.g. *The Morning Herald* for the *Morning Chronicle* on the false ground that the ordered paper was not published until late in the morning. John Bell was the first to declare his time of publication in *The Oracle*. It was printed between the name of the paper and the first paragraph of London intelligence—i.e. the position of the leading article. The 'Clock' device gave further authority to this, as the vital, position of the paper. The time of publication was first inserted in *The Times*, December 1803.

[2] These are the respective blocks. Neither lasted more than a few weeks, while the 'Clock' has held its position until the present day.

such as Astley's, appeared there, though the Royal Theatres invariably took precedence. The transfer was made in order to help the printer, for the outside of the sheet was printed first. Delay in the receipt of the playbills made the entire paper late, a danger lessened by the transfer to a position on the inside of the sheet. Notification of the transfer was given on March 31, 1794:

Notwithstanding the arrangements we have made to obtain early publication by printing the Paper at three Presses instead of two, we still find complaints are made of the lateness of its delivery in some parts of the Town. This arises from the sale of the Paper having continued to increase daily, in proportion as the delivery has been more early than it was formerly. The impossibility of obtaining an accurate copy of the PLAY-BILLS of the day, at an early hour on the preceding evening, has frequently delayed the outside pages of the Paper from being sent to Press; in future, therefore, the PLAY-BILLS will be inserted immediately preceding the *London News*.[1]

The theatres today occupy an inside position in *The Times* and they even succeeded in keeping their position over the leader until the close of Mr Moberly Bell's management of the paper.

The paper developed in the course of two decades into the fully grown early Victorian newspaper which it resembled until twenty years ago. With the issue of June 13, 1805, the necessity for reporting in full the impeachment of Viscount Melville forced the paper into the unprecedented dimensions of three sheets, each stamped and each selling for sixpence. This was the sort of emergency which made the blanket-folio so desirable, and which finally brought it about after stages in 1806, 1813, 1819 and 1822. Printing House Square went in for speed as well as bulk. On Sunday, November 3, 1805, an 'Extraordinary' was issued. The sheet makes an elegant appearance. I do not know of similar extraordinaries issued by journals other than *The London Gazette*. In the following year (October 28, 1806) a double number of *The Times* bore on its front page 'PRICE ONE SHILLING' instead of the previous legend 'PRICE SIXPENCE EACH SHEET'. A spectacular development occurred on April 7, 1806, when *The Times* printed on its front page two wood engravings, one a diagram of the ground plan and the other an elevation of the house of Mr Blight whose murder by Richard Patch was the sensation of the day.[2] A fifth column was incorporated with the issue

[1] Even so, there were delays. On January 6, 1796, we read that 'The Drury Lane playbill was not received when this paper went to press'.

[2] *The Times* at this period shewed a greater interest in illustration than any other newspaper. Richard Austin cut a picture of Lord Nelson's funeral car for the issue of January 10, 1806. It is a decent cut but lacking authority. 'The only difference in the appearance of the funeral car from the engraving', says *The Times*, 'is that contrary to what was at first intended, neither the pall nor the coronet

The Times.

NUMBER 6704 | **LONDON, MONDAY, APRIL 7, 1806.** | **PRICE SIXPENCE.**

TRIAL OF RICHARD PATCH.

ADJOURNED SURRY ASSIZES, HORSEMONGER-LANE
SATURDAY, APRIL 5.

The prisoner had been indicted for the murder of ISAAC BLIGHT; and in consequence of the rumours which were supposed to have prejudiced the public mind, it was not thought fit that he should be tried at the Assizes for the County of Surry, and the investigation of his case was removed, that it might be decided by a Special Jury, in the neighbourhood of the Capital. The following were the Gentlemen, who, after several objections taken by the prisoner, were sworn upon the Jury:—

THE JURY.

TYSON CHAPMAN, of Putney.	JOHN WEDGE, of Wandsworth.
THOMAS BARTLET, of Merton.	GEORGE MOORE, of Putney.
CHARLES SMITH, of Merton.	GEORGE SMITH, of Ditto.
THOMAS DALBY, of Barnes.	DANIAL LANGTON, of Wandsworth.
JOHN LEIGHTON, of Putney.	THOMAS CHAPMAN, of Putney.
JOHN CAPP, of Ditto.	
ISAAC HILLIER, of Merton.	

Six other Gentlemen, approved by the prisoner, were also desired to remain, to be put upon the Jury, in case their assistance should be required.

After Mr. KNAPP had arraigned the prisoner, and had received the plea of Not Guilty, he read the indictment in the usual abridged form, which stated, that *Richard Patch*, not having the fear of God before his eyes, did, on the 23d of September, feloniously and wilfully make an assault upon ISAAC BLIGHT; that with his right hand he did discharge a pistol, the contents of which entered the right side of the said Isaac Blight, and did penetrate and wound him, giving him a mortal wound on the right side of his body, of which he languished and died, on the 24th of the same month. The indictment further charged, that he did kill and murder the said Isaac Blight, &c.

Mr. POOLEY, Junior Counsel for the prosecution, then opened the pleadings, and was followed by

Mr. GARROW, who said: "I have the honour to attend on this occasion, in order to discharge a painful duty incident to my situation as Counsel for the Crown. We are to be engaged, Gentlemen, in an awful and important examination into the conduct of the prisoner, which will require your best and undivided attention. You will not expect from me, in opening the case, to enter into an elaborate argument on the nature of the offence, or to attempt, by subtile reasoning, to lead you to the conclusion to which I must have arrived—that the justice due to the country will require that you should pronounce the prisoner guilty. It is for you, Gentlemen, to direct your minds to the evidence, as it will be progressively laid before you; and it is for me, in the present stage of my duty, merely to supply you with the index to that evidence. I ought to preface what I have to offer in this place, and at this time, with one observation, which, I am sure, both you and his Lordship will excuse my introducing. I ought, not only in the name of the prosecution, but in the behalf of the prisoner himself, to offer my thanks to the Learned Judge who presides, for the accommodation he has procured us in this edifice, for the conduct of the enquiry. It is too true, that, on this subject, of so much magnitude to the interests of the community, there have been many details indiscreetly given in the periodical prints, in consequence of which the public mind has received a bias, unfavourable to the natural course of justice; and it is well known that at the assizes, the facts of the case, real or supposed, were the general topic of conversation; so that it became expedient to remove the scene of enquiry, that the prisoner and the public might have the benefit of a fair and satisfactory trial. By you, Gentlemen, I have reason to hope, that any previous conjectures you may have indulged, will be expelled from your minds. If you have had the misfortune, before you came here, to have read these imperfect details, being now upon the Jury engaged in this solemn business, I am convinced you will do your best to dismiss them from your minds. I cannot hesitate for a moment to suppose, but that you will remember the oath you have taken, and that the public will be satisfied, and not less your own consciences, with the result of your present labours.

"I shall have occasion to state to you the relative situation of the prisoner and the deceased, and also the scite of the premises, and the form and position of the buildings, where the crime is alledged to have been perpetrated. The facts themselves, which involve the guilt or innocence of the prisoner, will either be found to confirm, or to invalidate, my representations; and I shall not designedly utter a syllable to inflame your passions, or mislead your judgment, although it must necessarily happen, that, having attended to the commencement, the advance, and the conclusion of the affair, my mind is, unavoidably, powerfully impressed with the persuasion with which I expect you will terminate your duties.

"With respect, then, to the relative situation of these parties, it will shew that the prisoner, if indeed he be guilty of this act of atrocity, was the worst man in the world. He took occasion to entangle his generous friend and benefactor in the toils of mischief, with the determined purpose of destroying him; a case, which if not indeed itself petty treason, is next of kin to that offence. When I explain the structure of the premises, and the inclosure with which it is surrounded, you will see, that it is not only impossible that any other person should have occasioned the death of Mr. Blight, but you will learn, that it was from the hand of the prisoner that he received the fatal stroke. I shall unveil before you the demeanour, the conduct, and the conversation of the prisoner, and I shall then produce some peculiar circumstances in evidence, in which, without the assistance of any superstitious prepossessions, I have convinced myself that you will discern the awful hand of Providence employed to arrest guilt in its career, and to bring the criminal to condign punishment.

"Mr. Blight lived in the neighbourhood of Greenland Dock, where he followed the business of a ship-breaker. He had in his family, in the condition of a menial servant, the sister of the prisoner, and the latter, in the spring of 1803, came to the house of Mr. Blight to see his relation. On this occasion, he intreated that he might be permitted to remain

Mr. BLIGHT's HOUSE.

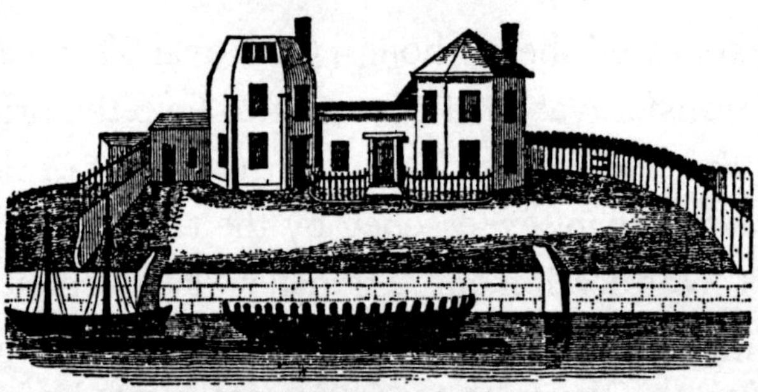

Ground Plan of Mr. BLIGHT's House.

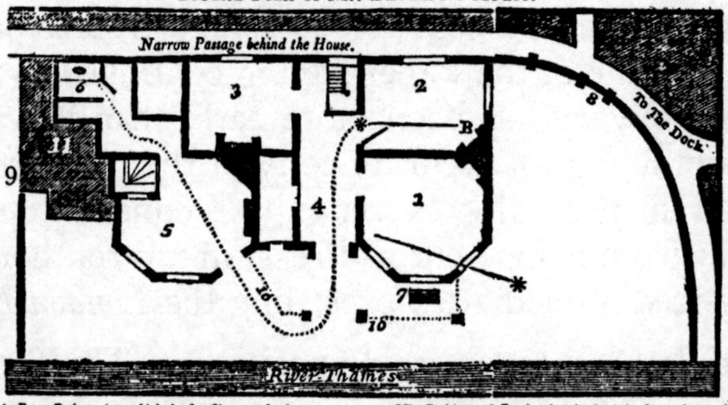

1. Front Parlour, into which the first Shot was fired.
2. Back Parlour, in which Mr. Blight was shot.
3. Kitchen, from the Window of which the Maid Servant jumped into the narrow Passage.
4. Entrance.
5. Counting-house.
6. Privy.
[The Way from the Privy to the back Parlour is described by a dotted line.]

[The Positions of *Patch* when he fired the first and second Shots are marked by stars.]
[The situation of Mr. Blight when shot is marked B]

7. Cellar-door.
8. Wicket-gate.
9. Stone-Mason's-yard.
10. Railing in front of the House.
11. Outhouses.

some days in the house, which being granted, he took an opportunity of representing himself to Mr. Blight as a distressed man, adding, that he had been obliged to leave the West of England on account of some importunate demand for tithes, and that if the deceased would employ him, he would engage in the lowest situation to obtain a livelihood. In consequence of this offer, he was taken into the service of Mr. Blight, without any salary, his victuals being the only return for his industry. He had continued for some time in this state of dependence, when Mr. Blight, finding him, I will acknowledge, a valuable servant, agreed to give him 30*l*. a year in addition to his board.

"He went on for some time in this way, until it was found more convenient that he should board elsewhere, and his remuneration was advanced to 100*l*. a year. Thus you see, Gentlemen, that he leaves this house in 1803, and after a short interval, by hard labour, is enabled to acquire an income sufficiently comfortable. In 1805, the affairs of Mr. Blight became embarrassed; he called his creditors together, and a deed of composition was prepared, by which the wreck of his property was to be made over to the claimants, and he was to be exonerated from their demands. The prisoner took an active part in this arrangement, and here we first discover the clue which terminated in this indictment. You know, Gentlemen, that it is a usual condition in such deeds, that if all the creditors do not accede to them, they should be void. In this case one of the creditors objected, and all was thrown into confusion. In this situation, pressed on every side, Mr. Blight thought it necessary to extricate himself in a way, which those who survive him may have reason to lament. An instrument was drawn up, by which he meant to transfer to the prisoner all his property, which amounted to two thousand and odd hundred pounds; and there will be produced to you, Gentlemen, a letter to the prisoner, stating, that the lease of the premises in question, should, if possible, by the interposition of Mr. Blight, be renewed for his benefit. This transaction was in July, 1805, about two months before the fatal event.

"A short time afterwards, the family of Mr. Blight went to Margate; but before he proceeded to join them, he entered into a new agreement with the prisoner. The other, you see, was merely colourable, and intended to be withdrawn altogether; or, in plain English, the object between them both was to defraud the creditors. The new agreement will be found of the last importance in the consideration of this case. By this contract, it was stipulated, that after some arrangement had been made with the creditors, Mr. Blight should return, should be interested to the reach of 2-3ds, and the prisoner to the extent of 1-3d of the business, for which he was to pay 1250*l*. It will naturally occur to you, Gentlemen, that the raising of this sum was no inconsiderable difficulty to the prisoner. He had nothing but his hundred a year, and he had not been a sufficient time in the service of Mr. Blight, to have raised an amount approaching to that he was to pay as the condition of his new engagement. You will find, in point of fact, that he did not pay it, but that he managed to raise 250*l*. leaving the sum of 1000*l*. undischarged. On neglect of payment, it was required that he should give security, at least in return for this surrender of one-third interest in the trade. He did give what he passed off as valuable security, and it was in the shape of a bill drawn by Mr. Goom, a glue-maker, for 1000*l*. falling due on the 16th of September following, or a week only prior to the commission of the crime. The enquiry was natural: 'How did you come by this bill?' The prisoner said, that he had sold an estate in the West, that he had lent the produce of it to Goom, and this was the return for it. You will expect, Gentlemen, that this bill was not paid at the time of its maturity. Mr. Blight said, in allusion, perhaps, to the trade of the borrower, 'It is a little odd that you should have glued up the money, but the thing is done, and cannot now be avoided.' Under pretencee of accommodating Mr. Goom, a check was given in return for the dishonoured bill, purporting to be drawn by Mr. Goom, and demandable on the 20th of September. We approach now very near to the time of the fatal event. On the Thursday, the day before the draft became due, Mr. Blight left his house, to pay a temporary visit to his wife at Margate. The important concern he left behind him, respected only this payment, which was to be made on the day of his joining his family. Gentlemen, the prisoner accompanied his friend on his journey, as far as Deptford; but as soon as he had taken his leave hastened to his bankers, and said, that Mr. Goom would not be able 'to face the draft upon the 20th,' and therefore he desired them not to present it for payment, adding, that the drawer had given him a security, with which he was perfectly satisfied.

"Now, Gentlemen, on the 19th (which is a day of vast importance), we find the prisoner at home, in the house of Mr. Blight, with a female servant only, of the name of Esther Kitchiner. You will learn, that the family usually spent the evening in a parlour facing the Thames, which, for the sake of distinctness, I shall call the front parlour. On this evening, he desired the servant to procure him sixpenny worth of oysters for supper. She had not far to go; but before she returned, a musquet had been fired, the ball of which had entered the window of this room. Mr. Patch said, that, immediately on hearing the report, he jumped up, and went out, but could find nobody, until he went to the gate, and there he met with a man and his wife, who will be produced to you as witnesses. I charge this prisoner with having fired the gun, at a time when no person was on the premises but the prisoner, and that this was a part of the deliberate scheme which he afterwards so unhappily accomplished. Having examined the place myself, I assert this with perfect confidence. In the front of this room, appears the wharf and timber, and the great depth of the river below the wharf makes it impossible that this shot should have entered the window fired by any person on the surface of the stream. The shutter and window will both be produced for your inspection, and you will discover by the manner in which the ball entered, the muzzle from which it was emitted, must have been higher than the aperture, and with an inclined direction from the butt end of the weapon to the other extremity. If any stranger had fired from the wharf, there was no opportunity of escaping, but from the gate where two persons were standing; yet they will tell you, that they saw no one walking or running, although they heard the report on the spot where the prisoner discovered them. In addition to this, the depth of the wharf was greatly increased, as it was low water, and a thick impassable sludge prevented the possibility of approach to the premises from the river. The explosion occasioned an alarm in the neighbourhood, and a publican of the name of Frost, who will also appear before you, hastened to the spot. 'What,' exclaimed he, 'does all this mean?' and being told the cause, he attributed it immediately to the malicious intentions of some persons unknown. Now, it is material to see, what was the conduct of the prisoner when interrogated by his neighbours; and in determining on his motives, we can only reason according to the common feelings of mankind, for God alone, from whom no secrets are hid, and to whom the guilt or innocence of this prisoner is known, can penetrate into the recesses of the human heart. Mr. Frost offered to continue with the prisoner, who coldly replied, that the assassins would not come again that night. 'Why not guard against it?'—'No, they will not return.'—'Are you provided with arms, have you pistols?'—'Yes, I have pistols, but I have no ammunition.'—Shall I provide you with some?'—'No, I will return home, and go to bed.'

"Thus, Gentlemen, concluded the 19th of September. The next day, he writes a letter to Mr. Blight, and gives him some account of the affair. That letter will also be produced to you. He says, he hopes that the discharge of the gun at the premises was the mere effect of accident, but if intended, he wishes to know whether Mr. Blight or himself were the objects of malignity; and concluding, he observes, that he shall be glad to have a line, but he should be much better pleased to see Mr. Blight, as he was the only one with whom he could counsel. I admit, that the communication of this circumstance to Mr. Blight was proper, but I perhaps do not see the necessity of inducing him immediately to hasten to the scene of danger. We should have expected, in a letter of this kind, an intimation at least, that Goom had taken up the note, or, in the event of his not doing so, that he had given security for it. The letter is not short: it enters into a detail of circumstances, yet it is wholly silent upon the subject of Goom's money, which, I said before, was the great object of importance with Mr. Blight. The deceased, on receiving this letter, set out from Margate, and arrived at home on Monday, the 23d of September. Perhaps the first subject of conversation was the supposed attempt on his life; the next, the payment of the thousand pounds in question. The latter was the subject of their conversation, and the prisoner went to London, with an absolute prohibition to return, unless he should procure the money. He did not succeed, but he returned, and this eventful day passed onward to the evening, when they drank tea together, and afterwards took their grog until the fatal hour of eight o'clock approached. It is remarkable, that on this occasion, for the first time, they passed the evening in the back parlour, where by some one, whoever it may be, Mr. Blight received his death wound. You will recollect, that the person who fired before, concluded they were in the front room. At this time, the prisoner said he was attacked by a pain in his stomach, and explaining his situation, which is not very usual, to a female, he desired Esther Kitchener to give him a candle. He leaves the parlour door open, proceeds to the street door, that also remaining open, he throws wide the gate, turns in the direction of the counting-house, the door of which he unlocks, and through this apartment he passes to the privy. Presently the privy door is heard to slam, and instantly afterwards Esther Kitchener says, she observed the flash of a pistol. Before Esther Kitchener could quit the place where she was sitting, Mr. Blight had entered the kitchen, and supported himself on the dresser. She hears him exclaim, 'I am a dead man,' and then instantly rushes past her master, and, as if impelled by instinct, she claps too the street door. By the time she had returned to the wounded man, the prisoner is knocking loud for admission. Gentlemen, you have just heard the circumstance which occasions the only doubt on this extraordinary case; in other respects, complete in all its parts, and redundant in all its circumstances. The doubt to which I refer is, that this female witness heard the door of the privy slam, and then says, she immediately after saw the flash. I shall be able to explain to you the exact distance between the privy door and the parlour (Mr. Serjeant Best afterwards stated it to be twenty yards.) But, is there any thing, Gentlemen, which we measure so unsuccessfully as time, especially when the mind is under the influence of violent agitation? Do you not find that on the most common occasions, whether in the pursuit of business or pleasure, the measure of time of persons even engaged in the same objects is very different. I admit that this testimony, if taken in the strict letter, cannot be correct, but on a thousand occasions we cannot receive the depositions according to the strict letter, when opposed by a host of contradictory statements; yet in this part of the case, it is your peculiar province to exercise your discretion, and I have thus pointedly directed your attention to it for this express purpose.

"In the front of the house, there is a paved court, and beyond that, a yard, where a great quantity of dirt is collected by the scraping of ship timber, and you will hereafter see that this is an important observation. The prisoner having knocked as I noticed, he was admitted, when Esther Kitchener explained to him the attempt that had been made upon her master, and he saw the dreadful situation of his friend. He instantly gave way to the affectionate expressions which the occasion seemed to call for, desired assistance might be procured, and the woman went instantly to Mr. Frost, who will describe what passed in his presence. Gentlemen, my view of this case, I have said, excludes the possibility of the crime having been committed by any other person excepting the prisoner. What was the condition of the premises at this time? The gates of the yard were shut; the state of the tide was such, that no one could have escaped by the river; and to remove all doubt, there were within view, several persons assembled; one of them, by a singular felicity for the success of this prosecution, bearing a torch in his hand, who will most positively depose, that no one escaped from the premises. Are there not circumstances now supplied amply sufficient to support this case? The apprehension of Mr. Blight was so great, in consequence of the former accident, that having occasion to go out of the door for a single minute in an earlier part of the evening, even

natural

Fig. 98. *Front page of* The Times (*April* 7, 1806) *with the illustration of the Blight murder* of May 30, and with one or two issues during June. The additional column disappeared until September 17, but thereafter made a more regular appearance, bringing the paper to a normal size of 14⅝ in. × 18¼ in. The five-column page became permanent in 1811. In the following year, the column was widened and lengthened.

In the matter of headings, *The Times* was less enterprising—for the good reason that the price being what it was, Walter II took it for granted that the paper was read from beginning to end, as a matter of course. The displayed headings noticeable in the paper between 1800 and 1808 were satisfactory enough for those days and upon Walter II's hypothesis, by no means as short of the mark as it would seem to our eyes. But even these were considered, in 1820, as being too expensive of space. The smallest and simplest lines of capitals were the rule until 1840.

On January 29, 1808, new italic capitals for heading such departments of the paper as the 'Law Report', 'Correspondence', etc. were used. It is a pleasanter, larger letter, a welcome exchange for a very tiny italic predecessor. Originally, the italic capital heading was, as already noted, taken from John Bell's setting for *The World*. It survived over the small paragraphs of *The Morning Chronicle* until the end of its career in 1862, and it still has a place in the present day dress of *The Times*.

An expedient occasionally resorted to in earlier years became, in 1808, a regular feature of the paper—a short 'take' led off with a line of long primer and continued to its conclusion in nonpareil.

In 1813 the front-page title was recut in the slightly heavier large style which, with only the slightest variation, has survived to our own day.

The Times for November 29, 1814, the first newspaper in the world—in fact the first job—printed 'by a mechanical apparatus.' We are met, not to discuss printing methods but to describe the product, and must content ourselves with pointing out that the new invention made immediate acceleration by printing the entire edition and ultimately enabled *The Times* to use a much larger sheet. It was the greatest boon to the craft, since its original invention.

In 1816 the type of the size known as nonpareil (i.e. 6-point) was first used in newspapers, causing a dispute with the employers, who expected it

appeared on the coffin...we had not time to make the alteration.' There was a map half a page in measure in the issue of July 16, 1809; a singularly attractive cut of the illuminations in St James's Park in 1817. In 1817, after a half-page illustration to a letter from Robert Owen had appeared, the enthusiasm of *The Times* for illustration seems to have ceased—until 1914.

The Times.

EXTRAORDINARY.

NUMBER 7434. LONDON, MONDAY AFTERNOON, AUGUST 8, 1808. PRICE SIXPENCE

THE TIMES OFFICE, Four o'Clock, P M.

We cannot restrain ourselves from communicating to the Public, with the utmost celerity, the pleasure with which we have been ourselves transported, on receiving this moment the Official Dispatches of the two Generals Castanos and Tilli, notifying to the Supreme Junta of Seville the full surrender of Dupont, and all his forces, as well those that had not been brought into action, as those who had fought and been conquered—as well those in the plain, as those who occupied the summits and passes of the mountains, together with all their baggage, arms, ammunition, and the fruits their rapacity—their plunder. It is not the least gratifying article of this capitulation, they are to conveyed back to France by sea, a performance in which we hall probably bear some part.

• MOST SERENE SEIGNIOR.

" I have the satisfaction to communicate to your Highness the most complete victory which has followed the battle of Baylen. General Dupont, and the whole of his division, with arms, artillery, baggage, &c are prisoners of war Those troops which had not entered into the action, although they had sustained no disaster, are included in the capitulation, and obliged to return to France by sea, so THAT THERE DOES NOT REMAIN A SINGLE FRENCHMAN IN ANDALUSIA. The general details will be communicated by my Nephew, Colonel Don Pedro Augustin Giron, Adjutant-General of the Infantry; and whilst the circumstantial details of the whole are preparing, I think it proper to inform your Highness, that the bravery of the troops and Officers, their constancy, suffering and privations, correspond with the just opinion which your Highness entertains of them, and to the conception which I had formed of their patriotism and zeal for the public cause.

" I take the liberty of requesting of your Highness to perform for me the vow which I had made of dedicating this action to the glorious St. Ferdinand.

" God preserve your Highness many years.

" The Most Serene Signor XAVIER de CASTANOS."

" Head-Quarters, at Andujar, July 21."

" To the Most Serene, the President of the Supreme Junta of Government."

The following is a dispatch from his Excellency Signor Count Tilli :—

" Yesterday the 20th instant, Spain, or to speak more properly, the army of your Highness, gained the most complete victory which this nation has witnessed for many ages. The result is an exact copy of the action of Pavia. In a moment, the Andalusias were freed from the French armies. The Division of Dupont, with all its baggage, booty, and all its Generals, are prisoners of war; and besides these the divisions which occupied his Majesty's dominions, from the summit of the Sierra, as far as Boylen, are bound to evacuate the peninsula by sea. This is in brief the sum of the Treaty, which I and his Excellency Signor Castanos had last night the happiness of signing; and as we retired from the field of battle at twelve o'clock at night, without sleep, and exhausted, it is not possible to send to your Highness a detail of the capitulation, and of the military atchievements that have been performed, which shall be done as soon as time will permit.

The bearer of this agreeable intelligence, is the Lieutenant-Colonel of the Column of Provincial Grenadiers, Don Pedro Augustin Giron, Brevet-Colonel, and Adjutant-General, an Officer of the greatest merit, who, by the talents and valour which he has displayed in many actions, and particularly since he has been with this army, has shewn himself worthy of every favour which your Highness can bestow upon him.

" I have this day given orders for taking the oath of allegiance to our Sovereign Don Ferdinand VII. which proceeding had not previously taken place in this city; and also that *Te Deum* shall be sung, and that there shall be an illumination for three nights successively.

" May God preserve your Highness many years.

Head-Quarters, at Andujar, July 21, 1808

" The Most Serene Senor Count TILLI."

To the Most Serene Senor the President, and Members of the Supreme Junta of Spain and the Indies.

Printed and published at the Office in Printing-house-square, near Apothecaries' Hall, Blackfriars, by C. Bell, Brunswick-street.

Fig. 99. *An afternoon 'Extraordinary' issue of* The Times *of* 1808 to be composed at the same rate as the minion or 7-point. Finally an extra penny per 1000 was conceded. The presswork, whether hand or machine, deteriorated with the increase in circulation; both before and after Waterloo, the paper presents a disagreeably unkempt appearance. On February 6, 1816, however, a new fount of type, which unlike previous installations came in unheralded, gave the paper a relatively decent appearance. Had it been possible to give some of the columns the benefit of at least a little leading, the dress of this issue could rank as one of the most satisfactory in the paper's career. The type, excellent in detail, makes up very economically; and, what is by no means the case in successive dressings of the paper, exhibits a pleasant relation between the small pica, long primer, bourgeois, minion and nonpareil sizes. The design is lighter, of greater evenness in line than any of its modern predecessors, resembling the tone of the old-face used for *The Universal Register*.

In 1816 the column depth became $21\frac{1}{8}$ in. The front page was vitiated, towards the end of the same year, by the introduction of two-line initials of a peculiarly clumsy and forbidding cut into the 'classified' advertising. By 1816 also the front page included 'personal' advertisements. Notwithstanding the fact that many advertisements were of minimum extent—i.e. of two lines—sheer force of that habit which we have noticed in *The World* and *The Oracle* gave each a two-line initial, an idle custom which obtains in every London newspaper to this day.

Initials to the news disappeared in the early years of the century. It is common in the period 1817 to 1820 to find the whole of one column on the front page devoted to small advertisements introduced with a coarsely cut letter T covering two lines. In order that columns should start with a strong black head and end with a weak grey tail, the shortest advertisements topped the column. There was considerable variation in the weight of these initials between the years 1817 and 1820; but often as handsome light initials were restored they were superseded by heavy, coarse characters which, it must be presumed, gave greater satisfaction to the advertisers.

On June 7, 1817, an extra *two* sheets were published, i.e. the paper consisted in all of three sheets. The price of each sheet was 7*d.* and each was headed with a displayed title in blackletter text, '**Supplement to The Times**',[1] these being the first supplements to be so distinguished. In the same year other enterprises, major and minor, were begun. A supplement covering a State

[1] Earlier supplements (e.g. in 1806–14) had been given a small column-wide heading.

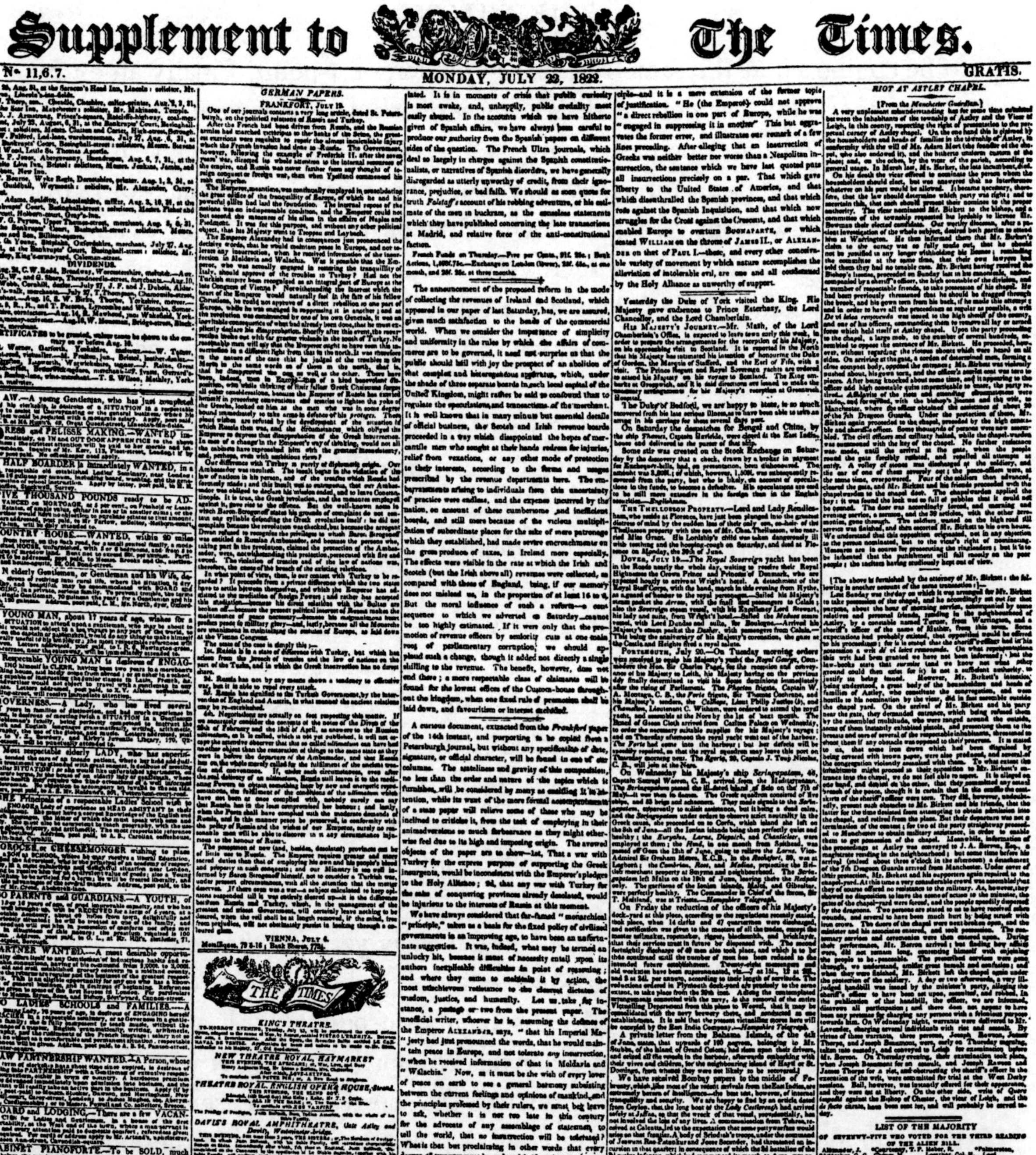

Supplement to The Times.

No. 11,6.7. MONDAY, JULY 29, 1822. GRATIS.

GERMAN PAPERS.

FRANKFORT, July 19.

LONDON, MONDAY, JULY 29, 1822.

RIOT AT ASTLEY CHAPEL.

LIST OF THE MAJORITY

LIST OF THE MINORITY

LIST OF THE MINORITY

Fig. 100. Supplement to The Times, 1822

trial was issued on October 25; a very intricate piece of tabular composition illustrated a manifesto by Robert Owen appearing on September 10; the deaths of Princess Charlotte and her infant were signalised by the printing of black borders round the whole four pages of the issue for November 7, and *The Times* so appeared for thirteen consecutive days between the 7th and the 20th—the day of the burial at Windsor.

Such expressions of mourning were carefully calculated. King George III was given the benefit of black rules as well as black borders; commencing with the paper for January 21, 1820, the paper so appeared for eighteen consecutive days. When on August 7, however, the death of the Duchess of York was announced, black borders surrounded all four pages of the issue, but they were not repeated until the 15th on the occasion of the funeral.

As, at the opening of the 'twenties, the pressure on the space of the paper became still more acute, the height of the italic capitals was again reduced. The make-up seems hurried. The issue for April 4, 1821, for instance, took the liberty of beginning the leader with one line at the bottom of the fifth column on page 3, turning over to page 4 to finish.

What we call a 'leader' had still not yet arrived at full stature, there being, in its position under the Clock device, nothing more than a fairly short and opinionated narration of an important event not chronicled elsewhere in the paper.

In 1822, increasing demand for space led *The Times* to take the left and right outside columns to the top of the type-area and range them with the head of the device. The transverse rules were cut to the measure of four columns and the heading thus confined in the barest minimum of space. This expedient permitted the paper to squeeze every drop of revenue out of its front page advertising, but it gave the paper a very disagreeable appearance. The practice was not introduced by *The Times*, but, it seems, by William Clement, the proprietor of *The Observer* and *Bell's Life in London*, who regularly printed such 'ears' round the heading of his paper. There was, however, no sort of typographical assimilation by *The Times* of the black egyptian headings made fashionable in the Sunday press by *The Dispatch*, *Bell's Life*, *The Sunday Monitor*, etc. The cleavage between the daily and the Sunday press was complete, in matter as in manner.

A new evening journal initiated for the purpose of blocking Catholic Emancipation made its appearance in 1827. No. 1 of *The Standard* was published on May 21, and was a sad-looking sheet. Some healthy black egyptian capitals were used in the first number but were dropped in favour of orthodox body capitals as the paper became established and the need was felt to give subscribers, in tiny type, all the no-popery ammunition which the paper could carry[1].

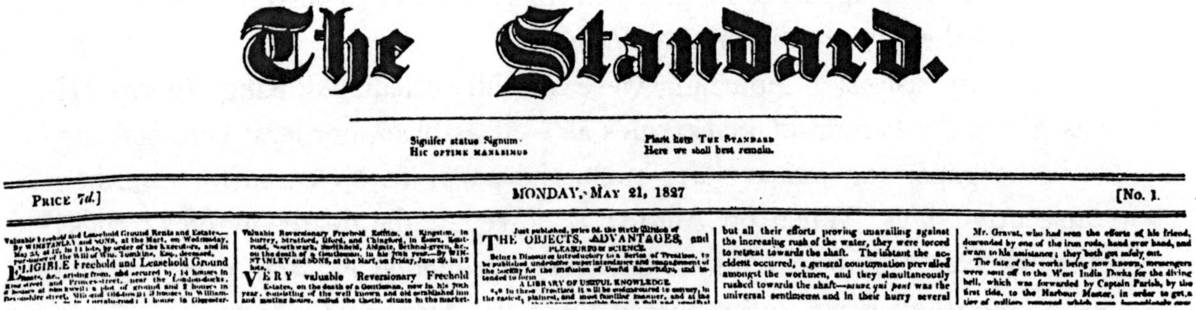
The Standard.

Signifer statue Signum · Hic optime manebimus

Plant here The Standard Here we shall best remain.

Price 7d.] MONDAY, MAY 21, 1827 [No. 1.

Fig. 101

The determination of the proprietor to have *The Times* supremely inclusive, made desirable, when the increasing advertising revenue made possible, the regular provision of supplements. During the period 1826 to 1829 such supplements were a constant feature, the legend 'Price with the Supplement 7*d.*' being the standard notification printed with the date at the head of the first page. On January 1, 1829, a four-page paper printed, as an entire final page, a reader-advertisement, set entirely in nonpareil, of Edmund Lodge's *Portraits and Memoirs of the most illustrious Personages of British History*. This work, which is, of course, well known to collectors, deserved the 'puff' printed at the foot of a news column: 'A whole page of *The Times* today is filled with an advertisement containing a detailed description of one of those magnificent enterprises of individual labour and talent which so proudly distinguishes this country'. This, the first whole page advertisement in *The Times*, was repeated on the following May 1.

A running headline appears for the first time over a rule covering the six columns and reading 'THE TIMES, MONDAY, FEBRUARY 9, 1829'. This was an eight-page paper. No running head was given to four-page papers. There is a large and increasing amount of nonpareil in the news of paragraphs of this period, but the New Press[2] gave excellent presswork. Eight-page papers, as a result of the expeditious mechanical presswork, predominated in the 'thirties. With the increased space thus afforded, the features of the paper began to occupy a more or less regular position: thus in 1832 the

[1] Later *The* (evening) *Standard* became a morning; which, in our own generation, was converted into the present *Evening Standard*.

[2] Invented for *The Times* by Applegath and Cowper in 1827.

Clock generally appears on the left-hand opening, as a rule page 4 of an eight-page paper. Small paragraphs as 'fill-ups' began to appear in 1828, and by 1833 assumed some importance as a regular element in the paper.

The 'Money Market' became a fully developed department during the 'thirties. The establishment of an eight-page paper as a normal issue was a possibility when, in 1833, the duty on advertisements was reduced from 3*s.* 6*d.* each to 1*s.* 6*d.* each. With the consequent expansion, racing appears regularly and is given good positions.

In 1836, the newspaper stamp which had been fourpence (less discount of 20 per cent.) since 1815 was reduced to one penny. The tax on paper was also brought down. The proprietors, rather than the public, gained, for the price to readers was revised from 7*d.* to 5*d.* only.

The Times now vastly exceeded in bulk and enterprise all its contemporaries. Even the new paper, announced (in 1843) as 'the novelty of nations and the wonder of the world', and entitled *The News of the World*, boasted that it was the size of *The Times*.[1] *The Times* type—set solid—varied in design only slightly from that used since 1799. A new fount was laid in and used for the issue of February 20, 1838, when the paper was also given a newly engraved text for its heading, the previous device being retained.[2]

On January 1, 1840, the minion size of type which continued to prevail throughout the paper was opened with consistent leading—a device to which the reader must have given a hearty welcome. A slight and very elementary form of news-display makes its appearance in connection with the first communications received by telegraph. When the news of a Royal accouchement in 1844 was thus communicated from Windsor, *The Times* mentioned the 'electro-magnetic telegraph' above the printed despatch and the paragraph was dignified with main and sub-headings in bold capitals.

[1] For *The News of the World* of 'size equal to the immense double sheet of *The Times*', see p. 252.

[2] A piece of 'daily' enterprise on the part of *The Sun* (founded in 1798) might be noted. By way of commemorating the coronation of Queen Victoria, the paper commissioned a large portrait, 12 in. × 11 in., of Her Majesty, engraved by Edward Wyon. The block is superbly cut, and was printed in black, while the letterpress of the outside forme was worked in gold ink by the special exertion of 'M. De La Rue'. This issue was published June 28, 1838. *The Sun* printed more than a score of re-impressions of the edition. There was a poem by the editor Murdo Young, entitled 'All hail, Queen Victoria'. He was an active journalist and, on occasion, availed himself of heavier founts for headings than most of his contemporaries. *The Sun* for January 24, 1844, carried three portraits and an architectural piece occupying in all more than half a page. For a daily, this was then no mean feat.

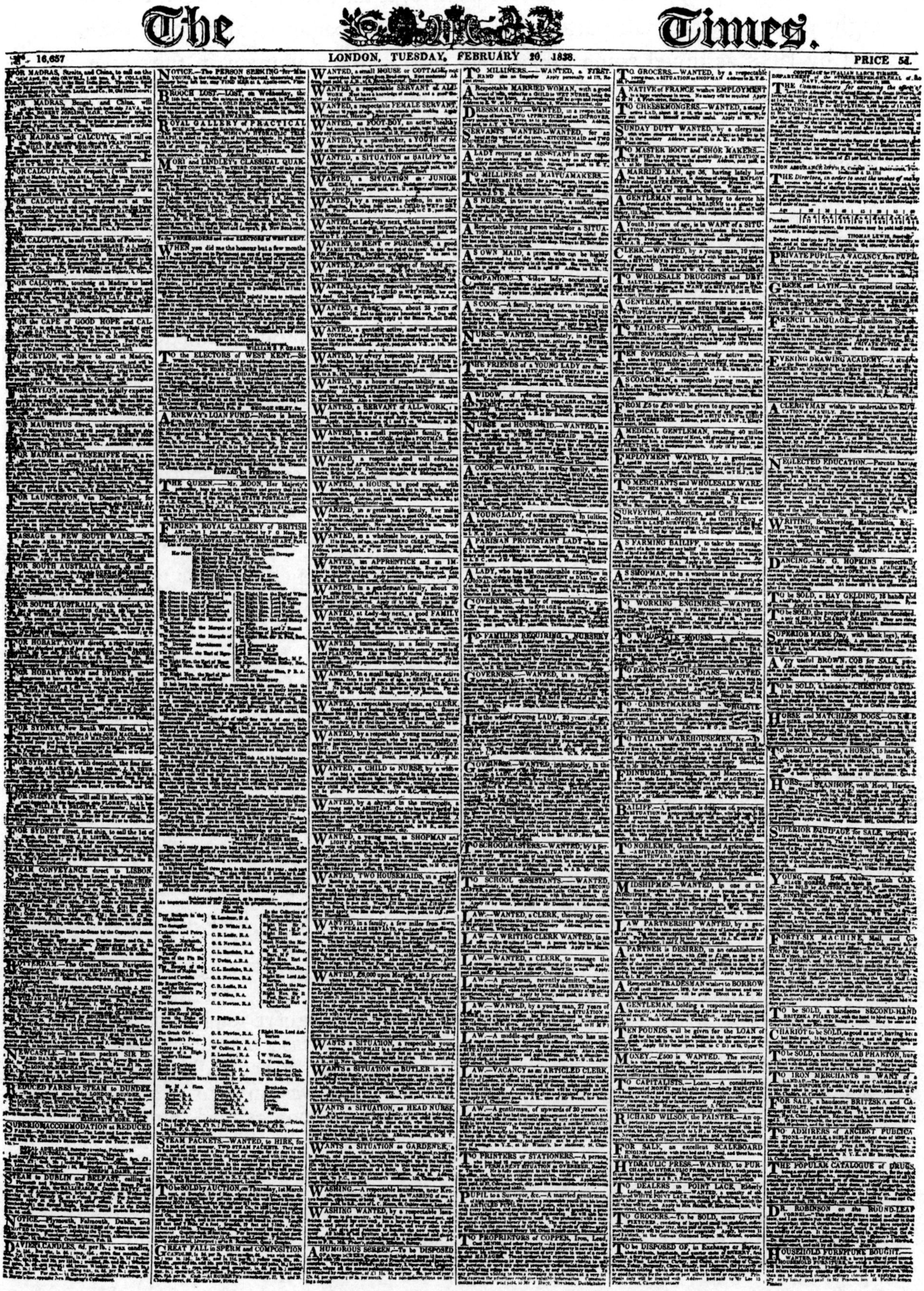

The Times.

No. 16,657 LONDON, TUESDAY, FEBRUARY 20, 1838. PRICE 5d.

Fig. 102. *The "classic" front-page of* The Times. *The Births, Marriages and Deaths were transferred from the back of the paper to the first column of the front page in* 1854

Telegraphed news from India and China is printed later in the same year. With these modern transmission methods, bolder headings (in 14-point titling, as we should say nowadays) were given to certain important home and foreign articles, though the customary old-style small italic heads over subsidiary matter were retained (see Fig. 103).

From 1849 onwards the regular heading 'THE LATEST FROM PARIS' in 14-point bold face was given a sub-heading in small capitals 'by electro-telegraph'. The other newspapers carried similar announcements.

In 1850 the agitation against the remaining tax of one penny per newspaper showed signs of succeeding in removing the last vestige of this barrier to progress first imposed by Queen Anne. The high-priced papers were content to bear the penny, or, rather, they knew their readers were able to bear it. A cheap press was not the best thing for the country, thought *The Times*. In other directions, too, the attitude of mind changed little. The sub-head 'by electro-telegraph' in connection with the royal accouchement was not merely the result of editorial excitement at the use of the new mechanism: its inclusion meant that the old habit of cramming small text type into every available pica of white space was at last beginning to break up. After 1844, double headings occur with greater frequency—though they were always exceptional. But the emancipation from the convention, more than a generation old, was difficult to attain, and in the case of *The Times* came slowly.

In the score of years from 1830 to 1850 the type remains small in every department of the paper except in the leading article and perhaps one other. Four-page supplements to an eight-page paper occur with increasing frequency between 1840 and 1850; by the end of the decade appearing every other day with the exception of three issues (April 18, 22, and May 2, 1850). *The Times* established a new record for bulk on February 10, 1851, when an eight-page paper was provided with an eight-page supplement. This expansion was several times resorted to during the year of the Great Exhibition.

By 1852 the text type of certain more important articles was enlarged; as these were headed with capitals of their own body, the number of large headings throughout the paper became proportionately greater. In no case, however, were these headings very large except on the occasion of a sensational event, when a 14-point bold face was requisitioned. Railway intelligence, railway finance, and railway shares were given prominence between 1849 and 1852, but, in accordance with *The Times* policy of restraining the

SDAY, AUGUST 6, 1844.

THE

ACCOUCHEMENT

OF

HER MAJESTY.

BIRTH OF A PRINCE.

THE TIMES-OFFICE, Tuesday Morning,
Half-past 8 *o'Clock.*

We have the happiness to announce that the Queen has been safely delivered of a PRINCE.

We are happy to state that Her Majesty is doing well.

We are indebted to the extraordinary power of the Electro-Magnetic Telegraph for the rapid communication of this important announcement.

COURT CIRCULAR.

WINDSOR, MONDAY.

The Queen and Prince Albert walked this morning in the pleasure grounds of the Castle. Her Majesty and his Royal Highness also took an airing in a pony phaeton.

Their Royal Highnesses the Prince of Wales and the Princess Royal were taken a drive in an open carriage in the forenoon. Her Royal Highness the Princess Alice was taken an airing in the gardens and slopes of the Castle.

Sir Henry Wheatley arrived at the Castle this afternoon on a visit to the Queen.

His Royal Highness Prince Albert, attended by Major-General Wemyss, rode out on horseback to-day.

The unfavourable state of the weather during the whole of the afternoon prevented Her Majesty and Prince Albert taking their accustomed airing.

Her Royal Highness the Duchess of Kent dined with the Queen and Prince Albert at the Castle this evening.

The Duchess of Cambridge and the Hereditary Grand Duchess of Mecklenburgh Strelitz paid a visit yesterday to

SECOND EDITION.

THE

ACCOUCHEMENT

OF

HER MAJESTY.

EXPRESS FROM WINDSOR.

THE TIMES-OFFICE, Tuesday Morning,
Half-past 10 *o'Clock a.m.*

In addition to the intelligence of the auspicious event which we published at half-past 8 o'clock, we have just received the following

OFFICIAL DESPATCH.

" WINDSOR CASTLE, AUGUST 6, 1844.
" *Half-past* 8 *o'Clock a.m.*

"The Queen was safely delivered of a PRINCE this morning at 50 minutes past 7 o'clock.

" Her Majesty and Infant are perfectly well.

"JAMES CLARK, M.D.
"CHARLES LOCOCK, M.D.
"ROBERT FERGUSON, M.D."

Intimation of Her Majesty's illness was forwarded from Windsor Castle to town at 6 o'clock this morning. The Lord Chancellor, the Duke of Buccleuch, Lord Privy Seal, Sir James Graham, Secretary of State for the Home Department, the Earl Delawarr, Lord Chamberlain, and the Earl of Jersey, Master of the Horse, were the first to arrive, having left town by a special train, which arrived at the Slough terminus of the Great Western Railway at 25 minutes past 8 o'clock. The Ministers and Officers of State immediately

Fig. 103. *Displayed headings in* The Times, 1844

crazy speculations of a romantic investing mania, these never received more than an italic headline.

Curiously enough, the new half-century permitted fewer displayed headings than are to be found in the paper of 1800–5. Foreign news of unaccustomed

INDIA.

BY EXPRESS FROM MARSEILLES.

THE TIMES-OFFICE, Friday Morning, Half-past 4 o'clock.

We have received by express from Marseilles our despatches in anticipation of the overland mail, which left Bombay on the 4th ult. and Calcutta on the 22d of January.

The chief event of the fortnight which has elapsed since our last intelligence has been the Governor-General's visit to Bombay. Having journeyed from Simla through the Punjab and Scinde, he arrived there on the night of the 26th of January, and left on the 2d of February, having during his stay won golden opinions of all sorts of people.

The Chief of Baroda, his Highness the Guicowar —the first Prince in Western India—was at Bom-

1850

LATEST INTELLIGENCE.

THE WAR IN ITALY.

[A portion of the following appeared in our second edition of yesterday:—]

The following telegram was received at Mr. Reuter's office May 24:—

"PARIS, TUESDAY, MAY 24.

"The *Moniteur* of this morning publishes the following telegram:—

"'ALESSANDRIA, MAY 23, EVENING.

"'Yesterday the Emperor attended mass in the Cathedral.

"'His Majesty everywhere receives testimonies of the public sympathy.

"'His Majesty enjoys perfect health.'"

THE BATTLE OF MONTEBELLO.

The *Moniteur* of yesterday publishes General Forey's official report of the battle of Montebello,

1859

LATEST INTELLIGENCE.

THE WAR.

THE

CAPITULATION OF PARIS.

(BY TELEGRAPH.)

(FROM OUR SPECIAL CORRESPONDENT.)

VERSAILLES, JAN. 24, 2 P.M.

M. Jules Favre is now here with proposals for Capitulation.

He proposes that the garrison shall leave Paris with honours of war.

This is quite inadmissible.

The attack on St. Denis and the great defeat of the 19th have mainly led to the resolution to ask for terms.

Trochu is ill.

Vinoy commands.

M. Favre has seen Count Bismarck.

1871

IMPERIAL AND FOREIGN INTELLIGENCE.

ASSASSINATION OF THE KING OF PORTUGAL AND THE CROWN PRINCE.

BRAVERY OF THE QUEEN.

(FROM A CORRESPONDENT.)

LISBON, FEB. 2.

When driving through Black Horse Square from the landing-stage on their return from Villa Viçosa, at 5 o'clock yesterday evening, the King and the Crown Prince were killed by assassins

1907

Fig. 103*a*. *Development of headings in* The Times, 1850–1907

importance is headed in 14-point capitals in accordance with a division into countries—e.g. America, Austria, France—but there is no 'picking out' with small bold-face headings. The Court news, cut away from the head or tail of the section below the Clock device, has achieved a separate existence,

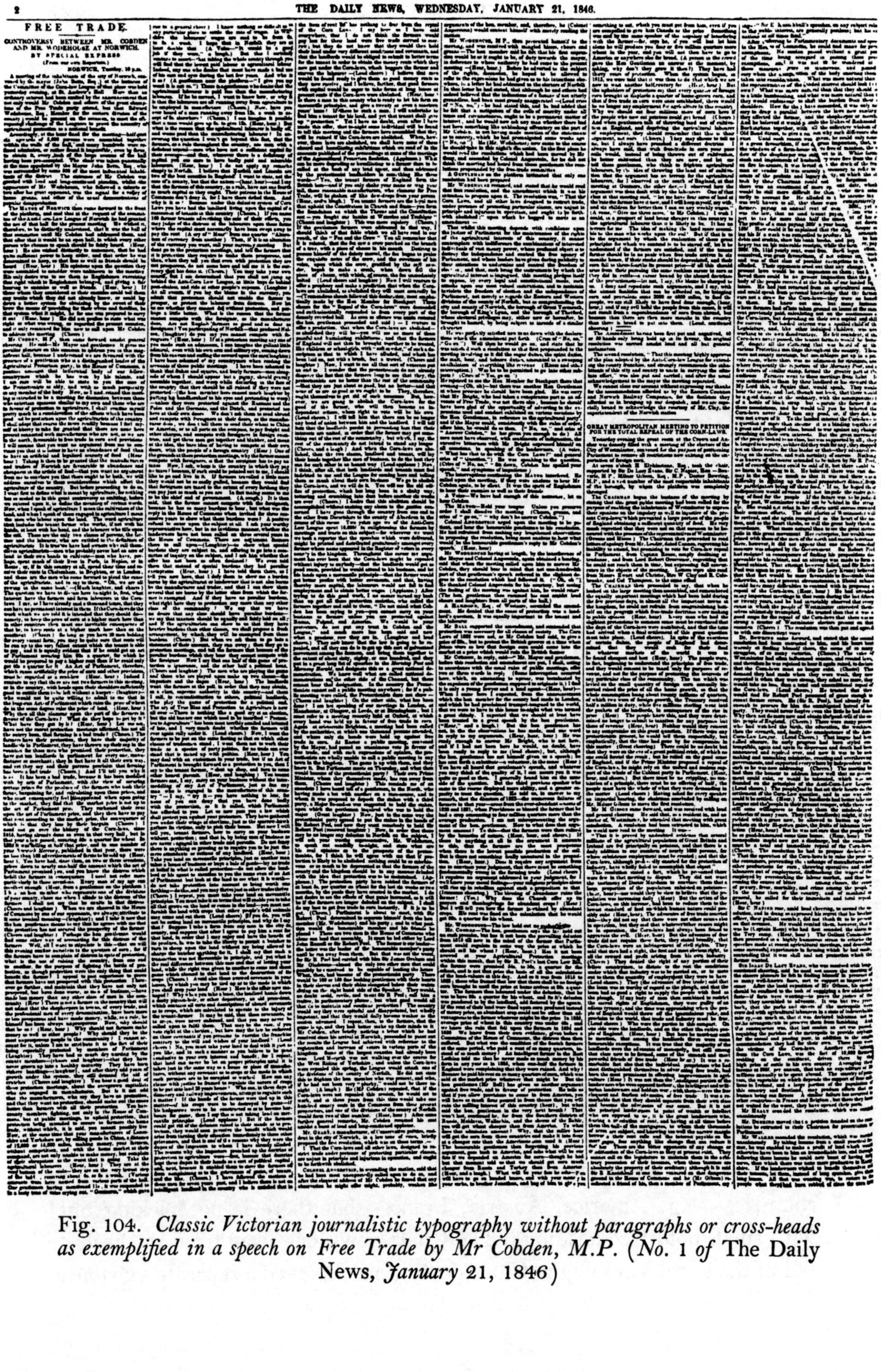

2 THE DAILY NEWS, WEDNESDAY, JANUARY 21, 1846.

FREE TRADE.

CONTROVERSY BETWEEN MR. COBDEN AND MR. WODEHOUSE AT NORWICH.

BY SPECIAL EXPRESS

(From our own Reporter.)

NORWICH, Tuesday, 10 p.m.

Fig. 104. *Classic Victorian journalistic typography without paragraphs or cross-heads as exemplified in a speech on Free Trade by Mr Cobden, M.P.* (*No.* 1 *of* The Daily News, *January* 21, 1846) regularly appearing at the end of the final leader under its own head 'Court Circular'. The remaining articles are headed with the small italic titling capitals; in fact the very size which has descended from 1788.

The lists of Births, Marriages, and Deaths were still printed at the very end of the news, just as they had been in *The Universal Register* and in still earlier papers. On occasion, when there was a supplementary sheet to *The Times*, these announcements ran over to the first page of such supplement. On April 20, 1854, the whole of the Births, Marriages, and Deaths were for the first time removed to their permanent and present position in the upper portion of the first column of the front page. The same year witnessed the inauguration of a submarine and European telegraph service, and messages thus originating were so indicated in small capitals. During this period the leader or leaders—now invariable—were restricted to the

The Daily News.

No. 1 LONDON, WEDNESDAY, JANUARY 21, 1846 PRICE 5d.

Fig. 105. *Heading of No.* 1 *of* The Daily News. *For a page of text see opposite,* Fig. 104

discussion of political and foreign topics. The Court items, as has already been pointed out, had been re-grouped under the heading 'Court Circular'; the late foreign news, formerly given precedence over the first leader, was removed to a column headed 'Latest Intelligence'—a title often set in bold face. Playbills, notices to correspondents, prices of public funds, and a summary of the Parliamentary speeches and business in the House of Lords and the House of Commons absorbed the space between the Clock and the first leader. The Parliamentary summary occasionally absorbed an entire column, and, by way of exception, even more; thus on August 9, 1854, the leader on the Crimean operations is separated from the Clock device by two or three columns. These were great days for *The Times*, now possessing, with its 50,000 circulation, a sale six or seven times that of any rival old or new.

The Morning Post had dropped behind during the years 1820–30. It was inferior in bulk to *The Herald*, and *The Chronicle* as well as *The Times*. *The Morning Herald* was a considerable paper in the 40's and 50's and even at its demise in 1869. It early followed the example of *The Times* in issuing supplements, equally headed in text **Supplement to the Morning Herald.**

The text of the *Herald*—closely set except in the leading articles—exactly followed the example of the all-powerful *Times*.

The Daily News of 1846 was the newest, *The Morning Chronicle* the most vigorous, of its competitors. The orthodox Victorian method of reporting and setting was continued in the *Daily News* as is testified by Fig. 104. Two columns of the speech by Cobden received "By Special Express" are printed without paragraphs and there are, of course, no cross-heads.

In 1855 *The Daily Telegraph* came out, failed at 2*d*., and was transferred to another proprietor. He had the courage to make it London's first penny daily, and to make a new idea look a new idea. The modern period of newspaper history seems at length to have arrived. But the halfpenny paper was not yet thought of, and modern journalism, as we know it, dates from the halfpenny *Daily Mail* which, in most typographical essentials, began as a substantial shadow of *The Times*. The order of these changes must be described in a final lecture.

CHAPTER XIII

THE NINETEENTH CENTURY

SUNDAY NEWSPAPERS TO 1861

British Gazette, and Sunday Monitor	1779
The London Recorder	1783
Sunday London Gazette	1783
The Review, and Sunday Advertiser	1789
The Observer	1791
Bell's Weekly Messenger	1796
Bell's Weekly Dispatch	1801
The News	1805
The Albion	1807
Bell's Life in London	1828
Bell's New Weekly Messenger	1831
Bell's Penny Dispatch	1841
The News of the World	1843
Lloyd's Penny Sunday Times	1843
Reynolds's Weekly Newspaper	1850
The London Halfpenny Newspaper	1861

CHAPTER XIII

THE NINETEENTH CENTURY

SUNDAY NEWSPAPERS to 1861

THE nineteenth century developed its dailies at the expense of its thrice-a-week newspapers. One by one, the older 'alternates'—such as *Lloyd's Evening Post*, *The London Evening Post* (d. 1806), and *The General Evening Post* (1813)—published in the evening died, and the newer papers of the same sort, for instance J. B. Bell's *The Inquisitor* (1809), failed more or less promptly.

By 1815 the only eighteenth-century tri-weeklies still in progress were *The London Chronicle* (f. 1757) and *The St James's Chronicle* (f. 1761). Of the old weeklies of the Mawson-Mist type, Read's was the longest lived, publishing until 1761. *The Westminster Journal* of 1742, which had had anything but an uninterrupted career, finally gave up in 1870. The weekly publication for the leisured classes interested in literature, the theatre and in politics, developed out of *Cobbett's Weekly Political Register*, an agreeable sixteen-page quarto issued on Saturdays from January 1, 1802, well printed[1] in double-column (and numbered in columns instead of being folioed in pages) with a good running headline. Cobbett occasionally gave his readers the benefit of a good whole-page map.[2] His paper was a first-class piece of up-to-date craftsmanship in printing.

Cobbett was followed by half-a-dozen National and Weekly Registers of brief career and little importance. As we are taking for our subject only the more strictly journalistic type of publication, we must pass by these political weeklies as well as the later *Examiner*, edited by Leigh Hunt, which was both interesting and important.

It is essential, however, that we notice the type of popular weekly newspaper which, originated in the eighteenth, was brought in the nineteenth century to a very high point of technical development, i.e. the publication known in the vernacular as 'The Sunday Paper'.

The seven-day newspaper has never been an English tradition. Whereas

[1] By Cox and Baylis, 75 Great Queen Street. Cox was a descendant of Edward Cox who printed the false *Morning Post* in 1776. The firm still brought out the *Courrier Politique et Littéraire Or, French Evening-Post*, a twice-a-week evening paper in French, founded 1777.

[2] See April 24, 1802.

E. Johnson's British Gazette, and Sunday Monitor.

Printed by E. JOHNSON, in Ludgate Place, (the Entrance between No. 4 and 5, Ludgate Hill) where LETTERS and ADVERTISEMENTS are taken in.

Price Three-Pence Halfpenny.] S U N D A Y, January 2, 1791. [No. DLXXXIII.

For the SUNDAY MONITOR.

THE work of creation is the display of supreme wisdom. It carries no character more conspicuous than this. If, from the structure and mechanism of some of the most complicated works of human art, we are led to high admiration of the wisdom of the contriver, what astonishment may fill our minds, when we think of the structure of the universe! It is not only the stupendous building itself, which excites admiration; but the exquisite skill, with which the endless variety of its parts are adapted to their respective purposes. Insomuch that the study of nature, which, for ages, has employed the lives of so many learned men, and which is still so far from being exhausted, is no other than the study of divine wisdom displayed in the creation. The farther our researches are carried, more striking proofs of it every where meet us. The provision made for the constant regularity of the universe, in the disposition of the heavenly bodies, so that in the course of several thousand years, nature should ever exhibit the same useful and grateful variety, in the returns of light and darkness, of summer and winter; and ever furnish food and habitation to all the animals that people the earth; must be a lasting theme of wonder to every reflecting mind.

But they are not only the heavens that declare the glory of God, and the firmament that sheweth forth his handy-work. In the most inconsiderable, as well as in the most illustrious works of the Creator, consummate art and design appear. There is not a creature that moves, nor a vegetable that grows, but, when minutely examined, furnishes materials of the highest admiration. The same wisdom that placed the sun in the centre of the system, and arranged the several planets around him in their order, has no less shown itself, in the provision made for the food and dwelling of every bird that roams the air, and every beast that wanders in the desert; equally great, in the smallest, and in the most magnificent objects; in the star, and in the insect; in the elephant, and in the fly; in the beam that shines from heaven, and in the grass that cloaths the ground. Nothing is over-looked. Nothing is carelessly performed. Every thing that exists, is adapted with perfect symmetry to the end for which it was designed. All this infinite variety of particulars must have been present to the mind of the Creator; all beheld with one glance of his eye; all fixed and arranged, from the beginning, in his great design, when he formed the heavens and the earth.

This wisdom displayed by the Almighty in the creation, was not intended merely to gratify curiosity, and to raise wonder. It ought to beget profound submission, and pious trust, in every heart. It is not uncommon for many who speak with rapture of creating wisdom, to be guilty, at the same time, of arraigning the conduct of Providence. In the structure of the universe, they confess that all is goodly and beautiful. But in the government of human affairs they can see nothing but disorder and confusion — Have they forgotten, that both the one, and the other, proceed from the same Author? Have they forgotten, that he who balanced all the heavenly bodies, and adjusted the proportions and limits of nature, is the same who hath allotted them their condition in the world, who distributes the measures of their prosperity and adversity, and fixes the bounds of their habitation? If their lot appear to them ill-sorted, and their condition hard and unequal, let them only put the question to their own minds, Whether it be most probable, that the great and wise Creator hath erred in his distribution of human things, or that they have erred in the judgment which they form concerning the lot assigned to them? Can they believe, that the divine Artist, after he had contrived and finished this earth, the habitation of men, with such admirable wisdom, would then throw it out of his hands as a neglected work; would suffer the affairs of its inhabitants to proceed by chance; and would behold them without concern, running into misrule and disorder? Where were then that consistency of conduct, which we discover in all the works of nature, and which we cannot but ascribe to a perfect Being!— My reader! when thy plans are disappointed, and thy heart is ready to despair; when virtue is oppressed, and the wicked prosper around thee; in those moments of disturbance, look up to him who created the heaven and the earth; and confide, that he who made light to spring from primæval darkness, will make order at last to arise from the seeming confusion of the world.

Had any one beheld the earth in its state of chaos; when the elements lay mixed and confused; when the earth was without form and void, and darkness was on the face of the deep; would he have believed, that it was presently to become so fair and well-ordered a globe as we now behold; illumined with the splendor of the sun, and decorated with all the beauty of nature? The same powerful hand, which perfected the work of creation, shall, in due time, disembroil the plans of Providence. Of creation, we can judge more clearly, because it stood forth at once; it was perfect from the beginning. But the course of Providence is progressive. Time is required for the progression to advance; and before it is finished, we can form no judgment, or at least a very imperfect one, concerning it. We must wait until the great æra arrive, when the secrets of the universe shall be unfolded; when the divine designs shall be consummated; when Providence shall be brought to the same completion which creation has already attained. Then, we have every reason to believe, that the wise Creator shall appear in the end, to have been the wise and just ruler of the world. Until that period come, let us be contented and patient; let us submit and adore.

Fig. 106

the French and the American capitals, to name only the most familiar foreign examples, are accustomed to a *Petit Parisien* or a *New York Times* every day, including Sunday, no such custom has ever taken root in London. On occasions, e.g. during 1805 and in 1915, *The Times* published a Sunday issue. In 1899 the *Sunday Daily Mail* and a *Sunday Daily Telegraph* (I quote the exact titles) evoked much protest—and not only from the Rev. Dr Clifford and the Rev. Dr Parker—and were abandoned. The Sunday paper was a badge of secularism from its institution and, in many quarters, is so still. In the result, the papers of the period from 1820–40 were radical in politics. *The Weekly Dispatch* was long a champion of freethought—even saying, on more than one occasion, that it was no worse to be an infidel than a clergyman. The Sunday paper was bound to be a thing apart when newsagents refused to 'handle' it. Some still refuse; hence the streets of central London are almost fuller of newsmen on Sundays that upon weekdays, for it has become an established custom of the Sunday newspaper bosses to rely for their distribution upon men rather than upon shops, even though Sunday opening of shops is in progress of becoming the rule rather than the exception.

The first London Sunday newspaper was the venture of Mrs E. Johnson of Ludgate Hill. The paper is a very rare one, and although it is known that it must have been founded about the year 1779, the earliest extant issue is No. 121, July 14, 1782.[1] *E. Johnson's British Gazette, and Sunday Monitor* was in general effect a daily paper published on Sundays, having all the usual sections: Home and Foreign Affairs, an epitome of the week's news from the daily papers, acknowledged or unacknowledged and, very important, a Postscript (on back page) for latest news. It used triple rules, french rules, in fact, exactly the typography and format of *The Morning Chronicle* or of *The Morning Post*. The heading of the paper followed the latter precisely. The one distinctive textual feature—headed 'For the Sunday Monitor', and introduced with a decent 12-line factotum of a preacher—was a column devoted to religious instruction. This instruction was printed in the first column of the front page in the place usually reserved, by the week-day papers, for the theatres. The format was kept very stable while the paper was doing well—and it did well for a long time.

On this point, the proprietress's address for the New Year 1791 (cf. issue for January 2) is worth quoting. She prints it over the Postscript at page 4:

It is with the most grateful acknowledgment that the Printer returns her

[1] In the Huntington Library (cf. Gabler's *Check List of English Newspapers before* 1801 *in the Huntington Library*, 1931).

Thanks to the Public for the very great and generous support she has experienced in this the *Original Sunday Newspaper*. The same line of conduct which has obtained, she hopes will preserve, the reputation which has been gained; and every endeavour on her part, with proper assistants shall be exerted to merit the continuance of the extensive encouragement with which this Paper has been honoured. She also takes this opportunity to inform the Public, that Four Thousand Papers are published every Sunday morning in the Cities of London, Westminster etc which circumstance must give a most pleasing sensation to all Advertising Customers.

A certain 'S. Johnson' succeeded to the direction of the paper in 1798, but there was no change in the style, the matter, the typography, or the address

THE SUNDAY MONITOR.

SUNDAY, APRIL 28, 1816. Price Seven-pence

Fig. 107

of the office. Even in 1812, when Draper Brewman, member of a family well known in the newspaper trade, acquired the property, it was still printed in the old face type with long ſ. In a year or two the paper changed hands to a successor of Brewman's. At the beginning of 1814, *The Sunday Monitor*, as the title became in the hands of a new proprietor, John Stokes, was admittedly in need of reconstruction. Stokes was constrained to write in one of his early issues that

...The Sunday Monitor after existing in high repute for near half a century had certainly through bad management and neglect declined considerably in public estimation. But since it came under the control of its present Proprietor and Editor it has attained a far greater altitude than it had ever before experienced, and although we do not proclaim, like the people of *The Times*, that we print it with a steam engine, yet we flatter ourselves that it will soon arrive at that point which will render our utmost effort necessary to supply the demand for it by the ordinary means.

The format of the paper was completely changed by Stokes, the new types for the body being of the latest fashion, heavy but readable. The front-page heading and other column-heads were set in large sizes of the then novel fat-face capitals. *The Sunday Monitor*'s was one of the earliest uses I have seen of these faces.[1] The religious article which came first, on Mrs Johnson's front page, from the very beginning held its position—until November 23, 1817, when it was removed to the inner forme for practical reasons. The paper so continued until 1829.

By this time *The Sunday Monitor* was far from being the only Sunday journal, but it had incorporated in 1795 the second foundation, *The London Recorder* of 1783, which had itself incorporated *The Sunday Reformer* of 1793. The typographic style of *The London Recorder* was similar to that of its predecessor, but more ambitious and, as it had a right to be, in view of Mrs Johnson's paper, competitive. A notice to the public—placed, at the usual

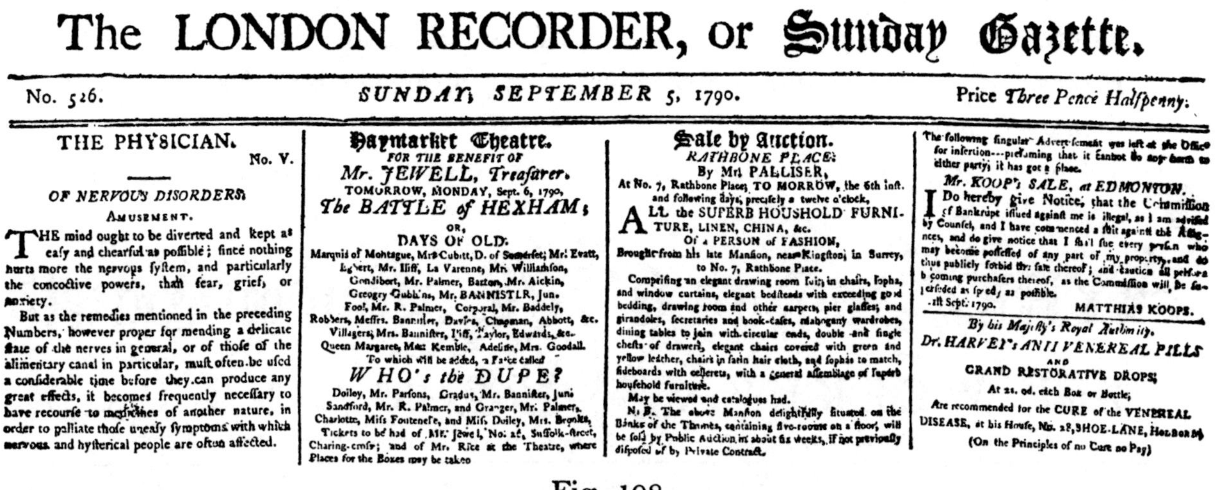

The LONDON RECORDER, or Sunday Gazette.

No. 526. *SUNDAY, SEPTEMBER* 5, 1790. Price *Three Pence Halfpenny.*

THE PHYSICIAN. No. V.

OF NERVOUS DISORDERS.

AMUSEMENT.

THE mind ought to be diverted and kept as easy and chearful as possible; since nothing hurts more the nervous system, and particularly the concoctive powers, than fear, grief, or anxiety.

But as the remedies mentioned in the preceding Numbers, however proper for mending a delicate state of the nerves in general, or of those of the alimentary canal in particular, must often be used a considerable time before they can produce any great effects, it becomes frequently necessary to have recourse to medicines of another nature, in order to palliate those uneasy symptoms with which nervous and hysterical people are often affected.

Haymarket Theatre.

FOR THE BENEFIT OF

Mr. JEWELL, Treasurer.

TOMORROW, MONDAY, Sept. 6, 1790,

The BATTLE of HEXHAM;

OR,

DAYS OF OLD.

Marquis of Montague, Mr. Cubitt, D. of Somerset, Mr. Evatt, Egbert, Mr. Iliff, La Varenne, Mr. Williamson, Gondibert, Mr. Palmer, Barton, Mr. Aickin, Gregory Gubbins, Mr. BANNISTER, Jun. Fool, Mr. R. Palmer, Corporal, Mr. Baddely, Robbers, Messrs. Bannister, Davies, Chapman, Abbott, &c. Villagers, Mrs. Bannister, Iliff, Taylor, Edwards, &c. Queen Margaret, Mrs. Kemble, Adeline, Mrs. Goodall.

To which will be added, a Farce called

WHO's the DUPE?

Doiley, Mr. Parsons, Gradus, Mr. Bannister, Jun. Sandford, Mr. R. Palmer, and Granger, Mr. Palmer, Charlotte, Miss Fontenelle, and Miss Doiley, Mrs. Brooks, Tickets to be had of Mr. Jewel, No. 26, Suffolk-street, Charing-cross; and of Mr. Rice at the Theatre, where Places for the Boxes may be taken

Sale by Auction.

RATHBONE PLACE.

By Mr. PALLISER,

At No. 7, Rathbone Place, TO MORROW, the 6th inst. and following days, precisely at twelve o'clock,

ALL the SUPERB HOUSHOLD FURNITURE, LINEN, CHINA, &c.

Of a PERSON of FASHION,

Brought from his late Mansion, near Kingston, in Surrey, to No. 7, Rathbone Place.

Comprising an elegant drawing room suit in chairs, sopha, and window curtains, elegant bedsteads with exceeding good bedding, drawing room and other carpets, pier glasses, and girandoles, secretaries and book-cases, mahogany wardrobes, dining tables to join with circular ends, double and single chests of drawers, elegant chairs covered with green and yellow leather, chairs in satin hair cloth, and sophas to match, sideboards with cellerets, with a general assemblage of superb household furniture.

May be viewed and catalogues had.

N. B. The above Mansion delightfully situated on the Banks of the Thames, containing five-rooms on a floor, will be sold by Public Auction in about six weeks, if not previously disposed of by Private Contract.

The following singular Advertisement was left at the Office for insertion---presuming that it cannot do any harm to either party, it has got a place.

Mr. KOOP's SALE, at EDMONTON.

I Do hereby give Notice, that the Commission of Bankrupt issued against me is illegal, as I am advised by Counsel, and I have commenced a suit against the Assignees, and do give notice that I shall sue every person who may become possessed of any part of my property, and do thus publicly forbid the sale thereof; and caution all persons becoming purchasers thereof, as the Commission will be superseded as speedy as possible.

1st Sept. 1790. MATTHIAS KOOPS.

By his Majesty's Royal Authority.

Dr. HARVEY's ANTI VENEREAL PILLS

AND

GRAND RESTORATIVE DROPS;

At 2s. 9d. each Box or Bottle;

Are recommended for the CURE of the VENEREAL DISEASE, at his House, No. 28, SHOE-LANE, HOLBORN.

(On the Principles of no Cure no Pay)

Fig. 108

position for such pronouncements, over the Postscript on the back page—gave its programme. It was dated 'Sunday Morning' and printed in the first issue (January 27, 1783):[2]

The Paper today offered to the Public, under the title of the *London Recorder and Sunday Gazette*, shall always be found to contain a better selection of the seven days events, foreign and domestic, than has ever yet been compiled by any publication of the kind in England. It will consist of something more than the insertion of those tedious reprinted paragraphs and essays for the antecedent week from the *General Advertiser* to the *Ledger*, from the *Ledger* to the *Morning Herald*, from the *Herald* to the *Chronicle*, from the *Chronicle* to the *Post*, from the *Post* to the *Gazetteer*, from the

[1] The front page of *The Sunday Monitor* (under Stokes) was much favoured as an advertising space by McBish, the Lottery agent, whose settings are very intelligent displays in various sizes of the then latest fat-faced types.

[2] The imprint of the paper ran: 'London Printed by *William Adlard*, No. 10 Salisbury Square, Fleet street, for the Proprietor, S. Pope and published at No. 48 the Corner of Ludgate Hill, Fleet Market, where Essays and Articles of Intelligence are received'.

Gazetteer to the *Public Advertiser*, from the *Public Advertiser* to the *Daily*, from all these Morning prints to the Evening Papers, and from both into the Sunday publications.

The London Recorder claimed to be an enterprising paper, and there were one or two creditable headlines to certain 'scoops' secured by a later proprietor. Being a Sunday paper, it took tactful notice of the 'Supreme Being', but pressure of space frequently resulted in preference being given to secular news. Excuse was made at the top of the first column of the front page; e.g. of the paper for January 15, 1786: 'The important occurrences of the week has prevented the *Moralist's* Lucubrations appearing in his favourite corner this Day'. Notwithstanding—or perhaps because of—this indifference to the religious character of its publishing day, *The London Recorder* did not last out the century, being absorbed by Mrs Johnson's *Sunday Monitor* in 1795.

One R. Ayre was the next to adventure into Sunday journalism. His

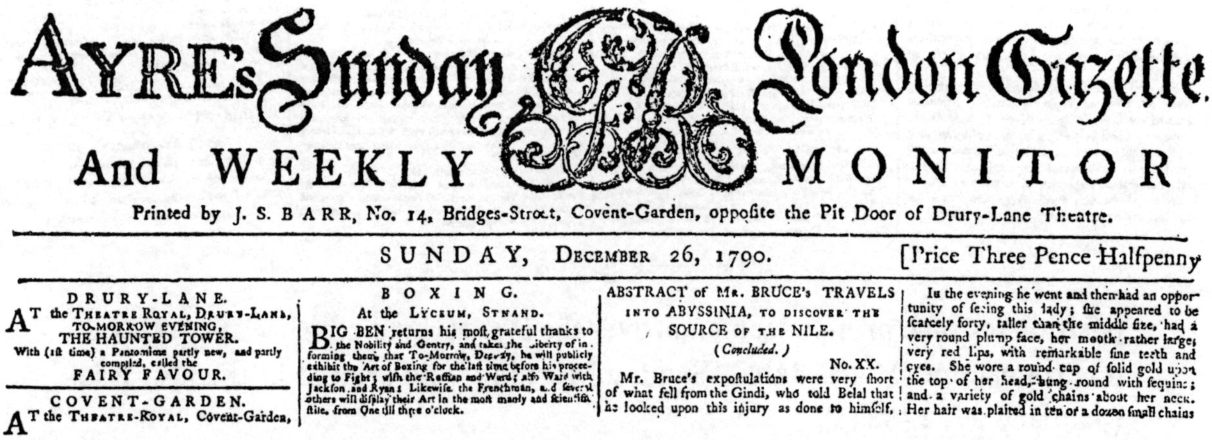

AYRE's Sunday London Gazette

And WEEKLY MONITOR

Printed by J. S. BARR, No. 14, Bridges-Street, Covent-Garden, opposite the Pit Door of Drury-Lane Theatre.

SUNDAY, DECEMBER 26, 1790. [Price Three Pence Halfpenny

DRURY-LANE.

AT the THEATRE ROYAL, DRURY-LANE, TO-MORROW EVENING, THE HAUNTED TOWER. With (1st time) a Pantomime partly new, and partly compiled, called the FAIRY FAVOUR.

COVENT-GARDEN.

AT the THEATRE-ROYAL, Covent-Garden,

BOXING.

At the LYCEUM, STRAND.

BIG BEN returns his most grateful thanks to the Nobility and Gentry, and takes the liberty of informing them, that To-Morrow, Deeday, he will publicly exhibit the Art of Boxing for the last time before his proceeding to Fight; with the Ruffian and Ward; also Ward with Jackson and Ryan; Likewise the Frenchman, and several others will display their Art in the most manly and scientific stile, from One till three o'clock.

ABSTRACT of MR. BRUCE's TRAVELS INTO ABYSSINIA, TO DISCOVER THE SOURCE OF THE NILE.

(Concluded.)

No. XX.

Mr. Bruce's expostulations were very short of what fell from the Gindi, who told Belal that he looked upon this injury as done to himself,

In the evening he went and then had an opportunity of seeing this lady; she appeared to be scarcely forty, taller than the middle size, had a very round plump face, her mouth rather large, very red lips, with remarkable fine teeth and eyes. She wore a round cap of solid gold upon the top of her head, hung round with sequins; and a variety of gold chains about her neck. Her hair was plaited in ten or a dozen small chains

Fig. 109

paper, *AYRE's Sunday London Gazette And Weekly Monitor*, made no concessions to piety but printed theatrical news and did not scruple to mitigate its news with entertainment. Parliamentary intelligence also formed a strong feature. The heading carried a large cipher device GR, set in double pica close up, which parted the main line of the title. The titular lettering was a good piece of gothic. A serial number was never used and the paper cannot be traced before May 4, 1783.

John Almon of *The Gazetteer*, on returning from a well-timed flight to France, to his business of bookselling, founded in the spring of the year 1788—the date is uncertain as the paper published no serial number—a journal entitled *The Sunday Chronicle* which, in the style of Mrs Johnson's paper, printed an ethical instruction (but of no more than half the column) on the front page. Theatrical news was also given, and the weekly occurrences sectionalised according to the days of the week, in the manner of *The*

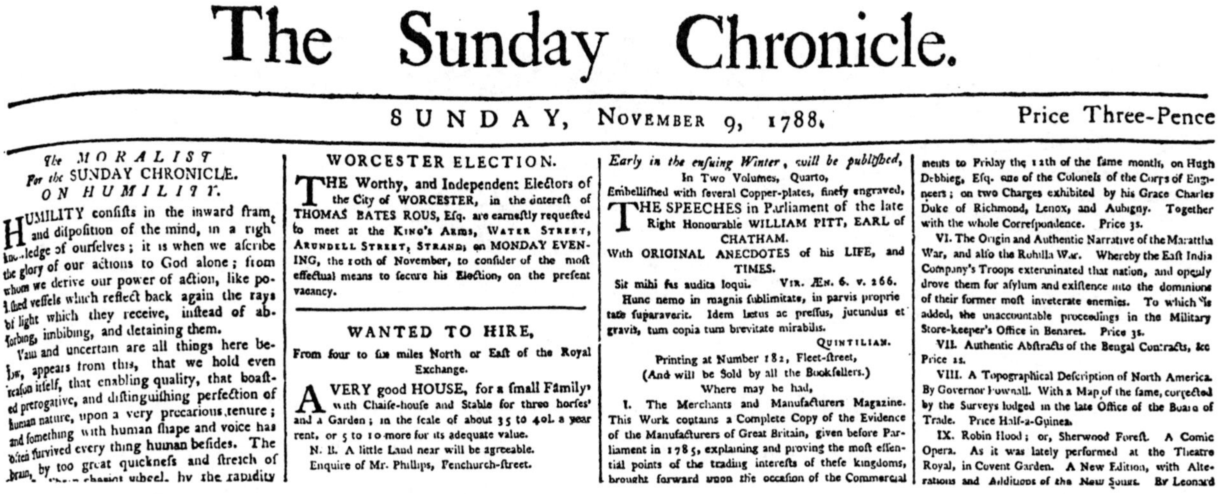

The Sunday Chronicle.

SUNDAY, NOVEMBER 9, 1788. Price Three-Pence

The MORALIST
For the SUNDAY CHRONICLE.
ON HUMILITY.

HUMILITY conſiſts in the inward frame and diſpoſition of the mind, in a right knowledge of ourſelves; it is when we aſcribe the glory of our actions to God alone; from whom we derive our power of action, like poliſhed veſſels which reflect back again the rays of light which they receive, inſtead of abſorbing, imbibing, and detaining them.

Vain and uncertain are all things here below, appears from this, that we hold even reaſon itſelf, that enabling quality, that boaſted prerogative, and diſtinguiſhing perfection of human nature, upon a very precarious tenure; and ſomething with human ſhape and voice has often ſurvived every thing human beſides. The brain, by too great quickneſs and ſtretch of ... chariot wheel, by the rapidity

WORCESTER ELECTION.

THE Worthy, and Independent Electors of the City of WORCESTER, in the intereſt of THOMAS BATES ROUS, Eſq. are earneſtly requeſted to meet at the KING'S ARMS, WATER STREET, ARUNDELL STREET, STRAND, on MONDAY EVENING, the 10th of November, to conſider of the moſt effectual means to ſecure his Election, on the preſent vacancy.

WANTED TO HIRE,

From four to ſix miles North or Eaſt of the Royal Exchange.

A VERY good HOUSE, for a ſmall Family, with Chaiſe-houſe and Stable for three horſes' and a Garden; in the ſcale of about 35 to 40l. a year rent, or 5 to 10 more for its adequate value.

N. B. A little Land near will be agreeable.

Enquire of Mr. Phillips, Fenchurch-ſtreet.

Early in the enſuing Winter, will be publiſhed,
In Two Volumes, Quarto,
Embelliſhed with ſeveral Copper-plates, finely engraved,

THE SPEECHES in Parliament of the late Right Honourable WILLIAM PITT, EARL of CHATHAM.

With ORIGINAL ANECDOTES of his LIFE, and TIMES.

Sit mihi fas audita loqui. VIR. ÆN. 6. v. 266.

Hunc nemo in magnis ſublimitate, in parvis proprie tate ſuparaverit. Idem lætus ac preſſus, jucundus et gravis, tum copia tum brevitate mirabilis.

QUINTILIAN.

Printing at Number 182, Fleet-ſtreet,
(And will be Sold by all the Bookſellers.)
Where may be had,

I. The Merchants and Manufacturers Magazine. This Work contains a Complete Copy of the Evidence of the Manufacturers of Great Britain, given before Parliament in 1785, explaining and proving the moſt eſſential points of the trading intereſts of theſe kingdoms, brought forward upon the occaſion of the Commercial

... ments to Friday the 12th of the ſame month, on Hugh Debbieg, Eſq. one of the Colonels of the Corps of Engineers; on two Charges exhibited by his Grace Charles Duke of Richmond, Lenox, and Aubigny. Together with the whole Correſpondence. Price 3s.

VI. The Origin and Authentic Narrative of the Marattha War, and alſo the Rohilla War. Whereby the Eaſt India Company's Troops exterminated that nation, and openly drove them for aſylum and exiſtence into the dominions of their former moſt inveterate enemies. To which is added, the unaccountable proceedings in the Military Store-keeper's Office in Benares. Price 3s.

VII. Authentic Abſtracts of the Bengal Contracts, &c Price 1s.

VIII. A Topographical Deſcription of North America. By Governor Pownall. With a Map of the ſame, corrected by the Surveys lodged in the late Office of the Board of Trade. Price Half-a-Guinea.

IX. Robin Hood; or, Sherwood Foreſt. A Comic Opera. As it was lately performed at the Theatre Royal, in Covent Garden. A New Edition, with Alterations and Additions of the New Songs. By Leonard

Fig. 110

London Recorder. There was also a Postscript. The paper seems to have had a short life. The last copy I have seen is dated 1790. This was the fourth Sunday foundation.

A fifth foundation of the century, *The Review, and Sunday Advertiser*, was established on June 21, 1789. It was a handsome production in characteristic Bell style, printed by C. Macrae. It was without pretence to piety, but rather

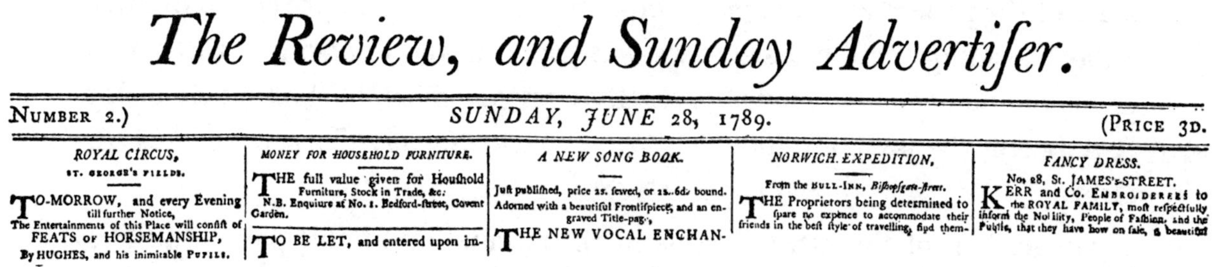

The Review, and Sunday Advertiſer.

NUMBER 2.) *SUNDAY, JUNE* 28, 1789. (PRICE 3D.

ROYAL CIRCUS,
ST. GEORGE'S FIELDS.

TO-MORROW, and every Evening till further Notice,
The Entertainments of this Place will conſiſt of
FEATS OF HORSEMANSHIP,
By HUGHES, and his inimitable PUPILS.

MONEY FOR HOUSEHOLD FURNITURE.

THE full value given for Houſhold Furniture, Stock in Trade, &c.
N.B. Enquiure at No. 1. Bedford-ſtreet, Covent Garden.

TO BE LET, and entered upon im-

A NEW SONG BOOK.

Juſt publiſhed, price 2s. ſewed, or 2s. 6d. bound. Adorned with a beautiful Frontiſpiece, and an engraved Title-page,

THE NEW VOCAL ENCHAN-

NORWICH EXPEDITION,

From the BULL-INN, *Biſhopſgate-ſtreet.*

THE Proprietors being determined to ſpare no expence to accommodate their friends in the beſt ſtyle of travelling, find them-

FANCY DRESS.

No. 28, St. JAMES'S-STREET.

KERR and Co. EMBROIDERERS to the ROYAL FAMILY, moſt reſpectfully inform the Nobility, People of Faſhion, and the Public, that they have now on ſale, a beautiful

Fig. 111

calculated to please the worldling. There is much theatrical and literary gossip, although the parliamentary proceedings are well summarised. Early numbers of the paper had a title in Fry's italic upper- and lower-case (48-point). I have not been able to see the first issue, but, following custom, it probably contains an interesting prospectus. There is one point which calls for mention: *The Review, and Sunday Advertiser*[1] dated June 28, 1789, is five columns. My own copy of the next available date, October 10, 1790, is in

[1] In the collection of the St Bride Foundation.

four columns with a new heading of Bell's gothic, with flourishes. In 1794 the titular lettering was again changed—to large roman capitals. A star device was also added and a notice at the head of the front page to indicate that

The Review, Sunday Advertiser.

NUMBER 69.) SUNDAY, OCTOBER 10, 1790. (PRICE 3D. Halfpenny.

BY PARTICULAR DESIRE,
YOUNG ASTLEY
Will appear (To-morrow evening, Monday the 11th inst. only) on Horseback, and also in the favourite Pantomime of the DEATH of GENERAL WOLFE.

ROYAL GROVE,

FORTUNATE NUMBERS SELECTED,

And Shares of Tickets, Two and half per Cent. cheaper than at any other Office,

AT the Licensed State Lottery - Office. of

LONDON AND MIDDLESEX UNIVERSAL
TONTINE SOCIETY,
For the BENEFIT of SURVIVORS, at the Expiration of SEVEN YEARS.

GOVERNMENT SECURITY.

ROSS,
LADIES' HAIR-DRESSER,
At his original Ornamental Hair and Perfume Warehouse,
(Late VICKERY'S)
No. 119, Bishopsgate-street, Three Doors from the London Tavern,

Fig. 112

the printer was Daniel Bond. The paper was again made up in five columns of 14½ ems. *The Review* survived the end of the century, but in 1804 became *The Sunday Review* in the hands of John Martin of 32 Holywell Street.

Thus, before 1795, there were five Sunday papers, i.e. *The British Gazette*, *The London Recorder*, *The Sunday London Gazette*, *The Sunday Chronicle*, and *The Review*[1], printed in the regular format of the dailies and, as a group, purporting to be little more than extra dailies. The Sunday feature of a religious exercise was confined to *The Gazette* and *The Recorder*, although there was a short and faintly ethical piece in Almon's *Sunday Chronicle*. Mrs Johnson's *Monitor* and *The Recorder* gave a summary of the week's news. The scale of the papers gave the proprietors no opportunity to provide more than a day's reading matter. Late news was given in the Postscript. Until 1790 or so the Sunday papers were actually printed and published on Saturday. A notice in the issue for June 20, 1790, of *The Sunday Chronicle* makes this clear:

> On account of the *rapid increase* in the circulation of this *paper*, the *Proprietors* are under the necessity of altering the Time of Publication, from Saturday Evening until Four o'clock on Sunday Morning, at which hour the Publication will in future regularly begin.

In a decade or two, sabbatarian protests succeeded in getting the time of publication altered to Saturday.

The Observer, first published on December 4, 1791, is our oldest Sunday paper. In its early years it conformed to the precedents set by Mrs Johnson or by John Almon. There was no particular enterprise about it, typo-

[1] Dr Trusler's list in his *London Adviser* mentions also a *Sunday Herald*. This I have not been able to trace.

graphically or otherwise. The individual name, however, was new, or at any rate was a new form of the old title 'Observator', to be found in 1654, 1681 and, at latest, in 1724. The name was a good one and it has not been varied during the paper's ample life. Originally, set between the two words of the name, there was the device of a human eye engraved upon an oval ground. *The Observer* became a strong paper after 1815 when it was controlled by William Clement, who for an unexplained reason preferred to adorn his other property, *Bell's Life*, with this same device of an eye. In its early days *The Observer* was a feeble-looking sheet. The Sunday papers, as a whole, had not realised their function, as they were bound to do later. The rising costs and the increased subscription prices placed the dailies and even thrice-weeklies out of the reach of many, interested in affairs, who either could not afford *The Times* at 4*d*. in 1792, 4½*d*. in 1796, or lived out of reach of inns or coffee-houses where these were to be seen. A weekly which would give more than a day's reading would be a boon even if the price exceeded that of the dailies by a penny. In 1796 such a paper came out: *Bell's Weekly Messenger*, 'London: Printed for the Proprietors by J. Bell. British Library, No. 90, opposite Southampton-street, Strand'. It appeared on a sheet which, folded twice, gave four pages 10½ in. × 15 in. All the existing papers were printed on a smaller sheet folded once to produce two pages 12½ in. × 19½ in. Bell's page was in three 18-em columns of a type which, at first Fry's old face, was soon exchanged for a smaller size of 'modern' which allowed Bell to claim that 'by printing in this mode, we are enabled to afford more interesting information than is contained in any other *two* newspapers'. There is a running headline such as *The Cabinet* had introduced in 1792. The title is in roman capitals with a central device of a mounted postman blowing his horn. No advertisements appeared in the early numbers and none ever appeared on the front page until after 1836. Hence, Bell's front page, with its ancient device of a mounted postman and absence of theatrical or other advertisements, recalled the papers of the first part of the eighteenth century. The rest of the Sunday papers, in full folio, all carried advertisements on their front pages—except such as yielded a portion of the first column to a religious instruction. Bell, therefore, had invented a new type of Sunday journalism. In setting, it was a strictly utilitarian and not in any sense an aesthetic piece of typography. If the typography was ever altered, it was always for the purpose of making the *Weekly Messenger* supremely inclusive.

Towards the end of 1801 a new type was announced as 'making', and, in January 1802, there appeared a notice that

BELL'S WEEKLY MESSENGER.

No. 1.] SUNDAY, MAY 1, 1796. [PRICE 6D.

SUNDAY, 1

FIFTH SUNDAY AFTER EASTER.
Rogation Sunday.
St. Philip and St. James.

CHURCH SERVICE.
Morning, 1st Lesson, Ecclesias. chap. vii.
2d Lesson, John i. ver. 43.
Evening, 1st Lesson, Ecclesias. chap. ix.
2d Lesson. Rom. chap. i.
Psalms for this Day of the Month.

HIGH WATER at LONDON BRIDGE.
Morning, 38 min. after 8—Evening, 10 min. after 9.
Half Year's Interest due on the Imperial Loan 3 per Cent. guaranteed by England.
Collar Day at St. James's, without Offering.

MOND. 2

Easter Fourth Return.
Sun rises 34 minutes after 4.
Empress of Russia born, 1729.
High Water—Mor. 44 m. aft. 9—Night, 6 m. aft. 10.

TU. 3

Invention of the Cross.
High Water—Mor. 47 m. af. 10—Night, 19 m. af. 11.

WED 4

Day 15 hours 10 minutes long.
Twilight ends 7 minutes after 10.
High Water—Mor. 51 m. af. 11—Night, 47 m. af. 12.

THURSDAY, 5

Collar-Day at St. James's, and Offerings.
Ascension-Day.
Holy Thursday.
Holliday at the Public Offices.
This being Ascension-Day, no Sittings at Westminster.
High Water—Mor. 21 m. af. 12—Night, 4 m. af. 12.

FRI. 6

St. John the Evangelist.
On the Morrow of Ascension 5th Return.
High Water—Mor. 24 m. af. 1—Afternoon, 4 m. af. 1.

SAT 7

New Moon 45 minutes after 8 in the Morning.
Sun sets 35 minutes after 7.
High Water—Mor. 8 m. af. 2—Afternoon, 3 m. af. 2.

FAIRS THROUGHOUT ENGLAND AND WALES
FOR THE ENSUING WEEK.

MONDAY, 1

FIXED FAIRS.

HaileyRidge	Cleobury-Mortimer	Hurstperpoint	N. Petherton	Shoreham
[illegible]	Fowey	Leighton (Hun.)	Oldham	Stansted
Brickhill	Green-st.	Lancaster	Orton	Stockport
Burnham	W. Haddon	Lichfield	Philips-Norton	Stonehouse
[illegible]	Hammersmith	Lashfield	Penryn	Stogursey
[illegible]-Cary	Harwich	Leominster	[illegible]	Tatterly
Carleon	[illegible]	Towcester	Read. g	Totness
Staling	Ross	Melbroke	Redruth	[illegible]
[illegible]	Hope		Burford	Wighton
[illegible] Hampton				Withyam
Coventry				

MOVEABLE FAIRS.

Cockermouth	Guisburn	Overton (Flints.)	Pelham St. Mary	Roach
[illegible]borough	Ingleswhite			

TUESDAY, 2

FIXED FAIRS.

Aldeburgh	Broadclist	Castle Hemingham	Colnbrook	Poulton
Acton U n-derwood	Broadward	Chard	Highhickington	Tidswell
	Bury (Lanc.)			Tregony

MOVEABLE FAIRS.

Farmergreen	Hambledon	Mattishall	Radnor	Somerton

WEDNESDAY, 3

FIXED FAIRS.

Ampthill	Cheadle	Guildford	Modbury	Tenby
Emey	Chesterfield	Harling	North Herts.	Thrapstone
Boston	Chichester	Henfield	Northampton	Ticehurst
Preston	Earith	Hodnett	N. Duffield	Torrington
Hitchcock	Edgware	Ipswich	Nutley	Wilton
Brenton	Elmstead	Kellington	Overton	Woburn
Badington	Frampton	Likney	Stobus	Wooler
[illegible]combe	Frodsham	Maiden-Newton	Shapp	Wotton Bas.
Chagford	Gosport		Tamworth	Wrotham

MOVEABLE FAIRS.

Abergeley	King's Brumpton	Ryegate	Sherborne	Workington
Dorking				

THURSDAY, 4

FIXED FAIRS.

Caston	Llanrhiader	Marlow	Pentraeth-Mon	Thaxted
Chorley				

MOVEABLE FAIRS.

Alresford	Bures	Grantham	Melton-Mowbray	Stortford-Bishop's
Attleboro'	Burton	Hallaton	Mendlesham	Stone (Kent)
Banbury	Caerphilly	Hanslope	Middlewich	Summercourt
Bawtry	Capper-Cunnon	Hawkshead	Montgomery	Throckfords
Beaconsfield	Cerne-Abby	Henley (O on.)	St. Neot's	Trew
Beaumaris	Chapel-le-Firth	Higham-Ferrers	Newbury	Ulverstone
Beeston	Cheadle	Hundon	Newport (Monmou.)	Weldon
Beverley	Cheltenham	Kidderminster	N. Walsham	Wellington (Somerset)
Bildestone	Dane-hill	Kilkhampton	St. Osyth	Wem
Bingham	Devizes	Kirby Lonsdale	Pepanston	Weobly
Bishop Auckland	Ditcher	Llanelly	Pickock	Wetherby
Bowstead	Eccleshall	Llangadock	Petworth	Wigan
Blyth	Ely	Litton	Rippon	Winslow
Botesdale	Eglwyswrw	Luton	Ross	Woodnesboro
Broughton	Farnham	Liverard	Saxmundham	Wrexham
Bovey Tracey	Fenden	Loughboro'	Scarboro'	Yarum
Bridport	Faversham	Lutterworth	Seglang	Yaxley
Brighton	Garstang		Stockbridge	

FRIDAY, 5

FIXED FAIRS.

Aldermaston	Coleshill, W.	Knaresbro'	Oakham	Tavistock
Booth	Dunmow	Knighton	Penford	Tregarneha
Brigstock	Dursley	Lewes	Pensley	Uttoxeter
Buckingham	Eatonbridge	Liss	Pocklington	Wem
Calne	Garligan	Llanner-chymedd	Peterborough	West-Looe
Castle-town	Halsford	Macclesfield	Stanbridge	Wigmore
Chawley	Hunmanby	Marlow	Brigstock	Wymondham
Chipping-Norton	Ivinghoe	Nangiyn	Stratton	
Corton	Kendall		[illegible]	

MOVEABLE FAIRS.

Bishop Auckland	Bishop's-Castle	Crowcomb	Derby	Southampton	Stevenage

SATURDAY, 6

FIXED FAIR
Traybont

MOVEABLE FAIR.
Howef [illegible] [illegible]

BELL'S WEEKLY MESSENGER.

NUMBER I.

GOOD MAY ARISE OUT OF EVIL, and happy shall I be if the MESSENGER shall hereafter entitle me to acknowledge the verity of this maxim.

The WORLD is no stranger to my name—nor to my pretensions: my *new Case*, however, is singular, and it shall be briefly stated.

It is but twelve months since I first had the Misfortune to see *George Cawthorne*; a Partnership was entered into between us in the Concern of THE BRITISH THEATRE *only*, on certain conditions, as may be seen by a reference to the Articles, and for a few months I had reason to consider him as friendly to my General Interests—but, alas! a short time proved, that, like a KITE, he was only hovering round me, until an opportunity should offer when he might pounce upon, and destroy me as his unsuspecting prey.

He purchased my Premises under a pretence of serving me; but before the Bargain was confirmed, and during my Absence from Home, he took premature and violent Possession of them—turned my Family out of doors by Force—detained *all my Property* and Books then on the Premises, excepting the Books which constitute the BRITISH LIBRARY—converted all my extensive Establishment to his own Use—detained, and still detains my Books of Accounts—unwarrantably collected the Debts due to me, in his own name, and audaciously threatened, and even sued, Parties indebted to me as Debtors to himself. Having, by these means, been kept for seven months without access to my Property or Books of Accounts, I was consequently deprived of every Resource which could enable me to satisfy my Creditors; and I have been in every other respect subject to the utmost Distress, without any other remedy than an appeal to the Laws of my Country, which Appeal is now in Process, and, I trust, in train to render me ample Justice, whenever the Law's Delay will admit of a final Issue.

That Process has already obtained me an Injunction from the Court of Chancery against his proceeding any farther in Printing the BRITISH THEATRE, until he shall have satisfactorily answered my Charges against him ON OATH. If oaths are sacred, as I think they are—cursed will he be if he dare to controvert even one of my assertions!

Whatever may be the result of these Litigations, I wish ever to remain, as long as I live, the obedient Servant of the Public. These Litigations, however, have been the Parent of the present Project. My Declarations to the WORLD have been candid, and I was young enough to imagine, that, in consequence, my Plan would have been much sooner brought to maturity. EXPERIENCE, however, a bitter cup of which I have drunk deeply, has convinced me, more fully than ever, that I am to look forward only to Good Fortune through the medium of renovated Resolution and Perseverance.

When I tell the World, that till within seventy-eight hours of the appearance of the present MESSENGER, my Printing Arrangements were not compleated, owing to the disappointments of Mechanics, they will not wonder at receiving an imperfect Work. Such as it is, it will indicate, I hope, a good Intention, and justify my pretensions to that which I shall ever wish to aspire to—the PATRONAGE OF THE PUBLIC. The future Numbers, I flatter myself, will be looked for with some anxiety. —Resources are open—Talents are engaged—and my Experience shall be actively employed to render the MESSENGER hereafter a welcome Visitor at the SUNDAY Breakfast-table of every Person who wishes to be informed or amused.

JOHN BELL.

DESCRIPTION OF THE ADMIRALTY TELEGRAPH

The above Cut represents the frame of the Telegraph with six moveable octagonal frames, by changing the position of which, any letter may be made, and in certain positions, a variety of things may be signified at pleasure. Thus one frame being placed horizontally, and the others shut, or in a perpendicular situation, may denote the letter *a*; two frames only being in an horizontal position may give the letter *b*; three the letter *c*; and so on. As there may be made as many changes with these frames as with the same number of bells, the letters of the alphabet may be made with ease, and a sufficient number of signals may be formed for extraordinary purposes.

In the above Sketch the Octagons marked 1 to 6, all move on an axis, are raised perpendicular, as 1, 2—5, 6, and returned to their original station, as 3, 4, by means of the ropes *A* fixed at the ends of the cross bars *B*, which are attached to the extremities of the axles *C*, on which the octagons move; to each cross bar there are attached two ropes, one at each extremity; at one end to raise the octagon perpendicular, and at the other to return; and these ropes pass through the roof of the house into the room *D*, where persons are stationed continually to watch and work the machine.—Similar frames are erected on a chain of posts from London to Deal.

RETROSPECT
OF THE
POLITICAL EVENTS,
THAT HAVE OCCURRED SINCE THE BEGINNING OF THE PRESENT YEAR.

As the French Nation has been accustomed, from the beginning of the War, to carry the Campaign with the most bloody perseverance into the very heart of Winter, it was natural to expect that the New Year would have been ushered in by similar scenes of havock and desolation, especially as the unusual mildness of the season seemed to invite to a prolongation of hostilities: but just before its commencement, the Austrian and Republican Armies desisted on a sudden from their daily conflicts, so unavailing was the slaughter, and so impartially were the smiles and frowns of Fortune dispensed, after PICHEGRU had receded entirely from the right bank of the *Rhine*, and JOURDAN had retreated from post to post, till he made good his position in the vicinity of *Dusseldorff*.

This unexpected Armistice was hailed by all parties as the harbinger of Peace; but the agreeable delusion was of short duration; for scarcely had a single month elapsed when a Message was sent by the French Directory to the Council of Five Hundred, declaring the pacific language of their enemies to be perfidious, and proposing the levy in kind of horses, and such other articles as might be called for by the exigencies of the War.

In spite, however, of the inferences thence to be drawn, and of the Foreign Gazettes, which continued to "give note of dreadful preparation," the rumour of a general Pacification was revived, and was fondly entertained by the Public, till all our hopes were effectually destroyed by the appearance of two Official Notes that had recently passed between Mr. WICKHAM, the English Resident, and M. BARTHELEMI, the French Ambassador, at *Basle*. In answer to his enquiry, whether any disposition towards Peace prevailed in *France*, Mr. WICKHAM was given to understand, that the French Nation was ready to treat with its enemies; but that the Cession of all the Countries incorporated with its own, must necessarily form the basis of the Negociation. As these comprize the whole of the *Austrian Netherlands*, all *Savoy*, *Avignon*, the *Comtat Venaissin*, and several smaller districts, such a preliminary was declared absolutely inadmissible by the English Cabinet, in a Note addressed to all the Foreign Ambassadors resident in London.

The determination of the Minister to resist the pretensions of the enemy, met with approbation, even among those who are in the habit of censuring his measures; so injurious did it seem to English honour, interest, and security, to suffer the new Republic to receive such a formidable accession to its strength. It was deemed probable that the continued pressure of the War might occasion the breaking up of the French Finances, or produce some new convulsion, which, by increasing their embarrassment at home, might render them less haughty in their behaviour to Foreign Powers.

These sentiments, however, were by no means general among those who oppose the warlike system pursued by the present Administration. Many of them remarked, that the question was not, Whether the proffered preliminaries were such as suited us, but whether, by a further expence of blood and treasure, better were likely to be obtained. America, they said, had carried on the war for years after her paper-money had sunk to total insignificance; and so might the French; nor did it follow that a new convulsion, or even the overthrow of the Government, would render them less formidable; since, during the whole contest, they had regularly exhibited the curious phænomenon of the greatest weakness and vacillation in the centre, accompanied by the most tremendous force and the most unremitting energy at the extremities of the political machine.

It might even have been said, that the Government itself had assumed greater consistency since the establishment of the New Constitution.—The Council of Elders generally approved of the proceedings of that of Five Hundred; the Council of Five Hundred submitted with a good grace to the few instances of opposition it met with from the Council of Elders; and the Executive Directory cordially seconded the views of the Legislative Bodies. Ere long, however, a spark from the warm regions of the South seemed likely to raise the flame of contention anew between the discomfited band of Terrorists and the triumphant party of the *Moderes*. The horrible excesses committed in the Departments adjacent to the *Rhone*, by the hangmen, head-loppers, and

Fig. 113

Bell's Weekly Messenger is now printed in a New Type cast by Mr Thorne,[1] the graceful formation and present Arrangement of which enables us to introduce Intelligence equal to One-Eighth more than we have formerly done, and with a more distinct and agreeable effect to the eye of the Reader than is observed in any other newspaper.

Maps and other illustrations were included from time to time. Bell's plan of giving his news on the front page allowed him to illustrate a description of the new Admiralty telegraph with a cut of column-width and 3½ in. in depth. With such enterprise, the *Weekly Messenger* succeeded rapidly. Commencing with the year 1799, a Monday edition, for the express benefit of persons in the country, containing the state of the London Markets and any late news, was published in time to go out by the evening posts. Bell's efforts and example did not pass without notice from his rivals in the Sunday newspaper trade. *The Observer*, then in four large pages of four columns, went to a 'modern' type some months before *The Messenger*, i.e. on June 30, 1797, announced in the previous week's issue as having been 'some months in preparation, and is so constructed that, having a considerable encreased face, and the same sized body as at present, an equal quantity of matter will be given in improved and perfectly legible characters'. A fount of type seems then to have been renewed every other year. The expense was considerable and the newspaper always 'took credit' for some time before its use in the paper. A notice in some such terms as the following (from *The Observer* of June 30, 1799) was usually printed:

The Patrons of *The Observer* will, in the new type used in this impression, receive an humble offering of our Gratitude, and a respectful assurance of a Continuance of our utmost Exertion to merit the distinguished favours we have received."

The distribution of the Sunday papers was by means of the 'horn boy', a lad, who, equipped with a cap bearing the name of his paper, with a quire of them under his arm, announced them by the aid of shrill voice and trumpet —to the disturbance of the whole neighbourhood. The papers were, as we have noticed, published in the early mornings, at a time afterwards abandoned on sabbatarian protest. In 1799 there was a service of coaches on Sundays. *The Observer* respectfully informed its patrons, in a notice dated June 30 of that year, that:

This Paper continues to be forwarded *on the Days of Publication* to every part of Great Britain and Ireland, with the same regularity as if there were

[1] Mr Thorne was at this time the most fashionable founder in Europe. In 1818 he cut a fat face for the Imprimerie Nationale.

THE WEEKLY DISPATCH

SUNDAY, JAN. 22, 1804.

123.

On Saturday will be published, Price 9d

NUMBER III,

THE ROYAL STANDARD and LOYAL POLITICAL REGISTER; a Periodical Paper, published weekly, in answer to COBBETT'S WEEKLY POLITICAL REGISTER, containing also a digested Series of Foreign and Domestic Intelligence, Essays on Various Political, Military, and Literary Subjects, with an Occasional Effusion of Poetry, appropriate to the Present Times ... Parsons, Bookseller, Ludgate-hill; and sold by ... Strand; and by all Newsmen in Town and ...

THREE DAYS NEXT WEEK.

Public are respectfully acquainted that the Lot. ... Three Days next week ... under

FAMILY LINEN and FURNITURE, WAREHOUSE, No 104, Corner of New Bridge-street, Fleet-street

WAITHMAN and EVERINGTON respectfully inform the Nobility and Public, that they have now on SALE, a fresh and extensive assortment of Irish Linens, Hollands, Sheetings, and Table Linen, of the primest fabrics; on elegant selection of Furniture and Garment Prints, mostly of their own engaged Patterns; India and British Muslins of every description; Chambray, Italian, and French Cambrics; Dimities, Counterpanes, Quilts, &c. &c. Each article will be charged, by the single Piece, at the very lowest Wholesale Price.

††† Agreeable to their usual Plan, at the conclusion of each Season, they have selected such part of their Stock as are out of condition, which they are now disposing of at considerable reduced prices; among which are, a large quantity of ell-wide Town-printed Furniture, from 2s. 6d. to 3s. 6d. per yard, usually sold ...

made preparations for his reception. On the approach of the General and his suite towards the camp, the Sheike el Arab, accompanied with the other Sheikes went to meet them, and conducted them to his tent. When they had seated themselves on a carpet spread for that purpose, the Sheike's son presented a large sieve made of sheep-skin, laden with fruits of various kinds, and a delicious sweet-meat composed of a rich pastry and preserved dates, to each of the guests; and pressed him to take what he liked best. After the first course was removed, ...

noble than any of the other Tribes. They scorn to cultivate the land, they think that every other occupation, except that of plunder, is degrading to them. Their flocks, camels, and asses, are few in proportion to the population of their tribe. But their cavalry amounts to more than 600. They constantly reside in the interior parts of the desert, where they find scrap of pasturage, and where they can retire in safety with their booty. Not only the cultivators of land; but the Tribe of Hanadis pay a tribute to the Walled Ali's, whose power ...

THE WEEKLY DISPATCH;

SUNDAY, MARCH 12, 1815.

No. 701. *Printed and Published by G. KENT, 164, Strand.* *Price* 8d.

HISTORY AND POLITICS.

WESTMINSTER MEETING.

DIRELICTION AND SEDITIOUS SPEECH OF BURDETT—THE RIOTS, AND THE CORN BILL.

It would hardly be possible to find so complete a practical illustration of the mischiefs which would arise out of a Parliamentary Reform, founded on the principles of ge-

had let for 1,500*l.* a-year, and for which there was now paid a rent of 7,000*l.*—(*Loud huzzas.*)—He also knew of another estate which would have been well paid for by the sum of 20,000*l.* which had been, some time ago, sold for the sum of 80,000*l.* In fact, the most enormous prices had been paid, and contracted to be paid, during the war, for lands; and, because the persons who carried on this traffic were, on the return of peace, disappointed in their grasping views and speculations, they came to Parliament to ask for relief; they now came whining and crying to Parliament, setting forth that they had made bad speculations, and

Members was to enforce a military despotism in the country; and they might be considered as a chamber of taxation, whose business it was to register tax-edicts, issued by the Ministers of the Crown, in order that they themselves may come in for a share of the money plundered from the people. He did not think it proper to meet that Assembly any more—he did not choose to carry on the mockery of debate in that House—he was not fond of keeping bad company or bad hours.—(*Loud shouts from the populace*)—The Members of that assembly had become bankrupt in character and talent, and had brought the country

WEEKLY DISPATCH.

VOL. 22.—No. 1204.] SUNDAY, SEPTEMBER 26, 1824. [PRICE 8½d

PRINTED, PUBLISHED, AND EDITED BY ROBERT BELL, AT THE OFFICE, NO. 139, FLEET-STREET.

HISTORY AND POLITICS.

HOW ARE CANTING ENTHUSIASTS & FANATICS TO BE DEALT WITH?

Having in last Sunday's DISPATCH, and in several former numbers at various times, animadverted on the canting mania that has become almost universal throughout the kingdom; we may be asked by some one who entertains the same disgust for it, and views it in the same mischievous light that we

lyte-making Sectarians have pursued:—that of acquiring an absolute dominion over the purses, the minds, and bodies of their followers. Fortunately, however, the Methodists are not yet in possession of the field of power: and we are confident they never will be. To be sure there is no Act of Parliament—no law to check their progress; they are at full liberty to cant, and rant, and brawl as much as they please; and that is the very reason why they will never gain the ascendancy they aim at. If any law were passed to silence or restrain those conceited ...

FOREIGN & COLONIAL AFFAIRS

FRANCE.

PARIS, SEPT. 21.—All the pensions granted by the late King out of the Civil List, will be provisionally continued by His Majesty, from the 16th instant.

According to his Majesty's intention, the Museum and other public places, which have been closed, will be re-opened on Friday, the 24th of this month.—The Council of State, the clergy of Paris, the clerks in the several ministerial offices, the Municipal Body, the National Guard, the Courts and Tribunals have been to-day successively to the Tuileries, to throw holy water on the corpse of the late king.

WEEKLY DISPATCH

SUNDAY, FEBRUARY 28, 1836.

No. 1793] PRINTED AND PUBLISHED AT NO. 139, FLEET-STREET, LONDON. [PRICE 8½d

HISTORY AND POLITICS.

CHURCH PLUNDER.—THE BISHOPRICK OF DURHAM.

The Whig Ministers have not been very fortunate in wind falls, or in opportunities of appointing their friends to good livings, upon vacancies occasioned by the demise of preceding occupants, and even when such vacancies have occurred they have committed the egregious sin of giving the prize to the enemy. They have now, however, the good fortune of having at their disposal the most enormous and the most villanous church job in all Europe, the Popedom alone excepted. Doctor Van Mildert, the Bishop of Durham, is dead, and the bench of Bishops are as eager as hungry terriers or starved cats in the

the County; and yet, when a question was put to Lord John Russell in the House of Commons, on Thursday night, he could only reply, that it was then under the consideration of his Majesty's Ministers, whether the new Bishop should be appointed with an understanding that if the good of the country required a separation of his warlike and political, from his sacred functions, he would submit to the disjunction. This is really carrying a respect for vested rights further than we have ever yet heard of. How can the people so blindly and tamely submit to such impositions? The day is gone by for Bishops to appear at the head of troops, clad in armour, and foremost in slaughter and plunder; and yet, for the sake of fees and immemorial usage, we continue all these functions to a

FRANCE.

The *Moniteur* of Monday at length contains the decree, nominating the five Ministers, M. Thiers, as President of the Council and Minister of Foreign Affairs; M. Montalivet, as Minister of the Interior; M. Sauzet, as Minister of Justice; M. Passy, as Minister of Commerce; and M. Pelet de la Lozere, Minister of Public Instruction. Messrs. Maison, Dupere, and D'Argout retain the places occupied by them in the last Ministry. Great efforts were made by the Court and the friends of the ex-Cabinet to keep M. Persil in office. MM. Thiers and Passy both positively objected; the former proposed that M. Martin du Nord, who may be called another Persil, should occupy a seat in the Cabinet, but not of Justice. M. Martin refused. The Court, however, insisted on two *King's friends* being in the Cabinet, to balance the two of the *Tiers Parti*; to meet which, M. Passy waived his claim to the Finance Department, which M. D'Argout retains.]

SPAIN.

IMPERIAL PARLIAMENT.

HOUSE OF LORDS.—MONDAY.

Lord ASHBURTON presented a petition from Nova Scotia on the subject of the timber duties. ...

Lord ELLENBOROUGH said he had several petitions to present on the subject of the Ecclesiastical Courts Consolidating Bill. ...

Lord WHARNCLIFFE postponed his motion for returns of Magistrates ...

Fig. 114. *Development of the headings of* The Weekly Dispatch, 1804–1836 established Post from London on Sundays. It is received at Bath, Bristol, Portsmouth etc. on Sunday evening; at Liverpool, Manchester etc. early on Tuesday morning; at Edinburgh, Glasgow, and when the wind answers, Dublin, early on Wednesday, and at all other places with proportionate celerity.

A foundation of the year 1801, which still appears on Sundays, is *The Weekly Dispatch*, established in September of that year and printed in the customary style of the dailies and of *The Observer*. The origins of the paper are unknown, but at some time (I think after 1815) it came under the control of one Robert Bell, an Irish barrister, who re-assembled the paper into conformity with the style of *The Weekly Messenger*, added a device of a Mercury flourishing a ribbon bearing the name 'Bell', and thus made the title read *Bell's Weekly Dispatch*.

THE NEWS.

No: 451. *SUNDAY, FEBRUARY 27, 1814.* *PRICE 8d.*

This Paper is Published at an early hour every SUNDAY Morning, at "THE NEWS" Office, No. 28, Brydges-street, and distributed throughout the Metropolis, and within the Two-penny Post District, by Nine o'Clock.—Communications (post-free) respectfully attended to.

LADY PERCEVAL AND THE EDITOR OF THE NEWS.

" You have proclaimed me a libeller: I have denied the charge, and *retorted the accusation*. Yet you avoid judicial inquiry, and shun the approach of that day, to which conscious innocence eagerly looks forward. Am I, then, silently and tamely to bear the stigma of "*libeller*," until it is your pleasure graciously to grant me

ters was from Mr. Phipps, who sent me his paper of the 4th of April, accompanied by a letter.

Q. Was Mr. Phipps in the habit of sending his paper *The News*?—A. I ordered the paper previous to the 4th of April, and it was regularly delivered.

Q. Did you ever use these expressions, "that the spirit of John Bull was dying away, but that this would make him clamourous?"—A. I never used that expression.

Q. Did you ever tell the Defendant, "that it was absolutely requisite for him to be out of the way for a

Mr. Hardcastle a second time to bring the Defendant down?—A. I think on the Monday morning.

Q. When next did you see the Defendant?—A. He was brought down to Blackheath on Wednesday evening—it was about 11 o'clock as I understood, but I did not see him. I am positively certain I did not see him from the 26th March till the 2d April.

Cross-examined by Mr. ALLEY.

Q. You have been for some time acquainted with the Defendant?—A. I have.

Fig. 115

The tax on each copy of a daily or weekly was raised to $3\frac{1}{2}d.$ in 1804. The price of *The Observer* went up accordingly, and, like *The Times*, to take the most conspicuous instance in the daily press, condensed its type still more, drove the columns as close as possible to the dividing rules. *The Times* set about the invention of a larger sheet, and in 1808 came out with a paper wider, by a full column, than any other paper. *Bell's Weekly Messenger* crammed more letterpress into its established format, and newly founded Sunday papers followed his, rather than *The Observer*'s, lead. The two papers represented two completely distinct traditions which never merged. In 1806 *The Observer* remained, more or less, a daily published on Sunday. At that time its heading was without any device, the lettering being redrawn in the gothic of *The World* of 1787. It cost 6*d.*, whereas *Bell's Messenger* was $7\frac{1}{2}d.$ When T. A. Phipps started *The News* in May 1805, he scrupulously followed

THE ALBION.

No. 15. SUNDAY, NOVEMBER 29. 1807. Price 7½.

This Paper is published early on Sunday Morning, at "THE ALBION" Office, No. 5. Russel-court, opposite the Box-Door of Drury-lane Theatre, London, distributed throughout the Metropolis, and within the Twopenny Post District, by Nine o'Clock.—Communications, (Post free) respectfully attended to.

FROM LAST NIGHT'S GAZETTE,

NOVEMBER 28, 1807.

The *Gazette* of last night contains a Proclamation for the Prorogation of Parliament to the 21st day of January next.

As likewise, an Order of Council that due Notice should be given to Neutral Vessels, with respect to the Order of General Blockade issued on the 11th of November last.

As likewise, an Order, permitting Neutral Vessels to carry East India Produce to the Enemies West India Colonies.

As likewise, an Order, regulating the Trade from Gibraltar to the Mediterranean, and other Ports under the Controul of the Enemy.

As likewise, an Order, exempting the Vessels of Prussia and Lubeck from the operation of the Order of Blockade.

As likewise, an Order, exempting the Portuguese Ships from the same operation.

As likewise, an Order, continuing certain Bounties on the Fisheries, &c.

BANKRUPTS.

William Dicks, of Frome-Selwood, Somerset, clothier, Dec. 8, at the Christopher Inn, Bath, 15, and Jan. 9, at eleven, at the George Inn, Frome-Selwood. Attorneys, Mr. J. Williams, Red Lion-square, London; and Mr. S. Williams, Trowbridge, Wilts.

William Mabbott, sen. of Nottingham, hosier, Dec. 7, 8, and Jan. 9, at one, at the Blackmoor's Head, Nottingham. Attorneys, Messrs. H. Ince, Nottingham; and Messrs. Kinderley, Long, and Ince, Gray's-Inn, London.

Thomas Lees, of Hebden-bridge, York, cotton-spinner, Dec. 9, 10, and Jan. 9, at ten, at the Talbot Inn, Halifax. Attorneys, Mr. Wigglesworth, Gray's-Inn, London; and Messrs. Wigglesworth and Thompson, Halifax.

William White, of Apperley-Bridge, York, merchant, Dec. 21, 22, and Jan. 9, at eleven, at the Star and Garter Inn, Leeds. Attorneys, Mr. Scott, Leeds; and Messrs. Exley and Stocker, Furnival's-Inn, London.

George Watts, sen. of Chichester, hatter, Dec. 7, at three, 8, at eleven, and Jan. 9, at the Dolphin Inn, Chichester. Attorneys, Mr. R. Dally, Chichester; and Mr. Few, Great James-street, London.

James Oldfield, of Liverpool, merchant, Dec. 28, 29, and Jan. 9, at eleven, at the Globe Tavern, Liverpool. Attorneys, Mr. Davies, Liverpool, and Messrs. Meddowcroft and Stanley, Gray's-Inn, London.

Robert Winter, of Islington, Middlesex, factor, Dec. 1, 15, and Jan. 9, at ten, at Guildhall. Attorney, Mr. Tarn, Gloucester-street, Queen-square.

Thomas Beale Taylor, Coventry-street, Haymarket, ladies shoemaker, Dec. 1, 8, and Jan. 9, at Guildhall, London. Attorney, Mr. Allen, Carlisle-street, Soho.

Lance Bentley, of High-street, Lambeth, cheesemonger, Nov. 30, Dec. 15, and Jan. 9, at twelve, at Guildhall. Attorney, Mr. Lankow, Wardrobe Place, Doctors' Commons.

John Gresham, of Gale's Wharf, Lambeth, timber-merchant, Dec. 5, 12, and Jan. 9, at twelve, at Guildhall. Attornies, Messrs. Tilbury and Bedford, Bedford Row, London.

John Hunter, of Great Newport-street, London, haberdasher, Dec. 1, 12, Jan. 9, at one, at Guildhall. Attorney, Mr. Parnell, Church-street, Spitalfields.

William Jones, of Liverpool, stationer, Dec. 22, 26, and Jan. 6, at one, at the Globe Tavern, Liverpool. Attornies, Mr. Thos. Bowkteck, St. Mildred's Court, Poultry, London; or Messrs. Eardswell and Stephenson, Drury-lane, Liverpool.

Charles Bithery Sharp and Israel Pitt, of Birmingham, factors, Dec. 12, 14, and Jan. 9, at eleven, at the Shakspeare Tavern, Birmingham. Attornies, Messrs. Devon and Tooke, Gray's Inn, Square, London; and Mr. George Barrish, Temple Row, Birmingham.

Samuel Walker, of Leeds, Yorkshire, maltster, Dec 21, 29, and Jan. 9, at eleven, at the Golden Lion, Leeds. Attornies, Messrs. Upton, Nicholson, and Hemingway, Leeds; and Mr. J. Lambert, Hatton Garden, London.

James Battershell, of Portsmouth, ship-chandler, Dec. 11, at one, Dec. 12, at ten, and Jan. 9, at one, at the Royal Oak Inn, Portsea. Attorney, Mr. W. Messum, of St. James's-street, Portsea.

William Sisson, of Whitehaven, Cumberlandshire, wine and spirit-merchant, Dec. 17, 18, and Jan. 9, at eleven, at the Globe, Cockermouth. Attornies, Mr. Chambre, Inner Temple Lane, London; and Messrs. Benson and Nicholson, Cockermouth.

Louis Firebont, jun. of Fort-street, London, silk-manufacturer, Dec. 5, 12, and Jan. 9, at twelve, at Guildhall, London. Attorney, Mr. Edmonds, Crane-court, Fleet-street.

DIVIDENDS.

Dec. 19. Christain John Adam Witke, of Coleman-street, London, merchant, at one, at Guildhall, London.

Dec. 22. John Tench, of Tokenhouse-yard, London, merchant, at ten, Guildhall, London.

Dec. 22. William Hopkins, of Leman-street, silk-thrower, at ten, Guildhall, London.

Dec. 22. Patrick Boyle, of Vine-street, Middlesex, printer, at ten, Guildhall, London.

Dec. 19. Thomas Withers, and Penry Browne Withers, of Greenhill's-rents, Middlesex, merchants, at one, Guildhall, London.

Jan. 30. John Carleton, of Hilbeck-hall, Westmoreland, cotton-spinner, at one, Guildhall, London.

Feb. 6. Thomas White, Southwark, haberdasher, at one, Guildhall, London.

Dec. 29. John Bleasc, of Manchester, innholder, at three, Palace Inn, Manchester.

Dec. 22. John Wright, of Newgate-street, London, grocer, at twelve, Guildhall, London.

Dec. 22. William Hoard, Lower East Smithfield, Middlesex, victualler, at eleven, Guildhall, London.

Dec 22. William Disting, of Plymouth, tallow-chandler, at ten, Guildhall, London.

Dec. 22. John Clarke, of Long-lane, Bermondsey, hide salesman, at twelve, at Guildhall, London.

Dec. 19. Thomas Tiplady Rowe, of Chelmsford, linnen-draper, at ten, at Guildhall, London.

Dec. 22. William Branwhite, of Tobacco-roll-court, London, warehouseman, at ten, at Guildhall, London.

Dec. 22. John Bundock, of Great East Cheap, London, corn-factor, at eleven, at Guildhall, London.

Dec. 19. William Valentine Scotney, of Oxford-street, Middlesex, linen-draper, at one, at Guildhall, London.

Feb. 2. James Burgess of Coventry-street, Haymarket, military hatter, at ten, at Guildhall, London.

Dec. 1. James Cotter Bigshaw, of Savage-Gardens, London, corn-factor, at one, at Guildhall, London.

CERTIFICATES, Nov. 28.

Samuel Lawton, of Grappenhall, Chester, butcher.—Anthony Thomas, of Duke-street, Westminster, feather-manufacturer.—Matthew Bennett, of St. Thomas the Apostle, Devonshire, yarn manufacturer.

FROM THE AMERICAN PAPERS.

NEW-YORK, OCTOBER 22.

LETTER STEALING.

The Editor of the *Aurora*, in attempting to explain, in this morning's paper, that ugly affair about the British Minister's Dispatches, says, he believes the packet to have been a political contrivance here, a trick invented on purpose to entrap and expose him. It would seem, therefore, that he supposes the British Minister to be perfectly acquainted with that unfortunate propensity which renders it impossible for *some folks*, having once got possession of another person's letter, to let it go again with an unbroken seal!

We do not believe the inference to be just. Mr. ERSKINE was not here at the time that certain letters, directed from Washington to the Editor of this Gazette, came to hand through the medium of the *Aurora*. We presume, therefore, that he was not at all aware that placing a letter belonging to another man within the reach of Mr. DUANE, would lay him under any extraordinary temptation, or that it would prove a sure means of drawing him into disgrace. But whatever the fact may be, the Editor takes great credit to himself for having suspected the trick, and for effectually resisting the temptation, strong as it was. Though he does not absolutely say that he did not open the packet, he plainly insinuates that he did not, by expressing a doubt as to the contents of it, and by the exulting manner in which he announces his fortunate escape from the trap thus artfully and temptingly laid for him. The following are his words:

"The adherents of the British Government have now the whole advantage of the trick, for such we must still believe it to be. But the trap did not catch—they must try another trick, or give it another turn."—*United States Gazette.*

In relating the affair of Mr. ERSKINE's Dispatches, we stated erroneously that they were demanded in form by the British Consul, or by his orders. Mr. BOND did not apply for the Packet, either in person or by order. It was, however, applied for by a Gentleman of this city, who received the answer stated in our last.—*Ibid.*

OCT. 23.—The Editor of the *Aurora* has commenced a formal Defence of the letter-stealing Affair which came to light a few days ago. The strong point of his defence is, that it was a Measure of Retaliation for the interception and publication of Admiral WILLAUMEZ's Dispatches to the French Ambassador. We subjoin his words, that we may not be accused of misinterpreting his meaning:

"We cannot pass the subject over without calling to the recollection of the public, a damning proof of the base depravity of the British Adherents and Tories.

"It is but a few months ago, that in a Federal Paper at Norfolk, there was published various Letters and Papers said to be the Contents of a Dispatch addressed to the French Ambassador resident at Washington.

"When the Dispatches addressed to the French Ambassador were intercepted, they were not forwarded to the Ambassador—they were not forwarded to the Executive of the United States, the only legitimate channel of communication of public concerns between Citizens of the United States and Foreign Ministers: the first intimation of their existence was their Publication in a Newspaper.

"The Dispatches to the Minister of this friendly Power were stopt!

"Not alone stopt, but the American Government was treated with studied insult, by the publication of those Papers openly avowed to be intercepted."

Such is the defence set up by a private man, claiming to be an American Citizen, for intercepting and detaining Letters addressed to the British Minister. A moment's examination will be sufficient to convince any one that if this is all that he can say in justification of his conduct, he would much better remain silent. The Dispatches of the French Minister were intercepted on the high seas by a British Officer—an Officer of a hostile Nation. They were therefore a good prize; they became the property of the captor, who had a perfect right to break the seals, and to publish the contents. A belligerent has a right by the laws of war, to seize and appropriate every species of the property of his enemy wherever he can find it. There was no violation, therefore, of either law or honour, in the seizure and publication of French Dispatches by the British. It is true, the *Aurora* would have it believed, that Americans, that federalists, intercepted and published those Papers; and, perhaps, to carry on the parallel, he expects to have it believed that they were embezzled and opened within the United States by the Editor of a Paper. Unfortunately for his defence, the well-known fact is, that the papers were seized and opened by an avowed enemy, upon the high seas, and were published both at Halifax and in the West Indies before they appeared in any Paper printed in the United States.

The sole argument, therefore, on which Mr. DUANE rests his defence is in itself baseless and visionary, unless he stands in the same relation to the British Government as exists between the Commander of a British Ship of War on the high seas and the French Government. Now, though we have long perceived his warm attachment to the cause and Government of France, we did not suppose that he would avow such an allegiance and subserviency as would entitle him to the rights of a Belligerent, and justify him in seizing and detaining British property. As he has chosen, however, to take this ground, it is not for us to say that he is not entitled to it. But he must excuse us for objecting to his making use of our neutral territory as the theatre of his warfare against the seals of English dispatches. If he is a liege subject of BONAPARTE, or one of his mercenaries, he is fully entitled to intercept British letters, or any other British property upon British territory, or on the high seas, but not in the streets of Philadelphia.—*U. S. Gazette.*

A Telegraph Order was some days ago received at Plymouth, to apprehend a man passing through that place, supposed to be a swindler or a spy—but he could not be found. A letter from Marazion inclines us to believe that he passed through Cornwall unsuspected, and escaped to sea. A man of genteel appearance, calling himself CAMPBELL, arrived at Marazion on Tuesday last, and hired a small sloop for the ostensible purpose of conveying him to Cork, where he said he was going to join the Expedition under Sir SIDNEY SMITH, and was charged with dispatches for that officer. He left his signature as "J. D. CAMPBELL, Commissioner;" spoke English fluently, but with something of the Irish accent; his person, however, appeared to resemble the French. He got clear off.

Mrs. DICKONS, it is with infinite sorrow we mention, was at the close of the New Opera, last Thursday Evening, so suddenly indisposed, as to be conveyed home in a dangerous state. This misfortune will cause the postponement of the next performance of "*Two Faces under a Hood*," in which the vocal powers and excellent acting of Mrs. DICKONS were so deservedly admired.

PRICE OF BREAD.—Tuesday the LORD MAYOR, having inspected the Mealweighers' Reports, ordered the Price of Bread to be raised Half an Assize, or one Penny in the Peck Loaf, to commence to-morrow: the Price of the Quartern Loaf of Wheaten will then be tenpence halfpenny, and household ninepence.

BOXING.—Notwithstanding *Gregson*, the Lancashire bruiser, was so severely beaten in his late contest with *Gulley*, that his life was despaired of, he is still confident that, in the event of another battle, he will prove victorious. His friends encourage him in this opinion, as he is under the tuition of *Dan Mendoza*, and they have prevailed upon him to challenge his late opponent for £200 a-side.

Fig. 116

the quarto format of *The Messenger*, only substituting a horn boy for the postman as the heading device. *The Albion* 'printed in *quarto*, containing Eight Pages, on paper of superior Texture, and the *largest Size* that can be used' delivered 'within seven miles of London and Westminster, by Nine o'clock on Sunday morning' was, in general, a paper of our *New Statesman* class, but more detailed in its plan, printing the text of despatches as well as offering reflections thereon, and giving also the police, law and theatre news besides touching upon 'every subject connected with the refined and elegant pleasures of life'. The first number appeared on August 23, 1807, some months before John Hunt brought out *The Examiner*. On January 3, 1808, *The National Register*, printed by John Browne Bell, future founder of *The News of the World*, was published. It was 'splendidly printed on yellow-woven paper of the largest size that ever was manufactured' and, at the price of 8*d*., J. B. Bell's was a sixteen-page paper, exactly the same size as his father's eight-page *Weekly Messenger* when given one more fold.

These were the three chief formats used in the first decade of the nineteenth century. Up to 1810 the full-folio *Sunday Monitor* and *The Observer* represented one, the quarto *Bell's Weekly Messenger* a second, and *The Albion*, also a quarto, a third category of text. All were serious papers and intended for family reading—though some of the text would not be tolerated in the newspapers of this generation, commonly regarded as lax. The political papers increased in number, if not in circulation, as schisms occurred,[1] or the political situation grew strained,[2] but we must omit them in the interest of our main consideration: newspapers in the strict sense. The French wars prospered all the newspapers and, as time passed, these took on a conversation style. The journal which best displays the tendencies of the time is *Bell's Weekly Dispatch*. The style of the *Weekly Messenger* shewed little change except in bulk. It was enlarged from June 24, 1810, when it announced that it contained a greater quantity of news than any other paper, though costing only 8*d*., whereas some were 8½*d*., 9*d*. and 10*d*. It was extended again in 1828 to provide thirty-two instead of twenty-four columns as previously. Opportunity was taken to reaffirm a determination to progress as a family journal, excluding all articles which might 'offend the decency of private life'. This may be interpreted as

[1] The editor of *The News*.

[2] The prospectus of *The Constitution* (No. 1, January 5, 1812), price 6½*d*., indicates that the paper was the property of a state prisoner for alleged libels. I have not been able to see any issue.

a warning to those likely to be led astray by the *Dispatch*, regarded by all conservative minds as a scurrilous paper.

Bell's Weekly Dispatch, although, like the *Messenger*, interested to 'expatiate with truth, boldness and independence, upon every subject of common interest', introduced copious reports of seductions, rapes, murders and any other sort of horror. This tendency began to shew itself soon after 1815. At about the same time, Pierce Egan began to contribute his characteristic descriptions of wrestling and racing to the columns of what had been a

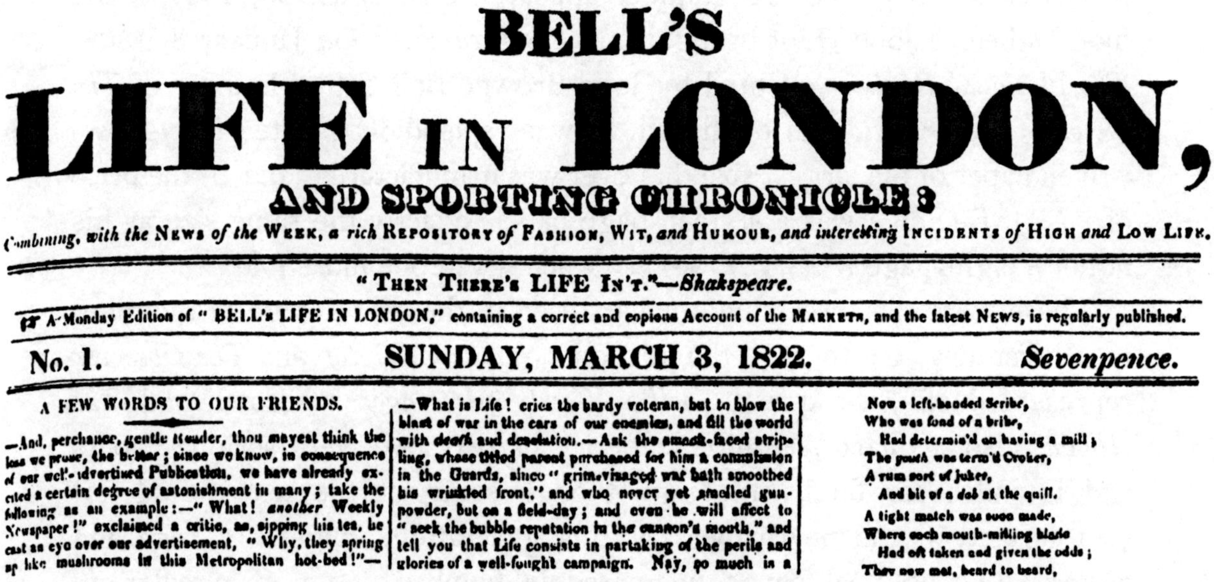

BELL'S

LIFE IN LONDON,

AND SPORTING CHRONICLE:

Combining, with the NEWS *of the* WEEK, *a rich* REPOSITORY *of* FASHION, WIT, *and* HUMOUR, *and interesting* INCIDENTS *of* HIGH *and* LOW LIFE.

"THEN THERE'S LIFE IN'T."—*Shakspeare.*

☞ A Monday Edition of "BELL's LIFE IN LONDON," containing a correct and copious Account of the MARKETS, and the latest NEWS, is regularly published.

No. 1. SUNDAY, MARCH 3, 1822. *Sevenpence.*

A FEW WORDS TO OUR FRIENDS.

—And, perchance, gentle Reader, thou mayest think the less we prose, the better; since we know, in consequence of our well-advertised Publication, we have already excited a certain degree of astonishment in many; take the following as an example:—"What! *another* Weekly Newspaper!" exclaimed a critic, as, sipping his tea, he cast an eye over our advertisement, "Why, they spring up like mushrooms in this Metropolitan hot-bed!"—

—What is Life! cries the hardy veteran, but to blow the blast of war in the ears of our enemies, and fill the world with *death* and desolation.—Ask the smooth-faced stripling, whose titled parent purchased for him a commission in the Guards, since "grim-visaged war hath smoothed his wrinkled front," and who never yet smelled gunpowder, but on a field-day; and even he will affect to "seek the bubble reputation in the cannon's mouth," and tell you that Life consists in partaking of the perils and glories of a well-fought campaign. Nay, so much in a

Now a left-handed Scribe,
Who was fond of a bribe,
Had determin'd on having a mill;
The youth was term'd Croker,
A rum sort of joker,
And bit of a *dab* at the quill.

A tight match was soon made,
Where each mouth-milling blade
Had oft taken and given the odds;
They now met, beard to beard,

Fig. 117. *Head of* [*Robert*] Bell's Life in London, *successor to* [*W. R. Macdonald's*] Life in London *founded January* 13, 1822

merely political and general paper of *The Observer* class. *The Weekly Dispatch* quickly became of national importance—as it had never before been. The editor, Robert Bell, with his new power, proceeded to attack the newly established police, the established church, and anything else established. Thus, while the *Dispatch* continued to deal seriously with serious affairs, it made better and more varied, and more unconventional, reading than any other paper. There began a new tradition in Sunday journalism and, in twenty years, the authorities recognised that radical opinions were too widely held to be safely interfered with. The Sunday press was, in fact, one of the greatest of the forces lying behind the Reform Bill. All the big circulations—except *Bell's Weekly Messenger*—were on the side of the Reform. *The Weekly Dispatch* of 1820–30 was not all atheism and scurrility as some of its opponents pretended, and Pierce Egan's contributions alone shewed the opposite. But at last there was a quarrel and Egan was dismissed, with such resulting confusion in the newspaper world that we need to clear up its bibliographical uncertainties.

Life in London, or the Day and Night Scenes of Jerry Hawthorne esq., and his elegant friend, Corinthian Tom, accompanied by Bob Logic, the Oxonian, was the lengthy title of the very first example of an important work to be issued in monthly parts.[1] It was illustrated by George Cruikshank and was completed in 1821. The author was Pierce Egan. On January 13, 1822, when the popular cult of Tom and Jerry was at its highest, one William R. Macdonald brought out the first number of a new Sunday paper under the title *Life in London.* On March 3 one Bell, Robert, but not the Robert Bell[2] of *Bell's Weekly Dispatch* (for whom Pierce Egan was then writing), brought out *Bell's Life in London*, which, on June 23, incorporated the earlier newspaper of the same name. In January 1824, Egan was dismissed from the *Dispatch* and at once set about a rival paper; he brought out the first number of *Pierce Egan's Life in London, and Sporting Guide*, on February 1, 1824. By then, *Bell's Life* was in difficulties, and was bought by William I. Clement[3], who had already secured *The Observer*, retaining the name 'Bell' in the title. From 1824 to 1827, therefore, *Pierce Egan's*, and *Bell's*, *Life in London* as two similarly named Sunday papers, of similar aspect, bid for the favour of those who liked their

[1] No parts are known. The next issue was illustrated boards.

[2] This is made certain by a controversy which sprang up in November 1823 between 'Mr Robert Bell formerly a Member of the University of Dublin and of the Society of the Middle Temple, London', editor and proprietor of the *Weekly Dispatch* 'upwards of 20 years', who issued a circular 'in consequence of certain piratical attempts made by the conductors of a lately established journal to impress on the public that the two Papers belong to the same parties', and *Bell's Life in London* (cf. the issue for November 9, 1823). The latter, in claiming 'not to vie with any contemporary in mere cant and balderdash', regarded it as unnecessary to 'remind our Readers that we do not allude to OUR OWN Mr Robert Bell—he is altogether a different sort of man'. In proceeding, the *Bell's Life* writer states that: 'With Mr. Egan, we have at present nothing further to do—nor do we intend to have; and much should we regret, if, by the title of our Paper, (which has been explained in our early Numbers,) a thought should be conveyed to our Readers that we ever *had* any thing to do with him. We want no names but our own, and repeat, that it is by the merits or demerits of our publication that it shall ever stand or fall.

'As we have been forced upon this subject we must address a word or two to another Mr. Bell, (we trust our friends will not thing we are ringing a *peal*)—of the *Messenger*. At our commencement, he in the most open and candid manner published a notice to his readers, stating, that although he wished it to be understood that we had no connection with his Journal, yet he considered that every man had an undoubted right to bring out a Newspaper in his own name who thought proper to do so. We have not the paragraph before us, but recollect it was such as any man would have written who wished plain dealing, and we thank him for it'.

[3] Of this important character, my first note is that he received the advertisements for *The Weekly Dispatch* in 1806.

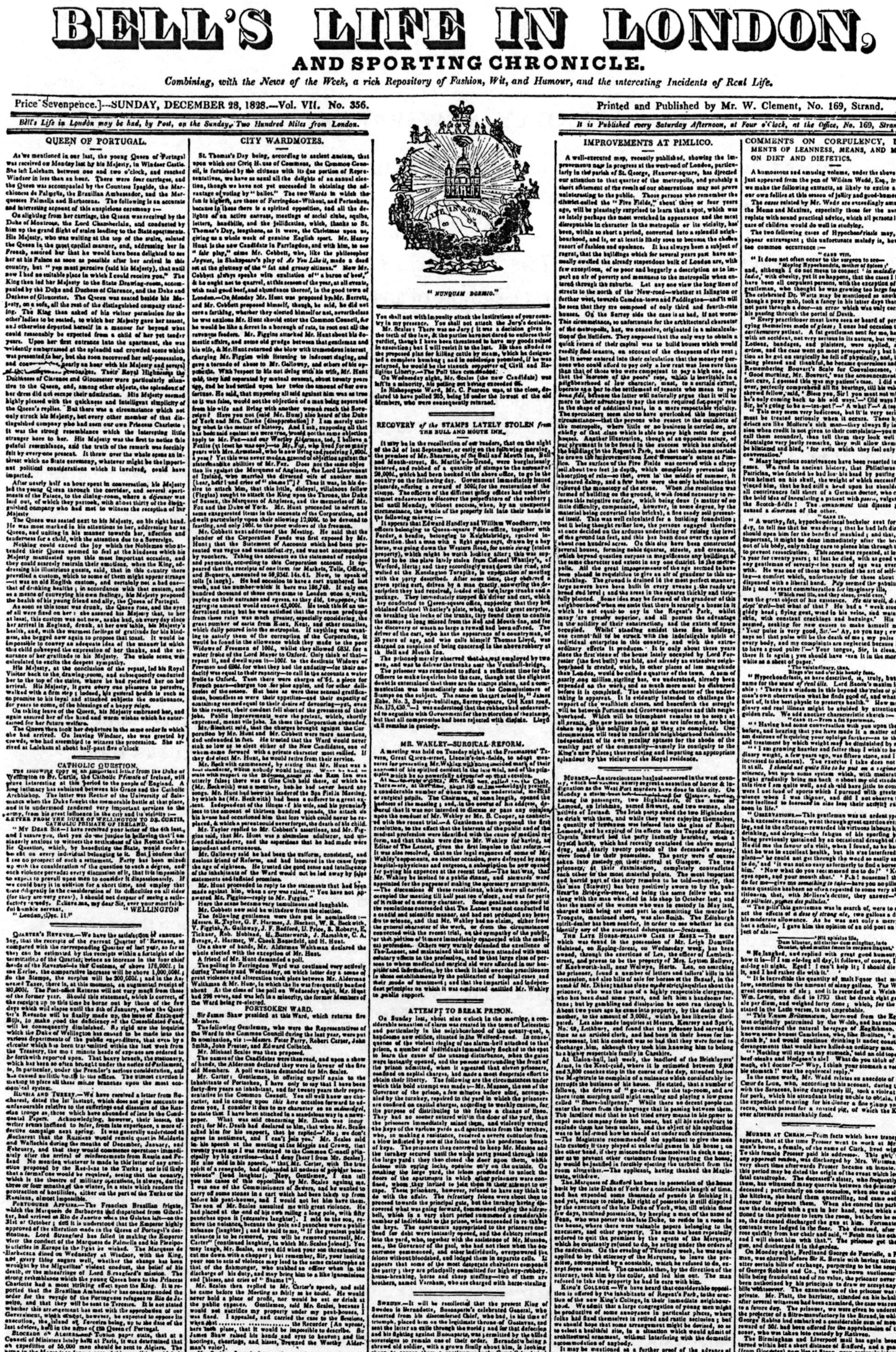

BELL'S LIFE IN LONDON,

AND SPORTING CHRONICLE.

Combining, with the News of the Week, a rich Repository of Fashion, Wit, and Humour, and the interesting Incidents of Real Life.

Price Sevenpence.]—SUNDAY, DECEMBER 28, 1828.—Vol. VII. No. 356.

Printed and Published by Mr. W. Clement, No. 169, Strand.

Bell's Life in London may be had, by Post, on the Sunday, Two Hundred Miles from London.

It is Published every Saturday Afternoon, at Four o'Clock, at the Office, No. 169, Strand.

QUEEN OF PORTUGAL.

CATHOLIC QUESTION.

CITY WARDMOTES.

PORTSOKEN WARD.

"NUNQUAM DORMIO."

RECOVERY OF THE STAMPS LATELY STOLEN FROM THE BULL AND MOUTH INN.

MR. WAKLEY—SURGICAL REFORM.

ATTEMPT TO BREAK PRISON.

IMPROVEMENTS AT PIMLICO.

COMMENTS ON CORPULENCY, LINEAMENTS OF LEANNESS, MEANS, AND MAXIMS, ON DIET AND DIETETICS.

Fig. 118. *Front page of* Bell's Life *in its fully developed format*

THE TURF.

LATEST STATE OF THE ODDS.

The betting since our last has been unimportant, and would hardly justify a quotation, but for some heavy bets on three or four South-country horses for the St. Leger, and for which Merchant and Ultimatum promise to become good favourites. The following is the fullest statement we can give :—

TO CORRESPONDENTS.

QUESTIONS ANSWERED.

DRIVING FROM NOTTINGHAM TO NEWARK.—A Correspondent has kindly favoured us with the following answer to the question in our last, upon this subject :—

"At page 137 of Vol. 44 of the Sporting Magazine for June, 1814, is the following passage :—'On Tuesday, the 21st, a match for one hundred

THE AQUATIC REGISTER.

HIGH WATER AT LONDON BRIDGE.

	FORENOON.	AFTERNOON.
Sunday (this day)......	14 min. past 4	31 min. past 4
Monday	49 min. past 4	8 min. past 5
Tuesday	29 min. past 5	51 min. past 5
Wednesday..............	14 min. past 6	39 min. past 6

SPORTING CHRONICLE.

SPARRING AT THE TENNIS COURT.

BENEFIT OF JEM BUNN, "THE BOW BOY."

JEM BUNN (the Bow Boy), who has long retired from the Prize Ring, but who has all his life been a *trump* in the Sporting Circles of the East, and very generally esteemed by all classes, took his benefit on Tuesday at the Tennis Court, in

THE FASHIONABLE WORLD.

THE KING'S COURT.

On Thursday, his Majesty, attended by the Lord Steward of the Household, arrived at his Palace in St. James's, in his travelling carriage and four, escorted by a party of Lancers, from the Royal Lodge in Windsor Park. The King was received by the numerous spectators assembled in the Park by every demonstration of respect; the Gentlemen all uncovering and cheering his Majesty as the carriage passed through the

The Drama.

DRURY LANE.

Miss LOVE, for the first time, appeared as *Ophelia*, in *Hamlet*, on Wednesday night, not, we suppose, because she is particularly qualified for the part, nor because she imagined she could make any very novel impression in it, but in default of any female in the company, since the departure of Miss FOOTE, who was at

ORIGINAL CORRESPONDENCE.

TO THE EDITOR OF BELL'S LIFE IN LONDON.

SIR—Allow me, through the medium of your Paper, to return my most grateful thanks to the numerous sporting and private friends who attended my benefit at the Tennis Court, on Tuesday last. To those Members of the P. R. whose offers of support and

THE CHASE.

HUNTING APPOINTMENTS.

His Majesty's stag-hounds meet to-morrow, at Laleham, near Staines; and Friday, at Farnham Common, Bucks, at half-past 10.

The Brighton harriers meet to-morrow, near Patcham; Wednesday, near the Race Course; and Friday, near the Dyke, at a quarter before 11.

Fig. 119. *Headpieces (original size) to the columns of* Bell's Life, 1828 general news varied with lively sporting reports. In November 1827 Pierce Egan was in straitened circumstances, his paper was sold by auction and knocked down to Clement, who amalgamated it with the *Bell's Life* he had bought in 1824. W. R. Macdonald was appointed to the editorial chair of the sole surviving paper which ran, in an enlarged format, under the title of *Bell's Life in London* until its end in 1886.[1]

Throughout this time *Bell's Weekly Messenger* remained in the original format. A block stamped on the front page to distinguish his own from other papers claiming the use of his surname made known John Bell's *Messenger*

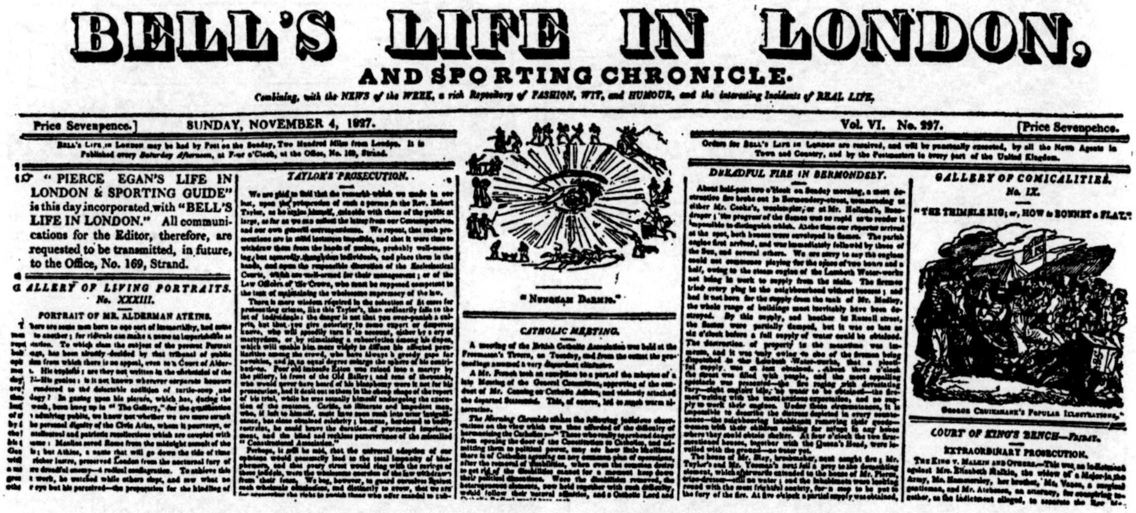

BELL'S LIFE IN LONDON,
AND SPORTING CHRONICLE.
Combining, with the NEWS of the WEEK, a rich Repository of FASHION, WIT, and HUMOUR, and the interesting Incidents of REAL LIFE,

Price Sevenpence.] SUNDAY, NOVEMBER 4, 1827. Vol. VI. No. 297. [Price Sevenpence.

"PIERCE EGAN'S LIFE IN LONDON & SPORTING GUIDE" is this day incorporated with "BELL'S LIFE IN LONDON." All communications for the Editor, therefore, are requested to be transmitted, in future, to the Office, No. 169, Strand.

GALLERY OF LIVING PORTRAITS. No. XXXIII.

PORTRAIT OF MR. ALDERMAN ATKINS.

TAYLOR'S PROSECUTION.

CATHOLIC MEETING.

DREADFUL FIRE IN BERMONDSEY.

GALLERY OF COMICALITIES. No. IX.

"THE THIMBLE RIG; or, HOW to BONNET a FLAT."

GEORGE CRUIKSHANK'S POPULAR ILLUSTRATIONS.

COURT OF KING'S BENCH—FRIDAY.

EXTRAORDINARY PROSECUTION.

Fig. 120. Bell's Life *and* Pierce Egan's Life *incorporated*

as 'the paper with the black patch'. In the course of time the front page heading of the *Weekly Dispatch* changed. Originally a meek setting in italic capitals, Robert Bell first added a Mercury within a floral border (cf. Fig. 114). In this form the *Dispatch* heading became an influence in the Sunday newspaper style of the next score of years. It seems to have symbolised at first a radical political programme, and later an anti-clerical and anti-newspaper tax attitude.[2] The *Dispatch* remained in the same size and number

[1] A certain W. Chambers published *High Life in London: A Political, Sporting, Literary, Scientific and General Newspaper* in eight pages quarto form from December 23, 1827. The paper, transferred to A. Maddocks with No. 7 and to J. Smith with No. 12, became a folio. 'It has likewise been objected that the title of High Life in London being somewhat exclusive in its meaning—as in a manner shutting out intelligence connected with the *haut ton* of the world at large—we have substituted that of "High Life"....'

[2] See *infra* for mention of *Penny Weekly Dispatch* (1840), *Clark's Weekly Dispatch* (1841), *Bell's Penny Dispatch* (1842).

of pages. It headed its racing column with a block of a horse and rider taking a five-barred gate,[1] a poor echo of the fine series of headpieces drawn by G. Cruikshank for Pierce Egan's Sunday paper and which, turned over to Clement, were employed to good advantage to top the columns of *Bell's Life in London* every Sunday.[2] This was an inheritance and one of the paper's best and most permanent features of its long career. When, under Clement's active management, *The Observer* became a pioneer in pictorial journalism, *Bell's Life* made further use of the satirical genius of George Cruikshank, and others. Each number of the year 1827, for instance, carried an engraving by one of the Cruikshanks and later by John Leech which were republished in *The Gallery of Comicalities*, a *Times*-size four-pager covered

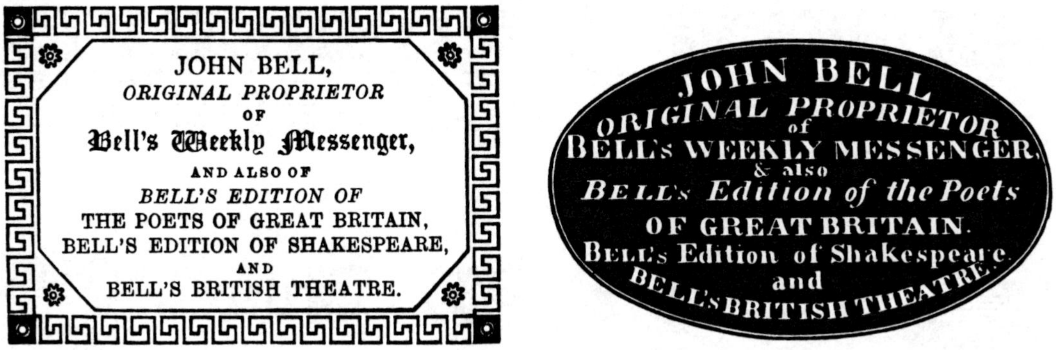

(*a*) (*b*)

Fig. 121. Bell's Messenger *devices:* (*a*) *temporary,* (*b*) *the permanent 'black patch'*

with a mass of cuts. The three such collections of *Bell's Life* blocks issued were printed and reprinted over and over again. The tops of the paper's columns of Fashionable Intelligence, the Drama, the Ring, Racing, etc., were adorned with lively engravings after the same artists. The reporting style was a compound of slang, back-slang and the wise-crack, the whole well-done and making excellent reading. *Bell's Life* contained much general news. It is the most interesting of all the papers of its class, requiring more study than we can here give to it.

We need to pass on to *The Independent Whig*, as its name implies, a political sheet. It was set up in the style of *Bell's Messenger* and of the

[1] Probably this block was introduced by Egan in his time as the *Dispatch*'s special sporting writer. The subscribers to *Bell's Weekly Dispatch* were given, with their annual index, a mezzotint plate 'Robt. Cruikshank, fecit' shewing five old English sports, with the lettering 'The Only Sporting Newspaper, Bell's Weekly Dispatch'.

[2] Pierce Egan made another unsuccessful attempt to found a sporting Sunday newspaper in *Pierce Egan's Weekly Courier*, No. 1, Sunday, January 4, 1829. It expired April 26 of the same year.

Albion. The editor of *The Independent Whig* left that paper at the beginning of 1821 and brought out a new Sunday journal dated February 18, 1821. He chose for the title '*The New* [device of a human eye] *Observer*'[1], set in large egyptian capitals. In a month or two the paper was reconstructed, with new serial numeration and in the same typographical style, as '*The Independent* [same device] *Observer*' (No. 1, April 21, 1821). In October 1822, as if convinced that the goodwill of the name 'Observer' was not what it had been, another change in the title was decided upon. On October 20 the journal appeared with gothic lettering for its new title '*Sunday* [royal device] *Times*' which it carries at the present day. A notice in the interior

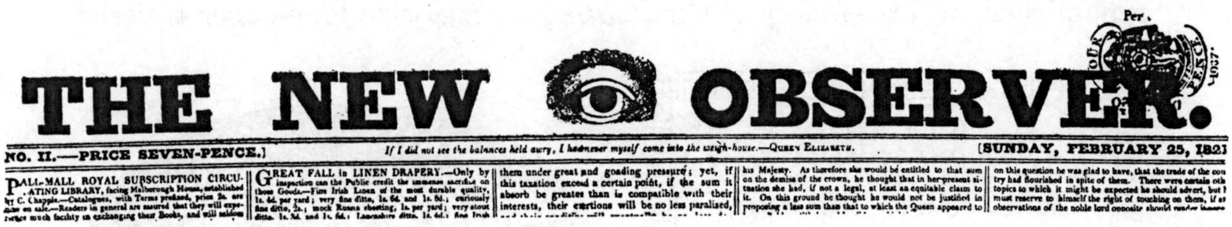
THE NEW OBSERVER.
NO. II.—PRICE SEVEN-PENCE.] *If I did not see the balances held awry, I had never myself come into the weigh-house.*—QUEEN ELIZABETH. [SUNDAY, FEBRUARY 25, 1821

PALL-MALL ROYAL SUBSCRIPTION CIRCULATING LIBRARY, facing Malborough House, established by C. Chapple.—Catalogues, with Terms prefixed, price 2s. are now on sale.—Readers in general are assured that they will experience much facility in exchanging their Books, and will seldom

GREAT FALL in LINEN DRAPERY.—Only by inspection can the Public credit the immense sacrifice on those Goods.—Fine Irish Linen of the most durable quality, 1s. 4d. per yard; very fine ditto, 1s. 6d. and 1s. 8d.; curiously fine ditto, 2s.; mock Russia sheeting, 1s. per yard; very stout ditto, 1s. 3d. and 1s. 6d.; Lancashire ditto, 1s. 4d.; fine Irish

them under great and goading pressure; yet, if this taxation exceed a certain point, if the sum it absorb be greater than is compatible with their interests, their exertions will be no less paralised,

his Majesty. As therefore she would be entitled to that sum on the demise of the crown, he thought that in her present situation she had, if not a legal, at least an equitable claim to it. On this ground he thought he would not be justified in proposing a less sum than that to which the Queen appeared to

on this question he was glad to have, that the trade of the country had flourished in spite of them. There were certain other topics to which it might be expected he should advert, but he must reserve to himself the right of touching on them, if the observations of the noble lord opposite should render

Fig. 122

Sunday Times.
Established in 1822.
This Paper may be received in the Country by Saturday night's Post on Sunday morning, at any distance within 170 miles, free of postage. It may also be sent to the West Indies and Colonies for 1½d.—Advertisement are inserted in the whole impression, which is not the case with most other Sunday Papers.
No. 349.] LONDON, SUNDAY, JUNE 28, 1829. [Price 7d.

MATRIMONY.—A GENTLEMAN of 25, of hereditary title, is desirous of forming a Matrimonial Alliance with a LADY of fortune. Any respectable and wealthy citizen wishing to procure rank for his daughter may, perhaps, find the present a suitable opportunity. Should any lady or gentleman be disposed to answer this advertisement, they may depend upon

MONEY.—Several SUMS are ready for immediate investment, on approved security. Apply personally, or by letter (post-paid), to Messrs. Carr and Kirby, 2, Churchyard-court, Inner Temple.

FROM £8,000 to £10 000 to be LAID OUT.—

JOURNAL of a PASSAGE from the PACIFIC to the ATLANTIC, crossing the Andes in the Northern Provinces of Peru, and descending the River Marañon or Amazon. By HENRY LISTER MAW, Lieut. R.N. John Murray, Albemarle-street.

LITERATURE.
Life and Correspondence of John Locke. By Lord King. Colburn.
A valuable collection of papers connected with the name of one of the most celebrated philosophers

Fig. 123. *The* Sunday Times, *formerly* The Independent, *formerly* The New, Observer

of the paper reads '*The Sunday Times* | *The Independent Observer* is incorporated with the *Sunday Times*'. A royal device in the style of that of *The Times* was added on November 3, 1822. The typography itself, in using the egyptian capitals in the heading and in the text, drew away from *The Weekly Dispatch* style and assimilated, deliberately, one supposes, the standards of Printing House Square. The only serious variation from the Walter style was the running gothic headline on the inside pages. For the rest, the *Sunday Times*, like many another London paper, Sunday or other, looked as if it might have been produced in the office of *The Times*.

The Sunday paper tradition maintained by *Bell's Weekly Messenger* was supported in the main by *Bell's Weekly Dispatch*, but with a difference that the latter, while giving general news, specialised in sport both before and

[1] Clement had abolished this device and transferred it to *Bell's Life* in place of the older device of St Paul's.

after *Bell's Life in London*. *The Observer* and the *Sunday Times* differed from both the *Messenger* and the *Dispatch* by ignoring their domestic character. There was nothing of the magazine quality about *The Observer* and the *Sunday Times*. Nor was *The Observer* in 1822 what it was when it was founded—a daily paper published on Sundays. That tradition had died. *The Selector, or Say's Sunday Report*, published in 1806, *The Sunday Paper* of 1807 had no long existence, and, like *The London Recorder* which had already absorbed the old *Sunday Reformer*, were all defunct in 1820. There had been several weekly reviews, epitomes, or what you will, published on Sundays—such as *The Champion* (formerly Drakard's, 1814–22), *The British Neptune* (1805–23) which approximated to the *Messenger*. *The Sunday Monitor* dragged on until 1829 under a proprietor who, as a convinced supporter of Joanna Southcott, alienated readers by the space he gave to Joanna's Box.

In 1824, the experiment of reviving a typical morning paper, to be published on Sundays, was made in *The Sunday Morning Herald*. Though only thirteen issues are known, it is as well, since no similar attempt was made for more than a generation, to quote the statement of its aims:

> We have no Sunday paper. The numerous publications called Sunday papers are in reality Weekly Papers, containing as far as relates to Intelligence nothing more than an abstract of what had appeared in the Daily Papers of the Six preceding days. It is therefore proposed to establish *A Real Sunday Paper*. A paper which, instead of repeating in an abridged form the News which has appeared in the Morning Papers of the Six Preceding Days, shall itself be a Morning Paper of the seventh day, containing a full and accurate account of every interesting occurrence whether Domestic or Foreign which may transpire from the publication of Daily Papers on Saturday morning up to the latest hour on Saturday night.[1]

The failure of this paper left in possession the three types of Sunday journal, i.e. the political, the family, and the sporting papers. It seems clear that the bulk of the circulation of the most important conservative family paper, *Bell's Weekly Messenger*, was in the country; it was at its best between 1810 and 1820. *Bell's Weekly Dispatch*, as the chief general news compendium affected by lovers of sport and of radical politics, was at its highest point between 1820 and 1840. *Bell's Life in London* was the favourite sporting weekly. *The Observer* set out to give news and, if the public appetite required it, news of crime; it was at its best between 1820 and 1830. The public

[1] From No. 1, March 2, 1824 (Robert Appleyard, 297 Strand), *The Real John Bull* was incorporated with *The Sunday Morning Herald*. The paper has a black-letter title and resembled *The Times* in style.

interest in murder was exploited by Pierce Egan, but the activity of William Clement, proprietor of *The Observer*, surpassed all records, notably in the reporting of the Weare murder. Clement was a syndicate. He built up a newspaper trust which excited the suspicions which were attached to the Northcliffe press of our own time. Clement's purchases included, besides *The Observer* and *Bell's Life*, a third paper, entitled *The Englishman* (founded 1803, purchased 1821), in all three of which his large expensive wood engravings and relevant text appeared *seriatim*. Finally Clement burnt his fingers over *The Morning Chronicle* for which he paid a then unheard-of sum, and was later glad to sell it for a tithe. During the years 1820–40, however,

GRATIS!!! GRATIS!!! ON SUNDAY, JUNE 10, 1832, A PORTRAIT, AN ACCURATE LIKENESS OF EARL GREY, WILL BE DELIVERED GRATIS WITH "THE BELL'S NEW WEEKLY MESSENGER."

AND IN A FEW WEEKS WILL ALSO BE DELIVERED GRATIS, A JUBILEE PLATE, BEING A MEMENTO OF THE GREAT PUBLIC QUESTION OF REFORM, WHICH WILL CONTAIN ABOUT TWENTY PORTRAITS, AND AN EMBLEMATICAL VIGNETTE REPRESENTING THE DISPERSAL OF THE ENEMIES OF REFORM. IMMEDIATE ORDERS SHOULD BE GIVEN TO YOUR NEWSMEN, OR TO THE OFFICE OF THIS PAPER, 2, SURREY STREET, STRAND, LONDON.

THE BELL'S NEW WEEKLY MESSENGER. 64 COLUMNS

VOL. 1. No. 20. SUNDAY, MAY 13, 1832. PRICE {Newspaper 4½d. Tax... .... 4d.} 8½d.

THE WEEKLY PRESS.

FROM THE EXAMINER OF THIS DAY.

[Perhaps it is not too bold an assertion—that the Sunday Press alone is a power sufficient to withstand all the combined villanies which an Oligarchical Government could possibly now attempt in England. At all events, the following article must be a more effectual force with the Nation, than any Tory coup d'état of The Duke, or the Tame Elephant.]

"THE DESPOTISM.

"Mischief is swift. We reckoned on the event. … duties would also be withheld, and one example has in this case the most powerful effect; for the manufacturer or dealer who brings his goods into the market without paying the excise, commands the market by the lowness of his prices, and forces others in self defence, if for no other cause, to adopt his course. Constitutionally, the power of stopping supplies belongs to the Commons; and if, owing to the admitted corruption of the House, the people cannot have the benefit of this measure through their representatives, they will compass it by their own resolutions. They know full well that the roots of Government are in … couched in the genuine language of an Anglo-Saxon patriot:—"WITH UNBROKEN FAITH, THROUGH EVERY PERIL AND PRIVATION, WE HERE DEVOTE OURSELVES AND OUR CHILDREN TO OUR COUNTRY'S CAUSE!" how impressive must have been the scene—how glorious the spectacle! Here words have millions of lives—each sentence swarms with consequence. Remember, it was given out word by word, as an oath, and each word followed by an echo from hundreds of thousands of voices: conceive the effect of a quarter of a million of Britons proclaiming their UNBROKEN FAITH, mouth after mouth, with hand and

FROM THE ATLAS OF THIS DAY.

[The veil has at length been forcibly dragged from before the people's eyes, and they have indeed found that the newspapers alone made his Majesty "a Patriot King." Our contemporary is rather sharp this week, as the following article from his columns will testify.]

"THE DECEIVER AND THE DECEIVED!

"The events of the past week are the most important that have occurred since the introduction of the Reform Bill; the opposition in the House of Lords having succeeded in defeating Ministers,

Fig. 124. *John Browne Bell's aggressive publicity as shewn in a heading to his* New Messenger

his Sunday papers achieved handsome circulations. His importance is greatest in the history of pictorial journalism, for he did not establish any new journal.

In 1828 John Bell died at the age of 86. His son, born in 1779, achieved temporary success with *Le Beau Monde* and *The National Register*, but his father's death and his own disinheritance gave him the motive to start a journal in opposition to John Bell's former property. *The Bell's New Weekly Messenger* was a lively periodical and it made considerable progress at the expense of the old *Messenger*. It began by cutting its price and enlarging its size. *The Bell's New Weekly Messenger* more nearly resembled *The Weekly Dispatch* than any other weekly. It made quite clear that it had 'no connection with that old journal, commonly called in the country "My Grandmother's Newspaper"'. The heading of the new paper had a floral centre-piece in the style of the *Dispatch*. In lieu of a Mercury, the new Messenger set the sign '64 |

COLUMNS'. The extent of the paper was, indeed, unique among weeklies. Two supplements, *The Reviewer* (a literary affair) and *The Commercialist*, with separate titles in large capitals, gave the reader the conviction that he was getting more than twice as much for his money than any other paper provided. Assistance in the right manœuvring of the paper was needed and was thus offered:

To the Reader:—Open the paper to its fullest extent, and cut it in halves:—the First Half forms the Newspaper:—then, divide the Second Half in the middle:—and the two parts of it will severally constitute the Reviewer and the Commercialist.

The paper progressed under the vigorous direction of John Browne Bell. The young Bell's advertisements exhibited a degree of hyperbole which would have filled his father with admiration. Extra inducements were provided 'at enormous expense'. A caricature appeared in the second number. 'Elegant, comic, amusing and original' title-pages were presented with the final number of the year in the interests of those who bound their sets in the eighteenth-century habit. The circulation was considerable. At the end of the first year, advertisers were assured (in egyptian type) that '60,000 persons read it every week—contradict it who can!'

Special attention was paid to type. A new face 'cast expressly for *The Bell's New Weekly Messenger*, at the foundry of Messrs Vincent and James Figgins' was procured for use in the paper of January 1, 1843. Throughout its career the *New Messenger* was agreeably printed in a business-like fashion. The lines were well spaced and leaded.

The same publisher established on Sunday, October 4, 1843, *The News of the World*, of a size equal to that of the immense double sheet of *The Times*. The paper was indeed a novelty for Sunday in size and in price. The reduction of the newspaper tax in 1836 to 1*d.* made some such adventure as J. B. Bell's *News of the World*. Why he preferred to establish a new paper rather than reconstruct *The Bell's New Weekly Messenger* is not clear. One guesses that then, as now, the standing trade terms made the lowering of the price impossible without trouble with the newsagents. And trouble there was enough with *The News of the World*. As a 3*d.* paper, it was attacked by what Bell referred to in his general thundering denunciation (printed on his leader page) as 'an infamous conspiracy against cheap knowledge'. Bell, in his first number affirmed that 'we most positively and distinctly state that upon no account shall any alteration ever be made in the price of the *News of the World*. We intend and are resolved that it shall be sold for threepence only',

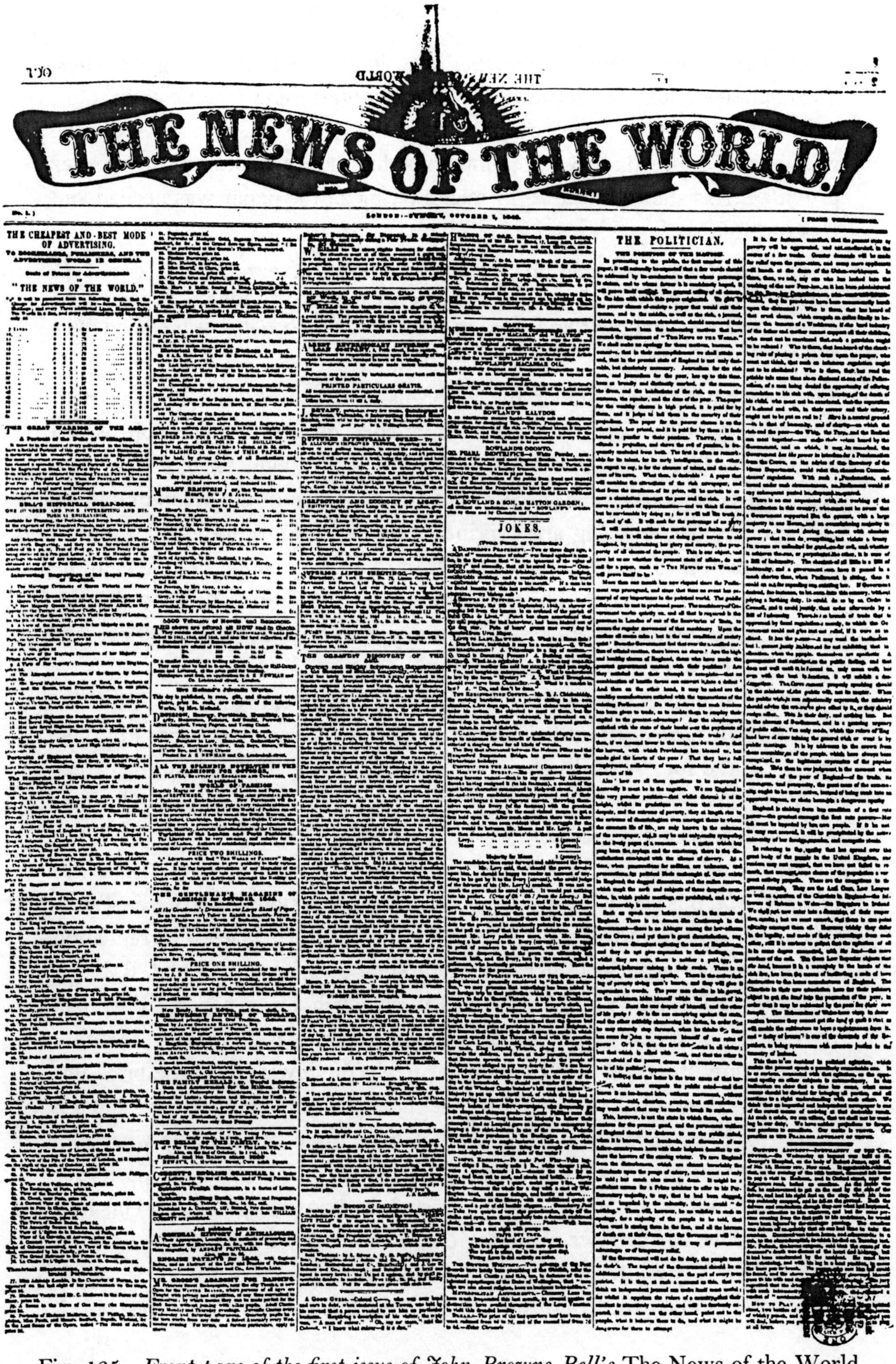
THE NEWS OF THE WORLD

THE CHEAPEST AND BEST MODE OF ADVERTISING.

"THE NEWS OF THE WORLD."

THE POLITICIAN.

JOKES.

Fig. 125. *Front page of the first issue of John Browne Bell's* The News of the World, *October* 4, 1843

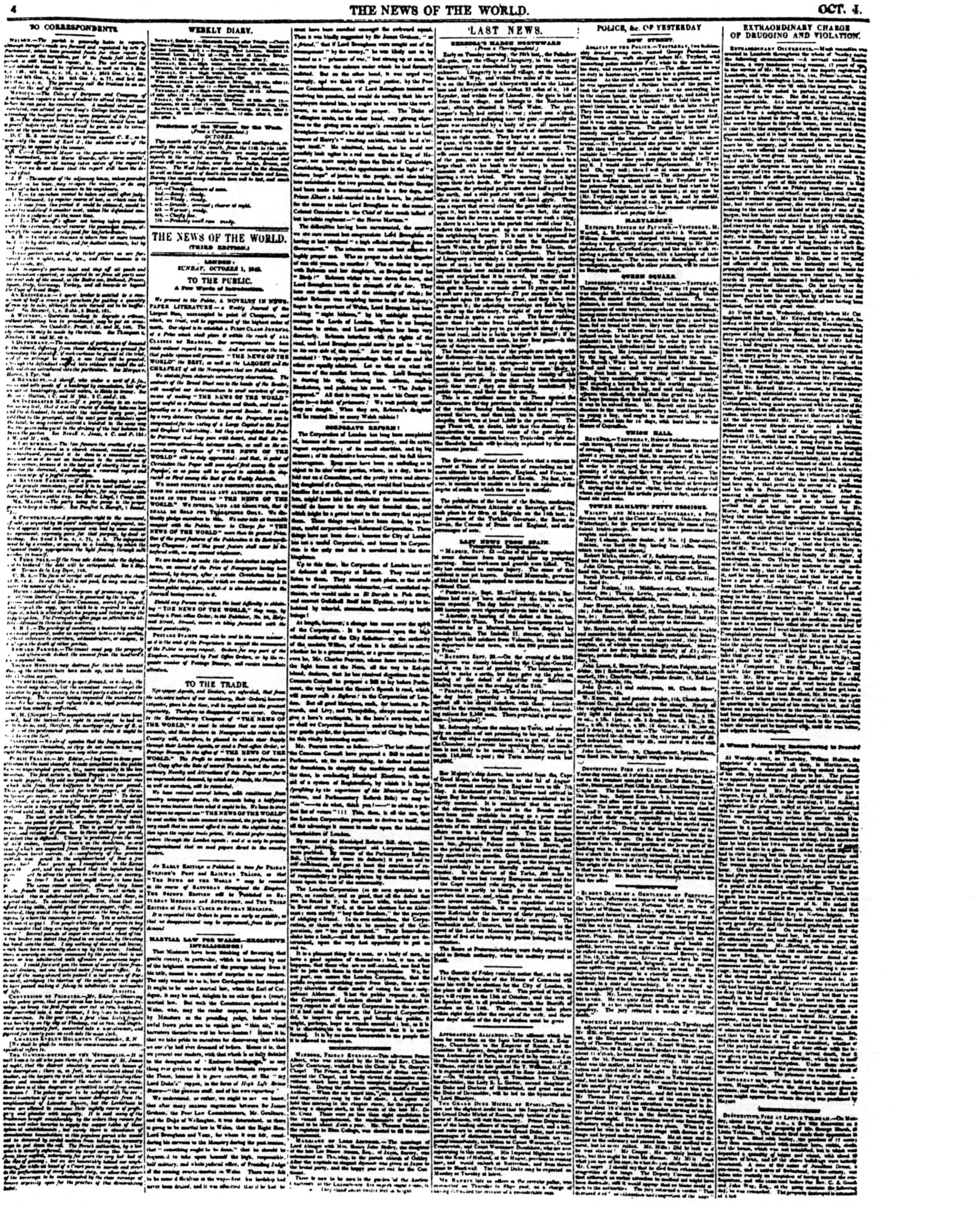
4 THE NEWS OF THE WORLD. OCT. 4.

TO CORRESPONDENTS.

WEEKLY DIARY.

THE NEWS OF THE WORLD.

TO THE PUBLIC.

TO THE TRADE.

LAST NEWS.

POLICE, &c. OF YESTERDAY

EXTRAORDINARY CHARGE OF DRUGGING AND VIOLATION.

Fig. 126. *Leader page from the first issue of* The News of the World, *October* 4, 1843

LLOYD'S PENNY

Sunday Times

AND PEOPLES' POLICE GAZETTE.

No. 179. LONDON: SUNDAY, SEPTEMBER 3, 1843. **Vol. 4.**

Police.

MANSION-HOUSE.

William Light, alias "Touting Bill," a sort of amphibious fish broker, was charged with having diddled James Linsey out of 3s. 6d., by the following process: —The defendant, it appeared, was one of those accomodating gentry, termed "bobbers;" a class of persons who hang about the avenues of Billingsgate to pick up countrymen or strangers who come to the market to buy fish, in order to put them in the way of buying them, by which means a large quantity of unsaleable fish is disposed of at somewhere about double the market value. The defendant in the exercise of his "touting" vocation—viz., looking out for "flats"—that morning fell in with the complainant, and after some conversation was empowered to purchase six cod fish from the boat. "Bill" asserted that "nine bob was the werry lowest figure," though the price was actually but seven shillings; and upon being furnished with the money, he promised to pick out some "reg'lar rum uns." The defendant, however, saw no more of his broker, but after waiting some time a basket, containing only four cod fish, was handed to him as his purchase, which fish were, indeed, "reg'lar rum uns," for the fish were all broken, and in a state to have required a strong stomach to digest them.—Mr. Goldham, the Superintendent of the Market, hearing of the circumstances, caused "Bill," for whom he had been for some time on the look out for similar practices, to be taken into custody.—Please your Lordship, said Bill in defence, that ere good gentleman accostes me in the market and says, young man (says he), vill you buy me six cod fish? Yes (says I), I vill, and get you some as shall do me credit; so he hands me over the dumps, and I goes right away into the boat, but ven I seed as how the fish vorn't in no state to do no credit to my carakter, I says, says I, I von't have told up no more nor four into the basket; vell, some von gets the basket unperceived on shore, and ven I vant to look arter it I vas taken into custody, quite at a nonplush.—The Lord Mayor, after a suitable caution, allowed the defendant to leave the office upon returning the money he had attempted to appropriate.

BOW-STREET.

Lusus Naturæ.—Application was made to the magistrate upon an occasion of a very uncommon description.

Some time ago, a poor woman, the wife of a person who resides at Bath, was delivered of two still-born children united, as were the Siamese twins, in such a manner that if they had lived, they would probably have been no greater incumbrance to each other than the extraordinary children who had filled the town not long ago with curious speculations were known to be. The parents of the twins being indebted to a surgeon in the sum of 17*l.* or 18*l.*, the bodies were placed among his curiosities, we understand, as a sort of security for the amount of the debt. Some time afterwards the strange birth having excited a great deal of interest and inquiry, the surgeon sold the bodies for a more considerable sum than that which would have discharged his bill. The purchase was made by a person who was also a professional man, and as the fame of the conjoined bodies increased, the new buyer thought it would be advisable to convey his bargain to London, where curiosity was often indulged at a most extravagant price, and either to exhibit them to the public, or dispose of them to one of the great institutions of the metropolis. This, at least upon the part of the family who might be supposed to have the highest claim to the profits derivable from the *lusus naturæ*, was conjectured to be the case, and up to town came the father and mother, and grandfather and grandmother, and uncles and aunts of the twins, in order to contend for the restitution of what they considered to be their property. They soon ascertained that the gentleman who was in possession of the bodies, was involved in pecuniary embarrassments, out of which he was endeavouring to extricate himself by the sale of this remarkable kind of treasure, and they were most anxious to know from the magistrate whether he could not adjudicate in such a case of hardship, and restore the twins to their hands?

The magistrate begged to know who had been so kind as to consider him qualified to act as an intercessor or referee on so unusual a matter?

The applicants stated, that they had mentioned the circumstance to a solicitor, upon whose counsel they waited upon his worship. They had reason to suppose that the curiosity was extremely valuable, for, upon inquiring at the College of Surgeons or Physicians, they heard that the twins had been exhibited and offered for sale to the members, and that the sum required amounted to some hundreds.

The magistrate declared that the subject happened to be at as remote a distance as possible from his jurisdiction. He had, however, an opinion upon this subject, to which the applicants were quite welcome, and that was, that as far as he could collect from what had been stated, the party by whom the bodies were placed in a state of preparation was the only one who could make a legal claim, and that he, of course, had a legal right to dispose of them. That party, however, was in honour bound to give up the difference between the sum he had received and the amount of his bill, the expense of the preparation deducted.

The applicants appeared to be much disappointed at this intelligence. The magistrate endeavoured to console them by stating that the sum which the Siamese twins had had was no argument of the probable success of a speculation upon the comparatively insignificant curiosity of still-born twins.

Libellous Drama.—On the 6th of January, 1607, a farce was acted at Paris, before Henry IV., his Queen, and the greater part of the princes, lords, and ladies of the court. The subject of the piece was a quarrel between a married man and his wife. The wife told her husband, that he stayed tippling at the tavern, while executions were daily laid upon their goods for taxes, which must be paid to the king; and that all their substance must be carried away. During this dialogue, three officers of justice came in and demanded the payment of some taxes, and in default of payment, prepared to carry away their furniture. The wife began a loud lamentation, and at length the husband asked them who they were. "We belong to justice," said the officers. "They who belong to justice," replied the man, "act in another manner; I do not believe you." During this altercation the wife seized a trunk, upon which the officers commanded her, "in the King's name," to open it, and after much dispute the trunk was opened, and, out jump three devils, who carried away the three officers of justice. The magistrates conceiving themselves to have been insulted by this performance caused the actors to be arrested, and committed them to prison. On the same day they were discharged by express command of the King, who magnanimously told those that complained of the affront, "you are fools! if any one has a right to take offence it is I, who have received more abuse than any of you. I pardon the comedians from my heart, for the rogues made me laugh till I cried again."

HORACE VIVYAN DISCOVERING UNA CONVERSING WITH ASHLEY BELGRAVE.

THE WALTZ OF DEATH.

A TRUE STORY.—BY C. C. AINSWORTH, AUTHOR OF "THE FORSAKEN," "EUSTACE EGERTON," &c. &c.

A week or two ago I took my sisters, Alice and Beatrice, down to Basmere in Kent, to pay old Uncle Horace a visit, which was certainly, if truth be spoken, more of a duty than inclination, for though as worthy a man as ever lived, yet the good gentleman's eccentricities are somewhat too numerous to be borne with patience.

When we arrived at the house, which is as quaint as to its pointed gables, oval windows, and twisted chimnies as Uncle Horace himself, we learned from old Charity Dobson, the housekeeper, that "master was main poorly, and sometimes quite fierce-like with the gout!"

Alice and Beatrice involuntarily turned a look of dismay on me, which, however, I could not help returning with a mischievous smile.

"Well, Charles," said Alice, "I really wish papa had come with us, for I quite dread meeting this grim uncle of ours."

"And only fancy," said Beatrice, with a mysterious glance round the old hall, worthy of Emily St. Aubert herself, in the castle of Udolpho, "only fancy having to pass a whole week in this gloomy, haunted-looking place! Oh! Charles, I wish we had never come."

But by this time we had reached the door of Uncle Horace's *sanctum*, which Mistress Charity Dobson throwing open, with all that majestic dignity which always seems innate in an old single gentleman's housekeeper, announced us in a kind of *rustico-Siddonian* voice, as "Master Charlie *hand* the young ladies."

"Well, Charles, my boy," exclaimed the old gentleman, who was sitting in the most luxurious of luxurious easy chairs, his right leg supported on a gout stool, "I'm devilish glad to see you once more at Basmere Grange. And you too, girls, bless you both! why don't you come and give old nunky a kiss? for though he's a savage old dog sometimes, he never snarls at a pretty girl! Whew! whew!—this gout—this d—d gout! it'll be the death of me! Now mind, Charles—and you too, Alice—and you too, little Miss Miranda—Euphemia—what the deuce is your name?"

"Beatrice, uncle," replied the half-frightened girl.

"Well, Beatrice," said the old gentleman, "why the devil couldn't your silly mother have called you Mary or Betsy, or some such name, fit for a Christian! I hate your humbugging Adelinas, and Aramintas, and Beatrices. But let that pass, and mind, all three of you, if Sir Earnest Fitzhenry should ask you to dinner while you're here, mind you beware of turtle soup, fat venison, and punch a la Rom.—Hang it! why can't they call good things by some good old English name, that it won't split your windpipe to pronounce!"

Alice and I laughed out, and even poor little Beatrice seemed inclined that way, when Uncle Horace again broke out.

"Ah!" he exclaimed, peevishly, "you may laugh at an old man's advice, Miss Alice, but I should very much like to know what kind of a figure you think you would cut at Almack's with a leg like this! How many quadrilles would you be able to dance, I say?"

"Not many, I fear," replied Alice, laughing most heartily, "but that would not grieve me, uncle."

"Not grieve you!" repeated Uncle Horace, "what do you mean, child?—What do you go to balls for, if it's not to dance?—Why, arn't you fond of dancing?—Why, don't you go to quadrilles?—You don't mean to say, Alice Ainsworth, that you sit by [illegible] one corner of a ballroom, as Lady Grace Kingstone [illegible] to do in my day for the sake of flirting and talkin[g] rubbish with all the empty-headed Lord Johns and Honourable Williams, who may please to—"

"No, no, uncle," interrupted Alice, "but I do not see that because I am not fond of dancing quadrilles, I must be a second edition of Lady Grace Kingstone."

"Very good! very good, Miss Ainsworth!" said the old gentleman, testily, "but once for all, I do not see what in the world you go to balls for, if you are not fond of dancing."

"Oh! but I *am* fond of dancing," cried Alice, smiling.

"Why, what the deuce do you mean, Miss Ainsworth?" exclaimed Uncle Horace, working himself up into a regular pet, as a fresh twinge shot through the unfortunate leg; "just this moment you said you didn't care for quadrilles?—Did she not, Charles?—Did she not, little Lucinda—Minerva—whatever your name is?"

"She certainly did, sir," I replied, "but then my sister did not say that she disliked the mazurka, galop, or the *waltz*."

"Exactly," added Alice, beginning to fancy the old man was not quite in his right mind, "Beatrice and I are both extremely fond of waltzing; and besides, you know every one waltzes now."

"Do they; do they?" cried my uncle, convulsively grasping my arm, and gazing at me with a wild stare of agony. "Oh, God! Charles, this has quite unmanned me!"

"My dear, sir!" I exclaimed, becoming no less alarmed than Alice and Beatrice, who stood trembling by my side. "My dear uncle, let me ring for Charity—you are ill, I am sure you are!"

The old man buried his face in his handkerchief, and sobbed aloud—the deep groan-like sob of a proud, stern man.

I shall never forget how that broad, manly chest heaved with emotions not to be resisted. Poor Uncle Horace! I forgave him all his eccentricities, all his petulence, all his bachelor whims, when I saw him thus *unexpectedly*—thus wofully subdued in spirit.

After a minute or two had elapsed he again raised his head; but now we saw not the same face we had seen before. No! now all was calm, sadly calm! and there was an expression of the deepest, most profound misery in those usually quick, flashing eyes.

"My children," he murmured, in a low, broken voice, "pardon an old man's weakness;—but—but—you shall hear all by-and-bye. I cannot tell it now! Now go Charles, take your sisters into the dining-room, where you will find lunch, and after that you can amuse yourselves in the grounds. I am better alone at present."

* * * * *

The next day Uncle Horace, to account for his strange conduct, told me the following circumstances, which, however, for the sake of brevity, I shall relate in my own words:—

My mother's uncle, Horace Vivyan, was, in his young days, one of the most elegant and fascinating men about town; and besides his personal appearance, which of course captivated the *daughters*, he possessed a fortune and estates which had their due affect on the *mammas*. But Horace Vivyan flirted, danced, and sentimentalized with his eyes open, and escaped *Scot-free* all the attacks made upon his heart or fortune, inasmuch that the manœuvring Countess of J——y at last gave it as her opinion to her daughters, the Ladies Laura, Matilda, and Narcissa P——l, that they might spare themselves the trouble of trying to catch Mr. Vivyan, for he was decidedly not a *marrying man*.

But about this time, Sir Ernest Fitzhenry, an old schoolfellow of Horace Vivyan's, introduced to the world of fashion his only sister, who, as an heiress and a *debutante*, was of course immediately all the rage. But had Una Fitzhenry *not* been the sister of a wealthy baronet of ancient family, she would have been no less sought after. The sweetness of her manners, and the extreme loveliness of her person could not fail to attract admirers wherever she appeared.

I have seen a portrait of this beautiful being, which still hangs in the oak gallery at Vivyan Hall, and never shall I forget the touching beauty of those pale Grecian features, those soft dark eyes, shaded by long silken lashes, and the glossy tresses of rich brown hair braided on either side the noble forehead. There is, however, a kind of innate pensiveness in the expression of that face, as though the fair girl had already learned her early doom. But I am digressing from my narrative, which is indeed a sad one, and, as Lucentio says, in the drama of "The White Fiend"—

"A sad tale should always be short, I say;—
A merry one as long as pleases you!"

I will not detain my readers by entering into minute details concerning how Horace Vivyan loved Una Fitzhenry, and how she chose him from among the noble and great who sought her hand; and how Sir Ernest joyed to behold his earliest, dearest friend, the affianced husband of his only sister. These are pleasing themes, but ere long we must come to sadder.

Fitzhenry and Una were at Paris for the season, and Horace Vivyan had followed them there. In six months the projected marriage was to take place.

One evening there was a splendid ball, at the house of the Marquis de V——, and Sir Ernest and Una were there. Horace, who was engaged to dine with the ambassador, was to join them in the course of the evening.

The first thing which met the eyes of Vivyan, on entering the brilliant *salon*, was Una Fitzhenry, waltzing with Lord Ashley Belgrave.

At another time Horace would, of course, not have thought anything of so natural a circumstance, but now being somewhat heated with wine, he was totally unable to control the jealous feeling which had entered his heart; and there he stood, sullen and gloomy, in a corner of the *salon*, with his eyes fixed on the forms of Una and Lord Ashley, as they floated along to the enchanting sounds of the best band in Paris.

The waltz was over.

Una Fitzhenry sat down, Ashley Belgrave by her side, and they were soon enjoying a seemingly interesting conversation; at least interesting to Una, though perhaps not quite so much so to Lord Ashley; for Horace Vivyan was the subject of it. A quadrille was danced, and another waltz commenced, and still Belgrave sat beside Miss Fitzhenry.

Horace suddenly crossed the apartment to where they sat, and in a sharp, hurried manner, so unlike his usually mild, courteous style, requested, or rather demanded, Una's hand for the waltz.

"Indeed, Horace" said she, "you must excuse me. I am sadly fatigued, and not quite well this evening."

Belgrave moved away.

"It seems you were well enough to waltz with that fop," said Vivyan, angrily; "and, therefore you *shall* waltz with me."

"Now, dear Horace, pray do not press me," entreated Una. "I am very—very tired; and the room is excessively warm."

The sweet girl did indeed, look pale and fatigued; but Vivyan was too excited to notice anything of the kind, and exclaimed—

"Nonsense, Una! I will not thus be denied. You have been waltzing twice with that Ashley Belgrave, and waltz with me you *shall!*"

Una said not another word, but immediately rising, she took Horace's arm. Her hands trembled—her eyes were cast on the ground. Away they went, whirl!—whirl!—whirl!—

But suddenly Vivyan felt the form which he supported grow heavier and heavier. He stopped—and oh!—Heaven!—it was a *corpse* that he held in his arms, amid the merry waltzers.

Yes!—Una Fitzhenry was dead, and a stream of blood flowed from her pale lips down upon her white garments. A large artery about the heart had burst, and — but sad tale is already told.

* * * * * * * *

A few nights since I was at a party with my sisters at Sir Ernest Fitzhenry's. A *waltz* was playing, and Alice was the partner of Cecil Douglas—*my favorite sister, and my chosen friend*—and *engaged to be married too!*

A thrill ran through my frame, as Alice suddenly paused in the dance. Our eyes met; hers were filled with tears. I know that she was thinking of uncle Horace, and the "Waltz of Death!"

GENEVEVE; OR, THE MYSTERIES.

The parents of Geneveve were poor, industrious, honest people, and resided in a small cottage near the Black Forest, in Germany. They cultivated a small bit of land with a garden attached, which produced them many of the necessaries, if not the luxuries of life; and their highest ambition was to see their only daughter married to some respectable youth in their own sphere, who would continue the same kindness with which they had so long cherished her.

Geneveve from her youth upwards had assisted her parents in every domestic duty, and had imbibed those strict notions of order and cleanliness which so peculiarly mark the character of a rustic life, and beget in the mind those tranquil joys which nothing can subvert if unalloyed by ambition or inordinate desire. Happy and cheerful, her countenance bespoke the feeling of her heart; the rich glow of health beamed in every feature, and nought of care or anguish had yet assailed her. Scarce a shade of thought had crossed her placid brow to give that character of pensiveness so much admired by some, for her life had been one of unclouded serenity, while her laughing eye and ruby lip breathed and spoke of nought but joy and good will to all.

When the duties of the day were passed, this rustic beauty might be seen neatly and prettily dressed, seated beneath the cottage porch (around which the honeysuckle and woodbine twined and diffused their fragrance) assisting her aged mother in some lighter employ, or tending the flowers in her little garden, which were her peculiar care, and amply rewarded the trouble lavished on them; or, when some festival was to be kept, dancing with the maidens of the neighbouring hamlet to the pipe of some rural swain who sat beneath the shade of an aged tree to screen him from the glare of the setting sun. Amongst her companions, none excelled her in the dance or personal beauty, or attempted to dispute with her the palm of merit, but secretly envied that excellence which drew so many admirers, and threw their own budding charms so much into the shade, and as devoutly wished her married as her parents, that she might no longer rival them in the affections of their several admirers.

Geneveve could not be insensible to the admiration which she excited, or the preference which was always shown by the youths of the village over her companions; and, notwithstanding her numerous virtues (finding she had many hearts at her disposal, that she could enlist them in her service when she pleased, and discard them at her pleasure) she thought lightly of them, and became a coquette, flirted with all, and in the twilight of a summer's eve often might her merry laugh be heard echoing along the borders of the forest, as she strayed with some ardent suitor, who pleaded his cause in vain.

* * * *

Notwithstanding all this, however, there was one that troubled her heart a little; but he was too shy to make the first advance, and although she gave him all the encouragement her modesty would admit of, their love progressed but slowly; he saw he had many rivals to contend with, and he knew that Geneveve was in better circumstances than himself, and this disarmed him. He saw, too, that she gave him encouragement, but so she had to many; and, being poor, Guillaume feared being trifled with, or scorned.

The manly form of Guillaume was one that pleased the eye of Geneveve, but his shyness piqued her, and upon reflection she thought it would be as well that he did not make further overtures, for pride whispered that possibly she might be laughed at by her companions for making an ill-judged match, and give them secret cause to triumph over her. Again, this would satisfy the revenge of the men, as she had refused several of the handsomest and most wealthy—to say nothing of the number of hearts she had broken.

* * * * *

Geneveve was now eighteen; she had never been a dozen miles from her paternal roof, and it was with the greatest joy that she received an invitation to spend a few months with an aunt and cousins who resided at Friburg, a town in Suabia, and some miles distant from the Black Forest.

All the necessary preparations were soon completed, and after a long journey she arrived at her destination, where she was received with the greatest kindness by her relatives. Never having been in a large town before she was surprised at its magnificence—the steeple of the great church excited her admiration, while the colleges came in for their share of applause; nor was this the only source of amusement, for being an university, the number of students soon afforded her the means of gratifying the vanity which had been excited in her native village.

Her uncle was a lapidary, with which that city abounds, and here she first became acquainted with the value of the glittering ornaments that constantly displayed their polished surfaces to her dazzled sight.

Here too, the profligate students who frequently came to her uncle's shop to purchase some article of jewellery for their mistresses, would cast the bauble around her neck or head (under pretence of seeing how it looked) and at the same time would whisper some complimentary nothing into her willing ear.

Day after day the gorgeous equipages of the nobility rolled through the city, and she gazed upon the beauty and richness of the liveries; she lamented for the first time that she had not a carriage; or, as some wealthy dame entered the shop, whose satin rustled as it swept the floor, she sighed deeply to think of the lowliness of her home near the Black Forest.

Her beauty soon became known, and numbers of dash-

THE BARR-BELLE.

Of all the fish that sportsmen love,
In River Lea, or well,
There's none to my mind can compare
With a gentle fair *Barr-Belle.*

THE PERCH.

'Tis not so pleasant when we sport,
To be left in the lurch;
But e'er if such should be the case,
We can always take a *perch.*

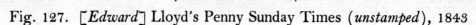

Fig. 127. [*Edward*] Lloyd's Penny Sunday Times (*unstamped*), 1843

etc. And it would seem that John Browne Bell had determined to fight the trade. The progress of the quarrel belongs to the history of journalism. By the end of the year, the paper was established in spite of the newsagents' refusal to handle it otherwise than at an increased selling price to the public. Typographically the pages of *The News of the World* are excellent.

That portion of the community known to the select committees of the House of Commons, in those days, as 'the lower classes', had neither the time nor the money to read the daily press, and could not, as they were expected, follow a *Times*' 'leader', either at home, or in the barber's shop, while their chins were being lathered on the Sunday mornings, customarily set aside for this operation. The 'lower classes' looked forward to the week-end press. *The News of the World* was no exception to a tendency which began twenty years earlier, and which was well established in *The Bell's New Weekly Messenger*. *The News of the World*, moreover, being comparatively free from advertising, depended for its income upon a mass circulation. Hence the paper embodied more and more news of interest to the increasing audience of comparatively uncritical readers brought into existence by a rapidly expanding industrialism. In fact, the Sunday reading public of the London market had been expanding for some years. There had been innumerable radical unstamped papers which led the possessing classes to feel that the abolition of the newspaper tax would mean the instantaneous multiplication of seditious journalism. So far as *The News of the World* was concerned, no such objection could be made. Although much space was given to murders and crime of every kind, the paper was less Radical than *The Weekly Dispatch* of twenty years earlier.

The News of the World, though radical, did not intend to antagonise the opposite sentiment. It had to succeed upon the broadest possible basis, upon its low price, and upon its comprehensiveness. Throughout its founder's life, the paper was printed, if not handsomely, straightforwardly, with accuracy and clearness. The first heading, a poor but flamboyant design, differs only slightly from that of the present paper. Its design was without precedent—and without progeny. The ornamental lettering on a waved ribbon has been slightly simplified, but the style is still what it was in 1843, namely, a common sign-writer's lettering such as would have been familiar to the patrons of the old London music halls. It may be seen occasionally today on the side of pantechnicons or a circus van. If the design of the title was poor, it cannot be denied that it was apt. It could be understanded of the people. The paper itself was unquestionably a benefit to everybody. Even the

THE PENNY

Sunday Times, AND PEOPLES' POLICE GAZETTE.

No. 2. LONDON:—SUNDAY, APRIL 12, 1840.

Police.

BOW STREET.

A LAWYER BIT.

MARLBOROUGH STREET.

THE INQUEST AT THE BARNSBURY CASTLE.

THE LATE MR. TEMPLEMAN RECEIVING THE MONEY FROM HIS TENANT ON THE DAY OF HIS MURDER.

MRS. TEMPLEMAN SEEKING PERMISSION TO VIEW THE REMAINS OF HER MURDERED HUSBAND.

HATTON GARDEN.

UNION HALL.

WONDERFUL DISCOVERY OF MURDER.

MELANCHOLY LOSS OF LIFE.

DREADFUL ACCIDENT TO AN OFFICER.

Fragments for the Curious.

TO PITY.

Fig. 128. [*Edward Lloyd's*] The Penny Sunday Times, *an unstamped Sunday paper*

Government must have been pleased that the provision of such a tremendous three penn'orth should drive out the illegal unstamped penny papers which had been multiplying in London for years, and which, when driven out of London, were printed in Birmingham and Liverpool in increasing numbers. These penny papers caused great scandal to the authorities, who were compelled to equip the Stamp Office with a special staff of detectives to hunt them down. *The Penny Satirist* (No. 1, April 22, 1837) had for sub-title the description that it was 'A cheap substitute for a weekly newspaper'. The names and formats of established papers were imitated without scruple. *The Penny Weekly Dispatch* (J. S. Frampton, 1840) and *Clark's Weekly Dispatch* (1841) were both tantamount to copies of Bell's paper of that name. *The Penny Sunday Times, and Peoples' Police Gazette*[1] was more original in form. The title of *Bell's Penny Dispatch. Sporting and Police Gazette, and Newspaper of Romance, and Penny Sunday Chronicle* (1842) adequately explains itself.

All such papers were four-page folios carrying, on the upper half of the front page, a wood engraving of an average size of 8 in. × 6½ in. The subject of the cut was generally a topical one, such as the court scene of a murder trial, or, in default, a romantic design, e.g. of a 'daring conspiracy and attempted violation'. The first page of No. 179 of *Lloyd's Penny Sunday Times* prints a striking cut of Horace Vivyan discovering Una Fitzhenry conversing with Lord Ashley Belgrave—an episode in its serial story entitled "The Waltz of Death".

Another tribute, by imitation, to the prestige of *The Weekly Dispatch* came from *Comic News: A Droll Dispatch and New Weekly Messenger of Fun*, whose heading reproduced the floral centre-piece which the Sunday paper had used for a quarter of a century.

These, with other unstamped papers considered subversive, were driven out of existence by the miraculous cheapness of such a paper as *The News of the World*. This paper long maintained its success. It incorporated the *Bell's New Weekly Messenger* in March 1855 for the obvious reason that the newcomer at 3*d*. was bound to attack the position of dearer papers. Three months later, John Browne Bell died; but *The News of the World* continued successfully for some time, and, like the other Sunday papers, gradually adjusted its setting to the orthodox morning paper standards.

Edward Lloyd came into prominence as a publisher in connection with a work entitled *The Penny Pickwick* which was edited by 'Bos' and illustrated

[1] Later (from No. 174, August 14, 1842) entitled *Lloyd's Penny Sunday Times*, etc.

CLARK'S

WEEKLY DISPATCH.

SUNDAY, SEPTEMBER 12, 1841.

No. 17. PRINTED AND PUBLISHED BY W. M. CLARK, 17, WARWICK-LANE, LONDON. Price 1d.

A GHOST STORY OF OLD TIMES.

(From the German of Baron A. Von Sternberg.)

(Continued.)

At the termination of the thirty years' war, the narrator began, the family of the Counts of Hohen Rolandseck possessed this memorial castle; there are still extant, documents, signed by the Imperial Generalissimo, securing this possession to the noble family, with the remark—"For special services rendered to the Imperial House."

There were some, however, in those days, who asserted, that the Duke of Friedland had found a certain Count Von Hohen Rolandseck so serviceable to his ambitious schemes, that the clause should have run—"For treason to the Emperor," &c. Be that as it may, certain it is, the counts were true and admiring adherents of the duke; and, on the occasion of his subsequent sudden death at Eger, privately pursued his murderers to the death. As ill luck would have it, a certain Count Von Hoya was also named amongst those who had conspired against the life of the duke, in chastisement for his treason. This circumstance caused the most vehement rupture between the kindred lines of Hoya and Rolandseck, and made them vow eternal hatred to each other.

It may be easily imagined that, in those wild and stormy times, in which the national strife, descending into the affairs of private life, subdivided itself into all sorts of family feuds, and in which the most multifarious interests were at mortal issue; that, in those times, the gentle voices of nature and of love must have been smothered and ineffectual in the discordant din. Bohemia was overrun by foreign troops, after the death of her ambitious and sumptuous prince; devastated by her own children; her national unity almost extinguished; while, on every side, appeared aspiring princes, numbering counts and barons in their party: and thus it came to pass, that the two hostile cousins adopted the cause of different leaders, and stood opposed in open warfare to each other.

Now old stories love to tell how the children's love counteracts the rancour of the parents: and so it was here. The particulars of this amour have escaped my memory; but, assuredly, it was as enthusiastic and glowing as ever could have been the loves of *Romeo* and *Juliet*. The young Count Von Hoya, as long as he lay with his regiment at Prague, found a thousand ways and means to come here to this castle, with his faithful 'squire; sometimes disguised as Bohemian jugglers, sometimes as Hungarian soothsayers, sometimes even as gipsies; but the Lady Elizabeth was, according to the manner of those times, watched with conventual strictness; and she could do nothing but cast glances at her lover, when opportunity allowed; or, at most, make him furtive signs. A scanty nurture this, but still a nurture for their love, which grew even stronger and stronger upon it, till it wholly ruled the two young hearts, and prepared them to brave, unflinchingly, all that humanity shrinks appalled from.

The Count was ordered to quit Prague: he was to [illegible] the enemy, and knew not whether he should ever again behold the blue eyes of his beloved. He resolved, though it should cost him his life, to spend, at least, one uninterrupted hour with his Eliza; and, to effect this, he devised a strange and fearful plan. Just then there had died in this castle a female relation of the family, who was yet young, and had been abbess of a neighbouring convent. The corpse had been laid out in the hall yonder; but as she had died of a pestilential malady, it was carried hither to this isolated tower, and even the watchers, usual on such occasions, were dispensed with. All that had life in the castle fled that chamber, where only the corpse lay with its lonely-burning taper: nought but the death-bell above her smote, with its mournful sounds, the ear of midnight.

Dark rumours whispered that, in the hours when sleep is deepest, the chamber was filled with forms pertaining to another world. Love shrinks before no horrors: through the long and lonely passages, when all were asleep, stole Elizabeth's rapid step; up the rugged walls clambered the bold youth, and, in presence of the corpse, sounded the whispers and the kisses of ecstatic loves. When the hour of parting arrived, the maiden was broken-hearted; she assented to her lover's proposal to quit with him, for ever, the home of her parents. The youth clasped her in his arms with a burning kiss. "But a few hours more, and thou art mine," he whispered: "Elizabeth! if thou couldst deceive me; if thou shouldst fail to appear when I fix the helpful ladder to-morrow, at midnight!"

"I will come," cried the excited girl: "though my mother lie dying, I will quit her and come to thee; sooner will this corpse rise to life than I break my oath to thee."

"Enough!" said the youth, shuddering at the words of her vow: "I trust thee."

A gloomy morning succeeded this night; storm followed storm; the thunder resounded in the sullen hills, repeated a thousand-fold by the echoes; the rain poured down in torrents, and darkness fell earlier than usual upon the earth.

At twelve that night a travelling-carriage stopped at the entrance of the park; and two muffled men made their way, softly, towards the tower, from which the lights shone; applied a ladder to it, and cautiously ascended. No star shone from above; the storm swept in deep-toned gusts round the old walls; the clock struck twelve; the climber softly opened the well-known window, and, lo! wrapt in her veil, stood the loved one, close before him; he threw his strong arm round her, and descended the ladder with his prize. With hasty steps he thought to return to the carriage; but it seemed as if the locality had been transformed; seek as he would, no carriage was to be seen, and the path was lost in wild tangled thickets. The unfortunate youth laboured through, till his breath failed him, but in vain. The thick darkness prevented his recognizing any object; it was to no purpose that he shouted out his servant's name; all around him was dark and silent as the grave. His strength threatened to fail him, he sank on his knees, and, bending over her, he sought to inspire his beloved with a confidence he did not himself possess. But she gave him, in return, no sign of life; he sought her lips—they were closed and cold. He kissed her eyes—they were shut, and deep in their sockets. A fearful apprehension came over him: just then the castle clock struck one; with the sound appeared lights, and his servant approached him with a torch. The first thing the Count did was to hold the light to the countenance of his fainting mistress; but, hardly had he done so, when, with a dull cry of horror, he fell to the ground.

In the night when this occurred, all was confusion and dismay in the castle. Elizabeth had been seized with a sudden attack of illness: as it struck twelve she lay insensible on her bed, the physician, her parents, and her brothers and sisters, around her. She awoke in the wildest delirium, struggled forcibly from her bed, and with maniac eyes fixed upon the window, she screamed, in a voice that pierced the souls of the hearers with dread, "Look, look! there he stands! he is waiting for me! I have sworn to him! fearful oaths have I sworn, to follow him! See how he beckons with his bare skull! how he raises his withered and bleached dead hand through the black sky! Let me out!"

As the first beams of morning shone through the closed curtains, she lay cold and dead. The following night she lay in the place of the buried nun, in the tower chamber. The young Count was never again seen in the vicinity of the castle: it is said he died mad.

Shuddering vehemently, the narrator here broke off, buttoned his coat closer round him, and cast a sombre look upon the ground. The Count, who had listened attentively, now said—"Is your story done?"

"Not yet," replied the stranger, in a hollow voice; "the sentence is still to be told: we were condemned, for our guilty enterprise, to find no rest in the grave, until—"

"What!" cried the Count, starting back upon his seat. —"Who are you, sir?"

The stranger smiled, with averted face. "I have so possessed myself with this story, and recounted it so often, that it sometimes really seems to me that I am recounting my own history."

Count Alexander forced himself to laugh, but in reality felt anything but an inclination to do so. A pause ensued: both sat still; the stranger with his face still turned away. At last, to break the silence, the Count threw out a few remarks on fear of ghosts.

The stranger made some reply, the meaning of which the Count did not catch; then rose, and turned to depart.

"Stop!" cried the Count; "one question more: I interrupted you as you were about to name the conditions on which the unhappy souls may be set at rest."

"This is no other than that two lovers of the respective races should watch for one night together in the tower over our heads."

"Nothing more!" said the Count, cutting a flourish with his cane; "how gladly would I take upon me to appease the shade of my venerable ancestor, but, unfortunately, I want the main thing for the purpose—a mistress. I have no mind, for the sake of securing his repose, to forego my own. It would be a sorry exchange."

The stranger smiled, made a slight bow, and withdrew.

The Count looked after him, and noticed how the faded black velvet coat he wore had the nap pressed flat on the back, and was marked all over with yellowish creases, as if its proprietor had [illegible] Count hurried out of the shade, and was glad at heart when he found himself again in the clear sunshine, and only heard from a distance the rustling of the pines.

At dinner, he burned with impatience to relate his adventure; but, just as if on purpose, it happened on this day that the Countess Elizabeth was slow in making her appearance. He asked after her, and her mother apologized for her: he asked a second time, and this was a cordial to the Dowager's heart: lastly, he asked a third time —such a phenomenon had never before occurred; the Countess could not conceal her joy. At length the young Countess entered. She had this day, whether from caprice or for want of something to do, devoted more than usual care to her toilet, and was really as elegant and finished a figure as ever the sun looked down on, amongst the fair promenaders of the Prater. Her cousin now came out with his ghost tale, piping hot; delivered it, with an animation and feeling never before witnessed in his style of narration; and, in conclusion, failed not accurately to describe the extraordinary stranger. The ladies were filled with wonder; there was no end to their conjectures and discussions respecting this mysterious visitor; and all this while the Castellan rubbed his hands with a chuckle of secret satisfaction.

"I see," said the delighted old gentleman, in reply to a question from the Dowager Countess, "that the notices I have had inserted in several papers have produced their effect. Strangers—strangers whom we so long hope—there they go, walking about the castle garden; and story-telling strangers, too—an excellent kind, now nearly extinct, since it is grown the fashion to plod through the world in mute and brown study-like profundity."

"Mute!" cried the Count; "I wish my stranger had been mute; but he talked such a deal of strange and bewildering matter, I was downright uncomfortable, I assure you. I have him this moment before my eye, as he walked off with his long back as straight and stiff as a ramrod, like a corpse long cold in the grave."

"Oh, hush! what a figure!" cried the young Countess, with both her little hands before her eyes.

The Castellan again chuckled, and rubbed his hands.

"Well," said the Dowager, "what do you know of this matter?"

"Please your worship, I know the stranger: he is the Advocate Ulrich, son of the clergyman in the next town. Every child knows him and his threadbare black coat."

The Count rewarded this explanation with an ugly look: it was very mortifying to have this prosaic Advocate thrust into his adventure, to the great discomfiture of its romance.

The shrewd Castellan perceived his mistake, and to repair it, hastened to subjoin—"For the rest, it is very true that a part of the castle, and especially the tower-chamber, is haunted."

"Have you ever seen anything?" said the Dowager.

"Nothing, my lady."

"Then how did you know it?"

"My niece, a girl of twelve years, tells me that her aunt had it from her grandmother, and that her step-father's sister—"

"Oh, for pity's sake, Castellan, let us have no more of this story."

"For my part," said the Countess Elizabeth, "so little timorous am I, that I declare myself quite ready and willing to offer one sleepless night to the repose of my good ancestress."

"If you will accept me as your companion," cried the Count, eagerly, "I am quite ready, for the sake of my worthy ancestor."

The Dowager made a slight sign to her daughter.

"No," said the young Countess, sharply, and playing with her plate; "I have no idea of imposing on you the part of a lover."

[illegible] turning his dark eyes full upon her.

"You are too good," said the young beauty, laughing; "when such a bold deed is to be done, thank my stars, I need not be at a loss for a gallant knight; if I rightly interpret, for instance, the obliging glance our worthy Castellan this moment bestows upon me."

"Your ladyship"—stammered forth the modest and glorified Castellan.

The Count burst into a loud laugh. "Capital!" he exclaimed; "I will fall in, too, with the exchange: you choose the Castellan, and I will kneel to his good lady. The only question is, whether the ghost can be satisfied in a lawful way by two lovers whose passion rests on so unlawful a foundation."

The Dowager put an end to the conversation: in her heart, however, she resolved not to let this godsend of a ghost-story fall to the ground. She looked upon it as an innocent pastime, which yet, rightly directed, might lead to a substantial and desirable result. "It would really be curious," she thought to herself, "if fear should generate love; and if a ghost should reach the point after which the author of the fair 'Clarissa' has striven in vain." But is not love, too, a strange unearthly apparition? she might have added, had not not such a thought tended to lead her far from her purpose.

(To be continued.)

A SLIGHT MISTAKE.

CLERK.—Let us sing the 9th Hymn, uncommon measure.

"If I had a donkey vot vouldn't go—"

Oh! dear me! here's a go! If I haven't pulled out the *Pocket Songster* instead of the Hymn Book!

BONAPARTISM.—A courtier of the imperial regime, conversing with some ladies who obstinately refused to share his admiration for the emperor, expressed his overflowing zeal in rather a novel manner. "Ladies," said he, "I have such perfect confidence in the emperor, that were he to call me knave, I might at first humbly remonstrate; but were he a second time to say, with an air of conviction, 'I assure thee, thou art a knave!'—as I am a man of honour, I would take his majesty's word for it!"

THE PARISIAN BARBER'S BOY.

There was once a gentleman in Paris, who was the terror of all the barbers' boys, as one whom it was next to impossible to shave, and who was yet so extremely fastidious about his beard, that he would have killed any barber who left a single hair standing on his chin. As he paid largely, the master barber whom he generally employed was anxious to keep his custom. But then he could scarcely get a garçon who had a heart stout enough to encounter a task which threatened such consequences. A Gascon at length presented himself, who, being informed of the great difficulty of the business, and the wrath which the gentleman generally fell into on being ill-shaved, declared lustily that, though he were the devil himself, he would not be afraid to try his hand upon him. He went to the gentleman, who, opening his great eyes upon him, saw a man of good stature, and who had all the appearance of one who had seen much of the world. Indeed, the gentleman was a good deal struck at first with the mien and countenance of the Gascon.

"My good fellow," said he, "are you aware that I am very ill to shave?"

"Oh, yes," said the Gascon readily; "but I also know that I am a thousand times more expert than you are difficult."

So, without giving his customer time to think further, he applied the napkin to his neck, laid his razors on the table, and began to shave with such exquisite nicety that the patient scarcely felt him touch the skin. From time to time he [illegible] and raised his eyes to heaven, [illegible] work.

The gentleman was surprised at his conduct, and asked what a prayer to God should signify in shaving.

"A prayer," said the pious barber, "is a good thing at all times."

"Very true," said the gentleman bluntly; "but I wish you would remit your prayer till another time."

"No time so good," said the Gascon, "as when one feels he has need of it."

"How," cried the gentleman, more bluntly still; "how can there be need for praying just now?"

"If you really wish me to tell you," said the shaver, "I will. It is because I feel at this moment a temptation which I can scarcely get the better of—a temptation to cut your throat."

"The devil!" exclaimed the patient; "a temptation to cut my throat!" and his colour rose to a pitch unexampled on even that fiery countenance. "Get you gone, you rascal, if you do not wish to be thrown over the window."

"Softly, softly," said the Gascon, with great coolness; "I have overcome the temptation, and will now proceed with my work without more disturbance."

"You scoundrel!" cried the shaver, his rage still increasing; "begone, if you wish to save your life."

The Gascon only replied with greater coolness than before, "I am not afraid of you; if I pleased, I could shave you in spite of yourself. But what signifies it after all? If you wish to have only the half of your beard done, I bid you good day."

The gentleman was actually so much subdued by the firmness of the man, as to permit him to depart with the last word.

When the Gascon got back to the shop, he said to his master, "You told me that this gentleman would storm if a single hair was left on his visage; I found him quite in another humour to-day; he has made me leave half of his beard unshaven."

RUNNING A MUCK.

One of the greatest objections in India is the almost certainty of every young man forming those *liaisons* which are not only dangerous in a moral point of view, but often destructive in our worldly career. Encouraged by example, shut out by the more refined society of European ladies, without a hope of marrying, and unchecked by the laws of society, the young soldier or civilian in India, stationed in some dreary spot, removed from the awe which the presence of virtuous females inspires, is apt to form a connexion as revolting to European taste as opposed to every moral precept.

Mr. A—— was unmarried, young, and handsome; he had won and carried off a lovely girl of sixteen (that is to say, if loveliness can be imagined with a dark skin). He had lived with her about three years, and had by her two children, whom he in after-life acknowledged and cherished. In him the act was wrong; in her it was excusable, since the form of marriage, the mere thought of such a thing, had never entered her head; her very parents were proud of the honour done her; her rude ignorance blotted out the blame that would otherwise have attached to her: while the only excuse he could offer for the seduction of a mere child was the force of example —the custom of the country.

Ayah (so will I call her) was in the bath with her two little babes, amused with their infantine screams, as they nestled closer to her bosom, and shunned the water she occasionally immersed them in: her brother held a post in the house; her sister was her companion; her father held the situation of porter in the outer lodge-gate.

The first of these was a religious enthusiast; he had been wrought on by certain Brahmins; he had committed many faults; he determined at once to expiate them. One way only is thought by the pious Malay to lead straight to heaven, and on this he resolved; he offered up his prayers, performed his ablutions, and prepared to run a muck.

The fanatic who thus determines, first vows to his God to destroy every living thing he may meet on his path; to spare neither sex nor relationship, to turn neither to the right nor the left, but to sacrifice all indiscriminately, till he himself in turn be sacrificed. He first proceeds to oil his body all over to elude capture as long as possible (for the more victims he makes, the more certain is his road to heaven); he casts off everything that may be caught at; shaves his head, lest he should be seized by the hair; takes a large potion of opium, or some other maddening poison; then arming himself with a knife or creese in either hand, he rushes forth to immolate all he may encounter.

Ayah was leaving the bathing-room, with her children in her arms, her sister and attendants were following her, laughing and playing with her little babes; a more innocent, a more happy group could not have been found. They were already in the passage, when a sudden noise made the young mother turn round; in another instant she fell a corpse, struck down by her own brother—that brother she had loved so tenderly. A single blow had nearly severed her head from her body, and as she fell the blood gushed over the unconscious little ones that fondled in her bleeding breast; a scream burst from all, as the madman bounded away, triumphing in the act. He fled along the passage; an old bearer met him—in less than time for thought his head was nearly split in two, and his grey beard deluged in blood. The surviving sister rushed after him to stay him in his wild career; he repulsed her; turned to look at her for an instant; he hesitated—he doubtless repented? No, he paused but to make his aim more sure; the creese he carried in his left hand was buried in her breast; he smiled as an exulting demon, and rushed on; the alarm was given; a general pursuit took place without effect; the porter was called to close the gates; he came out, and saw his infuriated son; he read his purpose; he hesitated for a moment, and as the parricide sprang towards him, the father stepped back and discharged the contents of his musket into the heart of his child, who, quivering, fell, still grinning in diabolical agony: he died at the foot of him who gave him birth, impotently attempting still to strike those who dared not approach to succour him.

One of the two bereaved children, fostered by the generous woman who afterwards married their father, died in action, a major in the British army; the other was for a short period the beauty of Dublin; but, unfortunately, after a masquerade at Lady B.'s, where she had gone, dressed as a Sultana, she imprudently washed her face with cold water, and a few hours afterwards was a corpse. —*Bentley's Miscellany.*

EASTERLY WINDS.—The late Mr. Hall, author of the "Crazy Tales," notwithstanding all his wit and humour, was often oppressed with very unpleasant hypochondriac affections. In one of these fits, at Skelton Castle, in Yorkshire, he kept his chamber, talked of death and the *east* winds in synonymous terms, and could not be persuaded by his friends to mount his horse, and dissipate his blue demons by air and exercise. Mr. Sterne, who was at this time one of his visitants, finding that no reasons could prevail against the fancies of his friend, bribed an active boy to scale the turret of the castle, turn the weathercock due [illegible] rose from his bed as usual, oppressed and unhappy, when casting his eyes through a bay-window to the turret, and seeing the wind due west, he immediately joined his company at breakfast, ordered his horse to be saddled, and enlivened the morning's ride with his facetious humour, execrating *easterly* winds, and launching forth in praise of western breezes. This continued for three or four days, till, unfortunately the cord breaking which fastened the weathercock, it returned at once to the easterly position, and Mr. Hall retreated to his chamber, without having the least suspicion of the trick which his cousin Shandy had played upon him.

CONVERSION OF RAGS INTO SUGAR!—Dr. Volgel, Member of the Royal Academy of Sciences, has submitted to a careful examination in the Laboratory of the Academy of Munich the surprising discovery of Braconnet, of Nancy, of the effects of concentrated sulphuric acid on wood and linen. He has not only fully confirmed this discovery, but also extended his own experiments, with equal success, to other similar vegetable substances, such as old paper, both printed and written upon, and cut straw. By diluting the sulphuric acid with a due addition of water, saw-dust, cut linen, paper, &c. were converted into gum and saccharine matter. It must excite great interest in reflecting minds, to see an indissoluble tasteless substance, like the filaments of wood, converted, by chemical reaction, into new bodies; and chemistry thus exercise a power, which, till lately, appeared to belong to nature alone, and in particular to vegetation. For this artificial formation of sugar and gum, now discovered, must not be confounded with the extraction of these two substances from bodies in which they already existed, a process which has been known from time immemorial. What has now been discovered, is a transformation—a metamorphosis, of which the most ingenious chemist had previously no idea; and it affords a new proof of the boundless extent of the domain of practical chemistry.

Fig. 129. [*W. M.*] Clark's Weekly Dispatch

BELL'S

PENNY DISPATCH.

SPORTING AND POLICE GAZETTE, AND NEWSPAPER OF ROMANCE,

AND

PENNY SUNDAY CHRONICLE.

No. 66. SUNDAY, FEBRUARY 27, 1842. PENNY.

DARING CONSPIRACY — ATTEMPTED VIOLATION.

([illegible], 1841.)

(See plate.)

In the *Globe* of Tuesday appears the following, under the head of "Paris":—

A curious circumstance lately occured here in one of the principal hotels. A party, consisting of an English nobleman and his wife, a gentleman of some fortune and his wife, a gentleman who has been living in considerable style at the west end of London, and a young lady of beauty and fortune in the West of England, were all residing in the house. The young lady had accompanied the married ladies alluded to to Paris, and had been enjoying all the gaities of this gay city. The unmarried gentleman already noticed had paid his addresses to the young lady before their arrival here, although unsuccessfully, and was busy in renewing his protestations. All on a sudden, however, a few mornings ago the whole hotel were roused out of their beds by the shrieks of the young lady, who immediately charged the gentleman alluded to with an attempt to violate her person by entering her bedroom. The greatest ferment reigned over the whole establishment until the following morning, when the young lady sought the advice of the Ambassador. A challenge was sent by a friend of the young lady to the offender, who immediately produced a note, as he represented, written to him by her, inviting him to come to her bed-room on the night in question; and to such a degree had the culprit imposed on her friends seeking satisfaction, that they were led to believe that she had really been guilty; and it is said that the Ambassador concurred in the advice which had been given by her friends, namely, that she should at once marry the gentleman, her former suitor. To this she most resolutely replied, she would sooner die; that the letter was a forgery, and that no power on earth could prevent her from going home and consulting with her family on this affair, so serious to her character. She left for London, and on the day she left it was accidentally discovered in *Galignani* that the gentleman who intruded himself into the lady's room had been declared a bankrupt as a broker in the city. Finding himself blown on, he immediately repaired to the Ambassadors, asked for a fresh passport, and was actually on his way to Belgium when arrested on a charge of fraud on the police. He was sent to the prison La Force, where we believe he is at present. No idea can be formed of the great excitement amongst the English in Paris about this most extraordinary affair. There are a great many awkward rumours afloat on the subject which I will refrain from giving, as doubtless the affair will undergo some farther investigation.

In explanation of the above we have been furnished with the following statement, from a correspondent, on whose veracity we can place the utmost reliance:—

A person well known, of the name of Douglas, a "Captain" by courtesy, and his wife were at Exeter, where they became acquainted with a Miss H———, a young lady of large fortune, a native of Devonshire, who resided in that city. Douglas, actuated by the most philanthropic motives, on ascertaining that she had the control of her property, lost no time in looking about for some respectable man to whom he might introduce her—with, of course, a view to ulterior benefit to himself. He at length found, in the person of Mr. George Berkeley [illegible]

DARING CONSPIRACY AND ATTEMPTED VIOLATION.

[illegible]

The marriage of Charles Kean with Miss Tree has led some people to compare the bridegroom to Charles the Second after the Battle of Worcester. Why, may be readily guessed by our readers, who bear in mind the monarch's adventures in the oak tree.

THE GREEN MAN.

BY M. JULES JANIN.

CHAPTER I.

[illegible]

CHAPTER II.

[illegible]

Fig. 130

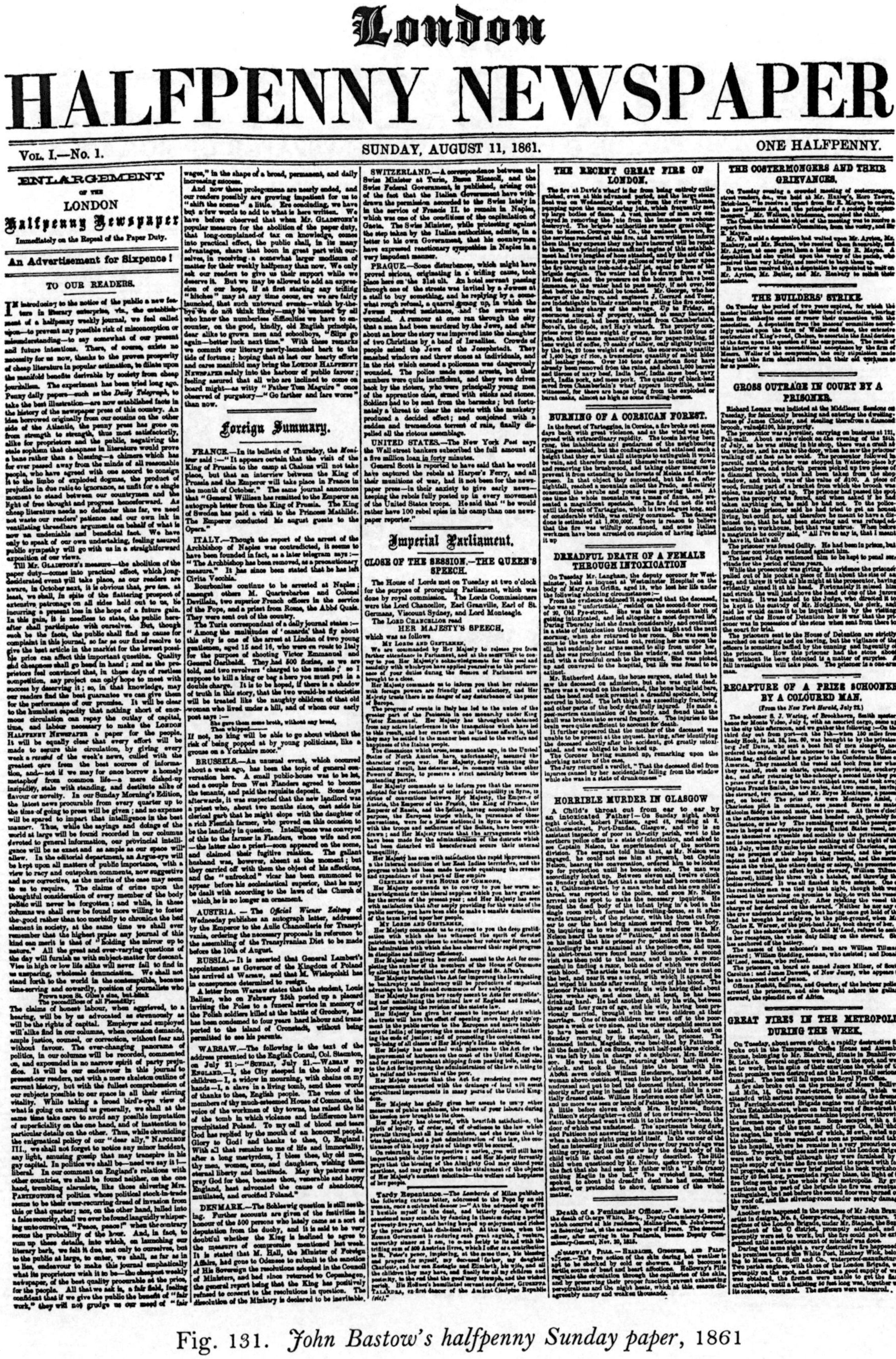
London
HALFPENNY NEWSPAPER

VOL. I.—No. 1. SUNDAY, AUGUST 11, 1861. ONE HALFPENNY.

ENLARGEMENT OF THE LONDON Halfpenny Newspaper Immediately on the Repeal of the Paper Duty.

An Advertisement for Sixpence!

TO OUR READERS.

Foreign Summary.

Imperial Parliament.

CLOSE OF THE SESSION.—THE QUEEN'S SPEECH.

HER MAJESTY'S SPEECH.

THE RECENT GREAT FIRE OF LONDON.

BURNING OF A CORSICAN FOREST.

DREADFUL DEATH OF A FEMALE THROUGH INTOXICATION

HORRIBLE MURDER IN GLASGOW

THE COSTERMONGERS AND THEIR GRIEVANCES.

THE BUILDERS' STRIKE.

GROSS OUTRAGE IN COURT BY A PRISONER.

RECAPTURE OF A PRIZE SCHOONER BY A COLOURED MAN.

GREAT FIRES IN THE METROPOLIS DURING THE WEEK.

Fig. 131. *John Bastow's halfpenny Sunday paper*, 1861

by 'Phis'. Tupman was Tupnall, Snodgrass, Snodgreen. Dickens brought an unsuccessful action and the parties were reconciled. Lloyd, after publishing *The Penny Sunday Times* brought out in the year (1842) of the foundation of *The Illustrated London News* his own paper entitled *Lloyd's Illustrated London Newspaper* at the price of twopence, stamped. The first issue was dated November 27, 1842. With the eighth number, the illustrations were dropped, the size of the paper reduced, and the title changed to *Lloyd's Weekly London Newspaper*, later abbreviated to *Lloyd's Weekly News*, under which title the paper continued until recent years.[1] *Lloyd's Penny Sunday Times*, Figs. 127 and 128, was continued until 1844, when it was apparent that *Lloyd's Weekly* was a success.

In 1860 John Bastow brought out *The Penny Newsman and Sunday Morning Mail and Telegraph* as a penny paper—with excellent bold egyptian headings[2] in the old style of *The Weekly Dispatch*. Though the venture did not have any particular success, it had the effect of reducing the price of the other Sunday papers to 1*d*.

Reynolds's Weekly Newspaper, 'A Journal of Democratic Progress and General Intelligence', began publication on Sunday, May 5, 1850. Like *The News of the World*, it was printed in blanket folio, six columns to each of its eight pages; and, again like its predecessors, it gave much space but little love for parsons. The paper carried small fat-egyptian headlines and, on occasions larger (12-point appearing) lines in clarendon. The price of *Reynolds's*, originally 4*d*., went to 5*d*., and back to 3*d*. in 1855.

The next development was the same publisher's reconstruction of his previous foundation into a new sheet of four large pages, with headlines in bold type, entitled the *London Halfpenny Newspaper*. This journal, the first of the halfpenny papers, ante-dating *The Echo* by some seven years, had a brief career. I have succeeded in tracing only four issues, of which the first is dated August 11, 1861. The paper made a point of taking advertisements at the price of 16 records for sixpence.

The important Sunday papers of the period, in growing out of their popular origins, had abandoned bold headlines. The *London Halfpenny News-*

[1] The biography of Edward Lloyd in the *D.N.B.* needs correction from the account by the editor, Thomas Catling, in *Lloyd's Weekly News*, November 30, 1902.

[2] The text was in the usual modern face. A note over the leader reads: 'Good News! Glorious News!! The present number of THE PENNY NEWSMAN IS SET UP IN NEW TYPE cast at the celebrated Foundry of H. W. Caslon and Co., Chiswell Street, and is printed on the new and fast perfecting machines erected for the purpose by Messrs Bradbury & Evans of Blackfriars.'

paper is the last attempt to maintain the old tradition set up by *The Weekly Dispatch* forty years before. The task of developing the clearly visible headline was thus resigned—and in favour, as we shall see in the next lecture, of the popular halfpenny evening press.

CHAPTER XIV

THE MID-VICTORIAN PENNY AND HALFPENNY PAPERS

1855–1881

The Daily Telegraph	1855
The Pall Mall Gazette	1865
The Echo	1868
The St James's Gazette	1880
The Evening News	1881

CHAPTER XIV

THE MID-VICTORIAN PENNY AND HALFPENNY PAPERS

1855–1881

THE total abolition of the so-called taxes on knowledge entirely altered the economics of newspaper distribution. So slow was time, in the newspaper offices of the period, that the emancipation did not, for many years, affect the appearance of any other paper than the *Daily Telegraph and Courier*. Everything, from the point of view of the student of typographical arrangement, went on precisely as before, and for reasons which are clearer now than they were then.

In the seventeenth and for the first half or more of the eighteenth century, the newspapers were under the control of men who were nothing if not printers. During the nineteenth century they had drifted into the hands of men who were nothing if not journalists. The typographical style followed during the period in which the Stamp Act pressed most hardly, necessarily ignored the advantages of displayed headings in favour of utilising every atom of available space in favour of what was then regarded as a greater benefit, i.e. the maximum quantity of text. That the newspaper tax was the ultimate cause of the rigidity and solidity of the English daily between 1820 and 1850 may be proved by placing the London newspapers beside the contemporary New York productions. There had been no Stamp tax in the American colonies, and there was none in the early Republican period. Almost from the beginning, therefore, the American newspapers, with the greater elbow room at their command, were able to include more and larger headings in the news columns as well as in the advertising. Cobbett's *Porcupine's Gazette*, Philadelphia, 1797, carried larger heading types in its news and in its advertisements than Cobbett's *The Porcupine*, London, 1800. The stamp made the difference and did so for generations. Hence, to take an instance from the year 1857, two years after the abolition of the tax in England, the headings of *The Times* on the one hand, and *The Daily News* as a modern but *pre-abolition* foundation on the other, cannot be compared with the headings of such contemporary American journals as *The New York Herald* under James Gordon Bennett. In England the control of the news-

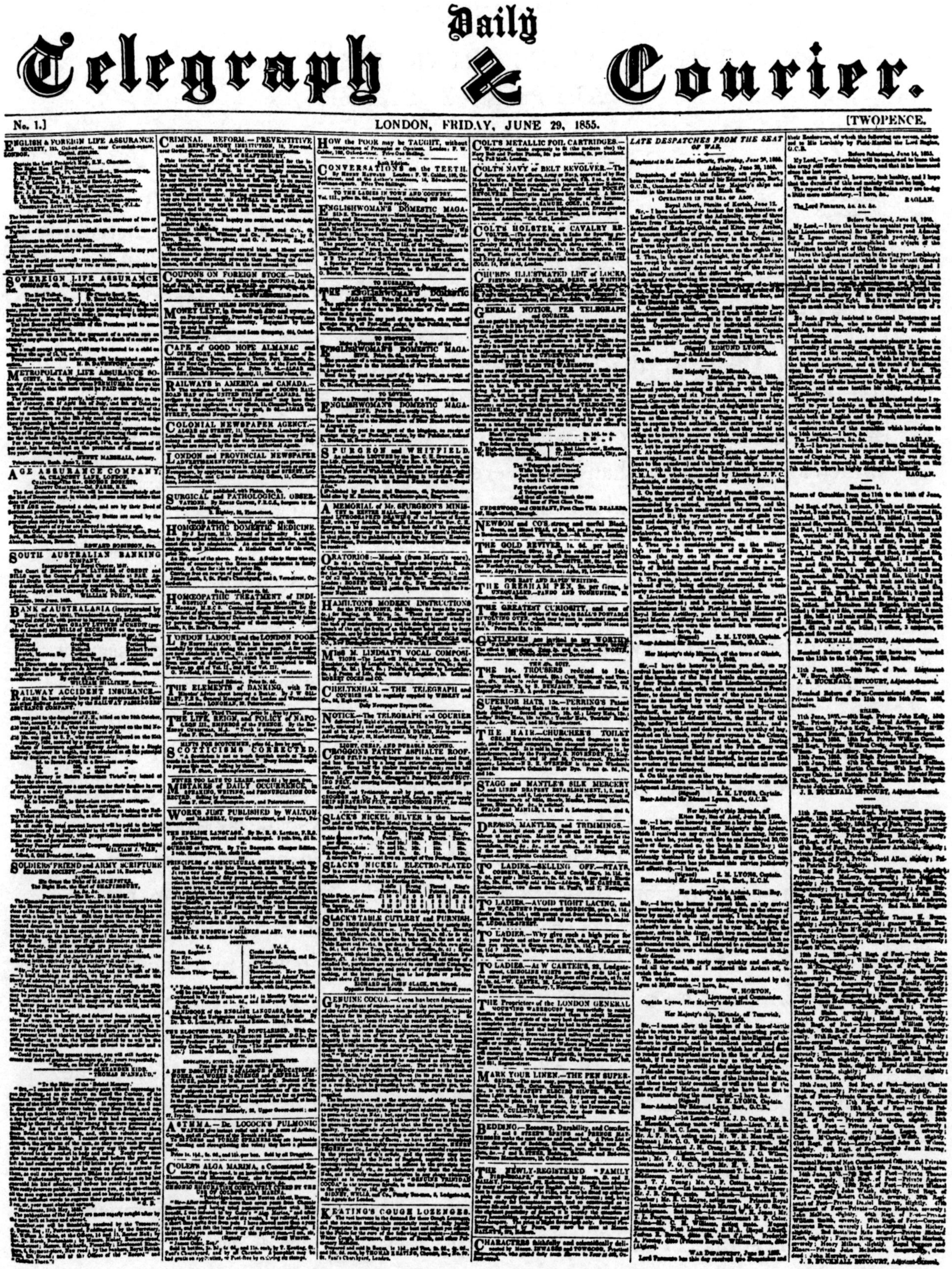

Daily Telegraph & Courier.

No. 1.] LONDON, FRIDAY, JUNE 29, 1855. [TWOPENCE.

ENGLISH & FOREIGN LIFE ASSURANCE SOCIETY

SOVEREIGN LIFE ASSURANCE COMPANY

METROPOLITAN LIFE ASSURANCE SOCIETY

AGE ASSURANCE COMPANY

SOUTH AUSTRALIAN BANKING COMPANY

BANK of AUSTRALASIA

RAILWAY ACCIDENT INSURANCE

SOLDIERS' FRIEND and ARMY SCRIPTURE READERS SOCIETY

CRIMINAL REFORM.—PREVENTITIVE and REFORMATORY INSTITUTION

COUPONS ON FOREIGN STOCK

MONEY LENT

CAPE of GOOD HOPE ALMANAC and DIRECTORY

RAILWAYS in AMERICA and CANADA

COLONIAL NEWSPAPER AGENCY

LONDON and PROVINCIAL NEWSPAPER ADVERTISEMENT OFFICE

SURGICAL and PATHOLOGICAL OBSERVATIONS

HOMŒOPATHIC DOMESTIC MEDICINE

HOMŒOPATHIC TREATMENT of INDIGESTION

LONDON LABOUR and the LONDON POOR

THE ELEMENTS of BANKING

THE LIFE, REIGN, and POLICY of NAPOLEON III

SCOTTICISMS CORRECTED

MISTAKES of DAILY OCCURRENCE

WORKS JUST PUBLISHED BY WALTON and MABERLY

ASTHMA.—Dr. LOCOCK'S PULMONIC WAFERS

HOW the POOR may be TAUGHT

CONVERSATIONS on the TEETH

ENGLISHWOMAN'S DOMESTIC MAGAZINE

SPURGEON and WHITFIELD

A MEMORIAL of Mr. SPURGEON'S MINISTRY

ORATORIOS

HAMILTON'S MODERN INSTRUCTIONS

MISS M. LINDSAY'S VOCAL COMPOSITIONS

CHELTENHAM.—THE TELEGRAPH and COURIER

NOTICE.—The TELEGRAPH and COURIER

CROGGON'S PATENT ASPHALTE ROOFING FELT

SLACK'S NICKEL SILVER

SLACK'S NICKEL ELECTRO-PLATED

SLACK'S TABLE CUTLERY and FURNISHING IRONMONGERY

GENUINE COCOA

KEATING'S COUGH LOZENGES

COLT'S METALLIC FOIL CARTRIDGES

COLT'S NAVY or BELT REVOLVER

COLT'S HOLSTER, or CAVALRY REVOLVER

CHUBB'S ILLUSTRATED LIST of LOCKS

GENERAL NOTICE, PER TELEGRAPH

NEWSOM and CO'S

THE GOLD REVIVER

THE GRESHAM PEN

THE GREATEST CURIOSITY

GENTLEMEN are invited

THE 14s. TROUSERS

SUPERIOR HATS

THE HAIR.—CHURCHER'S TOILET CREAM

STAGG and MANTLE'S SILK MERCERY

DRESSES, MANTLES, and TRIMMINGS

TO LADIES.—SELLING OFF.—STAYS

TO LADIES.—AVOID TIGHT LACING

TO LADIES.—Why give such a high price

TO LADIES.—At W. CARTER'S

THE Proprietors of the LONDON GENERAL

MARK YOUR LINEN.—THE PEN SUPERSEDED

BEDDING

THE NEWLY-REGISTERED "FAMILY

CHARACTERS faithfully and scientifically delineated

LATE DESPATCHES FROM THE SEAT OF WAR.

Fig. 132. *First heading of the* Daily Telegraph (*price 2d.*)

papers by newspaper men meant an ignorant or timid printing policy, bound up with the enforced space-saving habits of the taxation era. Provided they could get printed what they wanted to write in the manner to which they had accustomed their readers, they were not prepared to admit any but the slightest change. Even when one man backed his belief in the existence of an entirely new public, his heading technique was timid in the extreme. Indeed, there is but a very slight degree of freshness in the headlines of *The Daily Telegraph*. Lord Burnham recalls that his grandfather used to say 'I like a black paper'. As the newspaper progressed it grew blacker in its text and more reserved in its headlines. The opportunity of designing a fresh headline technique was ignored by those who liked a 'black' paper. But the early years of the paper were slightly less 'black' than the rest of the mornings, as the block (cf. Fig. 133) shews when compared with a page from *The Daily News* of 1846 (cf. Fig. 131).

The first effect of emancipation from the fetters of the Stamp Act was seen in the *Daily Telegraph and Courier* in its penny stage. Originally the *Daily Telegraph and Courier* was printed by David Aird and Edwin Tunstall for Colonel Sleigh. The first issue was dated Friday, June 29, 1855, and it gave four six-column pages for twopence. The matter was good, the paper was good, the type was good. The paper is more readable to our eye than any of its contemporaries as the type of the body is not set solid. The paper must have looked a little strange at the time, but it looked anything but 'cheap'. True, the type being large, gave less actual reading matter, but the proprietors had resolved that advertisements should be confined to the front page. Theatres were tacitly exempted from this rule, and placed in the now traditional position, directly over the leader. Telegraphed news was so indicated in a line of small capitals. There was a large running page-headline, but no other novelty than the, to that generation, unaccustomed lightness made by leading the lines. The front page title was a new, rather spectacular, but very incorrect piece of romantic blackletter, much larger in size than that of the old foundations whose headings, one and all, had been reduced during the taxation years. With No. 45 (August 20, 1855), when the paper was still twopence, the heading was simplified into one main line, *The Daily Telegraph*. With No. 57 the paper was transferred to another printer and publisher and on September 16, 1855 (No. 69), London was given its first morning paper at the sensational price of one penny.[1] A double-leaded pro-

[1] A month previously there was published the first issue of *The London Evening News*. I have not been able to find an earlier copy of this paper than that for

THE DAILY TELEGRAPH, THURSDAY, SEPTEMBER 20, 1855. 3

TO THE TRADE.

TO ADVERTISERS.

TERMS FOR ADVERTISEMENTS.

TWO LINE ADVERTISEMENTS, ONE SHILLING.

Offices: 253, STRAND, near Temple Bar.

The Daily Telegraph.

LONDON, THURSDAY, SEPT. 20.

HOW TO ESTABLISH A CHEAP PRESS.

WIFE-BEATING.

THE MARRIAGE VOW AMONGST THE WORKING CLASSES.

KING BOMBA.

ADMIRALTY TELEGRAPHIC DESPATCHES.

LOSS OF THE SHIP OF WAR WOLVERINE.

EXCHANGE OF THE HANGO OFFICERS AT ODESSA.

LATEST TELEGRAPHIC DESPATCHES.

THE EXPECTED DESPATCHES.

HEALTH OF LONDON DURING THE WEEK.

THE MURDER IN SPITALFIELDS.

ELECTION OF AN ALDERMAN.

Fig. 133. *Text page of the penny* Daily Telegraph, *September* 20, 1855 nouncement in the form of a leading article announced the change to the readers of the paper, but no trace of economising in the quality of the paper was noticeable for some time. In September, *The Daily Telegraph* was able to claim that it had 'a circulation greater than any four morning newspapers put together', making in all a figure which was only exceeded by *The Times*. 'As an advertising medium this journal stands second only to that of *The Times.*' Its policy was to attract readers unattached to other journals; it made its appeal to those whose minds and reading appetites had not been formed upon the contents and style of the older and more expensive national papers—which now profoundly despised their low-priced contemporary. It was easier for such a paper to set its important news with important-looking headlines. The Crimean news was so distinguished, but the use of large headlines did not become general throughout the paper. This is the more curious, for Mr Levy, the conductor of the paper, had an eye on New York. The early issues of *The Daily Telegraph* under his control reviewed a recent life of James Gordon Bennett; the leading article announcing the reduction to a penny adduced the example of America in general, New York in particular, and gave special mention to *The New York Herald*—price two cents. Nevertheless, although the Crimean War gave the new paper the chance to use two-, three- and even five-line headings, they did not develop into a permanent feature. The peace saw *The Daily Telegraph* preferring to relapse into the passive announcement of, rather than to proceed with the task of dramatising, its news. It became more and more orthodox as its bulk increased. In other words, the headlines of *The Daily Telegraph*, like those of the Sunday papers, became a conventional, as it became an established, property. On March 17, 1856, it went to a larger sheet of seven columns, but was unable to retain the increased size beyond June, when a notice was published that the old size was to be reinstated pending the acquisition of new machinery. The original size remained and *The Daily Telegraph* relied upon the brevity, colloquialism and wit of its writing to make its reputation. It also invented the 'Box' system, by which replies were sent to the newspaper office, and had specialised in 'Apartments to Let', 'Situations Vacant' and other popular wants and sales. These advertising successes brought *The Daily Telegraph* to a permanent eight pages for a penny from 1857. Until 1888 there was little general advance in news-display. An addition to London's cheap press

January 31, 1856. An advertisement (repeated daily in the issues for February of that year) asserts a claim to be 'the First Daily Newspaper published in London at the novel price of one Penny. Established 14 August, 1855'.

was made on the morning of March 17, 1856, by *The Morning Star*, a penny paper on orthodox lines, i.e. with a title in shadow-gothic (but it carried an eight-rayed star right and left of the text) over a front page of 'classified' advertisements each set with a two-line drop-letter initial. The body of the paper is less open than *The Daily Telegraph* but it is nevertheless clear and attractive. The headlines are in italic capitals of the body fount except those over the news received by means of the electric telegraph. The latter were headed in large display sizes of the common newspaper text fount. A companion paper, *The Evening Star*, also priced at a penny, came from the same office, in the same style, on the same day. Both survived until 1869, a year after *The Daily News* had gone to a penny. All were good examples of the classic Victorian typographical style created by, and still sponsored by, *The Times*. *The Standard*, a power in the 'seventies, conformed to the same model. During the 'eighties, formats underwent little or no change. *The Times*, *The Standard*, *The Morning Post*, *The Daily News*, *The Daily Telegraph* differed but slightly. New methods of transmission, rather than new methods of display, were agitating the staffs. There was no time in such circumstances to revise the typography of any one of these journals. The body type faces and headings which had been inherited by the post-tax generation were virtually those of 1820. *The Daily News* followed the lead of *The Daily Telegraph* and had interspaced its lines with advantage to the reader, but the heads of important despatches were clogged with small capital lines reading 'BY SUBMARINE TELEGRAPH' and 'FROM OUR OWN CORRESPONDENT'. No attempt was made to digest the text in the interest of rapid reading. In 1860, 1870 and 1880 it was still assumed that the papers were taken by earnest-minded seekers after news to whom search was part of the discipline which they readily exacted from themselves. And the assumption was that readers were interested above all in political news, political speeches and political leading articles. The vast mass of what the seventeenth and eighteenth centuries described as 'Occurrences, Domestick' possessed no political significance, and it was below the dignity of the great papers of the nineteenth century to print much of it. The 'gossip' of the eighteenth century found no counterpart in the nineteenth; pictures were regarded either as technically impossible or as vulgar and undesirable. The non-political news and illustrations were thus left to the Sunday journals. The situation could not last, for nothing 'lasts', even in so conservative a trade as journalism. The dailies, eventually bound to learn their job, could never reconstitute their technique of presentation without risking the alienation of some portion of their subscribers. The history of journalism proves, as we shall see, that not to take this risk is suicide. It is clear that, up to 1855, the Stamp Acts had made it impossible to spend space upon news-display; and that in the result, fresh foundations were cast precisely in the mould of the old-fashioned journals. But although the tendency in newly-founded dailies of the second half of the century was definitely against the old methods, we cannot find in the 'quality' press of the 1860's, '70's and '80's anything like the bold, intelligent, but economical liberality, of the headlines in papers like *The News of the World* in 1856. It had become a prime dogma of journalists that for a morning paper to be a morning paper it must look like a morning paper. According to these fundamentalists, it follows that if a certain headline technique is appropriate to a Sunday paper, it is a thousand to one against its being in place in a daily. Moreover, in 1856, a penny daily was only more respectable than a Sunday journal, and *The Daily Telegraph* relapsed into the use of the conventional headlines when its success gave it the institutional status which permitted it to be bought by gentlemen.

This upper- and middle-class typographical orthodoxy, good enough for its leisured generation, could not expect—as it did expect—to be good enough for the lower middle-class generation which grew up after the Education Act of 1870. Yet, another news-market was at hand—the working-class readers who impatiently waited until the week-end for their *News of the World* or *Weekly Dispatch*. Finally there was a new army of clerical workers for whom provision could be made—and was soon to be made. By 1889 there were female typists and female telegraphists in the City; and they had no interest in political alignments. These large masses of readers remained outside, uncatered for by any newspaper.

Naturally, the omnipotence in sheer circulation of *The Times* was inevitably menaced by the emergence of these new classes. Another force to be reckoned with at Printing House Square was the establishment of *The Pall Mall Gazette | An Evening Newspaper and Review* | No. 1, Tuesday, February 7, 1865, price 2*d*. This was an evening paper on the lines of Canning's *Weekly Jacobin* and the *Saturday Review* and printed as such.[1] It addressed itself to the leisured classes, and, by its inclusiveness, its comparative lightness of touch and openness of setting, rapidly achieved an influential position which could not but reduce the lead of *The Times*. Established above all as a 'paper written by gentlemen for gentlemen', it was deliberately set in 'old style'—i.e. a book type cut in the tradition of the early and not the late eighteenth century—which had not been seen in newspapers for sixty years. *The Pall*

[1] See Frederick Greenwood in the *P.M.G*'s 10,000th issue (April 14, 1897).

THE

PALL MALL GAZETTE

An Evening Newspaper and Review.

No. 1.—Vol. I. *TUESDAY, FEBRUARY 7, 1865.* *Price Twopence.*

THE QUEEN'S SECLUSION.

A LITTLE paragraph appeared in the newspapers lately, to revive a hope which was to have been fulfilled to-day, and has not. "We " are informed that Her MAJESTY the QUEEN will open Parliament " in person next session:" this was the little paragraph—printed, too, in that authoritative large type which carries conviction straight into the minds of most newspaper readers. But somehow the herald who brought such good tidings from Court was little credited. The trumpet sounded—that we all heard; but no confirming echo answered it—not even in those hollow places in our own hearts where dwells the hope of what we much desire. The most timid inquirer hesitated to believe; and he whose faith in editorial announcements had hitherto been complete, found himself disturbed by a strangely courageous scepticism. Was the announcement authorized at all by any one? Had we not been told of journalists and politicians who endeavoured to achieve what they wished by declaring it already certain? These questions were asked by many people. The answer to the first one is that the QUEEN never at any moment intended to open Parliament this session—(here is our own authoritative large type to prove it)—and to the conscious of an observation which is scarcely the less painful for being sympathetic. Therefore we say Her MAJESTY'S seclusion is exactly what might have been expected of her position and her virtues; and that inasmuch as we respect them we must respect their natural consequences, nor forget that her retirement is the most natural one of all.

But this is not saying we wish the seclusion to continue. What we do say is, that with the fullest sense of what is due to Her MAJESTY, with the strongest inclination to take no part in the discussion of this subject, we cannot resist the suggestions of the ceremony of to-day. In brief, we cannot help speculating, not upon the regret or the disappointment of the nation at large on seeing another fair occasion for the QUEEN'S re-appearance amongst us pass by, but upon the satisfaction it may give that small, determined coterie of Americanized politicians who are so particularly active just now, and whom we shall behold still more active before another Parliament can be assembled. Who can doubt that they *do* find satisfaction in the QUEEN'S absence, once more, from the most important and significant of all State ceremonials? To be sure, they are not likely to acknowledge such sentiments. There are many bold speakers amongst them, and a carnival of

Fig. 134. *Upper portion of* The Pall Mall Gazette

THE

ST. JAMES'S GAZETTE

An Evening Review and Record of News.

No. 1.—Vol. I. MONDAY, MAY 31, 1880. Price Twopence.

BIRTH.

ROBERTSON, the wife of R. B., Esq., Glasgow, at Montgreenan, Ayrshire, May 24—of a son.

Fig. 135. *Upper portion of* The St James's Gazette

Mall's choice, later adopted by *The St James's Gazette* (1880), passed on to *The Westminster Gazette* (1893). It was a distinguished-looking paper, but, with the adoption of the 'old style' type, there was, as yet, no abrupt departure from the standardised relation of the headlines to the text as exemplified in the morning press. Of course, it would be unnecessary for a newspaper published in the form of a weekly review to use tall or heavy capitals. They would be appropriate, even necessary, on a blanket sheet; but London had to wait for a score more years for them. Journalists, more and more afraid of taking risks, became correspondingly enamoured of precedent. *The Pall Mall Gazette* was started in 1865. *The Echo* was founded by Mr Cassell, of Messrs Cassell, Petter and Galpin, as an evening paper at the sensational price of one-halfpenny,[1] yet it was in substance a *Pall Mall*, for a quarter of

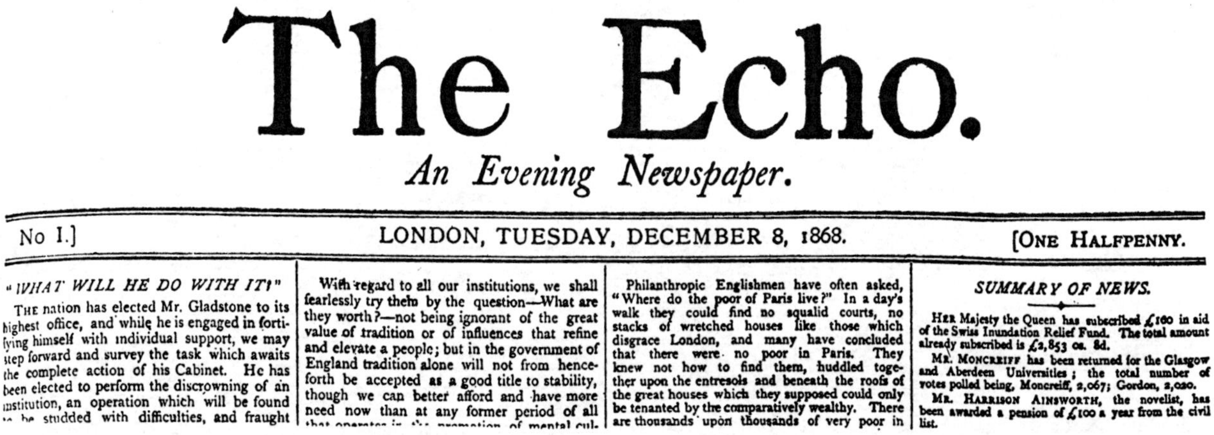

The Echo.

An Evening Newspaper.

No I.] LONDON, TUESDAY, DECEMBER 8, 1868. [ONE HALFPENNY.

"*WHAT WILL HE DO WITH IT?*"

THE nation has elected Mr. Gladstone to its highest office, and while he is engaged in fortifying himself with individual support, we may step forward and survey the task which awaits the complete action of his Cabinet. He has been elected to perform the discrowning of an institution, an operation which will be found to be studded with difficulties, and fraught

With regard to all our institutions, we shall fearlessly try them by the question—What are they worth?—not being ignorant of the great value of tradition or of influences that refine and elevate a people; but in the government of England tradition alone will not from henceforth be accepted as a good title to stability, though we can better afford and have more need now than at any former period of all that operates in the promotion of mental cul-

Philanthropic Englishmen have often asked, "Where do the poor of Paris live?" In a day's walk they could find no squalid courts, no stacks of wretched houses like those which disgrace London, and many have concluded that there were no poor in Paris. They knew not how to find them, huddled together upon the entresols and beneath the roofs of the great houses which they supposed could only be tenanted by the comparatively wealthy. There are thousands upon thousands of very poor in

SUMMARY OF NEWS.

HER Majesty the Queen has subscribed £100 in aid of the Swiss Inundation Relief Fund. The total amount already subscribed is £2,853 0s. 8d.

MR. MONCREIFF has been returned for the Glasgow and Aberdeen Universities; the total number of votes polled being, Moncreiff, 2,067; Gordon, 2,020.

MR. HARRISON AINSWORTH, the novelist, has been awarded a pension of £100 a year from the civil list.

Fig. 136

the price. It was set in 'old style' type and put together with the same dignity. It had a roman head on the front page. It made its way by providing evening reading matter for intelligent business folk unable to spend the time or money upon the penny morning press. *The Echo* was hardly a 'popular' paper. Hence, when the telegraph gave a great impetus to betting by flashing the results all over the country, an evening paper for the 'masses,' with a strong sporting side, became desirable. Moreover, football increased in popularity during the 1880's, and the provincial press was already publishing special Saturday night football editions. London's popular evening paper at last made its appearance in *The Evening News* (No. 1, July 26, 1881), and secondly, and more successfully, in *The Star* (No. 1, January 17, 1888). Without scorning politics, both gave sporting intelligence priority

[1] The first morning newspaper at a halfpenny came from Printing House Square. *The Summary* lasted for 381 numbers from July 26, 1883—October 11, 1884 (cf. infra, p. 293).

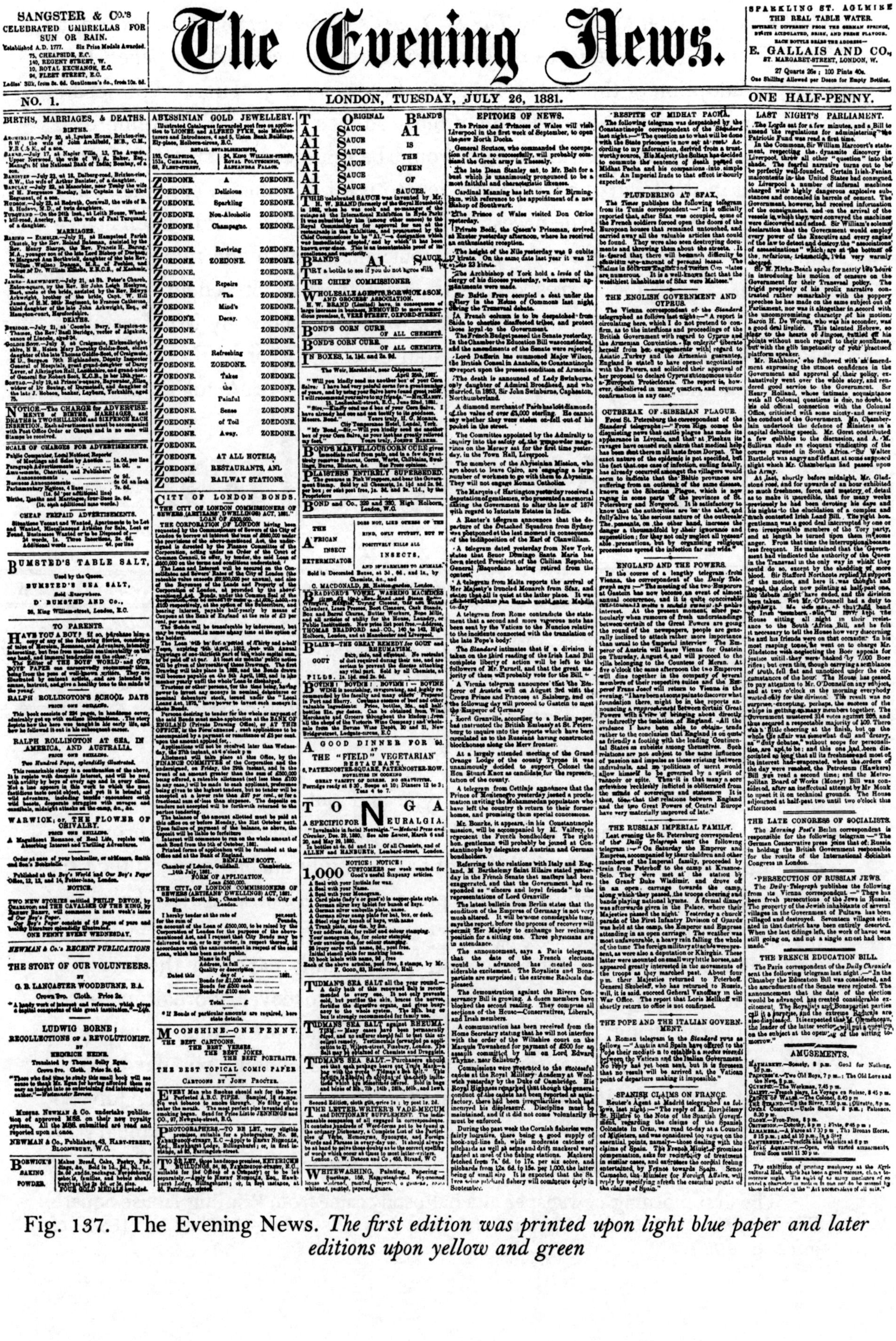
SANGSTER & CO.'S
CELEBRATED UMBRELLAS FOR
SUN OR RAIN.

The Evening News.

SPARKLING ST. AGLMIER
THE REAL TABLE WATER.
E. GALLAIS AND CO.,
ST. MARGARET-STREET, LONDON, W.

NO. 1. LONDON, TUESDAY, JULY 26, 1881. ONE HALF-PENNY.

BIRTHS, MARRIAGES, & DEATHS.

ABYSSINIAN GOLD JEWELLERY.

ZOEDONE.

EPITOME OF NEWS.

"RESPITE OF MIDHAT PACHA."

LAST NIGHT'S PARLIAMENT.

PLUNDERING AT SFAX.

THE ENGLISH GOVERNMENT AND CYPRUS.

OUTBREAK OF SIBERIAN PLAGUE.

ENGLAND AND THE POWERS.

THE RUSSIAN IMPERIAL FAMILY.

THE POPE AND THE ITALIAN GOVERNMENT.

SPANISH CLAIMS ON FRANCE.

THE LATE CONGRESS OF SOCIALISTS.

PERSECUTION OF RUSSIAN JEWS.

THE FRENCH EDUCATION BILL.

AMUSEMENTS.

CITY OF LONDON BONDS.

BUMSTED'S TABLE SALT.

TO PARENTS.

RALPH ROLLINGTON'S SCHOOL DAYS

RALPH ROLLINGTON AT SEA, IN AMERICA, AND AUSTRALIA.

WARWICK; or, THE FLOWER OF CHIVALRY.

NEWMAN & Co.'s RECENT PUBLICATIONS

THE STORY OF OUR VOLUNTEERS.

LUDWIG BORNE; RECOLLECTIONS OF A REVOLUTIONIST.

MOONSHINE.—ONE PENNY.

TONGA

A SPECIFIC FOR NEURALGIA.

Fig. 137. The Evening News. *The first edition was printed upon light blue paper and later editions upon yellow and green* over the City. The first number of *The Evening News*, printed upon blue paper, has an appearance which the morning papers would have considered as at least decent for an evening paper. Unlike *The Echo*, which, following *The Pall Mall Gazette*, carried a roman title, the title of the first *Evening News* was drawn in text, i.e. a solid piece of blackletter. The white-line of orthodox newspaper-gothic was added later when the paper came into the hands of Alfred Harmsworth and Kennedy Jones. *The | St James's Gazette | An Evening Review and Record of News* | established on May 31, 1880, at twopence, was titled in roman 'old-style' type in *The Pall Mall Gazette* fashion. The text followed the same precedent, except that unlike either *The Pall Mall Gazette* or *The Echo*, the whole of the front page was occupied with advertisements—theatres occupying the first of the four narrow columns, their old traditional eighteenth-century position. The news was in the two agreeably wide-measured columns to which evening readers had been accustomed by *The Pall Mall Gazette*.

In the body of *The Evening News* there was little novelty. The largest headlines were at the most three-deckers. One of these in five-lines is the main item on the main page of the first issue:

THE DISCOVERY OF
INFERNAL MACHINES

PRECAUTIONS AT THE HOUSES
OF PARLIAMENT

STATEMENT OF O'DONOVAN ROSSA

As such headlines were set in graded sizes of the same design as the body face, the paper retained a uniformly grey colour. The text of the important news and the leading article was set in a large size (10-point). In 1882, following a change of proprietorship which seems to have occurred (I am not certain of this point), the headlines were set in bold condensed sans-serif capitals. This practice, making possible the instant reference to any favourite portion of the paper, had been employed in the Sunday journals of 1820. So complete was the separation of Sundays from dailies that so obvious a boon as a clear bold heading was not extended to the reader of the classic morning papers until a few years ago.

As the dogmatic typography of the daily journalists excluded consideration of the experience of their fellows on the Sunday journals, a similar insularity developed between the new evening papers and the old mornings. One by one the old evening papers, e.g. *The Express* in conjunction with

The Daily News, had ceased publication, and it was evident to the conductors of the morning papers that evening newspapers had somehow drifted out of hand and had become a different, a separate, business. *The Echo* proved it first and *The Evening News* pressed home the lesson. The elderly and dignified morning papers which had regarded even the early *Pall Mall Gazette* with suspicion were utterly scandalised by what happened to the *Pall Mall Gazette* when John Morley was succeeded by W. T. Stead in 1880. Within ten years it became obvious that the evening papers had taken the lead in London journalism. The fundamentalists of Printing House Square and Bouverie Street long stood firmly against the tendencies which Stead was the first London editor to sponsor. Ultimately, a new and less conservative generation succeeded in effecting a revolution in the headlining practice of *The Times*. This revolution, and it was nothing less, was not the work of a year or two. *The Times* took approximately a generation to isolate the modern headline from journalistic tendencies, with which it could neither temporise nor sympathise, and to assimilate it with its own traditions, and to create its present individual style. Such a development, either in *The Times* or out of it, would hardly have been possible without the justification of far-reaching social changes. Sport was not the only interest followed by the 'million', nor was it followed only by the 'million'. At last there was a population which could mark and learn and, finally, read; and it was only a matter of time before the evening papers which were closest to the masses educated the classic 'mornings' towards an editorial programme and policy adapted to human beings rather than to political camp-followers. But the approved threepenny, twopenny or penny journalism, of the period from the coronation to the jubilee of Queen Victoria, was completely isolated from the interests of the generation which grew up after the Great Exhibition of 1851 and the Education Act of 1870. To serve this new generation of readers, a new generation of editors, authors, critics, gossip-writers, interviewers and illustrators was required. And these required a new typography for their 'new journalism'.[1]

[1] The plan of these lectures excludes the treatment of illustration, but *The Evening Illustrated Paper* ought not to pass unrecorded. It is absent from *The Times Handlist*, but was first published October 25, 1881, printed in 'old-style' type on cream paper. 'Of late years, the preparation of journals for printing has undergone a great evolution: wood engraving, except for such purposes as those in which time is of no consequence, has lapsed into dessuetude (*sic*) and a process known as zinco-typography has assumed a supremacy it seems likely to maintain.' Three out of the eight folio pages are of blocks. The text consists of reports of shootings, wrecks, fenian outrages, railway disasters, the trial of a perjurer and similar ingredients of the modern New York 'Tabloid'.

CHAPTER XV

THE 'NEW JOURNALISM'

1883–1896

The Pall Mall Gazette 1883
(under W. T. Stead)

The Star 1888
(under T. P. O'Connor)

The Times
(under G. E. Buckle)

The Morning 1892

The Morning Leader 1892

The Evening News
(under Kennedy Jones)

Daily Mail 1896

CHAPTER XV

THE 'NEW JOURNALISM'

1883–1896

THE 'New Journalism', so called by Matthew Arnold, made its entry into the English newspaper world by way of the evening papers, to be precise, in the later *Pall Mall Gazette* under Stead; and it made itself at home in *The Star*, from its beginning under T. P. O'Connor in 1888. So far as headline typography is concerned, the Sunday papers of 1820 and after tended in the right direction. *The Weekly Dispatch* consistently used a good black **EGYPTIAN** and, on occasion, used cross-heads. These appear to good advantage in the very lengthy report of the execution of William Corder who murdered Maria Martin in 1828. The *Dispatch* devoted a column leader, a column and a half of 'remarks' on Corder's motives, and eight ghastly columns describing the execution. Page 258 of the issue for August 17 (reproduced in Fig. 138) employs three cross-heads for '**CONFESSION**', '**EXECUTION**' and '**DISSECTION**' respectively. The same issue of the *Dispatch* presented its readers with a representation of the execution of Corder, together with a very correct portrait of the head of that miserable man as it lay on the dissecting board, and a drawing of the Red Barn; the whole printed by lithography on two separate sheets. *The News of the World* in the 'sixties and *The London Halfpenny Newspaper* carried on what is to us the elementary practice of enabling the reader to pick out the headlines from the surrounding grey or black text. This can only be done by setting the headlines in a suitably large size of the type used for the text, or, better still (because less extravagant of space and yet more effective), a heavier type of another design. Such use of small but bold headline founts never made its way into the 'classical' daily papers; and as, later, the Sunday papers themselves became more respectable, they gradually adopted the monotone typography of the rest of the 'superior' press. In consequence, the principle of distinguishing the headlines from the text was forgotten. The theory of *The Times* was that as every reader knew by experience that every word in the paper was indispensable, he worked his way through the entire solid and black print, from the first page to the last. Dominated by *The Times*, the whole morning newspaper press con-

258 **THE WEEKLY DISPATCH.**

ed the utmost solicitude lest the sneers and contumely of the world should visit his transgressions upon her.—She entreated him to dismiss all reflections on her personal condition, not to disturb his mind, or distract his attention from the consolatory duties of religion; that matters of higher import than any which related to her should be at once attended to; "and," said she, "dear William, there is a good and merciful God, who will protect me: to him I look up, and from him in this calamitous hour I derive my support." She implored him to disregard all worldly affairs, and to consider and calmly reflect upon the heavy account he would be so soon called upon to deliver to the Almighty. Mr. Orridge was present while it continued, and at its close intimated to the prisoner and his unhappy partner, that they would again be permitted to see each other at eleven o'clock on Sunday morning; but that this they must consider as their final meeting in this life. Mrs. Corder and Mrs. Atherton walked both to and from the gaol: the former had a care-worn, melancholy, and dejected countenance; but yet, considering the severity of her afflictions, preserved a greater portion of self-possession than could naturally have been expected. She was dressed in a brown levantine silk pelisse, a straw bonnet, with a black veil, which was drawn down so closely over her face that it almost concealed it, and across her shoulders was thrown a blue English Cachemere shawl, with a coloured border. Mrs. Atherton's dress was equally plain, and though she did not see the culprit, while waiting in the Governor's room, she wept most bitterly.

After Mrs. Corder had taken leave of her husband, and had, in company with Mr. Orridge, joined her friend, Mrs. Atherton, she anxiously inquired of Mr. Orridge whether he thought an application to the throne for mercy was likely to be available, or that she could obtain even a short respite to the execution?—Mr. Orridge replied, that in a matter of so serious a nature, he hoped she would excuse him from offering any opinion or advice. She had better consult her friends and legal advisers, and pursue that course their and her own good judgment deemed the most eligible.

On Saturday a gateway was cut in the wall for the prisoner to advance to the fatal platform, along a stage to be erected for that purpose. Some of his fellow prisoners, who seemed to think that life is a jest, and that death is nothing but a drunken sleep, cut a joke upon this door-way, by giving it the nickname of "Corder's eternal way."

Corder, though much dejected at his approaching fate, slept soundly during the greater part of Saturday night. About eight o'clock in the evening, his mental exhaustion overcame his physical strength, and he dropped into a calm and undisturbed sleep, which lasted till three o'clock on Sunday morning. We have been given to understand, that though after sentence he appeared greatly dismayed at the approaching close of his mortal career, he never, from the first, expected any other termination to this trial. On hearing that his friends, some of whom are very opulent and respectable persons, were willing to make large pecuniary sacrifices to ensure him the benefit of all the assistance which could be derived from the talent and ingenuity of the most able and experienced advocates at the bar, he wrote a letter to them returning them thanks for their kindness, but at the same time declaring, that the evidence which had been taken at the inquest, would appear to all persons who were unacquainted with the real nature of the transaction, so strong against him, that it would answer no useful purpose to expend their money in his behalf. He also stated that he had made up his mind to meet with courage and fortitude the fatal destiny, which had befallen many other individuals who were as innocent as himself. It appears from the event, that he had miscalculated his own strength of nerve: for, it was quite clear that the elasticity of his spirit was entirely destroyed, and that he laboured under the most poignant distress of mind.

On Sunday morning the condemned Sermon was preached in the chapel attached to the gaol, by the chaplain, the Rev. W. Stocking. Shortly after nine, the chapel was opened; besides the inmates of the gaol, there were about twenty persons present. After the debtors confined in the county gaol had taken their seats, the different felons, who have been tried at the late assizes, were admitted to theirs. The latter were dressed in a coat and trowsers of grey frieze, striped at intervals with two bars of black, enclosing a broader stripe of yellow, which is the costume of this prison. After the chaplain had taken his station in the pulpit, Corder was led into the barred cell reserved for culprits under sentence of death, by Mr. Orridge and one of his attendants. He wept bitterly as he came along the passage; but buried his face in his handkerchief, as if anxious to withdraw himself from the gaze of the curious. His step was any thing but firm, and he had evidently lost a great part of that self command which he exhibited at the commencement of the trial. As soon as he was locked in the pew appointed for him, he heaved a deep sigh, sat himself down on one of the benches, and leant against the side of the pew; he then raised his foot on the bench before him, rested his elbow on his knee, and his face, which he covered with a white handkerchief, on his hand, and remained in that position during the greater part of the service. The Rev. Gentleman then read an excellent occasional prayer for persons in Corder's deplorable situation; he appeared much moved by it, and betrayed great agitation, when the Rev. Gentleman bade his congregation reflect that but for the mediating blood of Christ, they might have been shut up in hell instead of in that prison. In that part of the service of the day in which the clergyman prays that the rest of our lives may be pure and holy, Corder's emotion was excessive, owing, perhaps, to its exciting the painful reflection that the rest of his life was already numbered. The psalms which were selected for the occasion, were the 51st and the 130th. In that part of the 51st psalm in which the inspired writer implores God to deliver him from blood-guiltiness, Corder sighed deeply, and showed by the uplifted motion of his hands that he joined cordially in the prayer. These two psalms, which are very affecting, produced no other display of feeling from the prisoner, so deep and stupifying was the grief by which he was overwhelmed. The first lesson read was the usual lesson for the day; the second was selected with reference to the prisoner's situation, and was that part of the 15th chapter of St. Paul's First Epistle to the Corinthians, which the Church of England, from admiration of its deep and affecting sublimity, has incorporated into the burial service. The 30th verse, "Why stand we in jeopardy every hour?" affected him greatly. At the commencement of the Litany, he sighed deeply; and evidently joined in heart, though not in word, with the supplication to the Trinity to have mercy upon all miserable sinners. On coming to that clause in the Litany in which the preacher prays that God will show his pity upon all prisoners and captives, and especially on him who is now awaiting the execution of his sentence, he let his head fall against the wall with a heart-rending sigh. At the close of the Litany, the clergyman introduced a prayer for Corder, which affected him so much that he cried audibly. In the closing paragraph of it, in which God was implored to enable so heinous a sinner to cast himself wholly on his Redeemer, and, through the merits of his passion and death, to relieve himself from the pressure of his sins, he groaned aloud, and half whispered "Amen." This prayer appeared to make a greater impression upon him than any other portion of the service of the day. He changed his position repeatedly, but never abstained from keeping his handkerchief in front of his face. It was the only time in which he joined in the responses, though many of them were most suitable to his desperate condition. To the sermon he paid considerable attention. It was taken from the 41st verse of the 23d chapter of St. Luke, and was in these words:—"And we indeed justly, for we receive the due reward of our deeds, but this man hath not done amiss." The reverend preacher said that these were the words of the malefactor who was crucified with Jesus, and who, in consequence of his belief in the divine character of our Saviour, received from him a promise that he should be entitled with him to the joys of Paradise. He pointed out the happy result which the words of the text had produced to the person who uttered them, and said that he should take occasion from them to point out the state of mind which a malefactor appointed to die, ought to strive with all his soul to attain. The external demeanour of a person so circumstanced should be such as not to give offence to those who should watch his actions at the time of his death: for the damage he might then do was irreparable, and he could never have any opportunity to repair it by repentance. He ought to endeavour so to conduct himself at the close of his existence as to edify and improve by his death, those who could have received nothing but evil example from his life. A death on the scaffold excited great attention on the part of the spectators, and whatever was then said or done by the malefactor doomed to die, made an impression on their memories, which rendered it incumbent on him to say or do nothing which could weaken the respect due from us all to that God at whose tribunal he was going to appear. The inward demeanour of the prisoner was that, however, to which he ought to pay the greatest concern. He should endeavour to make his peace with God, and should repent of his sins with a repentance not to be repented of. As he could not expect to bring forward in his life fruits meet for repentance, it was incumbent upon him to reiterate his prayer for a change of mind, till he became certain that it was accepted. He should prepare himself for that awful occasion, when the dead in Christ should rise again, and when the great judgment of the Lord should pronounce absolution on the godly and condemnation on the wicked. He pointed out the distressing situation of those to whom God should say,—"Depart from me, ye wicked, into everlasting fire." [here Corder was violently affected, and sobbed convulsively,] and asked with great enthusiasm what would not the wicked give for one hour at that time to make their peace with their offended Creator. Then it would be too late to implore his mercy—their eternal state would be concluded on—and the certainty that there would be no change in it, would aggravate the intensity of their sufferings. [Here Corder's emotion was truly distressing—he moved about in his seat in great mental anguish.] Let those, who thought that they stood, take care lest they fell; and let them take warning from the death which was now impending over their fellow-prisoner, and endeavour not to do likewise, lest a worse fate should hereafter befall them.

The close of this sermon, of which we have given a very faint and imperfect sketch, was the close of the service for the day. Corder was led out by Mr. Orridge in almost a fainting condition. As soon as he reached his cell, he staggered to his bed, on which he flung himself, sobbing convulsively for many minutes. Nothing could be more altered than the cast of his countenance, since the Friday preceding. His cheeks had collapsed, his eyes were swollen greatly, and his whole appearance was most ghastly. He looked the picture of despair.

At noon Mrs. Corder had an interview with her wretched husband. It lasted from half-past twelve to two o'clock, and was to a spectator infinitely distressing. Mr. Orridge, who was present, and who is not unaccustomed to such scenes, was much affected by it. Corder particularly requested his wife not to marry again, or at least, if she did, not to obtain a husband, as she had obtained him, by means of an advertisement, for it was of all modes of getting a husband the most dangerous and imprudent. It is perhaps right to add, that one of the first questions which Corder asked his wife, on seeing her led into his cell by Mr. Orridge, had reference to the advertisement by which he gained her. Mr. Orridge appeared to have some doubt whether Corder had received so many answers as he said to his advertisement, and in order to remove them, Corder aked her how many letters she herself had seen? She replied immediately, 45. The advertisement is as follows:—

"A private gentleman, aged 24, entirely independent, whose disposition is not to be exceeded, has lately lost chief of his family by the hand of Providence, which has occasioned discord among the remainder, under circumstances the most disagreeable to relate. To any female of respectability, who would study for domestic comfort, and is willing to confide her future happiness to one in every way qualified to render the marriage state desirable, as the advertiser is in affluence. Many happy marriages have taken place through means similar to this now resorted to. It is hoped no one will answer this through impertinent curiosity; but should this meet the eye of any agreeable lady, who feels desirous of meeting with a sociable, tender, kind, and sympathizing companion, they will find this advertisement worthy of notice. Honour and secrecy may be relied on. As some little security against idle application, it is requisite that letters may be addressed, post paid, A. Z., care of Mr. Foster, stationer, 68, Leadenhall-street, with real name and address, which will meet with most respectful attention."

On leaving her husband's cell, Mrs. Corder was completely overcome by the violence of her feelings. She fainted away several times, and was with difficulty recovered by the restoratives administered to her by Mr. Orridge, who sincerely commiserated her sufferings. She was not able to walk to the gig which was waiting to convey her to her lodgings, but was carried into it by her friend Mrs. Atherton and one of the prison attendants. Corder, on her quitting him, said that the bitterness of death was now over, and was heard to express a wish that there was a less interval to the time of his execution. He likewise said that he found in Mrs. Corder one of the most tender, faithful, and affectionate of wives.

In the course of Sunday evening, Mr. Orridge addressed a paper to the prisoner, impressing upon him the duty of making a confession of his guilt, of which he said few people now entertained doubt. The unfortunate prisoner said that he did not see any reason why he should make it. Mr. Orridge then reminded him, that in his defence he had imputed to Maria Martin the commission of suicide; and if he left the world without contradicting that statement, he would be tainting her memory with the imputation of a dreadful crime. This argument appeared to make a deep impression on his mind, especially as it was strengthened by reference to the first duty of man, "to do unto another as he would wish others to do unto him." The Rev. Mr. Sheen, the chaplain to the High Sheriff, who saw him about half-past five o'clock, had previously addressed him also upon the same topics; and the consequence of these solicitations was, that he made the following—

CONFESSION.

"Bury Gaol, Aug. 10, 1828. Condemned Cell.

"I acknowledge being guilty of the death of poor Maria Martin, by shooting her with a pistol. The particulars are as follows:—When we left her father's house, we began quarrelling about the burial of the child, she apprehending that the place wherein it was deposited would be found out. The quarrel continued for about three-quarters of an hour upon this and about other subjects. A scuffle ensued, and during the scuffle, and at the time I think that she had hold of me, I took the pistol from the side pocket of my velveteen jacket and fired. She fell, and died in an instant. I never saw even a struggle. I was overwhelmed with agitation and dismay—the body fell near the front doors on the floor of the barn. A vast quantity of blood issued from the wound, and ran on to the floor and through the crevices. Having determined to bury the body in the barn (about two hours after she was dead), I went and borrowed the spade of Mrs. Stowe; but before I went there, I dragged the body from the barn into the chaff-house, and locked up the barn. I returned again to the barn and began to dig the hole; but the spade being a bad one, and the earth firm and hard, I was obliged to go home for a pick-axe and a better spade, with which I dug the hole, and then buried the body. I think I dragged the body by the handkerchief that was tied round her neck—it was dark when I finished covering up the body. I went the next day, and washed the blood from off the barn-floor. I declare to Almighty God, I had no sharp instrument about me, and that no other wound but the one made by the pistol was inflicted by me. I have been guilty of great idleness, and at times led a dissolute life, but I hope through the mercy of God to be forgiven.

"W. CORDER."

Witness to the signing by the said William Corder,
JOHN ORRIDGE.

Sunday evening, half-past twelve o'clock.

Condemned Cell, eleven o'clock, Monday morning, Aug. 11, 1828.

The above confession was read over carefully to the prisoner in our presence, who stated most solemnly it was true,—that he had nothing to add to or retract from it.

W. STOCKING, Chaplain.
T. R. HOLMES, Under-Sheriff.

In answer to a question from the Under-Sheriff, he said "that he thought the ball had entered the right eye." He said this in corroboration of his previous statement, that he had no sharp instrument with him in the barn at the time he committed the murder. The Under-Sheriff stated, that *Dr. Probart* was with him at the time when the prisoner made this last confession.

At half-past one o'clock on Sunday night, (or rather Monday morning) Mr. Orridge left Corder, and soon afterwards he fell asleep, and slept to all appearance calmly till six o'clock on Monday morning. He said, however, that his sleep was not sound, but disturbed by dreams. He acquired considerable firmness in the course of Sunday, in consequence of the spiritual consolation afforded to him, first of all by his wife, and next by the chaplain of the gaol, the Rev. Mr. Stocking, and the Rev. Mr. Sheen. Several Methodist preachers applied to be admitted to him, but were refused admission, in consequence of his having addressed a letter to the magistrates, requesting that they would not allow any such fanatics to come near him.

On Monday morning at half-past nine o'clock, Corder was, by his own request, taken into the prison chapel to attend for the last time divine service. He entered the chapel with a firm step, and took his seat in the condemned pew, as he did yesterday. He had, however, laid aside his prison dress, and had on the same clothes which he wore in court during the trial. His appearance was much more composed than could have been expected after the overwhelming sorrow and dismay by which he appeared overcome on the preceding morning. He did not hide his countenance in his handkerchief; nor did he shed a single tear. He exhibited a befitting and not unmanly sense of the awful situation in which he was placed. On sitting down he betrayed his inward feelings by a tremulous motion of his foot for some time, and then rested his head on his hand, supporting his elbow upon his knee. A part of the burial service was again introduced into the service of the day, and during several parts of it, he showed by his motions that he joined in it from his inmost soul. When the gracious invitation of God for all that were heavy laden to come to him and rest upon his mercy was read, he opened his hand slowly, pressed it to his head, and heaved a deep sigh. He likewise exhibited some emotion at an occasional prayer which was introduced into the service, in which the text of Scripture was introduced that says, "Whoso confesseth his sins and forsaketh them, shall have mercy." He joined with great fervour in a prayer which called upon God to spare him in the agonies of death, which he was presently to endure; and to extend to him that mercy which he had not extended to his departed sister. The latter allusion affected him deeply, for he raised up his left hand, gave a convulsive shudder, and struck it with some violence on his knee. During the rest of the service, which was nearly the same as that of the day before, he did not betray any extraordinary emotion. At the close of it, his pew was opened; on leaving it, he made a few steps by himself, and then tottered and seemed as if about to fall. One of the prison attendants then gave him his arm, and led him back to his cell. At eleven o'clock the chaplain was admitted into his cell, and administered to him the sacrament.

Some additional particulars of Corder's behaviour after receiving sentence, were furnished by Mr. Orridge, who after detailing some statements made by Corder relative to his marriage, &c., of which the public are already acquainted, goes on to say, "During Saturday the chaplain (Mr. Stocking) was several times with him. At other times I now and then hinted the necessity of confession. In the course of that day he said 'that confession to God was all that was necessary, and that confession to man was what he called Popedom or Popery, and he would never do it.' It was hinted to him, some time in the day, that he must have had great nerve, to dig the hole during the time the body lay in his sight. His reply was 'Nobody knows that the body lay in the barn and in sight whilst I dug the hole;' and would then say no more on the subject, but exclaimed, 'O God! Nobody will dig my grave!' His wife saw him in my presence for near an hour. He expressed much anxiety about her future welfare: she entreated him to forget her, and employ his few hours yet remaining in prayer for his salvation and eternal welfare. I went to his room on Saturday evening, about eight o'clock, with an intention of sitting an hour or two with him, but he had gone to bed, and was asleep, and my men told me the next morning, that he slept untill near three o'clock.

On Sunday morning Mr. Stocking was with him early, and endeavoured to lead his mind to the necessity of confession: he attended chapel and was very much affected; about half-past twelve his wife had her last interview: they were both very much affected. In the course of that interview he exclaimed, "Well might Mr. Orridge say, that I was a most fortunate man to meet with such a woman as you are!"

He then explained to her that he had told me the way in which they had come together, and that he had 45 applications to his advertisement; he entreated her not to answer any similar advertisement, as woful experience must have convinced her how dangerous a step it was. The parting scene was most affecting, the poor woman remained in a state of stupor for some time. Corder was much affected throughout the day, Mr. Stocking had several interviews with him, and in the evening the Sheriff's chaplain, the Rev. Mr. Sheen, attended him, for which attention he expressed himself as feeling very grateful.

Mr. Orridge here details the contents of a paper which he sent to Corder, enforcing the propriety of his making a confession, and proceeds as follows:—"I begged he would read it attentively, and that I would come to him soon; I went to his room a little before ten, and remained in earnest conversation with him till half-past eleven; that I well knew, from his letters that I had seen, and from other circumstances, that the line of defence he had adopted was not the dictates of his own mind, at least for a long time after his commitment; and that I was sure that he would not and dare not take the sacrament, and remain silent, or deny being the guilty cause of the death of poor Maria Martin. He then exclaimed, "Oh, Sir, I wish I had made a confidant of you before; I have often wished to have done it, but you know, Sir, it was no use employing a legal adviser, and then not follow his advice." I told him, that up to the time of his conviction it was proper, but that being over all earthly considerations must cease. He then exclaimed, "I am a guilty man!" I then went for a pen and ink, and began to ask him the particulars of the offence; which I told him the public had supposed him to be guilty of. He said, "Oh, spare me, I can only mention to you the particulars of how Maria came by her death; with this the public must be satisfied; I cannot say more."

Mr. Orridge proceeds to state, that he immediately wrote Corder's confession (as given above), merely in his own words, and adds:—"I read it to him attentively, and he signed it with a firm hand. I left him about half-past one o'clock, and my men tell me he lay very still, and appeared to sleep through the night. On Saturday he told a respectable individual whom I had asked to sit and read to him, that he was guilty of the forgery upon Messrs. Alexander's bank, and that he had been assured the money was paid: there are some parts of the foregoing statement which he also mentioned to the same individual. He also expressed much horror at the thoughts of being dissected and anatomized. He also stated, after he had signed the confession, that he felt great respect for the girl, but that he had no intention to marry her at that time."

About an hour before his execution, Corder wrote the following letter to his wife:—"My life's loved companion—I am now going to the fatal scaffold, and I have a lively hope of obtaining mercy and pardon for my numerous offences. May heaven bless and protect you through this transitory vale of misery; and which when we meet again may it be in the regions of everlasting bliss. Adieu, my love, for ever adieu. In less than two hours I hope to be in heaven; my last prayer's that God will endue you with patience, fortitude, and resignation to his will. Rest assured that his wise providence works all things together for good. The awful sentence which has been passed upon me, and which I am now summoned to answer, I confess is very just, and I die in peace with all mankind, truly grateful for the kindness I have received from Mr. Orridge, and the religious consolation from the Rev. Mr. Stocking, who has promised to take my last words to you."

(No Signature).

The above was written with pencil, on a blank leaf at the end of a volume of "Blair's Sermons," which appears to have been a gift of Mrs. Corder to her husband, from the following words written on another leaf at the beginning of the book:—"Mary Corder to her husband William Corder—a birth-day present, June 22, 1828."—(Corder attained his 24th year on that day).

THE EXECUTION.

From an early hour on Monday morning, the population of the surrounding districts came pouring into Bury; and the whole of the labouring classes in the town struck work for the day, in order that they might have an opportunity of witnessing the execution of this wretched criminal, which was appointed to take place at twelve o'clock at noon. As early as nine o'clock in the morning, upwards of 1,000 persons were assembled around the scaffold, in the paddock, on the south side of the gaol, and their number kept increasing till 12 o'clock, when they amounted to at least 7,000 persons. Nothing could be more decent and orderly than their conduct.—The majority consisted of men, but we observed a large number of females in the crowd. Two women must have been there at an extremely early hour, for they were close up to the wood-work which surrounded the fatal drop. They appeared to be of the lowest class; but many of the female spectators were of a much superior grade. Seated on a wall, which gave a commanding view of the whole scene, were several ladies, dressed in the first style of fashion. Every building in the neighbourhood was covered with occupants, and in one of the adjacent fields were several gentlemen on horseback, expecting the appearance of the prisoner.

At ten minutes before twelve o'clock, the prisoner was brought from his cell and pinioned by Foxton, the hangman, who was brought from London for the purpose. He appeared resigned, but was so weak as to be unable to stand without support; when his cravat was removed he groaned heavily, and appeared to be labouring under great mental agony. When his wrists and arms were made fast, he was led round towards the scaffold, and as he passed the different yards in which the prisoners are confined, he shook hands with them, and speaking to two of them by name, he said, "Good bye, God bless you." They appeared considerably affected at the wretched appearance which he made, and "God bless you!" "May God receive your soul!" were frequently uttered as he passed along. As a proof that he was at that time perfectly conscious of what he was doing, he singled out a prisoner of the name of Nunn, shook hands with him as well as his bandaged situation would allow, and said to him, "Nunn, God Almighty bless you." After he had gone round the entrance to the different wards of the prison, which are ranged round the Governor's house, which is built upon an octagonal base, he proceeded to the entrance of the debtor's yard, where he bade farewell to three individuals who came to the gate to shake hands with him. After he had performed this duty, which Mr. Orridge was of opinion might prove beneficial to the juvenile offenders in the prison, the procession to the scaffold was formed in the usual manner by the Under-Sheriff and his attendants. The Rev. W. Stocking, for whose attention the prisoner expressed himself most grateful, led the way, reading the commencement of the burial service, "I am the resurrection and the life, whosoever believeth in me shall not die, but have everlasting life." In a few minutes afterwards the procession reached the door-way which opened to the scaffold, and Corder was placed upon the floor which, when withdrawn, was to plunge him into eternity. The prospect from the place on which he stood is of the most beautiful description. The foreground consists of softly-swelling hills, bounded in the distance by extensive plantations, which form a sort of amphitheatre around the prison. But the loveliness of the scenery had for him no beauty; for the moment his eyes opened upon it they were to be closed for ever. After he was placed under the fatal beam, Mr. Orridge approached him, and asked whether he wished to address the multitude. He gave some indistinct answer, which we did not hear, and Mr. Orridge immediately said to the crowd, in a loud voice, "He acknowledges the justice of his sentence, and dies in peace with all mankind." The executioner then drew the cap over his face. The officer who supported him says that he afterwards added, when quite unable to stand, "I deserve my fate; I have offended my God. May he have mercy on my soul!" Within a minute afterwards, the deadly bolt was withdrawn, and he was cut off from the number of the living. The hangman, after the corpse had fallen, performed his disgusting but necessary task, of suspending his own weight around the body of the prisoner, to accelerate his death. At the same moment, the prisoner, who appeared to be in the last agonies, clasped his hands tighter together, as if he was forming his last prayer for the mercy and forgiveness of offended Heaven. Immediately afterwards his arms, which were raised a little, fell—the muscles appeared to relax—and his hands soon sunk down as low as their pinioned condition permitted. But life was not yet extinct; about eight minutes afterwards there was a heaving of the shoulders, a slight convulsion of the frame, an indistinct groan, and then all was still, and no further motion was observed.

A gentleman, who attended the execution for a Morning Paper, says, "It is an extraordinary fact, and certainly not to be accounted for on any principle of reason or common sense, that the rope with which Corder was hanged has become an article of arduous competition. It has been sold for a guinea an inch to the various parties who bade for it. One of the purchasers is said to have come to purchase the whole for the Cambridge Museum, but was deterred by the price. He reversed the common proverb; for he came for an ell, and went away contented with an inch. I give the story because I heard it, but I believe it myself to be a fiction. I heard, in the course of the day, that several labouring men had walked thirty miles to witness the execution; the account appears extremely probable; for on my return to London, the road was lined for several miles with persons returning from this melancholy spectacle."

Mrs. Corder (the mother of the deceased) has been so overcome by the disgrace which the misconduct of her son has brought upon her, that she has for some time been unable to leave her bed. Neither she nor her daughter held the slightest communication with Corder after his condemnation. His wife is in Bury, seriously indisposed.

THE DISSECTION.

About an hour after the execution, the body was removed to a private room in the Shire-hall, where Mr. Creed, the county surgeon, assisted by Mr. Smith and Mr. Dalton, made a longitudinal incision along the chest, as far as the abdominal parts, and deprived it of the skin, so as to exhibit the muscles of the chest. The anxiety to see Corder's body was as great as at his execution; crowds flocked round the doors. He was put in the Nisi Prius Court, and the people entered at one door and departed at another; he was placed on the table, and, with the exception of his trowsers and stockings, he was naked. The face and throat was somewhat swollen and discoloured, the right eye was open, and the left partially so; the mouth was also open sufficiently to show the teeth.

There were three scrofulous marks on the neck, two on the right side and one on the left. The latter was pressed by the rope, and had assumed a dark yellowish colour. The lower scrofulous mark on the right having been immediately covered by the knot, the cuticle had been partially separated, and a slight effusion of blood had taken place. The wound thus made apparent was about an inch and a half long, and appeared as if made with a sharp instrument. But there exists not the slightest ground for such a suspicion.

Such was the anxiety to see him, that we heard several females boasting that they had been in to see him five

Fig. 138. *Page of* The Weekly Dispatch, *August* 17, 1828, *shewing cross-heads in report of the execution of William Corder for the murder of Maria Martin at the Red Barn, Polstead* tinued to print its news and its headlines in a uniform tone. Even when extraordinary news came to hand, the headlines merged with the text so nicely that the despatch, however sensational its content, was, but for a slight increase in the height of the heading capitals, restrained within the limits of a typographical expression designed for conventional day-to-day happenings.

In the eighteenth century, newspaper men (e.g. John Bell) were experimenting with a type of headline which, but for the Stamp Acts, would undoubtedly have developed into a satisfactory modern English method. Any such development ceased in 1815. The reduction of headlines to the minimum made the papers more forbidding than they had ever been. There was no entertainment in the classic dailies. The unremitting preoccupation with politics, which the Victorian journalist ascribed to his public, necessarily excluded from the morning papers diversions which the eighteenth-century journalist regarded as essential to a self-respecting newspaper. Charles Lamb reminds his readers in his Elia essay on *The Newspapers of Thirty-five Years Ago* that at one time

every Morning Paper kept an author,...who was bound to furnish daily a quantum of witty paragraphs. Sixpence a joke—and it was thought pretty high too—was Dan Stuart's settled remuneration in these cases. The chat of the day, scandal, but above all, dress, furnished the material. The length of no paragraph was to exceed seven lines. Shorter they might be, but they must be poignant...The appointment of a regular wit has long ceased to be a part of the economy of a Morning Paper....Parson Este, and Topham, brought up the set custom of 'witty paragraphs' first in *The World*..., etc.

The desirability, obvious to newspaper-men today, of relieving the seriousness of 'Occurrences, Domestick and Foreign' with jokes or personal paragraphs was ignored by the Victorian journalists. Sport, excepting on big occasions, was likewise ignored, except the tedious game of Liberal and Conservative. Murder was an object of rightful human interest, but the rest was all foreign treaties and what Mr Gladstone (and others) said, all set solid, unbroken by cross-heads, without paragraphs. The evening papers, *The Courier*, *The Globe* and such later journals as *The Express* (founded by *The Daily News* in 1877), were conducted in precisely the same spirit. Some mornings and evenings were under the same conductors, and printed in the same heavy style upon the same presses. *The Pall Mall Gazette*, under W. T. Stead, was the first notable breakaway from mid-Victorian journalism, *The Daily Telegraph* having relapsed into orthodoxy. *The Pall Mall Gazette*

THE EVENING NE

SPECIAL EDITION.

CURRENTE CALAMO URBI ET ORBI

LATEST TELEGRAMS.

SEÑOR CASTELAR AND THE SLAVS.

[REUTER'S TELEGRAM.]

MADRID, Feb. 21.

Señor Castelar has published an article on General Skobeleff's recent speech to the Servian students in Paris. He expresses fears of a coming invasion of Europe by the Slavs, and declares that it behoves the Latin races, in the interests of civilisation, to enter into a close alliance with the German people.

THE CZAR AND GENERAL SKOBELEFF.

[REUTER'S TELEGRAM.]

ST. PETERSBURG, Feb. 22.

The *Journal de St. Petersbourg* to-day says: "The speech recently delivered by General Skobeleff, which has been much commented upon by the foreign press, forgets the principles proclaimed by the Emperor since his accession to the throne. These principles announced His Majesty's intention of pursuing a policy faithful to the historical traditions and friendships of Russia, a policy essentially pacific in character and devoted to the economical, civil, and social development of the country. "A declaration of this nature," adds the semi-official organ, "emanating direct from the Sovereign under such solemn circumstances, does not admit of doubt of any kind. It may therefore be regarded as certain that Russian policy remains, and will continue to remain, absolutely subservient to the supreme will which has been thus plainly expressed."

THE NEW FRENCH AMBASSADORS.

(REUTER'S TELEGRAM.)

PARIS, Feb. 22.

The appointments of M. Tissot and the Marquis de Noailles as French Ambassadors in London and Constantinople, respectively, are gazetted to-day.

COLLIERY STRIKES IN FRANCE.

[REUTER'S TELEGRAM.]

PARIS, Feb. 22.

The delegates of the Extreme Left appointed to inquire into the recent strikes in the coal mining districts have succeeded in obtaining some concessions in favour of the men on strike at Bességes, and work has now been partly resumed there.

To-day, the delegates will proceed to Molières, where a more serious strike has occurred.

STORMY WEATHER IN THE UNITED STATES.

GREAT LOSS OF CATTLE.

[REUTER'S TELEGRAM.]

NEW YORK, Feb. 22.

The recent stormy weather appears to have been

THIS DAY'S PARLIAMENT.

HOUSE OF COMMONS.

The SPEAKER took the chair at quarter-past two o'clock.

MR. BRADLAUGH'S OFFENCE.

In answer to a question from Mr. Gladstone,

The SPEAKER said: I am not prepared to say that any member not having signed the roll of members, after taking Oath, thereby invalidates the taking of the Oath.

Mr. GLADSTONE then said—Referring to the occurrences of last night, he thought it was quite time, after the scandalous matter that had occurred, the House would be of opinion that the Speaker should be armed with some authority which would prevent a repetition of scenes of that kind, and that power of this kind, which did not need to be enforced by a resolution of the House should be permanently vested in the Speaker. As to what took place last night, it was explicitly stated in the Proceedings of the House. After the division had been taken on the motion of the hon. member for Northampton, upon the numbers being declared, Mr. Bradlaugh suddenly advanced to the table, and read from a paper in his hand the words of the oath, and having kissed a copy of the New Testament which he had brought with him, signed the said paper. Mr. Speaker forthwith directed Mr. Bradlaugh to withdraw, in pursuance of the resolution of the House of the 7th February last. Mr. Bradlaugh thereupon withdrew below the Bar, leaving the said paper and copy of the New Testament upon the table, but immediately re-entered the House, and took a seat within the Bar. Mr. Speaker again directed Mr. Bradlaugh to withdraw below the Bar. And Mr. Bradlaugh, after stating that he had now taken the oath required by law, and had also taken his seat, again withdrew below the Bar. The scene which took place last night was painful in the highest degree. He pointed out that the motion made by Lord Randolph Churchill last night was open to objection, because the mere fact of sitting in the House without having taken the oath was not sufficient to vacate a seat unless the member sat during a debate. He was of opinion that the legality of the action of Mr. Bradlaugh was a question for the courts of law, and he deprecated the assumption of authority on the part of the House, and believed that in deciding the legality of Mr. Bradlaugh's claim to take the the oath the House had acted all along beyond its powers, and had all along been against the law. The case now before them was a case of disobedience and flagrant disodedience. He pointed out that on several former occasions resolutions had been proposed with regard to Mr. Bradlaugh. He would not go into the question of the consistency of those resolutions, but would only say that the Government had on each occasion been in a minority. The conclusions they had arrived at on former occasions was to allow the majority of the House to take its own course, and, having been a minority, the Government thought they should again, in this case, allow the majority, which was in reality the House of Commons, notwithstanding who might be the leader, of the House to take its own course in this matter, and the Government would on no account offer any obstruction to the wishes of the majority. He thought it was in accordance with the dignity of the House if he continued to take the course he had hitherto adopted. (Ironical Cheers). He would not disguise the fact that in his opinion there had been a flagrant disobedience to a resolution of the House which he believed to be opposed to law and it would be an act of inconsistency under the circumstances if he moved in this matter. ("Oh! oh!" and laughter.)

Sir STAFFORD NORTHCOTE rose, amidst great Opposition cheers, and asked the Speaker whether Mr. Bradlaugh was right in going through the form he did, while the Speaker had risen in his place, and called on him to withdraw?

The SPEAKER said he considered that for Mr. Bradlaugh to have gone through a form of taking the oath when he had risen and called order was a distinct disobedience to the chair. (Cheers.) He also pointed out that he had ordered Mr. Bradlaugh to retire below the Bar. Mr. Bradlaugh had done so, but had immediately afterwards returned within the Bar of the House. And he considered that also a distinct disobedience to the chair (loud cheers.

pleasure of the House, yes.")

The SPEAKER said House that Mr. Bradlau

SCENE IN

Sir STAFFORD NO his motion, and to sub sion of Mr. Bradlaugh.

Mr. Bradlaugh, wh a seat in the House.

Several Members ca this, and

The SPEAKER said that the member for N obeyed the Chair.

There were then loud eventually Mr. Gladsto

The SPEAKER, wh withdraw.

Mr. BRADLAUGH claimed his right to tak

Mr. GLADSTONE s on this subject before th to interfere.

Sir S. NORTHCOTE he could from taking up of the House; but his ha therefore, ask to withd another for the expulsi cheers.)

The motion was not al was negatived, and

Sir S. NORTHCOT Bradlaugh, amidst trem

Mr. GLADSTONE this motion was consequ of the House, taken in conduct, he should not

Mr. LABOUCHER was only to obtain a cas

D

The House then divid

Mr. BRADLAUGH against the motion.

For the motion

Against............

Majority

After the division Mr

(I

THE MACI

FORMA

To-day, at the Judicia judgment was given in Penzance, the Dean o Mackonochie, which journal on the 3d ins Jeune, and Mr. G. O. and the respondent, sented.

The appeal was hear Spencer (the Lord Pre Lord Blackburn, Lord James Hannen, and Si

The ecclesiastical Durham, Winchester, a

In order to underst has now entered in its state that the present against Mr. Mackonoc Alban's, Holborn. In menced; in May, 1874, t the third suit. In the sions for offences agai respondent was conde

Fig. 139. *Portion (original size) of* The Evening News, *Feb. 23, 1882, with bold headlines* was a very different evening journal from any of its twopenny, penny, or halfpenny predecessors. It had its witty paragraphs and causerie. More sensational still, it sponsored the interview, forthwith denounced by the old stagers, as an outrage upon the private life of the individual. It ran campaigns for or against a government policy in an entirely new way. When *The Pall Mall Gazette* developed into an eight-page full folio in place of the sixteen-page half-size paper it had been since 1865, the headings were increased. On one occasion the forthcoming government dissolution was headed in bold condensed sans serif over a text itself set in bold face.

The Echo, at a halfpenny, but in larger sheet and seven instead of four columns, was, even in 1889, a restrained, conservative piece of newspaper typography. Much the same style, though modern in type-face, was retained by *The Evening News*. This paper, as a whole, was lightened in its texture by the liberal insertion of leads and cut-offs between paragraphs. Only the first three of the six columns on the front page were classified advertisements. For some years *The Evening News* remained stable in format and finance. A summary of the news (one column), late telegrams and an epitome of the previous evening's parliament completed the front page. The rest of the make-up was traditional, i.e. the main news-page (including 'Sport', 'City') was a right-hand opening facing the leader page which comprised a column of classified advertisements outside the flag, the leaders, the causerie, etc. The 'modern-face' headlines gave place, in 1882, to a heavy condensed sans-serif throughout, and the use of a bold upper- and lower-case as introductory run-on lining titles to column fill-ups. This is the old Sunday newspaper style.

In 1887, a competitor, *The Evening Post*, was started. *The Morning Post* entered an action for infringement of title; won their injunction but lost on appeal. Yet *The Evening Post* failed and hence *The Evening News* was able to drop 'Telephone' and add 'Post' instead to its sub-title. Consolidation was indeed advisable. The year 1888 is memorable in the history of journalism. *The Star*, a competitor which nearly brought *The Evening News and Post* to its end, was founded by T. P. O'Connor in 1888. The paper, also a halfpenny, came out in a new style which may fairly claim to be regarded as the first whole-hearted determination to engraft the 'New Journalism' upon the stock of high Victorian tradition. Stead had, to a great extent, prepared the way with his gossip column, the interview and other features. These developments, which the early 'eighties had never heard of, were accompanied by headlines which they had never seen.

The reader of London morning newspapers had never seen that humble but vital aid to quick reading, the 'cross-head', until Stead used it in *The Pall Mall Gazette* during the year 1881. Typographically the cross-head is vastly more advantageous to the reader than any fat, heavy or condensed headline. It was the first sign of the coming of the 'New Journalism', and Stead was its prophet. When Matthew Arnold wrote his article in *The Nineteenth Century* for May 1887 he had W. T. Stead in mind. 'We have had opportunity', he said, 'of observing a new journalism which a clever and energetic man has invented. It has much to recommend it; it has ability, novelty, variety, sensation, sympathy, generous instinct; its own great fault is that it is *feather-brained*', etc. As we are not here to study journalism in itself, we may do no more than make this quotation for the purpose of establishing the date for the emergence of the name 'New Journalism' and for the type of writing which it describes. In view of the absence of any history of the journalism written by one who lived through this period, it would be rash to dogmatise, but my impression is that journalism owes more to W. T. Stead than it realises. Matthew Arnold's criticism of his methods made him, in some accidental sort, the prophet of the movement. Stead, hardly a journalist in the professional sense, was no more going to 'twaddle about chrysanthemums or spin rigmaroles about the dresses at the last drawing room, or the fashions at Goodwood', instead of campaigning, than he was going to accept the professionally competent journalist's idea of setting out what he did choose to write. As Stead intended his paper to be read, he made it readable by inventing the cross-head.

And Stead, as I have said, accidentally found himself the champion of the new methods in journalism, whether literary or typographical. The reply to Matthew Arnold's *Nineteenth Century* article was given in two articles by Stead in *The Contemporary Review*. In the *Pall Mall* itself, the editor made a typographical point when opportunity offered.

"Wonders will never cease," Stead once wrote, "one of the morning papers has today adopted the device, so familiar to our readers, of breaking up the solid columns of speeches by cross-heads. The new departure is wonderful indeed—wonderful in that it should have been adopted at last and by so conservative a journal as the *Morning Post*; wonderful in that it should not have been adopted before. What would have been thought of a publisher who should bring out a book, not only with no division into chapters, but even without the relief of so much as a single fresh paragraph from the first word to the last? Yet Mr Goschen's Budget Speech last night, covering, as it does, eight columns of *The Times*, has as much in it in mere matter of words as many books, and a great deal more in it in matter of sense than most books.

"In this, as in all things, we English present a curious combination of enterprise and lack of intelligence. Nothing can be less intelligent than the way in which English journals as a rule present their parliamentary reports; nothing more enterprising than the amount of them they amass. Last night, for instance, the report of Mr Goschen's speech was an extraordinary feat", etc.[1]

Stead's contentions are on the whole just—at any rate, subsequent practice of the conservative papers has definitely been in the direction he pointed out. At the time, however, the morning paper shewed an obstinate preference for the old ways of conducting and printing a paper. Yet there had been progress.

The issue of *The Times* for January 29, 1869, first increased the solemnity of the leader page, as the seat of authority, by particularising the contents of the paper in a two-column table of small roman upper- and lower-case under the heading of 'Table of Contents'. In the issue for February 8, 1868, this table spaced to the full measure, received greater prominence.

The Times cordially embraced the opportunity which the Franco-German War gave it to shew maps of the theatre of activities. A full-page wood engraving of the war area was printed roughly once a week during the opening months of 1871, and a half-page map of Paris, similarly engraved, appeared on January 7 and 13.

An important date in the history of the paper's pictorial development is April 13, 1875, which saw the daily substitution of a map of the weather for the purely typographical table which had been printed for some years. This map was apparently printed from a wood-engraved block. The first zincographic engraving, in association with the usual meteorological diagram, appeared in the paper for January 4, 1877. Zincographic maps became frequent in the 'seventies, and Stead was one of the first to use line-block portraits, cartoons (by F. C. G.) or maps every day.

A portent had appeared in the advertisement columns of *The Times* during the autumn of 1866: nothing less than the first 'displayed' advertisement. It took an elementary form—namely, the line-by-line repetition of the name of the firm or its product, or both. In 1868 there are numerous instances of

[1] *The Pall Mall Gazette*, March 27, 1888, p. 4. *The Times*'s first cross-headed speeches were by Joseph Chamberlain on April 21, 1890. On October 27, 1891, *The Pall Mall Gazette* remarked that '*The Times* is becoming quite smart as a headliner'.

JANUARY 31, 1894. PALL MALL GAZETTE. 7

IMPENDING RESIGNATION OF MR. GLADSTONE.

GRAVE POLITICAL CRISIS.

DISSOLUTION PROBABLE.

We have reason to know, from an authority which we are not able to disclose, but in which we have every confidence, that Mr. Gladstone has finally decided to resign office almost immediately. We understand that the letter announcing his resolution will be sent to the Queen before the reassembling of Parliament. This decision is due to a sense of his advanced age and to the great strain of the late arduous session. He is also deeply disappointed at the rejection of the Home Rule Bill, and at the opposition which the Parish Councils Bill has encountered. Domestic pressure, moreover, has not been without considerable influence in determining his mind at last. Who will succeed him? And what will be the result?

THE MATABELE CAMPAIGN.

SETTLEMENT ROUND BULUWAYO

BARBAROUS CRUELTY BY A WITCH DOCTOR

On the return of Sir John Willoughby and Hon. Maurice Gifford's from searching for Captain Williams's body, they met the Induna whose impi destroyed Major Wilson and his party, and received confirmation of the details already given of the gallant defence and death of Wilson and his men. Mr. Cecil Rhodes has promised that if the patrol party which has gone out under Colonel Goold-Adams to seek for the bodies of Wilson's party is successful in its search, he will bear the cost of the conveyance of the remains to Zimbabye, as well as of the burial and the erection of a monument to the memory of the gallant dead. Heavy rains have set in. Numerous settlements are being made round Buluwayo. Prospectors are active, and one claims the discovery of an alluvial field near Inyati. All the farms between Buluwayo and Tati have been secured. The Bechuanaland Police have been placed at the disposal of the Chartered Company, who are administering the whole country.

HORRIBLE TORTURE OF A WOMAN

Sir Henry Loch, the High Commissioner, has received a report from Colonel Goold-Adams announcing that he has captured a notorious witch-doctor who has visited the kraals in the vicinity of Shiloh and carried off many women and children. In one instance a woman who fell into his hands was murdered in the most horrible manner. Her hands and feet were bound together, and the doctor then pricked out her eyes with needles. She was afterwards thrown into the Khami river, where she was torn to pieces by crocodiles. On hearing of this atrocity, Colonel Goold-Adams ordered the arrest of the witch-doctor and the victim's husband, and they were both tried for murder and condemned to be shot. The other women and children seized by the witch-doctor were set at liberty. Colonel Goold-Adams states that the natives in the district are engaged in sowing.

LIEUTENANT MIZON BANQUETTED

THE DREAM OF OTHER DAYS REALIZED.

PARIS, Wednesday.—The Industrial and Commercial Society of the Colonies gave a banquet yesterday evening to Lieutenant Mizon, the explorer. Addressing those present, Lieutenant Mizon said what formerly had been regarded as a dream, had become a reality, and that was the junction in the vicinity of Lake Tchad, of the French African possessions of Algeria, Senegal, and the Congo. He briefly sketched the work of the French explorers, Monteil, Le Maistre, and De Brazza, and then referring to Adamawa, he stated that this kingdom had been placed by treaty under the protection of the Republic, and a military post had been established at Yola, while he himself had governed Mouri and Bachama for a year. The dream of other days had thus been realized. M. Mizon concluded by extolling the advantages of colonies for the mother country.—*Reuter.*

ENTRY OF THE DUKE OF COBURG INTO GOTHA.

GOTHA, Wednesday.—To-day being the day fixed for the State entry of the new Duke of Saxe-Coburg-Gotha into this capital, the town is everywhere gaily adorned with flags and banners, and decked with draperies of bunting in the German, Coburg, and British colours. The houses are almost without exception decorated with bright-coloured hangings of all kinds, and the whole presents a pretty spectacle. The streets to be traversed by the Ducal procession are lined by rows of tall Venetian masts, decorated with flags and streamers and joined one to another by garlands of fir-cuttings. From an early hour crowds of sightseers have been pouring into the town from the surrounding districts, and the streets are thronged with spectators in holiday attire. The sky is overcast, but there is no rain at present.—*Reuter.*

THE CAPTURE OF JABEZ BALFOUR.

DECISION OF THE NATIONAL GOVERNMENT

THE ACT OF INTERNATIONAL COURTESY.

(FROM OUR OWN CORRESPONDENT.)

[PER THE EASTERN TELEGRAPH COMPANY, LIMITED.]

BUENOS AYRES, Wednesday.—The National Government has ordered the Governor of Salta to send Jabez Balfour here.

LONDON OFFICER LEAVES FOR ARGENTINA.

All the additional warrants, documents, papers, &c., having now been prepared and completed, Sergeant Craggs, of the Criminal Investigation Department, will proceed from Liverpool to-day by the Pacific liner *Britannia.* So far as is at present known, no other officer of the Metropolitan Police will go to the River Plate.

TEXT OF THE EXTRADITION TREATY.

An Order in Council, dated "At the Court at Osborne House, Isle of Wight, the 29th day of January, 1894," is published in yesterday's *London Gazette.* The Order embodies the whole of the Extradition Treaty made with the Argentine Republic on the 22nd May, 1889, of which ratifications were exchanged at Buenos Ayres on the 15th December, 1893; and orders that, in accordance with this treaty, the Extradition Acts of 1870 and 1873 shall apply to the Argentine Republic from and after the 9th February, 1894. This date has obviously been fixed in compliance with an article of the treaty which provides that it shall come into force "ten days after its publication, in conformity with the forms prescribed by the high contracting parties." It is therefore evident that Jabez Balfour has not been arrested under the Extradition Treaty, and the original announcement is confirmed, that "the arrest was made, not as implying any right on the part of the British Government to demand it, but as an act of international courtesy." The question of retrospective action is not in any way referred to in the treaty.

LIABILITY OF THE CONVICT WRIGHT.

In the Queen's Bench Divisional Court, yesterday afternoon, Mr. H. S. Theobald applied in the matter of the Liberator Building Society and H. G. Wright, convict, to have an appeal put down as urgent in the paper for Thursday. Counsel said there were proceedings in the City of London Court against Wright, seeking to make him liable for a considerable sum of money. He had taken out an appeal for security for costs, and it was most desirable that the appeal should be heard at once. As was well known, Jabez Balfour was expected in England before long, and when he came it would be necessary for the books of the Liberator Society to be handed over to him so that he might have an inspection of them. That would practically be preventing them from getting a hearing, as the books could not in the event be produced in the City of London Court. The other side did not in terms object or consent. The appeal was for costs, while in the meantime the whole proceedings were hung up. The Court granted the application, with liberty to the other side to reply.

THE REVOLUTION IN BRAZIL.

INTERVIEW WITH ADMIRAL BENHAM.

RIO DE JANEIRO, Tuesday Evening.—Admiral Benham, in the course of an interview on yesterday's incident said: "On Friday the batteries on Cobras Island fired at an American ship. Admiral da Gama claimed in defence of this proceeding that blank shots were first fired, warning the vessel that it was within the danger line. I ordered him, however, to cease. Nevertheless, on Saturday the fort on Cobras Island and the cruiser *Trajano* both fired at the barque *Agate.* I warned Da Gama that if he repeated this firing on American vessels I would fire back. If Admiral da Gama touches an American ship or American goods he is pirate. I will protect American vessels absolutely except against chance shots. I also notified Admiral da Gama unofficially that firing at the wharves for the purpose of terrorizing traders, and enforcing a blockade would not be permitted as far as it affected Americans. Admiral da Gama returned no answer. Three American vessels afterwards wanted to go to the wharves. I notified Admiral da Gama that I meant to convoy them at sunrise on Monday, and

THE FLEET WAS CLEARED FOR ACTION.

Two of the vessels, after all, declined to come in, but the *Amy* did so, escorted by the *Detroit.* I thought a fight was possible, and made every preparation for one. The cruisers *New York*, *Charleston*, and *Newark* were assigned to deal with the ironclad *Aquidaban* and the cruiser *Almirante Tamandare*, and the cruisers *Detroit* and *San Francisco* with the cruisers *Trajano* and *Guanabara.* The last-named fired a musket shot at the *Amy* whereupon the *Detroit* fired two shots at the *Guanabara* and *Trajano* All opposition to the convoy of the *Amy* to the wharves at once ceased.

THERE WAS NO NECESSITY TO USE THE HEAVY GUNS.

The reason the other two vessels stayed out was that they were persuaded to do so by the captain of the *Julia Rollins*, who is believed to be the agent of an English firm which is furnishing the insurgents with money. Later in the day Admiral da Gama conferred with his officers on the question of surrendering to the *Detroit* in consequence of the musket shots fired at the *Guanabara* and *Trajano*, but it was decided not to do so. The insurgent leader may, however, surrender yet. Admiral da Gama is in a bad way. The compromise considered at the conference on board the *New York* was rejected by the Government. Admiral de Mello's prolonged absence has given rise to a rumour that he is dead There are sixteen foreign warships now here, of which five are American and four British. The French commander has congratulated Admiral Benham on the vigorous action taken by him yesterday. The Austrian commander cleared for action in readiness to assist Admiral Benham, in the event of an engagement with the insurgent warships.—*Reuter.*

REPORTED DEFEAT OF GOVERNMENT TROOPS.

BUENOS AYRES, Tuesday Night.—According to intelligence from Rio de Janeiro, Curutiba, Paranagua, and Antonina are in the hands of the insurgents. The Government troops are stated to have fled, abandoning their arms and ammunition. Admiral De Mello is at Curutiba, and is reorganizing the administration of the province.—*Reuter.*

THE INSURRECTION IN MEXICO.

DEFEAT OF THE REBELS.

MEXICO, Tuesday Night.—The insurrection in the northern part of the Mexican Republic has been crushed by the Federal troops. The filibusters Ochoa and Lugan were overtaken in the Sierra Negurachie where they made a determined stand. The fight between the insurgents and the Government forces lasted eleven hours. The rebels lost thirty men killed, and twenty-five wounded, while of the Government troops one officer and seven men were killed and twelve wounded. Ochoa escaped and fled.—*Reuter.*

THE REBELLION IN HAYTI.

NEW YORK, Wednesday.—A despatch from Port au Prince states that the Haytian revolutionists are despondent. General Manigat, the leader of the Haytian revolutionary cause, was arrested at Kingston as he was about to enter a boat to be rowed to a steamer of which he was to take command, and which had been purchased for him by his agents in America. The arrest of their leader upsets all the plans of the revolutionists for their contemplated invasion of Hayti.—*Dalziel.*

MILITARY INTELLIGENCE.

PORTSMOUTH, Wednesday.—The hired transport *Bothnia*, sailed at eight o'clock this morning for Karachi with military reliefs under Major Taylor, of the Derbyshire regiment, numbering 39 officers, 570 rank and file, 24 soldiers' wives, and 14 children. She will call at Queenstown, where she will embark 600 more troops.—*Reuter.*

CORDITE PATENT IN CHANCERY.

THE "PALL MALL'S" CHARGES TRIED.

Upon the resumption to-day of the hearing of the Nobel Explosives Company's action against the Government for the infringement of their ballistite patent in the Ordnance Department's manufacture of cordite, Sir Charles Russell continued to cross-examine Dr. Odling, the Oxford Professor of Chemistry, who had declared cordite and ballistite to be, as Mr. Noble alleges them to be, practically the same thing. But Sir Charles was not the cross-examining terror that he usually is on the Queen's Bench side of the courts. Sir Charles is a specialist in human nature, but in matters of patent law he is a child in comparison with Mr. Fletcher Moulton, who leads for the plaintiff, or with Sir Richard Webster, who, ex-Attorney-General as he is, has been briefed by the Government to reinforce the Attorney-General's own not very formidable forces. Sir Charles was as far away from home in this case as Mr. Moulton might be on a sporting trial; but of course so great an advocate was not and could not be at anything like a loss for tactics. He had been well crammed with the technicalities of the matters in dispute. It was only in resourcefulness and facility of handling that his leading opponent showed to so much greater advantage. Mr. Moulton could doubtless conduct the whole case without any documents to refer to, and did, indeed, open the case exhaustively without notes. Sir Charles Russell does not dare to take a single step without consulting his voluminous references, unless it was upon a whispered suggestion from Sir Richard Webster that he proceeded.

THE POINT OF DIFFERENCE.

It was difficult to follow the line of the cross-examination, but it seemed to suggest that the nitro-cellulose employed in the cordite was of a more soluble variety than that employed in ballistite, enabling cordite to be manufactured in a manner altogether different from that of ballistite. Witness admitted that, according to the specification of ballistite, it was an essential that the substance in course of manufacture should be pressed between heated rollers, while in the manufacture of cordite no heated rollers were used, nor was there any pressure at all in the same sense, although in the kneading process used in cordite-making there was necessarily and obviously a certain degree of compression.

So far from heat being used at Waltham Abbey, a contrivance is resorted to in order to avoid heat?—Yes.

While in the manufacture of ballisite the rollers are heated to 100 degs. Centigrade, or boiling point?—That is so.

Other distinctions which Sir Charles elicited from the witness were that in cordite there was no camphor, but there was vaseline; while in ballistite there was no vaseline, and the use of camphor in the manufacture was optional. Sir Charles also put to the witness that while immersion in alcohol would reduce ballistite to a jelly, the same treatment applied to cordite would leave sticks of insoluble gun-cotton. Witness believed this to be so, but had never made the experiments.

THE RE-EXAMINATION.

All this while Mr. Moulton, who is a Senior Wrangler with the uncultured habit of continually wetting his pencil on his tongue, had been making voluminous notes, and it was he who re-examined Dr. Odling. He did it with the air of one revelling in these abstruse and highly technical matters. The case seems to be a scientific debauch for Mr. Moulton. Witness stated that the camphor used in ballistite-making was merely to facilitate the combination of the other ingredients. In the specification, acetone was mentioned as an alternative to camphor, and acetone was used in making cordite. What was used was driven off in the final stages in the making of both cordite and ballistite. Vaseline was used in cordite making, but before it was added the ingredients were thoroughly incorporated for 3½ hours. The vaseline did not alter the character of the union of nitro-cellulose and nitro-glycerine. There was no essential difference between the method and the result of the manufacture of the two things, beyond the one difference of the high temperature rolling in ballistite making.

Much has been made of the different results obtainable by the solution of the two things in alcohol. Is the great object for which they are made to put them into alcohol?—No.

Their use is as propellers of projectiles?—Yes.

And the immersion in alcohol fulfils absolutely no use except for test purposes?—That is so.

THE CLOSING OF BRUSSELS UNIVERSITY

STUDENTS' DISORDERLY CONDUCT

BRUSSELS, Wednesday.—Three hundred of the students have addressed a protest to the Pro-Rector, expressing their sympathy with their expelled comrades, and declaring that they will not enter the University until the present Council is dismissed. The twenty-two students of the University who have been expelled gave the Pro-Rector a hostile reception yesterday, in which they, aided by about two hundred of their companions, hooted him vigorously. So threatening did their attitude become that the Pro-Rector had to be protected by the professors who accompanied him The Pro-Rector announced that the University would be closed until further notice, whereupon the students formed themselves into a procession and paraded the principal streets of the city, singing and shouting, and headed by a banner bearing the words "The Unemployed." The demonstrators strongly support the attitude taken by Dr. Denis, the late Rector, who resigned owing to the action of the Council, and Professor Greef. The latter, it is said, will hold his class outside the University, probably in the Freemasons' Hall. It is expected that when M. Elisée Reclus, the cause of all the trouble, comes to Brussels to deliver his lectures, his presence will give rise to Socialist disorders.—*Dalziel.*

A REGISTRATION AGENT'S DIVORCE SUIT

The further hearing of the case of White v. White and Bovington was resumed this morning before Sir F. Jeune in the Divorce Division, it being the petition of Mr. Edward White, a Liberal registration agent in London, for a dissolution of his marriage with the respondent on the ground of her misconduct with the co-respondent. Mrs. White, the respondent, entered the witness-box and denied that she had been guilty of adultery.

ATTEMPTED SUICIDE THROUGH LOVE.

A young man named Green attempted to commit suicide last night at Chatham by cutting his throat. When discovered he moaned, "It is all for the love of her." He now lies in St. Bartholomew's Hospital, Rochester, in a critical condition.

WRECKS AND CASUALTIES.

During last night's gale a large iron vessel, laden with a general cargo bound for Glasgow, struck on Thorn Island at the entrance to Milford Haven. The vessel is partly submerged, the bows alone being above water and the forecastle is on fire. The crew were saved by the *Angle* lifeboat and rocket apparatus.

The large steamer, *Henry Fisher*, which ran ashore at Hayle during Monday night's gale, remains high and dry, and it is feared that unless the weather abates it will be difficult to tow her off.

IN THE LONDON BANKRUPTCY COURT TO-DAY

JOHN LUTTMAN.

The Official Receiver reported to-day upon the affairs of John Luttman, who states that since 1871 he has carried on business as a financial agent, company promoter, and accountant, having an office from 1888 until October last at No. 1, Gresham-buildings, City. The liabilities amount to £9,890, and the assets are returned at £10. The debtor, who admits that he has been insolvent for some years past, has been adjudged bankrupt.

Fig. 140. *Typographical expression of a scoop by* The Pall Mall Gazette, 1894 columns being given to this form of advertising, set in all cases in the capitals of the news fount. These displays could not but affect the typography of the paper.

In 1884 Mr G. E. Buckle became editor. There was little change in the aspect of the paper. On April 14 John Stuart Blackie overthrew a hoary tradition by appending his signature to a review of sundry works on Goethe. The new editor went thus far with the 'New Journalism'. A decent 4-in. zinco over two columns of the new Forth Bridge was slipped into *The Times* on June 16, 1884.

The front page advertising, logically and consistently arranged since 1820, was divided into its respective sections by a column-wide thick and thin rule. The departmental headings, such as 'Entertainments', 'Art Exhibitions', 'Hotels', and so forth, were not printed until February 22, 1886. On February 11, 1887 the 'Table of Contents' was initiated, printed over the leader, and set out with lines of alternate roman and italic capitals. *The Pall Mall Gazette*'s comment upon this arrangement was not encouraging. One of the 'occasional' notes, doubtless written by Stead, was devoted to the innovation:

> Nothing like your good old Conservatives for sweeping reform when he once sets his mind to it. Here is the *Times*, for instance, which has always been regarded—not without some reason—as the slow coach of London journalism. But the 'demon of sensationalism' as people call it has been too much for the *Times* at last, and, lo and behold! it comes out this morning in the most important place in its issue with twenty headlines and more, piled one on the top of the other, with a diversity of type and a prodigality of capitals we sincerely admire, but can never hope to attain. It is the most daring attempt that has yet been made by a long way towards 'Americanising' London journalism: indeed there has been nothing like the *Times*' 'Contents' this morning since the palmy days of the Indianapolis *Snapping-Turtle*, or since the Chicago *Times* announced the execution of 'Doc' Smith in headlines never to be forgotten—nor quoted. The *Times* of Chicago, by the way, used to keep a special man on its staff to concoct headlines; we recommend the plan to the *Times* of London.[1]

It is hardly fair comment, for the headlines referred to are indications printed over the general contents arranged in paragraph form, and not headlines over a news-story as *The Pall Mall Gazette* suggests and even represents. Larger capitals were at the same time given to certain subdivisions of the

[1] *The Pall Mall Gazette*, February 12, 1887. It must be acknowledged that the alternation of lines of roman capitals with lines of italic capitals had never been done before—or since. Nor have I ever seen the thing done in any American paper.

The New-York Times.

VOL. XIII.—NO. 4039. NEW-YORK, SATURDAY, SEPTEMBER 3, 1864. PRICE FOUR CENTS.

ATLANTA.

Fall of the Rebel Stronghold.

A Great Battle on the Macon Railroad.

HOOD'S ARMY CUT IN TWAIN.

THE REBEL GENERAL HARDEE KILLED.

SHERMAN ENTERS THE CITY.

Official Bulletin from the War Department.

A THUNDERBOLT FOR COPPERHEADS.

THE APPROACHING DRAFT

Its Burdens Materially Lightened

Grant Wants but One Hundred Thousand More Men.

These to Finish the Rebellion and Restore Peace.

[OFFICIAL DISPATCH.]

WAR DEPARTMENT, WASHINGTON, Sept. 2—6 P. M.

To Maj.-Gen. Dix, New-York:

This Department has received intelligence this evening that Gen. SHERMAN'S advance entered Atlanta about noon to-day. The particulars have not yet been received, but telegraphic communication during the night with Atlanta direct is expected.

It is ascertained with reasonable certainty that the naval and other credits required by the act of Congress will amount to about 200,000, including New-York, which has not been reported yet to the Department; so that the President's call of July 10 is practically reduced to 300,000 men

entered Atlanta at 9 o'clock this morning. No further particulars have been received.

REPORTS FROM NASHVILLE.

NASHVILLE, Friday, Sept. 2.

Gen. SHERMAN'S advance entered Atlanta this morning at 11 o'clock. The whole Federal force will enter to-day.

Several miles of the Nashville and Chattanooga Railroad were burned by Gen. WHEELER'S forces yesterday. Gen. ROUSSEAU drove the rebel force within three miles of Lavange, late in the afternoon of yesterday. He met with a stubborn resistance.

Late intelligence reports that the head of WHEELER'S column left the Murfreesboro pike going to the right, at 10 o'clock, and the rear at 3 o'clock, the whole force moving from the Tennessee and Alabama Railroad in the direction of Franklin. ROUSSEAU is in close pursuit.

A person just in from Franklin reports that the town is in the hands of WHEELER'S forces, he having entered and captured it last night. Particulars have not yet been received.

Our casualties in yesterday's skirmishing were five killed and fifty or fifty-five wounded.

A small body of rebels fired on a train at Brentworth, eight miles from here.

The rebel loss yesterday was eight killed and fifteen wounded. We captured a number of prisoners. The river is falling.

THE MIDDLE MILITARY DIVISION.

Early Still in the Valley—His Headquarters at Bunker Hill.

He Repairs his Communications with Richmond.

BALTIMORE, Friday, Sept. 2.

A special dispatch to the American, dated Charlestown, Va., Sept. 2, says: "Reconnoissances have established the fact that EARLY has not left, and has no intention of leaving the Valley. His headquarters are at Bunker Hill, between Martinsburgh and Winchester.

He is busily engaged in repairing and putting up a telegraph line, and he has already telegraphic communication with Richmond from this side of Woodstock. He is also receiving reinforcements, and FITZHUGH LEE is known to have received 500 horses for his cavalry, which is said to number 10,000.

There is a regular stage from Winchester to Staunton which runs every day, and several officers and soldiers are receiving short furloughs to go home and return to Winchester, which does not look as though the enemy intend leaving the Valley.

NEWS FROM WASHINGTON.

Special Dispatches to the New-York Times.

WASHINGTON, Friday, Sept. 2.

INDIAN DEPREDATIONS.

Advices from the Northwest inform us of the continuance of Indian depredations in that quarter. Hostile tribes are taking pattern by the rebels, and have resolved themselves into small bands, and carry on a guerrilla warfare, killing white settlers and emigrants wherever they can be found singly or in small parties. It is said that the [illegible] if properly conducted, would have then and there ended all these Indian difficulties, but that many officers engaged in the expedition were too deeply interested in speculations growing out of the [illegible]

SURRENDER OF FORT MORGAN.

Official Dispatches from Admiral Farragut.

The Correspondence Preliminary to the Capitulation.

Wanton Destruction of Property by the Rebels.

WASHINGTON, Friday, Sept. 2.

The Navy Department to-day received the following from Admiral FARRAGUT:

FLAGSHIP HARTFORD, WEST GULF BLOCKADING SQUADRON, MOBILE BAY, Aug. 25, 1864.

SIR: I had the honor in my dispatch, No. 31, to state to the Department that Fort Morgan had surrendered on the 23d inst. to the army and navy, though at the time the dispatch was written and mailed the ceremony of surrender had not actually taken place.

The correspondence preliminary to that event is herewith forwarded, marked Nos. 1, 2, 3 and 4, and the department will perceive the terms of capitulation were the same as in the case of Fort Gaines. Gen. PAGE endeavored to obtain more favorable terms, but without success.

I regret to state that after the assembling of the rebel officers at the appointed hour, 2 P. M., for the surrender outside the fort, it was discovered on an examination of the interior that most of the guns were spiked, many of the gun carriages wantonly injured, the arms, ammunition, provisions, etc., destroyed, and there was every reason to believe this had been done after the white flag had been raised.

It was also discovered that Gen. PAGE and several of his officers had no swords to deliver up, and further that some of those which were surrendered had been broken.

The whole conduct of the officers of Fort Gaines and Fort Morgan presents such a striking contrast in moral principle, that I cannot fail to remark upon it. Col. ANDERSON, who commanded the former, finding himself in a perfectly untenable position, and incumbered with a superfluous number of conscripts, many of whom were boys, determined to surrender a fort which he could not defend, and in this determination was supported by all his officers, save one. But from the moment he hoisted the white flag, he scrupulously kept everything intact, and in that condition delivered it over, whilst Gen. PAGE and his officers, with a childish spite, destroyed guns which they said they would defend to the last, but which they never defended at all, and threw away or broke those weapons which they had not the manliness to use against their enemies, for Fort Morgan never fired a gun after the commencement of the bombardment, and the advance pickets of our army were actually on its glacis.

As before stated, the ceremony of surrender took place at 2 o'clock P. M., and that same afternoon all the garrison were sent to New Orleans in the United States steamers Tennessee and Bienville, where they arrived safely.

Very respectfully your obedient servant,

D. G. FARRAGUT [illegible]

having [illegible] there for that purpose from Baltimore by order of Gen. WALLACE.

Lieut. [illegible] arrived at Old Point, at 2:30 P. M., from City Point, on [illegible]

DEATHS IN THE HAMPTON HOSPITAL.

The following persons have died at the Hampton Hospital since the last report:

J. Wilkins, [illegible] U. S. Col'd.	E. A. Friday, 1st Ct. Vols.
Charles [illegible], 18th Penn.	F. Heggles, 2d Penn. Art.
Jas. B. Black, [illegible] Mass.	A. H. [illegible] Penn.
J. Thomson, 62d Ohio.	H. Newbury, 26th Mass.
J. Sel[illegible], 1st Conn. Art.	P. Henderson, 126th Ohio.
A. Hall, [illegible] Ohio.	Thomas Davis, 55th Penn.
Wm. Mattore, 62d Ohio.	Patrick Gallagher, 1st Md. Cavalry.
John [illegible], 16th Penn.	John A. Lyon, 55th Penn.
John Hamp, 16th N. H.	Peter Smith, [illegible] N. H.
James E. Boyd, 6th N. Y. Artillery.	J. E. Woodward, 3[illegible] New Jersey.
Thomas O'Neron, 10th N. Y. Artillery.	J. Johnson, 9th N. J.
Moses [illegible], 2d US colored.	Henry [illegible], 13th N. Y. Artillery.
Richard [illegible], 16th N. Y. Artillery.	John Wood, 98th N. Y.
R. G. [illegible], 1st D. C. Cav.	Lane Rooney, 13th N. Y.
Michael [illegible], 115th N. Y.	John B. Clayton, 55th Penn.
Jacob [illegible], 163d Ohio.	

Major [illegible] N. CLARK, 133d Ohio, died last night, at the Chesapeake Hospital.

THE WAR IN TENNESSEE.

Movements of the Rebel Forces Under Wheeler, Forrest and Roddy.

General Rousseau Starts Out to Meet Them.

A BATTLE IN PROGRESS.

FROM LOUISVILLE.

LOUISVILLE, Ky., Thursday, Sept. 1.

Passengers from Nashville say that the rebel forces under Gens. WHEELER, FORREST and RODDY, are engaged in tearing up the track of the Great Western Railroad between Nashville and the Tennessee.

The Nashville Union says that Gen. ROUSSEAU has made such a disposition of his forces, that these rebel commands cannot injure the railroad, and that he has gone out to give them battle.

FROM NASHVILLE.

NASHVILLE, Tenn., Thursday, Sept. 1.

A rebel force, estimated at ten thousand strong, with twelve pieces of artillery, was within seventeen miles of Nashville, on the Murfreesboro pike, at daylight this morning.

Maj.-Gen. ROUSSEAU, with a body of cavalry and infantry, started yesterday afternoon, and met the enemy's advance early this morning. Sharp skirmishing commenced, with varying success.

Later accounts Gen. ROUSSEAU had driven the rebels, under WHEELER, RODDY and FORREST, three miles toward Murfreesboro.

Messengers from our advance report that Gen. WHEELER'S whole force is now between this city and Murfreesboro'.

There is a considerable force of rebels also at Lebanon.

Prisoners and some wounded have been sent from [illegible] front.

[illegible]

LOUISVILLE, Ky., Thursday, Sept. 1.

Fifteen guerrillas under BILLY MCGANDER are reported to have thrown an engine off the track of

FIVE DAYS LATER FROM EUROPE

The Hecla at Halifax and the Caledonia Off Cape Race.

Orders Respecting National and Rebel Vessels-of-War in British Ports.

THE FRIGATE NIAGARA IN THE TAGUS.

The Niagara Correspondent of the Times on the Peace Negotiations:

RUMORS OF A NEW CONFEDERATE LOAN.

MOVEMENTS OF ROYAL PERSONAGES.

THE DIFFICULTIES WITH EGYPT ADJUSTED

HALIFAX, Friday, Sept. 2.

The steamship Hecla, Capt. MACAULEY, from Liverpool at 2 o'clock on the afternoon of the 23d, via Queenstown on the 24th ult., arrived here at 2 o'clock this morning. Her dates are three days later than those already received.

ST. JOHNS, N. F., Thursday, Sept. 1. via PORT HOOD, Friday, Sept. 2.

The steamship Caledonia from Glasgow on the 20th, passed Cape Race at 7:30 o'clock this evening. Her advices are two days later than those per the Hecla at Halifax.

No commercial advices have been received by the Caledonia.

OUR PARIS CORRESPONDENCE.

Splendid Decorations and Fireworks for the Fete Napoleon—As-tu-vu Lambert—The Husband of the Queen of Spain in Paris—Secession Rejoicings.

PARIS, Friday, Aug. 19, 1864.

The official decorators of the city of Paris again found something new this year in their marvelous art, for the national fête of Saint Napoleon and the Virgin Mary. In the middle of the Place de la Concorde they built or planted a charming garden reaching from fountain to fountain, and variegated with undulating grass plats, beds of rare flowers and luxuriant plants and trees. In the middle, around the famous old obelisk of Luxor, they built an imitation of the Palace of Montezuma at Mexico, now occupied by the Emperor MAXIMILIAN, and this and the garden were profusely furnished with jets of gas arranged in festoons, stars and devices. The fountains were made to vomit vast columns of illuminated water, which represented the boiling of lava from a crater. The Place had two circles of gas lights in unpolished glass globes of variegated colors an hung in garlands. The effect of all this, when brilliantly lighted, surpassed anything we have yet seen in the same place. The barren and severe aspect of the Place de la Concorde is so much improved by this artificial garden that most people would be glad to see it converted into a reality.

The illumination of the Champs Elysées, of the Garden of the Tuileries, and of the monuments and [illegible] of the city, was remarkably effective on the occasion. The fireworks were brilliant as usual, and in their political aspect, were Mexican, of course. It is the habit at the national

tions here over the situation at home, and the secession journals all claim that the campaign of GRANT is a failure.

MALAKOFF.

OUR LONDON CORRESPONDENCE.

The Riots in Belfast—The Confederate Organ on Peace—An Unequal Bargain—An Average Harvest—Mr. Roebuck—English Prosperity and Prudence—The World on its Travels—English in Paris—French and English Ships and Guns—French and English Policy—Extension of Commerce.

LONDON, Saturday, Aug. 20, 1864.

There is not very much news, but the world moves on. The great midsummer religious and national fête of France will find graphic record in your columns. In the United Kingdom, the event of the week has been the continuous, bloody and, to a considerable number, fatal riots of Belfast. For a week the whole population has been divided into two hostile camps—two mobs of furious zealots, who have destroyed property, taken life, and who have finally, been attacked by the police and military. Who began it? That depends a good deal upon whether your sympathies are with the green flag or the orange. It was the marching under the green flag and the laying a corner-stone for a monument of O'CONNELL in Dublin that roused up the Orangemen of Belfast to burn the Liberator in effigy. They found the burning such a success, that the next night they had a funeral, putting the ashes in a coffin, and carrying it to a cemetery. Then they wrecked a convent or so; but it is not likely that they would have done anything of the sort but for the demonstration in Dublin. Even then, if the Catholics would only have kept quiet, and allowed their buildings to be smashed and themselves beaten without resistance, the riot would have subsided. Their Bishop gave them good advice—to keep in their houses, and if attacked to retreat—but they would not take it. They began to retaliate, and the result has been ten days of furious riot and bloodshed, with hospitals filled with wounded and dying. The authorities proved as inefficient as usual in such cases. There is danger that the rioting may spread to other localities where the Orange faction has not so large a preponderance. If immediate trouble of this kind can be avoided, it will come in the future. You cannot conceive of the fury of hatred that breaks out between the conquerors and the conquered parties in the North of Ireland.

Even the Index—the Confederate official organ in England—announces a speedy peace. It has been slow to admit it, but yields to overwhelming evidence. North and South are tired of the war. Neither can conquer the other; neither can submit to the other; but they can make peace on terms of mutual respect and independence, and an identical foreign policy. The South owes nothing to England or France. The Government of England has been imbecile; that of France inconsistent, if not treacherous. The South would prefer her nearest neighbor for an ally. She will need a revenue, and has no special interest in free trade. If the North wants more territory, the South may also require expansion. Canada, the great Valley of the Red River of the North, and British Columbia, are on the one side, and Mexico and the West Indies on the other. The South is too strong to be conquered, but it is ready to divide the continent with its Northern ally.

This is the substance of a leader in the last Index, written by one of the ablest men connected with Confederate diplomacy—written to be read at Washington, at Richmond, in Downing-street, and in the Tuileries. It is an olive leaf held out to the North, and a threat to England. It says to England and France, give us recognition [illegible] war, or we will make terms with our enemy, and then look out for yourselves. The Index had not

Fig. 141. *American headlines in 1864*

THE NEW YORK HERALD.

NO. 1. LONDON EDITION, SATURDAY, FEBRUARY 2, 1889. PRICE ONE PENNY.

NEW YORK.

Mayor Grant Begins to Dismiss Hewitt's Appointees.

ZALINSKI'S WAR MONSTER.

Eastern Yachtsmen for a Large and Powerful Association.

THE GREAT TRAMWAY STRIKE.

[BY COMMERCIAL CABLE TO THE HERALD.]

NEW YORK, Feb. 1.

The sensation to-day is Mayor Grant's request for the resignation of all the members of the Board of Commissioners, which is composed of Everett P. Wheeler, E. L. Godkin, and Edmund Randolph Robinson. The resignations took place without any objection. Mayor Grant gave no reason to the officials, and refuses to explain to the public. Although this occurred a week ago, it only leaked out yesterday. The three Commissioners were in sympathy with Hewitt, and in opposition to Tammany, which is jubilant over the affair.

ARTIST LAMBDIN DEAD.

James R. Lambdin, the portrait and landscape painter, died at six o'clock yesterday evening from apoplexy, while travelling on a train from Philadelphia to Germantown.

MRS. SCOFIELD'S THREAT.

Mrs. Lilian Scofield, who was prominent in the mysterious death of Broker Nat Hatch, is now living at 217, West Forty-Third-street. Yesterday she was asked to leave, as her behaviour annoyed the other boarders. She said to the janitor who served her with the notice to quit: "I will make you do what I made Hatch do." The owner of the house has asked for a warrant.

cussed and decided at a meeting to be held on March 8th. Captain Joe Elsworth declared that it was high time that some simple and uniform system of measurement should be adopted, and hieroglyphics and mathematics discarded. It was evident that the chief bone of contention will be the measurement rule, but if the various clubs can agree upon this question the Association is bound to be highly successful.

THE FRENCH BALL CLOSED EARLY.

At the French Harmonic Ball yesterday, the police were present to prevent any indiscriminate sale of liquor. At one o'clock they stopped it altogether, and many people left the Opera House in disgust.

RICHARD STODDARD BETTER.

Richard Henry Stoddard has been successfully operated upon for cataract, and will soon be out.

CLEVELAND'S LAST DAYS.

Cleveland gave his last official hand shake to Congress and the Judiciary yesterday.

THE TRAMWAY STRIKE.

Cars are running to-day up to the schedule time. Nearly all roads affected by the "tie up." The Sixth Avenue, Forty-second, Crosstown and Boulevard lines are in full operation under police supervision. A striking Broadway car-driver was shot in a fight between two policemen and a mob between Broadway and Forty-ninth-street, in which pistols were used on both sides. One of the policemen was stabbed. Many strikers are returning to work. The Brooklyn strikers are quiet, and a few of Richardson's cars are running. There will be no general "tie up."

Theatres have been hard hit by the car strike, the Fifth Avenue losing 300 dollars, Palmer's 275 dollars, the Star 600 dollars, Daly's 225 dollars, the Grand Opera 400 dollars, and Niblo's 500 dollars a night.

AID FOR GENERAL LEGITIME.

Major David Essex Porter, the eldest son of the admiral, has offered his services to General Legitime, who claims to be the legitimate Hay-

WASHINGTON.

Shadows of General Harrison's Coming Administration.

SAMOA AND GERMANY

An Interesting Despatch from Mr. Charles Nordoff.

[BY COMMERCIAL CABLE TO THE HERALD.]

HERALD BUREAU, CORNER FIFTEENTH AND G STREETS, N.W., WASHINGTON, Feb. 1, 1889.

There have been very interesting phases of public opinion in America respecting the Samoan question. These changes illustrate in a vivid way the temperament of the American people.

When they first heard that the Germans had committed certain discourtesies they were curiously stolid and indifferent. They regarded it as a kind of thundershower that would blow over in an hour or two, and went about their business in the usual way.

Having rather hot tempers themselves, the American people were inclined to forgive any temporary ebullition on the part of the German Marines.

That was phase No. 1. Phase No. 2 soon trod on the heels of phase No. 1, and shoved it out of the way. The news came in detail, and was exasperating. The German gunboats were evidently acting under instructions, they formed a part of Bismarck's aggressive colonial policy.

BISMARCK'S LITTLE GAME.

Every mail, every new despatch confirmed this opinion that the Iron Chancellor edged in the little game of diplomatic chess, and proposed to use the factional fight among Samoans as an excuse to step in, settle the quarrel, and absorb a valuable

is nearly teased to death by this faction and that, but keeps awfully still and nobody knows what is going to happen until lightning strikes.

New York city is enjoying the luxury of a horsecar strike, not one of the European sort, but a very diluted imitation. Everybody is good natured except about a couple of hundred hot heads, mostly importations, and the affair will, we hope, be over in a day or two. In the meantime we are walking because we must, and thereby getting a good degree of health and very large amount of appetite.

CHARLES NORDHOFF.

HARRISON'S CABINET.

THIS TIME THE COMPLETE LIST OF ALL THE APPOINTMENTS GIVEN.

HERALD BUREAU, CORNER FIFTEENTH AND G STREETS, WASHINGTON, Feb. 1, 1889.

[BY COMMERCIAL CABLE TO THE HERALD.]

It is generally understood that Allison will refuse the Secretaryship of the Treasury. This may force Harrison to revise the whole of his list. McKinley, of Ohio, is spoken of if Allison refuses, but McKinley will also refuse. Charles Foster, of Ohio, expects a Cabinet place. Nothing is yet officially known, but Blaine and Wannamaker are considered certain. The latest list makes Blaine, Secretary of State, Allison, Secretary of the Treasury, Alger, Secretary of War; Wannamaker, Secretary of the Navy; Henderson of Missouri, Secretary of the Interior; Miller of New York, Postmaster-General; Estee of California, Attorney-General. If Alger is nominated, Sherman will oppose its confirmation.

AN EXTRA SESSION.

An extra Session is believed to be unavoidable, as no tariff or revenue reduction measure can pass before March. McKinley, Burroughs, Reed, Cannon, and Henderson, are all candidates for the Speakership. They are making an earnest canvass,

Americans have been injured, or any of their rights, as defined by law and treaty, taken away."

Senator Frye said in the debate that the German trading firm controlling the islands owns nearly all the real estate. It also gives orders to the German Consul and the German fleet. He did not believe that either Germany or Bismarck understood this.

"There is not a fourth-rate Power in Europe," he said, "that would not have risked its political life without hesitation if it had not been a party to a Conference with Germany in its own Courts about the autonomy of Samoa and its independance, and Germany, pending that conference, without any notice to such European Power, had deliberately ordered her ships to take possession and violate the autonomy and the independance of those islands. I say there is not a fourth-rate Power that would not have risked its national life on a demand made at once that the status quo existing at the time when that conference was in session, should be forthwith restored."

WHAT BLAINE'S FRIEND THINKS.

Senator Hale, who is supposed to represent Blaine, said: "I believe that whatever has been done in the Islands of Samoa in the direction of German interference, and German intervention there, has been done with deliberation, that while openly and apparently it may be of a Germany company, it is the act of the German Government, and in pursuance of a policy on the part of the German Government."

The Democrats took but a small part in the debate, seeing the Republicans disagreeing on the question.

GERMANY YIELDS.

FOREIGNERS TO BE EXEMPTED FROM MARTIAL LAW IN SAMOA.

The Times' excellent Philadelphia correspondent cables the following:—

The President this afternoon sent to Congress

Fig. 142. *American headline practice applied in London in 1889* general heading Foreign Intelligence. Three years later these larger capitals were extended to all subdivisions. At this time (October 24, 1887) *The Daily News* joined in the movement by giving its leaders cut-in shoulder-titles, but neither it nor *The Standard* revised its headline practice. The titles to leaders in *The Times* did not appear for another twenty years (July 15, 1907).

It has already been reported that *The Pall Mall Gazette* acclimatised the American journalistic invention, the 'interview'. On January 16, 1888, *The Pall Mall Gazette* published a lengthy report of an interview with Mr T. P. O'Connor. The occasion being the immediately prospective publication of the first number of *The Star*, the interviewer naturally reminded 'T. P.' that having been in America for some time, he probably had an intimate acquaintance with American newspapers. 'What do you think of them, and shall you imitate them?' he asked.—'Well', replied the editor of *The Star*, 'I am not a believer in half a column of headlines, because I think they are merely a waste of space; but in many respects the American paper will be my model'.

The 'Confession of Faith' which T. P. printed on his first page contained a couple of paragraphs aptly expressing the spirit of the new journalism:

We shall endeavour to present to our readers the best halfpenny journal in London or the provinces. The first necessity of a newspaper is news; and to news we shall give a larger amount of space than any other journal of equal size; not stinting money or labour in procuring it. In every department of a newspaper we hope to be equal to any journal published, resolved that though our limits forbid us giving everything at the length of larger journals, we shall by proper compression pass by nothing worth recording. Our commercial, our dramatic, our Parliamentary, and our sporting news have all been placed under the control of competent men. In our editorial department we shall find no place for the verbose and prolix articles to which most of our contemporaries still adhere. We shall have daily but one article of any length, and it will usually be confined within half a column. The other items of the day will be dealt with in notes terse, pointed, and plain-spoken. We believe that the reader of the daily journal longs for other reading than mere politics; and we shall present him with plenty of entirely unpolitical literature—sometimes humorous, sometimes pathetic; anecdotal, statistical, the craze of fashions, and the arts of housekeeping—now and then, a short, dramatic, and picturesque tale. In our reporting columns we shall do away with the hackneyed style of obsolete journalism; and the men and women that figure in the forum or the pulpit or the law court shall be presented as they are—living, breathing, in blushes or in tears—and not merely by the dead words that they utter. Our ideal is to leave no event unrecorded; to be earliest in

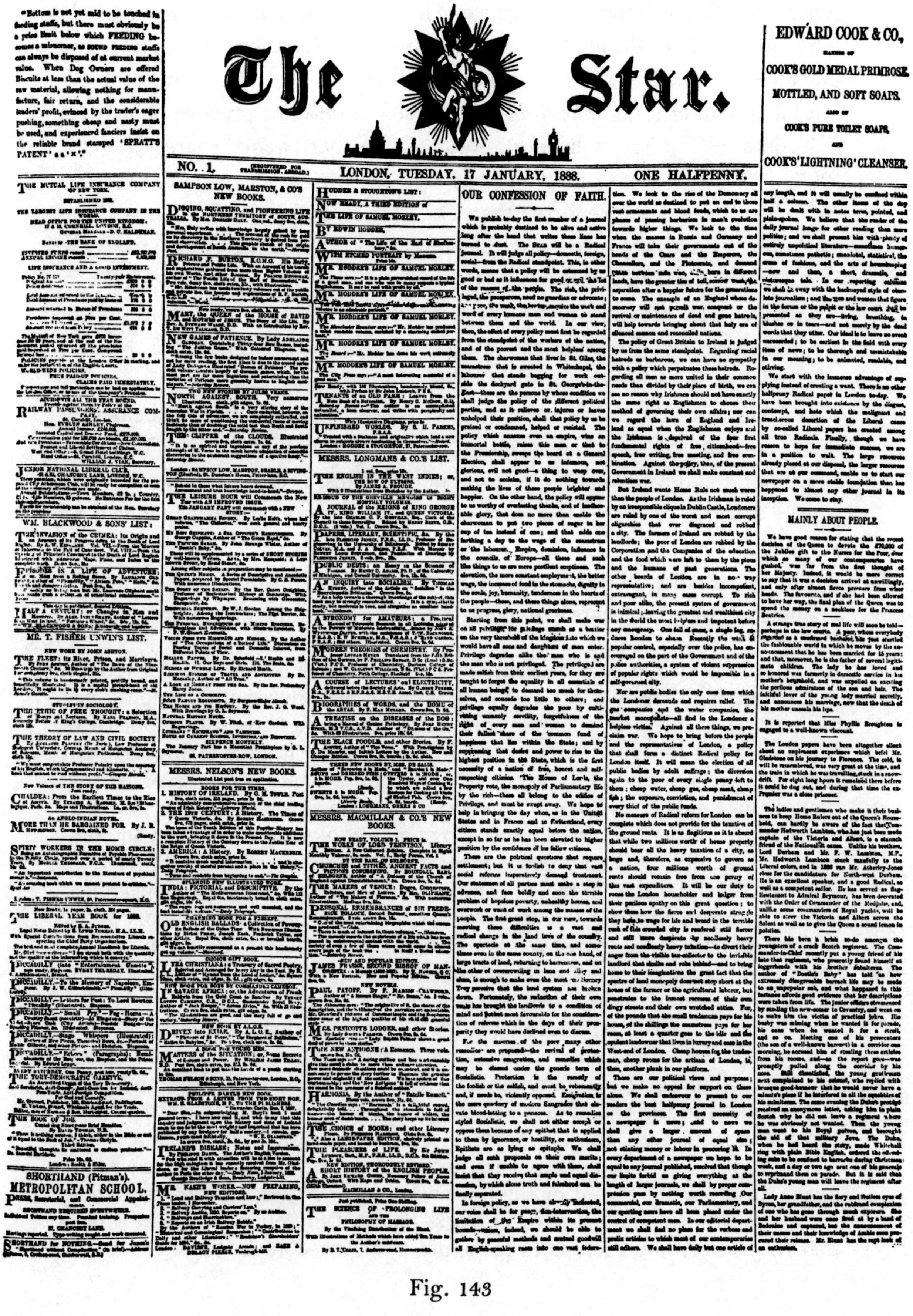

"Bottom is not yet said to be touched in feeding stuffs, but there must obviously be a price limit below which FEEDING becomes a misnomer, as SOUND FEEDING stuffs can always be disposed of at current market value. When Dog Owners are offered Biscuits at less than the actual value of the raw material, allowing nothing for manufacture, fair return, and the considerable traders' profit, evinced by the trader's eager pushing, something cheap and nasty must be used, and experienced fanciers insist on the reliable brand stamped 'SPRATT'S PATENT' and 'X'."

The Star.

EDWARD COOK & CO., MAKERS OF COOK'S GOLD MEDAL PRIMROSE, MOTTLED, AND SOFT SOAPS. ALSO OF COOK'S PURE TOILET SOAPS, AND COOK'S 'LIGHTNING' CLEANSER.

NO. 1. (REGISTERED FOR TRANSMISSION ABROAD.) LONDON, TUESDAY, 17 JANUARY, 1888. ONE HALFPENNY.

OUR CONFESSION OF FAITH.

We publish to-day the first number of a journal which is probably destined to be alive and active long after the hand that writes these lines has turned to dust. The STAR will be a Radical journal. It will judge all policy—domestic, foreign, social—from the Radical standpoint. This, in other words, means that a policy will be esteemed by us good or bad as it influences for good or evil the lot of the masses of the people. The rich, the privileged, the prosperous, need no guardian or advocate; the poor, the weak, the beaten, require the work and word of every humane man and woman to stand between them and the world. In our view, then, the effect of every policy must first be regarded from the standpoint of the workers of the nation, and of the poorest and the most helpless among them. The charwoman that lives in St. Giles, the seamstress that is sweated in Whitechapel, the labourer that stands begging for work outside the dockyard gate in St. George's-in-the-East—these are the persons by whose condition we shall judge the policy of the different political parties, and as it relieves or injures or leaves unhelped their position, shall that policy by us be praised or condemned, helped or resisted. …

… We look to the rise of the Democracy all over the world as destined to put an end to those vast armaments and blood feuds, which to us are phases of passing barbarism in man's evolution towards higher things. We look to the time when the masses in Russia and Germany and France will take their governments out of the hands of the Czars and the Emperors, the Chancellors, and the Plutocrats, and demand peace between men who, though born in different lands, have the greater ties of toil, sorrow, and the aspiration after a happier future for the generations to come. The example of an England whose democracy will not permit war, conquest or the revival or maintenance of dead and gone hatreds, will help towards bringing about that holy era of silenced cannon and reconciled nations.

The policy of Great Britain to Ireland is judged by us from the same standpoint. Regarding racial hatreds as barbarous, we can have no sympathy with a policy which perpetuates these hatreds. Regarding all men as more united in their common needs than divided by their place of birth, we can see no reason why Irishmen should not have exactly the same right as Englishmen to choose their method of governing their own affairs; nor can we regard the laws of England and Ireland as equal when the Englishman enjoys and …

MAINLY ABOUT PEOPLE.

Fig. 143

the field with every item of news; to be thorough and unmistakable in our meaning; to be animated, readable and stirring.

From its first day *The Star* was made easy by the cross-head. It was a help to circulation that *The Star*'s public—it was a radical paper—was interested in the trial of Messrs Graham and Burns for alleged riotous assembly 'to the terror and disturbance of Her Majesty's subjects' in Trafalgar Square. The trial began the day before the first number of *The Star* was issued—i.e. January 16, 1888. *The Evening News* of that day published a report in two columns solid under the headlines:

THE
TRAFALGAR SQUARE RIOTS

TRIAL OF
MR CUNNINGHAME GRAHAM, M.P.
AND
JOHN BURNS

SPECIAL DESCRIPTION

There was a triple heading, without turnover lines, to *The Star*'s report of the proceedings in its first issue of January 17, 1888. This also extended to two columns, of which the first was broken by five, and the second by four, cross-heads in the CAPITALS (not the SMALL CAPITALS) of the body fount. On the following day, seven cross-heads in small capitals lightened a single half-column of a leading article in *The Star* under the headlines: OUR FIRST DAY | AN EPOCH IN JOURNALISM | THE WORLD'S RECORD BEATEN | 142,600 COPIES SOLD.

On Monday, June 11, 1888, *The Star* adopted an entirely new method of displaying its heads, drawing directly upon American models. The historic method had been to centre the sub-heads, and, in the case of broken lines, to centre the conclusion upon the measure of the column. In the whole history of English newspaper typography headlines had never been set in anything else but capitals.

The Star adopted the practice and varied the position of the broken lines. The intention of the draughtsmanship of the more lengthy secondary headlines for which upper- and lower-case was used was to summarise the substance rather than to indicate the importance of the despatch. In *The Star* such secondary upper- and lower-case heads were more and more used alone, primary heads to small paragraphs in the centre two pages. They were com-

THE MORNING LEADER, LONDON, MONDAY, 23 MAY, 1892. 5

DEEMING

HAS PAID THE PENALTY OF HIS CRIMES.

HANGED AT SWANSTON TO-DAY.

HE MAINTAINED HIS DEFIANT DEMEANOR TO THE END, AND EMPLOYED HIS LAST HOURS IN DRAWING SKETCHES OF THE GALLOWS AND HIS COFFIN.

MELBOURNE, 23 May, (10.22 am.).—Frederick Bailey Deeming, who was condemned to death here on the 2nd inst. for the murder of his wife, Emily Mather, at 57, Andrew-st., Windsor, on or about Christmas Day last, was executed by hanging in Swanston Gaol this morning at one minute past ten o'clock.—*Reuter.*

MELBOURNE, 22 May.—The reason alleged by the Government for refusing to consent to the examination of Deeming's brain after death, is that they see nothing in the circumstances of the convict's case to justify an exceptional course being taken. All the preparations for to-morrow's execution are now complete, and very little change is observable in the convict's demeanor as the fateful hour draws nearer. A little additional nervousness is perceptible, but he says nothing indicative of remorse for his crime or of trepidation at his impending doom.—*Dalziel.*

MELBOURNE, 23 May, 4.30 a.m.—Deeming spent Sunday tranquilly. He read his Bible occasionally, and devoted the rest of the day to alternately writing and sketching gibbets and coffins. His mind appeared to dwell morbidly upon the details of his execution, in regard to which he made frequent inquiries, and upon receiving evasive answers he asked to be introduced to the hangman. This request was refused. In the evening it was thought that the doomed man showed some indications of a desire to relieve his mind by an avowal of his guilt, and the chaplain, the Rev. Mr. Scott, was sent for, but on the arrival of the reverend gentleman Deeming not only made no confession, but persisted in declaring himself innocent of the murders laid to his charge. He, however, intends to hand a statement to the governor of the gaol at the last moment, which is to be made public after his death.

Everything is now in readiness at the gaol for carrying out the last sentence of the law. The hangman, whose name is Jones, is already within the precincts, together with an assistant to help him in case of emergency. In two hours and a-half from now—namely, at 7 a.m.—Deeming's irons will be removed, and at 10 minutes past 10 this morning he will be led out to execution. Prior to going to the gallows he will be supplied with brandy, of which since his sentence he has been receiving an allowance three times a day.—*Dalziel.*

The curtain has now fallen upon one of the blackest tragedies of recorded crime—a sustained drama of villainy, in which the chief actor was of that type of embruted humanity which knows no remorse, no conscience. To Frederick Bayley Deeming conscience had no still small voice, no pleading note of pity. He killed with ferocious glee; an appetite, unsatiated with the blood of his victims, quickened only the zest of his demoniacal nature. The boy, who was father of the man in his case, gave an indication of his character at an early age; and with the strange traits of his boyhood developed the character of the cosmopolitan butcher whose deeds have now had their expiation on the scaffold. Deeming the boy was an ingenious liar; Deeming in his condemned cell was liar still.

DEEMING THE WANDERER.

The earliest accounts of Deeming represent him as a wanderer on the face of the earth. Whither he went, and what he did, nobody knew; and, unless the murderer's own biography throws light on his strange and devious ways, the secrets of his wanderings must be for ever unknown. Certain it is that he invented the wildest adventures ever dreamt of outside the range of the "Arabian Nights." His was an Oriental imagination. Was he the possessor of apparently unaccountable wealth? Assuredly his chameleon-like aptitude for changing the color of his circumstances at will was the operation of a moment. But the true story of his criminal career can never be written with any sequence of form. Something of the order of his Blue Beard amours is at least known. Deeming, the successful, married; and from that date his recorded career of infamy began. When he had made Miss Marie James a bride in 1881 his restlessness drove him forth a wanderer again. Behind him he left a long trail of impudent swindles, cunningly conceived, boldly carried out. His very brazen-facedness seems to have constituted his immunity from danger. He touched odd places in Australia, and his fingers, wherever they rested, seemed to have snatched ill-gotten gains.

AT JOHANNESBURG—TWO STRANGE MURDERS.

Then he flitted on his nomadic way to the Cape, and his stupendous impudence made havoc even in that home of wild and reckless spirits—the resort of adventurers as it was in those days. Johannesburg remembers him with good cause; but it was not until one startling day in March of this year, when all the world woke up to a new form of human butchery, that Johannesburg throbbed with a keen intensity concerning this wild, reckless man. People there revived the recollection of two black murders which had been grimly relegated to the gruesome catalogue of undiscovered crimes. Was Deeming the author of that mysterious blood-shedding? Whether he was or not, it is a curious correspondence of events that he flitted from the allurements of Johannesburg and its goldfields just about that time.

HIS RETURN—"HARRY LAWSON, OF BEVERLEY."

Not until 1889 had Deeming any desire to return to his native country, and even then it was rather as the hunted criminal than as an easy globe-trotting citizen of the world that he returned to his native soil. His wealth was as dazzling as of yore, and even as he ran he lied, defrauded, swindled. An aggressive display of jewelry, his familiar form of dazzling his victims, failed him not even in his rushing from justice. The chase waxed warm; the quarry doubled; in Monte Video he hoped to find a refuge. By this time he had become Harry Lawson, of Beverley, near Hull, who had squatted with advantage and profit in Queensland. He found time for fresh amour, won the affections of Miss Nellie Matheson, and deserted her on the very threshold of that domestic felicity which he had magnified with high-sounding phrases. Deeming was in all truth an ingratiating villain.

THE RAINHILL CRIME—HIS MARRIAGE.

But Monte Video proved no safe hiding-place. Nemesis ran him to earth. When the man was released from prison he might have been seized on another charge—the desertion of the woman he had so bigamously betrayed. But, without interruption, he recommenced his career of crime, and began to lay the train of those misdeeds for which Nemesis exacted a stern revenge on the Melbourne scaffold to-day. Within a week of his release he was revelling in his splendid assurance at Rainhill, laying the foundations of that deed of ghastliness, which has scarcely an equal for fiendish brutality in the annals of capital crime. He was grandiose as ever, and blossomed into Albert Oliver Williams, an "inspector of regiments." Part of his equipment, at any rate, was the cunning of the fox. By these he secured the now historical Dinham Villa, by these he inveigled Miss Emily Mather into his toils, and by these he lured his first wife and his four innocent children to their doom. All the world knows now how that deed was wrought, how mother and children were sepulchred in a cemented grave in that lonely house, how in the coolness of his stupendous audacity he finished his gruesome interment under the gaze of a casual acquaintance, and how, if rumor does not belie him, he danced on the spot beneath which his victims lay buried. This was his crime of 26 July. "Sister" (as he called his wife for public deception) and children dispatched, Williams plunged and continued his iniquitous career. By 22 Sept. Miss Mather had surrendered to his wiles, and on that day Deeming, in all the gorgeousness of hired regimentals, was a swaggering bridegroom at Rainhill's sequestered church. Then his spirit of unrest began to move again. He transferred himself to London with his latest bride, and thence he sped to Australia.

THE WINDSOR CRIME.

Of the adventures of the voyage, Miss Mather, in letters to her mother, was herself the historian. By the light of later events those epistles have now a pathetic interest. At Windsor, near Melbourne, the pair settled in the middle of December; before the month had fairly waned the miscreant had added another to his list of victims. His method in this last case was exactly similar in detail to the plan of his Rainhill butchery, and by the merest accident alone was the murder discovered. When the crime was out, and telegrams began to chase each other between England and Australia, the murderer was once more on the move. At Sydney he became "Baron Swanston," in which high-sounding title he was within an ace of securing another victim in the person of Miss Kate Rounsevell. On her he bestowed the rings of his murdered wife, even whilst he was begging Miss Matheson, whom he had basely deceived in 1890, to come out to him. But the meshes were closing around him. Even as Miss Rounsevell was on her way to join her lot with his he was arrested, and his murderous career was for ever stopped. The story of his trial and condemnation, and of the efforts made for a respite on his behalf, especially on the ground of insanity, is too fresh in the public mind to need recapitulation. Justice saw no reason to stay her retributive hand, and the criminal has at length expiated with his own life the long list of his cruel misdeeds.

CANADA AND NEWFOUNDLAND.

OTTAWA, 22 May.—The Dominion Government has accepted the offer of Newfoundland to admit Canadian fishermen to the ports of that colony upon the same terms as they admit American fishermen, and to reduce the duties on Canadian products on condition that the Dominion Government abolish the duties now imposed upon the products of Newfoundland.—*Dalziel.*

THE UNEMPLOYED IN SYDNEY.

SYDNEY, 22 May.—A deputation of unemployed yesterday waited upon the Hon. E. Barton, Attorney-General, and the Hon. W. J. Lyne, Secretary of Public Works, and urged the Government to provide them with work or bread, as the families of many of them were starving. Mr. Barton said that the Government fully sympathised with the men, but was unable greatly to relieve the distress in consequence of the difficulty of obtaining money. Mr. Barton refused to start relief works, but added that the productive works authorised by Parliament would be proceeded with as speedily as possible.—*Reuter.*

MAHER ADMITS HIS DEFEAT.

NEW YORK, 22 May.—Maher sailed by the Cunard steamer Etruria on Saturday, and before leaving he told a newspaper correspondent that he had expected to return to Dublin a victor, but he acknowledged he had been fairly defeated by Fitzsimmons. He added, "I will come back to show my friends that their confidence in me has not been misplaced. I will work hard and put myself in condition to meet a first-class man on my return."—*Dalziel.*

ANARCHIST ADVICE TO SOLDIERS.

PARIS, 22 MAY.—M. Pemjean, one of the leading members of the moderates in the Anarchist party, will be tried before the Assize Court of the Seine on the 8th prox. for issuing a proclamation to the army in which he called upon the soldiers to mutiny and lay down their arms. It is announced that M. Pemjean will summon as one of his witnesses a certain Major Labordere.—*Dalziel.*

ANNIVERSARY OF THE COMMUNE.

PARIS, 22 May.—The usual annual demonstration at the graves of those who lost their lives in the "bloody week" during the Paris Commune, that is to say the period from 22 May to 29 May, 1871, took place to-day at Père la Chaise. Notwithstanding an invitation issued by the various socialist committees to their members to muster in force, the attendance was much smaller than in previous years, and there was little speaking. No noteworthy incident occurred.—*Reuter.*

GAOLER'S MURDERER LYNCHED.

LITTLE ROCK, ARKANSAS, 22 May.—Charles Stuart, a colored man, killed Mr. Holmes, the gaoler here, this morning, and was lynched an hour afterwards by an infuriated mob, who had been apprised of the murder.—*Dalziel.*

AN APPEAL FOR NATIONALIST UNITY.

NEW YORK, 2 May.—The Irish National League of America have issued to the party at home an appeal for unity. The League declares that Irish-American support will only be given to a united party.—*Central News.*

THEFTS FROM A CEMETERY.

When Daisy Telfer and Mabel Holmes were charged at the West London Court with stealing flowers from graves in Brompton Cemetery, Mrs. Holmes, the mother of the latter, came forward crying, and said that she could not account for her daughter's presence in the cemetery. The girls were remanded to Kensington Workhouse, with a view to their being sent to a home.

The owners of the cargo which was lost with the German steamship Dexterro after a collision with the India brought in the Probate Division, on Saturday, an action to recover damages. The value of the lost cargo was £60,000. It was pleaded that the helm of the Indra was improperly ported, and was proceeding at too great a speed. On the other side, it was alleged that the Dexterro was going too fast, and that her engines were not stopped or reversed. The case was adjourned.

BY WIRE AND CABLE.

FIGHTING IN BRUSSELS.

POLICE SWORDS DISPERSE THE RIOTERS.

BRUSSELS, 23 May.—To-day the town was the scene of serious disturbances. The clerical party have gained the day at the elections, and obtained a majority of 176 Catholics to 147 Liberals. They were so intoxicated with their success that they proceeded in procession with their banners flying to their places of public meeting. The attitude they assumed so infuriated the populace and the Liberal party that they were received with groans and hisses as they marched through the streets. From shouts the mob soon proceeded to blows, until fighting became general, and a regular street riot ensued. The combatants gave the police a great deal of trouble. It was not until the latter had drawn their swords and inflicted many serious wounds that the rioters were dispersed.

LATER.—Order has not yet been restored. The disturbances took place in the Rue Wilhelm and in the Rue Terlement. In the latter street a Catholic was so seriously injured that his life is despaired of. Near the house of the Deputy M. de Trooz a veritable battle took place. Bands of Socialists are parading the streets and inciting to fighting and violence. The gendarmes have been called out. Numerous arrests have been made. The riots have not yet been quelled. The mob is growing.—*Dalziel.*

MURDERED BY CANNIBALS.

ENGLISHMAN'S TERRIBLE FATE IN THE NEW HEBRIDES.

Mail advices received at Queenstown from the New Hebrides contain intelligence of the murder of an Englishman named Lawers by the natives, who subsequently carried off the body, cooked it and ate it. Lawers, with another Englishman named Malcolm, early in the year arrived on the islands and purchased a plantation near the French settlement. He employed a number of natives, who, without the least provocation, killed Lawers at night, and also attempted to murder Malcolm; but he managed to escape. H.M.S. Cordilia was subsequently sent to investigate the murder; but the natives retreated to the bush, and as the commander had no instructions he did not send an armed force ashore to punish the cannibals. The Europeans on the island are said to be in a state of alarm.

LOSS OF AN IRONCLAD.

OVER 100 LIVES LOST—ONLY SIX MEN SAVED.

MONTE VIDEO, 21 May.—Intelligence has reached here of a terrible maritime disaster, involving great loss of life on the dangerous northern coast of the River Plate. The Brazilian war vessel Solimoes, one of the few seagoing armourclads possessed by the Republic, has been totally lost off Cape Santa Maria, the great majority of the crew being drowned. It is reported that only half a dozen men were saved, and the loss of life is estimated at considerably over 100. No particulars have yet reached here as to the manner in which the disaster occurred, but the entire coast eastwards from Colona abounds in shoals and sandbanks, while the currents are powerful and inconstant, and there are few landmarks. It is supposed, therefore, that the ill-fated vessel must have been driven aground during the prevalence of a southerly gale, and stranded too far from shore to establish communication. The Salimoes was one of the vessels which were recently despatched from Rio Janeiro with reinforcements for the province of Matto Grosso.—*Reuter.*

RIO DE JANEIRO, 22 May.—The news was received here to-day that the monitor Solimoes one of the vessels of the naval flotilla dispatched by the Brazilian Government to suppress the insurrection in the province of Matto Grosso, was wrecked last night off Cape Polonio, on the Uruguayan coast. It is reported that 125 of the crew were lost, and only five saved. Captain Castro, the commander of the Solimoes, is among the drowned.—*Reuter.*

SEVENTEEN LIVES LOST.

AUSTRALIAN FOOTBALL TEAM DROWNED AT PORT PHILIP.

MELBOURNE, 22 May.—What is feared to have been a sad boating fatality occurred in Port Phillip yesterday evening. Fifteen members of a football team secured the services of two fishermen to take them across the bay in an open boat. They never reached their destination, however, and this morning the boat was found floating bottom upwards, having evidently capsized. It is supposed, therefore, that all the occupants were drowned.—*Reuter.*

NEGROES BENT ON REVENGE.

BOSTON, 22 May.—The republican negro organ states that secret societies in Boston and Cambridge are earnestly discussing the recent lynching of negroes in the Southern States, and that certain of their members have been taking lessons in bomb-making from socialists and Russian refugees. These men purpose to go south very soon to revenge the deaths of their countrymen. It is feared that unless the outrages are stopped there will be serious trouble.—*Dalziel.*

SIX LIVES LOST IN A COLLISION.

NEW YORK, 21 May.—A passenger train and a freight train came into collision yesterday on the Cotton Belt Railway, in Arkansas, with disastrous results. The accident happened between Humphrey's and Golden Gate stations, and the force of the collision was so great that all the cars of the passenger train were thrown off the rails and upset, six of the occupants, including three women, being killed, while 18 others were injured. The accident is believed to be due to negligence on the part of those in charge of the passenger train.—*Reuter.*

FIGHT WITH TRAIN ROBBERS.

NEW YORK, 21 May.—A telegram from Jacksonville, Florida, states that four masked men attempted to plunder an express carriage attached to a train on the Jacksonville Tampa and Key West Railway, near Sanford, at two o'clock this morning. The train officials resisted the robbers, and in the pistol fight that took place the express messenger was killed. The robbers escaped, but without their intended booty.—*Dalziel.*

EIGHT KILLED BY AN EXPLOSION.

NEW YORK, 21 May.—A terrible explosion of gunpowder occurred at the Aetna Fireworks Company's factory at Hartford this afternoon. The building was completely wrecked, and eight persons were killed, while several others were injured.—*Reuter.*

For other Foreign Telegrams see page 6.

A DYING PARLIAMENT.

GOVERNMENT AND THE DISSOLUTION.

Our Special Parliamentary Correspondent writes:—It is in the lobby of the House of Commons, and not in the Chamber itself, that the real interst of Parliament at present centres. Members in these days are less concerned with the views of honorable and right honorable gentlemen on the intricacies of the Irish Local Government Bill, than with the latest authentic information about the final break-up. 'Tis the date of the Dissolution that everybody is talking about.

Mr. Labouchere has again and again tried to extract the fateful secret from Mr. Balfour's bosom, but up till now the leader of the House has fenced successfully the artfully contrived interrogatories that have been addressed to him. There is no doubt about the general feeling of the House as to the most likely time of the Dissolution. Mr. Gladstone has given a hint that it may be looked for by the end of June, and Mr. John Morley is bold enough to express the view that to give a hundred to one on its taking place before the middle of July would be a perfectly safe speculation. Of course, the report that the Cabinet had decided to dissolve on 20 June is, on the face of it, a pure invention. No decision of any kind has yet been arrived at, and the most that is known, even within the inner circle of the Government, is that business will be so arranged as to permit of the session coming to an end very early in July. It is possible that any day may produce a reason for the Government appealing to the country before that time, but, despite all rumors to the contrary, no such intention is at present seriously entertained. The rank and file of the Conservative party are believed to be favorable to the final plunge being taken sooner rather than later, but there is a strong disinclination not to unduly influence the Government on the point.

The fact that Her Majesty took special pains to let it be known at the Drawing Room the other day that she was opposed to an immediate Dissolution may carry some little weight with the Tory leaders, but even their disregard of Constitutional procedure will scarcely permit them to attempt an undue prolongation of Parliament. That Mr. Balfour considers there is an element of uncertainty in the situation is evident by a reply he gave privately a few days ago to a well-known Tory member, who, contemplating matrimony, ventured to ask his advice on the wisdom of fixing the interesting event for the middle of June, and allowing for a honeymoon of a fortnight's duration. With a caution that is not a little bit significant the leader of the House excused himself on the ground that it was a matter he would prefer not to offer any advice upon.

The truth is that at present Mr. Balfour knows very little more than the ordinary member of his party. In the course of the next few days the Cabinet will meet to consider the arrangement of business for the remainder of the session, and when we know what this is we will have no difficulty in fixing to within a week or two the date of the great exodus from Westminster. All that the best informed know at present is that the probabilities are that the General Election will be in active progress during the first week in July.

SIGNIFICANT COUNCIL AT HATFIELD.

The Press Association states that Lord Salisbury went to Hatfield on Saturday, where he was joined by Lord Wolmer, the chief Liberal Unionist Whip. Yesterday evening Mr. Balfour proceeded to Hatfield.

THE MEMBER FOR THE WARREN.

The constituency of Wilcannia, which Mr. Edward Bulwer Lytton Dickens represents in the Sydney Parliament, is not overburdened with electors—there are less than 500 of them—notwithstanding that its area is about half the size of England. But it is literally teaming with rabbits, a circumstance that gives rise to not a few parliamentary jokes at the expense of the youngest son of the novelist. Probably the rabbits have eaten the electors out of house and home. On 15 squatters' stations, the inspector says, 60 millions of rabbits have been destroyed by means of poisoned water and food. He furthermore estimates that for every rabbit deliberately killed in this fashion 30 have died from drought, disease, or other causes. And yet in spite of all this destruction the pest seems to be as numerous as ever. It is surely a reflection on the inventive ingenuity of our time that nobody has secured the handsome prize of £25,000 offered by the New South Wales Government for an effective means of ridding the colony of the rabbit plague.

THE WAY OF THE FINANCIAL AGENT.

Mr A. Macdonnell Grech, a financial agent and company promoter, carrying on business in the City, and residing at Broadstairs, was on Saturday made bankrupt with liabilities £9,030, and assets £105. No proposal was submitted.

Francis Cavaliere, a financial agent, and formerly part proprietor of the Junior Victoria Club, Westminster, was examined in the Bankruptcy Court on Saturday. He said he had no private means in 1884, and lived on his wits (a laugh). In 1887, in conjunction with two other gentlemen, he took premises in Victoria-st., Westminster, for the purpose of forming a club. He took the premises under the name of "Leigh." It was partly a betting club. He did not play baccarat there, and the police had never raided the club. All the books had been burnt. He had not speculated on the Stock Exchange, and had never backed a horse in his life. The examination was concluded.

CHILD KILLED WHILE AT PLAY.

A three-year-old child, the daughter of a laborer at Langhor, Carmarthenshire, was playing with an old knife on Saturday in the streets, when she fell forward on the point, which pierced her throat. She died immediately.

There was a deaf juryman at Battersea—or rather, he assured the coroner that he was deaf. "Eh, eh! what did you say, sir?" he repeatedly queried. "Well, you may go," said the coroner, convinced of his sincerity. "Thank you," said the juror with alacrity. "Oh, you heard that," sternly remonstrated the coroner; "I cannot excuse you." The juryman protested; the coroner had an excellent voice—clear and penetrating. How did he know that the jurymen were similarly blessed? Could the coroner withstand the compliment? The juryman was, of course, bowed out, eminently pleased with his success.

Irish solicitors may be interested to know that they cannot be admitted as legal practitioners in Melbourne. Two of them—Messrs. F. G. [illegible]erin and James Lynch—recently applied, and were refused by the full Court of Victoria on the ground that the qualification of Irish solicitors were not up to the standard required by the Local Legal Practitioners' Act, 1891. Roman, international, and constitutional law not forming subjects of the Irish examinations.

A FAMILY ATTACKED.

FATHER, WIFE, AND SON WOUNDED BY THE HUSBAND.

Huddersfield has been the scene of a deplorable tragedy. George Greaves, who had been out of work, called to see his wife, from whom he had been separated for some time, and who had been living under the protection of her father at Lockwood, a suburb of Huddersfield. Greaves was allowed to have an interview with his wife, with the result that they were soon engaged in a violent quarrel. Finally Greaves drew a six-chambered revolver and fired point-blank at his wife, severely wounding her in the right temple. The woman's screams brought her father and brother on the scene, but they had no sooner intervened when Greaves fired at them also. A desperate struggle ensued, but the two men were unable to secure Greaves, who, getting clear, fired two shots at the son, Albert Berry, one of which shattered the bridge of the unfortunate youth's nose and buried itself in his head, while the other bullet penetrated his chest. Albert fell to the ground, and Greaves then turned upon the old man, whom he shot through the body. Not content with that, the desperado took a butcher's knife from his pocket, and with that murderous weapon he stabbed his father-in-law under the left shoulder-blade, and right into the lung. The noise of the firing and the shrieks and shouts of the victims had, meanwhile, alarmed the whole neighborhood, and a number of men hastened to the spot and succeeded in overpowering and disarming Greaves, who was subsequently taken to Huddersfield borough police-station and charged with attempted murder. The three victims were conveyed to hospital, where they remain in a dangerous condition.

Greaves had been married three years and had two children. About six months ago, owing to continual ill usage, the wife left him, and went home with the children. As she did not return Greaves sold the furniture and left town. He returned very shortly afterwards, assured her of his repentance and persuaded her to go to his parents' house until he could refurnish a house. This was done, but Greaves abused her so much that she again left him. Subsequently an agreement was entered into whereby Greaves contracted to pay so much per week for wife and children's maintenance. This agreement he failed to comply with.

All six chambers of the revolver were emptied by Greaves, who, it is asserted, had declared his intention of killing all his wife's family and taking his own life.

FRAUDS ON THE WAR OFFICE.

Three Manchester laborers—Thomas Wilson, John Armstrong, and Robert Seymour—were convicted at the Manchester Assizes on Saturday on a charge of conspiring together, on 2 Oct. last and on 7 Jan. of this year, to fraudulently obtain from the War Office sums of £1 10s. 9d. and £4 11s. 4d. by personating Charles Jones, an army reserve man. It appears that Jones was sent to gaol in Nov., 1890, March, 1891, and Oct., 1891, for periods of three months, one month, and twelve months respectively; and the three prisoners conspired together to obtain Jones's army pay, such being forfeited according to army regulations. The three men were found guilty, and Mr. Justice Collins imposed a penalty of twelve months' hard labor upon each.

WARSHIP'S NARROW ESCAPE.

Advices received at Plymouth, from Cape Town, report that H.M.S. Mohawk recently had a narrow escape from foundering. Soon after leaving Durban a heavy gale sprang up from the westward, and washed away the stern boat, stove in the others, and flooded the cabins, besides doing other damage. Captain E. H. Bayley, who is well known in the Cape Peninsula, the navigating lieutenant, Mr. Clive, and the chief engineer, Mr. Burns, were down with intermittent fever, caused through severe exposure. The first lieutenant, Mr. Akers, who was suffering from a sunstroke, collapsed under the strain, and has been removed to the naval hospital at Cape Town, where he is now seriously ill. On Lieut. Philpotts fell the responsible duty of navigating the ship safely into port.

SERIOUS FIRE AT TOOTING.

At half-past five o'clock yesterday morning the firemen at Balham were called to the Broadway, Tooting, Graveney, when it was found that a destructive fire had broken out upon the premises of Mr. H. Brigden, contractor. Two brick and timber buildings, each of two floors, used as stables and hay stores, had caught fire from an unknown cause, and were ablaze from end to end. A third building, used as workshops and stores, also took fire, and all three were razed to the ground. Three horses which could not be moved were literally roasted to death, and the adjacent premises of Mr. J. Robertson, auction-room proprietor; Mr. J. H. Rowe, butcher; Mr. Taylor, confectioner; and Mr. J. Smith, florist, were badly damaged.

A STRUGGLE ON THE LINE.

When Maria Beadle, a Croydon laundress, announced her intention to commit suicide on Saturday last no heed was paid to her, but when the woman scaled a fence and proceeded in the direction of the railway, May Fisher, her stepdaughter, thought it time to interfere. The laundress had, it was then feared, determined to destroy herself, and her stepdaughter was determined to prevent her. A desperate struggle ensued between the two women, a struggle which continued until the arrival of John Hicks, a platelayer, who lent his aid to the stepdaughter. Arraigned at the Croydon Police-court later in the day, Maria Beadle was penitent, and the Bench allowed her to return to her husband.

SOLDIER STABBED AT ALDERSHOT.

A bricklayer named Whatcroft made a desperate attempt to murder Private M'Carthy, of the South Wales Borderers Regiment, on Saturday, just before midnight, in the streets at Aldershot by stabbing him in the left breast. He was arrested with a clasp knife in his hand. M'Carthy was taken to the Cambridge Hospital.

MR. J. PARNELL AS A CANDIDATE.

The Limerick Parnellites have adopted a resolution selecting Mr. John Howard Parnell, brother of the late chief of the Irish party, as the candidate for the representation of the city in opposition to the present member, Mr. Francis A. O'Keeffe, M.P. The choice is, however, subject to the approval of the Parnellite Parliamentary party.

THE WEATHER.

PROSPECTS FOR TO-DAY.

Appended is the forecast issued from the Meteorological Office at 8.30 last night:

Scotland (North), Scotland (East), and England (North-east): South-easterly and southerly winds; changeable, very unsettled and rainy.

England (East), Midland Counties, England (South) (London and Channel): Varying southerly winds; becoming unsettled; rain at times, possibly thunder.

Scotland (West), England (North-west and North Wales), England (South-west and South Wales), Ireland (North), and Ireland (South): Variable winds, mainly southerly or south-westerly; unsettled, rain at times.

The forecast for London and the Channel, issued at 8.30 p.m. last night, says:—"Varying south winds, becoming unsettled; rain at times; possibly thunder; no warnings issued."

Fig. 144. *Text page of the halfpenny* Morning Leader, 1892

posed from **small fat egyptians.** The front page avoided them. Condensed bolds were also used. An 18-point bold sans serif was used for departmental heads, e.g. for **SPORTING CHAT.**

By 1889 the 'New Journalism' became firmly established—and in this typographic fashion. The elder branch of journalism, controlled as it was by strongly entrenched professionalised journalists, shewed no signs of receiving any of the new practices into the canon. The personal paragraphs, the causerie, above all, the interview, were regarded as outside the pale of serious journalism, and as possible material only for the inferior evening sheets. *The Pall Mall Gazette* was regarded by the 'academic' critic, Andrew Lang, for example, as an Americanised sensational paper, hardly above the

EAGLE INSURANCE COMPANY
Head Office—79, PALL MALL, LONDON, S.W.
City Office—SOUTHSEA HOUSE, THREADNEEDLE STREET, E.C.
Chairman—SIR GEORGE RUSSELL, Bart., M.P.
Total Funds ... £2,760,000
Annual Income ... £300,000
Claims paid during past 44 years ... £11,000,000
The Company's Policies contain the latest MODERN and LIBERAL Conditions.
GEORGE HUMPHREYS, Actuary and Secretary.

The Morning

THE BEST MORNING DRINK IS BOVRIL.

NUMBER 1 | LONDON: SATURDAY, MAY 21, 1892. | PRICE ONE HALFPENNY

DEACON GETS A YEAR.

RESULT OF THE KILLING OF M. ABEILLE IN CANNES.

He Pleads Justification, but the French Judge says that One Shot and the Wounding of his Victim should have Sufficed.

From the Reuter Agency.

NICE, May 20.—The trial of Mr. Parker Deacon, who, on Feb. 18 last, shot a French gentleman named M. Abeille, whom he found at night in his wife's room at the Hotel Splendide at Cannes, began this morning, before the Nice Court of Assizes. The court was filled with people.

Mrs. Deacon was not in court, and a medical certificate was read declaring that the lady was not well enough to attend. The family of M. Emile Abeille did not bring any civil action, but were nevertheless represented, in

TERRIBLE DISASTER

A THOUSAND PEOPLE KILLED AT MAURITIUS.

Enormous Destruction of Property.—Thousands Rendered Homeless by a Storm.—Country Devastated and Crops Destroyed.

A hurricane, occasioning great damage to shipping and other property, is reported by Reuter and Lloyd's to have occurred at Mauritius on April 29. The hurricane is described in the despatches as one of the most disastrous on record, all business having been interrupted, and 90 per cent. of the crops damaged. It is authoritatively stated that the wind attained a velocity of 120 miles an hour. The havoc wrought in the capital and throughout the island is lamentable. No fewer than 900 persons have been killed, while thousands have been injured and rendered homeless. Port Louis

ECHOES FROM PARLIAMENT.

SLAVIN AND JACKSON

HOW PUGILISTS TRAIN WHEN THE PURSE IS LARGE.

The White Champion Exercises every Muscle—The Black Says He Does not Punch The Ball or Put on Gloves.

A MAGNIFICENT GIFT.

PRESENT OF AN ART GALLERY TO SOUTH LONDON.

Splendid Generosity of Mr. Passmore Edwards—The Gift Valued at £3,000.

The south side of London has no history, and rather is unhistoric, and its landmarks are public-houses and gin palaces, instead of ancient buildings such as we have in the West and East of the Metropolis.

Fig. 145. *Upper portion of* The Morning *shewing news on the front page, and headlines which should be compared with those of* The New York Herald (Fig. 142)

level of what we now call a 'tabloid'. The hierarchy of the morning papers would have none of the 'New Journalism'.

The rigidity of the ideas held by the conservative journalists is well brought out in the make-up of *The Summary* which was printed in the office[1] of *The Times*, whose pages were also the source of its news. The paper was published without any reference being made in *The Times*—a very curious circumstance since the new daily was issued at the unprecedented price (for a morning) of one halfpenny. *The Summary* was an eight-page paper, 12″ × 18″ in size, of four 14 em-columns. The first page consisted of classified advertisements set conventionally with 2-line 'drop' initials; page 2 gave law and police reports; page 3 a general news summary; page 4 publishers announcements and political speeches. There followed foreign telegrams, sport and court circular, finance, summary of letters to the editor of *The Times* and two final pages of advertising. The leading articles of *The Times* were summarised on page 5. *The Summary* was aptly

[1] Printed and published by George Edward Wright, Printer of No. 1 Printing-house-square, at the office in Printing-house-square and Playhouse-yard....

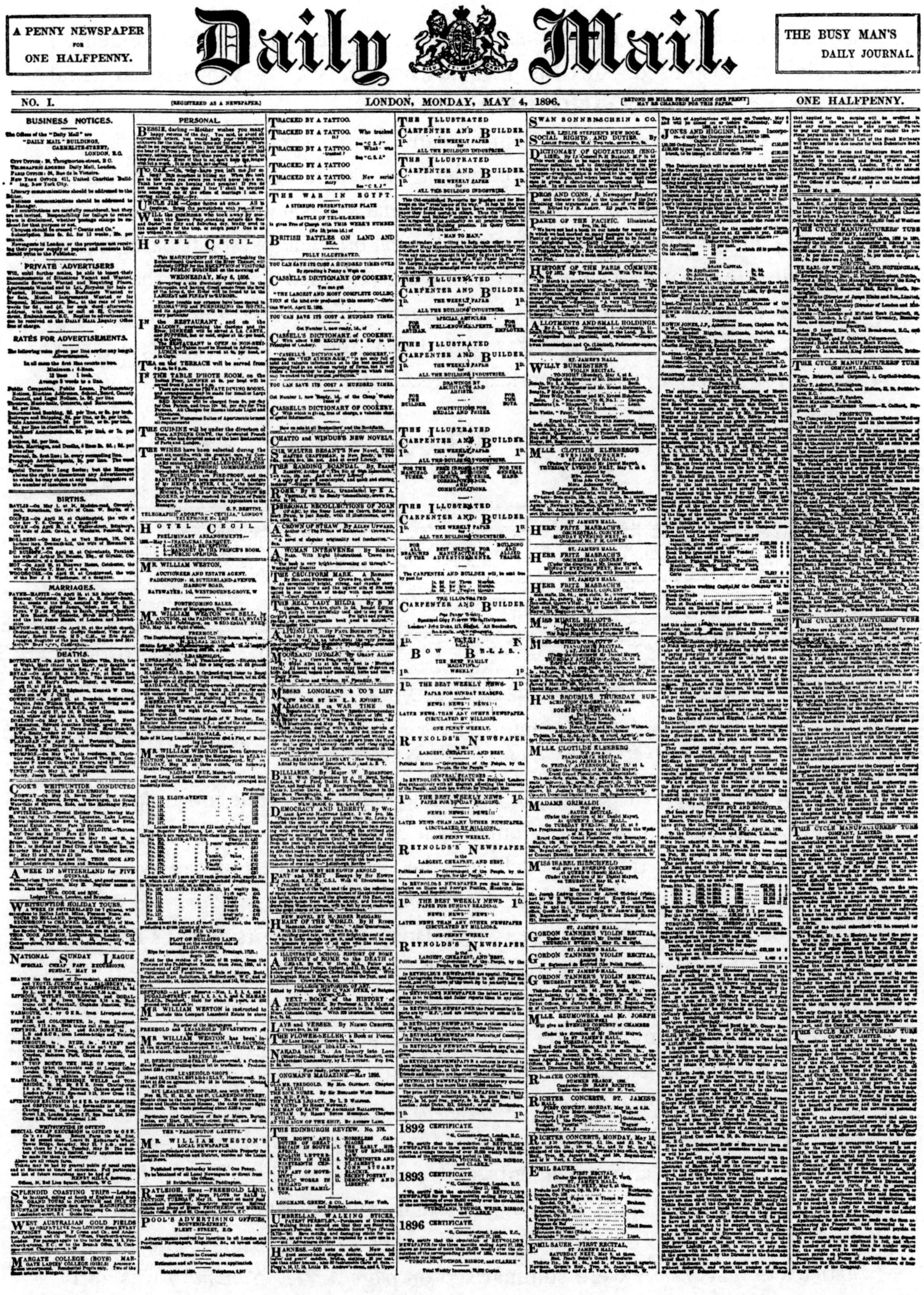

A PENNY NEWSPAPER FOR ONE HALFPENNY.

Daily Mail.

THE BUSY MAN'S DAILY JOURNAL.

NO. 1. [REGISTERED AS A NEWSPAPER.] LONDON, MONDAY, MAY 4, 1896. ONE HALFPENNY.

BUSINESS NOTICES.

PRIVATE ADVERTISERS

RATES FOR ADVERTISEMENTS.

BIRTHS.

MARRIAGES.

DEATHS.

PERSONAL.

HOTEL CECIL.

TRACKED BY A TATTOO.

THE WAR IN EGYPT.

THE ILLUSTRATED CARPENTER AND BUILDER.

REYNOLDS'S NEWSPAPER

BOW BELLS.

ST. JAMES'S HALL.

Fig. 146. *'Classical' reaction exemplified in the front page of the* Daily Mail, 1896 named but it had no success. Its career lasted from No. 1, July 26, 1883 to No. 381, October 11, 1884.

It could only be a matter of time, however, before some innovating outsider would try his hand at a cheap morning paper in the new style. The inevitable happened. *The Morning Leader* was projected and advertised. It was anticipated by *The Morning*; the former was published on May 23 and the latter on May 21, 1892. The two papers, though both sold at one halfpenny, were different in format, *The Morning Leader* being an eight-page folio and its competitor four-page blanket. *The Leader*, imitating *The Pall Mall Gazette*, carried thumbnail portraits printed from line blocks, even on its front page. This, under a badly drawn roman title, gave half its space to advertisements and half to gossip from club and stage. The main news-page was inside on the right-hand or the centre, opposite the leading article. The display headlines to news were small and simple, and all in type of the body fount. *The Morning* was, typographically, a far greater sensation. Its main news was concentrated upon its front page, and the main display headlines were in condensed light sans-serif capitals, with secondary headline in a wide light roman and a third in bold upper- and lower-case finishing with hanging indention. Both of these display faces are to be found in London editions of *The New York Herald* as published on February 2, 1889. This similarity is no accident, for the initiator and editor of *The Morning* was Chester Ives, formerly responsible for *The New York Herald* Paris edition.

There was, however, not enough cash behind it to enable *The Morning* to keep up its courage in the vital matter of placing the main news on the front page. As proprietors changed, advertisements began to appear, and *The Morning* assumed the appearance of a penny paper in accordance with the dogma that a morning paper cannot succeed unless it looks like a morning paper. Mr Kennedy Jones, who, with Alfred Harmsworth, made so much difference to London journalism, was a reactionary in this respect. He was on the staff of *The Morning*, and, leaving when the property changed hands, expressed his judgment that 'what was wrong with Chester Ives's venture was its appearance. It did not look like a morning paper'. Kennedy Jones considered that for a morning paper to look like a morning paper it must look like *The Times*. The evening paper had its own *tenu*, and an evening compared with a morning was as different as dress from undress. *The Evening News*, the early stages of which we have already described, came into the possession of Kennedy Jones and Alfred Harmsworth in 1894. Within two years there were vital developments in the headlines. Horizontal displays (i.e. headlines across two columns) or extended headlines in single columns were invented and used in the main news-page. This was still in the interior of the paper, the front page, following *The Star*, was confined to gossip. A banner (i.e. a legend running across the whole width of the page and enclosed between rules) across the front page was used for the first time on January 15, 1895. Such dramatisation of news, according to the Kennedy Jones-Harmsworth theories of those days, was appropriate or at least permissible only in an evening paper. Hence the first number of the *Daily Mail*, London, May 4, 1896, required its main news-page to face the leading article page, while the front page must be given to classified advertisements; otherwise the *Daily Mail* would not 'look' what it was intended to be, a penny morning paper for a halfpenny.

The headlines were all in the dignified morning-paper style and the make-up traditional in many important respects. The innovation was the woman's page. The success of the *Daily Mail* was in large part due to energetic distribution methods (and its first number sold 395,215 copies), but, most of all, to its realisation that, although women could also read, they were not the sole possessors of 'the meanest intelligence'.

Another evidence of the extension of curiosity to matters other than politics is to be found in *The Daily Courier* which made its appearance a fortnight before the *Daily Mail* first came into the hands of the public. *The Daily Courier*, built on the lines of a weekly review, was made up in sixteen three-column pages in small folio—the size of *The Spectator*. It gave most of its space to social, literary and sporting articles and a fraction only to occurrences foreign or domestic. As the outside sheets carried advertising, the text began on p. 5 with Court news, each paragraph of which was given a cut-in shoulder note set in bold sans-serif upper- and lower-case; but bold type was avoided elsewhere in the paper. It seems to us a huge, even cumbersome, pennyworth, but its ninety-eight issues (April 23–August 15, 1896) present an informing record of the social chat of the late 'nineties.

A notable creation of the 'nineties was "The Westminster". In 1892 when Mr Astor bought the *P.M.G.* and changed its politics, its editor, E. T. Cook, resigned with most of the staff. They founded, with the backing of Sir George Newnes, *The Westminster Gazette* in the following year, 1893. The paper continued the journalistic traditions of the *Pall Mall* and the bookish old style type and roman front page head. "The Westminster" was printed, for the better preservation of readers' sight, upon a green paper until its transformation into a morning paper in recent years.

THE WESTMINSTER GAZETTE

No. 1.—Vol. I. TUESDAY, JANUARY 31, 1893. Price One Penny.

NOTICES TO OUR READERS.

EVENING PAPERS AND THE EYESIGHT.

EVENING PAPERS are largely read by persons going home in badly-lighted railway carriages, omnibuses, &c. White paper and black ink may do very well for a reader sitting at home, on a steady floor and with sufficient light, But to try and read by the gloomy thing in the roof which railway companies are pleased to call a light, while one is jolted about in a railway carriage, is very injurious to the eyesight. It has, therefore, been decided to inaugurate the birth of THE WESTMINSTER GAZETTE *by trying to produce such a tint as will be restful to the eye and not injurious. In consultation with an oculist of great experience, we have decided to give a trial to the tint of paper which the reader now has before him—the tint of the fields, the trees, and the billiard-table.*

We shall be very glad to receive any opinions or suggestions with which our readers may be disposed to favour us on this subject. It is of course an experiment that we are making, and unforeseen objections may present themselves. But we would caution our readers against making too hasty criticism. Some allowance must be made for custom. A man has for years been reading his evening journal on white paper, and the strangeness of our innovation may at first sight surprise him. Custom and fashion count for so much in these matters. An édition de luxe nowadays is printed on the finest white paper. Among the old Romans white parchment was disliked, because it dazzled the eye; and their édition de luxe was written on purple or violet. But our modern reader is now confronted with something to which he is not accustomed, and the reason for which therefore he will probably not immediately appreciate. But that which surprises him on the spur of the moment he will perhaps—when he comes to realise the reason for the change, and the benefit (as it is hoped) to his eyesight—begin to recognise as a palpable improvement.

Meanwhile we invite correspondence on the subject. Our only desire is to conform to the comfort and convenience of our readers, and we shall not obstruct any change —whether it be a change to the old style, or to some different tint—which we have reason to believe the majority of them desire. In view of the fact that our innovation is introduced in the interest of the reader, and is supported by professional and expert opinion, we are confident that it will have a fair trial at the hands of the very large jury which it is hoped the popularity of THE WESTMINSTER GAZETTE *will be able to empanel on the question.*

Two other matters are of great importance in evening papers from the point of view of the eyesight. One is the matter of clear type. The types in use in THE WESTMINSTER GAZETTE *have been subjected by an expert to various tests, and are declared to be excellent for the purpose. The other point is thick paper, so that the print may not show through from one side to the other. This point has also been well considered, and the paper on which* THE WESTMINSTER GAZETTE *is printed is of a quality equal to that of the best printed of any of the morning papers.*

It is only right to add, with reference to the colour of the paper, one decidedly adverse opinion which we encountered in connection with the inquiry instituted before making this change. A spectacle maker, in a prominent thoroughfare in London, was asked his opinion, and he said that he objected to the change altogether, on the ground that it would take away a large part of his business.

NEW AND OLD.

Two things are, we believe, demanded by custom of those responsible for launching a new journal. One is an apology for the imperfections of the first number; the other, the promulgation of a new programme. We are making so large a departure from journalistic convention in another matter that we hardly dare at the same time to defy both of the requirements just alluded to. Let us say at once, therefore, that we have in no wise been exempt from the plentiful crop of difficulties which spring up in the path of all new enterprises. If any reader be disappointed with our first number, let him, in common charity, reflect how much more arduous it is to build up a complicated organism like a modern newspaper than to knock one down. And, after all, we shall so far venture to depart from usage as to maintain that our first appearance rather justifies gratification than calls for apology. To preserve the continuity of an old journal under a new name is not quite the same thing as to found a new journal. And the reappearance of the *Pall Mall Gazette* under its old management will not only, we hope, be welcomed by those who are in sympathy with our political and social principles; but also afford, as we venture to submit, grounds for satisfaction to all who are inclined to recognise the newspaper as among the serious and responsible factors in the modern world. From one point of view the purchase of a newspaper is no more of public importance or concern than the purchase of any other form of private property. Legally a newspaper proprietor has as much right to part with his paper as another man to sell his stud, and the outside public has no better warrant to pass judgment on the buying and selling in the one transaction than in the other. But morally there is a wide and obvious difference. The very phrase "the public Press" suggests the nature of it. For good or for evil, the Press is every day gaining greater power. Every day it claims to speak with higher authority; every day it finds, or reflects, the thoughts of a wider public. Such influence would be in the highest degree dangerous, such claims in the lowest degree absurd, unless the power of the Press begot, in the minds alike of writer and proprietors, a strong sense of public responsibility, a firm recognition of public duty. How ridiculous, for instance, becomes the assumption of the editorial "we," when a journal which for years has been advocating one policy begins some fine day—without any word of explanation or hint of substituted personality—to advocate the opposite; and when this stultification takes place, not as the result of any change of opinion, but as the journalistic equivalent for a transfer of gold. The evils of a venal Press are not limited to the grosser abuses revealed in the Panama scandals. The dignity of journalism as a profession, the seriousness of journalism as an influence, would no less be impaired if the transfer of a paper could avail either to convert hireling pens or to snuff out a public organ. It is for this reason that we venture to claim for the reappearance of the old *Pall Mall Gazette*, under the title of THE WESTMINSTER GAZETTE, the sympathy of all who are disposed to take journalism seriously. Those within the profession needed no fresh assurance; but to some others the first number of THE WESTMINSTER GAZETTE will come as a useful demonstration of the fact that a newspaper staff, if it may be sold, cannot be bought; and that, though a political organ may be silenced for a while, there is enough public spirit to ensure for it a speedy re-incarnation.

The foregoing explanation relieves us, it will be seen, from the conventional obligation of formulating, in our first number, any new programme for setting the world in order. We stand where we stood before; having changed our abode, not our minds; and begin again where we left off—with quite curious exactness, as the fortunes of politics and the virtues of her Majesty's Ministers have ordained. The *Pall Mall Gazette* was one of the earliest advocates of Home Rule; it was a Home Ruler, indeed, even before Mr. CHAMBERLAIN. But the Home Rule for which, until last October, it never ceased to plead was Home Rule on non-separatist lines. And the first duty of THE WESTMINSTER GAZETTE will be, we do not doubt, to support a Home Rule Bill in which the unity of the Kingdom and the sovereignty of Parliament are preserved by the retention of the Irish members. Home Rule for Ireland, we have always urged, should be regarded from the point of view of a possible Federation of the Empire. The maintenance and closer union of the Empire should in its turn be the governing idea in our foreign policy—a policy for which common ground has now been found between the renunciation of Jingoism by Lord SALISBURY and of Little-Englandism by the Liberals. The continuity of foreign policy, advocated for many years in the *Pall Mall Gazette*, has thus become possible: and here in THE WESTMINSTER we are not too late to congratulate Lord ROSEBERY on the signal proof he has afforded that the change of Government at home means no weakening of England's policy abroad. The retention of free markets and the provision of future breathing—spaces, which are now among the first essentials of England's Foreign Policy, stand in vital relation to "the condition of England question" at home. It was a saying of Cavour that "in whatever country, or in whatever social condition thou art placed, it is with the oppressed that thou shouldst live"; and to like effect Mr. MORLEY has "counted that day ill-spent in which some thought had not been given to the problem of the poor." THE WESTMINSTER GAZETTE will not forget the aphorism of the old editor of the *Pall Mall*. But, indeed, the claims of Labour are now so loudly vocal that every man must listen, whether he will or no; and the temptation against which a political editor has now to contend in relation to the working-classes is not so much to turn a deaf ear as to play the demagogue to them. The cause of Labour is in our belief bound up with the principles of Liberalism; and, writing in the *Pall Mall* on October 15, we pointed out how much might be done by Ministers before Parliament met to show that latter-day Liberalism is a frankly democratic force. Resuming to-day in THE WESTMINSTER, we have to note that her Majesty's Government—alike by their administration during the recess and in the legislative programme unfolded in the QUEEN'S Speech—have taken the sincere and courageous line which we ventured to recommend. To such a Government it is the bounden duty of every Liberal journalist to give the most cordial support. That the support of THE WESTMINSTER GAZETTE will at the same time be independent goes without saying; for no other kind of support is possible to an honest man, or acceptable to a wise one.

WELCOMES TO "THE WESTMINSTER."

From the Prime Minister.

In the course of a letter to the Editor of THE WESTMINSTER GAZETTE, dated from Downing Street, January, 1893, Mr. Gladstone writes as follows:—

Both on general grounds and from my lively recollection of you as Editor of the *Pall Mall Gazette*, I have truly desired to meet your wishes for some sort of literary or political contribution. But I have thought and thought and consulted the oracle within, which has made no response. From out of the silent cave I am obliged to answer, it is beyond my power. I have nothing but my heartiest good wishes to offer; combining with them the further wish that I had any means of showing how hearty they are. I stand upon a ledge which just gives me standing ground to resist old editors and friends.

From the Lord Chancellor.

Lord Herschell writes:—

I am glad to hear of the proposed addition to the London evening Press. There is nothing which Liberals desire more than the formation of public opinion by ample and free discussion of political questions. But to this end it is essential that opposing currents of political thought should both be adequately and fully presented, which, considering the number of evening newspapers advocating the cause of the Conservative Party, cannot be said to be the case at present. From this point of view, I regard your undertaking as likely to be of public service.

From the Chancellor of the Exchequer.

Sir William Harcourt, writing to the Editor *apropos* of the first appearance of THE WESTMINSTER GAZETTE, says:—

I heartily wish you success in your new enterprise. The ability and intelligence which you displayed in your former editorship are a guarantee that nothing will be wanting on your part which is required for the conduct of a first-rate Liberal journal.

From the Secretary of State for War.

The Right Hon. H. Campbell-Bannerman, M.P., writes:—

I have heard with great pleasure of the new evening paper, and feel no doubt that in your hands it will be worthy of the cause it will represent. Apart from the advocacy of right principles, which, of course, is the main object, you have always contrived to supply a readable newspaper, attractive to men of all opinions; and I believe the reappearance of a journal under your guidance will be welcomed on all sides.

From the President of the Board of Trade.

The Right Hon. A. J. Mundella, M.P., writes under date January 28:—

I learn with pleasure that the first number of THE WESTMINSTER GAZETTE will appear on Tuesday next under your able editorship, and I believe it will be welcomed by all readers of evening papers, irrespective of party, inasmuch as you and your staff heretofore supplied the most brilliant, interesting, and readable of newspapers. Another earnest Liberal evening paper, conducted on vigorous lines, is greatly needed, and will satisfy

CHAPTER XVI

THE NEWSPAPER OF TODAY

1898–1931

London Morning	1898
Morning Herald	1900
Daily Mail	
Daily Express	1901
The Tribune	1906
The Times	

CHAPTER XVI

THE NEWSPAPER OF TODAY

1898–1931

FOR some time after the opening of the twentieth century, the typography of the elderly, classical, London papers remained frankly mid-Victorian. Headlines were designed to be of the same colour as that of the text; and that notwithstanding concessions which had been made in the size of the letters themselves. Hence the pages of *The Times*, *The Morning Post* and *The Daily Telegraph* were uniformly grey. Contrariwise, the routine of *The Star* and *The Evening News* prescribed larger, heavier and, therefore, blacker headlines. The newest comer among mornings, the *Daily Mail*, was conservative in appearance from the beginning; and although it has since advanced the sizes, and displays its main headlines both perpendicularly and horizontally, it has never sponsored extreme American ideas. During the darkest days of the Boer War, the use, in the *Daily Mail*, of 'uncanonical' material, was only temporary, e.g. the report of the defeat of General Gatacre (*Daily Mail*, December 10, 1899) which was given ten headlines in alternate decks of modern and sans serif, was not allowed to be taken as a precedent. The Boer War, however, did develop a need for more expressive headlines and, simultaneously, the progress of advertising gradually forced the newspapers to supply their customers with a wider variety of sizes and designs of advertising founts; and these, whether suitable or not, were commandeered for headline use. Among other exceptional events which brought these advertising founts into the body of the paper was the death of Queen Victoria. This occurrence was reported in the penny press with the aid of a wide variety of depressing capitals. The *Daily Express*, in accordance with its early and consistent programme of not merely printing but dramatising the news, gave a display which must be seen to be believed. The front page of the paper was framed with what I believe are known as 'Oxford rules' and it carried seven inches of headlines across two columns. The *Daily Express* had evidently become determined to be first in adopting the latest American display methods, and to exceed all the rest of the halfpenny morning papers in its exploitation of the headline. It began by applying the evening newspaper practice to its own front page and it has, at

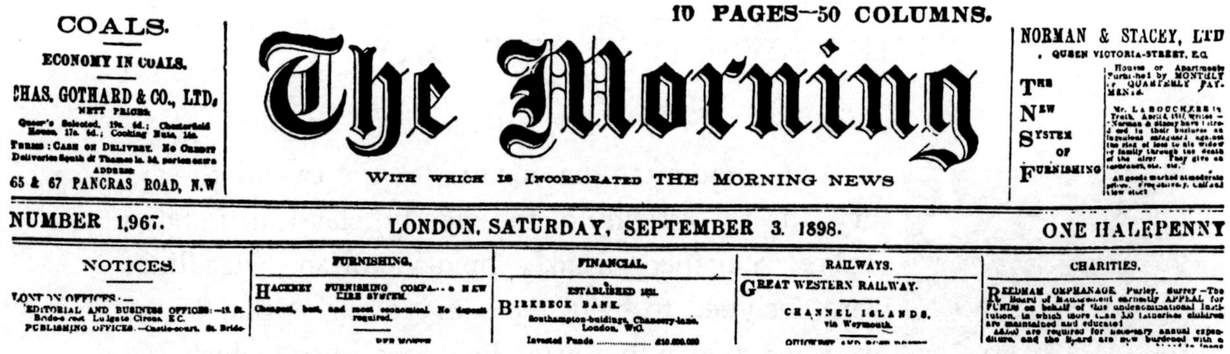

10 PAGES—50 COLUMNS.

COALS.

ECONOMY IN COALS.

CHAS. GOTHARD & CO., LTD.

NETT PRICES.

Queen's Selected, 19s. 6d.; Chesterfield House, 17s. 6d.; Cooking Nuts, 14s.

TERMS: CASH ON DELIVERY. NO CREDIT. Deliveries South of Thames 1s. 3d. per ton extra.

ADDRESS:

65 & 67 PANCRAS ROAD, N.W.

The Morning

WITH WHICH IS INCORPORATED THE MORNING NEWS

NORMAN & STACEY, LTD

QUEEN VICTORIA-STREET, E.C.

THE NEW SYSTEM OF FURNISHING

Houses or Apartments Furnished by MONTHLY or QUARTERLY PAYMENTS.

All goods marked at moderate prices. Frequently, call and view stock.

NUMBER 1,967. LONDON, SATURDAY, SEPTEMBER 3, 1898. ONE HALFPENNY

NOTICES.

LONDON OFFICES:—
EDITORIAL AND BUSINESS OFFICES:—19, St. Bride-street, Ludgate Circus, E.C.
PUBLISHING OFFICES.—Castle-court, St. Bride-

FURNISHING.

HACKNEY FURNISHING COMPANY'S NEW HIRE SYSTEM.

Cheapest, best, and most economical. No deposit required.

FINANCIAL.

ESTABLISHED 1851.

BIRKBECK BANK.

Southampton-buildings, Chancery-lane, London, W.C.

Invested Funds £10,000,000

RAILWAYS.

GREAT WESTERN RAILWAY.

CHANNEL ISLANDS, via Weymouth.

CHARITIES.

REEDHAM ORPHANAGE, Purley, Surrey.—The Board of Management earnestly APPEAL for FUNDS on behalf of this undenominational Institution, in which more than 300 fatherless children are maintained and educated.

Fig. 147. The Morning *reverts to orthodox make-up with 'classified' advertisements on the front page*

10 PAGES—50 COLUMNS.

SEE

THE DIFFERENCE

IN

THE MORNING.

London Morning

WITH WHICH IS INCORPORATED THE MORNING NEWS AND THE MORNING.

BIRKBECK BANK, Southampton-buildings, Chancery-lane, London, W.C.
Invested Funds .... £10,000,000.
Number of Accounts, 85,094.
TWO-AND-A-HALF per CENT. INTEREST allowed on DEPOSITS, repayable on demand.
TWO per CENT. on CURRENT ACCOUNTS, on the minimum monthly balances, when not drawn below £100.
STOCKS, SHARES, and ANNUITIES purchased and sold for customers.
SAVINGS DEPARTMENT.
Small deposits received, and Interest allowed monthly on each completed £1.
The BIRKBECK ALMANACK, with particulars, post free.
FRANCIS RAVENSCROFT, Manager.

NUMBER 1,968. LONDON, MONDAY, SEPTEMBER 5, 1898. ONE HALFPENNY

WHAT IS DOING TO-DAY.

BUSINESS—
Company Meeting. Ballarat Goldfields. Winchester House, 2.30.

PLEASURE.—
Yachting. Royal Corinthian Y.C., matches for 24 footers and 18-footers.
Lawn Tennis. At Brighton, Sussex Open Championships.
Cricket. At Hastings, Stoddart's XI. v. West of England.

"The Termagant," Her Majesty's Theatre, 8.
"The Little Minister," Haymarket Theatre, 8.30.
"The Gipsy Earl," Adelphi Theatre, 7.50.
"The Gondoliers," Savoy Theatre, 8.20.
"A Runaway Girl," Gaiety Theatre, 8.15.
"A Greek Slave," Daly's Theatre, 8.15.
"La Poupée," Prince of Wales's Theatre, 8.15.
"Lord and Lady Algy," Avenue Theatre, 8.30.
"Our Boys," Terry's Theatre, 8.45.
"Tommy Dodd," Globe Theatre, 8.
"The Dandy Fifth," Duke of York's Theatre, 8.
"Her Royal Highness," Vaudeville Theatre, 8.
Henry Irving and Lyceum Co., Borough Theatre, 7.30.
"Dangerous Women," New Imperial, 8.
"How London Lives," Lyric Opera House, 7.45.
"The Sign of the Cross," Britannia Theatre, 7.

Alhambra. New Ballet, "Jack Ashore," etc.
Empire. Ballet, "The Press," Mdlle. Jane Pierny, 8.
Palace. American Biograph, etc., 8.
Tivoli. Dan Leno, and long programme, 7.30.
Oxford: Varieties and Sketches, 7.30.
Middlesex. Varieties and Sketches, 7.30.
Canterbury. Paul Martinetti and Co., etc., 7.30.
Earl's Court Exhibition. 11 a.m. to 11 p.m.
Madame Tussaud's, open from 9 a.m. until 10 p.m.
Crystal Palace. Café Chantant, etc.
Royal Aquarium: Varieties all day.
Alexandra Palace, open from 11 a.m. till 10.30 p.m.
Queen's Hall Promenade Concert, 8.

NOTICES.

LONDON OFFICES:—
EDITORIAL AND BUSINESS OFFICES:—19, St. Bride-street, Ludgate Circus, E.C.
PUBLISHING OFFICES:—Castle-court, St. Bride-street, E.C.
PARIS OFFICES:—7, Rue du 29 Juillet, Paris.
TELEGRAPHIC ADDRESS:—THE MORNING, London.
Telephone—No. 961, Holborn.
Cheques and Post Office Orders should be made payable to JOSEPH COOKE, and crossed Lloyds Bank Limited.
The Editor will not be responsible for any rejected MS.
Newsvendors receiving an insufficient supply of Contents Bills or Papers, or having any complaints to make, are requested to communicate with the PUBLISHER.
Letters containing Advertisements, or having reference to same should be addressed to the ADVERTISEMENT MANAGER.
Replies to Advertisements can be received at THE MORNING Enquiry Department free of charge.

RAILWAYS.

PORTSMOUTH, RYDE, AND ROUND THE ISLE OF WIGHT, WEDNESDAY, SEPT 7th.
CHEAP DAY EXCURSIONS from London Bridge 7.0 a.m., Victoria 7.5 a.m., Clapham Junc. 7.10 a.m., New Cross 7.5 a.m. Fares, Portsmouth Town, 4s., Ryde 5s. 6d. Round the Island 6s.

EASTBOURNE REGATTA AND HASTINGS GRAND CRICKET MATCH, THURSDAY, SEPT. 8th.
CHEAP DAY EXCURSION from Victoria 8.10 a.m., Clapham Junction 8.15 a.m., London Bridge 8.5 a.m., New Cross 8.10 a.m., also from Shoreditch 7.56 a.m., calling at East London Line Stations. Fare 4s.
For Particulars see Bills, or address Superintendent of the Line, L.B. and S.C. Ry., London Bridge, S.E.

SHIPPING.

ORIENT LINE.—AUSTRALIA, NEW ZEALAND, TASMANIA FORTNIGHTLY MAIL SERVICE.—The following steamships will leave as under for ALBANY, ADELAIDE, MELBOURNE, and SYDNEY, with Her Majesty's Mails, calling at Plymouth, GIBRALTAR, Marseilles, Naples, Port Said, and Colombo, and taking passengers for all ports in Australasia.

	Tons	London	Plymo'th	M'rseilles	Naples
Oruba	5,857	—	—	Sep. 9	Sep. 11
Ormuz	6,387	Sep. 16	Sep. 17	Sep. 23	Sep. 25
Austral	5,524	Sep. 30	Oct. 1	Oct. 7	Oct. 9
Orient	5,354	Oct. 14	Oct. 15	Oct. 21	Oct. 23

First and Second Saloon Fares to Australia, £35 to £70, return, £65 to £110. Also Cheap Third class Tickets. Managers:—F. GREEN AND CO.; ANDERSON, ANDERSON AND CO.
Head Offices:—Fenchurch-avenue, London.
For passage apply to the latter firm, at 5, Fenchurch-avenue, E.C.; or to the Branch Office, 16, Cockspur-street, Charing Cross, S.W.

WEST AUSTRALIAN GOLDFIELDS by ORIENT LINE.
From London, Marseilles, and Naples, direct every fortnight. Fares from £15 15s. upwards. Apply as above.

CHEAP TRIPS to SCOTLAND.—London to Dundee in thirty hours, whence there are frequent trains daily to the Highlands and all parts of Scotland. The DUNDEE, PERTH, and LONDON SHIPPING COMPANY'S splendid Steamers leave NEW DUNDEE WHARF, 82, WAPPING, EVERY WEDNESDAY and SATURDAY. Fares: 1st cabin, 22s. 6d.; return tickets for twelve months, 35s., 2nd cabin, 16s.; return, 22s. 6d.—Apply for berths or full particulars to Geo. Wheatley and Company, 23, Regent-street, S.W., Cook's and Gaze's Booking Offices, the Company's City Offices, 75, Great Tower-street; and to James Mitchell, Agent, 82, Wapping, E. Cheap Circular Tours, via Grangemouth, Glasgow, Liverpool, and Bristol steamers.

AUSTRALIA, by the splendid Imperial Mail Steamers, of the NORTH GERMAN LLOYD.—FREMANTLE (for Perth and West Australian Goldfields), ADELAIDE, MELBOURNE, and SYDNEY.—Low Third-Class Fares from LONDON, regular Monthly Sailings. FRIEDRICH DER GROSSE (twin-screw), 10,531 tons, Sept. 26. Passengers taken free from Liverpool-street Station three days before sailing. Homeward tickets issued. Electric light throughout, and excellent accommodation for all classes. Apply to KELLER,

INSURANCE.

LIVERPOOL VICTORIA LEGAL FRIENDLY SOCIETY.
Established 1843.
Chief Office:—ST. ANDREW STREET, HOLBORN CIRCUS, LONDON, E.C.

PERFECT SECURITY TO THE ASSURED.
PROFITS DIVIDED AMONG THE POLICY HOLDERS ONLY. NO SHAREHOLDERS.
FREE POLICIES, REVERSIONARY AND CASH BONUSES, SURRENDER VALUES, ETC.

Accumulated Reserve Fund exceeds	£1,280,510
Insurance Claims and Grants paid to December 31, 1897	£3,579,270
Annual Income exceeds	£617,000
Gross Saving for 1897	£121,440
Cash Bonuses paid during past year	£34,000

ARTHUR HENRI, Secretary.

REFUGE ASSURANCE COMPANY, LIMITED.

CHIEF OFFICE—
OXFORD-STREET, MANCHESTER.
Branch Offices in all the principal towns throughout the Kingdom.

ANNUAL PREMIUM INCOME exceeds £1,096,000, showing an increase of £70,000 over the Income of 1896.
CLAIMS PAID in 1897, over £430,000.
TOTAL AMOUNT PAID on CLAIMS, over £4,285,000.

All claims are settled immediately on proof of death.
Prospectuses, Forms of Proposal, and every information may be obtained at the Chief Office or of the agents.
WILLIAM PROCTOR, Manager.

FINANCIAL.

ESTABLISHED 1851.
BIRKBECK BANK.
Southampton-buildings, Chancery-lane, London, W.C.
Invested Funds £10,000,000
Number of Accounts, 85,094.
TWO AND A HALF per CENT. INTEREST allowed on DEPOSITS repayable on demand.
TWO per CENT. on CURRENT ACCOUNTS on the minimum monthly balances when not drawn below £100.
STOCKS, SHARES, and ANNUITIES purchased and SOLD for customers.
SAVINGS DEPARTMENT.
Small deposits received and interest allowed monthly on each completed £1.
The BIRKBECK ALMANACK, with particulars, post free.
FRANCIS RAVENSCROFT, Manager.

THE TOPIC OF THE HOUR.

BY DAVID CHRISTIE MURRAY.

PERSONAL JOURNALISM.

It has been arranged that for one experimental half-year I shall "control and fill" this particular space in the columns of "The London Morning." I should like in these opening lines to get into a friendly understanding with my readers. Day by day—unless the experiment and I break down together—it will be my duty to stand up in this pulpit and preach my little sermon to the world at large. It is not to be doubted that I shall be sometimes in the wrong. With the best intention to be just, I shall sometimes take half-views of men and things. But at least the will to speak the truth shall not be wanting.

I do not know whether the experiment of a signed daily article by a single hand has ever been attempted in English journalism, and I confess to a certain fear as I contemplate the task which lies before me. There are dull days in the lives of all men. There are days when the nimblest fancy sleeps like a log, and refuses to be poked out of its kennel on any consideration. There are days when there is "nothing in the papers"—when the world is empty of stirring intelligence. At such times a writer for the press might well thank Heaven for the friendly shelter of anonymity, and it is at such times that the Personal Journalist finds himself at a painful disadvantage. He is there in his own proper person to be yawned at, and—perhaps—reviled. But it seems likely that this very danger will spur him to his best effort. You get more out of the average man who works in the open than you can out of the average man who works in the dark. And again, where a writer is known, the public learns how far it has a right to trust his judgment learning from our neighbours. As matters stand with us at present, the men who confer fame upon others belong to the only class in the liberal professions which is content to do work without taking credit for it. But the old-fashioned prejudice in favour of anonymity is dying, and the writer and reader are growing closer together—to their common advantage. The question of egotism may hint itself, but it can be dismissed in a moment. No entirely self-distrustful person will make it the business of his life to instruct and guide the public. The fact of wearing a mask affords no shelter for his modesty. The Veiled Prophet may even be a bit of a humbug.

And now for the policy which is to mark this column so long as it is under the present control. I believe that the game of purely party politics is nearly over. There have been so many breaches made in the Party wall, that, if it were not for the fossil old rules of the game, men might walk freely from one side to the other and back again. Ever since I have watched politics the strategy of Party has seemed to me be be rootedly dishonest. Had Home Rule been proposed by Beaconsfield, half the men who supported it would have stumped the country against it, and half the men who opposed it would have worked for it with all their energies. To belong to a party is to belong to a prejudice, to fetter intelligence to a preconception. The game played in all deliberative chambers nowadays is vicious—a waste of temper, time and energy, and it will be avoided here. But, leaving the arid regions of professional politics far aside, there are a hundred questions of Imperial and domestic interest about any one of which a human-natural word

Fig. 148. *New development of* The Morning *as* London Morning, *permitting signed article with double-column headlines on the front page* the present day, left the same papers behind. It is worth while noticing the steps by which the extreme 'ballyhoo' type of headline came into possession not merely of the columns of the *Express* but of the *Daily Herald* and the *Daily News-Chronicle*. It will be remembered that the first halfpenny daily was *The Morning* of 1892, founded by Chester Ives, formerly of the *New York Herald*. Agreeably with American ideas of a common-sense paper, the first page of *The Morning* began right away with news, so that the first page was a front page. This was regarded as 'un-English', and, when Chester Ives backed out from *The Morning*, his successors restored the *Times*-like classified advertising. This, and this alone, so they said, gave the paper the look of a morning paper. By the year of the Diamond Jubilee *The Morning* and the *Daily Mail* were very similar in appearance. The, to us very modest, headlines of *The Morning* had then been anglicised, that is to say, weakened, in accordance with Kennedy Jones's principle.

In 1898, the paper came into new hands; it went forward with the title of *London Morning*, carrying, as a novelty, a signed article written daily by one hand. This was an extension of the personal journalism which W. T. Stead had introduced ten years before; it was a new departure in journalism and it was a fine thing for successful journalists.

There are hundreds of scholarly, eloquent, clear-sighted men engaged at this hour upon the British press who, if they had chosen any other sphere in letters would have achieved distinction. Beyond their office door, their names are not known. For their reputation, anonymous journalism is a grave, and their genius lies buried beneath the gravestone of the editorial 'We'.

Thus the *London Morning* of September 5, 1898—and on the front page—under double-column headlines:

THE TOPIC OF THE HOUR.

BY DAVID CHRISTIE MURRAY.

PERSONAL JOURNALISM.

There was, however, a still further change of ownership in the following year—and a slight change of title. And what was now No. 1 of the *Morning Herald* (being No. 2165 of *The Morning*) chose to revert to the front-page style of the *Daily Mail*. A heavier top headline was introduced into the main news-page. There was a double column heading to a feature entitled 'In the Public Eye'. In August the property was bought by C. A. Pearson, and on Saturday, September 1, 1900, the *Morning Herald* changed its first page

GET IT TO-DAY,
READ IT TO-MORROW.
PEARSON'S MAGAZINE
FOR SEPTEMBER, 6d.

Morning Herald

GET IT TO-DAY,
READ IT TO-MORROW.
PEARSON'S MAGAZINE
FOR SEPTEMBER, 6d.

NO. 426. LONDON, SATURDAY, SEPTEMBER 1, 1900. ONE HALFPENNY.

To-day we present to readers of the MORNING HERALD the paper in the form in which it will appear in future, in the sincere hope that they will consider that the change is for the better.

On Monday the title will be altered to "The Daily Express and Morning Herald," and the succeeding issues of the paper will be published under this name.

Readers of the MORNING HERALD who have the paper delivered regularly are requested to be good enough to order their newsvendor to supply them in future with "The Daily Express and Morning Herald."

To-Day's Story.

PEKING IN SUNSHINE.

GRAPHIC STORY OF THE RELIEF.

SCENE IN THE LEGATION.

IT WAS LIKE A "GARDEN PARTY."

NEARING PEACE.

BRITISH PRISONERS

"BADLY CLOTHED AND HALF-STARVED."

BOER PRISONERS

"WELL TREATED, AND COMPLAIN OF GETTING TOO FAT."

WHERE IS KRUGER?

BOTHA'S REMNANT MAKES FOR BARBERTON.

POWERS AND PEACE.

GERMAN OPPOSITION WILL BE WITHDRAWN.

RUSSIA'S WINNING HAND.

ST. HELENA BOERS' GOOD TIME.

BOERS MASS NEAR FICKSBURG.

TROOPS MOVE TO MAFEKING.

"STOP THE WAR" MOTION.

THE SEIZED STEAMERS.

BRITISH WANTED IN AFRICA.

TO AVOID ANARCHISTS.

KING LEOPOLD TAKES A TRIP TO THE AZORES.

YVETTE GUILBERT

RECOVERING AFTER A CRUEL ILLNESS.

A CABLE FROM LI HUNG CHANG.

2,000 BOXERS MASSACRED.

SHAH AT MARIENBAD.

BRITISH PRISONERS.

TREK OF THE BOERS.

ENEMY WITHOUT AMMUNITION

THE PLAGUE AT GLASGOW

ANOTHER CASE REPORTED LAST NIGHT.

EFFECTS ON TRADE.

ENFORCEMENT OF QUARANTINE WILL CAUSE TROUBLE.

PRECAUTIONS ELSEWHERE.

THE FINAL FIGHT.

HOW CORBETT WON THE LAST GREAT BATTLE IN NEW YORK.

CORBETT'S CHALLENGES.

FIGHT ON THE FRONTIER

BULGARS AND ROUMANIANS IN FIERCE CONFLICT.

DUTCH QUEEN'S BIRTHDAY.

Fig. 149. *Final layout of the* Morning Herald, *formerly* The Morning, *with news on the front page* once more and for the last time. 'To-day', ran a notice over the news summary, printed in column 1, 'we present to readers of the *Morning Herald* the paper in the form in which it will appear in future, in the sincere hope that they will consider that the change is for the better. On Monday the title will be altered to *The Daily Express and Morning Herald*, and the succeeding issues...will be published under this name.' The setting of the front page is important for more reasons than we have the time here and now to specify. There is an admirable top headline with an indented turnover. The secondary headlines are alternately light venetian; and heavy, though not coarse, gallic old style. The early nineteenth-century modern face was entirely abandoned in the headlines. The text face, however, remained, and still remains, early or mid-Victorian. The cross-heads, not centred but ranged to the left, were in bold sans serif. In the *Daily Mail*, more conservative here as elsewhere, they were in the capitals and smalls of the body fount. Until 1901 there had been no horizontal double-column headlines in any London morning paper, threepenny, penny or halfpenny. More, the *Daily Express* was at that time the only daily with a front news-page. The dynamic setting with Oxford rules and double-column headlines of this paper's report of the death of Queen Victoria has already been noted. In the autumn of the same year the *Daily Express* carried further the principle of horizontal headline display. On September 9, 1901, the front page carried two such displays and thereafter on occasions of gradually increasing frequency and decreasing significance.

In 1904, on the emotion of his *Review of Reviews* success, W. T. Stead brought out *The Daily Paper* upon which he had long meditated—since 1893 in fact. It certainly was a queer paper: the first number carried a large design by Henry Holiday portraying the genius of *The Daily Paper* standing upon Pisgah, pointing the human race (with far greater confidence that the fully paid-up capital of the Company warranted) to the 'Homes, more Homes' in the fair vale below where stood the Garden City of the future. There followed page after page after page, 16 in all, of conscientious soul-saving journalism; and, such was the illusion of the half-size format of the paper, that the value for a copper seemed enormous. But *The Daily Paper* was a paper for the abnormally scrupulous, rather than for the normally curious reader. A census of the Sunday visitors to the public houses of Paddington, an interview with the Pope, were among the 'specials' which could hardly fail to alienate the general reader. These, oddly enough, were set in a style new even to those who were accustomed to the typographical rockets of the *Daily Express*. *The Daily Paper*'s special articles were topped with very large capitals, and with

To-day's League Games by
J. J. BENTLEY
and Gossip by
C. B. FRY,
ON PAGE EIGHT.

Daily Express

BEFORE YOU START
For the Holidays
send us your address and
SIXPENCE,

NO. 431. LONDON, SATURDAY, SEPTEMBER 7, 1901. ONE HALFPENNY

TO-DAY'S STORY.

PRESIDENT McKINLEY SHOT BY AN ANARCHIST

AT THE PAN-AMERICAN EXPOSITION.

TWICE WOUNDED.

STRUCK IN BREAST AND GROIN.

FATAL RESULT FEARED.

LORD MAYOR'S MESSAGE OF SYMPATHY.

THE NEWS IN LONDON.

"FATALLY INJURED."

PROBING FOR THE BULLET.

NIEMAN ATTACKED.

A PROFESSIONAL OPINION.

LORD MAYOR'S SYMPATHY.

THE NEWS IN LONDON.

SAD AND STRIKING SCENES IN THE WEST END.

MR. McKINLEY'S CAREER.

THE CHAMPION OF ULTRA-PROTECTION AND "IMPERIALISM."

ROOSEVELT WOULD SUCCEED.

OTHER SIMILAR ATTACKS

TWO UNITED STATES PRESIDENTS KILLED BY ASSASSINS.

IN THE UNITED STATES.

OTHER RULERS.

ANARCHIST WAVE.

HOW FRENCH POLICE PROVIDE AGAINST OUTRAGE.

LOTTER CAUGHT.

NOTABLE PRISONERS.

TWO NOTORIOUS CAPE REBELS KILLED.

HOW LOTTER WAS CAUGHT.

LOTTER AND HIS CAPTOR.

NATIVE TERRITORY INVADED.

CAPE M.P. ARRESTED.

CUP IN DANGER.

CURIOUS ACTION OF FIFTY BOSTON CITIZENS.

SHAMROCK TAKES A SPIN.

CHERRYSTONE CAUSES DEATH.

THE CZAR'S VISIT.

ENGLISH INTEREST.

THE KING'S JOURNEY.

MISHAP TO SANTOS-DUMONT.

PRINCE CHUN IN GERMANY.

THE MISSION TO JAPAN.

ANOTHER 5,000 FED.

A GIGANTIC TASK.

Fig. 150. *Early example of horizontal headline display in the* Daily Express, 1901, *successor to* The Morning Herald. *The following day's (Monday's) issue carried two such displays* secondary headlines in large upper- and lower-case, the whole well spaced and set over three of the six columns. This is the earliest example I have come across of the magazine make-up nowadays so conspicuous in the *Sunday Express*, the *Weekly Dispatch* and provincial week-end papers of the *Empire News* and the *Sunday Chronicle* class. Stead used pictures (line blocks, of course), he featured a bairns' page. His news-pages were well set out in the style of *The Morning*. *The Daily Paper* came to a sudden end on February 9, 1904. I see no reason to think that the make-up of the paper's special articles had immediate influence. The technique in the modern Sunday journals, though it is essentially identical, seems to me to be either independent—or derived from transatlantic sources. The 'gaga-maga-zine' make-up, with very big titling, unsuitably large half-tones, etc., is a post-war development.

Before the war, the *Daily Express* used 'streamer' headlines, in 36-point De Vinne, across the full measure of the front page, while the columns below were headed alternately in light and heavy founts. This was the most extreme piece of Americanism yet attempted here. After the declaration of war, the same paper became more and more extreme. The *Daily Mail* forbore to rival it in this respect. The *Daily News*, once or twice giving a seven-deck Cheltenham bold heading to its story of the Ulster crisis, used a 60-point streamer with a 48-point top headline for the declaration of war in its issue of August 5, 1914. Throughout the war, the *Daily News* was set in strong headlines, but these were necessarily condensed and reduced in 1917 when the paper went to the small-size *Star* format.

Both papers, similar in make-up, carried a daily streamer. The *News'* headlines were in elongated sans serif alternating with Caslon bold. All through, the *Daily Mail* continued to pursue a more moderate policy. The *Daily Express*, electing to maintain headline supremacy, printed the Armistice terms under a banner nearly 3 inches deep. For several years, whether week-day or Sunday, the *Daily Express* and the *Sunday Express*, respectively, has found news to justify a 'stunt' display in every issue. Today, the *Express* meets with competition from the 'stunt'-headline-minded *Daily Herald*, which is managed by a house possessing the most valuable of all newspaper-trade experience, that of running a Sunday newspaper. *The People* has provided Messrs Odhams with an insight into popular needs and tastes which political calculations or miscalculations can neither add to nor take from. The mass of the people never had any abiding interest in the game of Liberal *v.* Conservative. Today they care less for the game of Capitalist *v.* Socialist, than for the ease and pleasure of reading the special article, set in magazine

have received orders
e in South Africa.
Rifle Brigade stationed
ndergone medical in-
probably embark for
ber 10.
the First Army Corps
parture for the Cape
Parliament on Octo-

who leaves on Octo-
by the Mexican, but
ottar Castle.

MOVEMENTS.

mained at Highbury
ecial messenger was
despatches from the

ssary to add that the
changed, and as the
e adjourned there is
any new diplomatic
the present, unless
y to the new British
rded.
a partial lock in the

Bannerman arrived in
and it is understood
arly consultation with
e Front Opposition
bility of making some
on the crisis.

TS CHARTERED.

ls have been secured
e transport service:—
Star),
LE (Castle Line),
Castle Line),
(Castle Line),
(Castle Line),

),
O.),

will sail for the Cape
ut 1,600 officers and

had a notice posted at
in London inviting
take out to the Cape
., with the option of
no vessel is wanted by
st not be more than
passage from London

vernment in charter-
Mayathla, which were
, has been adversely
arters. Both vessels
docks at Birkenhead
r could be classed as

N VOLUNTEERS.

Correspondent.)

SYDNEY, Oct. 3.

Australian military
ommended that the
k Mr. Chamberlain
dent will accept Aus-
the threatened war
and if so, in what

first question be in
be decided whether
nt or whether the
parate offers. The
nce has not been

with the members

g on everywhere.

MILK TRAIN.

caused at King's-
on yesterday by the
son's messenger with
lisbury at Hatfield.
express train he
as this would have
ime to prepare the
they might expedite

UNFINISHED.

GREAT RACE FOR THE AMERICA CUP.

SHAMROCK'S SURPRISING FORM.

SPLENDID SPEED IN LIGHT BREEZES.

HOGARTH'S GRAND SEAMANSHIP.

ONLY THE TIME LIMIT PREVENTS BRITISH VICTORY.

GRAPHIC DESCRIPTIONS.

Shamrock and Columbia sailed the first of their five matches for the America Cup yesterday, and Shamrock was leading when the time limit expired.

The course was fifteen miles to leeward, down the coast of New Jersey, and back.

The official times of the start were:—

	H.	M.	S.
SHAMROCK crossed......	11	15	37
COLUMBIA „	11	16	20

There was a time limit of 5½ hours; if neither yacht finished within that period the race would be declared off.

The wind at the start was about nine miles an hour, and during the run to leeward the yachts passed and repassed one another several times.

Columbia led by two minutes rounding the mark, the official times being:—

	H.	M.	S.
COLUMBIA	1	37	57
SHAMROCK	1	39	58

On beating homeward the Shamrock made a series of short tacks, and finally obtained the windward position, drawing away a quarter of a mile from the Columbia.

The speed of the Shamrock in the light air which prevailed during the return was an unexpected revelation.

With six miles of the course still to be sailed, it became clear that owing to failure of the wind the race could not be completed within time.

At the call of time both yachts were making but little headway, and the Shamrock was leading a quarter of a mile.

A graphic descriptive article by our Special Correspondent, Mr. Charles E. Hands, will be found on page 4.

THE RACE.

HOW CAPT. HOGARTH HANDLED SHAMROCK.

WHERE THE GREAT RACE WAS SAILED.

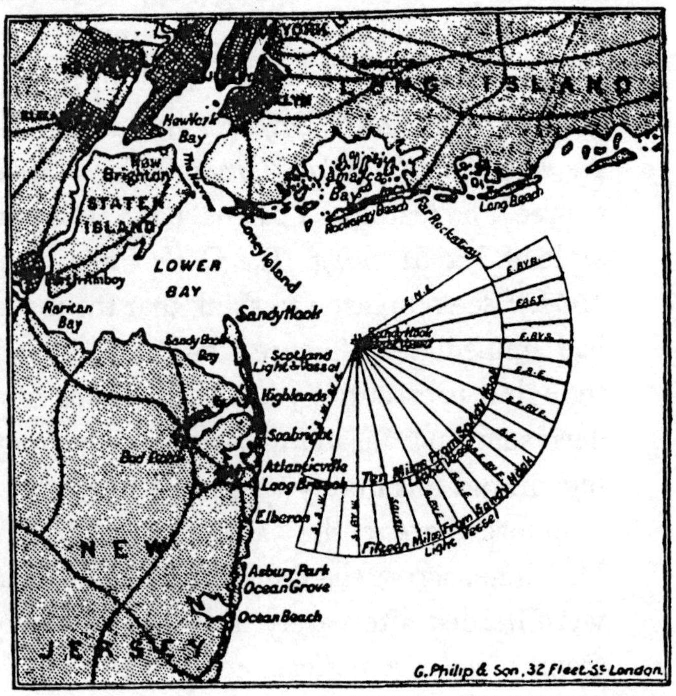

more than half covered, and Columbia was one minute ahead. And here Captain Hogarth made

AN ERROR OF JUDGMENT

in breaking out his spinnaker. But when the sail backed, checking Shamrock's speed, he saw his mistake, and immediately took the spinnaker in again.

Both yachts were now running ten knots an hour, but the Columbia was making less fuss, and continued to outfoot the challenger.

Owing to streakiness of the wind, the crews of both Shamrock and Columbia were compelled to be continually easing and trimming the main-sheets.

They were now approaching the end of the leg, and both yachts took in their spinnakers and gybed for a four-mile reach in making for the mark-boat. At 1hr. 15min. their spinnakers were reset for the run in to the mark, but Shamrock soon had to take hers in, owing to the wind veering towards the north-east.

The patrol boats kept the mark-boat well cleared from excursionist craft, and the yachts rounded it without the slightest interference. To do so they both took in their balloon jibs. Columbia

WAS FIRST ROUND

at 1hr. 37min. 57sec., and started on the homeward beat with a series of short tacks, setting all her lower sails and her club-topsail. Shamrock rounded the mark at 1hr. 39min. 58sec., Captain Barr with Columbia keeping the windward position.

At the outset the wind on the home stretch was very fickle. At this period Shamrock pointed distinctly the better of the two, and gradually cut down Columbia's lead. Later the wind grew more steady, and Columbia pointed the closer. Both yachts heeled to the same extent.

Captain Hogarth then endeavoured by a series of quick tacks to gain the windward position, but Captain Barr stuck to it stubbornly. All this time both yachts exhibited the most wonderful rapidity in stays, but at last Captain Hogarth was successful, and at 3hr. 22min. Shamrock took the windward position.

After this Shamrock drew ahead until she

ACROSS THE CABLE.

REPEATING THE RACE IN LONDON.

ENORMOUS CROWDS ON THE EMBANKMENT.

REMARKABLE SCENES OF ENTHUSIASM.

("Daily Mail" Special.)

The yacht race excited an interest in London quite unprecedented in the history of yacht racing.

As it proceeded, the race was pictorially represented on a large screen on the Embankment, which had been erected by the "Evening News" on the National Telephone Company's new building on the Thames-embankment. The device was known as a "cineyachtograph," and it indicated the varying fortunes of the race exactly as they were cabled to the "Daily Mail" from the special steamer off Sandy Hook.

The enterprise met with an extraordinary popularity. From four o'clock until ten the Embankment was crowded at that particular spot. People came and people went, but the crowd grew constantly larger, and from seven o'clock onwards it never numbered less than 20,000 people. At one time 40,000 or 50,000 must have been there.

The race was shown on a huge screen, painted to represent the New York seaboard and a stretch of the Atlantic Ocean. Grooves were cut in the screen out to the stakeboat and back, and along these grooves the boats travelled, one with green lights for the Shamrock, and the other with red lights for the Columbia. The screen was lit up with electricity.

Hundreds of people stood watching before the preparations were completed. When the boats were in position the number had swelled to a thousand. The first movement of the blocks sent the green boat nicely ahead.

The crowd became thicker and thicker, and the police sent for reinforcements. A large force came from Bridewell and Snow-

Fig. 151. *Upper right-hand portion of the main news-page of the* Daily Mail, *October* 4, 1899, *with alternate light and heavy headlines* style, written, or at any rate signed, by one or other of the names they know. And W. T. Stead and David Christie Murray were forerunners of 'Beachcomber' and the Dean; they prepared the way for personal journalism. The modern group comprising the *Sunday Dispatch*, the *Sunday Express* and *The People* divides popular support with the old-fashioned classical mid-Victorian Sunday paper, *The News of the World*. The last-named, specialising in human interest, is often taken as a supplement by subscribers to *The Observer* and the *Sunday Times* which specialise in literary and political news and views.

In sum, the post-war period has witnessed a gradual assimilation of nature, and of display, between certain dailies and the Sundays under the same ownership. The *Daily Mail* and the *Sunday Dispatch*, though under the same ownership, maintain their individuality unimpaired. The magazine make-up, regarded as essential except by *The News of the World*, has only lately—and slightly—been used in the pages of the *Daily Mail*. It seems likely that the next few years will bring the display methods of the *Mail* and the *Dispatch* into closer approximation. These dailies and Sundays, with articles and captions designed for the cinema- and magazine-minded generation, form a single group, possessing no meaning apart from circulation of a kind important only to any commercial undertaking selling mass-produced, branded goods. The revenue from the space sold to such undertakings forms the only immediate objective of the conductors of the group we have mentioned. Obviously, such influence upon thought and action as the printed word is capable of exercising cannot be expected from sheets deliberately written down to the lowest common intelligence.

The Evening News and *The Star*, possessing, by limitations of time and transport, circulations in the Home Counties only, form an important pair. Though affected by the 'Daily-Sunday' style of make-up, they give more local news in place of the interviews or special articles by, or on, cinema stars. The remaining link with the old evening-paper tradition initiated by *The Pall Mall Gazette*, *The St James's Gazette* and the early *Echo*, weakened when *The Globe*[1] was amalgamated with *The Pall Mall Gazette* in 1921, was finally severed when *The Westminster Gazette* became a morning later in the same year.

[1] *The Globe*, founded in 1803, was composed in five 16-em columns and printed on rose-coloured paper during the 'nineties and until its death in 1921. In 1896 the mast-head over the leader carried the legend '*The Globe* is set up on the Linotype Composing Machine'. Its politics were jingo, but it was a restrained-looking sheet. Theatrical news was printed on the left of the front page, on the right were gossip columns.

MAPLE'S BEDDING

WOOL MATTRESS from 9/9 HAIR MATTRESS „ 31/6

TOTTENHAM COURT RD LONDON

Daily Express

SHOOLBRED'S DAMASKS and TAPESTRIES

NO. 4,470. LONDON, WEDNESDAY, AUGUST 5, 1914. ONE HALFPENNY.

England Expects That Every Man Will Do His Duty.

TO-DAY'S WEATHER.

THE KING TO THE FLEET.

"THE SURE SHIELD OF BRITAIN."

"At this grave moment in our national history I send to you and through you to the officers and men of the fleets of which you have assumed command the assurance of my confidence that under your direction they will revive and renew the old glories of the Royal Navy and prove once again the sure shield of Britain and of her Empire in the hour of trial.

"GEORGE R.I."

FOR THE DEFENCE OF THE REALM.

THE KING'S INJUNCTION TO HIS SUBJECTS.

PRIVATE WAR NEWS FROM THE "DAILY EXPRESS."

TO-DAY'S DIARY.

WAR DECLARED ON GERMANY.

Great Britain declared war on Germany at eleven o'clock last night.

The Foreign Office issued the following statement at 12.15 a.m. this morning:—

Owing to the summary rejection by the German Government of the request made by His Majesty's Government for assurances that the neutrality of Belgium would be respected, His Majesty's ambassador in Berlin has received his passports, and His Majesty's Government has declared to the German Government that a state of war exists between Great Britain and Germany as from 11 p.m. on August 4.

GERMANY STRIKES FIRST BLOW.

MINE-LAYER SUNK.

SEA FIGHT REPORTED OFF ALGERIAN COAST.

ALL RAILWAYS IN GREAT BRITAIN TAKEN OVER.

THE SPIRIT OF LONDON.

IN THE CITY.

THE FOOD SUPPLY.

NEW SHIPS FOR ENGLAND.

ITALY'S ROLE.

THE RAILWAYS.

ACTS OF WAR.

FROM OVERSEAS.

BELGIUM.

IN SUPREME COMMAND.

SIR J. JELLICOE AT THE HEAD OF THE FLEET.

FIGHTING CAREER.

ADMIRAL SIR JOHN JELLICOE, Commander-in-Chief of the British Home Fleets.

GERMAN FLEET SINKS BRITISH SHIP.

DESTROYED WHILE ENGAGED IN LAYING MINES.

NO WOUNDED LANDED.

GERMAN CRUISER ATTACKS FRENCH PORT.

ENGAGED BY OUR FLEET IN THE MEDITERRANEAN.

LITTLE DAMAGE AT LIBAU.

ARMY BILLETS AND TRANSPORT.

A MORATORIUM?

WHAT THE GOVERNMENT SHOULD DO AT ONCE.

REDUCE THE BANK RATE.

GERMAN EMBASSY MOBBED.

HOSTILE DEMONSTRATION BY A CROWD.

MORE BATTLESHIPS.

NEW FOREIGN VESSELS BOUGHT BY BRITAIN.

ESPIONAGE ARRESTS.

THIRTY HOUSES RAIDED BY SCOTLAND YARD.

SIR JOHN FRENCH.

INSPECTOR-GENERAL OF THE FORCES.

WAR SPECIALS ON OTHER PAGES.

DASH AGAINST THE FRENCH.

THE KAISER'S TROOPS MARCHING THROUGH BELGIUM.

LIEGE GUNS HEARD.

ANOTHER BATTLE AT SEDAN?

THROUGH THE MEUSE VALLEY.

FIGHTING AT LIEGE.

CHECKED BY THE BELGIANS.

HISTORIC POINT INVADED.

RUSSIAN ADVANCE REPULSED.

LORD HALDANE AT THE WAR OFFICE.

GERMAN ATTACK BY LAND AND AIR (inset, the forts of Liege).

Fig. 152. Daily Express *front-page shewing streamer headline*

THE DAILY NEWS & LEADER Football Annual NOW READY. 1d. everywhere.

Daily News & Leader

4.30 EDN.

BRAND'S ESSENCE OF BEEF AND OF CHICKEN For Exhaustion and Weak Digestion.

No. 21,343. LONDON & MANCHESTER, WEDNESDAY, AUGUST 5, 1914. ONE HALF-PENNY.

GREAT BRITAIN & GERMANY AT WAR.

AT WAR!

Fateful Decision Last Evening.

KING'S MESSAGE TO NAVY.

"The Sure Shield of England and Empire."

FIRING IN THE NORTH SEA.

It was officially announced early this morning that war was declared between Great Britain and Germany last night.

This declaration followed a British ultimatum to which an answer was demanded by midnight.

The British action followed Germany's declaration of war on France and Belgium and the receipt of official news during the forenoon of the invasion of Belgian territory.

Germany is now at war with Great Britain, France, Russia and Belgium.

The Premier, in announcing the Government's momentous action to the House of Commons, stated that early yesterday morning Germany was asked for an assurance that her demand upon Belgium would not be proceeded with, and that her neutrality should be respected.

An immediate reply was asked for, and a message was received from the German Foreign Secretary to the effect that no Belgian territory would be annexed, but that Germany was compelled to disregard Belgian neutrality owing to fears of a French attack through that country.

News also reached London that the German Army was marching into Belgium.

Thereupon the British Government repeated its request for an assurance of Belgian neutrality on the same lines as that given by France, demanding that a satisfactory reply should reach London before midnight.

This grave announcement was received with loud cheers.

First news of Germany's declaration of war on Belgium reached London yesterday in a telegram from Mr. Ernest W. Smith, the special correspondent of "The Daily News" at Brussels. The German action was a reply to Belgium's firm refusal to allow the Kaiser's troops to cross her frontiers.

Great Britain is prepared for war. The Navy is mobilised and at sea; the Army is being mobilised. Men and youths are flocking to the colours, and crowds besiege the recruiting offices.

Admiral Jellicoe has been appointed to the supreme command of the Home Fleet, with Rear-Admiral Madden as his Chief of Staff. Sir John French has been reappointed to his former post as Inspector-General of the Forces.

The Admiralty has made a notable addition to the British Navy by the seizure of two battleships and two scouts, building in English yards. The battleships belonged to Turkey and the scouts to Chile.

The Lobby Correspondent of "The Daily News" says that Lord Haldane, the Lord Chancellor, is acting as Assistant Secretary for War, Mr. Asquith retaining the office of Secretary. Lord Kitchener's services, it is believed, will be available in this country.

The British railways have been taken over by the Government for military purposes, and it is notified that the ordinary services may be curtailed for some time.

Public fears as to food supply are groundless. An official statement by the Cabinet (See Page 5) shows that our supplies of corn and meat are ample, and that there is no justification for a rise in prices.

FIGHTING IN BELGIUM.

Germans Driven Back Near the Frontier.

BRUSSELS, Tuesday.

According to a wireless telegram received here, an engagement is said to have taken place near Liège between Belgian and German troops. The Germans were driven back. Numbers of Belgians were wounded, and will be brought to Brussels.—Reuter.

GERMANS TAKE VISE.

AMSTERDAM, Tuesday Night.

[illegible]

MOVING INTO FRANCE.

Three Columns Pressing Forward from Luxemburg.

BRUSSELS, Tuesday.

The German forces are advancing from Luxemburg in three columns, one towards Longwy, another towards Villerupt, and the third towards Thionville.

A telegram from Givet states that the French and German troops are blowing up the French and German frontier stations.—Central News.

[Villerupt is a French village situated eight miles east-north-east of Longwy. Thionville (German, Diedenhofen) is situated in Alsace-Lorraine, 15 miles north of Metz on the Moselle.]

NEAR MARS-LA-TOUR.

PARIS, Tuesday.

A German company is reported to be in French territory near Mars-la-Tour, the scene of one of the most sanguinary battles of the war of 1870.—Reuter.

[Mars-la-Tour lies close to the German frontier, eight-and-a-half miles west of Metz.]

THE DECLARATION

BRITISH DEMANDS REJECTED.

OFFICIAL MESSAGE.

AMBASSADOR HANDED HIS PASSPORTS.

The following statement was issued from the Foreign Office at 12.15 a.m. to-day:

Owing to the summary rejection by the German Government of the request made by his Majesty's Government for assurances that the neutrality of Belgium would be respected, his Majesty's Ambassador in Berlin has received his passports, and his Majesty's Government has declared to the German Government that a state of war exists between Great Britain and Germany as from 11 p.m. on August 4.

There was some confusion in earlier messages, the first being to the effect that Germany had declared war, while a second stated that Great Britain had taken the fateful step.

From the above official announcement it appears that Germany committed the act of war in rejecting the British ultimatum, while Great Britain, on receipt of this decision, declared the state of war.

WILD SCENES.

How News of Declaration was Received.

In anticipation of the receipt of Germany's reply, huge crowds gathered in Whitehall and outside Buckingham Palace, and extraordinary scenes of enthusiasm were witnessed.

[illegible]

AT THE PALACE.

[illegible]

THE NATIONAL ANTHEM.

[illegible]

THE GERMAN FLEET.

Bombardments in Baltic and Mediterranean.

[illegible]

The "Daily News" War Telegrams arriving during the day will be published in "The Star."

A MAP OF THE NORTH SEA, SHOWING THE GERMAN NAVAL BASES.

GERMANS SINK BRITISH SHIP.

Reported Loss of a Mine-Layer.

Late last night we received the following:

The Press Association learns that there is no truth in the report of a naval engagement in the North Sea.

It is understood that the British Government has received intimation of the sinking of a British mine-layer by the German Fleet.

KING'S MESSAGE TO ADMIRAL JELLICOE.

The Navy, the Sure Shield of the Empire.

The following message has been addressed by his Majesty the King to Admiral Sir John Jellicoe:

At this grave moment in our national history I send to you, and through you to the officers and men of the fleets of which you have assumed command, the assurance of my confidence that under your direction they will revive and renew the old glories of the Royal Navy, and prove once again the sure shield of Britain and of her Empire in the hour of trial.

GEORGE, R.I.

The above message has been communicated to the senior naval officers on all stations outside of home waters.

NEW HEADS OF NAVY AND ARMY

Admiral Jellicoe to Command the Fleet.

[illegible]

GERMAN ADVANCE.

Guns Heard Ten Miles Within the Belgian Frontier.

BRUSSELS, Tuesday.

[illegible]

WAR DECLARED ON BELGIUM.

German Army Enters Her Territory

KING'S SPEECH IN THE BELGIAN CHAMBER.

From Our Special Correspondent, ERNEST W. SMITH.

BRUSSELS, Tuesday.

[illegible]

KING GEORGE'S MESSAGE.

[illegible]

KING ALBERT'S CALL.

Every Citizen Required to Do His Duty.

BRUSSELS, Tuesday.

[illegible]

SEIZED FOR THE BRITISH NAVY.

Turkish Battleships and Chilian Scouts.

[illegible]

ADMIRALTY TAKES OVER LINERS.

[illegible]

CABINET & THE WAR.

Lord Haldane Assisting at War Office.

(By Our Lobby Correspondent.)

[illegible]

LIBERAL AND LABOUR FEELING.

[illegible]

CABINET RESIGNATIONS.

[illegible]

THE SESSION AND HOME RULE.

[illegible]

A. P. N.

STEPS WHICH LED TO THE WAR.

King of the Belgians' Appeal.

Mr. Asquith in the House of Commons yesterday made the momentous announcement that an ultimatum, expiring at midnight, had been presented to Germany in respect to the neutrality of Belgium.

Received with general cheers, the Premier said:

"In conformity with the statement of policy which was made by my right hon. friend the Foreign Secretary yesterday, a telegram was sent early this morning by him to our Ambassador in Berlin. It was to this effect.

[illegible]

We asked for an immediate reply (Renewed cheers.)

BELGIUM INVADED.

"We received this morning from our Minister at Brussels the following telegram:

[illegible]

"Simultaneously, or almost immediately afterwards, we received from the Belgian Legation here in London the following telegram from the Belgian Minister for Foreign Affairs:

[illegible]

THE GERMAN REPLY.

"We also received this morning from the German Ambassador here a telegram sent to him by the German Foreign Secretary, and communicated by the Ambassador to us, which is in these terms:

[illegible]

That is the end of the communication. I have to add this on behalf of his Majesty's Government:

[illegible]

TO-DAY'S WEATHER.

[illegible]

Fig. 153. *Streamer headline to the* Daily News & Leader

The *Evening Standard* is an evening newspaper in the *Sunday Express* style with headline typography and streamers and features to match. Its half-sheet size makes difficult the adoption of the magazine style for its special article, or it would doubtless approximate still further the 'gaga' style of the mammoth Sundays.

To complete this hurried inspection of the contemporary London press there remain the older morning journals. The *Daily News*, which absorbed *The Westminster Gazette* in 1928, though strongly influenced by the *Express* practice—on August 5, 1914, it had a 60-point streamer with a 48-point bold sans serif—now stands as a compromise between it and the more conservative practice of *The Daily Telegraph* and *The Morning Post*, proving that modern news display and magazine make-up for 'specials' need not be stupid and indiscriminate.

The Morning Post is the most 'advanced' of the classic dailies. It may be said to have become a modern newspaper when it reduced its price to a penny. The typography of the *Post* was archaic, like that of *The Daily Telegraph* when, at its new price, it came into friendly rivalry with it. The headlines of both were reserved; even after those of the *Post* were revised in 1925. The new headings were in the old-face tradition, and well cut; they were slightly heavier than those in *The Westminster* and in *The Pall Mall Gazette*. Their adoption was but the beginning of a series of experiments which has only lately reached finality in the choice of a conspicuously bold and readable series of headline founts. The paper has also adopted horizontal displays on the main news-page, still in its traditional position in the centre of the paper. There is a woman's page in which the magazine make-up with large italic headlines is allowed. *The Daily Telegraph*, which reverted to its original price of one penny in 1931, is now slowly adapting itself to a looser make-up. Double-column headlines have been admitted, and special articles are conspicuously headed with large founts. The *Telegraph*, in transition, is inferior to the *Post* in lucidity, as it is superior in bulk. It is no longer the fashion in these two conservative mornings to standardise a given fount for the headlines throughout. To maintain variety is an expense to newspapers, but their growth in volume from 8, 10, 12, 24 or even 32 pages made it desirable that the reader should be thus helped to find his way about. The *Daily Mail* of 1896 had pointed the way to this innovation.

All these revolutionary changes in headline technique and make-up practice are at last accepted in the most conservative papers. The changes, as we have proved, began in the despised evening papers and in the equally despised cheap mornings. Hence the present day headlines of *The Times*, to take the last and most significant example, have changed beyond recognition by the Victorians—and the Edwardians. Longer than any other journal, *The Times* had long kept at bay the new journalism. It did not permit any large display advertising face to be used until 1897. It used only one design throughout its editorial columns and by avoiding the use of any other in its advertising columns succeeding in maintaining that uniform colour on every page of the paper which pleased the mid-Victorian eye.

Early in the second half of 1904, job founts for displayed advertisements were evidently a regular holding in *The Times* case room. No control had yet been secured over these displays and they appeared all over the paper. Line blocks in the text of advertisements began to appear on October 17, 1904, with a Savoy Hotel announcement. These activities were confined to advertising. No change was visible in the editorial columns. The first instalment of an unpublished Beaconsfield novel appeared on January 20, 1905. This, the only serial fiction ever printed in *The Times*, was advertised extensively towards the close of 1904, but the headline remained insignificant when the instalments appeared. Things were better in the *Daily News*, but neither *The Daily Telegraph* nor *The Morning Post* shewed at this time any tendency to learn from the example of the halfpenny papers.

The Times, indeed, was at the least interesting point in its career; and at precisely the time when the rest of the London press was making most progress. Between 1904 and 1906, when *The Times* was at its weakest, the *Daily Mail*, *Daily Express* and the *Daily News* were, by their example, training the eyes of future *Times'* readers to demand much larger headlines than the mid-Victorian survivals at Printing House Square could then bear to think of. The great paper looked not only old-fashioned but unkempt. Between 1885 and 1905 the device in the front-page heading seems to have been used without any renewal, so that towards the end of this period it was worn almost entirely flat, appearing black and illegible. The same design was redrawn, and at length on February 8, 1905, the paper carried the new block. No other improvements were made. Grotesque advertising types were admitted on the front-page: bold elongated sans serifs advertising patent rat-killers, and slab-serifed egyptians bellowed the merits of strong beverages. This was a novelty, and literally with a vengeance; the classic front-page was as a devastated region. As to the text: in January 1906 a feature entitled 'Latest News' appears anywhere at the will of the printer, and headed at the will of the printer, in 24-point of a novel advertising face, Morland or

De Vinne. At last there was a little movement in the editorial headlining practice. In January of the following year the 'Imperial and Foreign Intelligence' page was reconstructed with a main heading in 14-point and subheadings in 12-point. The outside columns of the page retained the old light-faced 10-point italic capitals. The same year witnessed changes in the summary and index over the leader. Even so, *The Times* of 1906 was practically identical to the lay eye with *The Times* of 1850. Foreign news looked the most interesting, because it was the best displayed. The facing pages of an issue (cf. Figs. 155 and 156) fairly indicate the aspect of the paper at that time. It will be noted that the first three columns of what is now the main news-page are paragraphed but not cross-headed—in 1907. That

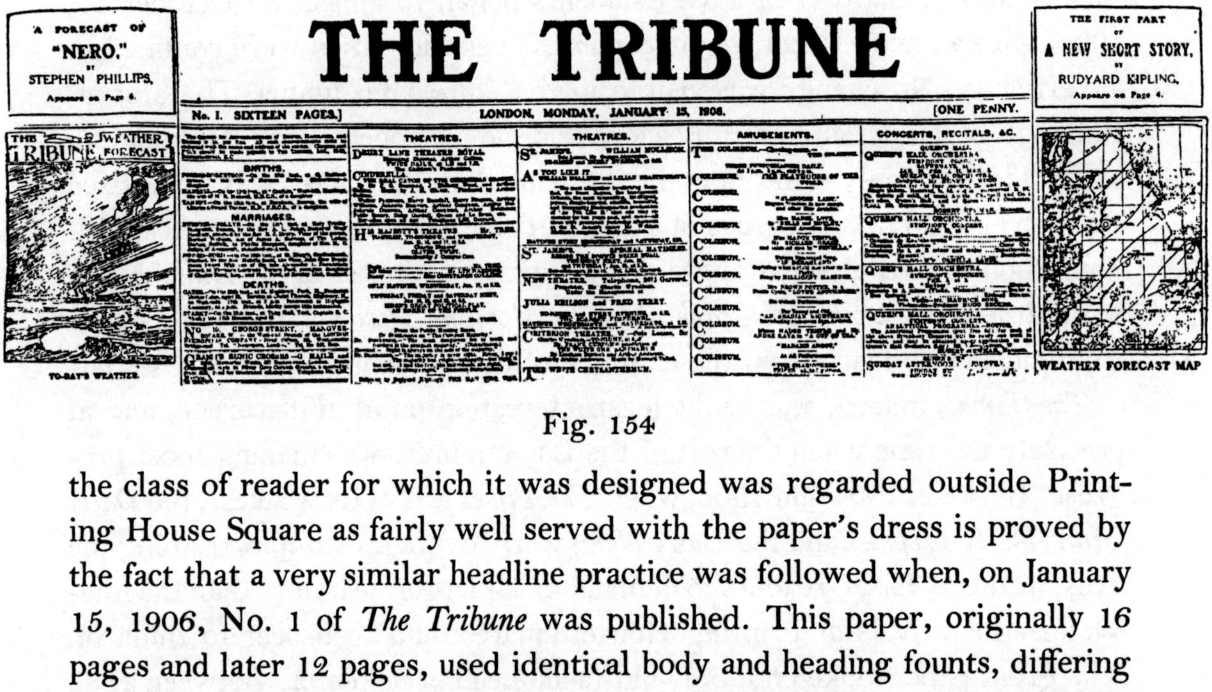
A FORECAST OF "NERO," BY STEPHEN PHILLIPS, Appears on Page 6.

THE TRIBUNE

THE FIRST PART OF A NEW SHORT STORY, BY RUDYARD KIPLING, Appears on Page 4.

No. I. SIXTEEN PAGES.] LONDON, MONDAY, JANUARY 15, 1906. [ONE PENNY.

THE TRIBUNE WEATHER FORECAST

BIRTHS. MARRIAGES. DEATHS.

THEATRES. THEATRES. AMUSEMENTS. CONCERTS, RECITALS, &C.

TO-DAY'S WEATHER. WEATHER FORECAST MAP

Fig. 154

the class of reader for which it was designed was regarded outside Printing House Square as fairly well served with the paper's dress is proved by the fact that a very similar headline practice was followed when, on January 15, 1906, No. 1 of *The Tribune* was published. This paper, originally 16 pages and later 12 pages, used identical body and heading founts, differing only from *The Times* (but imitating *The Daily Telegraph*) in being slightly more liberal with two- and three-decker headings. The leader page, unlike that of *The Times*, was on the left hand of an opening facing the main news-page, which thus had the advantage (denied to *The Times* of the present day) of overflowing to the verso. No English journalist ever dreamt of putting his leader in the first column of the front page—that is good French logic. The English tradition derives, as we saw when discussing *The Morning Chronicle* of 1770, from the traditional, accidental and happy-go-lucky make-up scheme which having insisted, since the beginnings of London journalism, upon London news always *following* foreign news, thus precipitated the latest town news in the centre, more or less, of the paper.

The example of *The Tribune* proves that journalists trained in the new school of Stead, T. P. O'Connor and Massingham, considered that the highbrow audience they were addressing was satisfied with the flat, monotonous typography of *The Times*. Every one of the sixteen pages of *The Tribune* was set in heading founts of the same design and colour. By way of novelty, the leaders were set under news-headings with a French rule inserted between them and their text. The theatre bills were printed in their traditional position over leaders, which extended to almost four columns, the seventh and final column of the page being given to 'A London Letter'.

As January 1906 was the month of an election, the results were strongly featured with a line of 24-point Cheltenham bold over the three centre columns of the main news-page. Such a display was naturally not required after the election, and the paper settled down to a normal single-column heading routine. By the time the paper failed (February 1908) there was a good deal of infusion of Cheltenham bold headings. The leaders were shorter. On the main news-page, 24-point modern was used, but the paper had become more of a paper when it was too late.

Even a new radical foundation of the same year, *The Majority, the Organ of All Who Work for Wage or Salary* (No. 1, July 10, 1906), was a conservative-looking paper. It was an eight-page halfpenny morning paper of seven columns in full blanket-folio. Its headings were light-faced moderns. News was on its front page, but it made the mistake of thinking that wage-slaves are interested enough in salvation to read about it. *The Daily Citizen* (No. 1, October 8, 1912), also a halfpenny of eight seven-column pages in *Daily Mail* style, shewed greater enterprise than *The Majority* in its headings (it carried Venetian tops to its entertainment features and streamers across five columns), but it failed to interest.

In the meantime, *The Times* had remained stationary. The chief news-page had not yet been built up. The theory that readers are more interested in comment than in news inevitably provided (and it still provides) *The Times* with leaders on the right-hand page.

In the summer of 1910, important letters to the editor and certain items of home news began to appear on what had hitherto been merely the page facing the leader. Political news also made its appearance in 1910 thereon and what is now the main news-page or 'bill' page came slowly into existence. The gradual ascendancy of this page began with the adoption of a suitably large fount of capitals for the headlines.

10 THE TIMES, SATURDAY, JULY 13, 1907.

THE MANŒUVRES IN SCOTLAND.

THE NEW REGULATIONS OF THE BOARD OF EDUCATION

INFANT ORPHAN ASYLUM, WANSTEAD.

LONDON ORPHAN ASYLUM.

THE LORD BISHOP OF LONDON

BRITONS FOR BRITISH SHIPS.

THEATRES.

OPERA

VARIETIES.

NOTICES.

Fig. 155. *Centre page of* The Times *in* 1907. *This is now the main news-page of the paper*

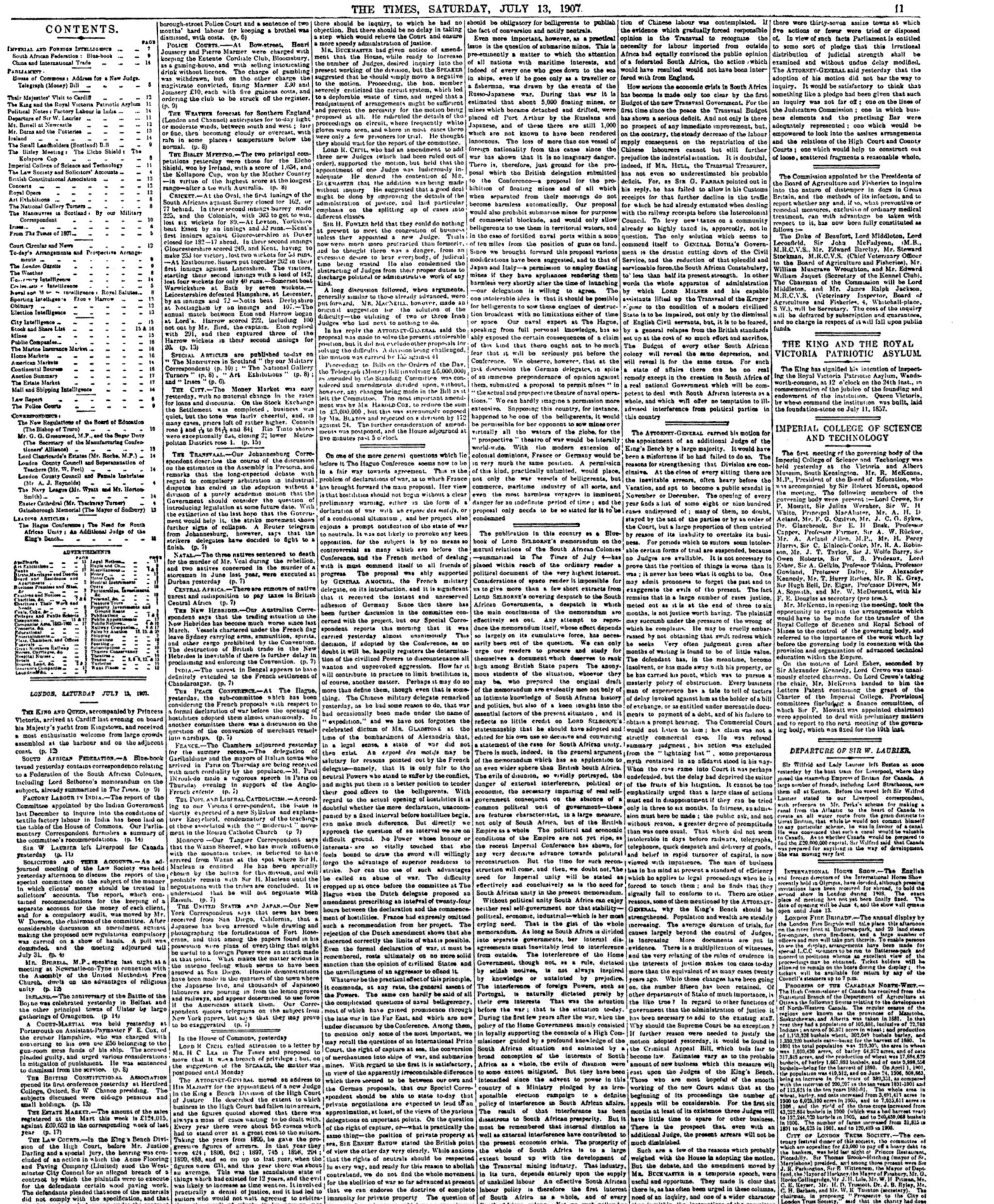
THE TIMES, SATURDAY, JULY 13, 1907. 11

CONTENTS.

LONDON, SATURDAY JULY 13, 1907.

THE KING AND THE ROYAL VICTORIA PATRIOTIC ASYLUM.

IMPERIAL COLLEGE OF SCIENCE AND TECHNOLOGY

DEPARTURE OF SIR W. LAURIER.

Fig. 156. *Leader page of* The Times, 1907

For example, on November 19, 1910, 'THE CRISIS' appears in 20-point modern, the largest type so far used in the editorial portion of the paper. The Sidney Street Siege was given an 18-point condensed modern heading and appeared on this 'bill' page, the italic heads being now taken down to the foot of all columns.

The heavy headings to the leaders first appeared on April 5, 1911; and what is now the 'turn-over' article developed on the leader-page, being headed with 18-point light condensed capitals. The heading of 'Imperial and Foreign Intelligence' was increased from 14-point capitals to two lines of 20-point upper- and lower-case, on October 10, 1912, a style which survives in the current issue.

A double-decker heading—of course in single-column—appeared to an article on the bill page on November 8, 1910; a triple heading on January 3, 1911. The Balkan Conference of 1913 gave the opportunity for a quadruple heading with the paper of January 4. On July 20, 1914, five headings were required to do justice to the Ulster crisis. It is clear at this point that *The Times* was at last committed to the adoption of the American headlines which had won their way into every other London journal from their original position at the top of the columns of *The Star* of 1888.

The early attempts by Printing House Square to re-model its headings were crude enough. But there was a war to excuse them. At the end of July 1914, the European situation had displaced the news of the Protestant rebellion in Ireland, causing its transfer to the turnover column; and on July 30 a main heading and five sub-headings, making a total of six, appeared on the 'bill' page. This looked like a piece of sheer sensationalism; but there was more to come as war approached.

A Sunday edition of *The Times* was published on August 2, 1914, looking uncommonly well; the news, displayed on its front page, gave the issue an admirably direct and clear title to the reader's attention that one was amazed on the Monday following to find that *The Times* had returned to the Victorian custom of printing the Births, Deaths and Marriages where the news was so logically placed on the Sunday. But on the Monday, the eve of the War, August 3, the paper broke with all its conventions and precedents by printing every one of its headings of the bill page and of the turnover page in condensed Venetian capitals. These new types, by their nature advertising letters, were supported from time to time by spirited designs of the same category. **Cheltenham bold condensed** is used in the first column of the main news-page for August 4, 1914, and for the turn-over article on the leader page, the bulk of the paper being headed with the condensed Venetian headings already noted.

Yet by the following year *The Times* went back to headlines in a fount designed before 1840. But unparalleled events were not to be expressed by tight-laced early Victorianisms. The march of events witnessed the ransacking of the type-cases and the eventual use, on the bill page, of every available category of type from Cheltenham bold condensed to bold condensed sans serif. The old-fashioned Caslon reappeared, and on another occasion a large condensed modern heading was combined with a condensed sans serif sub-heading—e.g. in the article on the Aegean danger, October 5, 1915.

The good crackling machine-made paper upon which *The Times* was printed gave way in the early part of 1915 to War paper. A change, however, would in any case have been made, since half-tones were to be received into the text of the paper. On March 11, 1914, an account of the suffragist slashing of the Rokeby Venus was illustrated with a half-tone block about 4 in. by 3 in. When on March 16, 1914, the price of the paper was brought to 1*d*. half-tones became increasingly frequent. Official photographs supplied by the Admiralty covering air raids were printed during the War, but it was not until the Peace that readers could depend upon finding half-tones in the day's paper. Lord Allenby's portrait is shewn in half-tone on November 7, 1921, and the Oxford and Cambridge Rugby teams shewn in the paper of December 8, 1921, but it was not until the spring of the following year that half-tones were given a page to themselves in every day's issue of the paper.

On March 1, 1916, a signal change in the construction of the paper made its first appearance—namely, the adaptation of the front page to a seven-column measure, a financial gain since it gave less space in the new column—at the old rate. This was carried out consistently through the outer sheet of four pages, but no changes were made in the editorial portion of the paper until February 19, 1921, when the entire paper was set to a seven-column width, with the single exception of the leader page, which retains its broad gauge until the present time. Fortunately the narrow measure—14 picas—is wide in comparison with the rest of the press. As a consequence, the headlines of *The Times* do not need to be either tortured into a high degree of condensation or to be flung across two columns.

The development of what is nowadays the main news-page was accelerated during 1922. The issue for Monday, January 29, 1923, is singular. All the heads in the main news-page are in light modern capitals of the same design as the body, the only feature headed with a blacker type being a letter to the

Editor from Mr St. Loe Strachey. The heading to the turn-over article is in the light capitals. On the following day, however, an article on the British debt to America, placed in the centre column of the bill page, is headed with condensed heavy modern capitals of the largest size, with two sub-heads; the turn-over article is also given the heavier headings. In March the light headings were restored. The alternating of columns with light and heavy headings became a regular practice towards the end of 1923. *The Times* of 1924 arrived at its present satisfactory legible and common-sensible headline.

There has never been a double-column heading in the paper. This is a point at which *The Times* is out of step with the entire London press without being out of step with right reason. The use of such a device inevitably introduces the habit of artificial display, "dressing the paper with an air of news when there is none"—to quote the writer in *The Daily Courant* of 1702. If *The Times* ever accepts double-column headings, it will not be because they are necessary but because a generation of readers has been habituated to them by reading journals less scrupulously conducted.

There is a point here worth examination; but there is only time to assert the obvious truth that the physical act of reading can only become tolerable when the deciphering of alphabetical symbols is performed without effort, when it has become, so far as may be, inherent in the mental constitution—in one word, *habit*. The reading habits of the people are based upon physical, ocular, laws; and, within those laws, upon the printed matter they experience. A considerable degree of similarity in the typography of newspapers argues originally a partial and, ultimately, a complete consent of readers. First, a new idea in layout is tried by an innovator, and competing papers follow when success rewards the new display with increased circulation or prestige. Thus *The Post-Man, The Weekly Journal, The Universal Chronicle, The St James's Chronicle* and *The Times* dominated the formats of old and new competitors during part of their respective periods. Smart imitators followed successful innovators; finally the conservatives changed—in the realisation that an old-fashioned layout acts like a tariff against the new readers who must be secured if the wastage of circulation by death of old readers is to be repaired.

Such 'new' readers have to be detached from other papers. In the final analysis, therefore, these young or new readers, with reading habits based upon the typography of the majority of papers, must ultimately prevail over the most rigidly conservative journal—or that journal will slowly but surely lose ground to its rivals. The circulation of *The Times* would be negligible today had it preserved the form in which it appeared in 1907. Hence, it is axiomatic that no journal, other than a gazette enjoying a privileged and uncompetitive status, can for any length of time isolate itself from the reading habits of prospective readers. When, therefore, *The Times* of the future accepts double-column headlines, it will indicate its conviction that such headlines have become permanently incorporated into the reading experience of the general public, and into its own particular public's idea of a newspaper.

It seems likely that a period of active headline experiment will follow the realisation by newspapers that the radio has undermined their old position as the sole exploiters of news. But our sufficient task has been to observe the major variations in form which the newspaper assumed in its evolution from the seventeenth-century quarto pamphlet to the present-day folio blanket, and we can leave the future to itself. Such speculations apart, there is justification for a plea, if not for a prophecy, that the newspaper should share in the interest and study which bibliographers and collectors have long lavished upon the manuscript codex and the printed book. The improved typography of books, with consequent enhanced pleasure of reading and world reputation of British craftsmanship, is due not only to the self-respect of publishers, the craft traditions of printers and the critical appreciation of readers, but also to the discrimination of bibliographers, whose part in forming the taste and guiding the experiments of typographical workers is less commonly realised. The community would unquestionably benefit if men of learning would extend their interest to the end that the tranquillity, exactitude, clarity and ease of reading, which have been secured in the English book, may also be obtained in that other category of printing, the fundamental economic character of which is more fully developed, and which is in consequence more widely distributed—the English Newspaper.

Self-Portrait of Francis Hoffman

APPENDIX

FRANCIS HOFFMAN

FRANCIS HOFFMAN, whose name is cited several times in Chapters III and V, was a craftsman whose range of activities entitles him to some mention in works of reference. This lacking, it seems justifiable to gather, in an appendix to a volume on newspapers, the available particulars of an artist much of whose work was done for newspaper printers. Hoffman cut heading-blocks for *The Post Man*, *The Post Boy*, *The Flying Post*, and Mist's *Weekly Journal*; his initial letters and factotums appeared in much of the book-printing of the time as well as in newspapers. Many of his pieces are signed, certain of them so conspicuously that it seems obvious that his reputation was considerable. To take one instance, in the 1722 blocks for *The Flying Post* the line 'F. Hoffman Fecit' assumes the function of a caption. The *F. H. fec* on the fame cut for *The Post Boy* (1722)

Heading-blocks from The Flying Post, 1722

are larger than the letters of the text *Viresque acquirit eundo.* Is it the implication that printers appreciated the co-operation of the artist and that it became a point of a newspaper manager's pride to equip his paper with a signed Hoffman heading and a Hoffman factotum? It seems likely. Nevertheless I have not stumbled across any personal mention of the artist in any of the books or papers of the period. The sole mention of him in the current reference books is in Thieme-Becker, *Allgemeines Lexikon der Bildenden Künstler* (1924, vol. XVII, 354), where he is credited with a portrait group of Henry St John (Viscount Bolingbroke), Wm Bromley (Speaker of the House of Commons) and Robert Harley, Earl of Oxford. This very crude affair (it is in the Print Room of the British Museum) is signed *Francis Hoffman fecit aquaforte* 1711.

The first trace of his other activities occurs in a *Pilgrim's Progress*, printed by R. Tookey 1706 'and now done into verse' by Francis Hoffman, who also contributed not merely a copper-plate frontispiece portrait of Bunyan, but woodcuts of Christian ascending Mount Zion, his being made righteous and relieved of his burdens, his being afflicted and persecuted by the world, and, finally, his overcoming Giant Temptation. These four blocks, some $2\frac{1}{2}$ in. × $4\frac{1}{8}$ in., reappear in the third edition of the work printed by John Marshal, Gracechurch Street, 1723. In the Museum copy, the frontispiece, if it was ever there, is lacking.

In 1707, a political sensation was caused by the arrest of a certain William Gregg, who had been Harley's confidential agent, for betraying documents to France. An outburst of pamphleteering occurred in which Francis Hoffman took part. William Gregg was hanged on April 28, 1708, after a committee of seven lords had examined him, which extraordinary proceeding was due to partisan allegations that Harley had all along been privy to Gregg's treason. Hoffman's contribution to the controversy is entitled: *Secret Transactions during the Hundred Days Mr William Gregg lay in Newgate under Sentence of Death for High Treason, from the Day of his sentence to the Day of his Execution*, printed in the year 1711. Although the author's name is not printed on the title-page of this piece, the dedication 'to our Queen' is signed by 'a most faithful and dutiful Subject, And of my Native Country, An affectionate Lover and Servant FRANCIS HOFFMAN'.

In the following year (1712) he made another contribution to Political controversy—on this occasion in verse—by issuing a folio broadside 'price one penny' under the title *Vulpoon in the Snare; Or, A Hue and Cry after Eight and Twenty Millions ſunk by the Hawkubite Crew*[1].

There is no trace of any other literary efforts until 1724, when Hoffman

[1] I owe my reference to this piece (in the University Library, Cambridge) to Mr G. R. Barnes.

published *The Testimony of Francis Hoffman concerning the Truth and Inoffensiveness, and for reasonable moderation in wearing Apparel.*

In the same year he appears as the author of *An Address to the Clergy concerning the First Article of the Church of England by a Person of Truly Scrupulous Conscience, almost persuaded to turn Dissenter. Unless seasonably relieved by Reasons more excellent and Divine than those herein made known.* This work is printed in some style with a headband and initial both signed F. H.

In the following year Hoffman brought out, 'printed for the author', *A Curious Uncommon Account of the Great Eclipse of the Moon, October the* 10*th*, 1725. *With a new Theory of all the Orbs in the Heavens, of the Stars, of the Earth and of the fixed Stars or Suns agreeing with Scripture, Love, Reason, Acts and Nature.* This work has two headbands and an initial, neither signed, but obviously by our artist. There is also a copper-plate of the eclipse which is not signed.

The British Museum preserves two broadsides, undated, but carrying blocks signed F. H.: *The Creed of Francis Hoffman Most Humbly dedicated to the Almighty Gorgos* and *The Real Door.* A large headpiece is common to both. A very fine tailpiece is appended to the *Real Door.*

The MS. Department of the British Museum preserves a letter from Francis Hoffman to Sir Hans Sloane, offering him a cordial calculated to cure him of every sort of effect of 'chill'. The cordial was obviously invented by himself. Hoffman fancied himself somewhat as an inventor. In the Record Office there is a petition to Queen Anne in which the artist claims to have discovered an invention whereby troops may be made more courageous than had ever been known and by means of which lives might be saved in battle. There is no indication on the document of any action being taken by the Queen in this matter. A more important claim is made in the portrait 'invented drawn Written & Engraved by Him' in which Hoffman puts forth a definite claim to being the first inventor of shipping with three bottoms, Anno 1709–10 'Propos'd by him to The Government. Also how near half of the Army might have been sav'd'.

As the histories of shipping give no support, it is more than likely that this was also given a disappointing reception.

Nevertheless, his claims, if not his achievements, must have been well known. The supersession of the original blocks of *The Post Boy, The Post Man,* and *The Flying Post* took place about the year 1722. Several of these are shewn on pp. 61, 64, 69 of the present work. In *The Post Man* the new blocks, not only designed but signed by Hoffman, include a fine packet with three decks. The blocks cut for Mist seem to date from 1718; they are illustrated on page 96.

Hoffman's factotums are found in use as initials by book printers. In 1728 Charles Ackers, of St John Street, Clerkenwell, printed Ralph's *Night* with a dedicatory epistle introduced with a factotum signed *F. H.* I have observed signed tailpieces in the books printed for Thomas Osborne, *ca.* 1723. A much used and much copied factotum by Hoffman is the 'fame' engraved originally for Mist. The factotum at the head of this appendix is recut from the signed block which Mrs Elizabeth Powell used for her *Orphan Reviv'd.*

Mist's 'fame' factotum

It has seemed desirable to include Hoffman's portrait in this appendix as giving the data for possible investigation by the curious into the career of this interesting, if minor, personality.

INDEXES

INDEX TO JOURNALS CITED

An asterisk after a page-number indicates reference to illustration on that page

ACCOUNT of Publick Transactions in Christendom, 58*
Account of two Great Battailes very lately Fought (1622), 11
Affairs of the World for this Present Week, 13
Albion, 193, 205, 240*, 241
Argus, 205
Aurora, 169, 172*
Ayre's Sunday London Gazette, 232*

BELL'S Life in London, 242*, 244*, 245*, 246*, 249
Bell's New Weekly Messenger, 250*
Bell's Penny Dispatch, 259*
Bell's Weekly Dispatch, 239, 241, 242, 249
Bell's Weekly Messenger, 169, 235, 241, 246, 247*, 249
Bingley's Journal, 154
British Apollo, 84
British Gazette, see *E. Johnson*
British Journal, 112
British Neptune, 249

CABINET, 197
Champion, 131, 249
Charitable Mercury, 85*, 100
Church-Man's Last Shift, 98*, 100
Citie Scout, 31, 35*
Citties weekly Post, 31, 34*
City Intelligencer, 84
Clark's Weekly Dispatch, 257, 258*
Cobbett's Weekly Political Register, 227
Comic News, 257
Commercialist, 251
Commonsense, 113
Compleate Intelligencer and Resolver, 29
Constitution, 241
Continuation... Speciall and Remarkable Passages, 22*, 23
Continued Journal, etc., 33
Coranto, A, 9, 10*
Country Journal, 109, 111, 114*
Courier, 169, 198
Courrier de Londres, 227
Craftsman, 105, 109, 110*
Craftsman (1739), 117
Currant Intelligence (Smith), 43, 45, 46*
Currant Intelligence (Banks), 45

DAILY Advertiser, 122*, 123, 124*, 143, 187
Daily Citizen, 313
Daily Courant, 70, 73, 74, 75, 85, 86, 111, 121
Daily Courier, 296
Daily Express, 299, 304*, 305, 308*
Daily Express and Morning Herald, 303
Daily Gazetteer, 126, 144
Daily Intelligencer of Court, City and County, 29
Daily Journal, 88, 105, 121
Daily Mail, 186, 189, 294*, 296, 299, 305, 306*, 307
Daily News, 205, 206, 222*, 223*, 270, 289, 305
Daily News and Leader, 309*
Daily Paper, 303, 305
Daily Post, 88, 121
Daily Register of Commerce and Intelligence, 151
Daily Telegraph, 223, 267, 310
Daily Universal Register, 180*, 181, 182
Dawks's News-Letter, 48, 49*, 50*, 75, 183
Day, 205
Diary or Woodfall's Chronicle, 193
Diurnall Occurrences or Heads, etc., 15
Diurnall Occurrences in Parliament, 15

E. JOHNSON'S British Gazette and Sunday Monitor, 61, 228*, 229
Echo, 261, 273, 283
English Chronicle, 175, 176*
English Courant, 47
Englishman, 250

Entertainer, 97
European Magazine, 193
Evening Advertiser, 133*
Evening Chronicle, 205
Evening Courant, 76, 131
Evening Illustrated Paper, 276
Evening Journal, 86, 131
Evening Mail, 192
Evening News, 273, 282*, 283, 295, 307
Evening Post (1706), 75, 131, 133
Evening Post (1709), 75, 76*
Evening Post (1887), 283
Evening Standard, 205, 310
Evening Star, 270
Evening Star, and Grand Weekly Advertiser, 189, 191
Exact Accompt...proceedings in Parliament, etc., 33, 35*
Exact Diurnall, 21
Examiner, 83, 84, 227, 241
Exchange Intelligence, 29
Express (1846), 205
Express (1877), 276, 281
Express and Evening Chronicle, 198

FAITHFUL Post, 31
Faithful Scout, 33
Female Tatler, 84
Flying Post (1644), 30, 31
Flying Post (1695), 31, 57, 68*, 69*, 86, 123, 321*
Flying Post and Medley, 70
Fog's Weekly Journal, 112
Freeholder's Journal, 109, 121

GALLERY of Comicalities, 247
Gazetteer, 144
Gazetteer and London Daily Advertiser, 145
Gazetteer and Public Advertiser, 147
General Advertiser, 126
General Evening Post, 131, 145
General Post, 76, 131
General Postscript, 83, 84
General Remark, 84
Generous London Morning Advertiser, 126
Genius, 153
Gentleman's Journal and Tradesman's Companion, 101
Globe, 205, 307
Grand Politique Post, 31
Great Britain's Post, 31
Grub-street Journal, 108*, 113

HEADS of Severall... Parliament... 1641, 14, 15
High Life in London, 246
Historical Account, 58

ILLUSTRATED London News, 261
Independent Chronicle, 154
Independent Observer, 248
Independent Whig, 247, 248
Intelligence: Domestick and Foreign, 45
Intelligencer, 37, 38*

JONES'S Evening News-Letter, 50

KINGDOMES Weekly Intelligencer, 29, 32*
Kingdomes weekly Post, 30

LE Beau Monde, 250
Life in London (1821), 243
Life in London (1822), 243
Literary Courier of Grub-street, 113
Lloyd's Evening Post, 187
Lloyd's Illustrated London Newspaper, 261
Lloyd's News, 48
Lloyd's Penny Dispatch, 257
Lloyd's Penny Sunday Times, 254*, 261
Lloyd's Weekly London Newspaper, 261
Lloyd's Weekly News, 261
London Chronicle, 50, 134*, 135
London Courant, 117, 118*
London Daily Post, 125
London Evening News, 267
London Evening Post, 131, 149
London Gazette, 42*, 43, 63
London Gazetteer, 126*, 141
London Halfpenny Newspaper, 260*, 261, 279
London Journal, 96*, 97, 101, 121
London Mercury (1671), 47
London Mercury (1681), 47
London Mercury (1720), 101
London Mercury or Moderate Intelligencer (1688), 47
London Morning, 300*, 301

London Morning Advertiser, 126
London Morning Penny Post, 127
London News Letter, 47
London Packet (1770), 145
London Packet, or New Evening Post (1771), 11, 183
London Post, 16, 31, 32*
London Post (1647), 57
London Post (1699), 57
London Recorder, 231*, 249
London Recorder (1783), 231*
London's Diurnal, 36
London Slip of News, 57
London Spy Revived, 86
Loyal London Mercury, 45
Loyal Observator Revived, 101
Loyalist's Weekly Journal, 100

MAIL (1868), 192
Majority, 313
Medley, 83, 84
Mercurius Academicus, 25, 26*, 29
Mercurius Anglicus, 44
Mercurius Aulicus, 24, 29
Mercurius Britannicus, 14, 27
Mercurius Civicus (1643), 25, 26*, 28*, 44
Mercurius Civicus (1679), 44
Mercurius Elencticus, 27
Mercurius Melancholicus, 27
Mercurius Politicus, 27, 30, 36, 39
Mercurius Pragmaticus, 27
Mercurius Publicus, 27
Mercurius Veridicus, 27
Middlesex Journal, 154, 155*, 157
Miscellany, 115
Mist's Weekly Journal, 102*
Moderate Intelligencer, 29
Moderne Intelligencer, 29
Monitor, 147
More Newes of this Present Week, 13
Morning, 293*, 295, 300*, 301
Morning Advertiser, 198
Morning Chronicle, 161, 162*, 163*, 165, 167, 179*, 193, 207, 223, 250
Morning Herald, 167, 169, 189, 222, 301, 302*
Morning Leader, 292*, 295
Morning Post, 55, 144, 164, 166*, 168*, 207, 310
Morning Post (Corrall), 175
Morning Star, 192*, 193, 270

NATION, 205
National Register, 241, 250
New Observer, 248*
New Times, 205
New Weekly Chronicle, 139
New York Herald, 265, 288*
New York Times, 288*
Newes, 37
Newes concernynge . . . Trydent (1549), 7, 9
Newes from France, 7, 8*, 9
Newes of this Present Week, 13
Newes out of Holland, 7, 8*
News, 239*
News Letter, 95
News of the World, 147, 217, 251, 252*, 253*, 257, 307
Night Post, 78, 131
Noon Gazette and Daily Spy, 170*, 172, 198
North Briton, 155

OBSERVATOR, 83, 84
Observer, 169, 249
Occurrences from Foreign Parts, etc., 36
Old Post-Master, 56*, 57
Oracle (1789), 169, 187, 193, 194*, 195*, 199, 200*
Original London Post, 99, 100
Original Star, 191
Orphan, 99
Orphan Reviv'd, 100
Our last Weekly Newes, 12*, 13
Owen's Weekly Chronicle, 138*
Oxford Gazette, 38

PALL Mall Gazette, 201, 271, 272*, 281, 286*
Parker's London News, 121, 123
Parker's Penny Post, 123
Parliament's Post, 31
Parliament Scout, 31
Parliamentary Intelligencer, 36
Payne's Universal Chronicle, 137
Pegasus, 51, 52*, 87
Penny London Post, 127*
Penny Newsman (1860), 261
Penny Pickwick, 257
Penny Satirist, 257
Penny Sunday Times, 256*, 257, 261
Penny Weekly Dispatch, 257

Penny Weekly Journal, 101
People, 305
People's Police Gazette, 257
Perfect Diurnall...Passages in Parliament (1643) (Coles & Blaikelock), 16, 17
Perfect Diurnall...Passages in Parliament (1641) (Cook & Pecke), 15, 18*
Perfect Diurnall...Passages in Parliament (Williamson), 17, 20*, 21
Perfect Occurrences of Every Daie Journall, etc., 29, 33, 34*
Perfect Occurrences of Parliament, etc., 16, 17, 19*
Perfect Passages of Each Dayes...Parliament, 22*, 24
Perfect Passages of Every Daies Intelligence, etc., 29, 33
Pierce Egan's Life in London, 243
Pierce Egan's Weekly Courier, 247
Play, 147
Politique Post, 31
Porcupine Gazette (Philadelphia, 1797), 265
Post Boy (Boyer), 60
Post Boy (James), 123
Post Boy (Roper), 57, 62*, 64*, 67, 70
Post Man (1695), 59
Post Man (Baldwin), 61*, 64–7, 70*
Post Man, 123
Protestant Post Boy, 84
Public Advertiser, 126, 187, 196
Public Ledger, 151*
Publick Intelligencer, 30
Publique Intelligence, 36

RAYNER'S Universal London Morning Advertiser, 126
Read's Weekly Journal, 80, 83
Real John Bull, 249
Reconciler, 86
Rehearsal, 84
Review 1712–13, 84
Review and Sunday Advertiser, 233*, 234*
Review of Reviews, 303
Reviewer, 251
Reynolds's Weekly Newspaper, 261
Robin's Last Shift, 95
Royal Westminster Journal, 118

ST JAMES'S Chronicle, 149, 150, 152*, 205
St James's Evening Post, 79*, 80, 105, 131
St James's Gazette, 272*, 273, 275
St James's Post, 73, 77*, 78
Saturday's Post, 97
Selector, or Say's Sunday Report, 249
Shift Shifted, 90*, 95
Shift's Last Shift, 92*, 95
Smith's Currant Intelligence, 45, 46*
Smith's Protestant Intelligence, 45, 46*
Some Speciall and Considerable Passages, 20*, 21
Spectator, 74, 83, 84
Spie, 31
Standard, 205, 215, 216*
Star (1788), 169, 188, 189, 190*, 191, 205
Star (1888), 273, 279, 283, 289, 290*, 291, 307
Statesman, 205
Stuart's Star and Evening Advertiser, 190*, 192
Summary, 293
Sun (1792), 198
Sun (1798), 217
Sunday Chronicle, 232, 233*
Sunday Daily Mail, 229
Sunday Daily Telegraph, 229
Sunday Dispatch, 307
Sunday Express, 305
Sunday Gazette, 169
Sunday Herald, 234
Sunday Monitor, 63, 189, 230*, 249
Sunday Morning Herald, 249
Sunday Paper, 249
Sunday Reformer, 231, 249
Sunday Review, 234
Sunday Times, 248*
Supplement, 84

THE Times, 146, 169, 184, 185*, 186*, 208*, 209, 210*, 211, 212*, 213, 214*, 215, 216, 218*, 219, 220*, 221, 239, 285, 287, 289, 311, 313, 314*, 315*, 316–19
Tatler, 57, 84, 109
Telegraph, 198, 199
Thursday Journal, 97, 101
Traveller, 205

Tribune, 312*
True Briton, 109
True Diurnall, 16
True Informer, 25, 28*
Tuesdaies Journall... Parliament (1649), 29

UNIVERSAL Chronicle, 88, 118
Universal Chronicle and Westminster Journal, 139
Universal Chronicle or Weekly Gazette, 136*, 137
Universal Journal, 109
Universal Spectator and Weekly Journal, 112

WEEKLY Account, etc., 16, 23, 30
Weekly Dispatch, 147, 229, 238*, 239, 279, 280*
Weekly Intelligencer, etc., 30
Weekly Journal (Applebee), 100
Weekly Journal (Heathcote), 99
Weekly Journal (Mawson), 88, 89*, 91, 95
Weekly Journal (Mist), 90, 95, 96*, 97, 102*
Weekly Journal (Read), 93*, 94*, 101, 104*
Weekly Medley, 99
Weekly Miscellany, 115, 116
Weekly Newes, 13
Weekly Newes from Italy, etc. (1622), 5, 9, 10*, 13
Weekly News Letter, 47, 48
Weekly Packet (1712), 84
Weekly Packet (1714), 87
Weekly Post, 31, 33, 55
Weekly Post Master, 31
Westminster Gazette, 201, 273, 296, 307
Westminster Journal, 116*, 117*, 139, 140
Whisperer, 84
Whitehall Evening Post, 131, 132*, 149*
World, 169, 177, 178*, 179*, 184

INDEX TO PROPER NAMES AND SUBJECTS

ACKERS, Charles, 323
Adlard, William, 231
Aird, David, 267
Allen, Ralph, 128
Almon, John, 11, 165, 169, 183, 232
Alsop, Bernard, 16, 23, 29, 30
Amhurst, Nicholas, 105, 109, 112, 117
Applebee, John, 97, 100, 121
Applegath, Augustus, 216
Appleyard, Robert, 249
Archer, Thomas, 9, 13, 14, 24
Arnold, Matthew, 279, 284
Astor, Mr Waldorf, 296
Austin, Richard, 185, 187, 209
Austin, Robert, 24, 30
Ayre, R., 232

BAKER, J., 78, 80
Baldwin, Charles, 153, 205
Baldwin, Henry, 153, 167
Baldwin, Richard, 47, 58, 59, 64
Banks, Allen, 45
Barnes, Thomas, 207
Barr, J. S., 175
Bastow, John, 261
Bate, Rev. Henry, 167, 169
Bates, Thomas, 25, 27, 44
Baylis, 227
Beardwell, B., 58, 59
Beardwell, L., 59
Beckford, William, 154
Bell, John, 97, 100, 155, 164, 167, 169, 175, 179, 187, 195, 199, 206, 235, 250
Bell, John Browne, 206, 241, 250, 257
Bell, Moberly, 209
Bell, Robert, 175, 206, 239, 242
Bellamy, 193
Bennett, James Gordon, 265, 269
Berington, E., 75
Bickerstaff, Isaac, 109
Bickerton, J., 88
Bickerton, Thomas, 100
Bigg, George, 164
Bingley, William, 154
Bishop, George, 16, 29, 30, 31
Bladon, John, 167
Blaikelock, Laurence, 17
Blunden, Henry, 21
Bond, D., 156, 234
Border, Daniel, 29
Boreham, 121
Bostock, R., 187, 198
Bourne, N., 9, 13, 14
Boyer, A., 60
Bragg, Mr, 57
Brewman, D., 118, 230
British Letter Foundry, 195
Brome, G., 47
Browne, J., 86
Buckle, G. E., 287
Buckley, A., 112, 121
Buckley, Samuel, 63, 74
Bulmer, William, 201
Burd, J., 175
Burnham, Lord, 267
Butter, Nathaniel, 9, 11, 13, 14, 16

CASLON (types), 40, 145, 155, 261
Caslon, Mrs Elizabeth, 199
Cassell, 273
Catling, Thomas, 261
Chambers, W., 246
Charlton, W., 97
Christie, 164
Cibber, T., 125
Clavel, R., 58
Clement, William, 235, 250
Cobbett, William, 265
Coe, A., 16
Coe, Jane, 17
Coles, F., 16, 17, 24
Cook, W., 17, 23, 24
Cook, William, 15, 17, 31
'Corantos,' 7–14
Corrall, George, 175
Cowper, 216
Cox, Edward, 164
Crofts, Captain, 169
Cruikshank, G., 243, 247

DALTON, Isaac, 93, 95
D'Anvers, Caleb: *see* Amhurst, Nicholas
Dawks, Ichabod, 48, 50
Dawks, Thomas, 37
Dickens, Charles, 261
'Diurnalls,' 14–21
Dodsley, Robert, 135
Downe, B., 14
Dunton, John, 51
Dury, G., 36

EGAN, Pierce, 242, 243
Evans, T., 167

FADEN, W., 118, 139
Fell, Isaac, 154
Fielding, Henry, 133
Figgins, Vincent, 251
Frampton, J. S., 257

GAYLARD, Doctor, 100
Gentletouch, Simon, 118
Goreham, H., 117
Gregg, William, 322
Griffin, William, 157
Griffith, John, 144
Griffiths, J., 126

HAMMOND, J., 30
Hardy, Thomas, 125
Harris, Benjamin, 45, 57
Haswell, Robert, 175
Hill, Sir John, 126
Hinton, James, 117
Hoffman, Francis, 97, 109, 321–3
Hooker, R., 115
Horton, G., 31, 55
Huggonson, J., 131
Hunt, John, 241
Hunt, Leigh, 227
Hurt, W., 69, 70

IBBITSON, Robert, 29
Imprimerie Nationale, 237
'Intelligencers,' 29–30
'Intelligences', 45–6
Ives, Chester, 295

JAMES, 63, 123
Jenour, J., 125
Jenour, M., 70, 123, 125, 187
Jephson, C., 115
Jerdan, William, 169
Johnson, Mrs E., 189, 191, 229
Johnson, H., 181
Johnson, Samuel, 137, 230
Jones, Kennedy, 295

KOENIG Press, 205

LAMB, Charles, 281
Lane, William, 191
Lang, Andrew, 293
Leach, Dryden, 123
Leach, F., 16, 24, 47, 66
Lee, 191
Leech, J., 247
L'Estrange, R., 37
Lichfield, L., 43
Lloyd, E., 48, 257
Logographic Press, 181

MACDONALD, W. R., 243, 246
Macrae, C., 233
Maddocks, A., 246
Mallet, E., 73
Manley, R., 112
Marshall, John, 322
Martin, John, 234
Martin, William, 201
Mawson, Robert, 88, 91, 93, 112
Meere, H., 121
'Mercuries', 24–9
Miles, Captain, 169
Millan, Buchanan, 198
Miller, John, 167
Mist, Nathaniel, 95, 97, 99, 112
Mitchell, Mr, 67
Monck, General, 36
Mooney, Mr, 112
Moore, T., 133
Morley, John, 276
Morphew, J., 75, 86
Moxon, James, 44, 58, 73
Muddiman, Henry, 36

NEEDHAM, Marchamont, 30, 36
Newbery, 139
Newbery, E., 155
Newbery, F., 151
Newbery, John, 144
Newbury, N., 9
Newcombe, T., 43
'New Journalism', 279, 287, 293
Newnes, Sir G., 296
News-letters, 47
News-pamphlets, 7–9, 12*, 14
Newspaper control: printer control, 143, 265; proprietor control, 144–5, 193
Newspaper features and typographical development:
Advertisements: theatrical, 146; 'Box' system, 269; displayed, 285
Bill page of *The Times*, 146, 313, 314*, 317
Blackletter headings, 44, 50, 165, 213, 216
Book reviewing, beginning of, 115
Caps and smalls for proper names, 13, 179
Children's page, 305
Commercial intelligence, 127
Contents table, 285, 287
Cross-headings, 279, 284, 286*, 291*, 312
Date-position on early papers, 13
Day of week in title, 29
Devices, development of, 16, 52*, 56*, 61*, 62*, 64*, 68*, 69*, 85*, 89*, 90*, 92–4*, 96*, 98*, 104*, 118*, 138*, 149*, 155*, 163*, 178*, 208*, 247*
'Ears', 22*, 23, 25
Essays, 87
'Evening': first use in title, 75
'Extraordinary' issues, 63, 209, 212*
Factotum, first use of, 16
Green paper, 296
Headline development, 78, 220*, 281, 282*, 287, 288*, 291*, 295, 299, 301, 303, 304*, 306*, 308*, 309, 310, 313, 316–19
'Idler' papers, 137
Illustrations, 16, 25, 33, 170*, 209, 210*, 211, 237, 238*, 254*, 256*, 258*, 259*
Interviews, 283
Italics, first use in newspaper, 179
Late news, early provision for, 63–8
Leading article, forerunner of, 163
Leading between pars, 179
Line blocks in advertisement text, 311
'London': first use in sub-title, 25
'Manifesto', 163
Maps, 199, 227, 237, 285
Music, 156
'New Journalism', 279, 287, 293
'Observations', 51
'Personal' journalism, 301, 307
'Postscripts', 61, 63, 64–5, 70, 76
Red-letter days, 183–4
Religious articles, 229, 231
Royal device, 43, 77*, 78, 79*, 80*, 176*, 180*, 185*, 186*, 195*
Rules, 17, 33, 43, 150, 177
Running headline, 197, 216
S, rejection of long ſ, 177, 185
Serial fiction in *The Times*, 311
Serial numbers, 11, 13, 23*, 25
Signed articles, 287, 301, 307
Steam printing, 207, 211
Sunday editions, 125, 209, 212*, 316
Supplements, 91, 213, 214*, 219
Table of contents, 285
Telegraphic transmission of news, 217
Time of publication, 208
Title to leading article, 289, 316
Titles—shortened in 1663, 37
Woman's page, 296
Nye (Mr), 65

O'CONNOR, T. P., 279, 283, 289
Okes, J., 16, 24
Osborne, Thomas, 323
Owen, R., 139, 213

PALMER'S Improved Mail Coach Plan, 189
Paper, 104, 201, 317; green, 296; tax, 207, 200*, 217; water-marked, 67
Parker, George, 121
Parry, J., 198
'Passages', 15, 21–4
Payne, John, 118, 133, 137

Payne, T., 109
Pearson, C. A., 301
Pecke, Samuel, 14, 15, 16, 23, 24
Peele, J., 101
Perry, James, 193
Phipps, T. A., 239
Pope, S., 231
Postal services—development, 128
'Posts', 30–1
Powell, Mrs Eliz., 85, 99, 100, 323
Printing presses—official control, 14, 21, 30, 36, 37, 39, 44, 51
'Public Register', 151

RAYNALDE, T., 7
Read, J., 80, 93, 95, 101
Redmayne, G., 117, 118
Rich, 47
Roberts, J., 88, 101, 115, 154
Roper, Abel, 57, 58, 59, 64
Royal Arms—absence of authority for use, 78
Rushworth, J., 30, 31

SALUSBURY, J., 31
Say, Charles, 145, 169
Say, Edward, 145
'Scouts', 31–6
Sharp of Ivy Lane, 121
Shefford, W., 9, 11
Skinner, Alderman, 164
Sleigh, Colonel, 267
Smith, Francis, 45
Smith, John, 45
'Spies', 31–6
Spilsbury, Thomas, 145
Stamp duty, 83, 85, 86, 103, 185, 201, 207, 217, 239, 251, 265
Stationers Company, 36
Stead, W. T., 276, 284, 301, 303, 307
Steele, Richard, 87
Stoddart, Dr, 205
Stokes, J., 230
Stonecastle, Henry, 112
Storer, Nathaniel, 95
Strahan, William, 135
Stuart, Daniel, 169, 198
Stuart, Peter, 189, 191, 196
Sunday newspaper, first London, 229

TATTERSALL, 164
Thomas, John, 15
Thorne, Robert, 237
Thurlow, J., 30
Tookey, R., 69, 322
Topham, Edward, 169, 177, 187
Touchit, Thomas, 116
Trehearn, Vincent, 172
Trenchard, J., 101
Trusler, Rev. Dr John, 164
Tunstall, E., 267

VILE, T., 47

WALKER, Henry, 29, 33
Walkley, T., 33
Walter, John (I), 169, 181, 182, 187
Walter, John (II), 167, 192, 207
War correspondent, first, 196, 200*
Webb, W., 112
West, A., 118
Wheble, John, 155, 164, 167, 175
White, R., 29, 31
Whitlock, J., 47, 58
Wilkes, John, 154, 155, 167
Wilkie, G., 137
Wilkie, J., 135
Wilkins, W., 101, 121
Wilkinson, E., 57, 59, 64
Williams, J., 155, 156, 175
Williams, O., 37
Williamson, R., 17, 21, 33
Wilson, R., 144
Wood, R., 17
Wood, Robt., 17, 23, 24
Woodfall, H., 125, 126, 147
Woodfall, W., 165, 167, 183, 193
Wright, G. E., 293
Wright, J., 25, 27
Wright, Thomas, 167

YOUNG, M., 217

Printed by W. LEWIS, M.A., *at the University Press, Cambridge*

Lightning Source UK Ltd.
Milton Keynes UK
UKOW03f1255020415

248997UK00005BA/218/P